Instant ASP.NET Applications

About the Author

Greg Buczek is a Microsoft Certified Solutions Developer and a Microsoft Certified Trainer working as an Independent Consultant in Flagstaff, Arizona, in addition to being the author of six previous titles. He has created and managed numerous web sites, where he strives to bring dynamic, data-driven content to the Internet. In his role as Webmaster, Greg has extensive experience with SQL Server. Greg also has extensive ASP, Visual Basic, and Access experience. He has developed numerous Visual Basic applications, ActiveX Components, and ActiveX Controls. As an MCT, Greg has taught and developed curricula for the MCSD courses. Greg's previous titles include *Instant ASP Scripts 1/e, Instant ASP Scripts 2/e, Instant Access Databases, Instant SQL Server 2000 Applications, Instant ASP Components,* and *ASP Developer's Guide.* You can e-mail Greg at books@netstats2000.com. When e-mailing, please include the title and edition of the book; do not send attachments. He also asks that, to avoid the spreading of viruses, you not add him to your e-mail address list.

Instant ASP.NET Applications

Greg Buczek

New York Chicago San Francisco
Lisbon London Madrid Mexico City Milan
New Delhi San Juan Seoul Singapore Sydney Toronto

Osborne/**McGraw-Hill**
2600 Tenth Street
Berkeley, California 94710
U.S.A.

To arrange bulk purchase discounts for sales promotions, premiums, or fund-raisers, please contact Osborne/**McGraw-Hill** at the above address. For information on translations or book distributors outside the U.S.A., please see the International Contact Information page immediately following the index of this book.

Instant ASP.NET Applications

1234567890 CUS CUS 01987654321

Book p/n 0-07-219293-3 and CD p/n 0-07-219292-5
parts of
ISBN 0-07-219291-7

Publisher	Brandon A. Nordin
Vice President & Associate Publisher	Scott Rogers
Acquisitions Editors	Jim Schachterle, Rebekah Young
Project Editors	Laura Stone, Monika Faltiss
Acquisitions Coordinators	Timothy Madrid, Paulina Pobocha
Technical Editor	Michael Adams
Copy Editor	Robert Campbell
Proofreaders	Mike McGee, Carroll Proffitt
Indexer	Jack Lewis
Computer Designers	Michelle Galicia, Jean Butterfield, George Toma Charbak
Illustrators	Michael Mueller, Lyssa Wald
Series Designer	Roberta Steele
Cover Designer	Greg Scott

This book was composed with Corel VENTURA™ Publisher.

This book is dedicated to my parents,
Bessie Georgeadis Buczek and
Henry Walter Buczek.
I have such wonderful memories of
the time we have spent together.

Contents at a Glance

Contents

Acknowledgments

As usual, I must start by acknowledging and thanking my wife, Joyce Buczek. She has supplied tremendous support and assistance during this project. I would also like to thank Michael Adams, my technical editor on this book.

In addition, my continued thanks to all the folks at McGraw-Hill, especially Rebekah Young and Paulina Pobocha, who have given me the opportunity to write this book and others over the past few years.

Introduction

This book is divided into two sections. The first two chapters introduce you to some of the topics in ASP.NET. The rest and bulk of the book presents ASP.NET solutions. Here you will learn through example how to use the numerous controls and techniques available in ASP.NET.

The presentation of the solutions within a chapter is consistent across the book. First, you see what the solution does through a sample walk-through. Figures display the different ASP.NET pages, and in the text you will learn about the tool's functionality. That is followed by a discussion of the back-end database used in the solution. There you will read about the structures of the tables and the relationships between tables. After that, the ASP.NET pages are viewed. There you will see what controls are used on each page, how they are implemented, and the code that drives them.

The CD-ROM that accompanies this book contains all the solutions discussed in Chapters 3–19. Please refer to Appendix B for a further discussion of the contents of the CD-ROM.

A final note: As you are reading, reviewing, and playing with the solutions presented in this book, always think about how you could modify the code to satisfy a different need. Don't pass by one solution because you think you will never use it. Open your mind and think about how you could mold it for your own needs or how you can use a procedure or technique within your specific situation.

CHAPTER

1

Introduction to ASP.NET

ASP.NET offers a whole new approach to developing your Web applications. Instead of a single code block that runs whenever the page is submitted, like we had in ASP, ASP.NET offers a richer programming model that emulates an event-driven programming environment.

Throughout this book, from Chapter 3 to Chapter 19, you will see through example how this programming model can be used to create varied applications for numerous purposes. But in these first two chapters, a brief introduction of ASP.NET is presented. You may want to read these chapters first to better understand the code presented later in the book. Or you may find that these first two chapters are best left as a reference when you need to review the functionality of a particular control.

In this chapter, we will start with a discussion of what ASP.NET is and how an ASP.NET page is processed. Then we will review the structure of an ASP.NET page through simple examples. That will be followed with a review of basic controls that you place on your ASP.NET pages. And toward the end of this chapter, we will review the validation controls that you can use to test the data entered by the visitors to your pages.

What ASP.NET Is

Static pages, Web pages that have the same content each time you view them, are more and more becoming a thing of the past. To encourage the development of your Web community and to get visitors to return to your site, you must provide them with a reason to come back. Probably the most compelling reason a person has for returning to your site is because you offer dynamic Web content.

Dynamic Web pages can change every time they are viewed, or they can offer ways for visitors to send information back to you. Examples of dynamic pages are pages that display the current weather, show today's sales items, tell how stocks are doing right now, enable a customer to place an item in their shopping cart, or allow visitors to search through your company's documentation. Each time the visitor revisits the pages, the site displays the most current information because the data behind the pages has been changed or because the information supplied by the visitor in preparing the page has changed. ASP.NET provides a way for you to create dynamic Web pages.

ASP.NET allows us to combine standard HTML elements (such as tables, text, text formatting, and title tags) with controls (such as Labels, DataGrids, and DropDownLists), along with event-driven code to produce a Web page that is dynamically generated every time your page is requested from a browser. The visitor, through their browser, requests the ASP.NET page—which if it hasn't already been compiled, is compiled at that point. The compiler then runs your page using your code and turns your controls into standard HTML tags and text. The resulting page contains none of your code or controls and is viewable by virtually any browser.

The only code that may be seen is client-side code that is generated by the compiler in combination with your events or controls. For example, later in this chapter we will look at the RequiredFieldValidator control. This control requires the visitor to enter a value before submitting the page. If they don't place a value in the field, they see a message you supply. The code that supplies this functionality is located on the client side. But you don't write the code; it is generated for you.

How an ASP.NET Page Is Processed

First, the visitor types in a request like http://www.a.com/sales.aspx to visit your site, or clicks a link that sends them to that page. Notice that the name of the page ends in .aspx. This is the file extension used by ASP.NET pages. The request for the page routes its way to your Internet Information Server (IIS).

IIS retrieves the requested file and notes that the request has the file extension of .aspx, which tells IIS that this is an ASP.NET page that contains code and controls that it must interpret. If the page has not been compiled, it is then compiled. Based on the visitor's request, the page is run. This may require IIS to launch other components such as ADO.NET, e-mail libraries, third-party components, or your own shopping-cart component.

Launching these other components and including these libraries really expands the capability of ASP.NET. Components and libraries allow you to read the contents of a current order from a database, use your UPS calculator to estimate shipping charges, and check to see if the person's browser supports frames before displaying them or displaying a custom layout for a particular visitor.

All of your code, the controls that you insert on the page, and the component code are converted into standard HTML that is sent back out through the Internet to the visitor's browser.

The compiler even looks at the visitor's browser to determine in what way the code should be generated. For example, if the visitor's browser supports client-side code, then that code is sent to the browser. Otherwise, further code will run on the server side.

In the final step, the visitor's browser receives the HTML and displays all of your Web site's dynamic content, helping you develop more robust applications that provide the needed functionality for your visitor or customer base.

ASP.NET Page Structure

Now, let's take a look at a few simple ASP.NET pages to better understand their structure. Here is the HTML for a very basic Web page (shown in Figure 1-1):

```
<html>
<head>
<title>Sample Page</title>
</head>
<body>
<p>Hello Web!</p>
</body>
</html>
```

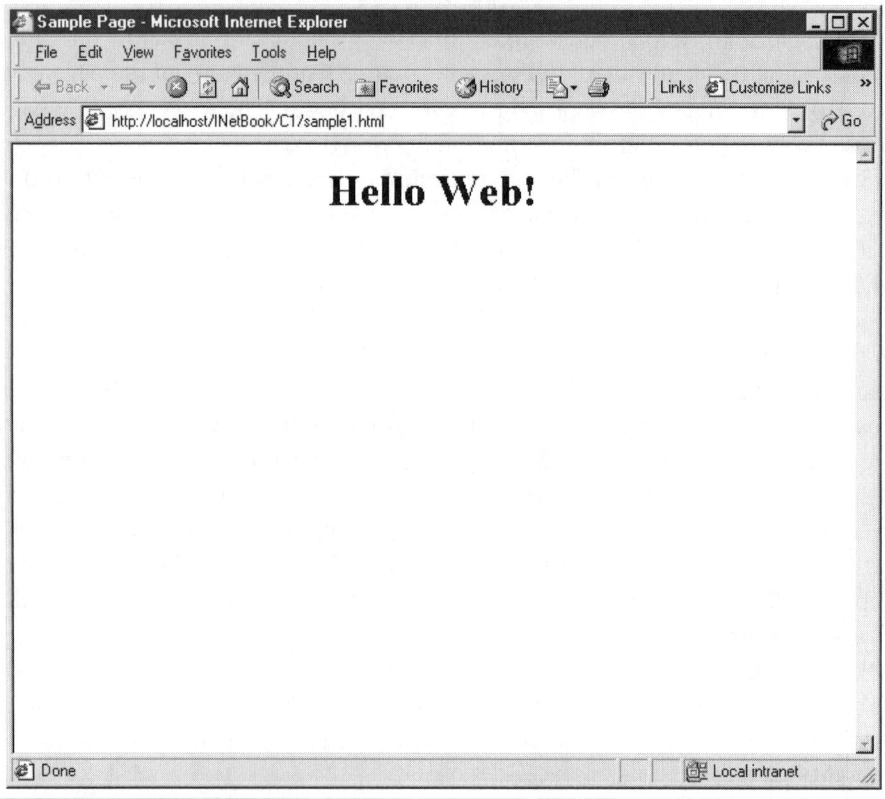

Figure 1-1 *Sample HTML page*

Here is how a very simple ASP.NET page that performs the same task would look

```
<html>
<head>
<title>Sample Page</title>
</head>
<body>
<form runat="server">
<asp:Label
    id="lblMessage"
    Font-Size="12pt"
    Font-Bold="True"
    Font-Name="Lucida Console"
    Text="<center><b><h1>Hello Web!</h1></b></center>"
    runat="server"
/>
</form>
</body>
</html>
```

The code has changed in two very important ways. The first is that the page contains a form tag:

```
<form runat="server">
```

This tag is typically placed on our ASP.NET page and tells the compiler to maintain the state of the controls within the page. Notice that the tag contains the property runat, which is set to “server”. Whenever you use that property, it means that you want the compiler to process the control instead of passing it on to the client.

The other big change to the page is that we have added a control to it—in this case, a Label control:

```
<asp:Label
    id="lblMessage"
    Font-Size="12pt"
    Font-Bold="True"
    Font-Name="Lucida Console"
    Text="<center><b><h1>Hello Web!</h1></b></center>"
    runat="server"
/>
```

A Label control is simply a way for you to place text, which can contain HTML tags, onto your page. Because it is a control, you can set properties of the control in a block or in your code.

The first line of the definition of the control tells the compiler what it is—in this case, a Label control:

```
<asp:Label
```

Now we can set the different properties of the control. Here we define the name of the control:

```
id="lblMessage"
```

Once that is established, we can use that in code to define the properties of the control or to invoke their methods.

Next, we set the size of the font,

```
Font-Size="12pt"
```

the fact that it is bold,

```
Font-Bold="True"
```

and the name of the font to be used

```
Font-Name="Lucida Console"
```

We then place text into the Label control. Note that because the text is rendered as HTML, it can contain HTML tags:

```
Text="<center><b><h1>Hello Web!</h1></b></center>"
```

We then inform the compiler that it should process this control:

```
runat="server"
```

That is followed by the closing tag of the control:

```
/>
```

The syntax of a control definition can also take this format:

```
<asp:Label
    id="lblMessage"
    Font-Size="12pt"
```

```
    Font-Bold="True"
    Font-Name="Lucida Console"
    Text="<center><b><h1>Hello Web!</h1></b></center>"
    runat="server"
>
</asp:Label>
```

Here, the closing tag is in a separate tag:

```
</asp:Label>
```

With some controls, you can use either version (with or without a separate closing tag), but other controls require a specific version.

Take a look at this next simple page. It takes the page one step further by programmatically setting the value of the text property in the Label control.

```
<%@ Page Language=VB Debug=true %>
<script runat=server>
Sub Page_Load(ByVal Sender as Object, ByVal E as EventArgs)
    lblMessage.Text = "<br><br><b><h2>The current time is: " _
        & TimeOfDay() & "</h2></b>"
End Sub
</script>
<html>
<head>
<title>Sample Page</title>
</head>
<body>
<form runat="server">
<asp:Label
    id="lblMessage"
    Font-Size="12pt"
    Font-Bold="True"
    Font-Name="Lucida Console"
    runat="server"
>
</asp:Label>
</form>
</body>
</html>
```

The output of this page is displayed in Figure 1-2.

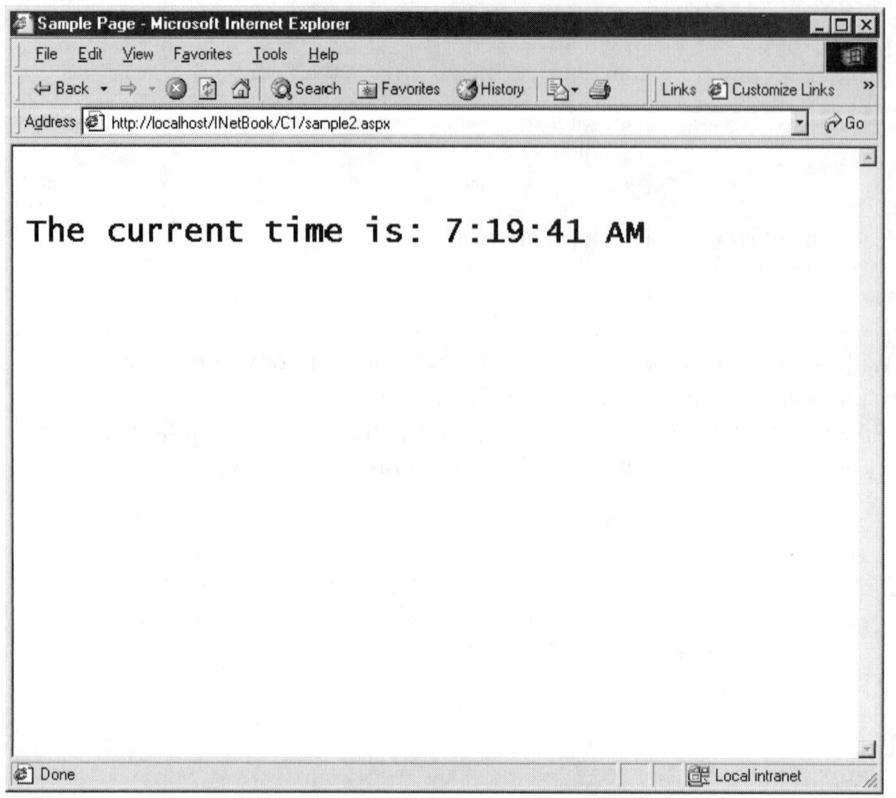

Figure 1-2 *Output of time of day code*

The page contains the same Label control as before, but now we have added a page directive and a code block at the top of the page:

```
<%@ Page Language=VB Debug=true %>
<script runat=server>
Sub Page_Load(ByVal Sender as Object, ByVal E as EventArgs)
    lblMessage.Text = "<br><br><b><h2>The current time is: " _
        & TimeOfDay() & "</h2></b>"
End Sub
</script>
```

Page directives offer us ways to tell the compiler to do something special with this page. In this example, we use a directive that tells the compiler that our coding language is Visual Basic. We also tell the compiler that we want the page to be run in debug mode. This allows us to see additional error messages when the page executes and has a run-time error:

```
<%@ Page Language=VB Debug=true %>
```

But you will also see a directive like this frequently used in the code in this book:

```
<%@ Import Namespace="System.Data" %>
```

This directive tells the compiler that when it runs this page, it should link to a Library called System.Data. We do that so that we can use the objects, methods, and properties contained within that library.

Next in our code block, we tell the compiler that what follows is code and that we want the server to run the code instead of passing it on to the browser to run

```
Sub Page_Load(ByVal Sender as Object, ByVal E as EventArgs)
```

This specific event is called the Page Load event. The code within this procedure will run every time the page is loaded. Within that code block, we simply set the Text property of our Label control to the current time, along with some HTML and fixed text:

```
lblMessage.Text = "<br><br><b><h2>The current time is: " _
    & TimeOfDay() & "</h2></b>"
```

We then end the procedure

```
End Sub
```

and end the script block:

```
</script>
```

Because ASP.NET is event-driven, we are not limited to placing all our code within a single code block. Take a look at this next simple page:

```
<%@ Page Language=VB Debug=true %>
<%@ Import Namespace="System.Data" %>
<%@ Import Namespace="System.Data.OLEDB" %>
<script runat=server>
Sub Page_Load(ByVal Sender as Object, ByVal E as EventArgs)
    If Not IsPostBack Then
        lblMessage.Text = "<br><br><b><h2>Please complete this " _
```

```
            & "page before pressing the button.</h2></b>"
    End If
End Sub
Sub SubmitBtn_Click(Sender As Object, E As EventArgs)
    lblMessage.Text = "<br><br><b><h2>Hello " & txtName.Text _
        & "</h2></b>"
End Sub
</script>
<html>
<head>
<title>Sample Page</title>
</head>
<body>
<form runat="server">
<asp:Label
    id="lblMessage"
    Font-Size="12pt"
    Font-Bold="True"
    Font-Name="Lucida Console"
    runat="server"
/>
<br><b>Name:</b><br>
<asp:TextBox
    id="txtName"
    Columns="25"
    MaxLength="30"
    runat=server
/>
<br><br>
<asp:button
    id="butOK"
    text="  OK  "
    Type="Submit"
    OnClick="SubmitBtn_Click"
    runat="server"
/>
</form>
</body>
</html>
```

This page adds an additional code block and two more controls. The output of the page after the button is clicked is displayed in Figure 1-3.

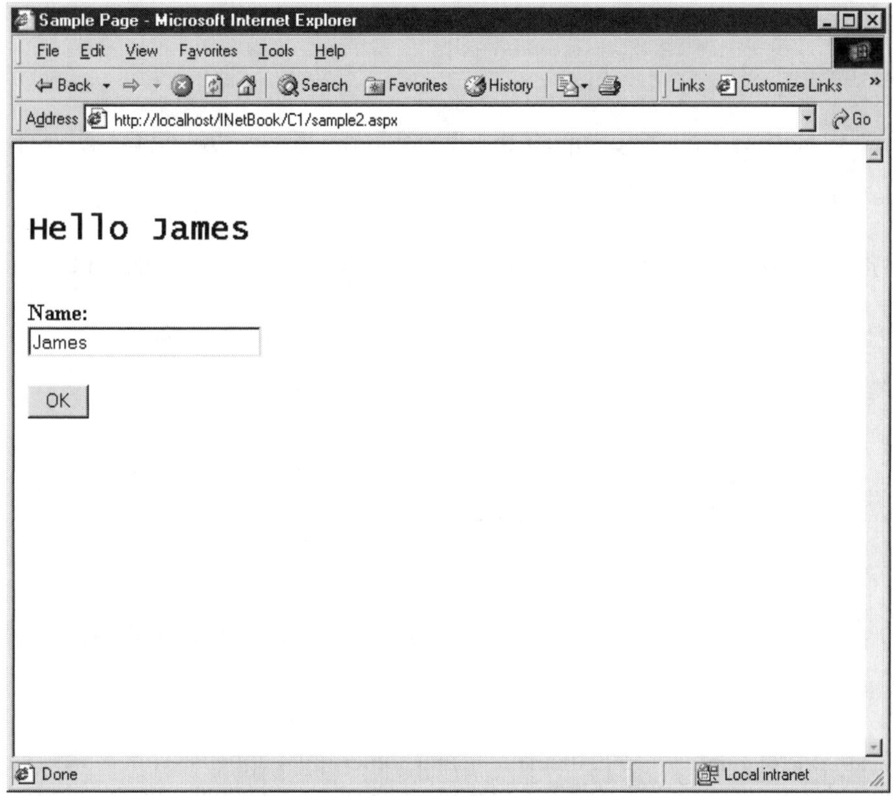

Figure 1-3 *Output of simple name page*

The first additional control is a TextBox control, which renders itself as an HTML Text tag when the page is run

```
<asp:TextBox
```

We set the ID property to txtName. This is how we will refer to the control in code:

```
id="txtName"
```

Next, we set the number of columns wide the control can be

```
Columns="25"
```

and the maximum number of characters that can be typed into the control:

```
MaxLength="30"
```

We also need to tell the compiler that it should run this control on the server side:

```
runat=server
```

The next control is a Button control. It is rendered as an HTML Submit tag:

```
<asp:button
```

Again, we give it a name:

```
id="butOK"
```

We set the text that we want to appear on it:

```
text="  OK  "
```

We tell the compiler the type that this should be—an HTML Submit tag:

```
Type="Submit"
```

This control can have code that runs when something happens. That is where the event-driven quality of ASP.NET comes in. Here we say when the visitor clicks the button, OnClick, we want the procedure called SubmitBtn_Click to run. Note that you must include a procedure with that name in your code for the page to run correctly:

```
OnClick="SubmitBtn_Click"
```

And we tell the compiler that we want this control to run on the server side:

```
runat="server"
```

As before, the first code block fires when the page is loaded

```
Sub Page_Load(ByVal Sender as Object, ByVal E as EventArgs)
```

However, the page will be loaded in two ways. The first way the page is loaded is when the visitor browses to our page. The second way the page is loaded is when the visitor has clicked the Button control. We only want the code in this procedure to run for the first scenario. So we check here to see if the form on the page was not submitted back, which means the page has been loaded but the button has not been clicked

```
If Not IsPostBack Then
```

If that is the case, we set the Text property of the Label control to the initial instructive text:

```
lblMessage.Text = "<br><br><b><h2>Please complete this " _
    & "page before pressing the button.</h2></b>"
```

The next procedure fires when the Button control is clicked. Note that the name of the event must match exactly what you placed in the OnClick property when you defined this control:

```
Sub SubmitBtn_Click(Sender As Object, E As EventArgs)
```

Here, we simply place the name entered into the TextBox control by the visitor into the Label control:

```
lblMessage.Text = "<br><br><b><h2>Hello " & txtName.Text _
    & "</h2></b>"
```

Basic Web Controls

In this next section, we will review the uses of some of the basic Web controls that you can insert onto your ASP.NET Web page. These controls are defined in the System.Web.UI.WebControls namespace, which is a new name for a library file.

Label Control

As you saw in the last section, the Label control provides a way for you to display HTML in the Web page that you can programmatically control through the Text property.

Beyond using the control to display a message as we did in the last section, it can also be used to display title text at the top of a page:

```
<asp:Label
    id="lblTitle"
    BorderWidth="7px"
```

```
        BorderStyle=9
        Width="90%"
        Font-Size="25pt"
        Font-Name="Arial"
        Text="TitleGoes Here"
        runat="server"
/>
```

We start by telling the compiler the type of control that we are using—a TextBox:

```
<asp:Label
```

Then we give our TextBox a name:

```
id="lblTitle"
```

To make it stand out more, we give the TextBox a thick border:

```
BorderWidth="7px"
```

We can also set the style of the border. Here we set it so that it stands out like a button:

```
BorderStyle=9
```

Next, we set the width of the TextBox so that it will be almost as wide as the whole page:

```
Width="90%"
```

We also can set the font properties:

```
Font-Size="25pt"
Font-Name="Arial"
```

We then place the text into the Label and have the compiler run it:

```
Text="TitleGoes Here"
runat="server"
```

TextBox Control

The TextBox control provides a way for you to retrieve information from the visitor that they enter free-form. Figure 1-4 shows a page that uses three TextBox controls, each a little different.

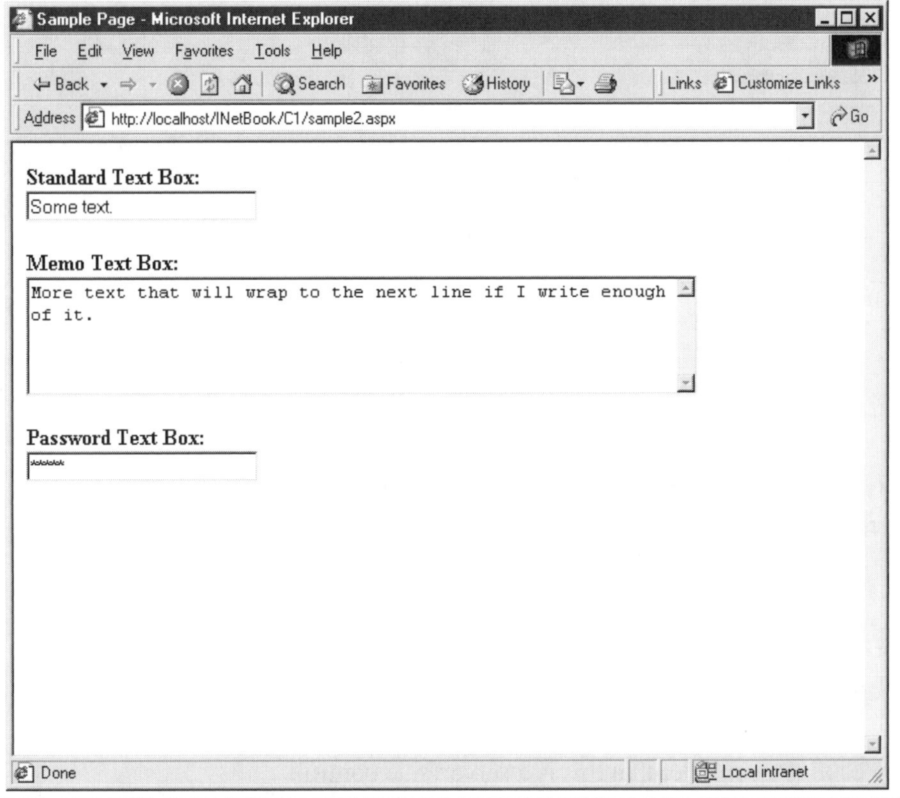

Figure 1-4 *TextBox control examples*

The code that defines these controls follows

```
<asp:TextBox
    id="txtStandard"
    Columns="25"
    MaxLength="30"
    runat=server
/>
<asp:TextBox
    id="txtMemo"
    Columns="60"
    Rows="5"
    runat=server
    TextMode="MultiLine"
/>
<asp:TextBox
```

```
    id="txtPassword"
    Columns="25"
    MaxLength="30"
    runat=server
    TextMode="Password"
/>
```

The first control is just a simple TextBox:

```
<asp:TextBox
```

As with all the other controls, we supply its name with the ID property:

```
id="txtStandard"
```

The Columns property is used to indicate how wide you want the control to appear on the Web page:

```
Columns="25"
```

You can also set the maximum number of characters that can be typed into the field:

```
MaxLength="30"
```

We tell the compiler that this is a server-side control:

```
runat=server
```

The next TextBox allows the visitor to type in much longer pieces of information, such as memos or notes. This version of the TextBox control is implemented as a TextArea HTML element:

```
<asp:TextBox
```

As before, we set the name of the control:

```
id="txtMemo"
```

We set the width of the control,

```
Columns="60"
```

but now we also need to define its height:

```
Rows="5"
```

The control will run server-side:

```
runat=server
```

We set the TextMode property to indicate that this should be rendered as a memo type of TextBox control:

```
TextMode="MultiLine"
```

The third control looks like a standard TextBox control, but the text that the visitor types is hidden. This type of control is typically used to enter a password. The only change needed for this type of control is to set the TextMode property to Password:

```
TextMode="Password"
```

Button Control

A Button control provides a way for you to have the form on the page submitted back for processing. When the visitor clicks the page, the code that you attach to the Button click event fires

```
<asp:button
    id="butOK"
    text="  OK  "
    OnClick="SubmitBtn_Click"
    runat="server"
/>
```

We start by telling the compiler that this is a Button control:

```
<asp:button
```

You then give it a name

```
id="butOK"
```

and set the text that will appear on the button:

```
text="  OK  "
```

Next, we define the procedure that should run when the button is clicked

```
OnClick="SubmitBtn_Click"
```

And we tell the compiler that the control is to be run on the server side:

```
runat="server"
```

Using the definition here, you must define a code block with a name like this:

```
Sub SubmitBtn_Click(Sender As Object, E As EventArgs)
```

HyperLink Control

The HyperLink control allows you to programmatically insert an HTML anchor tag in your code. The tag can be rendered either as just text or as an image that, when clicked, goes to the specified location.

Typically, the control is defined within your ASP.NET page. Then in code, you set the navigate and image location properties. Here are a couple of examples of the control:

```
<asp:HyperLink
    id="hypText"
    runat="server"
/>
<asp:HyperLink
    id="hypIcon"
    runat="server"
    Text="Click to view larger image"
    BorderWidth="7px"
    BorderStyle=7
/>
```

The first control is meant to just have text in it. First, we tell the compiler that this is a HyperLink control:

```
<asp:HyperLink
```

Then we set its name and tell the compiler to run it:

```
id="hypText"
runat="server"
```

Most likely, when the page is loaded, we would set the text property for the control, which is what the visitor sees

```
hypText.Text = "Click here for more information."
```

We would also set the location that the visitor would go to when they clicked the link through the NavigateURL property:

```
hypText.NavigateURL = "http://www.google.com"
```

Note that you wouldn't use fixed text, but would probably be using some value from a database.

The next example is also a HyperLink control:

```
<asp:HyperLink
```

We give it a name and have it run server-side:

```
id="hypIcon"
runat="server"
```

This HyperLink control will display a picture. The text property becomes the AltText in the HTML Image tag:

```
Text="Click to view larger image"
```

Because an image is going to be displayed, a border can look nice:

```
BorderWidth="7px"
BorderStyle=7
```

Then in code we set the location of the image that would be displayed. Here it is set to some field in a database:

```
hypIcon.ImageUrl = DSPageData.Tables("ProductData"). _
    Rows(0).Item("PathToIcon")
```

We also set the location to take the visitor to when they click the HyperLink control:

```
hypIcon.NavigateUrl = DSPageData.Tables("ProductData"). _
    Rows(0).Item("PathToFull")
```

Image Control

The Image control renders itself as an HTML Image tag. You can use the control to dynamically add an image to your page. For example, maybe you want an image to be randomly displayed. Or maybe you want to display a picture of a product. The Image control is useful in these instances.

```
<asp:Image
    id="imgStepPicture"
    runat="server"
/>
```

We start by defining the type of control:

```
<asp:Image
```

Then we give it a name

```
id="imgStepPicture"
```

and tell the compiler to run it:

```
runat="server"
```

Then, in code, we would set the AlternateText property, which is the text the visitor sees if they hover their mouse over the image:

```
imgStepPicture.AlternateText = _
    DSQuestion.Tables("CurrentQuestion").Rows(0).Item("PicAltText")
```

We also set the location of the picture. In both of these properties, we set the value according to data in a database:

```
imgStepPicture.ImageUrl = _
    DSQuestion.Tables("CurrentQuestion").Rows(0).Item("PicPath")
```

ImageButton Control

An ImageButton control is the combination of an Image control and a Button control. The control allows you to display an image that you want the visitor to be able to click. When they click it, an event is fired and code can run.

```
<asp:ImageButton
    id="imgButton"
```

```
    OnClick="SubmitPart1_Click"
    runat="server"
/>
```

We start by telling the compiler that this is an ImageButton control:

```
<asp:ImageButton
```

We then give it a name to be referred to in code:

```
id="imgButton"
```

We then define the name of the procedure that we want to run when the ImageButton is clicked

```
OnClick="SubmitPart1_Click"
```

and tell the compiler to run this control on the server side:

```
runat="server"
```

Notice that we haven't set the image that will appear in the control. We could do it here, or we can dynamically set it when the page is loaded

```
imgButton.ImageUrl="./pic1.gif"
```

We also must define a procedure that matches the name placed in the OnClick property:

```
Sub SubmitPart1_Click(Sender As Object, E As ImageClickEventArgs)
    'Place code here.
End Sub
```

Calendar Control

The Calendar control is one of the best new controls available to ASP.NET developers. Through a single control definition, you can render a calendar that the visitor can use to change months and days. And when the visitor selects a date, you have an event that code can run in.

Figure 1-5 displays the Calendar control with a Label control.

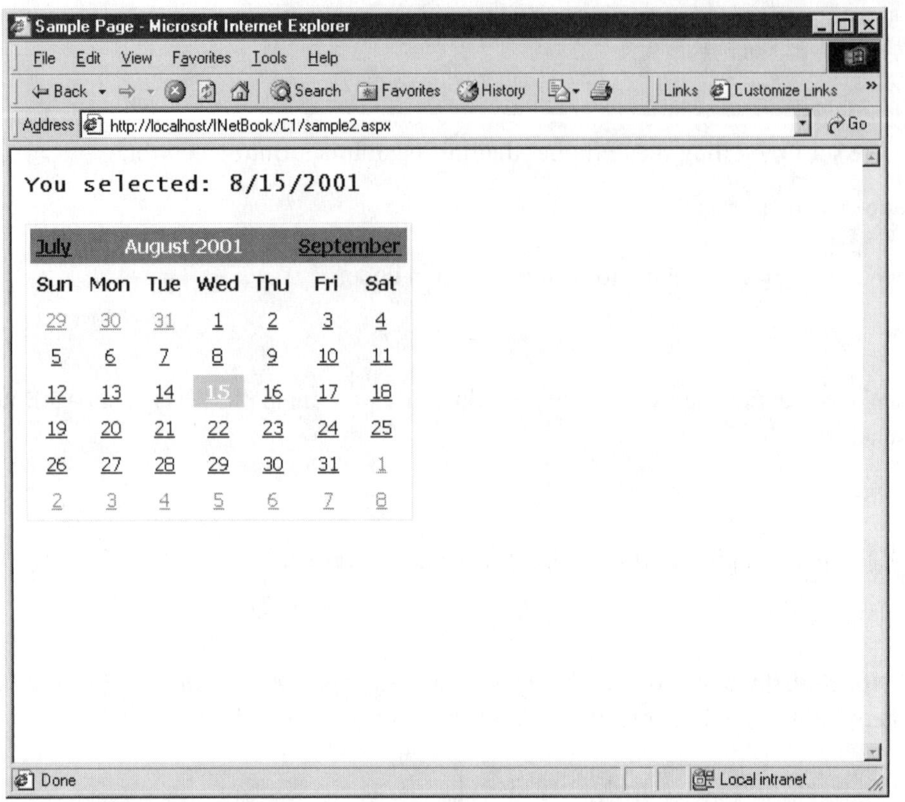

Figure 1-5 *Calendar control*

The definition that rendered that control follows

```
<asp:Calendar
    id="calDateToUse"
    runat="server"
    BackColor="ivory"
    CellPadding="3"
    CellSpacing="3"
    DayNameFormat="Short"
    FirstDayOfWeek="Default"
    NextPrevFormat="FullMonth"
    SelectionMode="Day"
    ShowDayHeader="True"
```

```
    ShowGridLines="False"
    ShowNextPrevMonth="True"
    ShowTitle="True"
    TitleFormat="MonthYear"
    TodayDayStyle-Font-Bold="True"
    DayHeaderStyle-Font-Bold="True"
    OtherMonthDayStyle-ForeColor="gray"
    TitleStyle-BackColor="#3366ff"
    TitleStyle-ForeColor="white"
    TitleStyle-Font-Bold="True"
    SelectedDayStyle-BackColor="#ffcc66"
    SelectedDayStyle-Font-Bold="True"
    Font-Name="Tahoma"
    Font-Size="14"
    OnSelectionChanged="calSelectChange"
/>
```

We start by telling the compiler that we are defining a Calendar control:

```
<asp:Calendar
```

Then we give the control a name

```
id="calDateToUse"
```

and tell the compiler to run it server-side:

```
runat="server"
```

Next, we set the background color for the weekday name row and the date rows of the calendar:

```
BackColor="ivory"
```

We also set the amount of space that we would like to have between the dates:

```
CellPadding="3"
CellSpacing="3"
```

We define that we want the short name for each weekday

```
DayNameFormat="Short"
```

and that the first day of the week should be set to the system default:

```
FirstDayOfWeek="Default"
```

Here we tell the compiler that we want the full names of the previous and next months to appear

```
NextPrevFormat="FullMonth"
```

and that we only want to allow the visitor to select a single day as opposed to a whole week:

```
SelectionMode="Day"
```

We want the weekday names to be displayed,

```
ShowDayHeader="True"
```

but we don't want to see grid lines between the dates:

```
ShowGridLines="False"
```

We do want the previous and next months,

```
ShowNextPrevMonth="True"
```

and we want a title to appear between those months

```
ShowTitle="True"
```

in the format of the month with the year:

```
TitleFormat="MonthYear"
```

We then set the bold style for the current selected date,

```
TodayDayStyle-Font-Bold="True"
```

as well as the days of the week:

```
DayHeaderStyle-Font-Bold="True"
```

Next, we set the color for dates that appear on the current month but are part of the next or last month:

```
OtherMonthDayStyle-ForeColor="gray"
```

We then set the text style for the title text

```
TitleStyle-BackColor="#3366ff"
TitleStyle-ForeColor="white"
TitleStyle-Font-Bold="True"
```

and the style for the selected date:

```
SelectedDayStyle-BackColor="#ffcc66"
SelectedDayStyle-Font-Bold="True"
```

Finally, we set the name and size for the font used in rendering the calendar:

```
Font-Name="Tahoma"
Font-Size="14"
```

We can then define the code that we want to run when the visitor selects a date:

```
OnSelectionChanged="calSelectChange"
```

In code, we can set the date that is the currently selected date. Here, we set it to today's date:

```
calDateToUse.SelectedDate = Today()
```

Then we must define a code block that has the same name that we placed in the OnSelectionChanged property. Here we do that and place the date that the visitor selected into the text of a Label control:

```
Sub calSelectChange(ByVal Sender as Object, ByVal E as EventArgs)
    lblMessage.Text = "You selected: " _
        & calDateToUse.SelectedDate
End Sub
```

Panel Controls

Panel controls are simply placeholders for other controls. When you define a Panel control, you typically place other controls within its definition. Typically you do this to make it easier to toggle the visibility of a group of controls. For example, you may have a form for the visitor to enter their personal information. When they click a Button control, you would want to add their information to a database table. Then you would want to display some success message and hide the form so that they can't enter another record. An easy way to do that is with a Panel control.

```
<asp:Panel
    id="pnlQuery"
    runat="server"
>
'controls go here
</asp:Panel>
```

We start by telling the compiler the type of control:

```
<asp:Panel
```

We give the control a name

```
id="pnlQuery"
```

and tell the compiler to run it server-side:

```
    runat="server"
>
```

Here is where we would insert controls that are to be placed within this panel:

```
'controls go here
```

After we are finished defining the controls or raw HTML that we want to render with this Panel, we close the control tag:

```
</asp:Panel>
```

Then, in code, we can hide all the controls and HTML within the Panel control like this:

```
pnlQuery.Visible = False
```

Validation Controls

ASP.NET offers a variety of validation controls that make it easy for you to make sure the visitor enters the correct type of information before the form on the page is submitted. Figure 1-6 demonstrates the use of some of the validation controls.

The page consists of four TextBox controls, four validation controls, and a Button control. Each of the TextBox controls has a validation control defined that checks its value when the visitor exits the field or when they click the Button control.

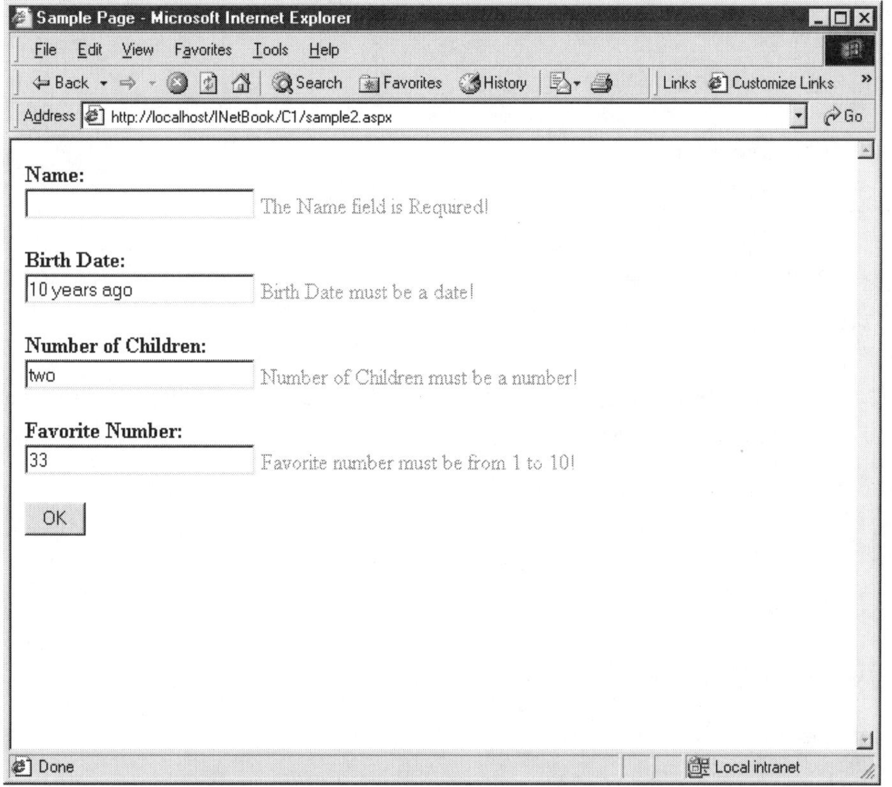

Figure 1-6 *Validation controls*

The first TextBox control must have a value in it because a RequiredFieldValidator control is used

```
<asp:RequiredFieldValidator
    id="rfvName"
    ControlToValidate="txtName"
    Display="Dynamic"
    runat=server>
    The Name field is Required!
</asp:RequiredFieldValidator>
```

We start by defining the type of control that we are using

```
<asp:RequiredFieldValidator
```

We then give it a name

```
id="rfvName"
```

and tell it which control to check:

```
ControlToValidate="txtName"
```

This next property tells the compiler not to allocate space for the error message until it needs to be displayed

```
Display="Dynamic"
```

The control is to be compiled on the server side:

```
runat=server>
```

This is the text that appears when the name field is left blank:

```
The Name field is Required!
```

We then close the control definition:

```
</asp:RequiredFieldValidator>
```

The next TextBox must be a date. A CompareValidator control checks that:

```
<asp:CompareValidator
    id="cvBirthDate"
```

```
    ControlToValidate="txtBirthDate"
    Operator="DataTypeCheck"
    Type="Date"
    Display="Dynamic"
    runat="server"
    >
    Birth Date must be a date!
</asp:CompareValidator>
```

We define the type of control

```
<asp:CompareValidator
```

and give it a name:

```
id="cvBirthDate"
```

Then we tell the compiler the name of the control that this control validates

```
ControlToValidate="txtBirthDate"
```

Next, we state that this control is to be checked for a data type

```
Operator="DataTypeCheck"
```

and that data type is a date:

```
Type="Date"
```

The space for the error message will be allocated, as it is needed,

```
Display="Dynamic"
```

and the control is to run on the server side:

```
runat="server"
```

This is the message the visitor sees if the value entered is not a date:

```
Birth Date must be a date!
```

Then we close the control definition:

```
</asp:CompareValidator>
```

The third TextBox must be a number. So we use another CompareValidator control.

```
<asp:CompareValidator
    id="cvNumChildren"
    ControlToValidate="txtNumChildren"
    Operator="DataTypeCheck"
    Type="Integer"
    Display="Dynamic"
    runat="server"
    >
    Number of Children must be a number!
</asp:CompareValidator>
```

This time the data type we are checking for is a number:

```
Type="Integer"
```

The fourth TextBox control must contain a number from 1 to 10. In this case, a RangeValidator control is used

```
<asp:RangeValidator
    id="rngFavNum"
    ControlToValidate="txtFavNum"
    Type="Integer"
    MinimumValue=1
    MaximumValue=9
    Display="Dynamic"
    runat="server">
    Favorite number must be from 1 to 10!
</asp:RangeValidator>
```

We start by defining the control type:

```
<asp:RangeValidator
```

We give the control a name

```
id="rngFavNum"
```

and specify the control that it is to validate

```
ControlToValidate="txtFavNum"
```

Next, we set the type of data that it should contain,

```
Type="Integer"
```

the minimum value it can have,

```
MinimumValue=1
```

and the maximum value:

```
MaximumValue=9
```

As with the other validation controls, this one will have its space allocated as needed,

```
Display="Dynamic"
```

and it will run server-side:

```
runat="server">
```

If the value entered by the visitor is not in the specified range, they will see this message:

```
Favorite number must be from 1 to 10!
```

CHAPTER

2

Beyond the Basics

In this chapter, we will continue our discussion of the language, controls, and environment that are used within ASP.NET applications. We will start with a discussion on Application and Session settings. After that we will review still-useful methods and collections within the Request and Response objects. Then we will review code used in this book to connect to and manipulate SQL Server and Access databases. After that, we will review Web controls that allow us to display this database information in a variety of formats.

Application and Session Settings

In this section, we will review how to create and use an ASP.NET application and how to store variables within the Application and Session scope.

Creating an ASP.NET Application

With some of the examples used in this book and for some of your own applications, you will need to tell IIS, the Internet Information Server, that you want your set of ASP.NET pages treated as a single application.

The advantage of doing this is that the pages can share application variables, share session variables, and use an application file to fire events. To set a folder as the root of an ASP.NET application, open IIS and browse to the location of the folder. Right-click that folder and select Properties. You should then see the dialog displayed in Figure 2-1.

Make sure you are on the Directory tab. In the bottom of the dialog, you will see a section labeled Application Settings. To create an ASP.NET application, click Create. The dialog should now look like what you see in Figure 2-2.

Now you can type in the name by which you want to refer to your application. Note that this name is just for your own recognition. You won't use it in code.

With this setting turned on, all the ASP.NET files located in this folder or any subfolders that are not marked as Applications are collectively referred to as an application. You can have all these pages share data through application and session variables, and you can use the Global.asax file to have code run when a visitor enters the application or when the application itself starts and stops.

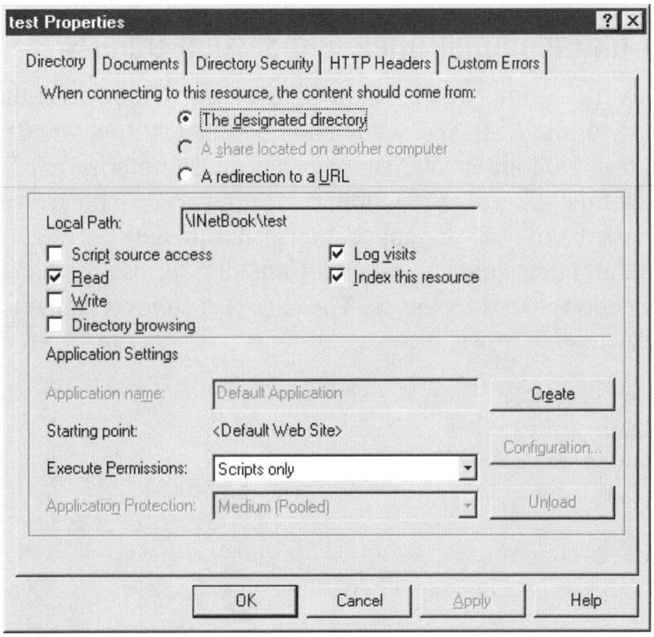

Figure 2-1 *Folder Properties*

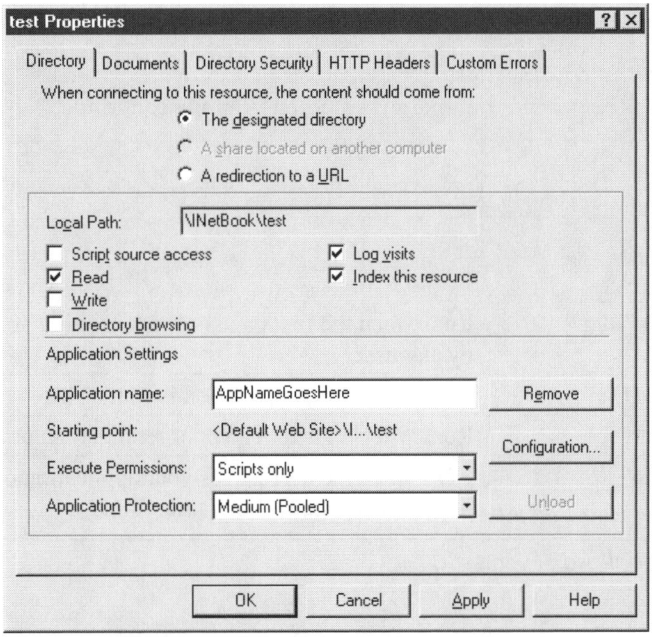

Figure 2-2 *Creating an ASP.NET application*

Global.asax and the Application and Session Objects

The Global.asax file is simply a text file with the name Global.asax that is placed in the root directory of the ASP.NET application. In this text file, you can place code that you want to run in four events. These events are summarized in Table 2-1.

The purpose of these events is to allow you to run code or create variables that will persist across the life of your application or during the stay of a visitor. Thus, you can store login information, constant information for use across your site, or dedicated connections to a data source. The code that follows contains a sample Global.asax file.

```
<script language=VBScript runat=Server>
Sub Application_OnStart
    Application("Discount") = .1
End Sub

Sub Application_OnEnd
    'Insert script to be executed when the application ends
End Sub

Sub Session_OnStart
    Session("LoginEmpID") = " "
End Sub

Sub Session_OnEnd
    'Insert script to be executed when a session ends
End Sub
</script>
```

Event	Purpose
Application_OnStart	Runs when the first page is opened within your application by any user
Application_OnEnd	Runs when your application is shut down
Session_OnStart	Runs when a visitor enters or returns to your application
Session_OnEnd	Runs when the user leaves your application or has not requested a page within a time frame

Table 2-1 *Global.asax Events*

The first thing you will notice about this listing is that we are using these tags to denote the beginning and end of the code block:

```
<script language=VBScript runat=Server>
</script>
```

Each of the events starts with the word "Sub" followed by the name of the event:

```
Sub Application_OnEnd
```

They end with:

```
End Sub
```

The importance of the application and session variables is their scope. *Scope* refers to where the variable can be seen, where we can retrieve the value of the variable. Say we create an application variable, as in:

```
Application("Discount") = .1
```

We have defined a variable for which the value is available anywhere within our ASP.NET application. This is very powerful because instead of defining a discount on ten different pages, we define it in one place and access the value in all of our pages. When it comes time to change the discount, we only have to change the information in one place. Similarly, we can define session variables for which the scope is only for a specific user's focus throughout the ASP.NET application. This allows us to keep track of an order as a visitor selects more items throughout our e-commerce site or to keep track of security as a user goes from page to page.

A session begins when a visitor first enters your site and ends when the session times out due to inactivity or you end the session in code. You can manage sessions with the TimeOut property and the Abandon method of the Session object. The TimeOut property is the number of minutes a session can be idle, during which the visitor makes no requests. Suppose we coded

```
Session.TimeOut = 30
```

A visitor's session will be considered over when they go through a period of 30 minutes without requesting a page. We can also explicitly end a session with the Abandon method:

```
Session.Abandon
```

We would use the Session.Abandon method when we wanted to give the user a button that allowed them to leave the application or once they placed their order and all processing for the order was complete. Once the session is abandoned or times out, the code in the Session_OnEnd event runs.

Request and Response Objects

Before ASP.NET, the Request and Response objects were used extensively to retrieve information from the visitor and to send them information. Most of that has been replaced with new techniques in ASP.NET, especially through its controls. But there still are a few instances when you need these objects. In this section, we will review those instances.

Response.Redirect Method

One functionality you still need within an ASP.NET page is to send a visitor to another page. For example, say that you have a site that requires visitors to first enter their name and password. To protect the other pages, you would check to see if they have logged in by looking at a session variable. If that variable were empty, you would need to send the visitor to the login page.

Or maybe you have a page that adds a product to the visitor's shopping cart. After the item has been added, you want to send the visitor to the Shopping Cart page so that they can check out. Frequently your programming model in ASP.NET is like this. You have one page that displays and processes information before sending the visitor on to another page.

To accomplish this task, you use the Redirect method of the Response object:

```
Response.Redirect("./login.aspx")
```

The visitor is sent to whatever page you specify in the first parameter of the method.

Request.QueryString Collection

Sometimes you need to pass information on to another page. For example, you may have one page where you list the names of courses that you offer at a school. When the visitor selects a course, you would want to send the visitor to a course page and pass to that page the course that the visitor selected. So, you would start by using the Redirect method of the Response object to send the visitor to that page with the ID of the course passed with the call:

```
Response.Redirect("./course.aspx?CourseID=4")
```

On the Course page, you would retrieve the value of the field passed in through the QueryString collection, like this:

```
Label1.Text = "You selected course: " _
    & Request.QueryString("CourseID")
```

Items are passed to a page through the QueryString collection with this format:

```
PageName.aspx?Field1=Value1&Field2=Value2&Field2=Value3
```

After the page name, a question mark is used to denote the parameter list. Each parameter is then paired with a value, and each pair is separated from the next pair through the ampersand character.

Request.Form Collection

Less often than in the days of ASP, you will want to use the Form collection of the Request object. The Form collection allows you to retrieve the values of fields passed to a page through the fields posted to it from another page.

For example, say that you had a page where the visitor supplied their name and e-mail address so that they could get on a distribution list. Say that you created that page with standard HTML. When the visitor clicks the Submit button on the page, you send the values that they entered to your ASP.NET page for processing.

On that ASP.NET page, you would use the Form collection of the Request object to retrieve the values passed in:

```
Label1.Text = Request.Form("EmailAddress")
```

Here we place the e-mail address entered by the visitor into the Text property of a Label control.

Data Objects and Code

In most of the examples in this book, we use code that connects to and manipulates data in a SQL Server or Access database. In this section, we will review what we are using these objects for.

Importing Libraries

At the top of each of the ASP.NET pages that connects to a database, you will see these two compiler directives:

```
<%@ Import Namespace="System.Data.OLEDB" %>
<%@ Import Namespace="System.Data" %>
```

These directives are Import directives. Generically, they tell the compiler to include these libraries with our ASP.NET page because we will use objects from them.

In this case, the directives import two data libraries. The first imports a library that lets us connect to an Access or a SQL Server database. It also allows us to create Command objects that we use to add, edit, or delete records directly through a SQL statement.

The second directive imports a library that allows us to retrieve data from a database and bind that data to controls on our ASP.NET page. Binding is the process whereby we link the values in a group of records so that they are displayed in the confines of a control.

Connecting to a Database

To connect to a SQL Server or Access database from our ASP.Net pages, we need code like this:

```
Dim DBConn as OleDbConnection
Dim DBConn2 as OleDbConnection
DBConn = New OleDbConnection("Provider=sqloledb;" _
    & "server=localhost;" _
    & "Initial Catalog=INETC9;" _
    & "User Id=sa;" _
    & "Password=yourpassword;")
DBConn2 = New OleDbConnection("PROVIDER=Microsoft.Jet.OLEDB.4.0;" _
    & "DATA SOURCE=" _
    & Server.MapPath("/INetBook/C9/" _
    & "Access/C9OnlineCampus.mdb;"))
```

We connect to an Access or SQL Server database using an OleDbConnection object:

```
Dim DBConn as OleDbConnection
Dim DBConn2 as OleDbConnection
```

This next line connects to the SQL Server database. In quotes, we pass the connect string. The first part of the connect string specifies the provider to use to connect to the database. Then we specify the name of the server that SQL Server is located on. That is followed by the name of the database within SQL Server. And the last part of the connect string is made up of the user name and password used to access the database:

```
DBConn = New OleDbConnection("Provider=sqloledb;" _
    & "server=localhost;" _
    & "Initial Catalog=INETC9;" _
    & "User Id=sa;" _
    & "Password=yourpassword;")
```

To connect to the Access database, we need to specify a different provider. That is followed by the physical path to the database. You could put in the full path. But here we use the path to the Web root on the server along with the rest of the path after that:

```
DBConn2 = New OleDbConnection("PROVIDER=Microsoft.Jet.OLEDB.4.0;" _
    & "DATA SOURCE=" _
    & Server.MapPath("/INetBook/C9/" _
    & "Access/C9OnlineCampus.mdb;"))
```

Directly Manipulating Data in a Database

Now that we have connected to the database, the procedure is the same when we want to change the data in the database. The only difference between using Access and SQL Server is the SQL syntax.

For example, here is a query that adds a record to a table called Courses:

```
Dim DBConn as OleDbConnection
Dim DBInsert As New OleDbCommand
DBConn = New OleDbConnection("Provider=sqloledb;" _
    & "server=localhost;" _
    & "Initial Catalog=INETC9;" _
    & "User Id=sa;" _
    & "Password=yourpassword;")
DBInsert.CommandText = "Insert Into Courses " _
    & "(CourseName, CourseDescription) values ('" _
    & "'" & txtCourseName.Text & "', " _
    & "'" & txtCourseDescription.Text & ")"
DBInsert.Connection = DBConn
DBInsert.Connection.Open
DBInsert.ExecuteNonQuery()
```

In addition to the OleDbConnection object, we also need an OleDbCommand object:

```
Dim DBInsert As New OleDbCommand
```

We then place the query that we want to run into the CommandText property of that object. In this example, it is an Insert statement:

```
DBInsert.CommandText = "Insert Into Courses " _
    & "(CourseName, CourseDescription) values ('" _
    & "'" & txtCourseName.Text & "', " _
    & "'" & txtCourseDescription.Text & "')"
```

The OleDbCommand object needs to connect to the database. Here, we tell it to use the OleDbConnection object that we established earlier in the code:

```
DBInsert.Connection = DBConn
DBInsert.Connection.Open
```

We can now run the query to insert the record:

```
DBInsert.ExecuteNonQuery()
```

Retrieving Data from the Database

To retrieve data from a SQL Server or Access database, we need to use DataSet objects. Take a look at this example, which retrieves the name of a course from a Courses table:

```
Dim DBConn as OleDbConnection
Dim DBCommand As OleDbDataAdapter
Dim DSPageData as New DataSet
DBConn = New OleDbConnection("PROVIDER=Microsoft.Jet.OLEDB.4.0;" _
    & "DATA SOURCE=" _
    & Server.MapPath("/INetBook/C9/" _
    & "Access/C9OnlineCampus.mdb;"))
DBCommand = New OleDbDataAdapter _
    ("Select CourseName from Courses Where " _
    & "CourseID = " & Session("CourseID") _
    , DBConn)
DBCommand.Fill(DSPageData, _
    "CourseName")
lblTitle.Text = "<center>Course " _
    & DSPageData.Tables("CourseName"). _
    Rows(0).Item("CourseName") _
    & "</center>"
```

In addition to the OleDbConnection object, we need an OleDbDataAdapter object, which will be used to retrieve data from the database:

```
Dim DBCommand As OleDbDataAdapter
```

We also need a DataSet object, which will store the data retrieved so that we can use it:

```
Dim DSPageData as New DataSet
```

After we connect to the database, we then use the SQL syntax to retrieve the desired data through our OleDbDataAdapter object:

```
DBCommand = New OleDbDataAdapter _
    ("Select CourseName from Courses Where " _
    & "CourseID = " & Session("CourseID") _
    , DBConn)
```

Now we execute that SQL statement by using the Fill method of the OleDbDataAdapter object. The method takes two parameters. The first is the name of the DataSet object that you want the data from the database to be placed in. The second parameter is the name that you want to use to define this record or group of records within the DataSet object:

```
DBCommand.Fill(DSPageData, _
    "CourseName")
```

The DataSet object now contains all the records that were retrieved through the SQL statement. Here, we place the name of the course into the Text property of a Label control:

```
lblTitle.Text = "<center>Course " _
    & DSPageData.Tables("CourseName"). _
    Rows(0).Item("CourseName") _
    & "</center>"
```

Data List Controls

Once we retrieve data from a database or have some other data that is in a column and row format, we need a way to display that information to the visitor. In this section, we will review a couple of controls that allow us to easily display that information.

DropDownList Control

The DropDownList control provides one of the simplest ways of displaying database or row/column data. It displays data into an HTML Select control. Take a look at Figure 2-3.

In addition to defining a Label control and a Button control, we define two DropDownList controls on the page:

```
<asp:dropdownlist
    id="ddlCourses"
    runat=server
    DataTextField="CourseName"
    DataValueField="CourseID">
</asp:dropdownlist>
<asp:dropdownlist
    id="ddlRating"
    runat=server>
    <asp:ListItem Value="Excellent">Excellent</asp:ListItem>
    <asp:ListItem Value="OK">OK</asp:ListItem>
    <asp:ListItem Value="Stinks">Stinks</asp:ListItem>
</asp:dropdownlist>
```

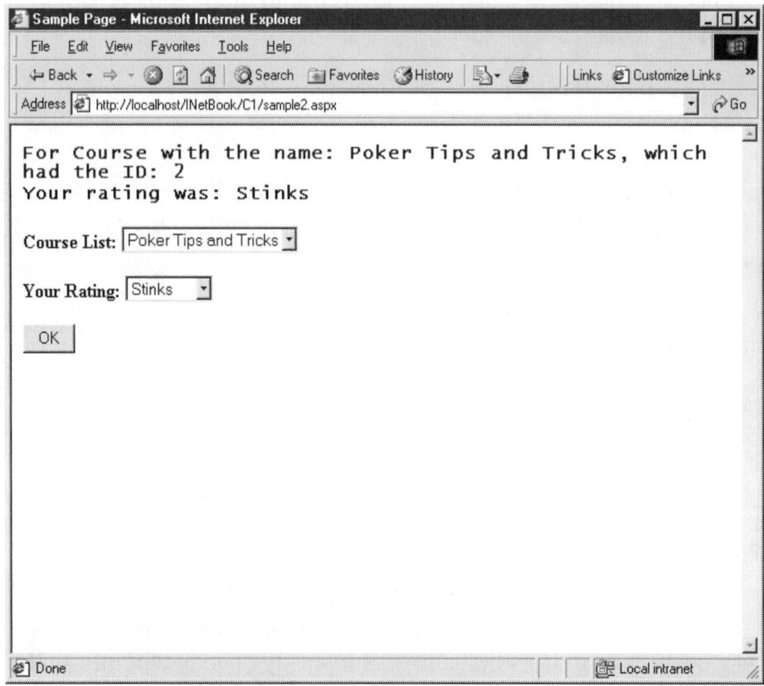

Figure 2-3 *DropDownList controls*

The first DropDownList will display the names of the courses with their IDs from the database. We start by telling the compiler that this is a DropDownList control:

```
<asp:dropdownlist
```

We then give the control a name so that we can reference it in code:

```
id="ddlCourses"
```

We tell the compiler to run the control server-side:

```
runat=server
```

Next, we specify the name of the field that is displayed in the DropDownList when the visitor views the page:

```
DataTextField="CourseName"
```

We can also specify a field that we can retrieve in code but that the visitor doesn't see

```
DataValueField="CourseID">
```

In other words, the visitor sees the name of the course, but we may want to retrieve the ID of the course. We then close the control's definition:

```
</asp:dropdownlist>
```

The other DropDownList control contains a fixed list of items. We start again with the control type,

```
<asp:dropdownlist
```

the name of the control,

```
id="ddlRating"
```

and that it should run on the server:

```
runat=server>
```

Next, we specify the items that we want displayed in the list as ListItem controls:

```
<asp:ListItem Value="Excellent">Excellent</asp:ListItem>
```

Here we use the same text for the Text property and the Value property:

```
<asp:ListItem Value="OK">OK</asp:ListItem>
```

But if we wanted to, we could make them different. The Value property is what we pass in code. The visitor does not see it. They see the text between the opening and closing tags:

```
<asp:ListItem Value="Stinks">Stinks</asp:ListItem>
```

We can now close that tag:

```
</asp:dropdownlist>
```

When the visitor first opens the page, we need to populate the first DropDownList by connecting to the database and retrieving data:

```
Sub Page_Load(ByVal Sender as Object, ByVal E as EventArgs)
    If Not IsPostBack Then
        Dim DBConn as OleDbConnection
        Dim DBCommand As OleDbDataAdapter
        Dim DSPageData as New DataSet
        DBConn = New OleDbConnection("Provider=sqloledb;" _
            & "server=localhost;" _
            & "Initial Catalog=INETC9;" _
            & "User Id=sa;" _
            & "Password=yourpassword;")
        DBCommand = New OleDbDataAdapter _
            ("Select CourseID, CourseName From Courses" _
            , DBConn)
        DBCommand.Fill(DSPageData, _
            "Courses")
        ddlCourses.DataSource = _
            DSPageData.Tables("Courses").DefaultView
        ddlCourses.DataBind()
    End If
End Sub
```

We only want this code to run the first time the page is loaded. If we don't add this line, the code will run even after the visitor clicks the Button control. That will then wipe out the selection made in the Courses DropDownList control by the visitor:

```
If Not IsPostBack Then
```

To populate the DropDownList, we will need to connect to the database and retrieve data:

```
Dim DBConn as OleDbConnection
Dim DBCommand As OleDbDataAdapter
Dim DSPageData as New DataSet
```

As you saw in the last section, we pass the connect string for the database:

```
DBConn = New OleDbConnection("Provider=sqloledb;" _
    & "server=localhost;" _
    & "Initial Catalog=INETC9;" _
    & "User Id=sa;" _
    & "Password=yourpassword;")
```

We then retrieve all the course records from a table called Courses:

```
DBCommand = New OleDbDataAdapter _
    ("Select CourseID, CourseName From Courses" _
    , DBConn)
```

Those records are placed into a table called Courses in the DataSet object:

```
DBCommand.Fill(DSPageData, _
    "Courses")
```

Now that we have all the course records, we need to place them into our DropDownList. We do this by binding the DropDownList control to the DataSet table. First, we specify the name of the DataSet table to use

```
ddlCourses.DataSource = _
    DSPageData.Tables("Courses").DefaultView
```

Then we bind to that table:

```
ddlCourses.DataBind()
```

When the visitor clicks OK, we place the value that they selected in the DropDownList controls into the Text property of a Label control.

```
Sub SubmitBtn_Click(Sender As Object, E As EventArgs)
    lblMessage.Text = "For Course with the name: " _
        & ddlCourses.SelectedItem.Text _
```

```
        & ", which had the ID: " _
        & ddlCourses.SelectedItem.Value _
        & "<br>Your rating was: " _
        & ddlRating.SelectedItem.Text
End Sub
```

We start with some fixed text:

```
lblMessage.Text = "For Course with the name: " _
```

Then we refer to the name of the course, which is available through the Text property of the SelectedItem object of the DropDownList control:

```
& ddlCourses.SelectedItem.Text _
& ", which had the ID: " _
```

Next, we refer to the ID of the course through the Value property:

```
& ddlCourses.SelectedItem.Value _
& "<br>Your rating was: " _
```

We also display the rating selected by the visitor:

```
& ddlRating.SelectedItem.Text
```

DataGrid Control

Typically, we need to display more information than just a single field in a DropDownList. A DataGrid allows you to display two-dimensional row and column data in a table format. Figure 2-4 shows a couple of examples of the control.

You can define a DataGrid in a couple of different ways. In the first example, we let the DataGrid control automatically generate columns for us. In the second instance of the control, we manually defined the columns.

Here are the control definitions:

```
<asp:DataGrid
    id="dgAuctionItems"
    Width="90%"
    BackColor="beige"
    AlternatingItemStyle-BackColor="cornsilk"
    BorderColor="black"
    ShowFooter="false"
    CellPadding=3
```

```
    CellSpacing="0"
    Font-Name="Arial"
    Font-Size="8pt"
    ForeColor="Black"
    HeaderStyle-BackColor="burlywood"
    HeaderStyle-Font-Bold="True"
    runat="server">
</asp:DataGrid>
<asp:DataGrid
    id="dgAuctionItems2"
    Width="90%"
    AutoGenerateColumns="false"
    BackColor="beige"
    AlternatingItemStyle-BackColor="cornsilk"
    BorderColor="black"
    ShowFooter="false"
    CellPadding=3
    CellSpacing="0"
    Font-Name="Arial"
    Font-Size="8pt"
    ForeColor="Black"
    HeaderStyle-BackColor="burlywood"
    HeaderStyle-Font-Bold="True"
    runat="server">
    <columns>
    <asp:HyperLinkColumn
        HeaderText="Name"
        DataNavigateUrlField="AuctionItemID"
        DataNavigateUrlFormatString="./item.aspx?ID={0}"
        DataTextField="ItemName"
        Target="_self"
    />
    <asp:BoundColumn
        HeaderText="Description"
        DataField="BriefDescription"
    />
    </columns>
</asp:DataGrid>
```

We start by defining the control type:

```
<asp:DataGrid
```

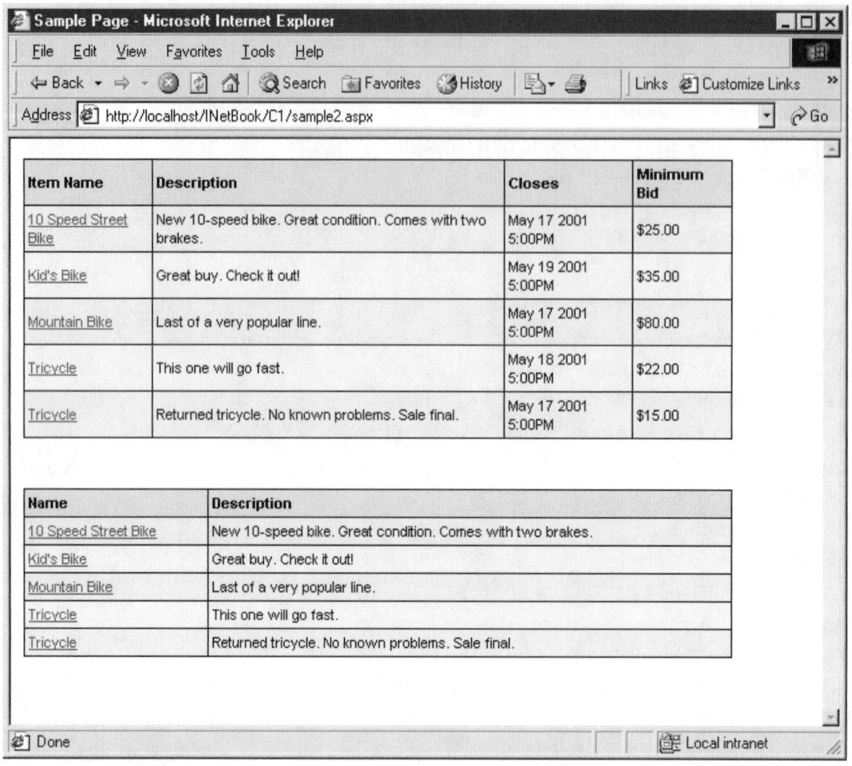

Figure 2-4 *DataGrid controls*

We then give it a name:

```
id="dgAuctionItems"
```

We can set the width that the control will occupy. In this case, the width is relative to the overall width of the browser window:

```
Width="90%"
```

Next, we set the background color for the odd-numbered rows

```
BackColor="beige"
```

and for the even-numbered rows:

```
AlternatingItemStyle-BackColor="cornsilk"
```

We can also give the border a color:

```
BorderColor="black"
```

Footers allow us to generate the field names at the bottom of the table. In this case, we choose not to do that:

```
ShowFooter="false"
```

We then define the amount of space between the cells in the table

```
CellPadding=3
CellSpacing="0"
```

and we establish the font properties:

```
Font-Name="Arial"
Font-Size="8pt"
ForeColor="Black"
```

Next, we set the background of the header column

```
HeaderStyle-BackColor="burlywood"
```

and have the font display the text in that row as bold:

```
HeaderStyle-Font-Bold="True"
```

Finally, we tell the compiler to run the control server-side

```
runat="server">
```

and we close the definition:

```
</asp:DataGrid>
```

The other grid is defined similarly. But with it, we don't want the columns to be generated automatically:

```
AutoGenerateColumns="false"
```

Instead, we will generate them through the Columns collection:

```
<columns>
```

The first column is a HyperLinkColumn control:

```
<asp:HyperLinkColumn
```

We can specify the text that we want to appear for that column:

```
HeaderText="Name"
```

Next, we specify the field that is used to indicate the ID of this record when it is passed on to another page as a link:

```
DataNavigateUrlField="AuctionItemID"
```

Here, we specify where in the link we want the ID field to go. The value in the preceding field will be placed where the {0} text is in this property:

```
DataNavigateUrlFormatString="./item.aspx?ID={0}"
```

Next, we supply the name of the field that is displayed in this column to the visitor:

```
DataTextField="ItemName"
```

And when the visitor clicks the link in this column, we specify that we want the current window to be used to display the page linked to:

```
    Target="_self"
/>
```

The next column is simply a BoundColumn control:

```
<asp:BoundColumn
```

We only need to provide the text for the column header

```
HeaderText="Description"
```

and the field to display:

```
DataField="BriefDescription"
```

When the page loads, we need to populate these DataGrid controls. The queries differ because in the first DataGrid, the control is automatically creating columns based on the fields retrieved, and in the second it is not:

```
Sub Page_Load(ByVal Sender as Object, ByVal E as EventArgs)
    Dim DBConn as OleDbConnection
    Dim DBCommand As OleDbDataAdapter
    Dim DSPageData as New DataSet
    DBConn = New OleDbConnection("Provider=sqloledb;" _
        & "server=localhost;" _
        & "Initial Catalog=INETC18;" _
        & "User Id=sa;" _
        & "Password=yourpassword;")
    DBCommand = New OleDbDataAdapter _
        ("Select '<a href=""./auction_item.aspx?AuctionItemID=' " _
        & "+ Convert(varchar(50), AuctionItemID) + '"">' + " _
        & "ItemName + '</a>' as [Item Name], " _
        & "BriefDescription as [Description], " _
        & "Convert(varchar(30), CloseDate, 100) as [Closes], " _
        & "'$' + Convert(varchar(30), MinimumBid, 1) " _
        & "as [Minimum Bid] " _
        & "From AuctionItems " _
        & "Order By ItemName", DBConn)
    DBCommand.Fill(DSPageData, _
        "AuctionItems")
    dgAuctionItems.DataSource = _
        DSPageData.Tables("AuctionItems").DefaultView
    dgAuctionItems.DataBind
    DBCommand = New OleDbDataAdapter _
        ("Select AuctionItemID, ItemName, " _
        & "BriefDescription " _
        & "From AuctionItems " _
        & "Order By ItemName", DBConn)
    DBCommand.Fill(DSPageData, _
        "AuctionItems2")
    dgAuctionItems2.DataSource = _
        DSPageData.Tables("AuctionItems2").DefaultView
    dgAuctionItems2.DataBind
End Sub
```

We will need data objects like those described earlier in this chapter:

```
Dim DBConn as OleDbConnection
Dim DBCommand As OleDbDataAdapter
Dim DSPageData as New DataSet
```

We start by connecting to the database:

```
DBConn = New OleDbConnection("Provider=sqloledb;" _
    & "server=localhost;" _
    & "Initial Catalog=INETC18;" _
    & "User Id=sa;" _
    & "Password=yourpassword;")
```

In this first query, we retrieve data for the first DataGrid. Because that DataGrid will display whatever we throw into it exactly as it is returned from the database, we need to format that data.

```
DBCommand = New OleDbDataAdapter _
```

In the first column, we want to place the name of the item and have it link to another page in the site. Therefore, within the query, we need to concatenate an HTML anchor tag with the ID and name of the item:

```
("Select '<a href="./auction_item.aspx?AuctionItemID=' " _
& "+ Convert(varchar(50), AuctionItemID) + '"">' + " _
& "ItemName + '</a>' as [Item Name], " _
```

In the second column, we want to display the description of the item. But the field name is made up of two words without spaces. We don't want that column name displayed in our DataGrid. Therefore, we output the field from the query with the name Description:

```
& "BriefDescription as [Description], " _
```

The next field to be displayed is a date. Without formatting, the date is displayed in a difficult-to-read format. Therefore, within our query we format the date:

```
& "Convert(varchar(30), CloseDate, 100) as [Closes], " _
```

We do the same for a money field:

```
& "'$' + Convert(varchar(30), MinimumBid, 1) " _
& "as [Minimum Bid] " _
& "From AuctionItems " _
& "Order By ItemName", DBConn)
```

We then retrieve the records into a DataSet table:

```
DBCommand.Fill(DSPageData, _
    "AuctionItems")
```

And as we did in the last section with the DropDownList control, we need to bind the DataGrid control to DataSet object table:

```
dgAuctionItems.DataSource = _
    DSPageData.Tables("AuctionItems").DefaultView
dgAuctionItems.DataBind
```

Next, we need to retrieve the data for the second DataGrid. Because the DataGrid control does not automatically generate columns, the query is much more basic:

```
DBCommand = New OleDbDataAdapter _
    ("Select AuctionItemID, ItemName, " _
    & "BriefDescription " _
    & "From AuctionItems " _
    & "Order By ItemName", DBConn)
DBCommand.Fill(DSPageData, _
    "AuctionItems2")
```

Once we retrieve the data, we bind the DataGrid to it:

```
dgAuctionItems2.DataSource = _
    DSPageData.Tables("AuctionItems2").DefaultView
dgAuctionItems2.DataBind
```

CHAPTER

3

Facilitating Customer Communication

In this chapter, we will review Web site tools that could be used by almost any company. These tools provide ways for you to communicate with your customers or for them to communicate with you.

First, we will review the Survey tool. The Survey tool dynamically creates a page of questions for the visitor that asks their opinion about some aspect of the company. The answers selected by the visitor are recorded by this tool.

After that, we will look at the Request for More Information tool. This simple, one-page tool provides a mechanism for visitors to your site to request additional information about a specific topic.

The third tool we will look at in this chapter is the Store Locator tool. This tool provides a simple way for visitors to locate your stores in their area.

Survey Tool

The Survey tool provides a way for you to query visitors on a variety of topics. The tool is flexible in that it can be used to generate different surveys, and each survey can have as many questions and answers as you want. One page allows the visitor to respond to questions. Another page allows the manager to view the results of the survey.

Sample Usage

This tool is made up of two pages. The first page is the one that the visitor sees. It is displayed in Figure 3-1.

The visitor is presented with a series of questions that display their choices with DropDownList controls. In this example, the visitor is presented with three questions. But take a look at Figure 3-2.

Now the same page is being used to display an entirely different survey. The title of the page is different, the instructions are different, the questions are different, and even the number of questions is different. As you will see when we review the code, we dynamically add controls to a panel according to the number of questions included for the survey.

Once the visitor is through with the survey, they click OK to submit their responses. When they do that, they see the message displayed in Figure 3-3.

The text displayed here also comes from the database. Therefore, you can specify different responses from one survey to another.

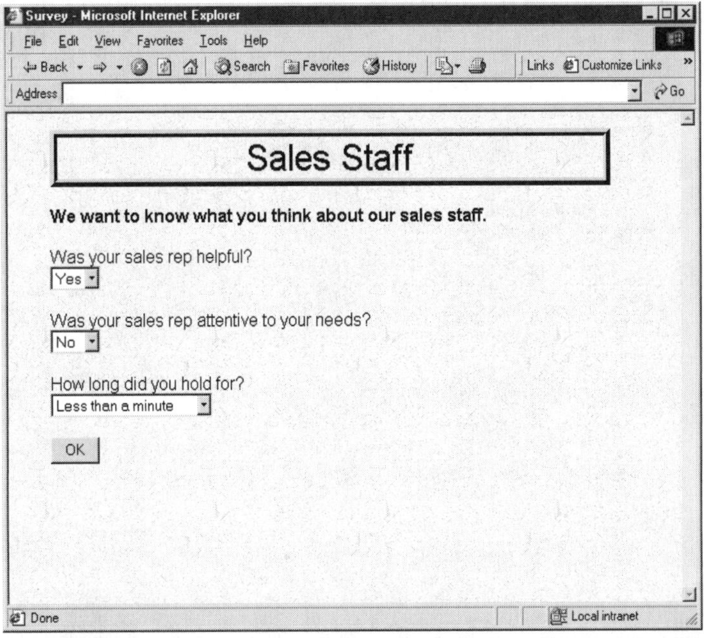

Figure 3-1 *Survey page displaying Sales Rep survey*

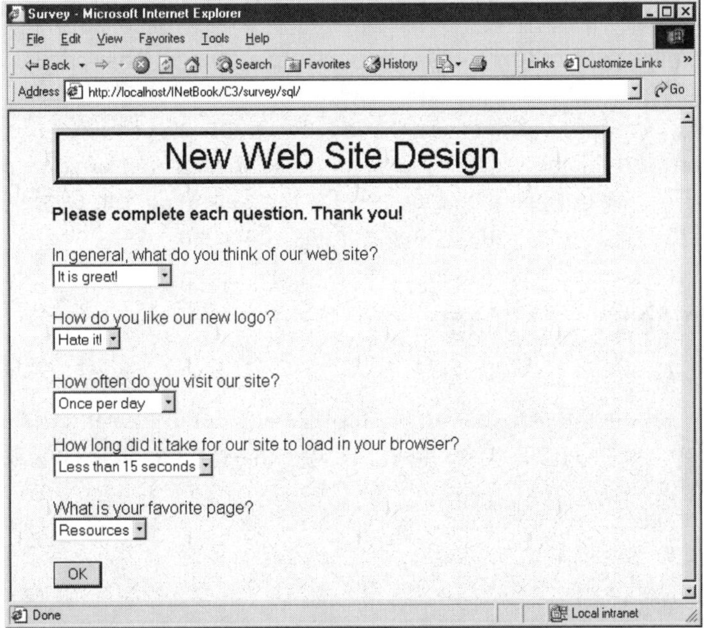

Figure 3-2 *Survey page displaying New Web Site Design survey*

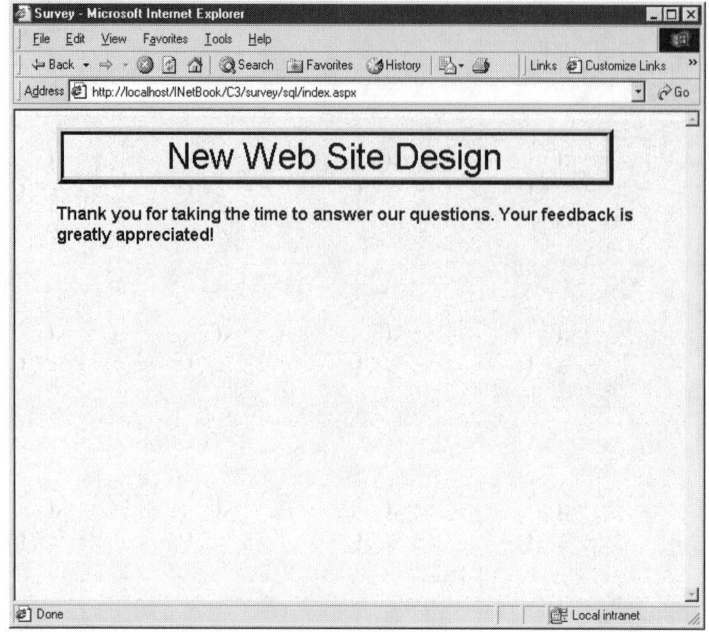

Figure 3-3 *Survey page after responses submitted*

The other page used in this tool is the Survey Says page. That page is displayed in Figure 3-4.

The Survey Says page allows you to view the results of a survey. The page shows each question with the total number of responses for each answer selected by at least one visitor. Here we see just the responses for the New Web Site Design survey. But you can use the page to view the results for any of the surveys.

Survey Database Component

C3Survey.sql

The database required to run the Survey tool is made up of four interrelated tables. In this section, we will look at the relationships between the tables and the fields that they contain.

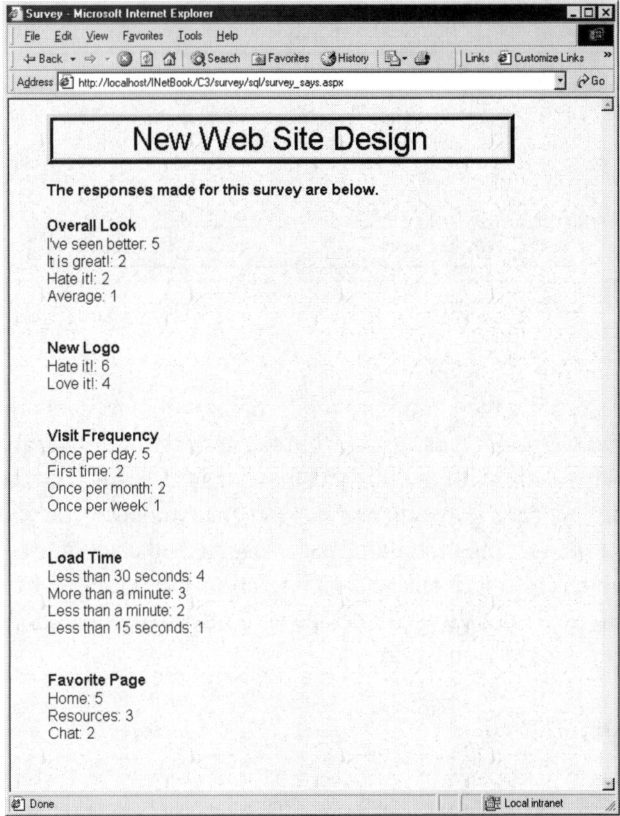

Figure 3-4 *Survey Says page*

Tables and Data Diagram

Figure 3-5 shows the relationship between the tables in the Survey database.

The top-level table in the Survey database is the Surveys table. It contains title and instruction information for the survey.

The SurveyQuestions table contains the text of each of the questions. It is in a one-to-many relationship with the Surveys table. Each survey can have many questions, but each question goes with a single survey.

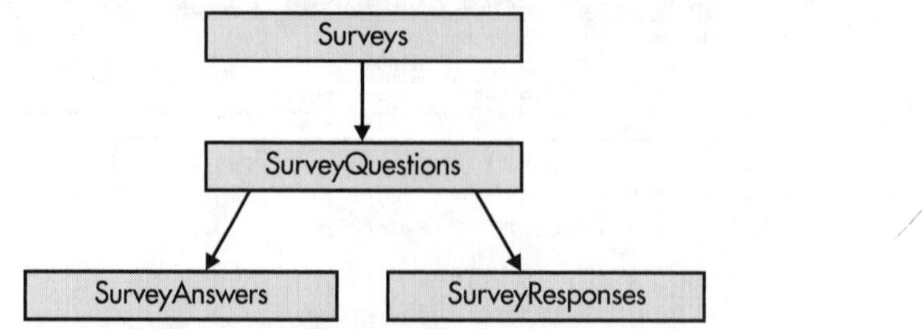

Figure 3-5 *Survey data diagram*

The SurveyAnswers table contains each of the possible answers to a question that are displayed in the DropDownList control for the question. That table is in a one-to-many relationship with the SurveyQuestions table. Each answer goes with a specific question, but each question can have as many answers as you like.

The SurveyResponses table contains each response to each question answered by a visitor. The table is also in a one-to-many relationship with the SurveyQuestions table, because the same question can be answered by many visitors, but each visitor selects a single answer to a question.

Survey Field Specifications

Survey.txt

The field specifications for the fields in the Survey table are displayed in Table 3-1.

The SurveyID field is the primary key in this table. It is automatically populated with a value when a new record is added to this table. The SurveyName contains the name of the survey and is displayed in the title label on both ASP.NET pages.

The SurveyInstructions field contains the text that the visitor sees when they first enter the survey before the questions are presented. And the SurveyResponse field contains the text that the visitor sees after they complete the survey.

Field Name	Field Type	Notes
SurveyID	int	Primary Key, Identity Column
SurveyName	varchar	Length = 50
SurveyInstructions	varchar	Length = 255
SurveyResponse	varchar	Length = 255

Table 3-1 *Survey Field Specifications*

Field Name	Field Type	Notes
SurveyQuestionID	int	Primary Key, Identity Column
SurveyID	int	Foreign Key
SurveyQuestionShort	varchar	Length = 50
SurveyQuestionLong	varchar	Length = 255

Table 3-2 *SurveyQuestions Field Specifications*

SurveyQuestions Field Specifications

SurveyQuestions.txt

The field specifications for the fields in the SurveyQuestions table are displayed in Table 3-2.

The SurveyQuestionID field is the primary key in the table. The other key field, SurveyID, links this table to the Surveys table.

The SurveyQuestionShort field is the text displayed for the question on the Survey Says page. The SurveyQuestionLong field contains the text of the question as it is displayed on the Survey page.

SurveyAnswers Field Specifications

SurveyAnswers.txt

The field specifications for the fields in the SurveyAnswers table are displayed in Table 3-3.

The SurveyAnswerID is the primary key in this table. The SurveyQuestionID field links this table to the SurveyQuestions table. The SurveyAnswer field contains the text of the answer.

SurveyResponses Field Specifications

SurveyResponses.txt

The field specifications for the fields in the SurveyResponses table are displayed in Table 3-4.

Field Name	Field Type	Notes
SurveyAnswerID	int	Primary Key, Identity Column
SurveyQuestionID	int	Foreign Key
SurveyAnswer	varchar	Length = 50

Table 3-3 *SurveyAnswers Field Specifications*

Field Name	Field Type	Notes
SurveyResponseID	int	Primary Key, Identity Column
SurveyQuestionID	int	Foreign Key
SurveyResponse	varchar	Length = 50

Table 3-4 *SurveyResponses Field Specifications*

The SurveyResponseID field is the primary key in this table. The SurveyQuestionID field links this table to the SurveyQuestions table. The SurveyResponse field contains the response selected by the visitor.

Survey ASP.NET Code

The Survey tool is composed of two ASP.NET pages. These pages both contain controls that are dynamically added to Panel controls. In this section, we will review the controls and the code on these pages.

Survey ASP.NET Page

Index.aspx

The code on the Survey page displays the questions to the visitor and adds their responses to the database. At the top of the page, we define three compiler directives.

```
<%@ Page Language=VB Debug=true %>
<%@ Import Namespace="System.Data" %>
<%@ Import Namespace="System.Data.OLEDB" %>
```

The first directive tells the compiler the language that we are using in our code and that we want to run the pages in debug mode. That gives us richer error messages in some cases, but remember to turn it off when you use this tool in production:

```
<%@ Page Language=VB Debug=true %>
```

The other two directives import libraries so that we can access the database and display data:

```
<%@ Import Namespace="System.Data" %>
<%@ Import Namespace="System.Data.OLEDB" %>
```

Within the body of the page, we declare a Label control that contains the title of the survey:

```
<asp:Label
    id="lblTitle"
    BorderWidth="7px"
    BorderStyle=7
    Width="90%"
    Font-Size="25pt"
    Font-Name="Arial"
    runat="server"
/>
```

Another label control displays the initial instruction text to the visitor and the response text after they complete the survey:

```
<asp:Label
    id="lblMessage"
    Font-Bold="True"
    runat="server"
/>
```

Next we define a Panel control:

```
<asp:Panel
    id="pnlQuestions"
    Width="90%"
    runat="server"
>
</asp:Panel>
```

Notice that the Panel control does not contain any of its own controls. Those will be added in code.

One final control on the page is a Button control that the visitor clicks when they want to submit their responses:

```
<asp:button
    id="butOK"
    text="   OK   "
    Type="Submit"
    OnClick="SubmitBtn_Click"
    runat="server"
/>
```

The code on the page runs in two events. The first fires when the page is loaded.

```
Sub Page_Load(ByVal Sender as Object, ByVal E as EventArgs)
    Dim DBConn as OleDbConnection
    Dim DBCommand As OleDbDataAdapter
    Dim DSPageData as New DataSet
    Dim I as Integer
    Dim J as Integer
    Dim TempID as String
    Application("SurveyID") = 1
    DBConn = New OleDbConnection("Provider=sqloledb;" _
        & "server=localhost;" _
        & "Initial Catalog=INETC3;" _
        & "User Id=sa;" _
        & "Password=yourpassword;")
    DBCommand = New OleDbDataAdapter _
        ("Select SurveyName, SurveyInstructions " _
        & "From Surveys Where SurveyID = " _
        & Application("SurveyID"), DBConn)
    DBCommand.Fill(DSPageData, _
        "SurveyInfo")
    lblTitle.Text = "<center>" _
        & DSPageData.Tables("SurveyInfo"). _
        Rows(0).Item("SurveyName") & "</center>"
    lblMessage.Text = DSPageData.Tables("SurveyInfo"). _
        Rows(0).Item("SurveyInstructions")
    DBCommand = New OleDbDataAdapter _
        ("Select SurveyQuestionID, SurveyQuestionLong " _
        & "From SurveyQuestions Where SurveyID = " _
        & Application("SurveyID"), DBConn)
    DBCommand.Fill(DSPageData, _
        "SurveyQuestions")
    For I = 0 to DSPageData.Tables("SurveyQuestions"). _
        Rows.Count - 1
        Dim lcHTML = New LiteralControl
        lcHTML.Text = DSPageData.Tables("SurveyQuestions"). _
        Rows(I).Item("SurveyQuestionLong") & "<br>"
        pnlQuestions.Controls.Add(lcHTML)
        Dim MyDDL = New DropDownList
        TempID = DSPageData.Tables("SurveyQuestions"). _
        Rows(I).Item("SurveyQuestionID")
        MyDDL.ID = "Q" & TempID
        DBCommand = New OleDbDataAdapter _
            ("Select SurveyAnswer " _
```

```
            & "From SurveyAnswers Where SurveyQuestionID = " _
            & TempID, DBConn)
        DBCommand.Fill(DSPageData, _
            TempID)
        For J = 0 to DSPageData.Tables(TempID). _
            Rows.Count - 1
            Dim MyItem = New ListItem
            MyItem.Text = DSPageData.Tables(TempID). _
            Rows(J).Item("SurveyAnswer")
            MyDDL.Items.Add(MyItem)
        Next
        pnlQuestions.Controls.Add(MyDDL)
        Dim lcHTML2 = New LiteralControl
        lcHTML2.Text = "<br><br>"
        pnlQuestions.Controls.Add(lcHTML2)
    Next
End Sub
```

Within this code block, we will need a Connection object to connect to our database:

```
Dim DBConn as OleDbConnection
```

We also need a Data Adapter object to retrieve data from the database:

```
Dim DBCommand As OleDbDataAdapter
```

and a DataSet object that will contain the retrieved data:

```
Dim DSPageData as New DataSet
```

Next, we declare two variables that will be used to iterate through records:

```
Dim I as Integer
Dim J as Integer
```

One more variable that stores the ID of the current question is declared

```
Dim TempID as String
```

Next, we set the ID of the current survey. This is the variable you would change if you wanted to display a different survey:

```
Application("SurveyID") = 1
```

Next, we connect to the database:

```
DBConn = New OleDbConnection("Provider=sqloledb;" _
   & "server=localhost;" _
   & "Initial Catalog=INETC3;" _
   & "User Id=sa;" _
   & "Password=yourpassword;")
```

Then we retrieve the name and instructions for the survey

```
DBCommand = New OleDbDataAdapter _
    ("Select SurveyName, SurveyInstructions " _
    & "From Surveys Where SurveyID = " _
    & Application("SurveyID"), DBConn)
```

and place that data into our DataSet object into a table called SurveyInfo:

```
DBCommand.Fill(DSPageData, _
    "SurveyInfo")
```

We then place the name of the survey into our title label:

```
lblTitle.Text = "<center>" _
    & DSPageData.Tables("SurveyInfo"). _
    Rows(0).Item("SurveyName") & "</center>"
```

We also need to place the instructions into the message label:

```
lblMessage.Text = DSPageData.Tables("SurveyInfo"). _
    Rows(0).Item("SurveyInstructions")
```

Next, we need to retrieve all the questions for this survey

```
DBCommand = New OleDbDataAdapter _
    ("Select SurveyQuestionID, SurveyQuestionLong " _
    & "From SurveyQuestions Where SurveyID = " _
    & Application("SurveyID"), DBConn)
```

and place them into our DataSet object:

```
DBCommand.Fill(DSPageData, _
    "SurveyQuestions")
```

We then enter the outer loop of our code block, which will allow us to process each of the questions on the survey:

```
For I = 0 to DSPageData.Tables("SurveyQuestions"). _
    Rows.Count - 1
```

Within that loop, we start by declaring a new LiteralControl. A LiteralControl is a very basic control that allows us to insert straight HTML dynamically onto our page:

```
Dim lcHTML = New LiteralControl
```

The text that we place into this control is the text for the current question:

```
lcHTML.Text = DSPageData.Tables("SurveyQuestions"). _
    Rows(I).Item("SurveyQuestionLong") & "<br>"
```

The LiteralControl is then added to our panel:

```
pnlQuestions.Controls.Add(lcHTML)
```

Now that we have the text of the question, we need a DropDownList for the answers to that question:

```
Dim MyDDL = New DropDownList
```

We then store the ID of the current question prefaced into our temporary variable

```
TempID = DSPageData.Tables("SurveyQuestions"). _
    Rows(I).Item("SurveyQuestionID")
```

and use it along with a "Q" as the name of our DropDownList control. Later, this will allow us to know what question the answer selected by the visitor goes with:

```
MyDDL.ID = "Q" & TempID
```

Next, we need to retrieve all the answers that go with the question

```
DBCommand = New OleDbDataAdapter _
    ("Select SurveyAnswer " _
    & "From SurveyAnswers Where SurveyQuestionID = " _
    & TempID, DBConn)
```

and place them into our DataSet object:

```
DBCommand.Fill(DSPageData, _
    TempID)
```

Now, we enter our inner loop in this code block so that we can process each of the answers that goes with the current question:

```
For J = 0 to DSPageData.Tables(TempID). _
    Rows.Count - 1
```

Each answer is added as a ListItem

```
Dim MyItem = New ListItem
MyItem.Text = DSPageData.Tables(TempID). _
    Rows(J).Item("SurveyAnswer")
```

to our DropDownList control:

```
MyDDL.Items.Add(MyItem)
```

We then move on to process the next answer:

```
Next
```

After completing the inner loop, we can add the DropDownList to our Panel control:

```
pnlQuestions.Controls.Add(MyDDL)
```

We also need to add additional HTML separator tags

```
Dim lcHTML2 = New LiteralControl
lcHTML2.Text = "<br><br>"
```

to our Panel control:

```
pnlQuestions.Controls.Add(lcHTML2)
```

We then move on to process the next question in our outer loop:

```
Next
```

The other code fires when the visitor submits their responses by clicking OK:

```
Sub SubmitBtn_Click(Sender As Object, E As EventArgs)
    Dim DBConn as OleDbConnection
    Dim DBInsert As New OleDbCommand
    Dim DBCommand As OleDbDataAdapter
    Dim DSPageData as New DataSet
    Dim MyControl as Control
    Dim MyDDL as DropDownList
    DBConn = New OleDbConnection("Provider=sqloledb;" _
        & "server=localhost;" _
        & "Initial Catalog=INETC3;" _
        & "User Id=sa;" _
        & "Password=yourpassword;")
    DBInsert.Connection = DBConn
    DBInsert.Connection.Open
    For Each MyControl in pnlQuestions.Controls
        If MyControl.GetType().FullName = _
            "System.Web.UI.WebControls.DropDownList" Then
            MyDDL = MyControl
            DBInsert.CommandText = "Insert Into SurveyResponses " _
                    & "(SurveyQuestionID, SurveyResponse) " _
                    & "values (" _
                    & Mid(MyDDL.ID, 2) & ", " _
                    & "'" _
                    & Replace(MyDDL.SelectedItem.Text, "'", "''") _
                    & "')"
            DBInsert.ExecuteNonQuery()
        End If
    Next
    DBCommand = New OleDbDataAdapter _
        ("Select SurveyResponse " _
        & "From Surveys Where SurveyID = " _
        & Application("SurveyID"), DBConn)
    DBCommand.Fill(DSPageData, _
        "SurveyInfo")
    lblMessage.Text = DSPageData.Tables("SurveyInfo"). _
        Rows(0).Item("SurveyResponse")
    pnlQuestions.Visible = False
    butOK.Visible = False
End Sub
</script>
```

Within this code block, we will need to connect to the database, retrieve data from it, and place data into it:

```
Dim DBConn as OleDbConnection
Dim DBInsert As New OleDbCommand
Dim DBCommand As OleDbDataAdapter
Dim DSPageData as New DataSet
```

Because we don't know how many questions are on the survey, we will need to iterate through all the controls on our Panel control:

```
Dim MyControl as Control
Dim MyDDL as DropDownList
```

We then connect to our database:

```
DBConn = New OleDbConnection("Provider=sqloledb;" _
    & "server=localhost;" _
    & "Initial Catalog=INETC3;" _
    & "User Id=sa;" _
    & "Password=yourpassword;")
```

Our Command object will use this Connection object:

```
DBInsert.Connection = DBConn
DBInsert.Connection.Open
```

Next, we enter a loop that will iterate through all the controls on our Panel:

```
For Each MyControl in pnlQuestions.Controls
```

We then check to see if the current control that we have iterated to is a DropDownList:

```
If MyControl.GetType().FullName = _
    "System.Web.UI.WebControls.DropDownList" Then
```

If it is, we assign it to our temporary DropDownList control:

```
MyDDL = MyControl
```

We then add the visitor's response to that question to our SurveyResponses table. Note that the ID of the question comes from the name of the DropDownList:

```
DBInsert.CommandText = "Insert Into SurveyResponses " _
    & "(SurveyQuestionID, SurveyResponse) " _
    & "values (" _
    & Mid(MyDDL.ID, 2) & ", " _
    & "'" _
    & Replace(MyDDL.SelectedItem.Text, "'", "''") _
    & "')"
DBInsert.ExecuteNonQuery()
```

We then move on to process the next control:

```
Next
```

Next, we need to retrieve the response text for the visitor,

```
DBCommand = New OleDbDataAdapter _
    ("Select SurveyResponse " _
    & "From Surveys Where SurveyID = " _
    & Application("SurveyID"), DBConn)
DBCommand.Fill(DSPageData, _
    "SurveyInfo")
```

which is placed into our message Label:

```
lblMessage.Text = DSPageData.Tables("SurveyInfo"). _
    Rows(0).Item("SurveyResponse")
```

Because the visitor has completed the survey, we can hide the questions Panel

```
pnlQuestions.Visible = False
```

as well as the Button control:

```
butOK.Visible = False
```

Survey Says ASP.NET Page

Survey_Says.aspx

The Survey Says page displays the results of the survey. At the top of the page, we declare the same compiler directives:

```
<%@ Page Language=VB Debug=true %>
<%@ Import Namespace="System.Data" %>
<%@ Import Namespace="System.Data.OLEDB" %>
```

Within the body of the page, we declare two Label controls. The first displays the title of the survey:

```
<asp:Label
    id="lblTitle"
    BorderWidth="7px"
    BorderStyle=7
    Width="90%"
    Font-Size="25pt"
    Font-Name="Arial"
    runat="server"
/>
```

The other label displays a description of the page's content:

```
<asp:Label
    id="lblMessage"
    Font-Bold="True"
    runat="server"
    Text="The responses made for this survey are below."
/>
```

The only other control on the page is a Panel control that will contain the results of the survey:

```
<asp:Panel
    id="pnlQuestions"
    Width="90%"
    runat="server"
>
</asp:Panel>
```

The only code block on the page fires when the page is loaded

```
Sub Page_Load(ByVal Sender as Object, ByVal E as EventArgs)
    Dim DBConn as OleDbConnection
    Dim DBCommand As OleDbDataAdapter
    Dim DSPageData as New DataSet
    Dim I as Integer
    Dim J as Integer
    Dim TempID as String
    Application("SurveyID") = 1
    DBConn = New OleDbConnection("Provider=sqloledb;" _
        & "server=localhost;" _
```

```
    & "Initial Catalog=INETC3;" _
    & "User Id=sa;" _
    & "Password=yourpassword;")
DBCommand = New OleDbDataAdapter _
    ("Select SurveyName " _
    & "From Surveys Where SurveyID = " _
    & Application("SurveyID"), DBConn)
DBCommand.Fill(DSPageData, _
    "SurveyInfo")
lblTitle.Text = "<center>" _
    & DSPageData.Tables("SurveyInfo"). _
    Rows(0).Item("SurveyName") & "</center>"
DBCommand = New OleDbDataAdapter _
    ("Select SurveyQuestionID, SurveyQuestionShort " _
    & "From SurveyQuestions Where SurveyID = " _
    & Application("SurveyID"), DBConn)
DBCommand.Fill(DSPageData, _
    "SurveyQuestions")
For I = 0 to DSPageData.Tables("SurveyQuestions"). _
    Rows.Count - 1
    Dim lcHTML = New LiteralControl
    lcHTML.Text =  "<b>" _
    & DSPageData.Tables("SurveyQuestions"). _
    Rows(I).Item("SurveyQuestionShort") & "</b><br>"
    pnlQuestions.Controls.Add(lcHTML)
    TempID = DSPageData.Tables("SurveyQuestions"). _
    Rows(I).Item("SurveyQuestionID")
    DBCommand = New OleDbDataAdapter _
        ("Select SurveyResponse, " _
        & "Count(SurveyResponseID) as TheCount " _
        & "From SurveyResponses Where SurveyQuestionID = " _
        & TempID & " Group By SurveyResponse " _
        & "Order By Count(SurveyResponseID) DESC" _
        , DBConn)
    DBCommand.Fill(DSPageData, _
        TempID)
    For J = 0 to DSPageData.Tables(TempID). _
        Rows.Count - 1
        Dim lcHTML2 = New LiteralControl
        lcHTML2.Text =  DSPageData.Tables(TempID). _
        Rows(J).Item("SurveyResponse") & ": " _
        & DSPageData.Tables(TempID). _
        Rows(J).Item("TheCount") & "<br>"
        pnlQuestions.Controls.Add(lcHTML2)
```

```
        Next
        Dim lcHTML3 = New LiteralControl
        lcHTML3.Text = "<br><br>"
        pnlQuestions.Controls.Add(lcHTML3)
    Next
End Sub
```

Within this procedure, we need data objects:

```
Dim DBConn as OleDbConnection
Dim DBCommand As OleDbDataAdapter
Dim DSPageData as New DataSet
```

We also need variables that allow us to loop through records within two nested loops:

```
Dim I as Integer
Dim J as Integer
```

One other variable, which will store the ID of the current question, is declared

```
Dim TempID as String
```

We then store the ID of the survey that is to be used for the current run of the page. You would change this value to show the results of a different survey:

```
Application("SurveyID") = 1
```

We start by connecting to our database

```
DBConn = New OleDbConnection("Provider=sqloledb;" _
    & "server=localhost;" _
    & "Initial Catalog=INETC3;" _
    & "User Id=sa;" _
    & "Password=yourpassword;")
```

and retrieving the name of the survey,

```
DBCommand = New OleDbDataAdapter _
    ("Select SurveyName " _
    & "From Surveys Where SurveyID = " _
    & Application("SurveyID"), DBConn)
DBCommand.Fill(DSPageData, _
    "SurveyInfo")
```

which is placed into the title Label control:

```
lblTitle.Text = "<center>" _
    & DSPageData.Tables("SurveyInfo"). _
    Rows(0).Item("SurveyName") & "</center>"
```

Next, we need to retrieve all the questions for the survey:

```
DBCommand = New OleDbDataAdapter _
    ("Select SurveyQuestionID, SurveyQuestionShort " _
    & "From SurveyQuestions Where SurveyID = " _
    & Application("SurveyID"), DBConn)
DBCommand.Fill(DSPageData, _
    "SurveyQuestions")
```

We then enter our outer loop that will allow us to process each of the questions:

```
For I = 0 to DSPageData.Tables("SurveyQuestions"). _
    Rows.Count - 1
```

The text of each question is placed into a LiteralControl object,

```
Dim lcHTML = New LiteralControl
lcHTML.Text =  "<b>" _
    & DSPageData.Tables("SurveyQuestions"). _
    Rows(I).Item("SurveyQuestionShort") & "</b><br>"
```

which is then added to our Panel control:

```
pnlQuestions.Controls.Add(lcHTML)
```

Next, we store the ID of the current question into our temporary variable:

```
TempID = DSPageData.Tables("SurveyQuestions"). _
    Rows(I).Item("SurveyQuestionID")
```

We retrieve all the responses to the current question. Note that we group them together so that we have a count of how many times each response was selected

```
DBCommand = New OleDbDataAdapter _
    ("Select SurveyResponse, " _
    & "Count(SurveyResponseID) as TheCount " _
    & "From SurveyResponses Where SurveyQuestionID = " _
```

```
    & TempID & " Group By SurveyResponse " _
    & "Order By Count(SurveyResponseID) DESC" _
    , DBConn)
```

We next place that into our DataSet object:

```
DBCommand.Fill(DSPageData, _
    TempID)
```

We then enter our inner loop so that we can process each of the response results:

```
For J = 0 to DSPageData.Tables(TempID). _
    Rows.Count - 1
```

The text of the response and the number of times it was selected are placed into a LiteralControl,

```
Dim lcHTML2 = New LiteralControl
lcHTML2.Text =  DSPageData.Tables(TempID). _
    Rows(J).Item("SurveyResponse") & ": " _
    & DSPageData.Tables(TempID). _
    Rows(J).Item("TheCount") & "<br>"
```

which is then appended to our Panel control

```
pnlQuestions.Controls.Add(lcHTML2)
```

before we move on to process the next response:

```
Next
```

After processing each of the responses, we add HTML separator tags

```
Dim lcHTML3 = New LiteralControl
lcHTML3.Text = "<br><br>"
```

to our Panel control

```
pnlQuestions.Controls.Add(lcHTML3)
```

before we move on to the next question:

```
Next
```

Access Code Changes

C3Survey.mdb

If you wish to use this solution with Access instead of SQL Server, you should only need to change the connect string from the one that points to the SQL Server database

```
DBConn = New OleDbConnection("Provider=sqloledb;" _
    & "server=localhost;" _
    & "Initial Catalog=INETC3;" _
    & "User Id=sa;" _
    & "Password=yourpassword;")
```

to one that points to your Access database:

```
DBConn = New OleDbConnection("PROVIDER=Microsoft.Jet.OLEDB.4.0;" _
    & "DATA SOURCE=" _
    & Server.MapPath("/INetBook/C3/Survey/" _
    & "Access/C3Survey.mdb;"))
```

Request for More Information Tool

One of the services you frequently must provide on your Web site is a way for your customers to request additional information regarding a topic. In this section, we will look at a page that provides that functionality. The Request for More Information tool uses the following files, which can be found on the CD-ROM:

- **Index.aspx** Request for More Information ASP.NET page
- **C3MoreInfo.sql** SQL Server table creation script
- **MoreInfoCategories.txt** Data for the MoreInfoCategories table
- **C3MoreInfo.mdb** Request for More Information Access database with data

Sample Usage

When the visitor first enters this page, they see what is displayed in Figure 3-6.

The first thing the visitor does is to select a topic. The topic list comes from a table in the database. Invisible to the visitor is the e-mail address that goes with the topic.

The visitor next enters their personal information. Note that they must enter something in the e-mail address field because of a RequiredFieldValidator control.

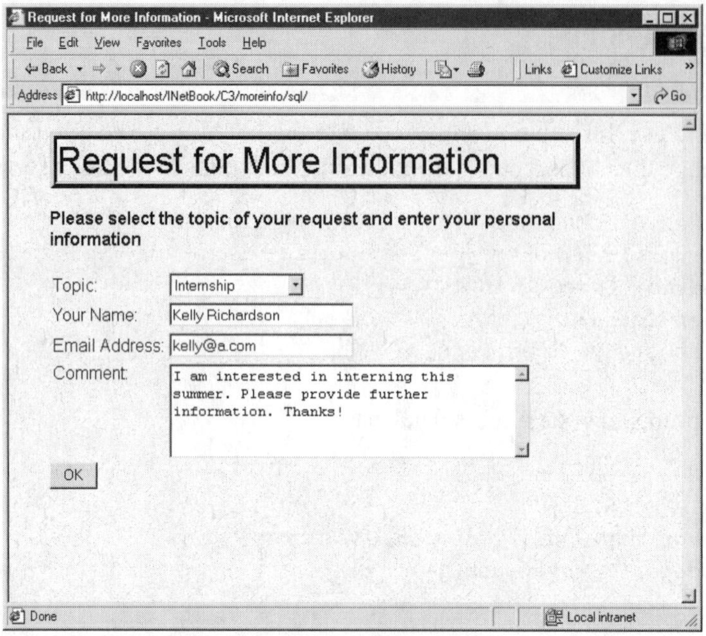

Figure 3-6 *Request for More Information page*

When the visitor clicks OK, their request is submitted and they see the page displayed in Figure 3-7.

The way the tool works is that an e-mail address is associated with each of the request categories. Therefore, each category or topic has a person who is responsible for filling the requests made by visitors. When the visitor clicks OK, that person receives an e-mail message such as the one displayed in Figure 3-8.

Note that the e-mail comes through as from the visitor to the page. Therefore, the person responding to the request could simply reply to this e-mail message to answer the request.

Request for More Information Database Component

C3MoreInfo.sql

For the Request for More Information tool to work, a single table is required. That table stores the information on the More Information categories. In this section, we will review the fields in that table.

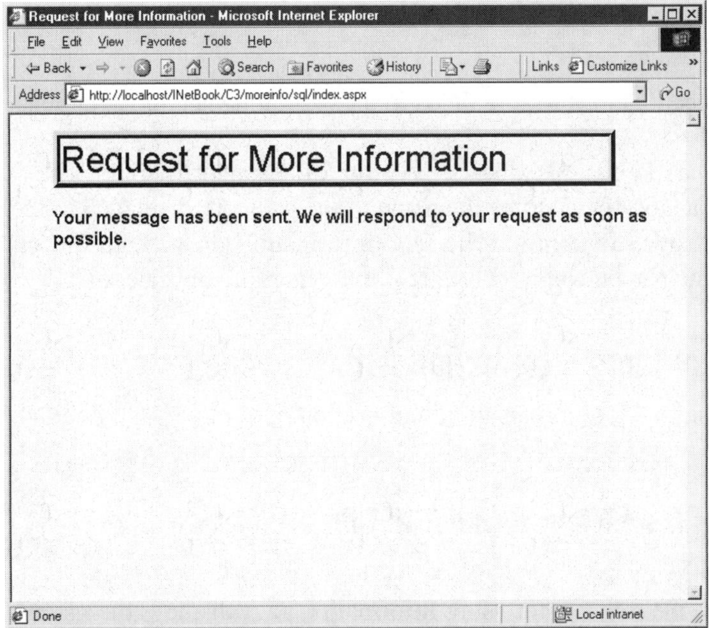

Figure 3-7 *Response displayed on Request for More Information page*

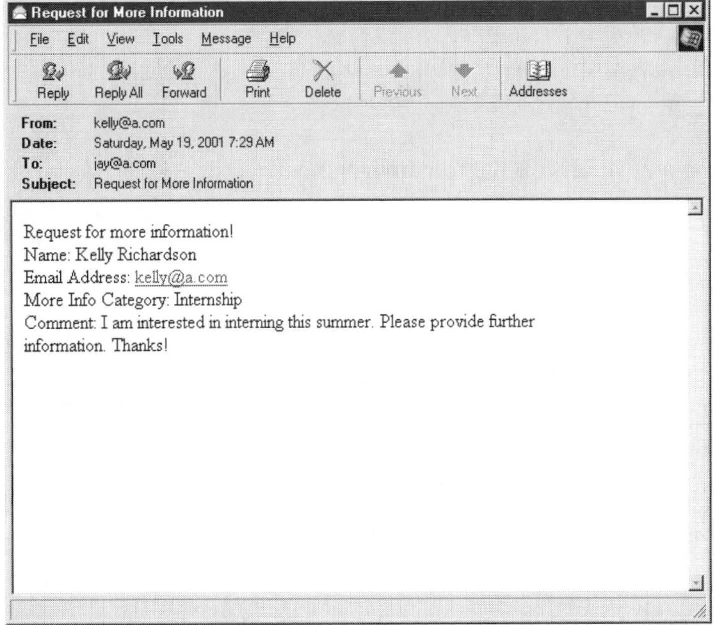

Figure 3-8 *E-mail sent by the Request for More Information page*

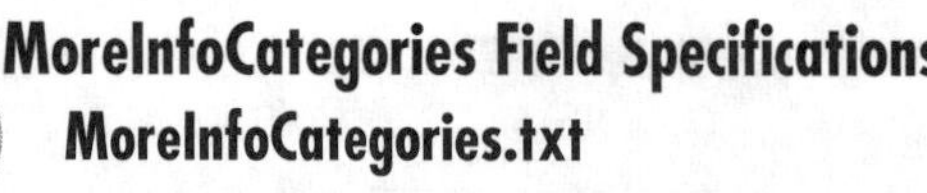

MoreInfoCategories Field Specifications

MoreInfoCategories.txt

The field specifications for the fields in the MoreInfoCategories table are displayed in Table 3-5.

The primary key in this table is the MoreInfoCategoryID field. The MoreInfoCategory field stores the name of the category displayed to the visitor in the DropDownList control. The MoreInfoEmailAddress field stores the e-mail address of the person who receives requests regarding the category.

Request for More Information ASP.NET Code

The Request for More Information tool is composed of a single ASP.NET page. In this section, we will review the controls and code on that page.

Request for More Information ASP.NET Page

Index.aspx

The code on the Request for More Information page displays the list of categories to the visitor and processes their request.

At the top of the page, four compiler directives are declared.

```
<%@ Page Language=VB Debug=true %>
<%@ Import Namespace="System.Data" %>
<%@ Import Namespace="System.Data.OLEDB" %>
<%@ Import Namespace="System.Web.Mail" %>
```

The first directive sets up the run environment:

```
<%@ Page Language=VB Debug=true %>
```

Field Name	Field Type	Notes
MoreInfoCategoryID	int	Primary Key, Identity Column
MoreInfoCategory	varchar	Length = 50
MoreInfoEmailAddress	varchar	Length = 100

Table 3-5 *MoreInfoCategories Field Specifications*

The next two are required so that we can retrieve data from the database and display it on our page:

```
<%@ Import Namespace="System.Data" %>
<%@ Import Namespace="System.Data.OLEDB" %>
```

The other directive imports a library that allows us to send e-mail out through our code:

```
<%@ Import Namespace="System.Web.Mail" %>
```

Within the body of the page, we have two Label controls. The first displays the title of the page:

```
<asp:Label
    id="lblTitle"
    BorderWidth="7px"
    BorderStyle=7
    Width="90%"
    Font-Size="25pt"
    Font-Name="Arial"
    Text="Request for More Information"
    runat="server"
/>
```

The other displays the instructions and response text after the form has been submitted

```
<asp:Label
    id="lblMessage"
    Font-Bold="True"
    Text="Please select the topic of your request and
    enter your personal information"
    runat="server"
/>
```

The other controls on the page are placed on a Panel control to make it easier for us to toggle their visibility:

```
<asp:Panel
    id="pnlRequest"
    Width="90%"
    runat="server"
>
```

The first control on the Panel is a DropDownList that displays the More Information categories:

```
<asp:dropdownlist
    id="ddlTopics"
    runat=server
    DataTextField="MoreInfoCategory"
    DataValueField="MoreInfoEmailAddress"
>
```

Note that the visitor sees the name of the category:

```
DataTextField="MoreInfoCategory"
```

But in code, we can also access the e-mail address for the category:

```
DataValueField="MoreInfoEmailAddress"
```

The next control is a TextBox that the visitor places their name into:

```
<asp:TextBox
    id="txtName"
    Columns="25"
    MaxLength="100"
    runat=server
/>
```

That is followed by a TextBox control for the visitor's e-mail address:

```
<asp:TextBox
    id="txtEmailAddress"
    Columns="25"
    MaxLength="100"
    runat=server
/>
```

This address is a required field, because this RequiredFieldValidator is linked to it:

```
<asp:RequiredFieldValidator
    id="rfvEmailAddress"
    ControlToValidate="txtEmailAddress"
    Display="Dynamic"
    Font-Name="Arial"
    Font-Size="10pt"
```

```
    runat=server>
    Email Address is Required!
</asp:RequiredFieldValidator>
```

Next, we have another TextBox where the visitor can add any comments:

```
<asp:TextBox
    id="txtComment"
    Columns="40"
    Rows="5"
    runat=server
    TextMode="MultiLine"
/>
```

Note that the TextBox is rendered as an HTML TextArea control because of the value in the TextMode property:

```
TextMode="MultiLine"
```

The only other control on the page is a button that fires an event when clicked, which processes the visitor's More Information request:

```
<asp:button
    id="butOK"
    text="  OK  "
    Type="Submit"
    OnClick="SubmitBtn_Click"
    runat="server"
/>
```

The code on the page is contained within two code blocks. The first runs when the page is loaded. It populates the DropDownList.

```
Sub Page_Load(ByVal Sender as Object, ByVal E as EventArgs)
    if Not IsPostBack Then
        Dim DBConn as OleDbConnection
        Dim DBCommand As OleDbDataAdapter
        Dim DSPageData as New DataSet
        DBConn = New OleDbConnection("Provider=sqloledb;" _
            & "server=localhost;" _
            & "Initial Catalog=INETC3;" _
            & "User Id=sa;" _
            & "Password=yourpassword;")
```

```
        DBCommand = New OleDbDataAdapter _
            ("Select MoreInfoCategory, MoreInfoEmailAddress " _
            & "From MoreInfoCategories " _
            & "Order By MoreInfoCategory", DBConn)
        DBCommand.Fill(DSPageData, _
            "Categories")
        ddlTopics.DataSource = _
            DSPageData.Tables("Categories").DefaultView
        ddlTopics.DataBind()
    End If
End Sub
```

We only want to populate the DropDownList when the page is first loaded

```
if Not IsPostBack Then
```

If that is the case, we need data objects to connect to the database and retrieve data:

```
Dim DBConn as OleDbConnection
Dim DBCommand As OleDbDataAdapter
Dim DSPageData as New DataSet
```

We start by making the connection to our database:

```
DBConn = New OleDbConnection("Provider=sqloledb;" _
    & "server=localhost;" _
    & "Initial Catalog=INETC3;" _
    & "User Id=sa;" _
    & "Password=yourpassword;")
```

We place text into our Data Adapter object to retrieve the category information,

```
DBCommand = New OleDbDataAdapter _
    ("Select MoreInfoCategory, MoreInfoEmailAddress " _
    & "From MoreInfoCategories " _
    & "Order By MoreInfoCategory", DBConn)
```

which is retrieved into our DataSet object:

```
DBCommand.Fill(DSPageData, _
    "Categories")
```

We then bind our DropDownList to that DataSet object:

```
ddlTopics.DataSource = _
    DSPageData.Tables("Categories").DefaultView
ddlTopics.DataBind()
```

The other procedure fires when the visitor clicks OK. It sends an e-mail message out to the person responsible for the request made by the visitor:

```
Sub SubmitBtn_Click(Sender As Object, E As EventArgs)
    Dim TheMessage as String
    Dim TheMailMessage as New MailMessage
    Dim TheMailConnection as New SmtpMail
    TheMessage = "Request for more information! "  & chr(13) _
        & "Name: " & txtName.Text & chr(13) _
        & "Email Address: " & txtEmailAddress.Text & chr(13) _
        & "More Info Category: " & ddlTopics.SelectedItem.Text _
         & chr(13) _
        & "Comment: " & txtComment.Text
    TheMailMessage.From = txtEmailAddress.Text
    TheMailMessage.To = ddlTopics.SelectedItem.Value
    TheMailMessage.Subject = "Request for More Information"
    TheMailMessage.Body = TheMessage
    TheMailConnection.Send(TheMailMessage)
    pnlRequest.Visible = False
    lblMessage.Text = "Your message has been sent. " _
        & "We will respond to your request as soon as possible."
End Sub
```

In this procedure, we need a few temporary variables. The first will store the text of our message:

```
Dim TheMessage as String
```

The next creates an Email object:

```
Dim TheMailMessage as New MailMessage
```

And the other allows us to send that Email object:

```
Dim TheMailConnection as New SmtpMail
```

We start by creating the text of the message, which is the combination of static text and the data selected or entered by the visitor on the page. Note the use of the Chr() function. That function, with the parameter 13, creates a new line within our e-mail message so that it is more readable:

```
TheMessage = "Request for more information! "  & chr(13) _
    & "Name: " & txtName.Text & chr(13) _
    & "Email Address: " & txtEmailAddress.Text & chr(13) _
    & "More Info Category: " & ddlTopics.SelectedItem.Text _
    & chr(13) _
    & "Comment: " & txtComment.Text
```

The message will be sent as if it is from the person making the request:

```
TheMailMessage.From = txtEmailAddress.Text
```

It is sent to the employee responsible for the category selected by the visitor:

```
TheMailMessage.To = ddlTopics.SelectedItem.Value
```

We place this text into the subject line of the message

```
TheMailMessage.Subject = "Request for More Information"
```

and use our temporary string variable as the text of the message:

```
TheMailMessage.Body = TheMessage
```

Our message is then sent

```
TheMailConnection.Send(TheMailMessage)
```

We then hide the Panel control that contains all the form elements from the visitor

```
pnlRequest.Visible = False
```

and present this acknowledgment message to the visitor:

```
lblMessage.Text = "Your message has been sent. " _
    & "We will respond to your request as soon as possible."
```

Access Code Changes

C3MoreInfo.mdb

If you wish to use this solution with Access instead of SQL Server, you should only need to change the connect string from the one that points to the SQL Server database

```
DBConn = New OleDbConnection("Provider=sqloledb;" _
    & "server=localhost;" _
    & "Initial Catalog=INETC3;" _
    & "User Id=sa;" _
    & "Password=yourpassword;")
```

to one that points to your Access database:

```
DBConn = New OleDbConnection("PROVIDER=Microsoft.Jet.OLEDB.4.0;" _
    & "DATA SOURCE=" _
    & Server.MapPath("/INetBook/C3/MoreInfo/" _
    & "Access/C3MoreInfo.mdb;"))
```

No other code changes should be necessary.

Store Locator Tool

The third tool we will review in this chapter is the Store Locator tool. This tool provides a simple way for your visitors to find the locations of your stores based on the ZIP code. The following files on the CD-ROM are associated with the Store Locator tool:

- **Index.aspx** Store Locator ASP.NET page
- **C3StoreLocator.sql** SQL Server table creation script
- **StoreLocations.txt** Data for the StoreLocations table
- **C3StoreLocator.mdb** Store Locator Access database with data

As you review this tool, note the use of the SelectedIndexChanged event that fires when the visitor changes the selection in the DropDownList, and the Sort event that fires when the visitor clicks a column in the DataGrid.

Sample Usage

When the visitor first enters this one-page tool, they see the view of the page displayed in Figure 3-9.

The visitor is presented with a sorted, distinct list of all the ZIP codes where you have stores, which comes from a database table. The visitor then selects the desired ZIP code and sees something like the page displayed in Figure 3-10.

First note that the visitor did not have to click a button to have the DataGrid appear. That is because code is supplied that runs when the visitor changes the DropDownList selection.

Within the DataGrid, the visitor sees the name, address, and directions to each store that is in the ZIP code they selected. Notice that the column headers are links. When the visitor clicks one of these links, the data is sorted by the field that they selected. For example, take a look at Figure 3-11.

Here the visitor has clicked the Address field, so now the records are sorted by that field.

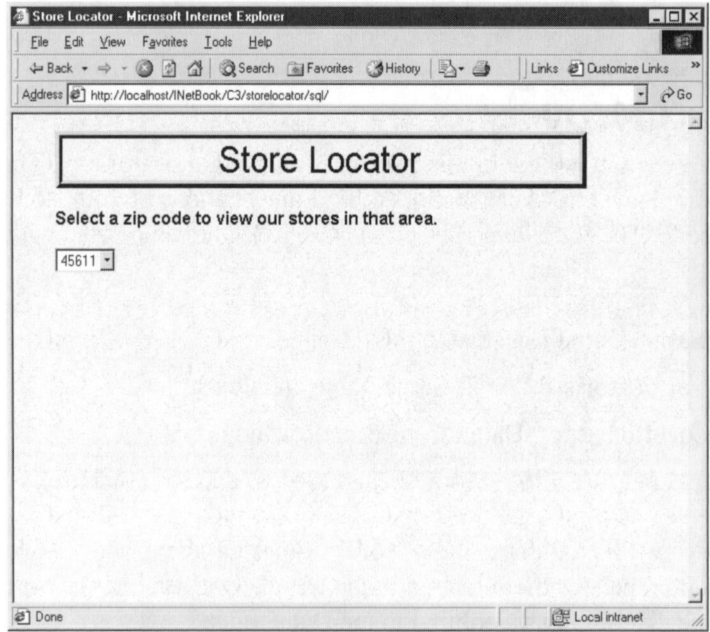

Figure 3-9 *Initial view of the Store Locator page*

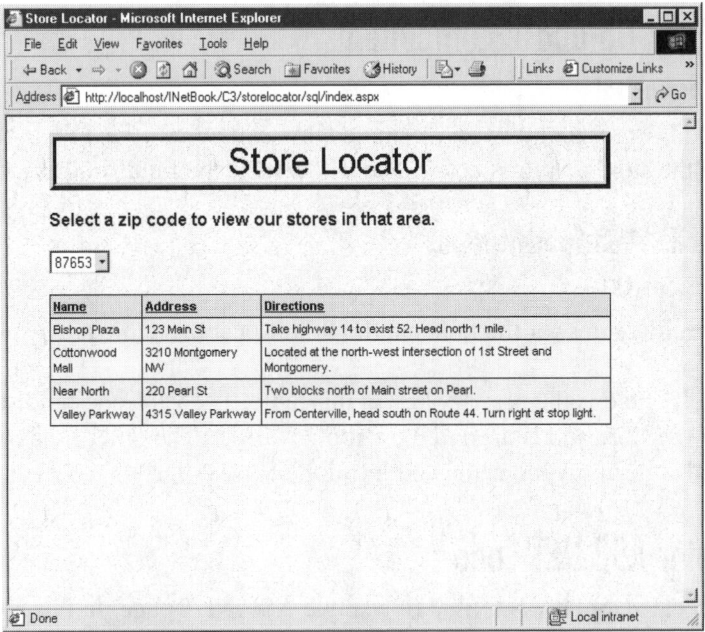

Figure 3-10 *Store Locator page with stores listed*

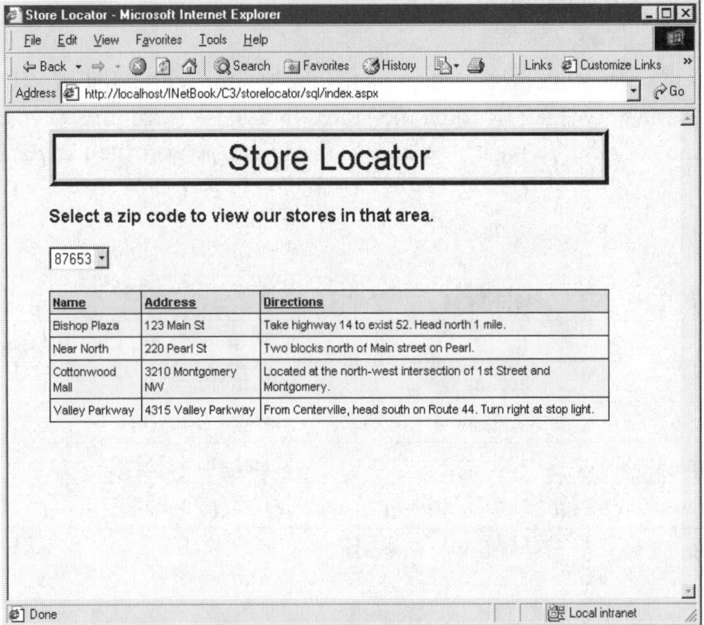

Figure 3-11 *Sorted data on the Store Locator page*

Store Locator Database Component

C3StoreLocator.sql

For the Store Locator tool to work, a single table is required. That table stores the locations of the stores. In this section, we will review the fields in that table.

StoreLocations Field Specifications

StoreLocations.txt

The field specifications for the fields in the StoreLocations table are displayed in Table 3-6.

The StoreID field is the primary key in this table. The ZipCode field stores the ZIP code of the store and is used in the DropDownList. The other fields appear in the DataGrid and supply the name and location of the store.

StoreLocator ASP.NET Code

The Store Locator tool is composed of a single ASP.NET page. In this section, we will review the controls and code on that page.

Store Locator ASP.NET Page

Index.aspx

The code on the Store Locator page presents the visitor with a list of ZIP codes. When the visitor selects a ZIP code, the stores in that area are presented in a DataGrid. The code in the page also allows the visitor to sort the DataGrid.

Field Name	Field Type	Notes
StoreID	int	Primary Key, Identity Column
ZipCode	varchar	Length = 50
FriendlyName	varchar	Length = 100
StoreAddress	varchar	Length = 150
StoreDirections	varchar	Length = 255

Table 3-6 *StoreLocations Field Specifications*

At the top of the page, we define three compiler directives, which set up the run environment and import needed data libraries:

```
<%@ Page Language=VB Debug=true %>
<%@ Import Namespace="System.Data" %>
<%@ Import Namespace="System.Data.OLEDB" %>
```

Within the body of the page, we define two Label controls. The first displays the title of the page:

```
<asp:Label
    id="lblTitle"
    BorderWidth="7px"
    BorderStyle=7
    Width="90%"
    Font-Size="25pt"
    Font-Name="Arial"
    Text="<center>Store Locator</center>"
    runat="server"
/>
```

The other displays instructions on the page:

```
<asp:Label
    id="lblMessage"
    Font-Bold="True"
    Text="Select a zip code to view our stores in that area."
    runat="server"
/>
```

The next control on the page is a DropDownList, which displays the ZIP codes to the visitor:

```
<asp:dropdownlist
    id="ddlZipCode"
    runat=server
    DataTextField="ZipCode"
    AutoPostBack="True"
    OnSelectedIndexChanged="ddl_Change"
>
</asp:dropdownlist>
```

Note that AutoPostBack is set to True:

```
AutoPostBack="True"
```

This is required so that their selection will be posted as soon as they change it without requiring them to click a button. When the visitor does change the selection, the procedure noted in this property fires

```
OnSelectedIndexChanged="ddl_Change"
```

The only other control on the page is a DataGrid that displays the stores corresponding to the ZIP code selected by the visitor:

```
<asp:DataGrid
    id="dgStores"
    Width="90%"
    BackColor="beige"
    AlternatingItemStyle-BackColor="cornsilk"
    BorderColor="black"
    ShowFooter="false"
    CellPadding=3
    CellSpacing="0"
    Font-Name="Arial"
    Font-Size="8pt"
    ForeColor="Black"
    HeaderStyle-BackColor="burlywood"
    HeaderStyle-Font-Bold="True"
    AllowSorting="true"
    OnSortCommand="Sort_Grid"
    runat="server">
</asp:DataGrid>
```

Note that we are allowing Sort,

```
AllowSorting="true"
```

which turns the column headers into links. And this procedure fires when they click one of those links:

```
OnSortCommand="Sort_Grid"
```

The code of the page is contained within three events. The first event fires when the page loads. It populates the DropDownList.

```
Sub Page_Load(ByVal Sender as Object, ByVal E as EventArgs)
    if Not IsPostBack Then
        Dim DBConn as OleDbConnection
        Dim DBCommand As OleDbDataAdapter
        Dim DSPageData as New DataSet
        DBConn = New OleDbConnection("Provider=sqloledb;" _
            & "server=localhost;" _
            & "Initial Catalog=INETC3;" _
            & "User Id=sa;" _
            & "Password=yourpassword;")
        DBCommand = New OleDbDataAdapter _
            ("Select Distinct ZipCode " _
            & "From StoreLocations " _
            & "Order By ZipCode", DBConn)
        DBCommand.Fill(DSPageData, _
            "ZipCodes")
        ddlZipCode.DataSource = _
            DSPageData.Tables("ZipCodes").DefaultView
        ddlZipCode.DataBind()
    End If
End Sub
```

We only want this code to run the first time that the page is loaded

```
if Not IsPostBack Then
```

If that is the case, we will need data objects:

```
Dim DBConn as OleDbConnection
Dim DBCommand As OleDbDataAdapter
Dim DSPageData as New DataSet
```

We start by connecting to our database:

```
DBConn = New OleDbConnection("Provider=sqloledb;" _
    & "server=localhost;" _
    & "Initial Catalog=INETC3;" _
    & "User Id=sa;" _
    & "Password=yourpassword;")
```

Next, we retrieve a distinct list of all the ZIP codes in our StoreLocations table:

```
DBCommand = New OleDbDataAdapter _
    ("Select Distinct ZipCode " _
    & "From StoreLocations " _
    & "Order By ZipCode", DBConn)
```

We then place that data into a table called ZipCodes in our DataSet object:

```
DBCommand.Fill(DSPageData, _
    "ZipCodes")
```

We then bind the DropDownList control to that DataSet table:

```
ddlZipCode.DataSource = _
    DSPageData.Tables("ZipCodes").DefaultView
ddlZipCode.DataBind()
```

The next procedure fires when the visitor changes the selection in the DropDownList. It populates the DataGrid according to the ZIP code selected in the DropDownList by the visitor.

```
Sub ddl_Change(Sender As Object, E As EventArgs)
        Dim DBConn as OleDbConnection
        Dim DBCommand As OleDbDataAdapter
        Dim DSPageData as New DataSet
        DBConn = New OleDbConnection("Provider=sqloledb;" _
            & "server=localhost;" _
            & "Initial Catalog=INETC3;" _
            & "User Id=sa;" _
            & "Password=yourpassword;")
        DBCommand = New OleDbDataAdapter _
            ("Select FriendlyName as [Name], " _
            & "StoreAddress as [Address], " _
            & "StoreDirections as [Directions] " _
            & "From StoreLocations Where " _
            & "ZipCode = '" & ddlZipCode.SelectedItem.Text _
            & "' Order By FriendlyName " _
            , DBConn)
        DBCommand.Fill(DSPageData, _
            "Stores")
        dgStores.DataSource = _
            DSPageData.Tables("Stores").DefaultView
        dgStores.DataBind()
End Sub
```

Within this procedure, we will need data objects:

```
Dim DBConn as OleDbConnection
Dim DBCommand As OleDbDataAdapter
Dim DSPageData as New DataSet
```

We start by connecting to the database:

```
DBConn = New OleDbConnection("Provider=sqloledb;" _
    & "server=localhost;" _
    & "Initial Catalog=INETC3;" _
    & "User Id=sa;" _
    & "Password=yourpassword;")
```

We then retrieve all the locations of all the stores in the ZIP code selected by the visitor

```
DBCommand = New OleDbDataAdapter _
    ("Select FriendlyName as [Name], " _
    & "StoreAddress as [Address], " _
    & "StoreDirections as [Directions] " _
    & "From StoreLocations Where " _
    & "ZipCode = '" & ddlZipCode.SelectedItem.Text _
    & "' Order By FriendlyName " _
    , DBConn)
```

and place those matching records into our DataSet object,

```
DBCommand.Fill(DSPageData, _
    "Stores")
```

which the DataGrid is bound to:

```
dgStores.DataSource = _
    DSPageData.Tables("Stores").DefaultView
dgStores.DataBind()
```

The other procedure on this page fires when the visitor clicks one of the column headers in the DataGrid. It sorts the DataGrid according to the column clicked

```
Sub Sort_Grid(ByVal Sender as Object, _
    ByVal E as DataGridSortCommandEventArgs)
        Dim DBConn as OleDbConnection
        Dim DBCommand As OleDbDataAdapter
        Dim DSPageData as New DataSet
```

```
        Dim SortField as String
        If E.SortExpression.ToString() = "Name" Then
            SortField = "FriendlyName"
        ElseIf E.SortExpression.ToString() = "Address" Then
            SortField = "StoreAddress"
        Else
            SortField = "StoreDirections"
        End If
        DBConn = New OleDbConnection("Provider=sqloledb;" _
            & "server=localhost;" _
            & "Initial Catalog=INETC3;" _
            & "User Id=sa;" _
            & "Password=yourpassword;")
        DBCommand = New OleDbDataAdapter _
            ("Select FriendlyName as [Name], " _
            & "StoreAddress as [Address], " _
            & "StoreDirections as [Directions] " _
            & "From StoreLocations Where " _
            & "ZipCode = '" & ddlZipCode.SelectedItem.Text _
            & "' Order By " & SortField _
            , DBConn)
        DBCommand.Fill(DSPageData, _
            "Stores")
        dgStores.DataSource = _
            DSPageData.Tables("Stores").DefaultView
        dgStores.DataBind()
End Sub
```

Within this procedure, we will need data objects:

```
Dim DBConn as OleDbConnection
Dim DBCommand As OleDbDataAdapter
Dim DSPageData as New DataSet
```

We also need a variable to store the name of the field that we need to sort by:

```
Dim SortField as String
```

We retrieve the name of the column clicked by the visitor through the SortExpression object. Here we check to see if the visitor clicked the Name column:

```
If E.SortExpression.ToString() = "Name" Then
```

If that is the case, we need to sort by the FriendlyName field:

```
SortField = "FriendlyName"
```

Next, we check to see if they clicked the Address column:

```
ElseIf E.SortExpression.ToString() = "Address" Then
    SortField = "StoreAddress"
```

Otherwise, they must have clicked the Directions column:

```
Else
    SortField = "StoreDirections"
```

Next, we need to connect to the database:

```
DBConn = New OleDbConnection("Provider=sqloledb;" _
    & "server=localhost;" _
    & "Initial Catalog=INETC3;" _
    & "User Id=sa;" _
    & "Password=yourpassword;")
```

We then retrieve the matching stores for the DataGrid, but this time we sort by whatever field the visitor clicked

```
DBCommand = New OleDbDataAdapter _
    ("Select FriendlyName as [Name], " _
    & "StoreAddress as [Address], " _
    & "StoreDirections as [Directions] " _
    & "From StoreLocations Where " _
    & "ZipCode = '" & ddlZipCode.SelectedItem.Text _
    & "' Order By " & SortField _
    , DBConn)
```

That data is placed into our DataSet object,

```
DBCommand.Fill(DSPageData, _
    "Stores")
```

and we bind the DataGrid to the DataSet:

```
dgStores.DataSource = _
    DSPageData.Tables("Stores").DefaultView
dgStores.DataBind()
```

Access Code Changes

C3StoreLocator.mdb

If you wish to use this solution with Access instead of SQL Server, you should only need to change the connect string from the one that points to the SQL Server database

```
DBConn = New OleDbConnection("Provider=sqloledb;" _
    & "server=localhost;" _
    & "Initial Catalog=INETC3;" _
    & "User Id=sa;" _
    & "Password=yourpassword;")
```

to one that points to your Access database:

```
DBConn = New OleDbConnection("PROVIDER=Microsoft.Jet.OLEDB.4.0;" _
    & "DATA SOURCE=" _
    & Server.MapPath("/INetBook/C3/StoreLocator/" _
    & "Access/C3StoreLocator.mdb;"))
```

No other code changes should be necessary.

CHAPTER

4

Creating Interactive Intranet Applications

In this chapter, we will look at solutions that are designed for a company's intranet, meaning that they are meant for internal company use. But as you review these solutions, think about how you could modify them for use even on your Internet site.

First, we will look at the Voting Booth solution. This tool allows employees to vote on topics and view the current results of the votes.

Then we will review the simple Birthday page. This page provides an easy way for employees to acknowledge the passage of their coworker's birthday.

The third example we will review in this chapter is the Email Blast tool. This tool allows employees in your company to easily send an e-mail out to a group of your customers.

Voting Booth Tool

The Voting Booth tool allows employees to vote on specific information. The tool allows you to specify which group of individuals can view a specific question and vote on that question. It also makes sure that the employee does not vote on a question more than once. The tool can contain as many voting questions as you want, each with as many possible answers as can be chosen for the voting question.

Sample Usage

When the employee first enters the Voting Booth tool, they see the page displayed in Figure 4-1.

The Sign-In page requires that the employee enter their name and password. We need to ensure that the employee only sees the questions that they are allowed to see and that they only vote once on each issue.

Note that a RequiredFieldValidator control is used to ensure that the employee does enter a name and password. If the employee enters an invalid name or password, they see the message displayed in Figure 4-2.

Once the employee enters a correct name and password, they see the page displayed in Figure 4-3.

The employee is taken to the Voting Booth page. Here they see a list of questions that are available to any of the groups that they belong to. For example, some questions may be asked of everyone; others questions may just be asked of managers or maybe just of employees in a particular department. However, the list displayed to the visitor contains all the questions asked for any of the groups that the employee belongs to.

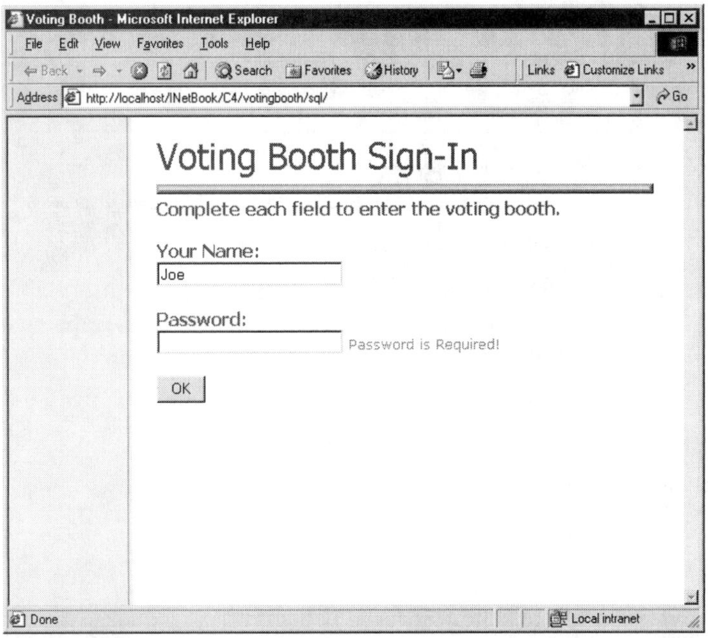

Figure 4-1 *Sign-In page*

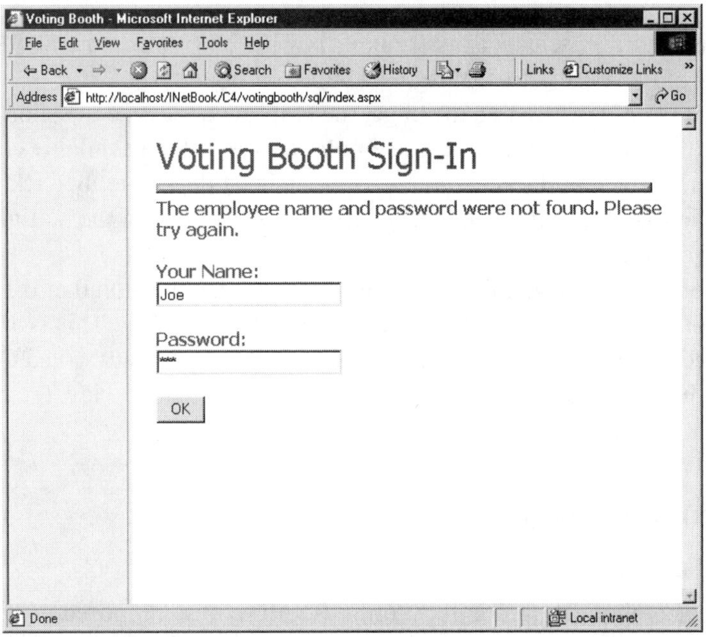

Figure 4-2 *Error message on Sign-In page*

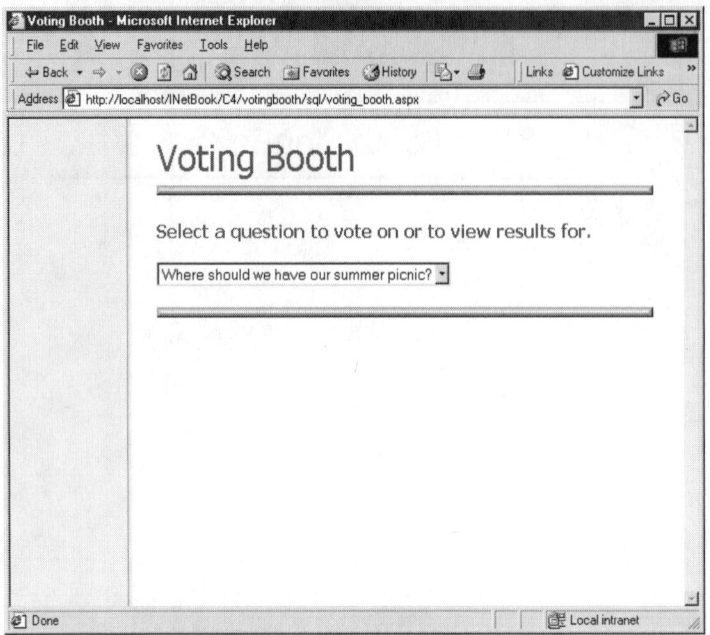

Figure 4-3 *Initial view of the Voting Booth page*

When the employee selects a question, if they haven't voted on that question, they see the view of the Voting Booth page displayed in Figure 4-4.

In the first DropDownList on the page, the employee sees the question that they selected. At the bottom of the page, the employee sees all the available choices for that question. They would select their answer and cast their vote by clicking OK. When they do that, the employee is taken to the results view of the Voting Booth page displayed in Figure 4-5.

In the top half of the page, the employee still sees the question that they selected, but in the bottom half, they see the current results of the voting. This is also what the employee sees when they select a question that they have already voted on, a feature that allows the employee to return to this page at a later date to view the current votes for this question.

Voting Booth Database Component

C4VotingBooth.sql

The database component used in the Voting Booth tool is composed of six interrelated tables. In this section of the chapter, we will review the relationships between the tables and the fields that they contain.

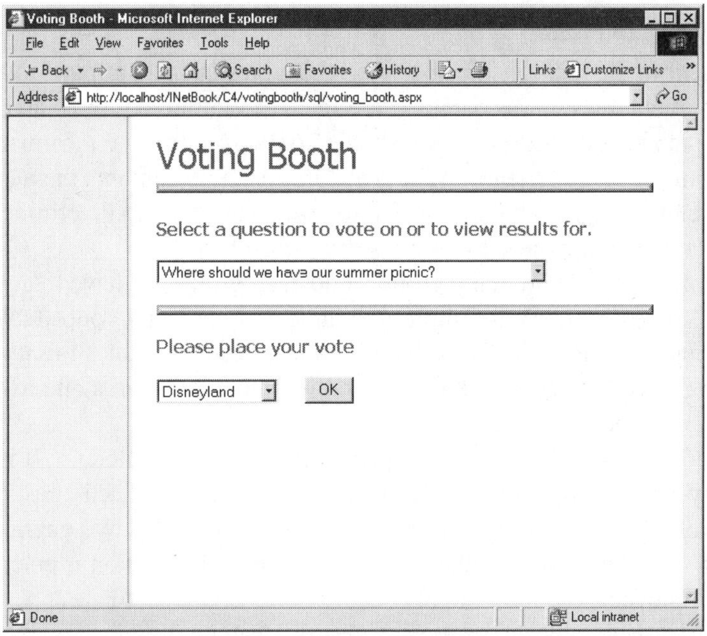

Figure 4-4 *Vote view of the Voting Booth page*

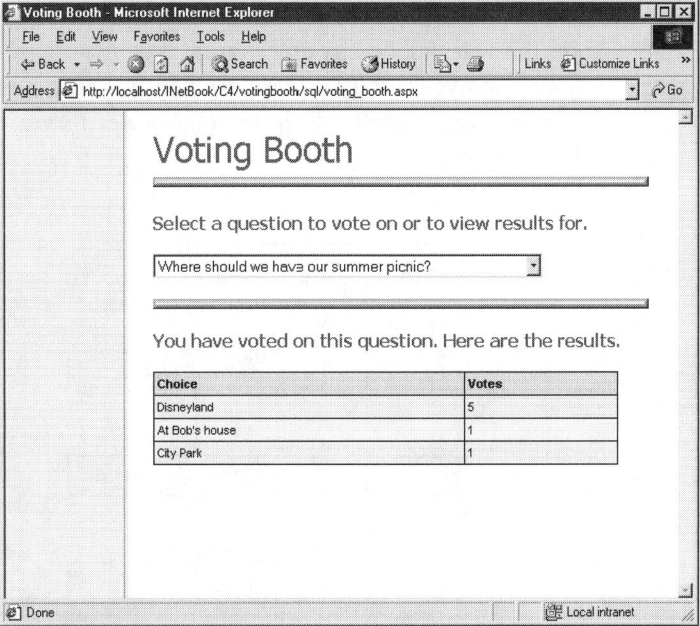

Figure 4-5 *Results view of the Voting Booth page*

Tables and Data Diagram

Figure 4-6 shows the relationships between the tables in the Voting Booth database.

Two top-level tables in this database are the VoteEmployees table and the VoteGroups table. The VoteEmployees table contains employee information used to sign the employee into the tool. The VoteGroups table contains the names of the groups that employees can belong to. These groups are used to determine the questions that the employee sees on the Voting Booth page.

Each employee can be in many groups, and each group can have many employees. Therefore, the VoteEmployees table and the VoteGroups table are in a many-to-many relationship. The table that links these two tables to satisfy their relationship is the VoteEmployeeInGroup table. That table is in a one-to-many relationship with the other two tables.

The VoteQuestions table stores the questions that can be voted on. It is in a one-to-many relationship with the VoteGroups table because each question can be answered by a single group of employees. The table is also in a one-to-many relationship with the VoteEmployees table because each question is entered by a specific employee.

The VoteAnswers table stores the answers that can be used in response to the vote questions. The table is in a one-to-many relationship with the VoteQuestions table because each question can have many answers, but each answer goes with a specific question.

The Votes table stores the votes placed by employees. It is in a one-to-many relationship with the VoteEmployees table because each employee can vote on many questions. It is also in a one-to-many relationship with the VoteAnswers table. Each answer can be used with many votes.

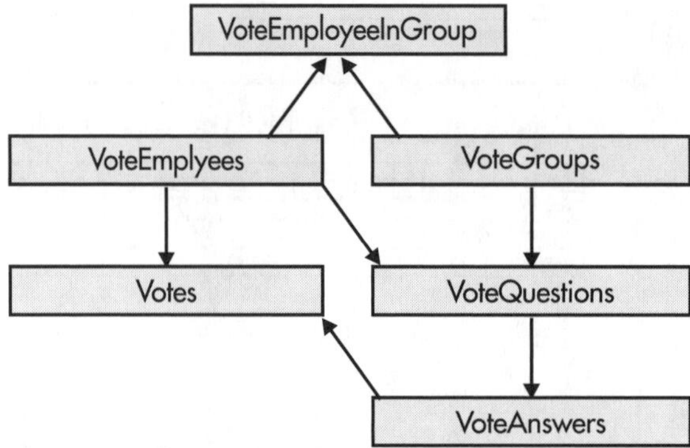

Figure 4-6 *Voting Booth data diagram*

Field Name	Field Type	Notes
EmployeeID	int	Primary Key, Identity Column
EmployeeName	varchar	Length = 100
Password	varchar	Length = 50
EmailAddress	varchar	Length = 100

Table 4-1 *VoteEmployees Field Specifications*

VoteEmployees Field Specifications

VoteEmployees.txt

The field specifications for the fields in the VoteEmployees table are displayed in Table 4-1.

The EmployeeID field is the primary key in this table. It is an identity column, so a value is automatically inserted into it when a new record is added. The rest of the fields store information about the employee.

VoteGroups Field Specifications

VoteGroups.txt

The field specifications for the fields in the VoteGroups table are displayed in Table 4-2.

The VoteGroupID field is the primary key in this table. The VoteGroup field stores the name of the group.

VoteEmployeeInGroup Field Specifications

VoteEmployeeInGroup.txt

The field specifications for the fields in the VoteEmployeeInGroup table are displayed in Table 4-3.

All the fields in this table are keys. The EmployeeInGroupID is the primary key. The EmployeeID field is a foreign key that links this table to the VoteEmployees

Field Name	Field Type	Notes
VoteGroupID	int	Primary Key, Identity Column
VoteGroup	varchar	Length = 50

Table 4-2 *VoteGroups Field Specifications*

Field Name	Field Type	Notes
EmployeeInGroupID	int	Primary Key, Identity Column
EmployeeID	int	Foreign Key
VoteGroupID	int	Foreign Key

Table 4-3 *VoteEmployeeInGroup Field Specifications*

table. The VoteGroupID field is another foreign key that links this table to the VoteGroups table.

VoteQuestions Field Specifications

VoteQuestions.txt

The field specifications for the fields in the VoteQuestions table are displayed in Table 4-4.

The QuestionID field is the primary key. The EmployeeID field links this table to the VoteEmployees table, and the VoteGroupID field links this table to the VoteGroups table. The other field, QuestionText, stores the text of the question as it appears to the employee in the DropDownList.

VoteAnswers Field Specifications

VoteAnswers.txt

The field specifications for the fields in the VoteAnswers table are displayed in Table 4-5.

In this table, the AnswerID field uniquely identifies each record. The QuestionID field links the answer to the VoteQuestions table. The AnswerText field stores the text of the answer as it is displayed in the DropDownList control.

Field Name	Field Type	Notes
QuestionID	int	Primary Key, Identity Column
EmployeeID	int	Foreign Key
VoteGroupID	int	Foreign Key
QuestionText	varchar	Length = 255

Table 4-4 *VoteQuestions Field Specifications*

Field Name	Field Type	Notes
AnswerID	int	Primary Key, Identity Column
QuestionID	int	Foreign Key
AnswerText	varchar	Length = 100

Table 4-5 *VoteAnswers Field Specifications*

Votes Field Specifications

Votes.txt

The field specifications for the fields in the Votes table are displayed in Table 4-6.

The VoteID in this table acts as the primary key. The QuestionID field links the table with the VoteQuestions table. The EmployeeID field links this table to the VoteEmployees table. The AnswerText field stores the text of the answer selected by the employee to the question.

Voting Booth ASP.NET Code

The Voting Booth tool is composed of two ASP.NET pages. These pages contain a variety of controls. In this section, we will review the controls and the code on these pages.

Sign-In ASP.NET Page

Index.aspx

The Sign-In page validates the employee's name and password before allowing them to enter the Voting Booth page. At the top of the page, we code three compiler directives:

```
<%@ Page Language=VB Debug=true %>
<%@ Import Namespace="System.Data" %>
<%@ Import Namespace="System.Data.OLEDB" %>
```

Field Name	Field Type	Notes
VoteID	int	Primary Key, Identity Column
QuestionID	int	Foreign Key
EmployeeID	int	Foreign Key
AnswerText	varchar	Length = 100

Table 4-6 *Votes Field Specifications*

The first control on the page is a Label control that displays the title of the page:

```
<asp:Label
    id="lblTitle"
    Font-Size="25pt"
    Font-Name="Tahoma"
    Text="Voting Booth Sign-In"
    runat="server"
/>
```

The next control is another label that displays instructions for the page and an error message if the employee does not enter a valid name and password:

```
<asp:Label
    id="lblMessage"
    Font-Size="12pt"
    Font-Name="Tahoma"
    Font-Bold="True"
    runat="server"
    Text="Complete each field to enter the voting booth."
/>
```

The next control on the page is a TextBox control that the employee uses to enter their name:

```
<asp:TextBox
    id="txtEmployeeName"
    Columns="25"
    MaxLength="100"
    runat=server
/>
```

That field is required because we link this RequiredFieldValidator to it:

```
<asp:RequiredFieldValidator
    id="rfvEmployeeName"
    ControlToValidate="txtEmployeeName"
    Display="Dynamic"
    Font-Name="Tahoma"
    Font-Size="10pt"
    runat=server>
    Your Name is Required!
</asp:RequiredFieldValidator>
```

The other TextBox control on the page allows the employee to enter their password:

```
<asp:TextBox
    id="txtPassword"
    Columns="25"
    MaxLength="50"
    runat=server
    TextMode="Password"
/>
```

That TextBox control is also required

```
<asp:RequiredFieldValidator
    id="rfvPassword"
    ControlToValidate="txtPassword"
    Display="Dynamic"
    Font-Name="Verdana"
    Font-Size="10pt"
    runat=server>
    Password is Required!
</asp:RequiredFieldValidator>
```

The only other control on the page is a Button control that the employee clicks when they want to submit their sign-in data:

```
<asp:button
    id="butOK"
    text="  OK  "
    Type="Submit"
    OnClick="SubmitBtn_Click"
    runat="server"
/>
```

The only code block on the page fires when that button is clicked.

```
Sub SubmitBtn_Click(Sender As Object, E As EventArgs)
    Dim DBConn as OleDbConnection
    Dim DBCommand As OleDbDataAdapter
    Dim DSPageData as New DataSet
    DBConn = New OleDbConnection("Provider=sqloledb;" _
        & "server=localhost;" _
        & "Initial Catalog=INETC4;" _
```

```
        & "User Id=sa;" _
        & "Password=yourpassword;")
    DBCommand = New OleDbDataAdapter _
        ("Select EmployeeID from " _
        & "VoteEmployees Where " _
        & "EmployeeName = '" _
        & Replace(txtEmployeeName.Text, "'", "''") _
        & "' and Password = '" _
        & Replace(txtPassword.Text, "'", "''") _
        & "'", DBConn)
    DBCommand.Fill(DSPageData, _
        "SignIn")
    If DSPageData.Tables("SignIn"). _
        Rows.Count = 0 Then
        lblMessage.Text = "The employee name and password " _
            & "were not found. Please try again."
    Else
        Session("EmployeeID") = DSPageData.Tables("SignIn"). _
            Rows(0).Item("EmployeeID")
        Response.Redirect("./voting_booth.aspx")
    End If
End Sub
```

The page requires that we connect to the database

```
Dim DBConn as OleDbConnection
```

and retrieve data:

```
Dim DBCommand As OleDbDataAdapter
Dim DSPageData as New DataSet
```

We start by connecting to our SQL Server database:

```
DBConn = New OleDbConnection("Provider=sqloledb;" _
    & "server=localhost;" _
    & "Initial Catalog=INETC4;" _
    & "User Id=sa;" _
    & "Password=yourpassword;")
```

We then attempt to retrieve the ID of the employee that matches the name and password they entered

```
DBCommand = New OleDbDataAdapter _
    ("Select EmployeeID from " _
    & "VoteEmployees Where " _
    & "EmployeeName = '" _
    & Replace(txtEmployeeName.Text, "'", "''") _
    & "' and Password = '" _
    & Replace(txtPassword.Text, "'", "''") _
    & "'", DBConn)
DBCommand.Fill(DSPageData, _
    "SignIn")
```

We then check to see if we found a matching record by looking at the number of records returned

```
If DSPageData.Tables("SignIn"). _
    Rows.Count = 0 Then
```

If the code flows here, it means the name and password were not found. In that case, we display this message:

```
lblMessage.Text = "The employee name and password " _
    & "were not found. Please try again."
```

Otherwise, we store the ID of the employee for retrieval on other pages

```
Session("EmployeeID") = DSPageData.Tables("SignIn"). _
    Rows(0).Item("EmployeeID")
```

and then we send the visitor to the Voting Booth page:

```
Response.Redirect("./voting_booth.aspx")
```

Voting Booth ASP.NET Page

Voting_Booth.aspx

The code on the Voting Booth page displays questions and answers, as well as the results of a question. The page uses Panel controls to control what elements of the page are displayed.

At the top of the page, we declare three compiler directives:

```
<%@ Page Language=VB Debug=true %>
<%@ Import Namespace="System.Data" %>
<%@ Import Namespace="System.Data.OLEDB" %>
```

The first tells the compiler that our code will be in Visual Basic and that we are in debug mode:

```
<%@ Page Language=VB Debug=true %>
```

The other two directives import libraries we need so that we can connect to our database and manipulate data:

```
<%@ Import Namespace="System.Data" %>
<%@ Import Namespace="System.Data.OLEDB" %>
```

Within the body of the page, we declare two Label controls. The first Label control displays the title of the page:

```
<asp:Label
    id="lblTitle"
    Font-Size="25pt"
    Font-Name="Tahoma"
    Text="Voting Booth"
    runat="server"
/>
```

The other Label control describes how to use the page:

```
<asp:Label
    id="lblMessage"
    Font-Size="12pt"
    Font-Name="Tahoma"
    Font-Bold="True"
    runat="server"
    Text="Select a question to vote on or to view results for."
/>
```

After that, we define a DropDownList that will display the text of the questions:

```
<asp:dropdownlist
    id="ddlQuestionID"
    runat=server
    DataTextField="QuestionText"
    DataValueField="QuestionID"
    AutoPostBack="True"
    OnSelectedIndexChanged="ddl_Change"
>
</asp:dropdownlist>
```

Note that the employee sees the text of the question,

```
DataTextField="QuestionText"
```

but in code we will be able to retrieve the ID of the question:

```
DataValueField="QuestionID"
```

When the employee changes the selection in this control, we automatically return the page so that we can process it

```
AutoPostBack="True"
```

through this event:

```
OnSelectedIndexChanged="ddl_Change"
```

Next, we define a Panel control that will contain the vote portion of the page. Note that it is initially invisible:

```
<asp:Panel
    id="pnlVote"
    runat="server"
    HorizontalAlign="Left"
    Visible="False"
>
```

Within that panel, we have another Label control that describes this section of the page:

```
<asp:Label
    id="lblMessageVote"
    Font-Size="12pt"
    Font-Name="Tahoma"
    Font-Bold="True"
    Text="Please place your vote"
    runat="server"
/>
```

Next, we define a DropDownList for the answers to the question:

```
<asp:dropdownlist
    id="ddlAnswers"
    runat=server
```

```
    DataTextField="AnswerText"
>
</asp:dropdownlist>
```

The other control on the panel is a button that the employee clicks to cast their vote:

```
<asp:button
    id="butOK"
    text="  OK  "
    Type="Submit"
    OnClick="SubmitBtn_Click"
    runat="server"
/>
```

The other Panel control on this page displays the results of a vote. Note that it, too, is initially invisible:

```
<asp:Panel
    id="pnlResults"
    runat="server"
    HorizontalAlign="Left"
    Visible="False"
>
```

Within this Panel control, we embed two controls. The first is a Label control that defines its contents:

```
<asp:Label
    id="lblMessageResults"
    Font-Size="12pt"
    Font-Name="Tahoma"
    Font-Bold="True"
    Text="You have voted on this question. Here are the results."
    runat="server"
/>
```

The other is a DataGrid that will display the current results of the vote for the current question after the employee has voted on it:

```
<asp:DataGrid
    id="dgResults"
    Width="90%"
```

```
    BackColor="beige"
    AlternatingItemStyle-BackColor="cornsilk"
    BorderColor="black"
    ShowFooter="false"
    CellPadding=3
    CellSpacing="0"
    Font-Name="Arial"
    Font-Size="8pt"
    ForeColor="Black"
    HeaderStyle-BackColor="burlywood"
    HeaderStyle-Font-Bold="True"
    runat="server">
</asp:DataGrid>
```

The code on the page is contained within three events. The first event fires when the page loads:

```
Sub Page_Load(ByVal Sender as Object, ByVal E as EventArgs)
    If Len(Session("EmployeeID")) = 0 Then
        Response.Redirect("./index.aspx")
    End If
    If Not IsPostBack Then
        Dim DBConn as OleDbConnection
        Dim DBCommand As OleDbDataAdapter
        Dim DSPageData as New DataSet
        DBConn = New OleDbConnection("Provider=sqloledb;" _
            & "server=localhost;" _
            & "Initial Catalog=INETC4;" _
            & "User Id=sa;" _
            & "Password=yourpassword;")
        DBCommand = New OleDbDataAdapter _
            ("select QuestionID, QuestionText " _
            & "from VoteQuestions Where VotingGroupID In " _
            & "(Select VoteGroupID from VoteEmployeeInGroup " _
            & "Where EmployeeID = " & Session("EmployeeID") _
            & ")", DBConn)
        DBCommand.Fill(DSPageData, _
            "Questions")
        ddlQuestionID.DataSource = _
            DSPageData.Tables("Questions").DefaultView
        ddlQuestionID.DataBind()
    End If
End Sub
```

The page should only be viewed if the employee has signed in:

```
If Len(Session("EmployeeID")) = 0 Then
```

If they haven't signed in, we send them to the Sign-In page:

```
Response.Redirect("./index.aspx")
```

The rest of the code should run only the first time that the page is loaded

```
If Not IsPostBack Then
```

If this is the first time the page is loaded, we will need data objects:

```
Dim DBConn as OleDbConnection
Dim DBCommand As OleDbDataAdapter
Dim DSPageData as New DataSet
```

We start by connecting to the database:

```
DBConn = New OleDbConnection("Provider=sqloledb;" _
    & "server=localhost;" _
    & "Initial Catalog=INETC4;" _
    & "User Id=sa;" _
    & "Password=yourpassword;")
```

We retrieve all the questions for the groups that the employee belongs to. Take a close look at this complex query. In the Where clause, we use a subquery to retrieve all the groups that the employee belongs to. That is matched against any questions that are in those groups:

```
DBCommand = New OleDbDataAdapter _
    ("select QuestionID, QuestionText " _
    & "from VoteQuestions Where VotingGroupID In " _
    & "(Select VoteGroupID from VoteEmployeeInGroup " _
    & "Where EmployeeID = " & Session("EmployeeID") _
    & ")", DBConn)
```

We then place the return of that query into our DataSet object:

```
DBCommand.Fill(DSPageData, _
    "Questions")
```

We bind the first DropDownList to that DataSet:

```
ddlQuestionID.DataSource = _
    DSPageData.Tables("Questions").DefaultView
ddlQuestionID.DataBind()
```

The next event fires when the employee changes the selection in the question DropDownList. It displays the possible choices for the question if the employee hasn't voted on the question. Otherwise, it displays the results of the question.

```
Sub ddl_Change(Sender As Object, E As EventArgs)
    Dim DBConn as OleDbConnection
    Dim DBCommand As OleDbDataAdapter
    Dim DSPageData as New DataSet
    DBConn = New OleDbConnection("Provider=sqloledb;" _
        & "server=localhost;" _
        & "Initial Catalog=INETC4;" _
        & "User Id=sa;" _
        & "Password=yourpassword;")
    DBCommand = New OleDbDataAdapter _
        ("Select VoteID from Votes " _
        & "Where QuestionID = " _
        & ddlQuestionID.SelectedItem.Value _
        & " and EmployeeID = " & Session("EmployeeID") _
        , DBConn)
    DBCommand.Fill(DSPageData, _
        "VotesCast")
    If DSPageData.Tables("VotesCast"). _
        Rows.Count = 0 Then
        pnlVote.Visible = True
        pnlResults.Visible = False
        DBCommand = New OleDbDataAdapter _
            ("Select AnswerText from VoteAnswers " _
            & "Where QuestionID = " _
            & ddlQuestionID.SelectedItem.Value _
            & " Order By AnswerText", DBConn)
        DBCommand.Fill(DSPageData, _
            "Answers")
        ddlAnswers.DataSource = _
            DSPageData.Tables("Answers").DefaultView
        ddlAnswers.DataBind()
    Else
        pnlVote.Visible = False
```

```
        pnlResults.Visible = True
        DBCommand = New OleDbDataAdapter _
            ("Select AnswerText as [Choice], " _
            & "Count(VoteID) as [Votes] From Votes " _
            & "Where QuestionID = " _
            & ddlQuestionID.SelectedItem.Value _
            & " Group By AnswerText Order By " _
            & "Count(VoteID) DESC", DBConn)
        DBCommand.Fill(DSPageData, _
            "VoteCount")
        dgResults.DataSource = _
            DSPageData.Tables("VoteCount").DefaultView
        dgResults.DataBind()
    End If
End Sub
```

Within this code block, we need to declare data objects:

```
Dim DBConn as OleDbConnection
Dim DBCommand As OleDbDataAdapter
Dim DSPageData as New DataSet
```

We connect to our database:

```
DBConn = New OleDbConnection("Provider=sqloledb;" _
    & "server=localhost;" _
    & "Initial Catalog=INETC4;" _
    & "User Id=sa;" _
    & "Password=yourpassword;")
```

We then place SQL text into our command object so that it will retrieve the vote made by the employee on this question:

```
DBCommand = New OleDbDataAdapter _
    ("Select VoteID from Votes " _
    & "Where QuestionID = " _
    & ddlQuestionID.SelectedItem.Value _
    & " and EmployeeID = " & Session("EmployeeID") _
    , DBConn)
```

The result of running that query is placed into our DataSet object:

```
DBCommand.Fill(DSPageData, _
    "VotesCast")
```

If we didn't find a record, it means the employee has not voted on this issue:

```
If DSPageData.Tables("VotesCast"). _
    Rows.Count = 0 Then
```

In that case, we display the Vote Panel control,

```
pnlVote.Visible = True
```

but hide the Results panel:

```
pnlResults.Visible = False
```

We then retrieve all the answers to the question

```
DBCommand = New OleDbDataAdapter _
    ("Select AnswerText from VoteAnswers " _
    & "Where QuestionID = " _
    & ddlQuestionID.SelectedItem.Value _
    & " Order By AnswerText", DBConn)
```

and place them into our DataSet object:

```
DBCommand.Fill(DSPageData, _
    "Answers")
```

We then bind our second DropDownList to this DataSet object:

```
ddlAnswers.DataSource = _
    DSPageData.Tables("Answers").DefaultView
ddlAnswers.DataBind()
```

If the code flows here, it means that the employee has voted on this issue:

```
Else
```

In that case, we hide the Vote panel,

```
pnlVote.Visible = False
```

but show the Results panel control:

```
pnlResults.Visible = True
```

In that case, we retrieve the total number of votes cast for this question, grouped by the answer selected to the question:

```
DBCommand = New OleDbDataAdapter _
    ("Select AnswerText as [Choice], " _
    & "Count(VoteID) as [Votes] From Votes " _
    & "Where QuestionID = " _
    & ddlQuestionID.SelectedItem.Value _
    & " Group By AnswerText Order By " _
    & "Count(VoteID) DESC", DBConn)
DBCommand.Fill(DSPageData, _
    "VoteCount")
```

Our DataGrid is then bound to the return of that query:

```
dgResults.DataSource = _
    DSPageData.Tables("VoteCount").DefaultView
dgResults.DataBind()
```

The other event on this page fires when the visitor clicks OK, casting their vote.

```
Sub SubmitBtn_Click(Sender As Object, E As EventArgs)
    Dim DBConn as OleDbConnection
    Dim DBInsert As New OleDbCommand
    Dim DBCommand As OleDbDataAdapter
    Dim DSPageData as New DataSet
    DBConn = New OleDbConnection("Provider=sqloledb;" _
        & "server=localhost;" _
        & "Initial Catalog=INETC4;" _
        & "User Id=sa;" _
        & "Password=yourpassword;")
    DBInsert.CommandText = "Insert Into Votes " _
        & "(EmployeeID, QuestionID, AnswerText) values (" _
        & Session("EmployeeID") & ", " _
        & ddlQuestionID.SelectedItem.Value & ", " _
        & "'" _
        & Replace(ddlAnswers.SelectedItem.Text, "'", "''") _
        & "')"
    DBInsert.Connection = DBConn
    DBInsert.Connection.Open
    DBInsert.ExecuteNonQuery()
    DBCommand = New OleDbDataAdapter _
        ("Select AnswerText as [Choice], " _
        & "Count(VoteID) as [Votes] From Votes " _
```

```
        & "Where QuestionID = " _
        & ddlQuestionID.SelectedItem.Value _
        & " Group By AnswerText Order By " _
        & "Count(VoteID) DESC", DBConn)
    DBCommand.Fill(DSPageData, _
        "VotesCast")
    dgResults.DataSource = _
        DSPageData.Tables("VotesCast").DefaultView
    dgResults.DataBind()
    pnlVote.Visible = False
    pnlResults.Visible = True
End Sub
```

In that case, we need data objects that allow us to add the vote record and retrieve the current vote tally:

```
Dim DBConn as OleDbConnection
Dim DBInsert As New OleDbCommand
Dim DBCommand As OleDbDataAdapter
Dim DSPageData as New DataSet
```

We start by connecting to the database:

```
DBConn = New OleDbConnection("Provider=sqloledb;" _
    & "server=localhost;" _
    & "Initial Catalog=INETC4;" _
    & "User Id=sa;" _
    & "Password=yourpassword;")
```

We then cast the vote entered by the employee

```
DBInsert.CommandText = "Insert Into Votes " _
    & "(EmployeeID, QuestionID, AnswerText) values (" _
    & Session("EmployeeID") & ", " _
    & ddlQuestionID.SelectedItem.Value & ", " _
    & "'" _
    & Replace(ddlAnswers.SelectedItem.Text, "'", "''") _
    & "')"
```

by adding it to our Votes table:

```
DBInsert.Connection = DBConn
DBInsert.Connection.Open
DBInsert.ExecuteNonQuery()
```

Next, we need to retrieve the current vote total for this question

```
DBCommand = New OleDbDataAdapter _
    ("Select AnswerText as [Choice], " _
    & "Count(VoteID) as [Votes] From Votes " _
    & "Where QuestionID = " _
    & ddlQuestionID.SelectedItem.Value _
    & " Group By AnswerText Order By " _
    & "Count(VoteID) DESC", DBConn)
```

and place that data into our DataSet object:

```
DBCommand.Fill(DSPageData, _
    "VotesCast")
```

The DataGrid is then bound to that DataSet:

```
dgResults.DataSource = _
    DSPageData.Tables("VotesCast").DefaultView
dgResults.DataBind()
```

We then hide the Vote panel

```
pnlVote.Visible = False
```

and display the Results Panel control:

```
pnlResults.Visible = True
```

Access Code Changes

C4VotingBooth.mdb

If you wish to use this solution with Access instead of SQL Server, you should only need to change the connect string from the one that points to the SQL Server database

```
DBConn = New OleDbConnection("Provider=sqloledb;" _
    & "server=localhost;" _
    & "Initial Catalog=INETC4;" _
    & "User Id=sa;" _
    & "Password=yourpassword;")
```

to one that points to your Access database:

```
DBConn = New OleDbConnection("PROVIDER=Microsoft.Jet.OLEDB.4.0;" _
    & "DATA SOURCE=" _
    & Server.MapPath("/INetBook/C4/VotingBooth/" _
    & "Access/C4VotingBooth.mdb;"))
```

Note that you would need to change the path to the location where you placed the Access database.

Birthday Page

The Birthday page provides a simple way for employees to find out whose birthday it is today according to the current system date. The tool uses a DataGrid to display all the employees whose month and date of birth matches the current month and date.

Sample Usage

Figure 4-7 shows the Birthday page.

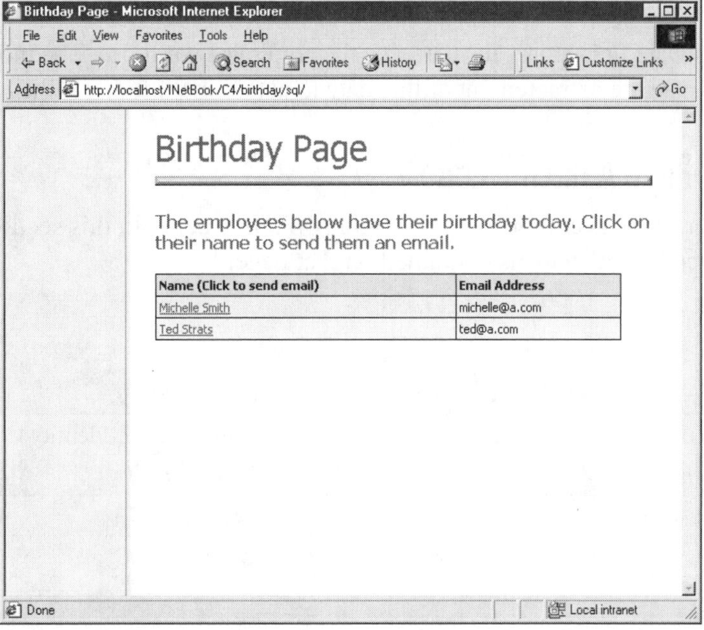

Figure 4-7 *Birthday page*

The page uses a DataGrid to display the names and e-mail addresses of all the employees born on the current system date. Note that the employee can click the name of the person to open an e-mail message to that person.

Birthday Database Component

C4Birthday.sql

The Birthday page requires just one table to accomplish its functionality. The table is the EmployeeBirthdays table, which stores information including birth dates of the employees used with this page. In this section, we will review the fields that make up that table.

EmployeeBirthdays Field Specifications

EmployeeBirthdays.txt

The field specifications for the fields in the EmployeeBirthdays table are displayed in Table 4-7.

The EmployeeID field is the primary key in this table. The name of the employee is stored in the EmployeeFirstName and EmployeeLastName fields. Those fields combined and the EmailAddress field are displayed on the Birthday page in the DataGrid.

The BirthDate field stores the date that the employee was born. The month and day of the birth date are extracted out of that date to determine if today is their birthday.

Birthday Page ASP.NET Code

The Birthday page is composed of a single ASP.NET page. In this section, we will review the code and controls contained on that page.

Field Name	Field Type	Notes
EmployeeID	int	Primary Key, Identity Column
EmployeeFirstName	varchar	Length = 50
EmployeeLastName	varchar	Length = 50
EmailAddress	varchar	Length = 100
BirthDate	datetime	

Table 4-7 *EmployeeBirthdays Field Specifications*

Birthday ASP.NET Page

Index.aspx

The code on the Birthday page displays all the employees born on this date as compared to the current system date. Information on those employees is displayed in a DataGrid.

At the top of the page, we define three compiler directives that set up the run environment and import needed data libraries:

```
<%@ Page Language=VB Debug=true %>
<%@ Import Namespace="System.Data" %>
<%@ Import Namespace="System.Data.OLEDB" %>
```

Within the body of the page, we insert two Label controls. The first displays the title of the page:

```
<asp:Label
    id="lblTitle"
    Font-Size="25pt"
    Font-Name="Tahoma"
    Text="Birthday Page"
    runat="server"
/>
```

The other displays a description of the page:

```
<asp:Label
    id="lblMessage"
    Font-Size="12pt"
    Font-Name="Tahoma"
    Font-Bold="True"
    runat="server"
    Text="The employees below have their birthday today.
    Click on their name to send them an email."
/>
```

The only other control on the page is a DataGrid that displays the employees whose birthday is today:

```
<asp:DataGrid
    id="dgBirthdays"
    AutoGenerateColumns="false"
    Width="90%"
    BackColor="beige"
```

```
    AlternatingItemStyle-BackColor="cornsilk"
    BorderColor="black"
    ShowFooter="false"
    CellPadding=3
    CellSpacing="0"
    Font-Name="Tahoma"
    Font-Size="8pt"
    ForeColor="Black"
    HeaderStyle-BackColor="burlywood"
    HeaderStyle-Font-Bold="True"
    runat="server">
    <columns>
        <asp:HyperLinkColumn
            HeaderText="Name (Click to send email)"
            DataNavigateUrlField="EmailAddress"
            DataNavigateUrlFormatString="mailto:{0}"
            DataTextField="FullName"
            Target="_self"
        />
        <asp:BoundColumn
            HeaderText="Email Address"
            DataField="EmailAddress"
        />
    </columns>
</asp:DataGrid>
```

Note that we will define our own columns instead of having the control automatically generate them for us:

```
AutoGenerateColumns="false"
```

The DataGrid contains two columns. The first is a HyperLinkColumn:

```
<asp:HyperLinkColumn
```

That means we need to specify a field that is linked to when clicked

```
DataNavigateUrlField="EmailAddress"
```

We need to specify that this is an e-mail link. Note that the text "{0}" will be replaced with the employee's e-mail address:

```
DataNavigateUrlFormatString="mailto:{0}"
```

The visitor will see the name of the employee in this column:

```
DataTextField="FullName"
```

The other column is a BoundColumn:

```
<asp:BoundColumn
```

It will display the employee's e-mail address:

```
DataField="EmailAddress"
```

The only code on the page fires when it is loaded.

```
Sub Page_Load(ByVal Sender as Object, ByVal E as EventArgs)
    Dim DBConn as OleDbConnection
    Dim DBCommand As OleDbDataAdapter
    Dim DSPageData as New DataSet
    DBConn = New OleDbConnection("Provider=sqloledb;" _
        & "server=localhost;" _
        & "Initial Catalog=INETC4;" _
        & "User Id=sa;" _
        & "Password=yourpassword;")
    DBCommand = New OleDbDataAdapter _
        ("Select EmployeeFirstName + ' ' + EmployeeLastName " _
        & "as FullName, EmailAddress From EmployeeBirthdays " _
        & "Where DatePart(mm, BirthDate) = " _
        & "DatePart(mm, GetDate()) and " _
        & "DatePart(dd, BirthDate) = " _
        & "DatePart(dd, GetDate()) " _
        & "Order By EmployeeLastName" _
        , DBConn)
    DBCommand.Fill(DSPageData, _
        "Birthdays")
    dgBirthdays.DataSource = _
        DSPageData.Tables("Birthdays").DefaultView
    dgBirthdays.DataBind()
End Sub
```

Within this procedure, we will need to connect to the database and retrieve data:

```
Dim DBConn as OleDbConnection
Dim DBCommand As OleDbDataAdapter
Dim DSPageData as New DataSet
```

We start by connecting to our SQL Server database:

```
DBConn = New OleDbConnection("Provider=sqloledb;" _
    & "server=localhost;" _
    & "Initial Catalog=INETC4;" _
    & "User Id=sa;" _
    & "Password=yourpassword;")
```

We then retrieve the names and e-mail addresses of employees born on this date. Note the use of the DatePart function in the Where clause to extract the month and date that the employee was born, as well as the month and date of the current system date, which is returned from the GetDate function:

```
DBCommand = New OleDbDataAdapter _
    ("Select EmployeeFirstName + ' ' + EmployeeLastName " _
    & "as FullName, EmailAddress From EmployeeBirthdays " _
    & "Where DatePart(mm, BirthDate) = " _
    & "DatePart(mm, GetDate()) and " _
    & "DatePart(dd, BirthDate) = " _
    & "DatePart(dd, GetDate()) " _
    & "Order By EmployeeLastName" _
    , DBConn)
```

We then place any records returned into our DataSet object,

```
DBCommand.Fill(DSPageData, _
    "Birthdays")
```

which our DataGrid is bound to:

```
dgBirthdays.DataSource = _
    DSPageData.Tables("Birthdays").DefaultView
dgBirthdays.DataBind()
```

Access Code Changes

C4Birthday.mdb

Two code changes are needed to get this page to work with Access instead of SQL Server. The first is to change the connect string

```
DBConn = New OleDbConnection("Provider=sqloledb;" _
    & "server=localhost;" _
    & "Initial Catalog=INETC4;" _
    & "User Id=sa;" _
    & "Password=yourpassword;")
```

so that it uses the correct provider and the proper path to the Access database:

```
DBConn = New OleDbConnection("PROVIDER=Microsoft.Jet.OLEDB.4.0;" _
    & "DATA SOURCE=" _
    & Server.MapPath("/INetBook/C4/Birthday/" _
    & "Access/C4Birthday.mdb;"))
```

The other change has to do with the SQL text to retrieve the employee birthday records. In SQL, we use the "+" as the concatenation character. We also used the DatePart function to extract parts of the date, and we used the GetDate function to retrieve the current system date:

```
DBCommand = New OleDbDataAdapter _
    ("Select EmployeeFirstName + ' ' + EmployeeLastName " _
    & "as FullName, EmailAddress From EmployeeBirthdays " _
    & "Where DatePart(mm, BirthDate) = " _
    & "DatePart(mm, GetDate()) and " _
    & "DatePart(dd, BirthDate) = " _
    & "DatePart(dd, GetDate()) " _
    & "Order By EmployeeLastName" _
    , DBConn)
```

In Access, the Date function returns the current system date, and we use the Month and Day functions to extract the needed parts of the date. Also, the "&" is the concatenation character:

```
DBCommand = New OleDbDataAdapter _
    ("Select EmployeeFirstName & ' ' & EmployeeLastName " _
    & "as FullName, EmailAddress From EmployeeBirthdays " _
    & "Where Month(BirthDate) = " _
    & "Month(Date()) and " _
    & "Day(BirthDate) = " _
    & "Day(Date()) " _
    & "Order By EmployeeLastName" _
    , DBConn)
```

Email Blast Tool

The next tool we will review is the Email Blast tool. It provides a simple way for employees at your company to send e-mail messages out to a group of customers or some other contact group from your intranet site.

Sample Usage

When the employee first enters this page, they see the view displayed in Figure 4-8.

At the top of the page, the employee sees the different groups that they can send an e-mail message to. This group list comes from a database table and has e-mail addresses associated with it.

In the bottom part of the form, the employee enters the details of their message. Note that each field is required. You can see here the message displayed when one of the fields is omitted.

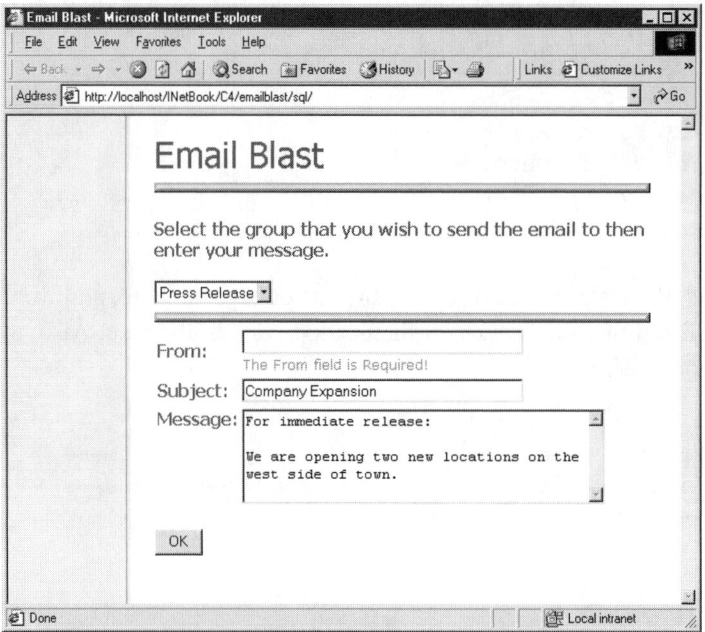

Figure 4-8 *Initial view of the Email Blast page*

Once the employee has entered all the required fields, they click OK and see the page displayed in Figure 4-9.

The employee now sees how many e-mail messages were sent out. They also have the opportunity of entering an additional message.

The recipient of the e-mail gets an e-mail message such as the one displayed in Figure 4-10.

Note that the message is based on the text entered by the employee on the Email Blast page.

Email Blast Database Component

C4EmailBlast.sql

The Email Blast tool requires a single table for its functionality. This table stores customer information used to send out the e-mail messages. In this section, we will review the fields in that table.

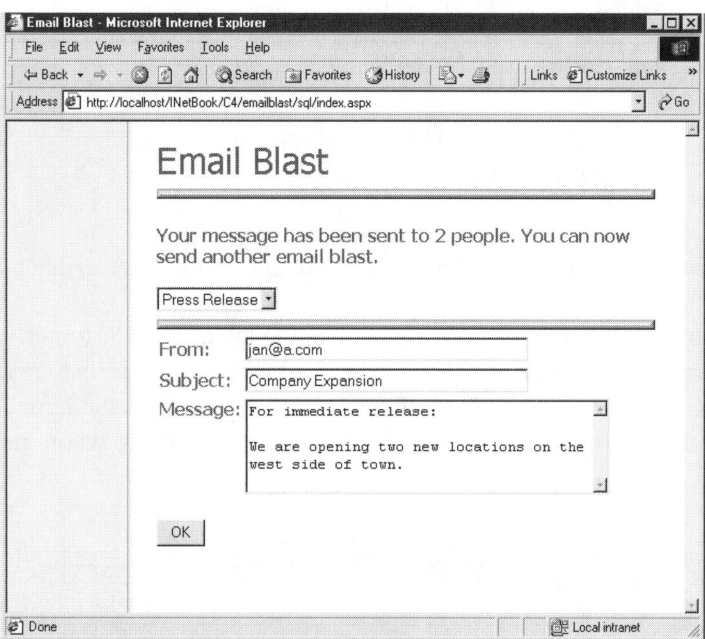

Figure 4-9 *View displayed after message is sent*

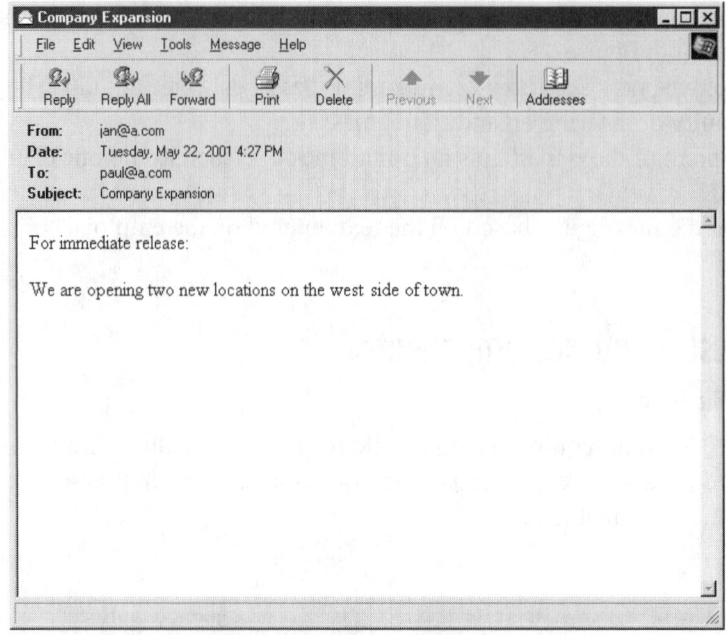

Figure 4-10 *E-mail message sent by the Email Blast page*

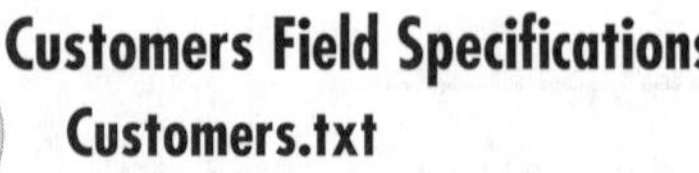

Customers Field Specifications

Customers.txt

The field specifications for the fields in the Customers table are displayed in Table 4-8.

The CustomerID field is the primary key in the table. The CustomerName and CustomerEmail fields store the name and e-mail address of the customer. The GroupName field stores the name of the group as it appears in the DropDownList on the Email Blast page. This field is then used to determine to whom the message is directed.

Field Name	Field Type	Notes
CustomerID	int	Primary Key, Identity Column
CustomerName	varchar	Length = 100
CustomerEmail	varchar	Length = 100
GroupName	varchar	Length = 50

Table 4-8 *Customers Field Specifications*

Email Blast ASP.NET Code

The Email Blast tool is composed of a single ASP.NET page. In this section, we will review the code and controls contained on that page.

Email Blast ASP.NET Page

Index.aspx

The code on the Email Blast displays a list of all the groups to the employee and sends out their message. To accomplish that functionality, we need these compiler directives:

```
<%@ Page Language=VB Debug=true %>
<%@ Import Namespace="System.Web.Mail" %>
<%@ Import Namespace="System.Data" %>
<%@ Import Namespace="System.Data.OLEDB" %>
```

The first directive tells the compiler that we will be using Visual Basic in our code and that we are in debug mode. Remember to turn debug mode off by removing that part of the directive when you move this tool to a production server:

```
<%@ Page Language=VB Debug=true %>
```

The next directive imports the library that allows us to create and send an e-mail message:

```
<%@ Import Namespace="System.Web.Mail" %>
```

The other two directives import libraries needed to retrieve data from the database:

```
<%@ Import Namespace="System.Data" %>
<%@ Import Namespace="System.Data.OLEDB" %>
```

Within the body of the page, we define a label for the title of the page:

```
<asp:Label
    id="lblTitle"
    Font-Size="25pt"
    Font-Name="Tahoma"
    Text="Email Blast"
    runat="server"
/>
```

Next, we define another label that displays the initial message and the message after an Email Blast has been sent

```
<asp:Label
    id="lblMessage"
    Font-Size="12pt"
    Font-Name="Tahoma"
    Font-Bold="True"
    runat="server"
    Text="Select the group that you wish to send the email to
        then enter your message."
/>
```

The next control is a DropDownList, which displays all the groups that the e-mail message can be sent to:

```
<asp:dropdownlist
    id="ddlGroupName"
    runat=server
    DataTextField="GroupName"
>
</asp:dropdownlist>
```

After that, we define a TextBox for the employee to enter their e-mail address, which is used to indicate whom the message is from:

```
<asp:TextBox
    id="txtFrom"
    Columns="40"
    MaxLength="100"
    runat=server
/>
```

That field is required because of this RequiredFieldValidator that is linked to it:

```
<asp:RequiredFieldValidator
    id="rfvFrom"
    ControlToValidate="txtFrom"
    Display="Dynamic"
    Font-Name="Verdana"
    Font-Size="10pt"
    runat=server>
    <br>The From field is Required!
</asp:RequiredFieldValidator>
```

The next TextBox control allows the employee to enter the subject of the Email Blast:

```
<asp:TextBox
    id="txtSubject"
    Columns="40"
    MaxLength="100"
    runat=server
/>
```

That field is also required

```
<asp:RequiredFieldValidator
    id="rfvSubject"
    ControlToValidate="txtSubject"
    Display="Dynamic"
    Font-Name="Verdana"
    Font-Size="10pt"
    runat=server>
    <br>The Subject field is Required!
</asp:RequiredFieldValidator>
```

The other TextBox on the page allows the employee to enter the text of the message. Note that it will be displayed as a TextArea HTML element because of the value in the TextMode property:

```
<asp:TextBox
    id="txtMessage"
    Columns="40"
    Rows="5"
    runat=server
    TextMode="MultiLine"
/>
```

We also require that the employee enter a value in this field:

```
<asp:RequiredFieldValidator
    id="rfvMessage"
    ControlToValidate="txtMessage"
    Display="Dynamic"
    Font-Name="Verdana"
    Font-Size="10pt"
    runat=server>
    <br>The Message field is Required!
</asp:RequiredFieldValidator>
```

The other control on the form is a button that the employee clicks to submit the e-mail message:

```
<asp:button
    id="butOK"
    text="  OK  "
    Type="Submit"
    OnClick="SubmitBtn_Click"
    runat="server"
/>
```

The code on the page runs in two blocks. The first procedure fires when the page is loaded.

```
Sub Page_Load(ByVal Sender as Object, ByVal E as EventArgs)
    If Not IsPostBack Then
        Dim DBConn as OleDbConnection
        Dim DBCommand As OleDbDataAdapter
        Dim DSPageData as New DataSet
        DBConn = New OleDbConnection("Provider=sqloledb;" _
            & "server=localhost;" _
            & "Initial Catalog=INETC4;" _
            & "User Id=sa;" _
            & "Password=yourpassword;")
        DBCommand = New OleDbDataAdapter _
            ("Select Distinct GroupName from Customers " _
            & "Order By GroupName", DBConn)
        DBCommand.Fill(DSPageData, _
            "Groups")
        ddlGroupName.DataSource = _
            DSPageData.Tables("Groups").DefaultView
        ddlGroupName.DataBind()
    End If
End Sub
```

We only want this code to run the first time that the page is opened

```
If Not IsPostBack Then
```

If this is the first time, we need data objects:

```
Dim DBConn as OleDbConnection
Dim DBCommand As OleDbDataAdapter
Dim DSPageData as New DataSet
```

In that case, we connect to our SQL Server database:

```
DBConn = New OleDbConnection("Provider=sqloledb;" _
    & "server=localhost;" _
    & "Initial Catalog=INETC4;" _
    & "User Id=sa;" _
    & "Password=yourpassword;")
```

We then retrieve a unique list of all the groups in the Customers table:

```
DBCommand = New OleDbDataAdapter _
    ("Select Distinct GroupName from Customers " _
    & "Order By GroupName", DBConn)
```

That data is placed in our DataSet object:

```
DBCommand.Fill(DSPageData, _
    "Groups")
```

We then bind our DropDownList to that DataSet object:

```
ddlGroupName.DataSource = _
    DSPageData.Tables("Groups").DefaultView
ddlGroupName.DataBind()
```

The other procedure on this page fires when the OK button is clicked. It sends out the Email Blast:

```
Sub SubmitBtn_Click(Sender As Object, E As EventArgs)
    Dim DBConn as OleDbConnection
    Dim DBCommand As OleDbDataAdapter
    Dim DSPageData as New DataSet
    Dim TheMailMessage as New MailMessage
    Dim TheMailConnection as New SmtpMail
    Dim I as Integer
    DBConn = New OleDbConnection("Provider=sqloledb;" _
        & "server=localhost;" _
        & "Initial Catalog=INETC4;" _
        & "User Id=sa;" _
        & "Password=yourpassword;")
    DBCommand = New OleDbDataAdapter _
        ("Select Distinct CustomerEmail from Customers " _
        & "Where GroupName = '" _
        & ddlGroupName.SelectedItem.Text & "'", DBConn)
    DBCommand.Fill(DSPageData, _
```

```
        "Emails")
    TheMailMessage.From = txtFrom.Text
    TheMailMessage.Subject = txtSubject.Text
    TheMailMessage.Body = txtMessage.Text
    For I = 0 to DSPageData.Tables("Emails"). _
            Rows.Count - 1
        TheMailMessage.To = DSPageData.Tables("Emails"). _
            Rows(0).Item("CustomerEmail")
        TheMailConnection.Send(TheMailMessage)
    Next
    if DSPageData.Tables("Emails").Rows.Count = 1 then
        lblMessage.Text = "Your message has been sent to 1" _
            & " person. You can now send another email blast."
    Else
        lblMessage.Text = "Your message has been sent to " _
            & DSPageData.Tables("Emails").Rows.Count _
            & " people. You can now send another email blast."
    End If
End Sub
```

Within this procedure, we need data objects,

```
Dim DBConn as OleDbConnection
Dim DBCommand As OleDbDataAdapter
Dim DSPageData as New DataSet
```

as well as e-mail objects

```
Dim TheMailMessage as New MailMessage
Dim TheMailConnection as New SmtpMail
```

and a variable to iterate us through a loop:

```
Dim I as Integer
```

We start by connecting to the database:

```
DBConn = New OleDbConnection("Provider=sqloledb;" _
    & "server=localhost;" _
    & "Initial Catalog=INETC4;" _
    & "User Id=sa;" _
    & "Password=yourpassword;")
```

We then retrieve all the e-mail addresses in the group selected by the employee in the DropDownList

```
DBCommand = New OleDbDataAdapter _
    ("Select Distinct CustomerEmail from Customers " _
    & "Where GroupName = '" _
    & ddlGroupName.SelectedItem.Text & "'", DBConn)
```

and place those e-mail addresses into our DataSet object:

```
DBCommand.Fill(DSPageData, _
    "Emails")
```

We then set the properties of the e-mail message, which won't change from message to message. First, we set whom the message is from:

```
TheMailMessage.From = txtFrom.Text
```

We then set the subject of the message

```
TheMailMessage.Subject = txtSubject.Text
```

and the text of the message:

```
TheMailMessage.Body = txtMessage.Text
```

We enter a loop so that we can send an e-mail message out to each customer record returned into our DataSet object:

```
For I = 0 to DSPageData.Tables("Emails"). _
    Rows.Count - 1
```

Within that loop we set whom the message is to

```
TheMailMessage.To = DSPageData.Tables("Emails"). _
    Rows(0).Item("CustomerEmail")
```

and then we send the message

```
TheMailConnection.Send(TheMailMessage)
```

before moving on to the next customer record:

```
Next
```

After the loop, we check to see how many e-mail messages were sent out:

```
if DSPageData.Tables("Emails").Rows.Count = 1 then
```

If it was one, we display this message:

```
lblMessage.Text = "Your message has been sent to 1" _
    & " person. You can now send another email blast."
```

Otherwise, the employee sees this message through the Label control:

```
lblMessage.Text = "Your message has been sent to " _
    & DSPageData.Tables("Emails").Rows.Count _
    & " people. You can now send another email blast."
```

Access Code Changes

C4EmailBlast.mdb

Just one code change is needed to get this solution to work with Access instead of SQL Server. We need to change the connect string

```
DBConn = New OleDbConnection("Provider=sqloledb;" _
    & "server=localhost;" _
    & "Initial Catalog=INETC4;" _
    & "User Id=sa;" _
    & "Password=yourpassword;")
```

so that it uses the correct provider and the proper path to the Access database:

```
DBConn = New OleDbConnection("PROVIDER=Microsoft.Jet.OLEDB.4.0;" _
    & "DATA SOURCE=" _
    & Server.MapPath("/INetBook/C4/EmailBlast/" _
    & "Access/C4EmailBlast.mdb;"))
```

No other code changes should be needed.

CHAPTER

5

Adding Functionality to an Intranet

In this chapter, we will continue our discussion on tools that would be useful for intranet web sites. Intranet sites are typically designed just for employees of your company. So adding tools to your intranet allows you to provide mechanisms for employees to complete their tasks.

We will start our discussion with a review of the Library application. This application allows employees to browse and search through book listings and to check books out. The tool also provides a screen for the librarian to add and remove books.

Then we will review the Incident Report tool. This tool allows employees to complete an incident report and lets managers comment on these reports.

Library Application

In this section, we will review the Library application. The tool allows employees at your company to search the company's book library or to browse the library by book categories. The employee can check books out of the library, and they can return books. The application also includes a page that allows managers to add and delete books from the library.

Sample Usage

When the employee first enters this application, they are asked to sign in using the page displayed in Figure 5-1.

The employee enters their username and password to gain access to the application. If they enter an invalid username or password, they are asked to try again. Once the employee enters a valid name and password, they are taken to the Menu page displayed in Figure 5-2.

The Menu page actually has two views, which are displayed depending on the employee who entered the application. The view displayed in Figure 5-2 shows the menu displayed to nonmanagers. But take a look at Figure 5-3.

The Menu page for managers has an additional link at the bottom of the page, which allows a manager to add and delete books. But also note another difference between these two menus. One displays a Return Book section; the other doesn't.

This is because the manager happens to have books currently checked out to their name. The employee returns a book by selecting the book in the DropDownList and

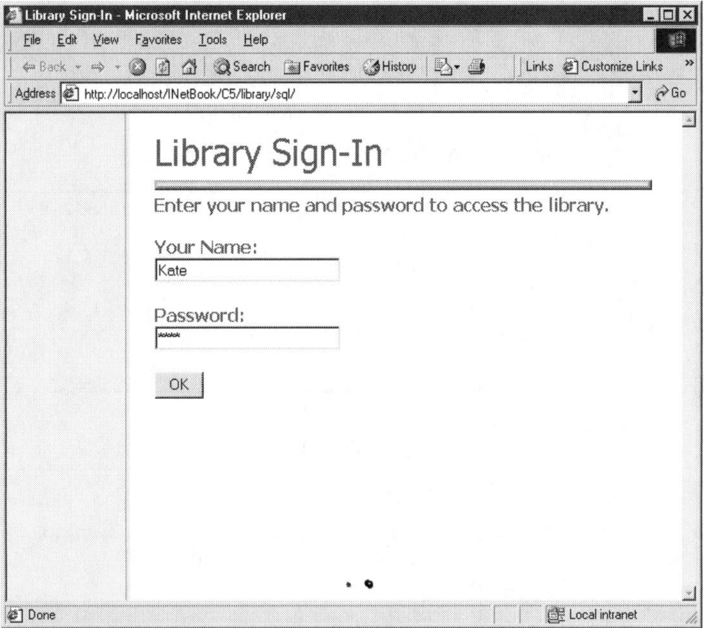

Figure 5-1 *Library Sign-In page*

Figure 5-2 *Menu page for a nonmanager*

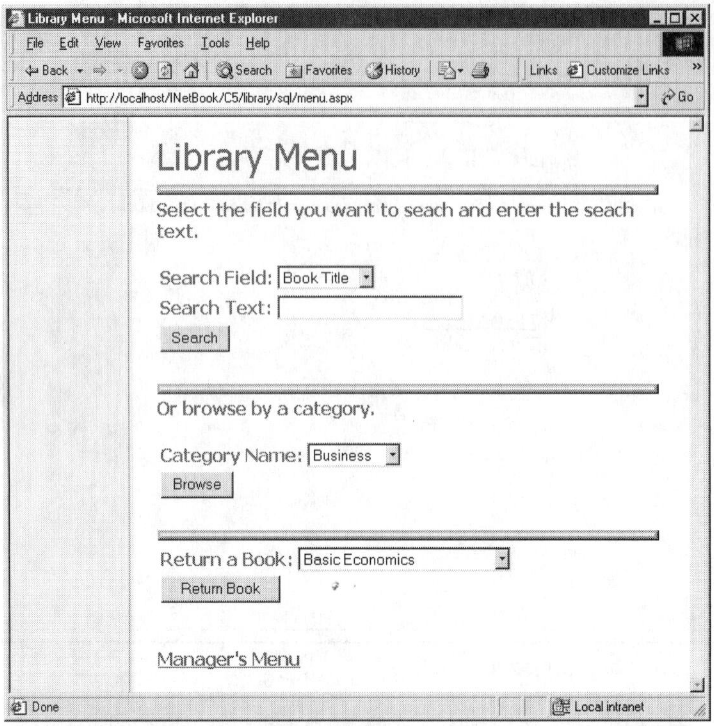

Figure 5-3 *Menu page for a manager*

clicking the Return Book button. If they have no other books checked out, that section of the page is hidden, as you can see in Figure 5-4.

The employee can use the menu page to search for books in the library. In the top section of the page, the employee selects the field that they want to search. They then enter a word or phrase that they wish to search for in that field. When they click the Search button, the employee sees the results of their search, as displayed in Figure 5-5.

In this example, the employee searches the book title for the word "Europe" and finds this one match. But the employee can also browse through books by category. Take a look at Figure 5-6.

In this case, the employee has selected the Business category. They now see, through the DataGrid, all the books that are in that category. Notice that the book titles are links in the DataGrid. When the employee clicks the title link, they see the full book listing, like the one displayed in Figure 5-7.

The employee sees the extended information on the book, including its status. If the book is available, they can click a button to check the book out. When they do that, the

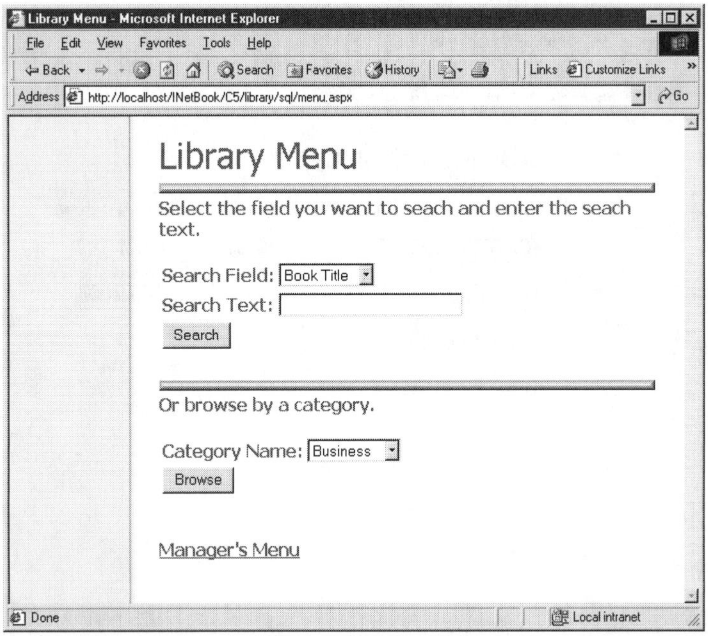

Figure 5-4 *Menu page without books checked out*

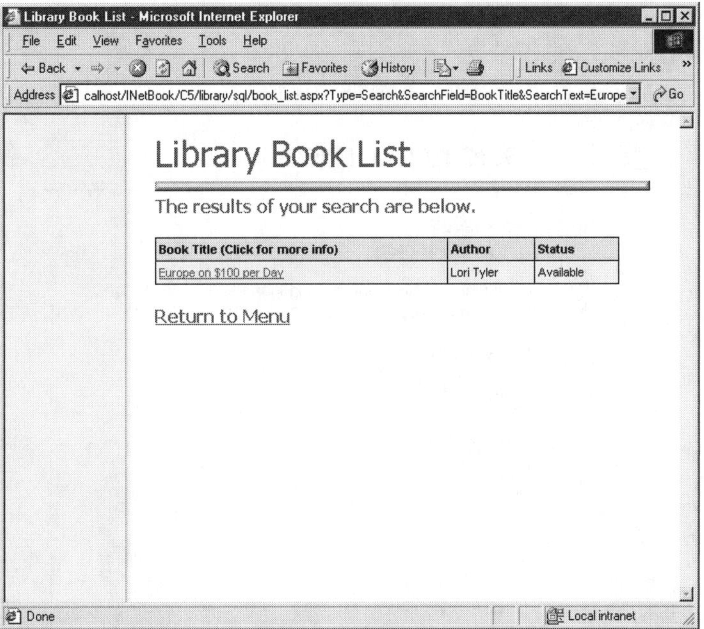

Figure 5-5 *Book List page after a search*

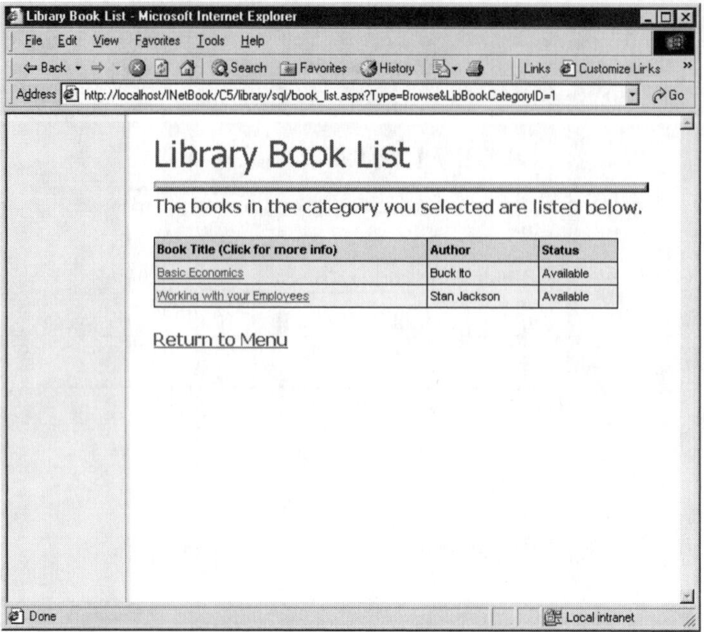

Figure 5-6 *Book List page displaying books in a category*

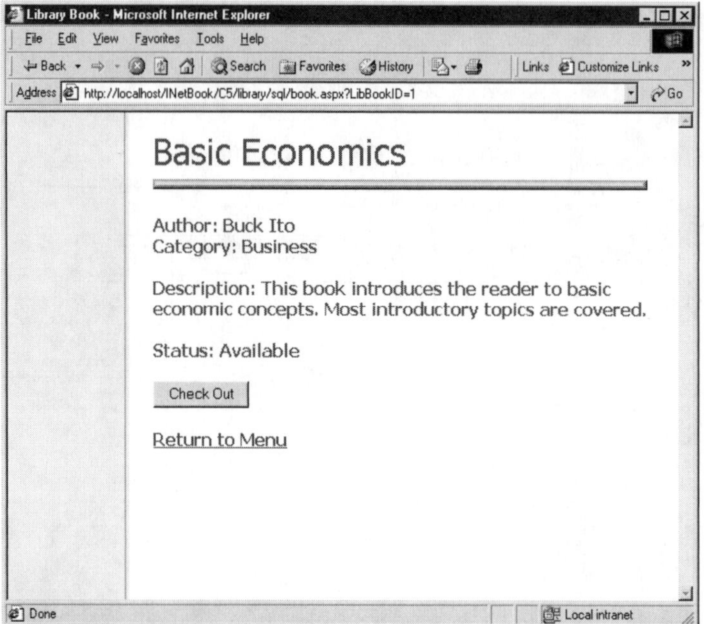

Figure 5-7 *Book page*

book is marked as checked out to them and they are returned to the Menu page. There they can see the book is checked out to them, as displayed in Figure 5-8.

At the bottom of the Menu page, the manager can click the link to be taken to the Manager's Menu page displayed in Figure 5-9.

The page is divided into two sections. The top part of the page provides a list of all the books. The manager can select a book and click the Delete button to remove the book from the database.

The other section of the page allows the manager to add a new book to the library. Here, they enter data into each field and click the Add button. Their book is then added to the database, as you can see in Figure 5-10.

Library Database Component

C5Library.sql

The database required for the functionality of the Library application includes three interrelated tables. In this section, we will review the relationships between the tables and the fields they contain.

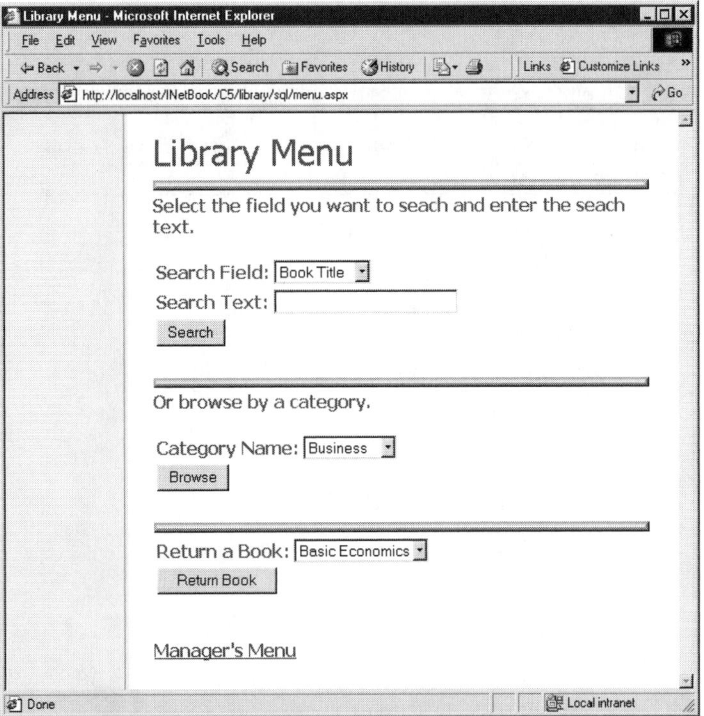

Figure 5-8 *Menu page after book has been checked out*

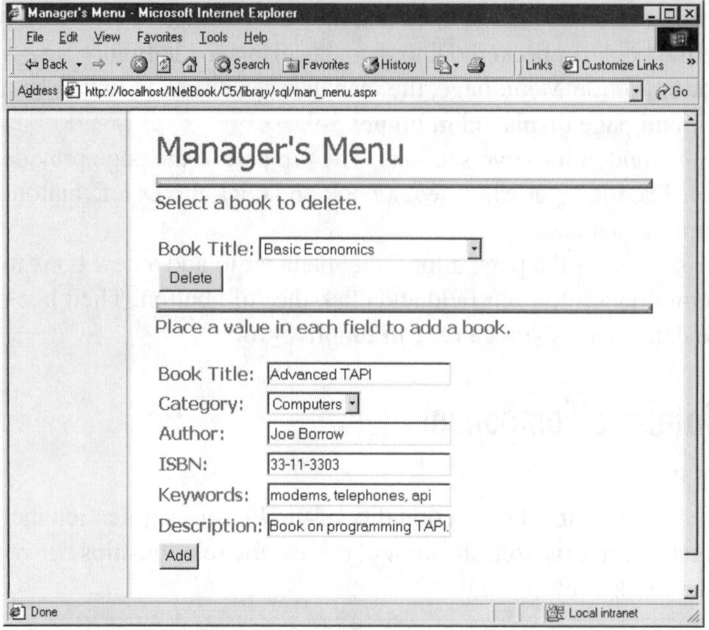

Figure 5-9 *Manager's menu*

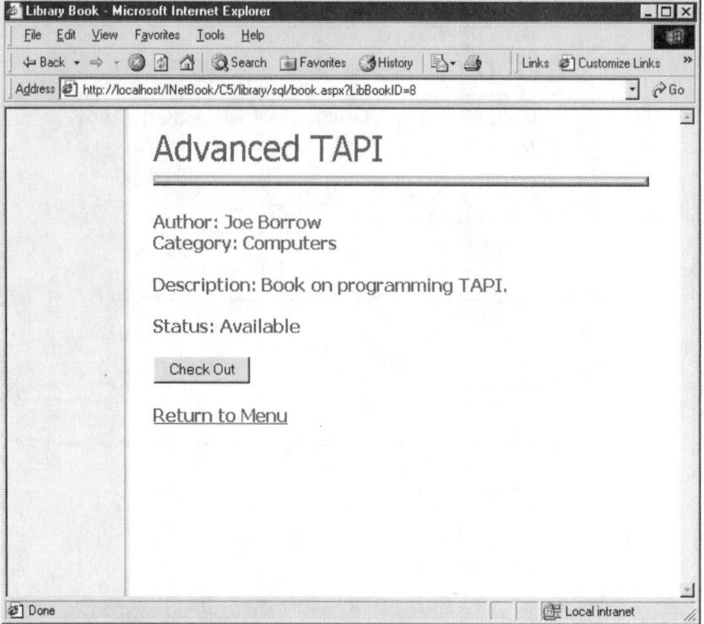

Figure 5-10 *New book displayed on the Book page*

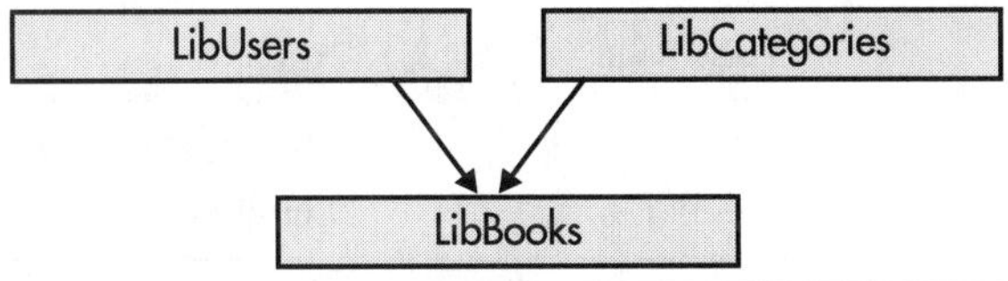

Figure 5-11 *Library data diagram*

Tables and Data Diagram

Figure 5-11 above shows the relationship between the tables in the Library database.

The Library database includes two top-level tables. One is the LibUsers table. This table contains information about the employees who can use the tool. The other top-level table is the LibCategories table. This table contains the names of the categories that a book can be in.

Both of those tables relate in a one-to-many relationship with the other table in the database, LibBooks. That table stores the information on the books.

LibUsers Field Specifications

LibUsers.txt

The field specifications for the fields in the LibUsers table are displayed in Table 5-1.

The LibUserID field is the primary key in the table. Since it is an identity column, it is automatically populated when a new record is added. The UserType field stores information regarding whether the user is a manager or not. The value in that field determines whether the employee can enter the Manager's Menu.

LibCategories Field Specifications

LibCategories.txt

The field specifications for the fields in the LibCategories table are displayed in Table 5-2.

Field Name	Field Type	Notes
LibUserID	int	Primary Key, Identity Column
UserName	varchar	Length = 50
Password	varchar	Length = 50
EmailAddress	varchar	Length = 100
UserType	varchar	Length = 50

Table 5-1 *LibUsers Field Specifications*

Field Name	Field Type	Notes
LibBookCategoryID	int	Primary Key, Identity Column
CategoryName	varchar	Length = 50

Table 5-2 *LibCategories Field Specifications*

The primary key in this table is the LibBookCategoryID field. The other field stores the name of the category and is used in DropDownList controls in the site.

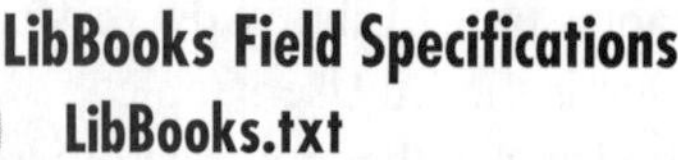

LibBooks Field Specifications

LibBooks.txt

The field specifications for the fields in the LibBooks table are displayed in Table 5-3.

The LibBookID is the primary key in this table. The LibBookCategoryID field is a foreign key that stores the ID of the category that the book is in. The other foreign key in this table, CheckedOutTo, stores the ID of the employee who has the book checked out.

The Status field contains either the text "Available" or "Checked Out" and is used to determine whether the employee can check out the book. The rest of the fields store general information about the book.

Library ASP.NET Code

The Library application is composed of five ASP.NET pages. The page employs a variety of controls to complete their functionality. In this section, we will review those five pages.

Field Name	Field Type	Notes
LibBookID	int	Primary Key, Identity Column
LibBookCategoryID	int	Foreign Key
CheckedOutTo	int	Foreign Key
BookTitle	varchar	Length = 100
Author	varchar	Length = 100
ISBN	varchar	Length = 50
Keywords	varchar	Length = 100
Description	varchar	Length = 255
Status	varchar	Length = 255

Table 5-3 *LibBooks Field Specifications*

Library Sign-In ASP.NET Page

Index.aspx

The Library Sign-In page is the entry-point into the application. The employee must successfully enter their name and password before being able to proceed to any of the other pages in the application.

At the top of the page, we declare three compiler directives.

```
<%@ Page Language=VB Debug=true %>
<%@ Import Namespace="System.Data" %>
<%@ Import Namespace="System.Data.OLEDB" %>
```

The first tells the compiler the language that we are using and also that we are in debug mode:

```
<%@ Page Language=VB Debug=true %>
```

The other two directives import libraries into our page, which allow us to connect to our database and manipulate data:

```
<%@ Import Namespace="System.Data" %>
<%@ Import Namespace="System.Data.OLEDB" %>
```

Within the body of the page, we declare a Label control that displays the title of the page:

```
<asp:Label
    id="lblTitle"
    Font-Size="25pt"
    Font-Name="Tahoma"
    Text="Library Sign-In"
    runat="server"
/>
```

Another Label is defined that initially displays instructions but can display an error message if the employee enters an invalid username and password pair:

```
<asp:Label
    id="lblMessage"
    Font-Size="12pt"
    Font-Name="Tahoma"
    Font-Bold="True"
    runat="server"
    Text="Enter your name and password to access the library."
/>
```

Next, we define a TextBox control that the employee enters their name into:

```
<asp:TextBox
    id="txtUserName"
    Columns="25"
    MaxLength="100"
    runat=server
/>
```

We require that field by linking a RequiredFieldValidator to it:

```
<asp:RequiredFieldValidator
    id="rfvUserName"
    ControlToValidate="txtUserName"
    Display="Dynamic"
    Font-Name="Tahoma"
    Font-Size="10pt"
    runat=server>
    User Name is Required!
</asp:RequiredFieldValidator>
```

One other TextBox is defined on this page for the employee's password:

```
<asp:TextBox
    id="txtPassword"
    Columns="25"
    MaxLength="50"
    runat=server
    TextMode="Password"
/>
```

That field is also required:

```
<asp:RequiredFieldValidator
    id="rfvPassword"
    ControlToValidate="txtPassword"
    Display="Dynamic"
    Font-Name="Verdana"
    Font-Size="10pt"
    runat=server>
    Password is Required!
</asp:RequiredFieldValidator>
```

The only other control on the page is a button that submits the form when it is clicked

```
<asp:button
    id="butOK"
    text="  OK  "
    Type="Submit"
    OnClick="SubmitBtn_Click"
    runat="server"
/>
```

The code on the page is contained within a single code block, which fires when the OK button is clicked.

```
Sub SubmitBtn_Click(Sender As Object, E As EventArgs)
    Dim DBConn as OleDbConnection
    Dim DBCommand As OleDbDataAdapter
    Dim DSPageData as New DataSet
    DBConn = New OleDbConnection("Provider=sqloledb;" _
        & "server=localhost;" _
        & "Initial Catalog=INETC5;" _
        & "User Id=sa;" _
        & "Password=yourpassword;")
    DBCommand = New OleDbDataAdapter _
        ("Select LibUserID, UserType from " _
        & "LibUsers Where " _
        & "UserName = '" _
        & Replace(txtUserName.Text, "'", "''") _
        & "' and Password = '" _
        & Replace(txtPassword.Text, "'", "''") _
        & "'", DBConn)
    DBCommand.Fill(DSPageData, _
        "SignIn")
    If DSPageData.Tables("SignIn"). _
        Rows.Count = 0 Then
        lblMessage.Text = "The user name and password " _
            & "were not found. Please try again."
    Else
        Session("LibUserID") = DSPageData.Tables("SignIn"). _
            Rows(0).Item("LibUserID")
        Session("UserType") = DSPageData.Tables("SignIn"). _
            Rows(0).Item("UserType")
        Response.Redirect("./menu.aspx")
    End If
End Sub
```

Within this code block, we will need data objects:

```
Dim DBConn as OleDbConnection
Dim DBCommand As OleDbDataAdapter
Dim DSPageData as New DataSet
```

We start by connecting to our SQL Server database:

```
DBConn = New OleDbConnection("Provider=sqloledb;" _
    & "server=localhost;" _
    & "Initial Catalog=INETC5;" _
    & "User Id=sa;" _
    & "Password=yourpassword;")
```

We then retrieve the ID and type of the user from the database as determined from the data they entered on the form

```
DBCommand = New OleDbDataAdapter _
    ("Select LibUserID, UserType from " _
    & "LibUsers Where " _
    & "UserName = '" _
    & Replace(txtUserName.Text, "'", "''") _
    & "' and Password = '" _
    & Replace(txtPassword.Text, "'", "''") _
    & "'", DBConn)
```

into our DataSet object:

```
DBCommand.Fill(DSPageData, _
    "SignIn")
```

We then check to see if a record was found that matches the name and password entered by the employee:

```
If DSPageData.Tables("SignIn"). _
    Rows.Count = 0 Then
```

If one wasn't found, we display this message to the employee through our Label control:

```
lblMessage.Text = "The user name and password " _
    & "were not found. Please try again."
```

Otherwise, we store the ID of the employee in a session variable

```
Session("LibUserID") = DSPageData.Tables("SignIn"). _
    Rows(0).Item("LibUserID")
```

We also store the type of user in a session variable:

```
Session("UserType") = DSPageData.Tables("SignIn"). _
    Rows(0).Item("UserType")
```

We then send the employee to the Menu page:

```
Response.Redirect("./menu.aspx")
```

Menu Sign-In ASP.NET Page

Menu.aspx

The Menu page allows the employee to search, browse, and check in books that are checked out. The page also supplies a link to the Manager's Menu page if the employee is a manager.

At the top of the page, we define the same three compiler directives:

```
<%@ Page Language=VB Debug=true %>
<%@ Import Namespace="System.Data" %>
<%@ Import Namespace="System.Data.OLEDB" %>
```

Within the body of the page, the first control you will find is a Label control that displays the title of the page:

```
<asp:Label
    id="lblTitle"
    Font-Size="25pt"
    Font-Name="Tahoma"
    Text="Library Menu"
    runat="server"
/>
```

The next control we declare is a DropDownList for the employee to select the field that they want to search:

```
<asp:DropDownList
    id="ddlSearchField"
    runat=server>
    <asp:ListItem
        Value="BookTitle" Selected="True">Book Title</asp:ListItem>
    <asp:ListItem Value="Author">Author</asp:ListItem>
```

```
    <asp:ListItem Value="ISBN">ISBN</asp:ListItem>
    <asp:ListItem Value="Keywords">Keywords</asp:ListItem>
    <asp:ListItem Value="Description">Description</asp:ListItem>
</asp:DropDownList>
```

We follow that with a TextBox for entering the search text:

```
<asp:TextBox
    id="txtSearchText"
    Columns="25"
    MaxLength="30"
    runat=server
/>
```

That is followed by a button that, when clicked, allows the employee to submit their search criteria:

```
<asp:button
    id="butSearch"
    text="Search"
    Type="Submit"
    OnClick="Search_Click"
    runat="server"
/>
```

Next, we need another DropDownList so that the employee can select a category

```
<asp:dropdownlist
    id="ddlCategory"
    runat=server
    DataTextField="CategoryName"
    DataValueField="LibBookCategoryID">
</asp:dropdownlist>
```

and a button that allows the employee to browse by category:

```
<asp:button
    id="butBrowse"
    text="Browse"
    Type="Submit"
    OnClick="Browse_Click"
    runat="server"
/>
```

In the next section of the page, we define a Panel control:

```
<asp:Panel
    id="pnlReturn"
    runat="server"
>
```

Within that control, we embed a DropDownList that displays all the books checked out by the employee

```
<asp:dropdownlist
    id="ddlBooks"
    runat=server
    DataTextField="BookTitle"
    DataValueField="LibBookID">
</asp:dropdownlist>
```

and a button so that they can check a book back in:

```
<asp:button
    id="butRetun"
    text="Return Book"
    Type="Submit"
    OnClick="Return_Click"
    runat="server"
/>
```

The only other control on the page is a HyperLink control, which displays the link to the Manager's Menu. We implement this as a control so that we can toggle its visibility:

```
<asp:HyperLink
    id="hypManagersMenu"
    runat="server"
    Text="Manager's Menu"
    NavigateUrl="./man_menu.aspx"
/>
```

The code on the page is contained within four procedures. The first procedure fires when the page is loaded.

```
Sub Page_Load(ByVal Sender as Object, ByVal E as EventArgs)
    If Len(Session("LibUserID")) = 0 Then
```

```
            Response.Redirect("./index.aspx")
        End If
        If Session("UserType") = "LibManager" Then
            hypManagersMenu.Visible = True
        Else
            hypManagersMenu.Visible = False
        End If
        If Not IsPostBack Then
            Dim DBConn as OleDbConnection
            Dim DBCommand As OleDbDataAdapter
            Dim DSPageData as New DataSet
            DBConn = New OleDbConnection("Provider=sqloledb;" _
                & "server=localhost;" _
                & "Initial Catalog=INETC5;" _
                & "User Id=sa;" _
                & "Password=yourpassword;")
            DBCommand = New OleDbDataAdapter _
                ("select LibBookCategoryID, CategoryName " _
                & "from LibCategories Order By CategoryName" _
                , DBConn)
            DBCommand.Fill(DSPageData, _
                "Categories")
            ddlCategory.DataSource = _
                DSPageData.Tables("Categories").DefaultView
            ddlCategory.DataBind()
            DBCommand = New OleDbDataAdapter _
                ("select LibBookID, BookTitle " _
                & "from LibBooks Where " _
                & "CheckedOutTo = " & Session("LibUserID") _
                & " Order By BookTitle", DBConn)
            DBCommand.Fill(DSPageData, _
                "Books")
            If DSPageData.Tables("Books").Rows.Count > 0 Then
                ddlBooks.DataSource = _
                    DSPageData.Tables("Books").DefaultView
                ddlBOoks.DataBind()
            Else
                pnlReturn.Visible = False
            End If
        End If
    End Sub
```

The employee can only access this page if they have signed in:

```
If Len(Session("LibUserID")) = 0 Then
```

If they haven't, we send them to the Sign-In page:

```
Response.Redirect("./index.aspx")
```

Next, we check to see if they are a library manager:

```
If Session("UserType") = "LibManager" Then
```

If that is the case, we display the link to the Manager's Menu page:

```
hypManagersMenu.Visible = True
```

Otherwise, we hide it:

```
hypManagersMenu.Visible = False
```

The rest of the code should only run when the page is initially loaded

```
If Not IsPostBack Then
```

If that is the case, we need data objects:

```
Dim DBConn as OleDbConnection
Dim DBCommand As OleDbDataAdapter
Dim DSPageData as New DataSet
```

We start by connecting to our database:

```
DBConn = New OleDbConnection("Provider=sqloledb;" _
    & "server=localhost;" _
    & "Initial Catalog=INETC5;" _
    & "User Id=sa;" _
    & "Password=yourpassword;")
```

And we retrieve the list of categories

```
DBCommand = New OleDbDataAdapter _
    ("select LibBookCategoryID, CategoryName " _
    & "from LibCategories Order By CategoryName" _
    , DBConn)
```

which are placed into our DataSet object:

```
DBCommand.Fill(DSPageData, _
    "Categories")
```

We then bind the category DropDownList control to that DataSet:

```
ddlCategory.DataSource = _
    DSPageData.Tables("Categories").DefaultView
ddlCategory.DataBind()
```

We also need to retrieve the books checked out by the employee:

```
DBCommand = New OleDbDataAdapter _
    ("select LibBookID, BookTitle " _
    & "from LibBooks Where " _
    & "CheckedOutTo = " & Session("LibUserID") _
    & " Order By BookTitle", DBConn)
DBCommand.Fill(DSPageData, _
    "Books")
```

We then check to see if they have any books checked out:

```
If DSPageData.Tables("Books").Rows.Count > 0 Then
```

If they do, we display that book list in a DropDownList:

```
ddlBooks.DataSource = _
    DSPageData.Tables("Books").DefaultView
ddlBOoks.DataBind()
```

Otherwise, we hide that section of the page:

```
pnlReturn.Visible = False
```

The next procedure fires when the employee clicks the Search button.

```
Sub Search_Click(Sender As Object, E As EventArgs)
    Response.Redirect("./book_list.aspx?Type=Search&" _
        & "SearchField=" & ddlSearchField.SelectedItem.Value _
        & "&SearchText=" & txtSearchText.Text)
End Sub
```

This procedure simply passes the search field and text on to the Book List page:

```
Response.Redirect("./book_list.aspx?Type=Search&" _
   & "SearchField=" & ddlSearchField.SelectedItem.Value _
   & "&SearchText=" & txtSearchText.Text)
```

Similarly, when the Browse button is clicked, we pass the ID of the category selected by the employee on to the Book List page:

```
Sub Browse_Click(Sender As Object, E As EventArgs)
    Response.Redirect("./book_list.aspx?Type=Browse&" _
        & "LibBookCategoryID=" & ddlCategory.SelectedItem.Value)
End Sub
```

The last procedure fires when the employee clicks the Return button. It allows the employee to check in a book.

```
Sub Return_Click(Sender As Object, E As EventArgs)
    Dim DBConn as OleDbConnection
    Dim DBCommand As OleDbDataAdapter
    Dim DSPageData as New DataSet
    Dim DBUpdate As New OleDbCommand
    DBConn = New OleDbConnection("Provider=sqloledb;" _
        & "server=localhost;" _
        & "Initial Catalog=INETC5;" _
        & "User Id=sa;" _
        & "Password=yourpassword;")
    DBUpdate.CommandText = "Update LibBooks set " _
        & "Status = 'Available', CheckedOutTo = 0" _
        & " Where LibBookID = " _
        & ddlBooks.SelectedItem.Value
    DBUpdate.Connection = DBConn
    DBUpdate.Connection.Open
    DBUpdate.ExecuteNonQuery()
    DBCommand = New OleDbDataAdapter _
        ("select LibBookID, BookTitle " _
        & "from LibBooks Where " _
        & "CheckedOutTo = " & Session("LibUserID") _
        & " Order By BookTitle", DBConn)
    DBCommand.Fill(DSPageData, _
        "Books")
    If DSPageData.Tables("Books").Rows.Count > 0 Then
        ddlBooks.DataSource = _
            DSPageData.Tables("Books").DefaultView
        ddlBOoks.DataBind()
    Else
```

```
        pnlReturn.Visible = False
    End If
End Sub
```

Within this procedure, we will need data objects:

```
Dim DBConn as OleDbConnection
Dim DBCommand As OleDbDataAdapter
Dim DSPageData as New DataSet
Dim DBUpdate As New OleDbCommand
```

After declaring those objects, we connect to our database:

```
DBConn = New OleDbConnection("Provider=sqloledb;" _
    & "server=localhost;" _
    & "Initial Catalog=INETC5;" _
    & "User Id=sa;" _
    & "Password=yourpassword;")
```

We then update the book selected by the employee, marking it as available:

```
DBUpdate.CommandText = "Update LibBooks set " _
    & "Status = 'Available', CheckedOutTo = 0" _
    & " Where LibBookID = " _
    & ddlBooks.SelectedItem.Value
DBUpdate.Connection = DBConn
DBUpdate.Connection.Open
DBUpdate.ExecuteNonQuery()
```

Next, we need to refresh the list of books still checked out by the employee

```
DBCommand = New OleDbDataAdapter _
    ("select LibBookID, BookTitle " _
    & "from LibBooks Where " _
    & "CheckedOutTo = " & Session("LibUserID") _
    & " Order By BookTitle", DBConn)
```

into a DataSet object:

```
DBCommand.Fill(DSPageData, _
    "Books")
```

We then check to see if they still have any books checked out:

```
If DSPageData.Tables("Books").Rows.Count > 0 Then
```

If they do, we rebind the DropDownList:

```
ddlBooks.DataSource = _
    DSPageData.Tables("Books").DefaultView
ddlBOoks.DataBind()
```

Otherwise, we hide the Return section of the page:

```
pnlReturn.Visible = False
```

Book List ASP.NET Page

Book_List.aspx

The code on the Book List page displays the results of the visitor's search for the contents of the selected category through a DataGrid. To accomplish that functionality, we need to declare these compiler directives:

```
<%@ Page Language=VB Debug=true %>
<%@ Import Namespace="System.Data" %>
<%@ Import Namespace="System.Data.OLEDB" %>
```

Within the body of the page, we define a Label control for the title of the page:

```
<asp:Label
    id="lblTitle"
    Font-Size="25pt"
    Font-Name="Tahoma"
    Text="Library Book List"
    runat="server"
/>
```

Another Label control will display a message about whether the visitor is searching or browsing

```
<asp:Label
    id="lblMessage"
    Font-Size="12pt"
    Font-Name="Tahoma"
    Font-Bold="True"
    runat="server"
/>
```

The only other control on the page is a DataGrid, which displays the matching book records:

```
<asp:DataGrid
    id="dgBooks"
    AutoGenerateColumns="false"
    Width="90%"
    BackColor="beige"
    AlternatingItemStyle-BackColor="cornsilk"
    BorderColor="black"
    ShowFooter="false"
    CellPadding=3
    CellSpacing="0"
    Font-Name="Arial"
    Font-Size="8pt"
    ForeColor="Black"
    HeaderStyle-BackColor="burlywood"
    HeaderStyle-Font-Bold="True"
    runat="server">
    <columns>
        <asp:HyperLinkColumn
            HeaderText="Book Title (Click for more info)"
            DataNavigateUrlField="LibBookID"
            DataNavigateUrlFormatString="./book.aspx?LibBookID={0}"
            DataTextField="BookTitle"
            Target="_self"
        />
        <asp:BoundColumn
            HeaderText="Author"
            DataField="Author"
        />
        <asp:BoundColumn
            HeaderText="Status"
            DataField="Status"
        />
    </columns>
</asp:DataGrid>
```

Note that we are displaying our own columns:

```
AutoGenerateColumns="false"
```

The first column is a HyperLinkColumn:

```
<asp:HyperLinkColumn
    HeaderText="Book Title (Click for more info)"
```

It will link to the Book page, passing to it the LibBookID field:

```
DataNavigateUrlField="LibBookID"
DataNavigateUrlFormatString="./book.aspx?LibBookID={0}"
```

But the employee will see the title of the book:

```
DataTextField="BookTitle"
Target="_self"
/>
```

The next column displays the author of the book:

```
<asp:BoundColumn
    HeaderText="Author"
    DataField="Author"
/>
```

The third column displays the status of the book:

```
<asp:BoundColumn
    HeaderText="Status"
    DataField="Status"
/>
```

The only procedure on the page fires when it is first loaded.

```
Sub Page_Load(ByVal Sender as Object, ByVal E as EventArgs)
    If Len(Session("LibUserID")) = 0 Then
        Response.Redirect("./index.aspx")
    End If
    Dim DBConn as OleDbConnection
    Dim DBCommand As OleDbDataAdapter
    Dim DSPageData as New DataSet
    DBConn = New OleDbConnection("Provider=sqloledb;" _
        & "server=localhost;" _
        & "Initial Catalog=INETC5;" _
        & "User Id=sa;" _
        & "Password=yourpassword;")
    If Request.QueryString("Type") = "Search" Then
```

```
        lblMessage.Text = "The results of your search " _
            & "are below."
        DBCommand = New OleDbDataAdapter _
            ("Select LibBookID, BookTitle, Author, Status " _
            & "From LibBooks Where " _
            & Request.QueryString("SearchField") & " Like '%" _
            & Replace(Request.QueryString("SearchText"), "'", "''") _
            & "%' Order By BookTitle", DBConn)
    ElseIf Request.QueryString("Type") = "Browse" Then
        lblMessage.Text = "The books in the category " _
            & "you selected are listed below."
        DBCommand = New OleDbDataAdapter _
            ("Select LibBookID, BookTitle, Author, Status " _
            & "From LibBooks Where " _
            & "LibBookCategoryID = " _
            & Request.QueryString("LibBookCategoryID") _
            & " Order By BookTitle", DBConn)
    Else
        Response.Redirect("./menu.aspx")
    End If
    DBCommand.Fill(DSPageData, _
        "Books")
    dgBooks.DataSource = _
        DSPageData.Tables("Books").DefaultView
    dgBooks.DataBind()
End Sub
```

The employee should only enter this page if they have signed in:

```
If Len(Session("LibUserID")) = 0 Then
```

If they haven't, we send them to the Library Sign-In page:

```
Response.Redirect("./index.aspx")
```

Next, we define needed data objects:

```
Dim DBConn as OleDbConnection
Dim DBCommand As OleDbDataAdapter
Dim DSPageData as New DataSet
```

We start by connecting to the database:

```
DBConn = New OleDbConnection("Provider=sqloledb;" _
    & "server=localhost;" _
    & "Initial Catalog=INETC5;" _
    & "User Id=sa;" _
    & "Password=yourpassword;")
```

We then check to see if the employee is searching the database:

```
If Request.QueryString("Type") = "Search" Then
```

If so, we display this message in our Label control:

```
lblMessage.Text = "The results of your search " _
    & "are below."
```

And we retrieve all the books that contain the text entered by the visitor in the field they selected

```
DBCommand = New OleDbDataAdapter _
    ("Select LibBookID, BookTitle, Author, Status " _
    & "From LibBooks Where " _
    & Request.QueryString("SearchField") & " Like '%" _
    & Replace(Request.QueryString("SearchText"), "'", "''") _
    & "%' Order By BookTitle", DBConn)
```

Next, we check to see if the employee is browsing a category:

```
ElseIf Request.QueryString("Type") = "Browse" Then
```

If that is the case, we display this message:

```
lblMessage.Text = "The books in the category " _
    & "you selected are listed below."
```

And select all the books in the selected category:

```
DBCommand = New OleDbDataAdapter _
    ("Select LibBookID, BookTitle, Author, Status " _
    & "From LibBooks Where " _
    & "LibBookCategoryID = " _
    & Request.QueryString("LibBookCategoryID") _
    & " Order By BookTitle", DBConn)
```

If the code flows here, it means that the employee did not enter this page through the Menu page:

```
Else
```

In that case, we send them to that page:

```
Response.Redirect("./menu.aspx")
```

Otherwise, we retrieve the matching book records

```
DBCommand.Fill(DSPageData, _
    "Books")
```

and bind our DataGrid to them:

```
dgBooks.DataSource = _
    DSPageData.Tables("Books").DefaultView
dgBooks.DataBind()
```

Book ASP.NET Page

Book.aspx

The Book page displays the full information on a book record. It also allows the employee to check a book out if the book is available. We start by defining our three compiler directives:

```
<%@ Page Language=VB Debug=true %>
<%@ Import Namespace="System.Data" %>
<%@ Import Namespace="System.Data.OLEDB" %>
```

On the page, we define a label that will display the title of the book

```
<asp:Label
    id="lblTitle"
    Font-Size="25pt"
    Font-Name="Tahoma"
    runat="server"
/>
```

and another label that will display the rest of the book information:

```
<asp:Label
    id="lblMessage"
```

```
    Font-Size="12pt"
    Font-Name="Tahoma"
    Font-Bold="True"
    runat="server"
/>
```

The only other control on the page is a Button control that allows the employee to check the book out if it is available:

```
<asp:button
    id="butOK"
    text="Check Out"
    Type="Submit"
    OnClick="SubmitBtn_Click"
    runat="server"
/>
```

The code on the page is contained within two procedures. The first fires when the page is loaded. It displays the contents of the book record.

```
Sub Page_Load(ByVal Sender as Object, ByVal E as EventArgs)
    If Len(Session("LibUserID")) = 0 Then
        Response.Redirect("./index.aspx")
    End If
    If Len(Request.QueryString("LibBookID")) = 0 Then
        Response.Redirect("./menu.aspx")
    End If
    Dim DBConn as OleDbConnection
    Dim DBCommand As OleDbDataAdapter
    Dim DSPageData as New DataSet
    DBConn = New OleDbConnection("Provider=sqloledb;" _
        & "server=localhost;" _
        & "Initial Catalog=INETC5;" _
        & "User Id=sa;" _
        & "Password=yourpassword;")
    DBCommand = New OleDbDataAdapter _
        ("Select BookTitle, Author, CategoryName, " _
        & "Description, Status From LibBooks Left Join " _
        & "LibCategories On LibBooks.LibBookCategoryID " _
        & " = LibCategories.LibBookCategoryID " _
        & "Where LibBookID = " _
        & Request.QueryString("LibBookID"), DBConn)
```

```
    DBCommand.Fill(DSPageData, _
        "Book")
    If DSPageData.Tables("Book"). _
        Rows(0).Item("Status") <> "Available" Then
        butOK.Visible = False
    End If
    lblTitle.Text = DSPageData.Tables("Book"). _
        Rows(0).Item("BookTitle")
    lblMessage.Text = "Author: " & DSPageData.Tables("Book"). _
        Rows(0).Item("Author") & "<br>" _
        & "Category: " & DSPageData.Tables("Book"). _
        Rows(0).Item("Categoryname") & "<br><br>" _
        & "Description: " & DSPageData.Tables("Book"). _
        Rows(0).Item("Description") & "<br><br>" _
        & "Status: " & DSPageData.Tables("Book"). _
        Rows(0).Item("Status") & "<br>"
End Sub
```

We first make sure that the employee has signed in to the database:

```
If Len(Session("LibUserID")) = 0 Then
```

If they have not, we send them to do so:

```
Response.Redirect("./index.aspx")
```

We also check to see if a LibBookID was passed into this page:

```
If Len(Request.QueryString("LibBookID")) = 0 Then
```

If it wasn't, we send the employee back to the Menu page:

```
Response.Redirect("./menu.aspx")
```

Otherwise, we define data objects

```
Dim DBConn as OleDbConnection
Dim DBCommand As OleDbDataAdapter
Dim DSPageData as New DataSet
```

and connect to our SQL Server database:

```
DBConn = New OleDbConnection("Provider=sqloledb;" _
    & "server=localhost;" _
```

```
    & "Initial Catalog=INETC5;" _
    & "User Id=sa;" _
    & "Password=yourpassword;")
```

We then retrieve most of the fields related to this book

```
DBCommand = New OleDbDataAdapter _
    ("Select BookTitle, Author, CategoryName, " _
    & "Description, Status From LibBooks Left Join " _
    & "LibCategories On LibBooks.LibBookCategoryID " _
    & " = LibCategories.LibBookCategoryID " _
    & "Where LibBookID = " _
    & Request.QueryString("LibBookID"), DBConn)
```

into our DataSet object:

```
DBCommand.Fill(DSPageData, _
    "Book")
```

We then check to see if the book is not available

```
If DSPageData.Tables("Book"). _
    Rows(0).Item("Status") <> "Available" Then
```

If that is the case, we hide the Check Out button:

```
butOK.Visible = False
```

Next, we place the title of the book in our Title Label control:

```
lblTitle.Text = DSPageData.Tables("Book"). _
    Rows(0).Item("BookTitle")
```

And the rest of the data on the book is concatenated with HTML tags and raw text into our other Label control:

```
lblMessage.Text = "Author: " & DSPageData.Tables("Book"). _
    Rows(0).Item("Author") & "<br>" _
    & "Category: " & DSPageData.Tables("Book"). _
    Rows(0).Item("Categoryname") & "<br><br>" _
    & "Description: " & DSPageData.Tables("Book"). _
    Rows(0).Item("Description") & "<br><br>" _
    & "Status: " & DSPageData.Tables("Book"). _
    Rows(0).Item("Status") & "<br>"
```

The other procedure fires when the employee clicks the Check Out button. It allows the employee to check out the book.

```
Sub SubmitBtn_Click(Sender As Object, E As EventArgs)
    Dim DBConn as OleDbConnection
    Dim DBUpdate As New OleDbCommand
    DBConn = New OleDbConnection("Provider=sqloledb;" _
        & "server=localhost;" _
        & "Initial Catalog=INETC5;" _
        & "User Id=sa;" _
        & "Password=yourpassword;")
    DBUpdate.CommandText = "Update LibBooks set " _
        & "Status = 'Checked Out', CheckedOutTo = " _
        & Session("LibUserID") _
        & " Where LibBookID = " _
        & Request.QueryString("LibBookID")
    DBUpdate.Connection = DBConn
    DBUpdate.Connection.Open
    DBUpdate.ExecuteNonQuery()
    Response.Redirect("./menu.aspx")
End Sub
```

To do that, we need these data objects:

```
Dim DBConn as OleDbConnection
Dim DBUpdate As New OleDbCommand
```

We start by connecting to our database:

```
DBConn = New OleDbConnection("Provider=sqloledb;" _
    & "server=localhost;" _
    & "Initial Catalog=INETC5;" _
    & "User Id=sa;" _
    & "Password=yourpassword;")
```

We then place an Update statement into our command object to update the current book, marking it as checked out to the signed-in employee:

```
DBUpdate.CommandText = "Update LibBooks set " _
    & "Status = 'Checked Out', CheckedOutTo = " _
    & Session("LibUserID") _
    & " Where LibBookID = " _
    & Request.QueryString("LibBookID")
```

The Command object will use our Connection object to connect to the database:

```
DBUpdate.Connection = DBConn
DBUpdate.Connection.Open
```

We then run our Update query

```
DBUpdate.ExecuteNonQuery()
```

and send the employee back to the Menu page:

```
Response.Redirect("./menu.aspx")
```

Manager's Menu ASP.NET Page

Managers_Menu.aspx

The Manager's Menu page allows a manager to add and delete books from the database. We start with our compiler directives, which import needed data libraries and set up the run environment:

```
<%@ Page Language=VB Debug=true %>
<%@ Import Namespace="System.Data" %>
<%@ Import Namespace="System.Data.OLEDB" %>
```

Within the body of the page, we define a Label control for the title of the page:

```
<asp:Label
    id="lblTitle"
    Font-Size="25pt"
    Font-Name="Tahoma"
    Text="Manager's Menu"
    runat="server"
/>
```

Next, we define a DropDownList that displays the names of all the books:

```
<asp:dropdownlist
    id="ddlBooks"
    runat=server
    DataTextField="BookTitle"
    DataValueField="LibBookID">
</asp:dropdownlist>
```

After that, we define a button, which the manager clicks to indicate that they want to delete the currently selected book:

```
<asp:button
    id="butDelete"
    text="Delete"
    Type="Submit"
    OnClick="Delete_Click"
    runat="server"
/>
```

The next section of the page is used to add new books. So we provide a TextBox for the title of the book

```
<asp:TextBox
    id="txtBookTitle"
    Columns="25"
    MaxLength="100"
    runat=server
/>
```

and a DropDownList for the category the book is in:

```
<asp:dropdownlist
    id="ddlibBookCategoryID"
    runat=server
    DataTextField="CategoryName"
    DataValueField="LibBookCategoryID">
</asp:dropdownlist>
```

Then we define a TextBox for the author of the book

```
<asp:TextBox
    id="txtAuthor"
    Columns="25"
    MaxLength="100"
    runat=server
/>
```

one for the ISBN of the book

```
<asp:TextBox
    id="txtISBN"
    Columns="25"
```

```
    MaxLength="50"
    runat=server
/>
```

another for the book keywords

```
<asp:TextBox
    id="txtKeywords"
    Columns="25"
    MaxLength="100"
    runat=server
/>
```

and one more for the book's description:

```
<asp:TextBox
    id="txtDescription"
    Columns="25"
    MaxLength="255"
    runat=server
/>
```

The last control on the page is a button that the manager clicks to add their book:

```
<asp:button
    id="butAdd"
    text="Add"
    Type="Submit"
    OnClick="Add_Click"
    runat="server"
/>
```

The code on the page runs in three procedures. The first runs when the page is loaded. It sets up the DropDownList controls.

```
Sub Page_Load(ByVal Sender as Object, ByVal E as EventArgs)
    If Len(Session("LibUserID")) = 0 Then
        Response.Redirect("./index.aspx")
    End If
    If Session("UserType") <> "LibManager" Then
        Response.Redirect("./menu.aspx")
    End If
    If Not IsPostBack Then
        Dim DBConn as OleDbConnection
```

```
        Dim DBCommand As OleDbDataAdapter
        Dim DSPageData as New DataSet
        DBConn = New OleDbConnection("Provider=sqloledb;" _
            & "server=localhost;" _
            & "Initial Catalog=INETC5;" _
            & "User Id=sa;" _
            & "Password=yourpassword;")
        DBCommand = New OleDbDataAdapter _
            ("select LibBookCategoryID, CategoryName " _
            & "from LibCategories Order By CategoryName" _
            , DBConn)
        DBCommand.Fill(DSPageData, _
            "Categories")
        ddlibBookCategoryID.DataSource = _
            DSPageData.Tables("Categories").DefaultView
        ddlibBookCategoryID.DataBind()
        DBCommand = New OleDbDataAdapter _
            ("select LibBookID, BookTitle " _
            & "from LibBooks Order By BookTitle" _
            , DBConn)
        DBCommand.Fill(DSPageData, _
            "Books")
        ddlBooks.DataSource = _
            DSPageData.Tables("Books").DefaultView
        ddlBooks.DataBind()
    End If
End Sub
```

We start by making sure that the manager has signed in:

```
If Len(Session("LibUserID")) = 0 Then
```

If they haven't, we send them to the Sign-In page:

```
Response.Redirect("./index.aspx")
```

Next, we make sure that they are indeed a manager:

```
If Session("UserType") <> "LibManager" Then
```

If they are not, we send them to the Menu page:

```
Response.Redirect("./menu.aspx")
```

The rest of the code on the page should run only the first time the page is loaded

```
If Not IsPostBack Then
```

If that is the case, we need data objects:

```
Dim DBConn as OleDbConnection
Dim DBCommand As OleDbDataAdapter
Dim DSPageData as New DataSet
```

We start by connecting to our database:

```
DBConn = New OleDbConnection("Provider=sqloledb;" _
    & "server=localhost;" _
    & "Initial Catalog=INETC5;" _
    & "User Id=sa;" _
    & "Password=yourpassword;")
```

We then retrieve a list of all the categories

```
DBCommand = New OleDbDataAdapter _
    ("select LibBookCategoryID, CategoryName " _
    & "from LibCategories Order By CategoryName" _
    , DBConn)
```

into our DataSet object:

```
DBCommand.Fill(DSPageData, _
    "Categories")
```

We then bind our first DropDownList to that DataSet object table:

```
ddlibBookCategoryID.DataSource = _
    DSPageData.Tables("Categories").DefaultView
ddlibBookCategoryID.DataBind()
```

Next we need to retrieve a list of all the books

```
DBCommand = New OleDbDataAdapter _
    ("select LibBookID, BookTitle " _
    & "from LibBooks Order By BookTitle" _
    , DBConn)
DBCommand.Fill(DSPageData, _
    "Books")
```

which are placed into our other DropDownList control:

```
ddlBooks.DataSource = _
    DSPageData.Tables("Books").DefaultView
ddlBooks.DataBind()
```

The next procedure fires when the Delete button is clicked.

```
Sub Delete_Click(Sender As Object, E As EventArgs)
    Dim DBConn as OleDbConnection
    Dim DBCommand As OleDbDataAdapter
    Dim DSPageData as New DataSet
    Dim DBDelete As New OleDbCommand
    DBConn = New OleDbConnection("Provider=sqloledb;" _
        & "server=localhost;" _
        & "Initial Catalog=INETC5;" _
        & "User Id=sa;" _
        & "Password=yourpassword;")
    DBDelete.CommandText = "Delete From LibBooks " _
        & "Where LibBookID = " & ddlBooks.SelectedItem.Value
    DBDelete.Connection = DBConn
    DBDelete.Connection.Open
    DBDelete.ExecuteNonQuery()
    DBCommand = New OleDbDataAdapter _
        ("select LibBookID, BookTitle " _
        & "from LibBooks Order By BookTitle" _
        , DBConn)
    DBCommand.Fill(DSPageData, _
        "Books")
    ddlBooks.DataSource = _
        DSPageData.Tables("Books").DefaultView
    ddlBooks.DataBind()
End Sub
```

Within this procedure, we will need these data objects:

```
Dim DBConn as OleDbConnection
Dim DBCommand As OleDbDataAdapter
Dim DSPageData as New DataSet
Dim DBDelete As New OleDbCommand
```

We will need to connect to our SQL Server database:

```
DBConn = New OleDbConnection("Provider=sqloledb;" _
    & "server=localhost;" _
    & "Initial Catalog=INETC5;" _
    & "User Id=sa;" _
    & "Password=yourpassword;")
```

We then delete the book selected in the DropDownList by the manager:

```
DBDelete.CommandText = "Delete From LibBooks " _
    & "Where LibBookID = " & ddlBooks.SelectedItem.Value
DBDelete.Connection = DBConn
DBDelete.Connection.Open
DBDelete.ExecuteNonQuery()
```

Now we need to refresh the DropDownList. So we grab the book list from the database

```
DBCommand = New OleDbDataAdapter _
    ("select LibBookID, BookTitle " _
    & "from LibBooks Order By BookTitle" _
    , DBConn)
DBCommand.Fill(DSPageData, _
    "Books")
```

and rebind our DropDownList:

```
ddlBooks.DataSource = _
    DSPageData.Tables("Books").DefaultView
ddlBooks.DataBind()
```

The other procedure on the page adds a new book to the database when the Add button is clicked.

```
Sub Add_Click(Sender As Object, E As EventArgs)
    Dim DBConn as OleDbConnection
    Dim DBInsert As New OleDbCommand
    DBConn = New OleDbConnection("Provider=sqloledb;" _
        & "server=localhost;" _
        & "Initial Catalog=INETC5;" _
        & "User Id=sa;" _
        & "Password=yourpassword;")
    DBInsert.CommandText = "Insert Into LibBooks " _
        & "(BookTitle, Author, LibBookCategoryID, ISBN, " _
```

```
        & "Keywords, Description, Status, CheckedOutTo) " _
        & "values (" _
        & "'" & Replace(txtBookTitle.Text, "'", "''") & "', " _
        & "'" & Replace(txtAuthor.Text, "'", "''") & "', " _
        & ddlibBookCategoryID.SelectedItem.Value & ", " _
        & "'" & Replace(txtISBN.Text, "'", "''") & "', " _
        & "'" & Replace(txtKeywords.Text, "'", "''") & "', " _
        & "'" & Replace(txtDescription.Text, "'", "''") & "', " _
        & "'Available', 0)"
    DBInsert.Connection = DBConn
    DBInsert.Connection.Open
    DBInsert.ExecuteNonQuery()
    Response.Redirect("./menu.aspx")
End Sub
```

Here, too, we need data objects

```
Dim DBConn as OleDbConnection
Dim DBInsert As New OleDbCommand
```

and we need to connect to the database:

```
DBConn = New OleDbConnection("Provider=sqloledb;" _
    & "server=localhost;" _
    & "Initial Catalog=INETC5;" _
    & "User Id=sa;" _
    & "Password=yourpassword;")
```

We then place a SQL Insert statement into the Command object

```
DBInsert.CommandText = "Insert Into LibBooks " _
    & "(BookTitle, Author, LibBookCategoryID, ISBN, " _
    & "Keywords, Description, Status, CheckedOutTo) " _
    & "values (" _
    & "'" & Replace(txtBookTitle.Text, "'", "''") & "', " _
    & "'" & Replace(txtAuthor.Text, "'", "''") & "', " _
    & ddlibBookCategoryID.SelectedItem.Value & ", " _
    & "'" & Replace(txtISBN.Text, "'", "''") & "', " _
    & "'" & Replace(txtKeywords.Text, "'", "''") & "', " _
    & "'" & Replace(txtDescription.Text, "'", "''") & "', " _
    & "'Available', 0)"
```

which, when executed, adds the new record to the database:

```
DBInsert.Connection = DBConn
DBInsert.Connection.Open
DBInsert.ExecuteNonQuery()
```

We then send the manager back to the Menu page:

```
Response.Redirect("./menu.aspx")
```

Access Code Changes

C5Library.mdb

If you wish to use this solution with Access instead of SQL Server, you should only need to change the connect string from the one that points to the SQL Server database

```
DBConn = New OleDbConnection("Provider=sqloledb;" _
    & "server=localhost;" _
    & "Initial Catalog=INETC5;" _
    & "User Id=sa;" _
    & "Password=yourpassword;")
```

to one that points to your Access database:

```
DBConn = New OleDbConnection("PROVIDER=Microsoft.Jet.OLEDB.4.0;" _
    & "DATA SOURCE=" _
    & Server.MapPath("/INetBook/C5/Library/" _
    & "Access/C5Library.mdb;"))
```

Note that you would need to change the path to the location where you placed the Access database.

Incident Report Tool

The other tool we will review in this chapter is the Incident Report tool. This one allows employees to report an incident. Depending on the department that they select for the incident, a manager receives an e-mail about the submission. The manager can then add comments to the incident report.

Sample Usage

When the employee wants to submit an Incident Report, they use the page displayed in Figure 5-12.

The employee first selects the department for the incident. They then supply answers to a series of questions. When they have completed their narrative, they click the Add button. Their report is added to the database, and the manager of the department receives an e-mail like the one displayed in Figure 5-13.

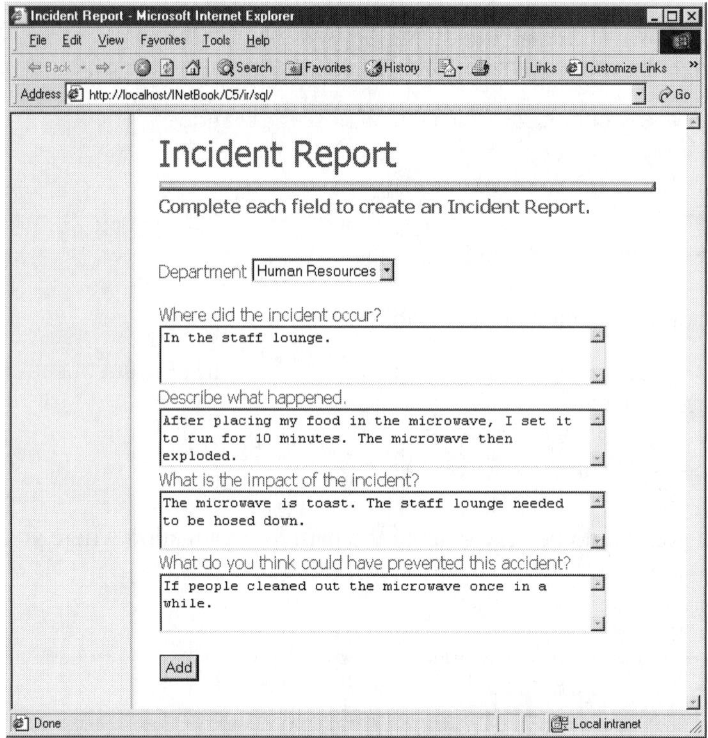

Figure 5-12 *Incident Report page*

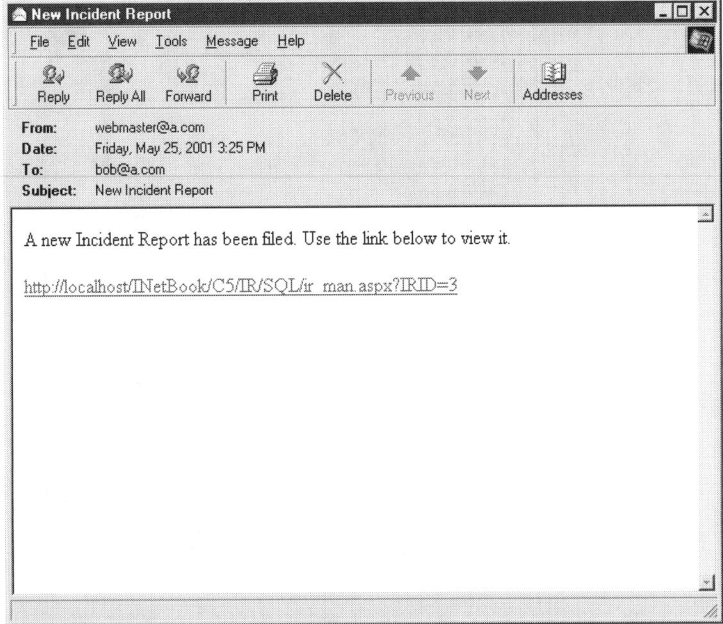

Figure 5-13 *E-mail sent by Incident Report page*

The manager is supplied, in that e-mail, with a link to a page where they can view and comment on the incident. That page is displayed in Figure 5-14.

At the top of the page, the manager sees the narrative entered by the employee. They can then add their comments to the record and change the status of the Incident Report through this page.

Incident Report Database Component

C5IR.sql

The database behind the ASP.NET Incident Report Application requires two tables. In this section, we will review the relationships between the tables and the fields they contain.

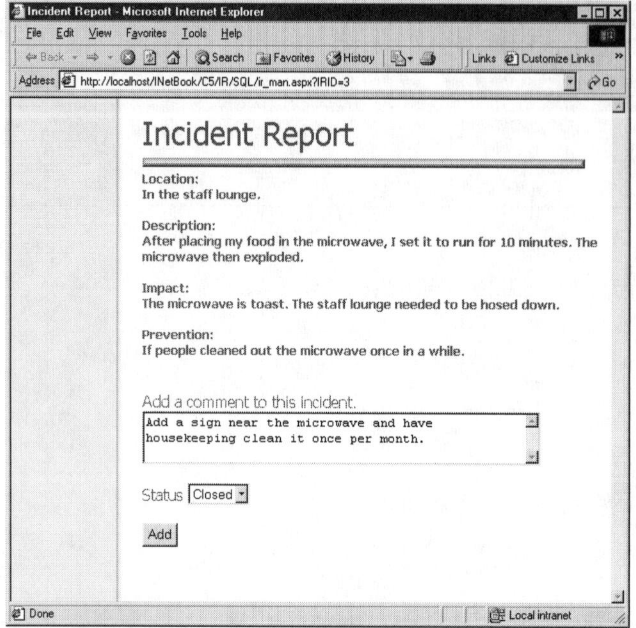

Figure 5-14 *Incident Report Management page*

Tables and Data Diagram

Figure 5-15 displays the relationship between the tables in the Incident Report database.

The top-level table is the IRDepartments table. It contains the list of departments and e-mail addresses used on the Incident Report page. The IRs table contains the incident report data. The two tables relate in a one-to-many relationship. Each department can have many reports, but each report is filed to a single department.

IRDepartments Field Specifications

IRDepartments.txt

The field specifications for the fields in the IRDepartments table are displayed in Table 5-4.

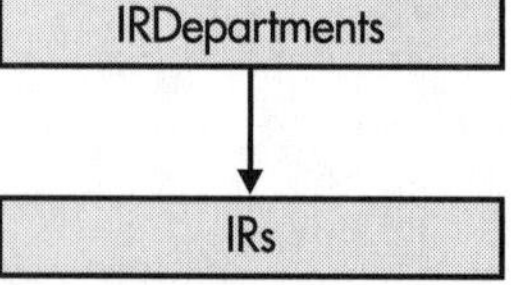

Figure 5-15 *Incident Report data diagram*

Field Name	Field Type	Notes
DepartmentID	int	Primary Key, Identity Column
DepartmentName	varchar	Length = 50
ContactEmailAddress	varchar	Length = 100

Table 5-4 *IRDepartments Field Specifications*

The primary key in this table is the DepartmentID field. The DepartmentName field stores the name of the department. The ContactEmailAddress field stores e-mail addresses that the message is sent to when an incident report is filed for the department.

IRs Field Specifications

IRs.txt

The field specifications for the fields in the IRs table are displayed in Table 5-5.

The IRID is the primary key in this table. The DepartmentID field links this table back to the IRDepartments table in a one-to-many relationship. The rest of the fields hold the data related to the incident report as entered by either the employee or the manager.

Incident Report ASP.NET Code

The Incident Report tool is composed of two pages. One is for the employee, and the other is for the manager. In this section, we will review those two pages.

Field Name	Field Type	Notes
IRID	int	Primary Key, Identity Column
DepartmentID	int	Foreign Key
Location	varchar	Length = 255
Description	varchar	Length = 255
Impact	varchar	Length = 255
Prevention	varchar	Length = 255
Status	varchar	Length = 50
Comments	text	

Table 5-5 *IRs Field Specifications*

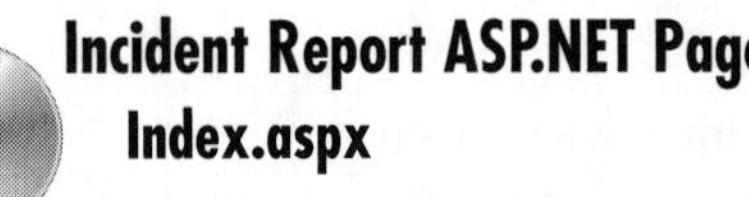

Incident Report ASP.NET Page

Index.aspx

The code on the Incident Report page displays a list of all the departments and allows the employee to send an incident report. At the top of the page, we have four compiler directives.

```
<%@ Page Language=VB Debug=true %>
<%@ Import Namespace="System.Data" %>
<%@ Import Namespace="System.Data.OLEDB" %>
<%@ Import Namespace="System.Web.Mail" %>
```

The first tells the compiler the language we are using and also that we are in debug mode:

```
<%@ Page Language=VB Debug=true %>
```

The next two import data libraries:

```
<%@ Import Namespace="System.Data" %>
<%@ Import Namespace="System.Data.OLEDB" %>
```

The last imports a library that allows us to define e-mail objects:

```
<%@ Import Namespace="System.Web.Mail" %>
```

Within the body of the page, we define a Label control that displays the title of the page:

```
<asp:Label
    id="lblTitle"
    Font-Size="25pt"
    Font-Name="Tahoma"
    Text="Incident Report"
    runat="server"
/>
```

Another Label control displays page instructions and a response after an incident report has been filed

```
<asp:Label
    id="lblMessage"
    Font-Size="12pt"
```

```
    Font-Name="Tahoma"
    Font-Bold="True"
    Text="Complete each field to create an Incident Report."
    runat="server"
/>
```

The rest of the controls on the page are contained within a Panel control to make it easier to toggle their visibility:

```
<asp:Panel
    id="pnlForm"
    runat="server"
>
```

On that Panel control, we place a DropDownList control for the employee to select the department:

```
<asp:dropdownlist
    id="ddlDepartments"
    runat=server
    DataTextField="DepartmentName"
    DataValueField="DepartmentID">
</asp:dropdownlist>
```

We then display a series of TextBox controls that are implemented as TextArea form elements on the page that allow the employee to enter their narrative. The first is for the location of the incident:

```
<asp:TextBox
    id="txtLocation"
    Columns="50"
    Rows="3"
    MaxLength="255"
    runat=server
    TextMode="MultiLine"
/>
```

The next allows the employee to enter a description of the incident:

```
<asp:TextBox
    id="txtDescription"
    Columns="50"
    Rows="3"
```

```
    MaxLength="255"
    runat=server
    TextMode="MultiLine"
/>
```

That is followed by a TextBox control for the impact of the incident

```
<asp:TextBox
    id="txtImpact"
    Columns="50"
    Rows="3"
    MaxLength="255"
    runat=server
    TextMode="MultiLine"
/>
```

and one for the prevention text:

```
<asp:TextBox
    id="txtPrevention"
    Columns="50"
    Rows="3"
    MaxLength="255"
    runat=server
    TextMode="MultiLine"
/>
```

The only other control on the form is a button that submits the form when it is clicked

```
<asp:button
    id="butAdd"
    text="Add"
    Type="Submit"
    OnClick="Add_Click"
    runat="server"
/>
```

The code on the page fires in two events. This first code block fires when the page is loaded.

```
Sub Page_Load(ByVal Sender as Object, ByVal E as EventArgs)
    If Not IsPostBack Then
        Dim DBConn as OleDbConnection
```

```
        Dim DBCommand As OleDbDataAdapter
        Dim DSPageData as New DataSet
        DBConn = New OleDbConnection("Provider=sqloledb;" _
            & "server=localhost;" _
            & "Initial Catalog=INETC5;" _
            & "User Id=sa;" _
            & "Password=yourpassword;")
        DBCommand = New OleDbDataAdapter _
            ("select DepartmentID, DepartmentName " _
            & "from IRDepartments Order By DepartmentName" _
            , DBConn)
        DBCommand.Fill(DSPageData, _
            "Departments")
        ddlDepartments.DataSource = _
            DSPageData.Tables("Departments").DefaultView
        ddlDepartments.DataBind()
    End If
End Sub
```

We only want this code to run when the page is first loaded

```
If Not IsPostBack Then
```

If that is the case, we need these data objects:

```
Dim DBConn as OleDbConnection
Dim DBCommand As OleDbDataAdapter
Dim DSPageData as New DataSet
```

We start by connecting to the database:

```
DBConn = New OleDbConnection("Provider=sqloledb;" _
    & "server=localhost;" _
    & "Initial Catalog=INETC5;" _
    & "User Id=sa;" _
    & "Password=yourpassword;")
```

And we retrieve a list of departments

```
DBCommand = New OleDbDataAdapter _
    ("select DepartmentID, DepartmentName " _
    & "from IRDepartments Order By DepartmentName" _
    , DBConn)
```

which are placed into our DataSet object:

```
DBCommand.Fill(DSPageData, _
    "Departments")
```

We then bind the Departments DropDownList control to that DataSet:

```
ddlDepartments.DataSource = _
    DSPageData.Tables("Departments").DefaultView
ddlDepartments.DataBind()
```

The procedure fires when the employee clicks the Add button. It adds their report to the database and sends out the e-mail.

```
Sub Add_Click(Sender As Object, E As EventArgs)
    Dim DBConn as OleDbConnection
    Dim DBInsert As New OleDbCommand
    Dim DBCommand As OleDbDataAdapter
    Dim DSPageData as New DataSet
    Dim TheMessage as String
    Dim TheMailMessage as New MailMessage
    Dim TheMailConnection as New SmtpMail
    DBConn = New OleDbConnection("Provider=sqloledb;" _
        & "server=localhost;" _
        & "Initial Catalog=INETC5;" _
        & "User Id=sa;" _
        & "Password=yourpassword;")
    DBInsert.CommandText = "Insert Into IRs " _
        & "(DepartmentID, Location, Description, " _
        & "Impact, Prevention, Status) values (" _
        & ddlDepartments.SelectedItem.Value & ", " _
        & "'" & Replace(txtLocation.Text, "'", "''") & "', " _
        & "'" & Replace(txtDescription.Text, "'", "''") & "', " _
        & "'" & Replace(txtImpact.Text, "'", "''") & "', " _
        & "'" & Replace(txtPrevention.Text, "'", "''") & "', " _
        & "'Open')"
    DBInsert.Connection = DBConn
    DBInsert.Connection.Open
    DBInsert.ExecuteNonQuery()
    DBCommand = New OleDbDataAdapter _
        ("Select Max(IRID) as TheID " _
```

```
        & "from IRs", DBConn)
    DBCommand.Fill(DSPageData, _
        "NewID")
    DBCommand = New OleDbDataAdapter _
        ("select ContactEmailAddress " _
        & "from IRDepartments Where DepartmentID = " _
        & ddlDepartments.SelectedItem.Value _
        , DBConn)
    DBCommand.Fill(DSPageData, _
        "Contact")
    TheMessage = "A new Incident Report has been filed. " _
        & "Use the link below to view it." & chr(13) & chr(13) _
        & "http://localhost/INetBook/C5/IR/SQL/ir_man.aspx" _
        & "?IRID=" & DSPageData.Tables("NewID"). _
        Rows(0).Item("TheID")
    TheMailMessage.From = "webmaster@a.com"
    TheMailMessage.To = DSPageData.Tables("Contact"). _
        Rows(0).Item("ContactEmailAddress")
    TheMailMessage.Subject = "New Incident Report"
    TheMailMessage.Body = TheMessage
    TheMailConnection.Send(TheMailMessage)
    lblMessage.Text = "The Incident Report you entered " _
        & "has been received."
    pnlForm.Visible = False
End Sub
```

Therefore, we will need data objects

```
Dim DBConn as OleDbConnection
Dim DBInsert As New OleDbCommand
Dim DBCommand As OleDbDataAdapter
Dim DSPageData as New DataSet
```

as well as a string to hold the e-mail message

```
Dim TheMessage as String
```

and e-mail objects:

```
Dim TheMailMessage as New MailMessage
Dim TheMailConnection as New SmtpMail
```

We start by connecting to our database:

```
DBConn = New OleDbConnection("Provider=sqloledb;" _
    & "server=localhost;" _
    & "Initial Catalog=INETC5;" _
    & "User Id=sa;" _
    & "Password=yourpassword;")
```

We then place an Insert statement into our Command object, which adds the data entered by the employee into the IRs table:

```
DBInsert.CommandText = "Insert Into IRs " _
    & "(DepartmentID, Location, Description, " _
    & "Impact, Prevention, Status) values (" _
    & ddlDepartments.SelectedItem.Value & ", " _
    & "'" & Replace(txtLocation.Text, "'", "''") & "', " _
    & "'" & Replace(txtDescription.Text, "'", "''") & "', " _
    & "'" & Replace(txtImpact.Text, "'", "''") & "', " _
    & "'" & Replace(txtPrevention.Text, "'", "''") & "', " _
    & "'Open')"
```

That Command object will connect to the database through our Connection object:

```
DBInsert.Connection = DBConn
DBInsert.Connection.Open
```

We then insert the record:

```
DBInsert.ExecuteNonQuery()
```

Next we need to retrieve the ID of the record we just added

```
DBCommand = New OleDbDataAdapter _
    ("Select Max(IRID) as TheID " _
    & "from IRs", DBConn)
DBCommand.Fill(DSPageData, _
    "NewID")
```

as well as the e-mail address of the person who should be notified that an incident has been reported

```
DBCommand = New OleDbDataAdapter _
    ("select ContactEmailAddress " _
```

```
    & "from IRDepartments Where DepartmentID = " _
    & ddlDepartments.SelectedItem.Value _
    , DBConn)
DBCommand.Fill(DSPageData, _
    "Contact")
```

The text of the e-mail message contains some raw text along with the ID of the record we just added to the IRs table:

```
TheMessage = "A new Incident Report has been filed. " _
    & "Use the link below to view it." & chr(13) & chr(13) _
    & "http://localhost/INetBook/C5/IR/SQL/ir_man.aspx" _
    & "?IRID=" & DSPageData.Tables("NewID"). _
    Rows(0).Item("TheID")
```

We then set who the e-mail message is from

```
TheMailMessage.From = "webmaster@a.com"
```

the manager who it is to be sent to

```
TheMailMessage.To = DSPageData.Tables("Contact"). _
    Rows(0).Item("ContactEmailAddress")
```

and the subject of the e-mail message:

```
TheMailMessage.Subject = "New Incident Report"
```

We next place the text of the message into the Body property:

```
TheMailMessage.Body = TheMessage
```

Now we can send the e-mail message:

```
TheMailConnection.Send(TheMailMessage)
```

We then display a success message to the employee

```
lblMessage.Text = "The Incident Report you entered " _
    & "has been received."
```

and hide the form on the page:

```
pnlForm.Visible = False
```

Incident Report Management ASP.NET Page
IR_Man.aspx

The Incident Report Management page allows the manager to view an incident report and to make comments on it. At the top of the page we define the environment and data library import directives:

```
<%@ Page Language=VB Debug=true %>
<%@ Import Namespace="System.Data" %>
<%@ Import Namespace="System.Data.OLEDB" %>
```

Within the body of the page we define a Label control that displays the title of the page:

```
<asp:Label
    id="lblTitle"
    Font-Size="25pt"
    Font-Name="Tahoma"
    Text="Incident Report"
    runat="server"
/>
```

Another Label control displays the contents of the incident report:

```
<asp:Label
    id="lblMessage"
    Font-Size="10pt"
    Font-Name="Tahoma"
    Font-Bold="True"
    runat="server"
/>
```

That is followed by a TextBox control where the manager can enter a comment for the incident report:

```
<asp:TextBox
    id="txtComments"
    Columns="50"
    Rows="3"
    MaxLength="255"
    runat=server
    TextMode="MultiLine"
/>
```

The next control on the page is a DropDownList control where the manager can enter the status of the incident

```
<asp:DropDownList
    id="ddlStatus"
    runat=server>
    <asp:ListItem Value="Open">Open</asp:ListItem>
    <asp:ListItem Value="Closed">Closed</asp:ListItem>
</asp:DropDownList>
```

and a button to submit the comments and status changes:

```
<asp:button
    id="butAdd"
    text="Add"
    Type="Submit"
    OnClick="Add_Click"
    runat="server"
/>
```

The code on the page fires in two events. The first event fires when the page is first loaded. It populates the page according to the incident report that is to be displayed.

```
Sub Page_Load(ByVal Sender as Object, ByVal E as EventArgs)
    If Len(Request.QueryString("IRID")) = 0 Then
        Response.Redirect("./index.aspx")
    End If
    If Not IsPostBack Then
        Dim DBConn as OleDbConnection
        Dim DBCommand As OleDbDataAdapter
        Dim DSPageData as New DataSet
        DBConn = New OleDbConnection("Provider=sqloledb;" _
            & "server=localhost;" _
            & "Initial Catalog=INETC5;" _
            & "User Id=sa;" _
            & "Password=yourpassword;")
        DBCommand = New OleDbDataAdapter _
            ("Select Location, Description, Impact, " _
            & "Prevention, Status From IRs " _
            & "Where IRID = " _
            & Request.QueryString("IRID"), DBConn)
        DBCommand.Fill(DSPageData, _
            "IR")
```

```
        lblMessage.Text = "Location:<br>" _
            & DSPageData.Tables("IR"). _
            Rows(0).Item("Location") & "<br><br>" _
            & "Description:<br>" _
            & DSPageData.Tables("IR"). _
            Rows(0).Item("Description") & "<br><br>" _
            & "Impact:<br>" _
            & DSPageData.Tables("IR"). _
            Rows(0).Item("Impact") & "<br><br>" _
            & "Prevention:<br>" _
            & DSPageData.Tables("IR"). _
            Rows(0).Item("Prevention") & "<br><br>"
        ddlStatus.SelectedItem.Text = _
            DSPageData.Tables("IR").Rows(0).Item("Status")
    End If
End Sub
```

The page should be opened only if an IRID was passed into it:

```
If Len(Request.QueryString("IRID")) = 0 Then
```

If one wasn't, we send the manager to the Incident Report page:

```
Response.Redirect("./index.aspx")
```

The rest of the code on the page runs only when the page is first opened

```
If Not IsPostBack Then
```

If that is the case, we need a data object so that we can retrieve the incident report record:

```
Dim DBConn as OleDbConnection
Dim DBCommand As OleDbDataAdapter
Dim DSPageData as New DataSet
```

We start by connecting to our database:

```
DBConn = New OleDbConnection("Provider=sqloledb;" _
    & "server=localhost;" _
    & "Initial Catalog=INETC5;" _
    & "User Id=sa;" _
    & "Password=yourpassword;")
```

We then retrieve the incident report corresponding to the ID passed into this page:

```
DBCommand = New OleDbDataAdapter _
    ("Select Location, Description, Impact, " _
    & "Prevention, Status From IRs " _
    & "Where IRID = " _
    & Request.QueryString("IRID"), DBConn)
DBCommand.Fill(DSPageData, _
   "IR")
```

The data in that record is placed with HTML tags into our Label control:

```
lblMessage.Text = "Location:<br>" _
    & DSPageData.Tables("IR"). _
    Rows(0).Item("Location") & "<br><br>" _
    & "Description:<br>" _
    & DSPageData.Tables("IR"). _
    Rows(0).Item("Description") & "<br><br>" _
    & "Impact:<br>" _
    & DSPageData.Tables("IR"). _
    Rows(0).Item("Impact") & "<br><br>" _
    & "Prevention:<br>" _
    & DSPageData.Tables("IR"). _
    Rows(0).Item("Prevention") & "<br><br>"
```

Next, we place the status of the incident into the DropDownList control:

```
ddlStatus.SelectedItem.Text = _
    DSPageData.Tables("IR").Rows(0).Item("Status")
```

The other event fires when the manager clicks the Add button.

```
Sub Add_Click(Sender As Object, E As EventArgs)
    Dim DBConn as OleDbConnection
    Dim DBUpdate As New OleDbCommand
    DBConn = New OleDbConnection("Provider=sqloledb;" _
        & "server=localhost;" _
        & "Initial Catalog=INETC5;" _
        & "User Id=sa;" _
        & "Password=yourpassword;")
    DBUpdate.CommandText = "Update IRs Set " _
        & "Status = '" & ddlStatus.SelectedItem.Text & "', " _
        & "Comments = '" _
```

```
        & Replace(txtComments.Text, "'", "''") & "' Where " _
        & "IRID = " & Request.QueryString("IRID")
    DBUpdate.Connection = DBConn
    DBUpdate.Connection.Open
    DBUpdate.ExecuteNonQuery()
End Sub
```

This procedure updates the incident report by inserting the comments and status entered by the manager into the record. Therefore, we will need data objects:

```
Dim DBConn as OleDbConnection
Dim DBUpdate As New OleDbCommand
```

We connect to the database

```
DBConn = New OleDbConnection("Provider=sqloledb;" _
    & "server=localhost;" _
    & "Initial Catalog=INETC5;" _
    & "User Id=sa;" _
    & "Password=yourpassword;")
```

and update the record that the manager is viewing as determined by the data they entered

```
DBUpdate.CommandText = "Update IRs Set " _
    & "Status = '" & ddlStatus.SelectedItem.Text & "', " _
    & "Comments = '" _
    & Replace(txtComments.Text, "'", "''") & "' Where " _
    & "IRID = " & Request.QueryString("IRID")
```

The Command object connects to the database through the Connection object:

```
DBUpdate.Connection = DBConn
DBUpdate.Connection.Open
```

We then update the record:

```
DBUpdate.ExecuteNonQuery()
```

Access Code Changes

C5IR.mdb

If you wish to use this solution with Access instead of SQL Server, you should only need to change the connect string from the one that points to the SQL Server database

```
DBConn = New OleDbConnection("Provider=sqloledb;" _
    & "server=localhost;" _
    & "Initial Catalog=INETC5;" _
    & "User Id=sa;" _
    & "Password=yourpassword;")
```

to one that points to your Access database:

```
DBConn = New OleDbConnection("PROVIDER=Microsoft.Jet.OLEDB.4.0;" _
    & "DATA SOURCE=" _
    & Server.MapPath("/INetBook/C5/IR/" _
    & "Access/C5IR.mdb;"))
```

No other code changes should be needed.

CHAPTER

6

Building a Sports Site

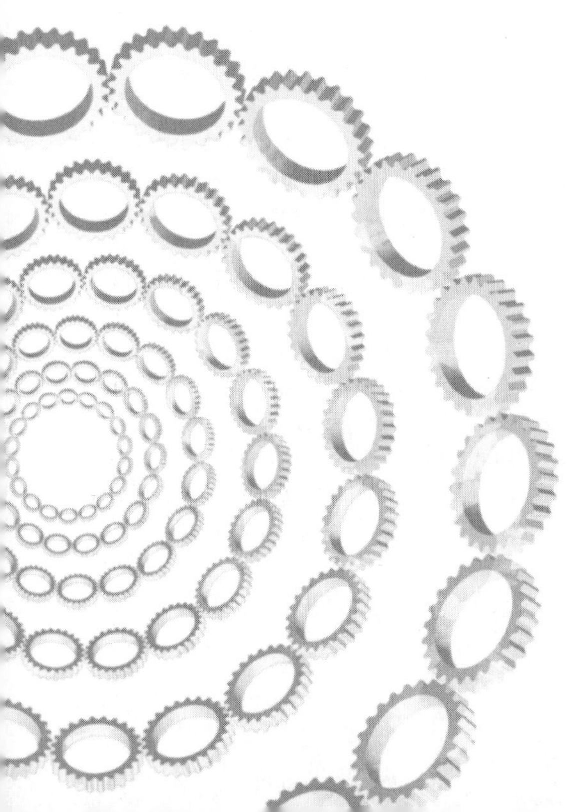

The solution presented in this chapter is a Sports site. The application allows you to manage teams within an imaginary basketball league. The teams participate in games with each other, and they have related news articles and players that are all viewable through the site.

Note that even though the tool is implemented as a basketball sports site, you could easily modify the tool to display information for some other sport or team activity.

Sample Usage

When the visitor first enters the site, they see the Standings page displayed in Figure 6-1.

The page displays all the teams in the league grouped by the conference that they are in. Each team is displayed with their record, wins, and losses.

The visitor can also view the team standings, based on the division that they are in, using the link at the top of the page. That view of the page is displayed in Figure 6-2.

As before, the teams are displayed in order of their records. But notice that each column header is a link. That means that we are allowing the visitor to sort the DataGrid on that column. Take a look at Figure 6-3.

Here the visitor has chosen to sort the DataGrid controls by a different column. The first is sorted by the team name, the second by the record, the third by the wins, and the fourth by the losses column.

The visitor can view results of games and the schedule of upcoming games by clicking the link at the bottom of the page. When they do that, they see the page displayed in Figure 6-4.

When the page first opens, the visitor is presented with the current date's games. In this case, the results of the games are not yet in, so the visitor does not see any scores.

But the visitor can use the calendar to view the games on any other date. Take a look at Figure 6-5.

Here the visitor has selected a date that games have been played on, so now they see the scores in that game.

Back on the Standings page, notice that the name of the team is a link. When the visitor clicks that link, they are taken to a Team page like the one displayed in Figure 6-6.

In the title text of the page, the visitor sees the team name. Below that, in a DataGrid, the visitor sees all the games played and scheduled for the current team.

At the bottom of the page, the visitor is presented with two lists. The first list displays the names of all of the players on this team. The second list displays the titles of news items that are related to this team.

When the visitor selects the name of a player and clicks View Player Info, they are taken to the Player page displayed in Figure 6-7.

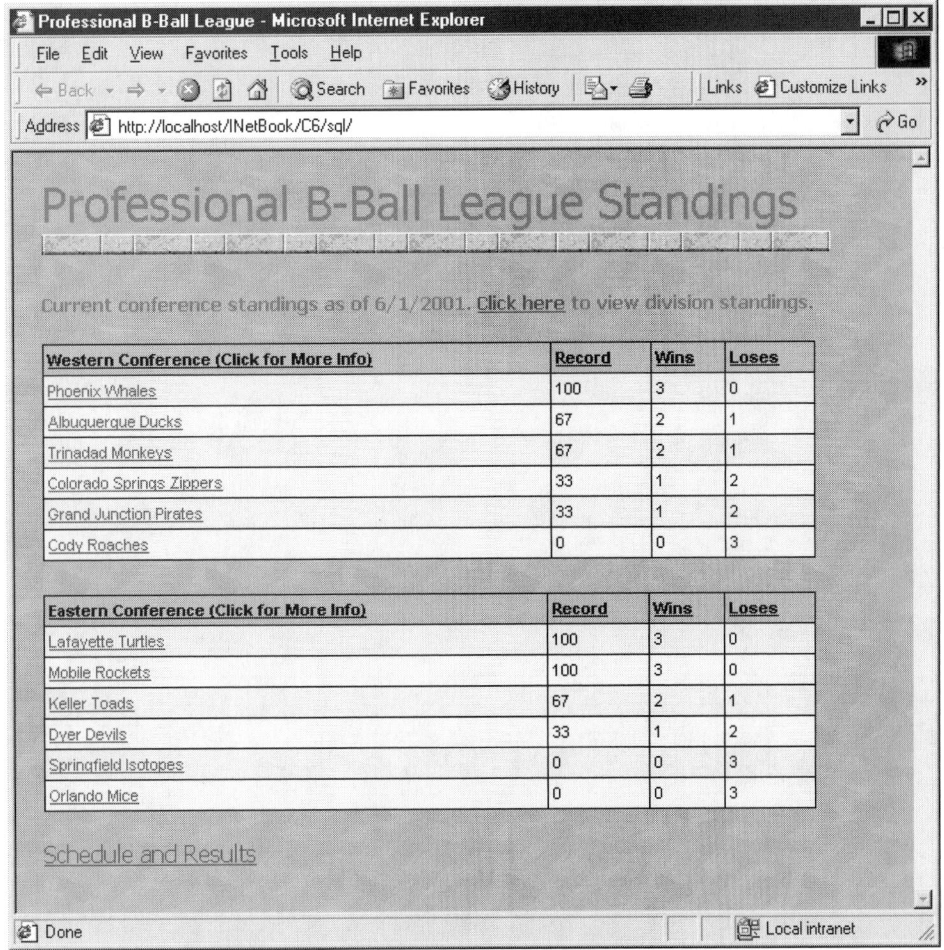

Figure 6-1 *Conference view of Standings page*

The page displays the name of the player, along with their number at the top of the page. Then in the body of the page, the visitor can see the player's game statistics as well as summary information about the player.

Back on the Team page, the visitor can view a news article by selecting it from the list and clicking the View Article button. The page the visitor sees is displayed in Figure 6-8.

The top of the page displays the headline for the article. Then in the body of the page, the visitor sees the date the article was entered and the text of the article. Note that since the text of the article is displayed as HTML, the author of the article could include HTML tags to format their text.

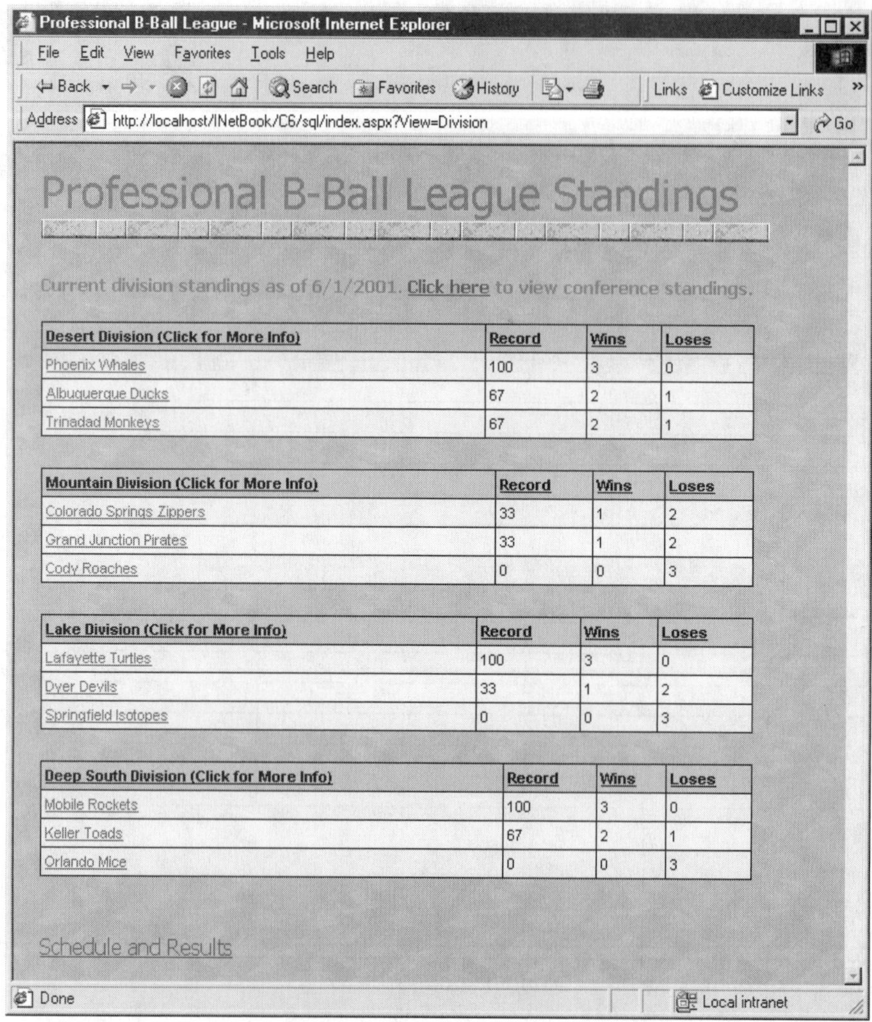

Figure 6-2 *Division view of Standings page*

Sports Site Database Component

C6.sql

The database required to run the Sports Site is composed of four related tables. In this section, we will look at the relationships between the tables and the fields that make up the tables.

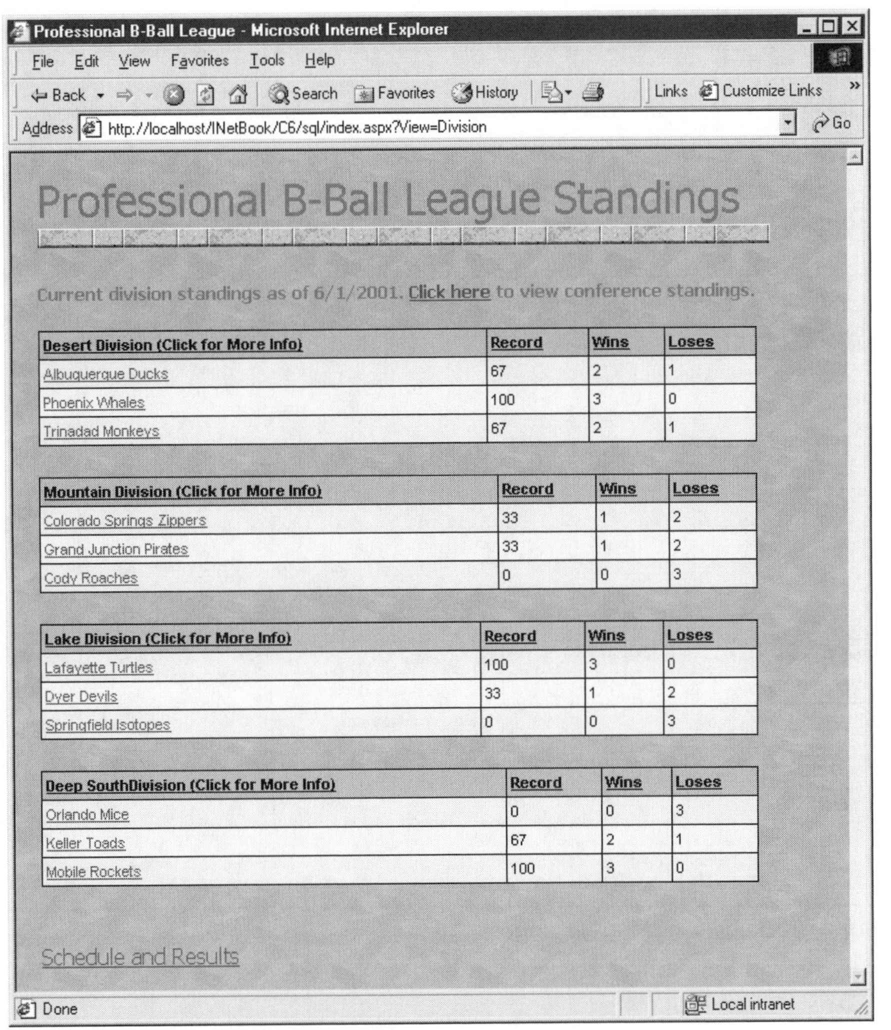

Figure 6-3 *Grids sorted on the Standings page*

Tables and Data Diagram

Figure 6-9 shows the relationships between the tables in the Sports Site database.

The top-level table in the database is the Teams table. That table stores the name and other singular information about the team. The table relates to all the other tables.

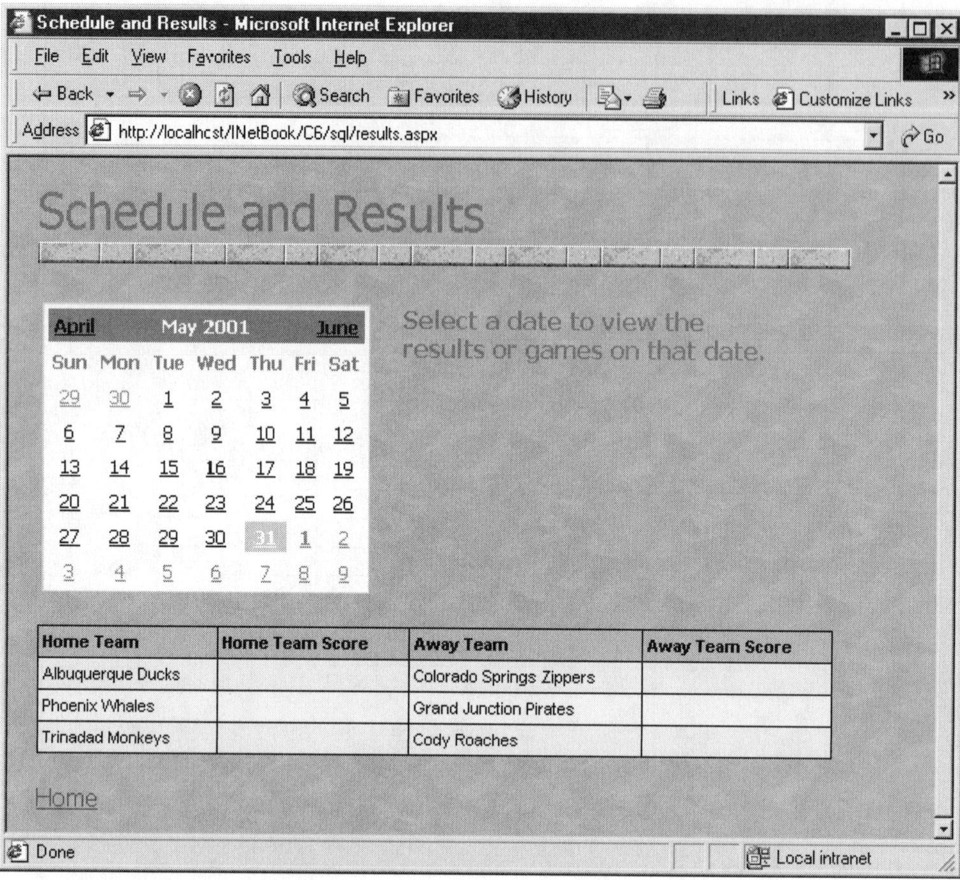

Figure 6-4 *Schedule and Results page*

In fact, it relates to the Games table twice. The Games table stores the teams and scores of each game. Since each game has two teams in it, the table relates to the Teams table twice in a one-to-many relationship.

The Players table stores data on each player. That table is in a one-to-many relationship with the Teams table. Each team can have many players, but each player plays on a single team.

The other table in the database, TeamNews, stores the news articles related to each team. The table is also in a one-to-many relationship with the Teams table. Each article goes with one team but each team can have many articles.

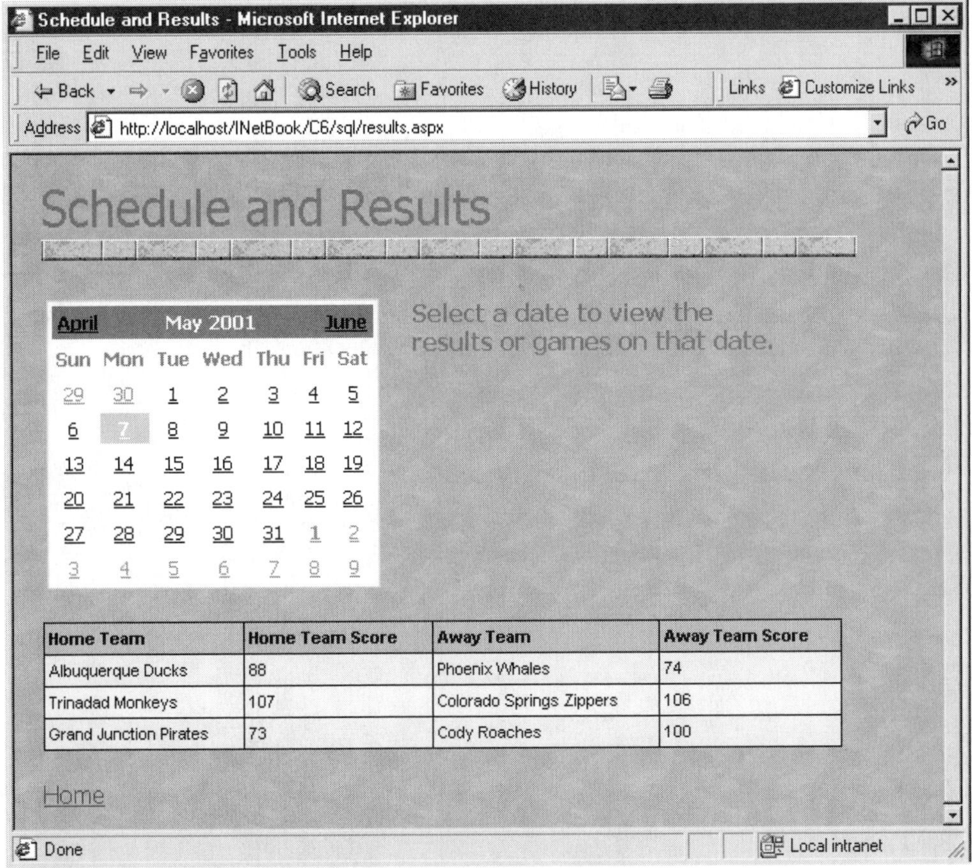

Figure 6-5 *Schedule and Results page displaying results of played games*

Teams Field Specifications

Teams.txt

The field specifications for the fields in the Teams table are displayed in Table 6-1.

The TeamID field is the primary key in the table and is automatically populated when a new record is added to this table. The TeamCity and TeamNickName fields are combined when displayed on the site to show the full team name.

The Conference and Division fields are used to determine which DataGrid the team should appear in on the Standings page. The other fields store the team's current record.

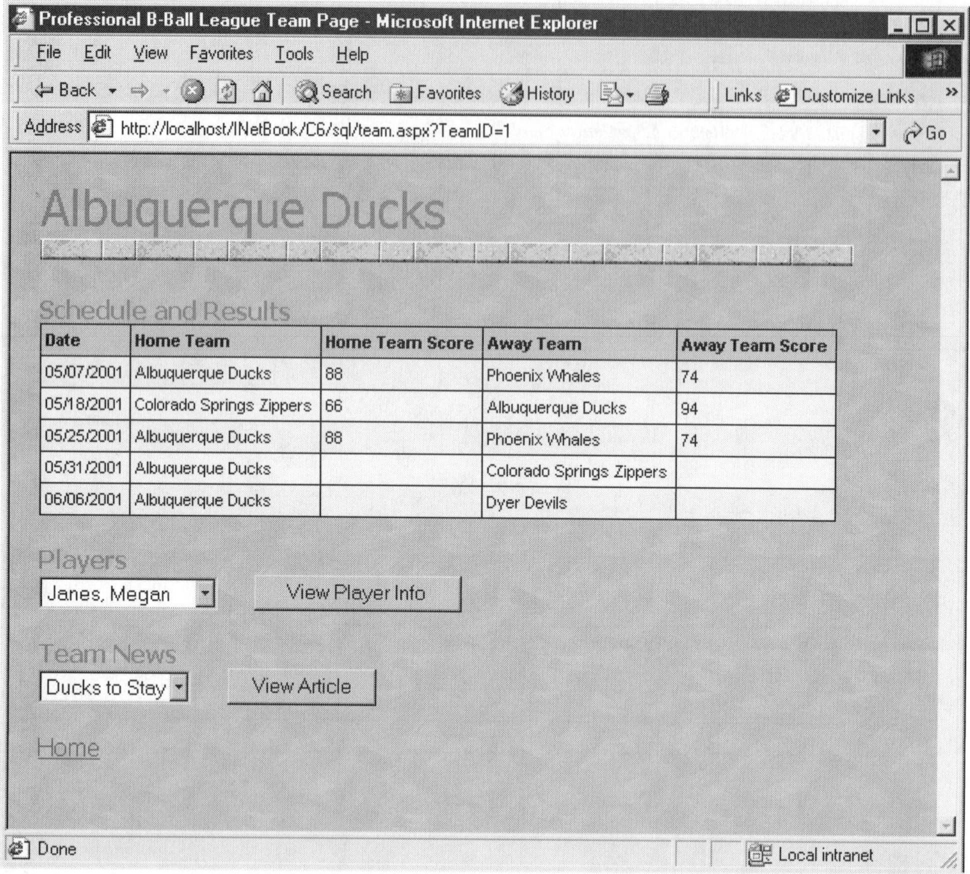

Figure 6-6 *Team page*

Games Field Specifications

Games.txt

The field specifications for the fields in the Games table are displayed in Table 6-2.

The GameID field is the primary key in this table. The TeamID1 field and the TeamID2 field are foreign keys that link this table to the Teams table. The first one stores the home team in this game, and the other one stores the away team in this

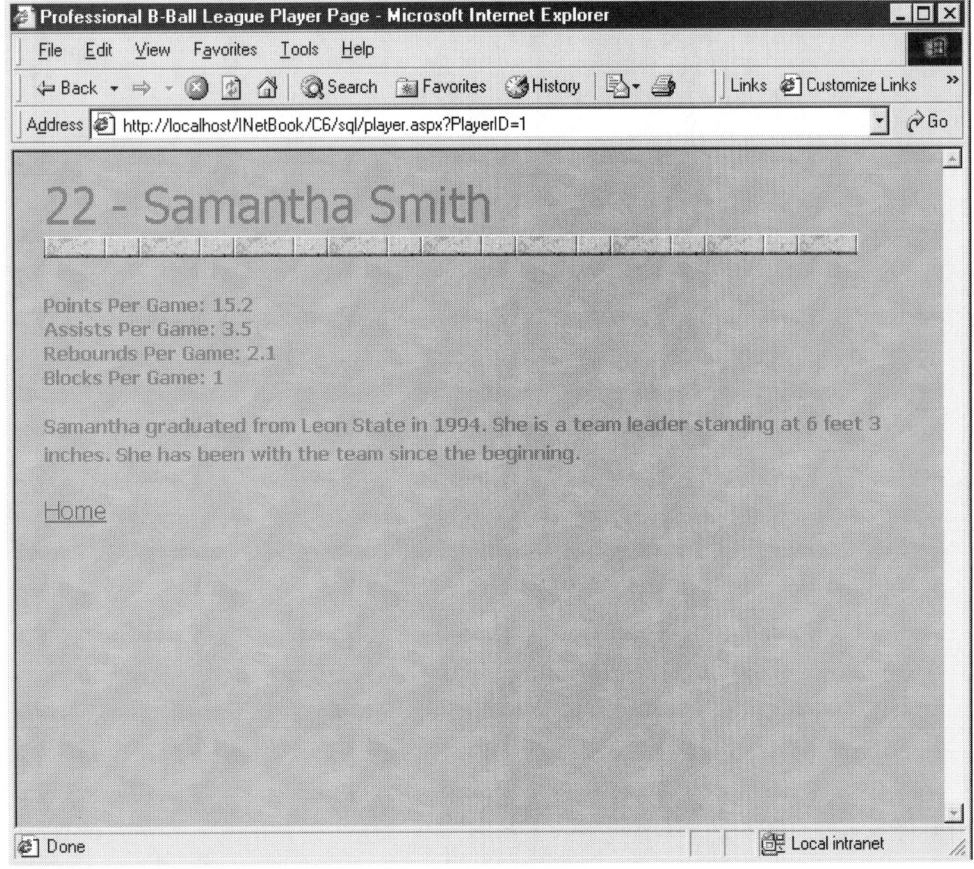

Figure 6-7 *Player page*

game. The two score fields, ScoreTeam1 and ScoreTeam2, store the score of the game for each team.

Players Field Specifications

Players.txt

The field specifications for the fields in the Players table are displayed in Table 6-3.

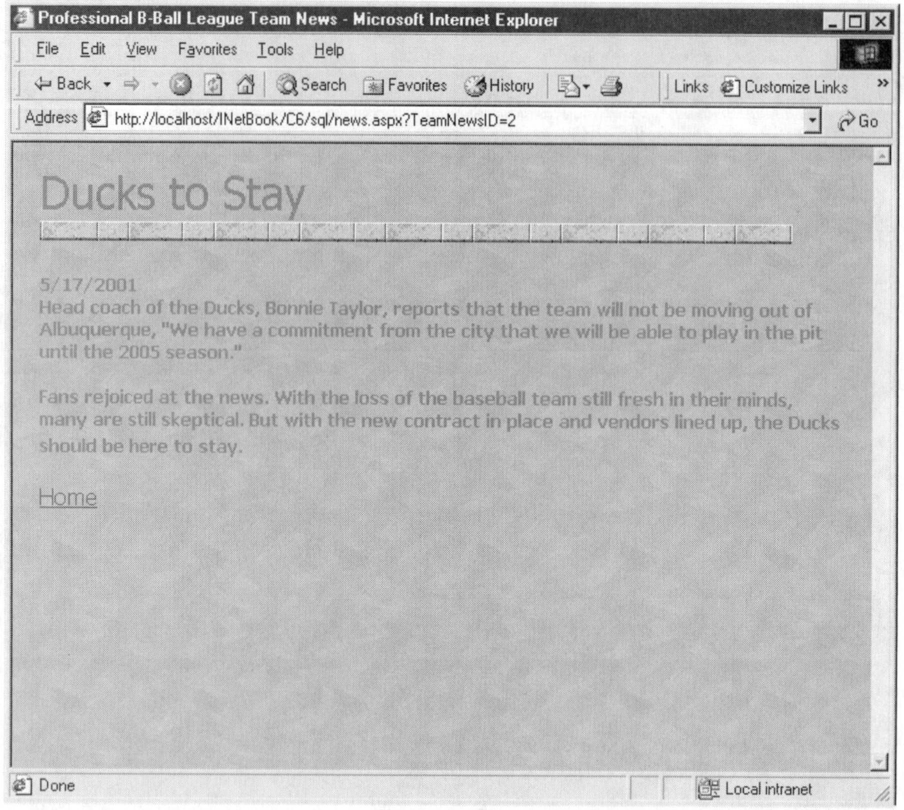

Figure 6-8 *News page*

The PlayerID field is the primary key in this table, uniquely identifying each record. The TeamID field links this table back to the Teams table.

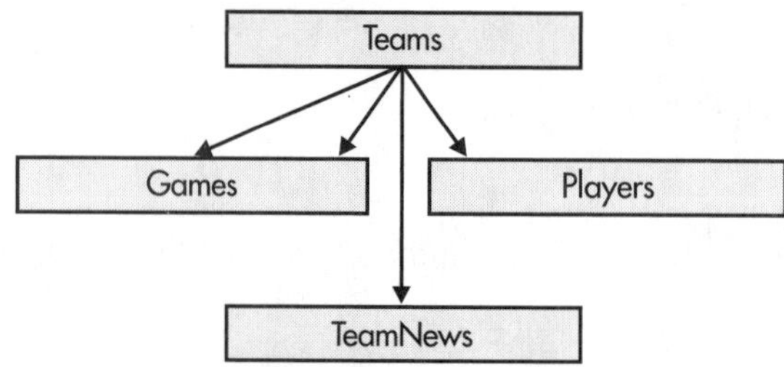

Figure 6-9 *Sports Site Data Diagram*

Field Name	Field Type	Notes
TeamID	int	Primary Key, Identity Column
TeamCity	varchar	Length = 50
TeamNickName	varchar	Length = 50
Conference	varchar	Length = 50
Division	varchar	Length = 50
NumWins	int	
NumLoses	int	

Table 6-1 *Teams Field Specifications*

The PPG field stores the number of points per game that the player averages. The APG field stores the number of assists per game. The RPG field stores the number of rebounds per game, and the BPG stores the blocks per game.

TeamNews Field Specifications

TeamNews.txt

The field specifications for the fields in the TeamNews table are displayed in Table 6-4.

The TeamNewsID field is the primary key. The TeamID field links the news article to a particular team. The rest of the fields store information on the news article.

Field Name	Field Type	Notes
GameID	int	Primary Key, Identity Column
GameDate	datetime	
TeamID1	int	Foreign Key
TeamID2	int	Foreign Key
ScoreTeam1	int	
ScoreTeam2	int	

Table 6-2 *Games Field Specifications*

Field Name	Field Type	Notes
PlayerID	int	Primary Key, Identity Column
TeamID	int	Foreign Key
PlayerNumber	int	
LastName	varchar	Length = 50
FirstName	varchar	Length = 50
PPG	float	
APG	float	
RPG	float	
BPG	float	
Description	text	

Table 6-3 *Players Field Specifications*

Sports Site ASP.NET Code

The Sports Site is made up of five ASP.NET pages. In this section, we will review the code and controls on each of these pages. As you review the pages, note the use of sorting on the DataGrid controls on the Standings page.

Standings ASP.NET Page

Index.aspx

The code on the Standings page displays the teams, grouped by either division or conference. The code also allows the visitor to sort the records by any of the fields in the DataGrid.

Field Name	Field Type	Notes
TeamNewsID	int	Primary Key, Identity Column
TeamID	int	Foreign Key
DateEntered	datetime	
Headline	varchar	Length = 50
News	text	

Table 6-4 *TeamNews Field Specifications*

At the top of the page, we declare three compiler directives.

```
<%@ Page Language=VB Debug=true %>
<%@ Import Namespace="System.Data" %>
<%@ Import Namespace="System.Data.OLEDB" %>
```

The first directive tells the compiler that we are using Visual Basic as our development language and that we want more error information to be displayed. Remember to change the Debug option to False when placing this page in a production environment.

```
<%@ Page Language=VB Debug=true %>
```

The other two directives import libraries that allow us to connect to either our Access or SQL Server database in our code:

```
<%@ Import Namespace="System.Data" %>
<%@ Import Namespace="System.Data.OLEDB" %>
```

Within the body of the page, we declare a Label control that will display the title of the page:

```
<asp:Label
    id="lblTitle"
    Font-Size="25pt"
    Font-Name="Tahoma"
    Text="Professional B-Ball League Standings"
    runat="server"
/>
```

Next, we define another Label control that displays a message to the visitor, which differs depending on whether the visitor is in Conference or Division view:

```
<asp:Label
    id="lblMessage"
    Font-Size="10pt"
    Font-Name="Tahoma"
    Font-Bold="True"
    runat="server"
/>
```

The rest of the controls on the page are contained within two Panel controls. The first Panel is for the Conference view:

```
<asp:Panel
    id="pnlConferenceView"
    runat="server"
>
```

It contains a DataGrid for the Western Conference teams

```
<asp:DataGrid
    id="dgWestConference"
    Width="90%"
    BackColor="beige"
    AlternatingItemStyle-BackColor="cornsilk"
    BorderColor="black"
    ShowFooter="false"
    CellPadding=3
    CellSpacing="0"
    Font-Name="Arial"
    Font-Size="8pt"
    ForeColor="Black"
    HeaderStyle-BackColor="burlywood"
    HeaderStyle-Font-Bold="True"
    AllowSorting="true"
    OnSortCommand="Sort_GridWestCon"
    runat="server">
</asp:DataGrid>
```

and one for the Eastern Conference teams:

```
<asp:DataGrid
    id="dgEastConference"
    Width="90%"
    BackColor="beige"
    AlternatingItemStyle-BackColor="cornsilk"
    BorderColor="black"
    ShowFooter="false"
    CellPadding=3
    CellSpacing="0"
    Font-Name="Arial"
    Font-Size="8pt"
    ForeColor="Black"
    HeaderStyle-BackColor="burlywood"
    HeaderStyle-Font-Bold="True"
```

```
    AllowSorting="true"
    OnSortCommand="Sort_GridEastCon"
    runat="server">
</asp:DataGrid>
```

The other Panel control displays the Division view of the page:

```
<asp:Panel
    id="pnlDivisionView"
    runat="server"
>
```

It contains four DataGrid controls. The first one displays the teams in the Desert Division:

```
<asp:DataGrid
    id="dgDesertDivision"
    Width="90%"
    BackColor="beige"
    AlternatingItemStyle-BackColor="cornsilk"
    BorderColor="black"
    ShowFooter="false"
    CellPadding=3
    CellSpacing="0"
    Font-Name="Arial"
    Font-Size="8pt"
    ForeColor="Black"
    HeaderStyle-BackColor="burlywood"
    HeaderStyle-Font-Bold="True"
    AllowSorting="true"
    OnSortCommand="Sort_GridDesertDiv"
    runat="server">
</asp:DataGrid>
```

The second displays the teams in the Mountain Division:

```
<asp:DataGrid
    id="dgMountainDivision"
    Width="90%"
    BackColor="beige"
    AlternatingItemStyle-BackColor="cornsilk"
    BorderColor="black"
    ShowFooter="false"
    CellPadding=3
    CellSpacing="0"
```

```
    Font-Name="Arial"
    Font-Size="8pt"
    ForeColor="Black"
    HeaderStyle-BackColor="burlywood"
    HeaderStyle-Font-Bold="True"
    AllowSorting="true"
    OnSortCommand="Sort_GridMountainDiv"
    runat="server">
</asp:DataGrid>
```

The third one displays the teams in the Lake Division:

```
<asp:DataGrid
    id="dgLakeDivision"
    Width="90%"
    BackColor="beige"
    AlternatingItemStyle-BackColor="cornsilk"
    BorderColor="black"
    ShowFooter="false"
    CellPadding=3
    CellSpacing="0"
    Font-Name="Arial"
    Font-Size="8pt"
    ForeColor="Black"
    HeaderStyle-BackColor="burlywood"
    HeaderStyle-Font-Bold="True"
    AllowSorting="true"
    OnSortCommand="Sort_GridLakeDiv"
    runat="server">
</asp:DataGrid>
```

And the last one displays the teams in the Deep South Division:

```
<asp:DataGrid
    id="dgDeepSouthDivision"
    Width="90%"
    BackColor="beige"
    AlternatingItemStyle-BackColor="cornsilk"
    BorderColor="black"
    ShowFooter="false"
    CellPadding=3
    CellSpacing="0"
    Font-Name="Arial"
    Font-Size="8pt"
    ForeColor="Black"
```

```
    HeaderStyle-BackColor="burlywood"
    HeaderStyle-Font-Bold="True"
    AllowSorting="true"
    OnSortCommand="Sort_GridDeepSouthDiv"
    runat="server">
</asp:DataGrid>
```

Notice that each of these DataGrid controls has sorting turned on:

```
AllowSorting="true"
```

This is what turns the column headers in the DataGrid controls into links. Each control also specifies an event to fire when the visitor clicks the link:

```
OnSortCommand="Sort_GridDeepSouthDiv"
```

The code on the page is contained within seven events. One of the events fires when the page is loaded.

```
Sub Page_Load(ByVal Sender as Object, ByVal E as EventArgs)
    if Not IsPostBack Then
        Dim DBConn as OleDbConnection
        Dim DBCommand As OleDbDataAdapter
        Dim DSPageData as New DataSet
        DBConn = New OleDbConnection("Provider=sqloledb;" _
            & "server=localhost;" _
            & "Initial Catalog=INETC6;" _
            & "User Id=sa;" _
            & "Password=yourpassword;")
        If Request.QueryString("View") = "Division" Then
            pnlConferenceView.Visible = False
            pnlDivisionView.Visible = True
            lblMessage.Text = "Current division standings as of " _
                & Today & ". <a HREF="" ./index.aspx?View=Conference"">"
_
                & "Click here</a> to view conference standings."
            DBCommand = New OleDbDataAdapter _
                ("Select '<a HREF=""./team.aspx?TeamID=' + " _
                & "Convert(varchar(10), TeamID) + '"">' " _
                & "+ TeamCity + ' ' + TeamNickName + '</a>' as " _
                & "[Desert Division (Click for More Info)], " _
                & "Round((Convert(float, NumWins) / " _
                & "(NumWins + NumLoses)) * 100, 0) as [Record], " _
                & "NumWins as [Wins], NumLoses as [Loses] " _
                & "From Teams " _
```

```
        & "Where Division = 'Desert' " _
        & "Order By Convert(float, NumWins) / " _
        & "(NumWins + NumLoses) DESC" _
        , DBConn)
    DBCommand.Fill(DSPageData, _
        "DesertDiv")
    dgDesertDivision.DataSource = _
                DSPageData.Tables("DesertDiv").DefaultView
    dgDesertDivision.DataBind()
    DBCommand = New OleDbDataAdapter _
        ("Select '<a HREF="" ./team.aspx?TeamID=' + " _
        & "Convert(varchar(10), TeamID) + '"">' " _
        & "+ TeamCity + ' ' + TeamNickName + '</a>' as " _
        & "[Mountain Division (Click for More Info)], " _
        & "Round((Convert(float, NumWins) / " _
        & "(NumWins + NumLoses)) * 100, 0) as [Record], " _
        & "NumWins as [Wins], NumLoses as [Loses] " _
        & "From Teams " _
        & "Where Division = 'Mountain' " _
        & "Order By Convert(float, NumWins) / " _
        & "(NumWins + NumLoses) DESC" _
        , DBConn)
    DBCommand.Fill(DSPageData, _
        "MountainDiv")
    dgMountainDivision.DataSource = _
                DSPageData.Tables("MountainDiv").DefaultView
    dgMountainDivision.DataBind()
    DBCommand = New OleDbDataAdapter _
        ("Select '<a HREF="" ./team.aspx?TeamID=' + " _
        & "Convert(varchar(10), TeamID) + '"">' " _
        & "+ TeamCity + ' ' + TeamNickName + '</a>' as " _
        & "[Lake Division (Click for More Info)], " _
        & "Round((Convert(float, NumWins) / " _
        & "(NumWins + NumLoses)) * 100, 0) as [Record], " _
        & "NumWins as [Wins], NumLoses as [Loses] " _
        & "From Teams " _
        & "Where Division = 'Lake' " _
        & "Order By Convert(float, NumWins) / " _
        & "(NumWins + NumLoses) DESC" _
        , DBConn)
    DBCommand.Fill(DSPageData, _
        "LakeDiv")
    dgLakeDivision.DataSource = _
                DSPageData.Tables("LakeDiv").DefaultView
    dgLakeDivision.DataBind()
```

```
    DBCommand = New OleDbDataAdapter _
        ("Select '<a HREF=""./team.aspx?TeamID=' + " _
        & "Convert(varchar(10), TeamID) + '"">' " _
        & "+ TeamCity + ' ' + TeamNickName + '</a>' as " _
        & "[Deep South Division (Click for More Info)], " _
        & "Round((Convert(float, NumWins) / " _
        & "(NumWins + NumLoses)) * 100, 0) as [Record], " _
        & "NumWins as [Wins], NumLoses as [Loses] " _
        & "From Teams " _
        & "Where Division = 'Deep South' " _
        & "Order By Convert(float, NumWins) / " _
        & "(NumWins + NumLoses) DESC" _
        , DBConn)
    DBCommand.Fill(DSPageData, _
        "DeepSouthDiv")
    dgDeepSouthDivision.DataSource = _
            DSPageData.Tables("DeepSouthDiv").DefaultView
    dgDeepSouthDivision.DataBind()
Else
    pnlConferenceView.Visible = True
    pnlDivisionView.Visible = False
    lblMessage.Text = "Current conference standings as of " _
        & Today & ". <a HREF=""./index.aspx?View=Division"">" _
        & "Click here</a> to view division standings."
    DBCommand = New OleDbDataAdapter _
        ("Select '<a HREF=""./team.aspx?TeamID=' + " _
        & "Convert(varchar(10), TeamID) + '"">' " _
        & "+ TeamCity + ' ' + TeamNickName + '</a>' as " _
        & "[Western Conference (Click for More Info)], " _
        & "Round((Convert(float, NumWins) / " _
        & "(NumWins + NumLoses)) * 100, 0) as [Record], " _
        & "NumWins as [Wins], NumLoses as [Loses] " _
        & "From Teams " _
        & "Where Conference = 'West' " _
        & "Order By Convert(float, NumWins) / " _
        & "(NumWins + NumLoses) DESC" _
        , DBConn)
    DBCommand.Fill(DSPageData, _
        "WestConf")
    dgWestConference.DataSource = _
            DSPageData.Tables("WestConf").DefaultView
    dgWestConference.DataBind()
    DBCommand = New OleDbDataAdapter _
        ("Select '<a HREF=""./team.aspx?TeamID=' + " _
        & "Convert(varchar(10), TeamID) + '"">' " _
```

```
                    & "+ TeamCity + ' ' + TeamNickName + '</a>' as " _
                    & "[Eastern Conference (Click for More Info)], " _
                    & "Round((Convert(float, NumWins) / " _
                    & "(NumWins + NumLoses)) * 100, 0) as [Record], " _
                    & "NumWins as [Wins], NumLoses as [Loses] " _
                    & "From Teams " _
                    & "Where Conference = 'East' " _
                    & "Order By Convert(float, NumWins) / " _
                    & "(NumWins + NumLoses) DESC" _
                    , DBConn)
                DBCommand.Fill(DSPageData, _
                    "EastConf")
                dgEastConference.DataSource = _
                            DSPageData.Tables("EastConf").DefaultView
                dgEastConference.DataBind()
            End If
        End If
    End Sub
```

We want the code in this event to fire only when the page is loaded

```
if Not IsPostBack Then
```

If the page is loaded, we will need data objects:

```
Dim DBConn as OleDbConnection
Dim DBCommand As OleDbDataAdapter
Dim DSPageData as New DataSet
```

We start by connecting to our database:

```
DBConn = New OleDbConnection("Provider=sqloledb;" _
    & "server=localhost;" _
    & "Initial Catalog=INETC6;" _
    & "User Id=sa;" _
    & "Password=yourpassword;")
```

Next, we check to see what view we are in:

```
If Request.QueryString("View") = "Division" Then
```

If the code flows here, it means that we are in Division view. In that case, we need to hide the Conference Panel control

```
pnlConferenceView.Visible = False
```

and display the Division one:

```
pnlDivisionView.Visible = True
```

We then put the division message in our message Label:

```
lblMessage.Text = "Current division standings as of " _
    & Today & ". <a HREF="./index.aspx?View=Conference"">" _
    & "Click here</a> to view conference standings."
```

Next, we retrieve the teams in the Desert Division sorted by their records:

```
DBCommand = New OleDbDataAdapter _
    ("Select '<a HREF=""./team.aspx?TeamID=' + " _
    & "Convert(varchar(10), TeamID) + '"">' " _
    & "+ TeamCity + ' ' + TeamNickName + '</a>' as " _
    & "[Desert Division (Click for More Info)], " _
    & "Round((Convert(float, NumWins) / " _
    & "(NumWins + NumLoses)) * 100, 0) as [Record], " _
    & "NumWins as [Wins], NumLoses as [Loses] " _
    & "From Teams " _
    & "Where Division = 'Desert' " _
    & "Order By Convert(float, NumWins) / " _
    & "(NumWins + NumLoses) DESC" _
    , DBConn)
```

And we place them into our DataSet object:

```
DBCommand.Fill(DSPageData, _
    "DesertDiv")
```

We then bind our DataGrid to that DataSet object:

```
dgDesertDivision.DataSource = _
    DSPageData.Tables("DesertDiv").DefaultView
dgDesertDivision.DataBind()
```

Next, we retrieve the teams in the Mountain Division. Notice that the name of the team will be displayed as a link to the Teams page:

```
DBCommand = New OleDbDataAdapter _
    ("Select '<a HREF=""./team.aspx?TeamID=' + " _
    & "Convert(varchar(10), TeamID) + '"">' " _
    & "+ TeamCity + ' ' + TeamNickName + '</a>' as " _
    & "[Mountain Division (Click for More Info)], " _
```

```
    & "Round((Convert(float, NumWins) / " _
    & "(NumWins + NumLoses)) * 100, 0) as [Record], " _
    & "NumWins as [Wins], NumLoses as [Loses] " _
    & "From Teams " _
    & "Where Division = 'Mountain' " _
    & "Order By Convert(float, NumWins) / " _
    & "(NumWins + NumLoses) DESC" _
    , DBConn)
DBCommand.Fill(DSPageData, _
    "MountainDiv")
```

Those records are then placed in another DataGrid:

```
dgMountainDivision.DataSource = _
    DSPageData.Tables("MountainDiv").DefaultView
dgMountainDivision.DataBind()
```

Next, we retrieve the Lake Division teams. Note that the fields are all outputted as aliased names. For example, the NumWins field will be displayed as Wins:

```
DBCommand = New OleDbDataAdapter _
    ("Select '<a HREF=""./team.aspx?TeamID=' + " _
    & "Convert(varchar(10), TeamID) + '"">' " _
    & "+ TeamCity + ' ' + TeamNickName + '</a>' as " _
    & "[Lake Division (Click for More Info)], " _
    & "Round((Convert(float, NumWins) / " _
    & "(NumWins + NumLoses)) * 100, 0) as [Record], " _
    & "NumWins as [Wins], NumLoses as [Loses] " _
    & "From Teams " _
    & "Where Division = 'Lake' " _
    & "Order By Convert(float, NumWins) / " _
    & "(NumWins + NumLoses) DESC" _
    , DBConn)
DBCommand.Fill(DSPageData, _
    "LakeDiv")
```

That DataSet table is used in the third DataGrid:

```
dgLakeDivision.DataSource = _
    DSPageData.Tables("LakeDiv").DefaultView
dgLakeDivision.DataBind()
```

One other DataSet table needs to be retrieved for the teams in the Deep South Division

```
DBCommand = New OleDbDataAdapter _
    ("Select '<a HREF="" ./team.aspx?TeamID=' + " _
    & "Convert(varchar(10), TeamID) + '"">' " _
    & "+ TeamCity + ' ' + TeamNickName + '</a>' as " _
    & "[Deep South Division (Click for More Info)], " _
    & "Round((Convert(float, NumWins) / " _
    & "(NumWins + NumLoses)) * 100, 0) as [Record], " _
    & "NumWins as [Wins], NumLoses as [Loses] " _
    & "From Teams " _
    & "Where Division = 'Deep South' " _
    & "Order By Convert(float, NumWins) / " _
    & "(NumWins + NumLoses) DESC" _
    , DBConn)
DBCommand.Fill(DSPageData, _
    "DeepSouthDiv")
```

which is bound to the fourth DataGrid on this Panel control:

```
dgDeepSouthDivision.DataSource = _
    DSPageData.Tables("DeepSouthDiv").DefaultView
dgDeepSouthDivision.DataBind()
```

If the code flows here, it means that the visitor wants to see the teams grouped by conference:

```
Else
```

In that case, we need to display the Conference Panel

```
pnlConferenceView.Visible = True
```

and hide the Division one:

```
pnlDivisionView.Visible = False
```

We also need to display a different message in our Label:

```
lblMessage.Text = "Current conference standings as of " _
    & Today & ". <a HREF="" ./index.aspx?View=Division"">" _
    & "Click here</a> to view division standings."
```

We then need to retrieve all the teams in the Western Conference

```
DBCommand = New OleDbDataAdapter _
    ("Select '<a HREF="" ./team.aspx?TeamID=' + " _
```

```
    & "Convert(varchar(10), TeamID) + '"">' " _
    & "+ TeamCity + ' ' + TeamNickName + '</a>' as " _
    & "[Western Conference (Click for More Info)], " _
    & "Round((Convert(float, NumWins) / " _
    & "(NumWins + NumLoses)) * 100, 0) as [Record], " _
    & "NumWins as [Wins], NumLoses as [Loses] " _
    & "From Teams " _
    & "Where Conference = 'West' " _
    & "Order By Convert(float, NumWins) / " _
    & "(NumWins + NumLoses) DESC" _
    , DBConn)
```

and place them in a DataSet table

```
DBCommand.Fill(DSPageData, _
    "WestConf")
```

which a DataGrid is bound to:

```
dgWestConference.DataSource = _
    DSPageData.Tables("WestConf").DefaultView
dgWestConference.DataBind()
```

Then we need to retrieve the Eastern Conference teams

```
DBCommand = New OleDbDataAdapter _
    ("Select '<a HREF=""./team.aspx?TeamID=' + " _
    & "Convert(varchar(10), TeamID) + '"">' " _
    & "+ TeamCity + ' ' + TeamNickName + '</a>' as " _
    & "[Eastern Conference (Click for More Info)], " _
    & "Round((Convert(float, NumWins) / " _
    & "(NumWins + NumLoses)) * 100, 0) as [Record], " _
    & "NumWins as [Wins], NumLoses as [Loses] " _
    & "From Teams " _
    & "Where Conference = 'East' " _
    & "Order By Convert(float, NumWins) / " _
    & "(NumWins + NumLoses) DESC" _
    , DBConn)
DBCommand.Fill(DSPageData, _
    "EastConf")
```

and bind the other grid to it:

```
dgEastConference.DataSource = _
    DSPageData.Tables("EastConf").DefaultView
dgEastConference.DataBind()
```

The other procedures on this page fire when the visitor sorts one of the DataGrid controls. The procedures are nearly identical other than that they retrieve records from a specific conference or division and that the team name column header is a little different. Therefore, we will review just one of those procedures here.

```
Sub Sort_GridWestCon(ByVal Sender as Object, _
    ByVal E as DataGridSortCommandEventArgs)
    Dim DBConn as OleDbConnection
    Dim DBCommand As OleDbDataAdapter
    Dim DSPageData as New DataSet
    Dim SortClause as String
    If E.SortExpression.ToString() = "Record" Then
        SortClause = "Order By Convert(float, NumWins) / " _
        & "(NumWins + NumLoses) DESC"
    ElseIf E.SortExpression.ToString() = "Wins" Then
        SortClause = "Order By NumWins DESC"
    ElseIf E.SortExpression.ToString() = "Loses" Then
        SortClause = "Order By NumLoses DESC"
    Else
        SortClause = "Order By TeamCity"
    End If
    DBConn = New OleDbConnection("Provider=sqloledb;" _
        & "server=localhost;" _
        & "Initial Catalog=INETC6;" _
        & "User Id=sa;" _
        & "Password=yourpassword;")
    DBCommand = New OleDbDataAdapter _
        ("Select '<a HREF=""./team.aspx?TeamID=' + " _
        & "Convert(varchar(10), TeamID) + '"">' " _
        & "+ TeamCity + ' ' + TeamNickName + '</a>' as " _
        & "[Western Conference (Click for More Info)], " _
        & "Round((Convert(float, NumWins) / " _
        & "(NumWins + NumLoses)) * 100, 0) as [Record], " _
        & "NumWins as [Wins], NumLoses as [Loses] " _
        & "From Teams " _
        & "Where Conference = 'West' " _
        & SortClause, DBConn)
    DBCommand.Fill(DSPageData, _
        "WestConf")
    dgWestConference.DataSource = _
              DSPageData.Tables("WestConf").DefaultView
    dgWestConference.DataBind()
End Sub
```

Within the procedure, we will need data objects:

```
Dim DBConn as OleDbConnection
Dim DBCommand As OleDbDataAdapter
Dim DSPageData as New DataSet
```

We also need a variable to store the sort clause that will be used

```
Dim SortClause as String
```

The name of the column clicked by the visitor is returned to us through the SortExpression object. Here we check to see if the visitor has clicked the Record column:

```
If E.SortExpression.ToString() = "Record" Then
```

If that is the case, we need to sort by the team's overall record:

```
SortClause = "Order By Convert(float, NumWins) / " _
    & "(NumWins + NumLoses) DESC"
```

Next, we check to see if the visitor wants to sort by the number of wins:

```
ElseIf E.SortExpression.ToString() = "Wins" Then
    SortClause = "Order By NumWins DESC"
```

Next, we check to see if they want to sort by the number of losses:

```
ElseIf E.SortExpression.ToString() = "Loses" Then
    SortClause = "Order By NumLoses DESC"
```

If the code flows here, it means that the visitor wants to sort by the name of the team:

```
Else
    SortClause = "Order By TeamCity"
```

Regardless of which sort is to be performed, we need to connect to the database:

```
DBConn = New OleDbConnection("Provider=sqloledb;" _
    & "server=localhost;" _
    & "Initial Catalog=INETC6;" _
    & "User Id=sa;" _
    & "Password=yourpassword;")
```

We then retrieve records from the database using the sort variable:

```
DBCommand = New OleDbDataAdapter _
    ("Select '<a HREF="./team.aspx?TeamID=' + " _
    & "Convert(varchar(10), TeamID) + '"">' " _
    & "+ TeamCity + ' ' + TeamNickName + '</a>' as " _
    & "[Western Conference (Click for More Info)], " _
    & "Round((Convert(float, NumWins) / " _
    & "(NumWins + NumLoses)) * 100, 0) as [Record], " _
    & "NumWins as [Wins], NumLoses as [Loses] " _
    & "From Teams " _
    & "Where Conference = 'West' " _
    & SortClause, DBConn)
```

And we place them into our DataSet object:

```
DBCommand.Fill(DSPageData, _
    "WestConf")
```

We then bind the DataGrid to that object:

```
dgWestConference.DataSource = _
    DSPageData.Tables("WestConf").DefaultView
dgWestConference.DataBind()
```

Schedule and Results ASP.NET Page

Results.aspx

The Schedule and Results page displays all the games on the current date or on the date selected by the visitor.

At the top of the page, we declare directives that establish the run environment and import needed data libraries:

```
<%@ Page Language=VB Debug=true %>
<%@ Import Namespace="System.Data" %>
<%@ Import Namespace="System.Data.OLEDB" %>
```

Within the body of the page, we declare a Label control for the title of the page:

```
<asp:Label
    id="lblTitle"
    Font-Size="25pt"
    Font-Name="Tahoma"
```

```
    Text="Schedule and Results"
    runat="server"
/>
```

The next control we define is a Calendar control:

```
<asp:Calendar
    id="calDateToUse"
    runat="server"
    BackColor="ivory"
    CellPadding="3"
    CellSpacing="3"
    DayNameFormat="Short"
    FirstDayOfWeek="Default"
    NextPrevFormat="FullMonth"
    SelectionMode="Day"
    ShowDayHeader="True"
    ShowGridLines="False"
    ShowNextPrevMonth="True"
    ShowTitle="True"
    TitleFormat="MonthYear"
    TodayDayStyle-Font-Bold="True"
    DayHeaderStyle-Font-Bold="True"
    OtherMonthDayStyle-ForeColor="gray"
    TitleStyle-BackColor="#3366ff"
    TitleStyle-ForeColor="white"
    TitleStyle-Font-Bold="True"
    SelectedDayStyle-BackColor="#ffcc66"
    SelectedDayStyle-Font-Bold="True"
    Font-Name="Tahoma"
    Font-Size="12"
    OnSelectionChanged="calSelectChange"
/>
```

When the visitor clicks a date in the calendar, this procedure is called

```
OnSelectionChanged="calSelectChange"
```

The only other control on the page is a DataGrid that displays the games on the selected or current date:

```
<asp:DataGrid
    id="dgGames"
    Width="90%"
    BackColor="beige"
    AlternatingItemStyle-BackColor="cornsilk"
```

```
    BorderColor="black"
    ShowFooter="false"
    CellPadding=3
    CellSpacing="0"
    Font-Name="Arial"
    Font-Size="8pt"
    ForeColor="Black"
    HeaderStyle-BackColor="burlywood"
    HeaderStyle-Font-Bold="True"
    runat="server">
</asp:DataGrid>
```

The code on the page is contained within two procedures. The first procedure fires when the page is loaded.

```
Sub Page_Load(ByVal Sender as Object, ByVal E as EventArgs)
    if Not IsPostBack Then
        Dim DBConn as OleDbConnection
        Dim DBCommand As OleDbDataAdapter
        Dim DSPageData as New DataSet
        DBConn = New OleDbConnection("Provider=sqloledb;" _
            & "server=localhost;" _
            & "Initial Catalog=INETC6;" _
            & "User Id=sa;" _
            & "Password=yourpassword;")
        DBCommand = New OleDbDataAdapter _
            ("SELECT Teams.TeamCity + ' ' + " _
            & "Teams.TeamNickName as [Home Team], " _
            & "Games.ScoreTeam1 as [Home Team Score], " _
            & "(Select TeamCity + ' ' + TeamNickName " _
            & "from Teams where TeamID = TeamID2) " _
            & " as [Away Team], " _
            & "Games.ScoreTeam2  as [Away Team Score] " _
            & "FROM Games INNER JOIN " _
            & "Teams ON Games.TeamID1 = Teams.TeamID " _
            & "Where Games.GameDate = '" _
            & Today() & "'", DBConn)
        DBCommand.Fill(DSPageData, _
            "Games")
        dgGames.DataSource = _
            DSPageData.Tables("Games").DefaultView
        dgGames.DataBind()
        calDateToUse.SelectedDate = Today()
    End if
End Sub
```

This procedure displays the games on the current date. Therefore, it should run only when the page is first loaded

```
if Not IsPostBack Then
```

If that is the case, we will need data objects:

```
Dim DBConn as OleDbConnection
Dim DBCommand As OleDbDataAdapter
Dim DSPageData as New DataSet
```

We start by connecting to the database:

```
DBConn = New OleDbConnection("Provider=sqloledb;" _
    & "server=localhost;" _
    & "Initial Catalog=INETC6;" _
    & "User Id=sa;" _
    & "Password=yourpassword;")
```

We then retrieve all the games according to the current system date. Note the use of a subquery to retrieve the name of the away team in the game:

```
DBCommand = New OleDbDataAdapter _
    ("SELECT Teams.TeamCity + ' ' + " _
    & "Teams.TeamNickName as [Home Team], " _
    & "Games.ScoreTeam1 as [Home Team Score], " _
    & "(Select TeamCity + ' ' + TeamNickName " _
    & "from Teams where TeamID = TeamID2) " _
    & " as [Away Team], " _
    & "Games.ScoreTeam2  as [Away Team Score] " _
    & "FROM Games INNER JOIN " _
    & "Teams ON Games.TeamID1 = Teams.TeamID " _
    & "Where Games.GameDate = '" _
    & Today() & "'", DBConn)
```

Those records are then placed into our DataSet object

```
DBCommand.Fill(DSPageData, _
    "Games")
```

which the DataGrid is bound to:

```
dgGames.DataSource = _
    DSPageData.Tables("Games").DefaultView
dgGames.DataBind()
```

Finally, we set the Calendar to the current date:

```
calDateToUse.SelectedDate = Today()
```

The other procedure fires when the visitor selects a date from the calendar.

```
Sub calSelectChange(ByVal Sender as Object, ByVal E as EventArgs)
        Dim DBConn as OleDbConnection
        Dim DBCommand As OleDbDataAdapter
        Dim DSPageData as New DataSet
        DBConn = New OleDbConnection("Provider=sqloledb;" _
            & "server=localhost;" _
            & "Initial Catalog=INETC6;" _
            & "User Id=sa;" _
            & "Password=yourpassword;")
        DBCommand = New OleDbDataAdapter _
            ("SELECT Teams.TeamCity + ' ' + " _
            & "Teams.TeamNickName as [Home Team], " _
            & "Games.ScoreTeam1 as [Home Team Score], " _
            & "(Select TeamCity + ' ' + TeamNickName " _
            & "from Teams where TeamID = TeamID2) " _
            & " as [Away Team], " _
            & "Games.ScoreTeam2  as [Away Team Score] " _
            & "FROM Games INNER JOIN " _
            & "Teams ON Games.TeamID1 = Teams.TeamID " _
            & "Where Games.GameDate = '" _
            & calDateToUse.SelectedDate & "'", DBConn)
        DBCommand.Fill(DSPageData, _
            "Games")
        dgGames.DataSource = _
            DSPageData.Tables("Games").DefaultView
        dgGames.DataBind()
End Sub
```

The procedure requires data objects:

```
Dim DBConn as OleDbConnection
Dim DBCommand As OleDbDataAdapter
Dim DSPageData as New DataSet
```

We start by connecting to the database:

```
DBConn = New OleDbConnection("Provider=sqloledb;" _
    & "server=localhost;" _
    & "Initial Catalog=INETC6;" _
```

```
    & "User Id=sa;" _
    & "Password=yourpassword;")
```

We then retrieve all the games according to the date selected by the visitor through the Calendar control:

```
DBCommand = New OleDbDataAdapter _
    ("SELECT Teams.TeamCity + ' ' + " _
    & "Teams.TeamNickName as [Home Team], " _
    & "Games.ScoreTeam1 as [Home Team Score], " _
    & "(Select TeamCity + ' ' + TeamNickName " _
    & "from Teams where TeamID = TeamID2) " _
    & " as [Away Team], " _
    & "Games.ScoreTeam2  as [Away Team Score] " _
    & "FROM Games INNER JOIN " _
    & "Teams ON Games.TeamID1 = Teams.TeamID " _
    & "Where Games.GameDate = '" _
    & calDateToUse.SelectedDate & "'", DBConn)
DBCommand.Fill(DSPageData, _
    "Games")
```

Those records are then placed in our DataGrid:

```
dgGames.DataSource = _
    DSPageData.Tables("Games").DefaultView
dgGames.DataBind()
```

Team ASP.NET Page

Team.aspx

The code on the Team page displays the schedule for the selected team as well as the players and news items associated with the team. At the top of the page, we have the three compiler directives, which import data libraries and set up the run environment:

```
<%@ Page Language=VB Debug=true %>
<%@ Import Namespace="System.Data" %>
<%@ Import Namespace="System.Data.OLEDB" %>
```

Within the body of the page we declare a Label control that displays the name of the team:

```
<asp:Label
    id="lblTitle"
```

```
    Font-Size="25pt"
    Font-Name="Tahoma"
    runat="server"
/>
```

Next, we define a DataGrid that displays all the games played and to be played by the selected team:

```
<asp:DataGrid
    id="dgGames"
    Width="90%"
    BackColor="beige"
    AlternatingItemStyle-BackColor="cornsilk"
    BorderColor="black"
    ShowFooter="false"
    CellPadding=3
    CellSpacing="0"
    Font-Name="Arial"
    Font-Size="8pt"
    ForeColor="Black"
    HeaderStyle-BackColor="burlywood"
    HeaderStyle-Font-Bold="True"
    runat="server">
</asp:DataGrid>
```

Next, we define a DropDownList that displays the names of the players on this team, as well as making their IDs available through the DropDownList:

```
<asp:dropdownlist
    id="ddlPlayers"
    runat=server
    DataTextField="PlayerName"
    DataValueField="PlayerID">
</asp:dropdownlist>
```

We then define a Button control that allows the visitor to view the player's page:

```
<asp:button
    id="butPlayerInfo"
    text="View Player Info"
    Type="Submit"
    OnClick="SubmitBtnPlayerInfo_Click"
    runat="server"
/>
```

We then define another DropDownList for the news items related to this team

```
<asp:dropdownlist
    id="ddlTeamNews"
    runat=server
    DataTextField="Headline"
    DataValueField="TeamNewsID">
</asp:dropdownlist>
```

and a Button control which, when clicked, displays the selected news item:

```
<asp:button
    id="butTeamNewsInfo"
    text="View Article"
    Type="Submit"
    OnClick="SubmitBtnTeamNews_Click"
    runat="server"
/>
```

The code on the page is contained within three events. The first fires when the page is loaded. It displays the DataGrid and populates the DropDownList controls.

```
Sub Page_Load(ByVal Sender as Object, ByVal E as EventArgs)
    If Len(Request.QueryString("TeamID")) = 0 Then
        Response.Redirect("./index.aspx")
    End If
    If Not IsPostBack Then
        Dim DBConn as OleDbConnection
        Dim DBCommand As OleDbDataAdapter
        Dim DSPageData as New DataSet
        DBConn = New OleDbConnection("Provider=sqloledb;" _
            & "server=localhost;" _
            & "Initial Catalog=INETC6;" _
            & "User Id=sa;" _
            & "Password=yourpassword;")
        DBCommand = New OleDbDataAdapter _
            ("Select TeamCity, TeamNickName from Teams " _
            & "Where TeamID = " _
            & Request.QueryString("TeamID"), DBConn)
        DBCommand.Fill(DSPageData, _
            "TeamInfo")
```

```
lblTitle.Text = DSPageData.Tables("TeamInfo"). _
    Rows(0).Item("TeamCity") & " " _
    & DSPageData.Tables("TeamInfo"). _
    Rows(0).Item("TeamNickName")
DBCommand = New OleDbDataAdapter _
    ("SELECT Convert(varchar(12), GameDate, 101) " _
    & "as [Date], " _
    & "Teams.TeamCity + ' ' + " _
    & "Teams.TeamNickName as [Home Team], " _
    & "Games.ScoreTeam1 as [Home Team Score], " _
    & "(Select TeamCity + ' ' + TeamNickName " _
    & "from Teams where TeamID = TeamID2) " _
    & " as [Away Team], " _
    & "Games.ScoreTeam2  as [Away Team Score] " _
    & "FROM Games INNER JOIN " _
    & "Teams ON Games.TeamID1 = Teams.TeamID " _
    & "Where TeamID1 = " _
    & Request.QueryString("TeamID") & " or " _
    & "TeamID2 = " & Request.QueryString("TeamID") _
    , DBConn)
DBCommand.Fill(DSPageData, _
    "Games")
dgGames.DataSource = _
    DSPageData.Tables("Games").DefaultView
dgGames.DataBind()
DBCommand = New OleDbDataAdapter _
    ("SELECT PlayerID, " _
    & "LastName + ', ' + FirstName as PlayerName " _
    & "From Players Where TeamID = " _
    & Request.QueryString("TeamID") _
    & " Order By LastName", DBConn)
DBCommand.Fill(DSPageData, _
    "Players")
ddlPlayers.DataSource = _
    DSPageData.Tables("Players").DefaultView
ddlPlayers.DataBind()
DBCommand = New OleDbDataAdapter _
    ("SELECT TeamNewsID, Headline " _
    & "From TeamNews Where TeamID = " _
    & Request.QueryString("TeamID") _
    & " Order By DateEntered DESC", DBConn)
```

```
            DBCommand.Fill(DSPageData, _
                "TeamNews")
            ddlTeamNews.DataSource = _
                DSPageData.Tables("TeamNews").DefaultView
            ddlTeamNews.DataBind()
        End If
End Sub
```

The page should be entered only if the ID of a team was passed into the page:

```
If Len(Request.QueryString("TeamID")) = 0 Then
```

If one wasn't, we send the visitor back to the Standings page:

```
Response.Redirect("./index.aspx")
```

The rest of the code fires only when the page is first loaded

```
If Not IsPostBack Then
```

If that is the case, we need data objects:

```
Dim DBConn as OleDbConnection
Dim DBCommand As OleDbDataAdapter
Dim DSPageData as New DataSet
```

We start by connecting to the database:

```
DBConn = New OleDbConnection("Provider=sqloledb;" _
    & "server=localhost;" _
    & "Initial Catalog=INETC6;" _
    & "User Id=sa;" _
    & "Password=yourpassword;")
```

We next retrieve the name of the team

```
DBCommand = New OleDbDataAdapter _
    ("Select TeamCity, TeamNickName from Teams " _
    & "Where TeamID = " _
    & Request.QueryString("TeamID"), DBConn)
DBCommand.Fill(DSPageData, _
    "TeamInfo")
```

so that it can be placed into a Label control:

```
lblTitle.Text = DSPageData.Tables("TeamInfo"). _
    Rows(0).Item("TeamCity") & " " _
    & DSPageData.Tables("TeamInfo"). _
    Rows(0).Item("TeamNickName")
```

Next, we need to retrieve all the games that the team has played or will play

```
DBCommand = New OleDbDataAdapter _
    ("SELECT Convert(varchar(12), GameDate, 101) " _
    & "as [Date], " _
    & "Teams.TeamCity + ' ' + " _
    & "Teams.TeamNickName as [Home Team], " _
    & "Games.ScoreTeam1 as [Home Team Score], " _
    & "(Select TeamCity + ' ' + TeamNickName " _
    & "from Teams where TeamID = TeamID2) " _
    & " as [Away Team], " _
    & "Games.ScoreTeam2  as [Away Team Score] " _
    & "FROM Games INNER JOIN " _
    & "Teams ON Games.TeamID1 = Teams.TeamID " _
    & "Where TeamID1 = " _
    & Request.QueryString("TeamID") & " or " _
    & "TeamID2 = " & Request.QueryString("TeamID") _
    , DBConn)
DBCommand.Fill(DSPageData, _
    "Games")
```

Those records are placed into our DataGrid object:

```
dgGames.DataSource = _
    DSPageData.Tables("Games").DefaultView
dgGames.DataBind()
```

Next, we need to retrieve the names and IDs of all the players on this team:

```
DBCommand = New OleDbDataAdapter _
    ("SELECT PlayerID, " _
    & "LastName + ', ' + FirstName as PlayerName " _
    & "From Players Where TeamID = " _
    & Request.QueryString("TeamID") _
    & " Order By LastName", DBConn)
DBCommand.Fill(DSPageData, _
    "Players")
```

Those are placed into the Players DropDownList control:

```
ddlPlayers.DataSource = _
    DSPageData.Tables("Players").DefaultView
ddlPlayers.DataBind()
```

We also need to retrieve the headlines and IDs of all the news articles related to this team

```
DBCommand = New OleDbDataAdapter _
    ("SELECT TeamNewsID, Headline " _
    & "From TeamNews Where TeamID = " _
    & Request.QueryString("TeamID") _
    & " Order By DateEntered DESC", DBConn)
DBCommand.Fill(DSPageData, _
    "TeamNews")
```

which are placed into the other DataGrid control:

```
ddlTeamNews.DataSource = _
    DSPageData.Tables("TeamNews").DefaultView
ddlTeamNews.DataBind()
```

The next procedure fires when the visitor clicks the Button next to the Players DropDownList control.

```
Sub SubmitBtnPlayerInfo_Click(Sender As Object, E As EventArgs)
    Response.Redirect("./player.aspx?PlayerID=" _
        & ddlPlayers.SelectedItem.Value)
End Sub
```

The procedure simply sends the visitor to the Player page, passing to it the ID of the player selected by the visitor:

```
Response.Redirect("./player.aspx?PlayerID=" _
    & ddlPlayers.SelectedItem.Value)
```

The procedure fires when the View Article button is clicked

```
Sub SubmitBtnTeamNews_Click(Sender As Object, E As EventArgs)
    Response.Redirect("./news.aspx?TeamNewsID=" _
        & ddlTeamNews.SelectedItem.Value)
End Sub
```

The procedure sends the visitor to the News page:

```
Response.Redirect("./news.aspx?TeamNewsID=" _
    & ddlTeamNews.SelectedItem.Value)
```

Player ASP.NET Page

Player.aspx

The code on the Player page displays all the information about the player matching the ID passed into the page.

The body of the page contains just two controls. The first will display the name and number of the player:

```
<asp:Label
    id="lblTitle"
    Font-Size="25pt"
    Font-Name="Tahoma"
    runat="server"
/>
```

The other displays the other information about the player:

```
<asp:Label
    id="lblMessage"
    Font-Size="10pt"
    Font-Name="Tahoma"
    Font-Bold="True"
    runat="server"
/>
```

The code on the page is contained within a single procedure, which fires when the page is loaded. The procedure displays the data on the selected player within the Label controls on the page.

```
Sub Page_Load(ByVal Sender as Object, ByVal E as EventArgs)
    If Len(Request.QueryString("PlayerID")) = 0 Then
        Response.Redirect("./index.aspx")
    End If
    If Not IsPostBack Then
        Dim DBConn as OleDbConnection
        Dim DBCommand As OleDbDataAdapter
```

```
            Dim DSPageData as New DataSet
            DBConn = New OleDbConnection("Provider=sqloledb;" _
                & "server=localhost;" _
                & "Initial Catalog=INETC6;" _
                & "User Id=sa;" _
                & "Password=yourpassword;")
            DBCommand = New OleDbDataAdapter _
                ("Select PlayerNumber, LastName, FirstName, PPG, " _
                & "APG, RPG, BPG, Description From Players " _
                & "Where PlayerID = " _
                & Request.QueryString("PlayerID"), DBConn)
            DBCommand.Fill(DSPageData, _
                "Player")
            lblTitle.Text = DSPageData.Tables("Player"). _
                Rows(0).Item("PlayerNumber") & " - " _
                & DSPageData.Tables("Player"). _
                Rows(0).Item("FirstName") & " " _
                & DSPageData.Tables("Player"). _
                Rows(0).Item("LastName")
            lblMessage.Text = "Points Per Game: " _
                & DSPageData.Tables("Player"). _
                Rows(0).Item("PPG") & "<br>" _
                & "Assists Per Game: " _
                & DSPageData.Tables("Player"). _
                Rows(0).Item("APG") & "<br>" _
                & "Rebounds Per Game: " _
                & DSPageData.Tables("Player"). _
                Rows(0).Item("RPG") & "<br>" _
                & "Blocks Per Game: " _
                & DSPageData.Tables("Player"). _
                Rows(0).Item("BPG") & "<br><br>" _
                & DSPageData.Tables("Player"). _
                Rows(0).Item("Description")
        End If
End Sub
```

The procedure should run only if the ID of a player was passed into the page:

```
If Len(Request.QueryString("PlayerID")) = 0 Then
```

If an ID was not passed in, we send the visitor back to the Standings page:

```
Response.Redirect("./index.aspx")
```

The rest of the code should run only when the page is first loaded

```
If Not IsPostBack Then
```

If that is the case, we need data objects:

```
Dim DBConn as OleDbConnection
Dim DBCommand As OleDbDataAdapter
Dim DSPageData as New DataSet
```

We start by connecting to the database:

```
DBConn = New OleDbConnection("Provider=sqloledb;" _
    & "server=localhost;" _
    & "Initial Catalog=INETC6;" _
    & "User Id=sa;" _
    & "Password=yourpassword;")
```

We then retrieve all the data on the player corresponding to the ID passed into the page

```
DBCommand = New OleDbDataAdapter _
    ("Select PlayerNumber, LastName, FirstName, PPG, " _
    & "APG, RPG, BPG, Description From Players " _
    & "Where PlayerID = " _
    & Request.QueryString("PlayerID"), DBConn)
```

and place it into the DataSet object:

```
DBCommand.Fill(DSPageData, _
    "Player")
```

The name and number of the player are placed into the title label control:

```
lblTitle.Text = DSPageData.Tables("Player"). _
    Rows(0).Item("PlayerNumber") & " - " _
```

```
    & DSPageData.Tables("Player"). _
    Rows(0).Item("FirstName") & " " _
    & DSPageData.Tables("Player"). _
    Rows(0).Item("LastName")
```

The rest of the data is combined with HTML tags and placed into the message label:

```
lblMessage.Text = "Points Per Game: " _
    & DSPageData.Tables("Player"). _
    Rows(0).Item("PPG") & "<br>" _
    & "Assists Per Game: " _
    & DSPageData.Tables("Player"). _
    Rows(0).Item("APG") & "<br>" _
    & "Rebounds Per Game: " _
    & DSPageData.Tables("Player"). _
    Rows(0).Item("RPG") & "<br>" _
    & "Blocks Per Game: " _
    & DSPageData.Tables("Player"). _
    Rows(0).Item("BPG") & "<br><br>" _
    & DSPageData.Tables("Player"). _
    Rows(0).Item("Description")
```

News ASP.NET Page

News.aspx

The code on the News page displays the contents of a news article corresponding to the ID passed into the page.

The page has two Label controls. The first control displays the headline for the article:

```
<asp:Label
    id="lblTitle"
    Font-Size="25pt"
    Font-Name="Tahoma"
    runat="server"
/>
```

The other Label control displays the date and text of the article:

```
<asp:Label
    id="lblMessage"
    Font-Size="10pt"
```

```
    Font-Name="Tahoma"
    Font-Bold="True"
    runat="server"
/>
```

The code on the page fires when the page is first loaded.

```
Sub Page_Load(ByVal Sender as Object, ByVal E as EventArgs)
    If Len(Request.QueryString("TeamNewsID")) = 0 Then
        Response.Redirect("./index.aspx")
    End If
    If Not IsPostBack Then
        Dim DBConn as OleDbConnection
        Dim DBCommand As OleDbDataAdapter
        Dim DSPageData as New DataSet
        DBConn = New OleDbConnection("Provider=sqloledb;" _
            & "server=localhost;" _
            & "Initial Catalog=INETC6;" _
            & "User Id=sa;" _
            & "Password=yourpassword;")
        DBCommand = New OleDbDataAdapter _
            ("Select DateEntered, HeadLine, News From TeamNews " _
            & "Where TeamNewsID = " _
            & Request.QueryString("TeamNewsID"), DBConn)
        DBCommand.Fill(DSPageData, _
            "News")
        lblTitle.Text = DSPageData.Tables("News"). _
            Rows(0).Item("Headline")
        lblMessage.Text = DSPageData.Tables("News"). _
            Rows(0).Item("DateEntered") & "<br>" _
            & DSPageData.Tables("News"). _
            Rows(0).Item("News")
    End If
End Sub
```

The page should be loaded only if an ID was passed into it:

```
If Len(Request.QueryString("TeamNewsID")) = 0 Then
```

If one wasn't, we send the visitor to the Standings page:

```
Response.Redirect("./index.aspx")
```

The rest of the code should run only when the page is loaded

```
If Not IsPostBack Then
```

If that is the case, we need data objects:

```
Dim DBConn as OleDbConnection
Dim DBCommand As OleDbDataAdapter
Dim DSPageData as New DataSet
```

We start by connecting to our SQL Server database:

```
DBConn = New OleDbConnection("Provider=sqloledb;" _
    & "server=localhost;" _
    & "Initial Catalog=INETC6;" _
    & "User Id=sa;" _
    & "Password=yourpassword;")
```

We then retrieve the news article matching the ID passed into the page

```
DBCommand = New OleDbDataAdapter _
    ("Select DateEntered, HeadLine, News From TeamNews " _
    & "Where TeamNewsID = " _
    & Request.QueryString("TeamNewsID"), DBConn)
```

and place it into our DataSet object:

```
DBCommand.Fill(DSPageData, _
    "News")
```

We then place the headline of the article into our title Label:

```
lblTitle.Text = DSPageData.Tables("News"). _
    Rows(0).Item("Headline")
```

And the date and text of the article are placed into our other Label control:

```
lblMessage.Text = DSPageData.Tables("News"). _
    Rows(0).Item("DateEntered") & "<br>" _
    & DSPageData.Tables("News"). _
    Rows(0).Item("News")
```

Access Code Changes

C6.mdb

A few changes are needed for this solution to run with an Access database instead of a SQL Server database. First, the connect string needs to change so that it uses the correct provider and points to the correct database:

```
DBConn = New OleDbConnection("PROVIDER=Microsoft.Jet.OLEDB.4.0;" _
    & "DATA SOURCE=" _
    & Server.MapPath("/INetBook/C6/" _
    & "Access/C6.mdb;"))
```

The concatenation character in Access is "&" instead of the "+" character used in SQL Server:

```
DBCommand = New OleDbDataAdapter _
    ("Select '<a HREF=""./team.aspx?TeamID=' & " _
    & "TeamID & '"">' " _
    & "& TeamCity & ' ' & TeamNickName & '</a>' as " _
    & "[Desert Division (Click for More Info)], " _
    & "(NumWins / " _
    & "(NumWins + NumLoses)) * 100 as [Record], " _
    & "NumWins as [Wins], NumLoses as [Loses] " _
    & "From Teams " _
    & "Where Division = 'Desert' " _
    & "Order By NumWins / " _
    & "(NumWins + NumLoses) DESC" _
    , DBConn)
```

On the Schedule and Results page, we look for games corresponding to a date. In SQL Server the date was surrounded with the " ' " character. In Access, we need to use the "#" character:

```
DBCommand = New OleDbDataAdapter _
    ("SELECT Teams.TeamCity & ' ' & " _
    & "Teams.TeamNickName as [Home Team], " _
    & "Games.ScoreTeam1 as [Home Team Score], " _
    & "(Select TeamCity & ' ' & TeamNickName " _
    & "from Teams where TeamID = TeamID2) " _
```

```
    & " as [Away Team], " _
    & "Games.ScoreTeam2  as [Away Team Score] " _
    & "FROM Games INNER JOIN " _
    & "Teams ON Games.TeamID1 = Teams.TeamID " _
    & "Where Games.GameDate = #" _
    & Today() & "#", DBConn)
```

On the Team page, we display the date of the games. In SQL Server, the date-only portion is extracted using the convert function. With Access, the format function is used

```
DBCommand = New OleDbDataAdapter _
    ("SELECT Format(GameDate, ""m/d/yyyy"") " _
    & "as [Date], " _
    & "Teams.TeamCity & ' ' & " _
    & "Teams.TeamNickName as [Home Team], " _
    & "Games.ScoreTeam1 as [Home Team Score], " _
    & "(Select TeamCity & ' ' & TeamNickName " _
    & "from Teams where TeamID = TeamID2) " _
    & " as [Away Team], " _
    & "Games.ScoreTeam2  as [Away Team Score] " _
    & "FROM Games INNER JOIN " _
    & "Teams ON Games.TeamID1 = Teams.TeamID " _
    & "Where TeamID1 = " _
    & Request.QueryString("TeamID") & " or " _
    & "TeamID2 = " & Request.QueryString("TeamID") _
    , DBConn)
```

No other code changes were needed.

CHAPTER

7

Managing Site Content

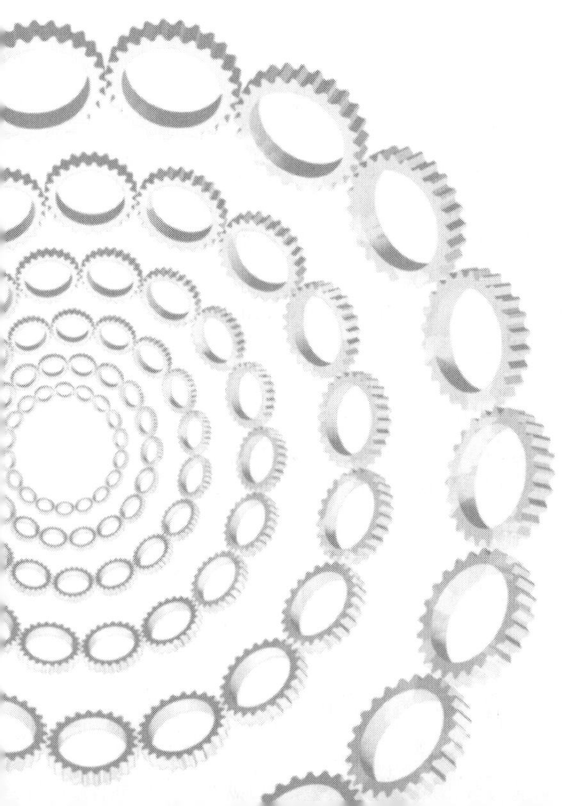

In this chapter, we will review tools that could be used on most sites. These tools add to the functionality of the site by providing the Webmaster with ways to manage the content of their site, or they provide functionality for visitors, and so assist in bringing more traffic to your site.

The first tool we will look at is the Ad Rotator tool. This tool shows you how to use the AdRotator control to manage banner ads on your site.

After that, we will review the Email File tool. Many companies need to be able to send documents such as catalogs, instruction manuals, or assorted forms to visitors. This tool makes it easy for a visitor to request and receive documents from your site.

The third tool we will look at in this chapter is the Message Board tool. With this one, visitors can view message threads, create message threads, or add a message to an existing thread.

Ad Rotator Application

The Ad Rotator tool demonstrates how you can use the AdRotator control to manage and display banner ads on your web site. As you review this tool, note the structure of the XML schedule file. Also note the use of the Ad Created event to fire code whenever a banner ad is displayed.

Sample Usage

When the visitor first views this page, they see a page like the one displayed in Figure 7-1.

Note the ad at the top of the page. The ad links to another site through a new window when the visitor clicks it. If the visitor were to refresh the page or another visitor were to come to this page, they might see a different banner ad, like the one displayed in Figure 7-2.

This ad links to a different site, and it has a different image and a different alternate text. As you will see when we look at the schedule file, you can control how often an ad is displayed compared to other ads.

Also note on the page that we display information about the ad as well as a count of the number of times that an ad has been displayed. Note that this is done to demonstrate the properties of the control. You would likely use this information to record an impression of the ad in your database.

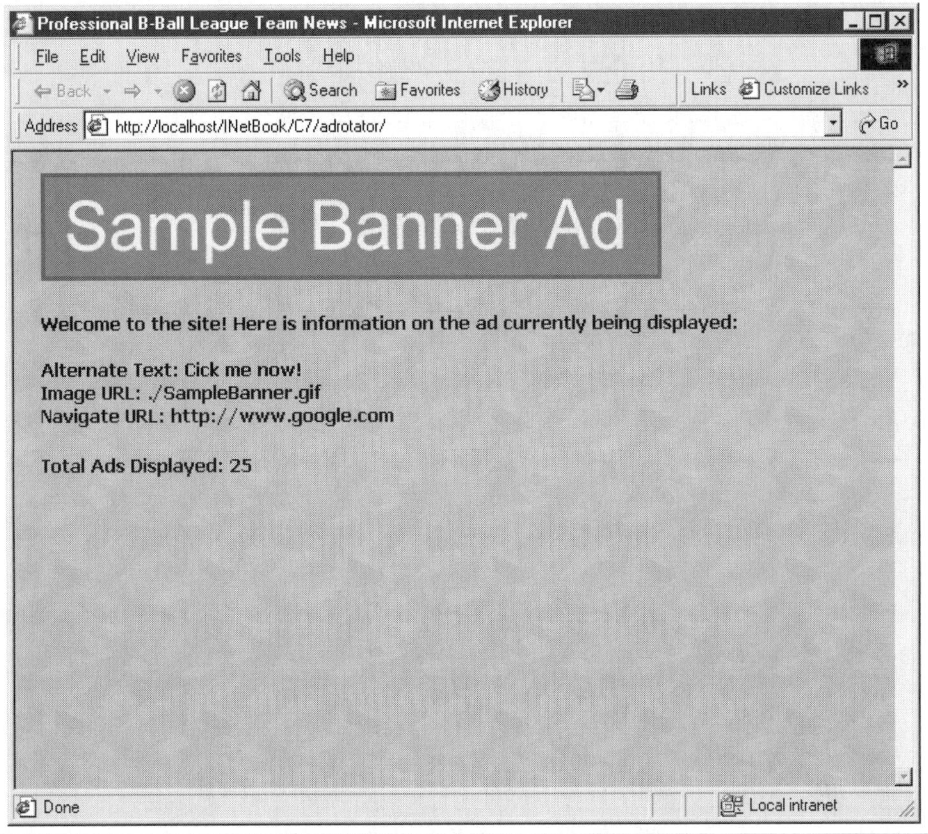

Figure 7-1 *Ad Rotator page displaying first ad*

Ad Rotator ASP.NET Code

The Ad Rotator tool is composed of two files. One is the ASP.NET page that displays the ads. The other page is the schedule file that determines what ads are displayed and how often they are displayed. In this section, we will review those two files.

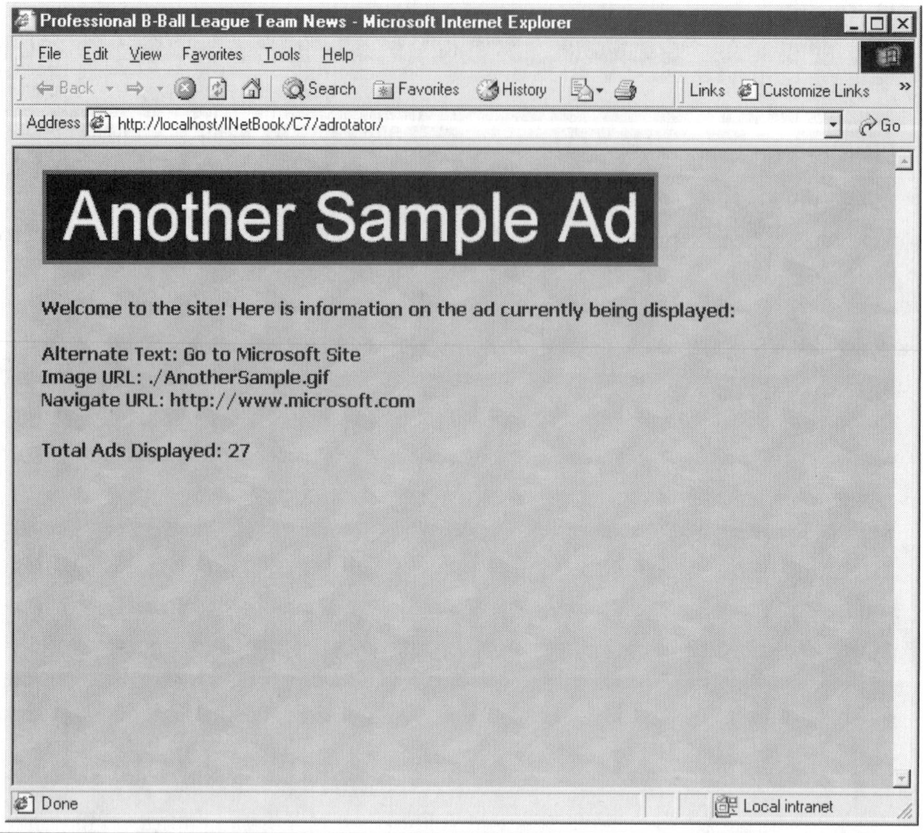

Figure 7-2 *Ad Rotator page displaying second ad*

XML Schedule File

BannerAds.XML

The schedule file contains a list of all the banner ads included with this site. The file is specified when we define the AdRotator control on our ASP.NET page. The file must be in a very specific format with corresponding opening and closing tags that define sections and properties. This is the schedule file used with this site:

```
<Advertisements>
   <Ad>
      <ImageUrl>./SampleBanner.gif</ImageUrl>
      <NavigateUrl>http://www.google.com</NavigateUrl>
      <AlternateText>Cick me now!</AlternateText>
      <Keyword>ShowMe</Keyword>
```

```
      <Impressions>71</Impressions>
   </Ad>
   <Ad>
      <ImageUrl>./AnotherSample.gif</ImageUrl>
      <NavigateUrl>http://www.microsoft.com</NavigateUrl>
      <AlternateText>Go to Microsoft Site</AlternateText>
      <Keyword>ShowMe</Keyword>
      <Impressions>70</Impressions>
   </Ad>
   <Ad>
      <ImageUrl>./DoesNotExist.gif</ImageUrl>
      <NavigateUrl>http://www.microsoft.com</NavigateUrl>
      <AlternateText>Won't see me</AlternateText>
      <Keyword>DoNotShowMe</Keyword>
      <Impressions>2000</Impressions>
   </Ad>
</Advertisements>
```

The file starts with an opening Advertisement tag:

```
<Advertisements>
```

Within that section, we define an Ad section:

```
<Ad>
```

The image displayed with this ad is set through the ImageURL property:

```
<ImageUrl>./SampleBanner.gif</ImageUrl>
```

Next, we set where the visitor will go when they click the ad:

```
<NavigateUrl>http://www.google.com</NavigateUrl>
```

The AlternateText property contains the text the visitor sees when they hover their mouse over the ad:

```
<AlternateText>Cick me now!</AlternateText>
```

Next, we define the keyword property. This property allows us to use the same ad file over many pages. Then on each page we can display a subset of the ads:

```
<Keyword>ShowMe</Keyword>
```

Next, we set the relative number of times that this ad is displayed compared to the rest of the ads in the file:

```
<Impressions>71</Impressions>
```

We then close this ad section

```
</Ad>
```

and start a second ad:

```
<Ad>
```

This ad uses a different image file:

```
<ImageUrl>./AnotherSample.gif</ImageUrl>
```

And the visitor is sent to a different site when the ad is clicked. Note that you could send the visitor to your own page, which could record a hit on that ad before redirecting the visitor to the target site:

```
<NavigateUrl>http://www.microsoft.com</NavigateUrl>
```

The ad will display this text when the visitor hovers their mouse over it:

```
<AlternateText>Go to Microsoft Site</AlternateText>
```

The ad uses the same keyword filter:

```
<Keyword>ShowMe</Keyword>
```

But it will be displayed slightly less frequently than the first ad:

```
<Impressions>70</Impressions>
```

We then close this ad

```
</Ad>
```

and start a third ad:

```
<Ad>
    <ImageUrl>./DoesNotExist.gif</ImageUrl>
```

```
    <NavigateUrl>http://www.microsoft.com</NavigateUrl>
    <AlternateText>Won't see me</AlternateText>
```

Note that this ad uses a different keyword:

```
<Keyword>DoNotShowMe</Keyword>
```

When we look at the ASP.NET page, you will see that we filter this file so that this ad is not displayed. Therefore, even though it has a much more likely chance of being displayed because of this impression level

```
<Impressions>2000</Impressions>
```

it will not be displayed on our sample site:

```
</Ad>
```

We then close the Advertisements section:

```
</Advertisements>
```

Ad Rotator ASP.NET Page

Index.aspx

The Ad Rotator page uses the schedule file to display banner ads. Within the body of the page, we define two controls. The first is the AdRotator control.

```
<asp:adrotator
    AdvertisementFile="bannerads.xml"
    KeywordFilter="ShowMe"
    Target="_blank"
    OnAdCreated="AdCreated_Event"
    BorderColor="blue"
    BorderWidth=3
    runat="server"
/>
```

We specify the name of the schedule file to be used with this control:

```
AdvertisementFile="bannerads.xml"
```

We then specify that we only want to use banner ads with the keyword "ShowMe." This means that the third ad will not be displayed. By defining keywords for your banner ads, you can have some pages that only show a subset of the banner ads and other pages that display any of the ads:

```
KeywordFilter="ShowMe"
```

Next, we specify that a new window should be opened when the visitor clicks an ad:

```
Target="_blank"
```

The default is for the same browser window to be used.

We then specify the name of the procedure that we want to run when an ad is displayed

```
OnAdCreated="AdCreated_Event"
```

Finally, we format the look of the image control:

```
BorderColor="blue"
BorderWidth=3
```

The other control on the page is a Label control that displays the properties of the current ad:

```
<asp:Label
    id="lblMessage"
    Font-Size="10pt"
    Font-Name="Tahoma"
    Font-Bold="True"
    runat="server"
/>
```

The only code on the page fires when an ad is displayed.

```
Sub AdCreated_Event(ByVal Sender as Object, ByVal E as
AdCreatedEventArgs)
    Application("TotalAds") = Application("TotalAds") + 1
    lblMessage.Text = "Welcome to the site! " _
        & "Here is information on the ad " _
        & "currently being displayed:<br>" _
        & "<br>Alternate Text: " & E.AlternateText _
        & "<br>Image URL: " & E.ImageURL _
        & "<br>Navigate URL: " & E.NavigateURL _
```

```
        & "<br><br>Total Ads Displayed: " _
        & Application("TotalAds")
End Sub
```

We start by incrementing an application variable that stores the number of times that banner ads have been used

```
Application("TotalAds") = Application("TotalAds") + 1
```

You may want to store a hit in a database indicating that the ad has been displayed to keep track of the number of impressions for each ad.

We then place into our Label control the properties of the current ad being displayed, which are passed into this procedure through the AdCreatedEventArgs parameter:

```
lblMessage.Text = "Welcome to the site! " _
    & "Here is information on the ad " _
    & "currently being displayed:<br>" _
    & "<br>Alternate Text: " & E.AlternateText _
    & "<br>Image URL: " & E.ImageURL _
    & "<br>Navigate URL: " & E.NavigateURL _
    & "<br><br>Total Ads Displayed: " _
    & Application("TotalAds")
```

Email File Tool

Frequently, companies have files that they need their visitors to be able to get copies of. These files might include product catalogs, rebate forms, instruction manuals, or product presentations. The Email File tool provides an easy way for visitors to access these files through your site and have a file e-mailed to them. Refer to the following files on the CD-ROM for use with the Email File tool:

- **Index.aspx** Email File ASP.NET page
- **C7EmailFile.sql** SQL Server table creation script
- **Files.txt** Data for the Files table
- **C7EmailFile.mdb** Email File Access database with data

Sample Usage

When the visitor first enters the Email File tool, they see the page displayed in Figure 7-3.

The visitor is presented with a list of files. They select one and enter their e-mail address. When they click OK, they see the message displayed in Figure 7-4.

The visitor can then check their e-mail. They are sent an e-mail message like the one displayed in Figure 7-5.

The body of the e-mail message includes the name of the file that they requested. Note that the message has an attachment. This attachment is the file that the visitor selected from the DropDownList on the Email File page.

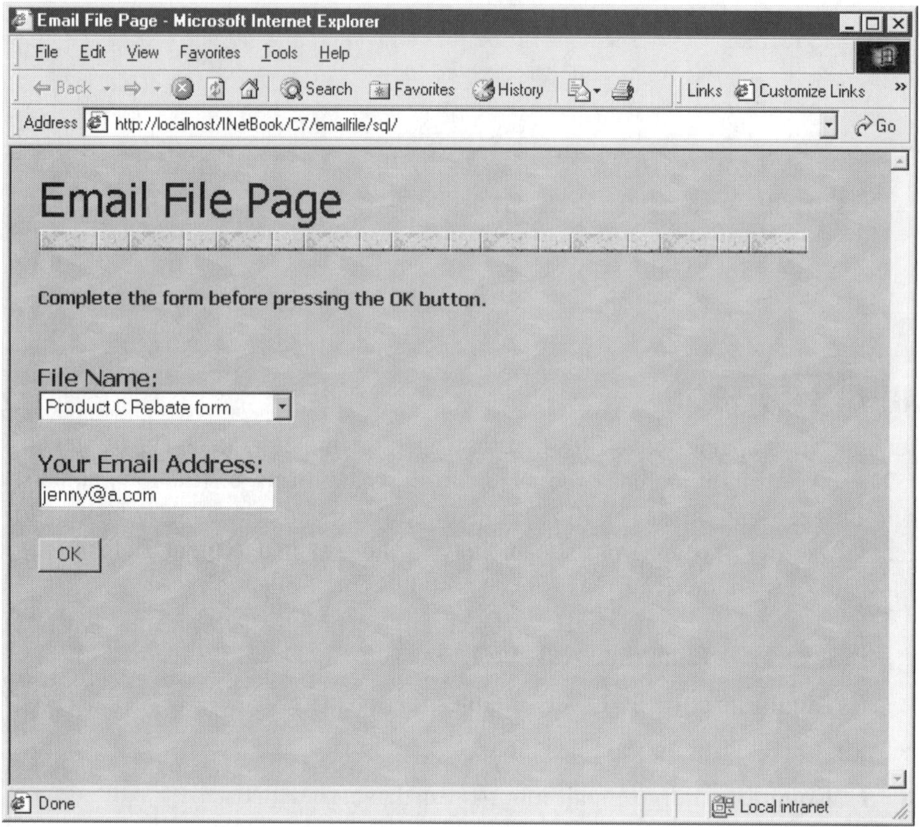

Figure 7-3 *Initial view of the Email File page*

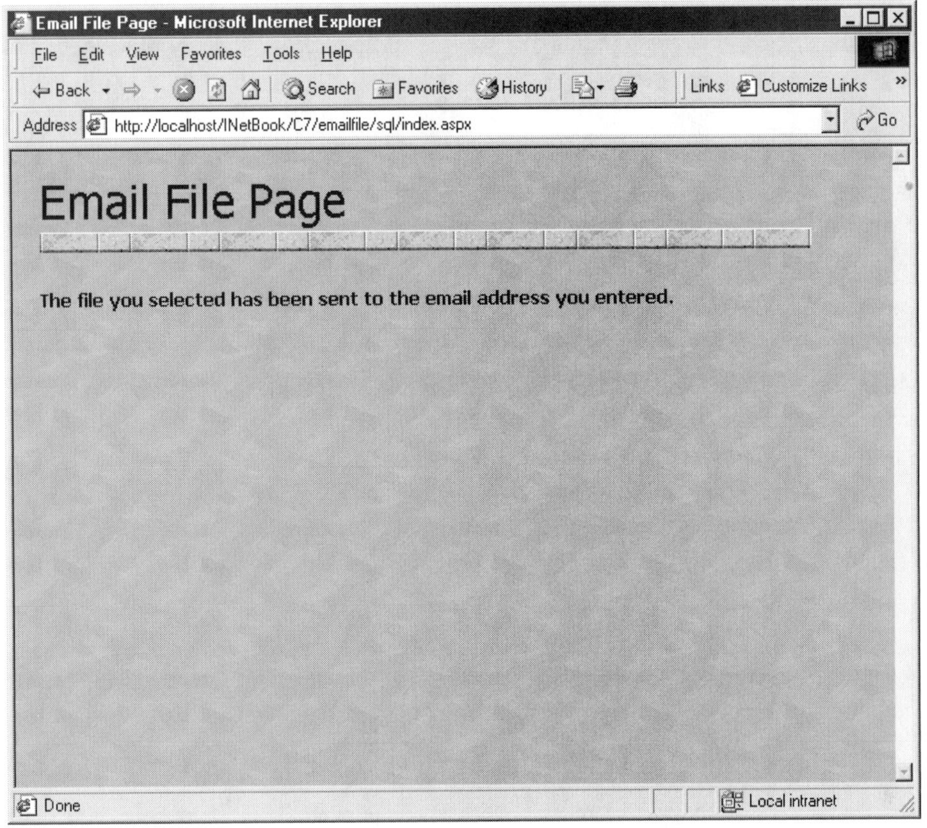

Figure 7-4 *Response view of the Email File page*

Email File Database Component

C7EmailFile.sql

The database required for use with the Email File tool has just one table in it. In this section, we will review the contents of that table.

Files Field Specifications

Files.txt

The field specifications for the fields in the Files table are displayed in Table 7-1.

The Files table stores the file information that is displayed in the DropDownList control on the Email File page. The FileID field is a primary key that uniquely identifies each record. The FileTitle field stores the name of the file as the visitor sees it in the DropDownList control and in the e-mail message.

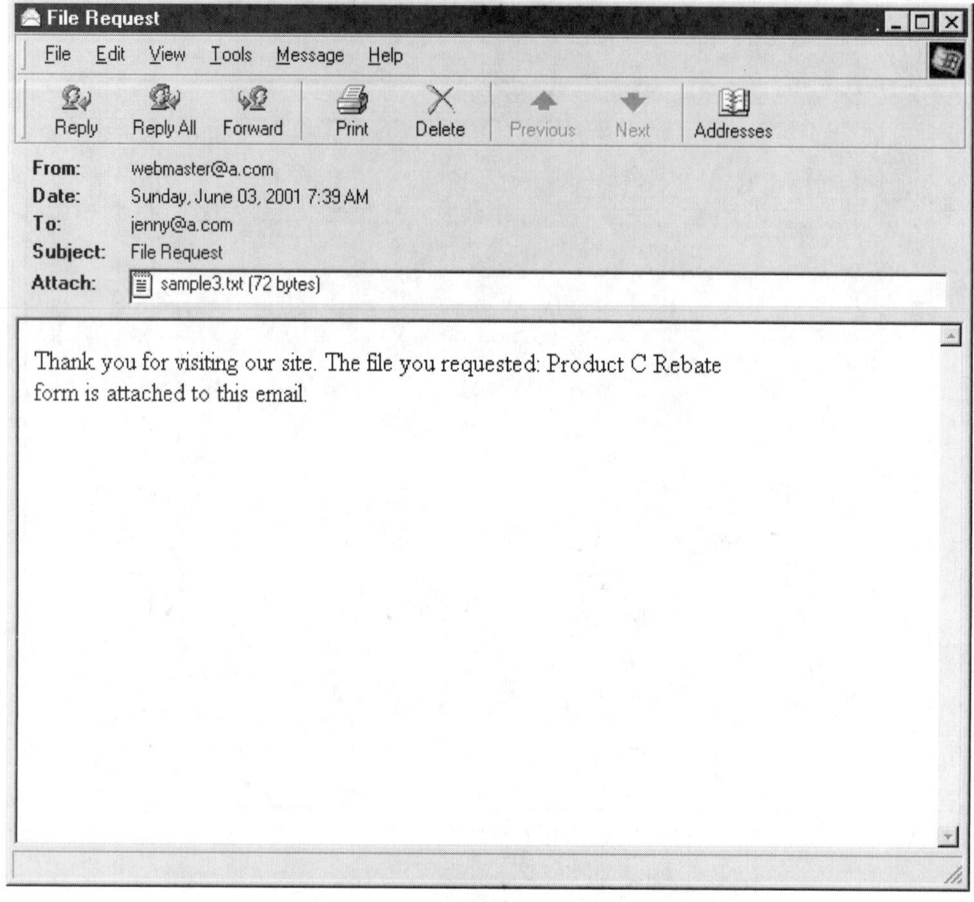

Figure 7-5 *E-mail sent from the Email File page*

Field Name	Field Type	Notes
FileID	int	Primary Key, Identity Column
FileTitle	varchar	Length = 50
FileName	varchar	Length = 50

Table 7-1 *Files Field Specifications*

The FileName field stores the physical name of the file that is to be attached to the e-mail message. Note that in this implementation the files must be in the same folder as the Email File page. But you could also put the full path of the file in this file and then modify the code so that it doesn't use the relative path of the Email File tool.

Email File ASP.NET Code

Only one ASP.NET page is used with the Email File tool. In this section, we will review the code on that page and the controls that it contains.

Email File ASP.NET Page

Index.aspx

The code on the Email File page displays a list of files from the Files table. The page also sends an e-mail message with an attachment based on the file selected by the visitor.

At the top of the page, we declare four compiler directives.

```
<%@ Page Language=VB Debug=true %>
<%@ Import Namespace="System.Data" %>
<%@ Import Namespace="System.Data.OLEDB" %>
<%@ Import Namespace="System.Web.Mail" %>
```

The first directive informs the compiler of the language that we are using and that we want to run the page in debug mode:

```
<%@ Page Language=VB Debug=true %>
```

The next two directives are required so that we can access and display data from our Access or SQL Server database:

```
<%@ Import Namespace="System.Data" %>
<%@ Import Namespace="System.Data.OLEDB" %>
```

The other directive is required so that we can create e-mail objects that allow us to send an e-mail message with an attachment to the visitor:

```
<%@ Import Namespace="System.Web.Mail" %>
```

Within the body of the page, we declare a Label control that displays the title of the page

```
<asp:Label
    id="lblTitle"
```

```
        Font-Size="25pt"
        Font-Name="Tahoma"
        Text="Email File Page"
        runat="server"
/>
```

Another Label control is defined that will display either page instructions or a confirmation message:

```
<asp:Label
        id="lblMessage"
        Font-Size="10pt"
        Font-Name="Tahoma"
        Font-Bold="True"
        runat="server"
/>
```

The rest of the controls on the page are contained within a Panel control to make it easier to toggle their visibility:

```
<asp:Panel
        id="pnlForm"
        runat="server"
>
```

On that Panel control, we place a DropDownList that will contain the files from the File table:

```
<asp:dropdownlist
        id="ddlFiles"
        runat=server
        DataTextField="FileTitle"
        DataValueField="FileName">
</asp:dropdownlist>
```

Note that the visitor will see the name of the file but that we place the physical name of the file in the Value property.

Next, we define a TextBox control for the visitor's e-mail address:

```
<asp:TextBox
        id="txtEmailAddress"
```

```
    Columns="25"
    MaxLength="50"
    runat=server
/>
```

The visitor must enter a value in the Email Address field because of this RequiredFieldValidator that is linked to it:

```
<asp:RequiredFieldValidator
    id="rfvEmailAddress"
    ControlToValidate="txtEmailAddress"
    Display="Dynamic"
    Font-Name="Verdana"
    Font-Size="10pt"
    runat=server>
    Email Address is Required!
</asp:RequiredFieldValidator>
```

The only other control on the page is a Button control that processes the visitor's request when it is clicked:

```
<asp:button
    id="butOK"
    text="  OK  "
    Type="Submit"
    OnClick="SubmitBtn_Click"
    runat="server"
/>
```

The code on this page is contained within two procedures. The first procedure fires when the page loads. This procedure sets up the DropDownList and displays instructions.

```
Sub Page_Load(ByVal Sender as Object, ByVal E as EventArgs)
    If Not IsPostBack Then
        Dim DBConn as OleDbConnection
        Dim DBCommand As OleDbDataAdapter
        Dim DSPageData as New DataSet
        DBConn = New OleDbConnection("Provider=sqloledb;" _
            & "server=localhost;" _
            & "Initial Catalog=INETC7;" _
            & "User Id=sa;" _
            & "Password=yourpassword;")
```

```
        DBCommand = New OleDbDataAdapter _
            ("SELECT FileTitle, FileName from Files " _
            & "Order By FileTitle", DBConn)
        DBCommand.Fill(DSPageData, _
            "Files")
        ddlFiles.DataSource = _
            DSPageData.Tables("Files").DefaultView
        ddlFiles.DataBind()
        lblMessage.Text = "Complete the form before pressing the " _
            & "OK button."
    End If
End Sub
```

We only want this code to run the first time the page is loaded

```
If Not IsPostBack Then
```

If this is the first time, we will need data objects:

```
Dim DBConn as OleDbConnection
Dim DBCommand As OleDbDataAdapter
Dim DSPageData as New DataSet
```

We start by connecting to our database:

```
DBConn = New OleDbConnection("Provider=sqloledb;" _
    & "server=localhost;" _
    & "Initial Catalog=INETC7;" _
    & "User Id=sa;" _
    & "Password=yourpassword;")
```

Then we retrieve all the file information from the Files table

```
DBCommand = New OleDbDataAdapter _
    ("SELECT FileTitle, FileName from Files " _
    & "Order By FileTitle", DBConn)
```

which is placed into our DataSet object:

```
DBCommand.Fill(DSPageData, _
    "Files")
```

The DropDownList is then bound to that DataSet table

```
ddlFiles.DataSource = _
    DSPageData.Tables("Files").DefaultView
ddlFiles.DataBind()
```

We also need to place instructions into our message label:

```
lblMessage.Text = "Complete the form before pressing the " _
    & "OK button."
```

The other procedure fires when the OK button is clicked. It sends an e-mail message with an attachment to the visitor.

```
Sub SubmitBtn_Click(Sender As Object, E As EventArgs)
    Dim TheMessage as String
    Dim TheMailMessage as New MailMessage
    Dim TheMailConnection as New SmtpMail
    Dim TheAttachment as New MailAttachment _
        (Server.MapPath("/INetBook/C7/EmailFile/SQL/" _
        & ddlFiles.SelectedItem.Value))
    TheMessage = "Thank you for visiting our site. The file " _
        & "you requested: " & ddlFiles.SelectedItem.Text _
        & " is attached to this email."
    TheMailMessage.From = "webmaster@a.com"
    TheMailMessage.To = txtEmailAddress.text
    TheMailMessage.Subject = "File Request"
    TheMailMessage.Body = TheMessage
    TheMailMessage.Attachments.Add (TheAttachment)
    TheMailConnection.Send(TheMailMessage)
    lblMessage.Text = "The file you selected has been sent " _
        & "to the email address you entered."
    pnlForm.Visible = False
End Sub
```

We will need a variable to store the text of the message:

```
Dim TheMessage as String
```

We also need to declare an e-mail object

```
Dim TheMailMessage as New MailMessage
```

an object so that we can send the e-mail message

```
Dim TheMailConnection as New SmtpMail
```

and a MailAttachment object. Note that when we declare it, we have to set the name of the file that the attachment contains. Also note that we are using the MapPath method to return the physical path to the folder that the Email File page is located in. If you wish to put the full paths of the files in the database, you would just use the Value property by itself:

```
Dim TheAttachment as New MailAttachment _
    (Server.MapPath("/INetBook/C7/EmailFile/SQL/" _
    & ddlFiles.SelectedItem.Value))
```

Next we concatenate text with the name of the file requested to form the body of the message:

```
TheMessage = "Thank you for visiting our site. The file " _
    & "you requested: " & ddlFiles.SelectedItem.Text _
    & " is attached to this email."
```

We set the e-mail message so that it appears as if from the Webmaster of our fictional site:

```
TheMailMessage.From = "webmaster@a.com"
```

The message will be sent to the e-mail address entered on the page by the visitor:

```
TheMailMessage.To = txtEmailAddress.text
```

We also set the subject of the message:

```
TheMailMessage.Subject = "File Request"
```

We then place the text of the message into the Body property:

```
TheMailMessage.Body = TheMessage
```

We also need to add the attachment to this message:

```
TheMailMessage.Attachments.Add (TheAttachment)
```

Now the e-mail message can be sent to the visitor:

```
TheMailConnection.Send(TheMailMessage)
```

The visitor will then see a confirmation message on the page:

```
lblMessage.Text = "The file you selected has been sent " _
    & "to the email address you entered."
```

Finally, we hide the Panel control that contains the form controls:

```
pnlForm.Visible = False
```

Access Code Changes

C7EmailFile.mdb

If you wish to use this solution with Access instead of SQL Server, you should only need to change the connect string from the one that points to the SQL Server database

```
DBConn = New OleDbConnection("Provider=sqloledb;" _
    & "server=localhost;" _
    & "Initial Catalog=INETC7;" _
    & "User Id=sa;" _
    & "Password=yourpassword;")
```

to one that points to your Access database:

```
DBConn = New OleDbConnection("PROVIDER=Microsoft.Jet.OLEDB.4.0;" _
    & "DATA SOURCE=" _
    & Server.MapPath("/INetBook/C7/EmailFile/" _
    & "Access/C7EmailFile.mdb;"))
```

Note that you would need to change the path to the location where you placed the Access database.

Message Board Tool

One helpful and useful addition to a Web site is a Message Board. A Message Board provides a way for visitors to your site to form their own community and communicate with each other.

In this section of the chapter, we will review a Message Board tool. This tool allows visitors to browse through existing message threads. The visitor can also add to an existing thread, or they can create their own thread. The Message Board tool is made up of the following files, which can be found on the CD-ROM:

- **Index.aspx** Message Board ASP.NET page
- **C7MessageBoard.sql** SQL Server table creation script
- **Messages.txt** Data for the Messages table
- **C7MessageBoard.mdb** Message Board Access database with data

Sample Usage

When the visitor first enters the Message Board, they see the welcome message displayed in Figure 7-6.

The welcome message is actually just another thread. The way the code works is that the first message in the database is displayed, so it may be helpful to make the first message one that is instructional or that welcomes the visitor.

But the visitor can view other message threads by selecting the title of the thread from the DropDownList control. Figure 7-7 shows the page after a thread has been selected.

At the top of the page, the visitor sees the name of the thread in title text. Then, below that, the visitor sees the entire message thread. Each message in the thread is composed of the name of the person who entered the message, the date it was entered, and the text of the message. Each message in the thread is separated by an HTML HR tag.

When the visitor wishes to create a new thread, they use the bottom part of this page. Here they enter their name, the title of the message, and the initial text of the thread. When the visitor clicks the Add Thread button, their message is added to the database and they see it as it is displayed in Figure 7-8.

Other visitors can now view this thread and add their own messages to the thread. This is done through the middle section of the page. Here the visitor just enters their name and the text of their message. They then see the addition of their text to the thread, as displayed in Figure 7-9.

Notice that the visitor who updated the thread included HTML <i> tags in their message, which makes the text italicized. Since the text is displayed as HTML, the visitor can add a variety of formatting tags such as these.

Message Board Page - Microsoft Internet Explorer

File Edit View Favorites Tools Help

Back Search Favorites History Links Customize Links

Address http://localhost/INetBook/C7/messageboard/sql/ Go

Message Board - Welcome

Welcome to the message board. Use this page to view existing messages, to add a message to a thread or to create a new thread.

Select a thread to view it: Marsha View Thread

Add a message to the current thread

Your Name:

Your Message:

Update Thread

Create a new thread

Your Name:

Message Title:

Your Message:

Add Thread

Done Local intranet

Figure 7-6 *Welcome message displayed on the Message Board page*

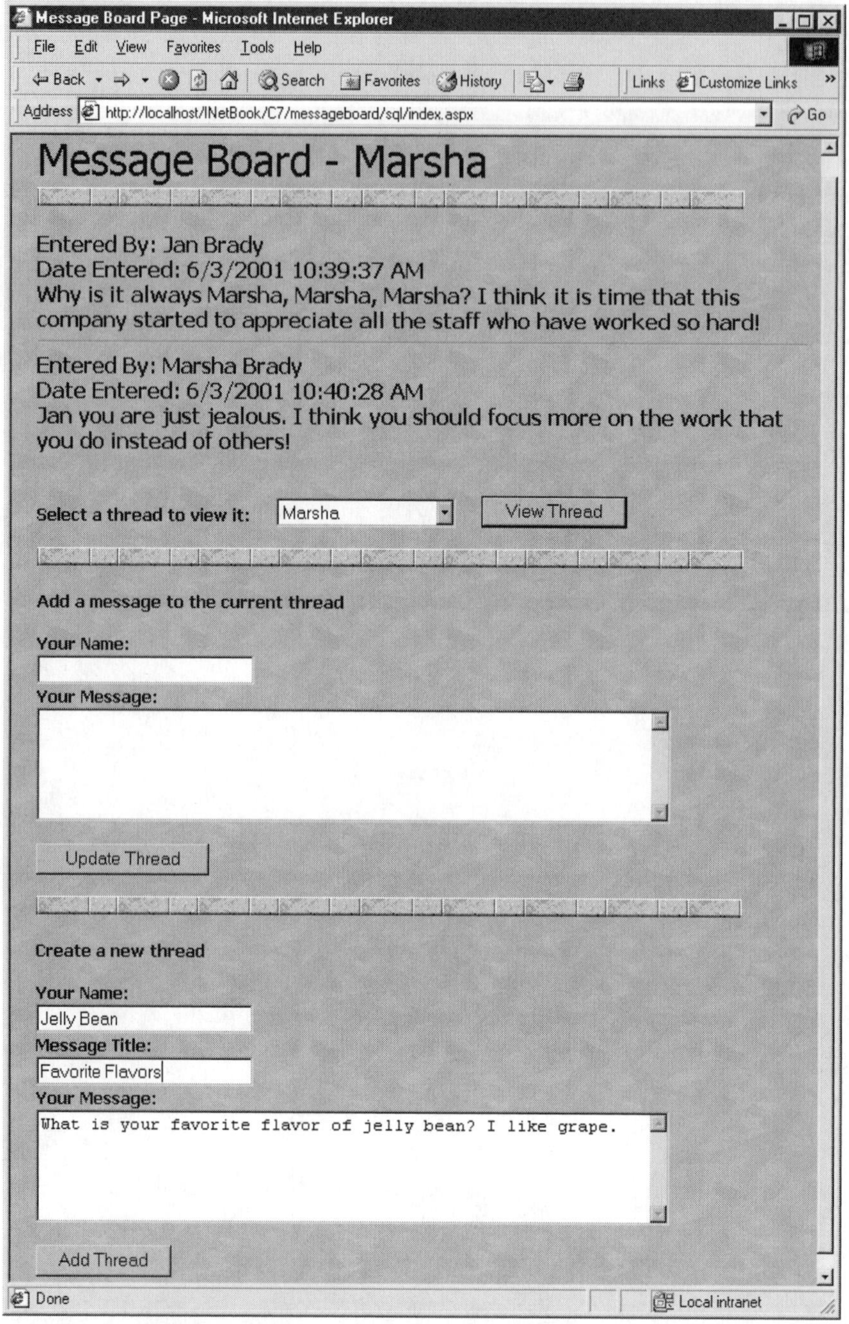

Figure 7-7 *Message Board displaying an existing thread*

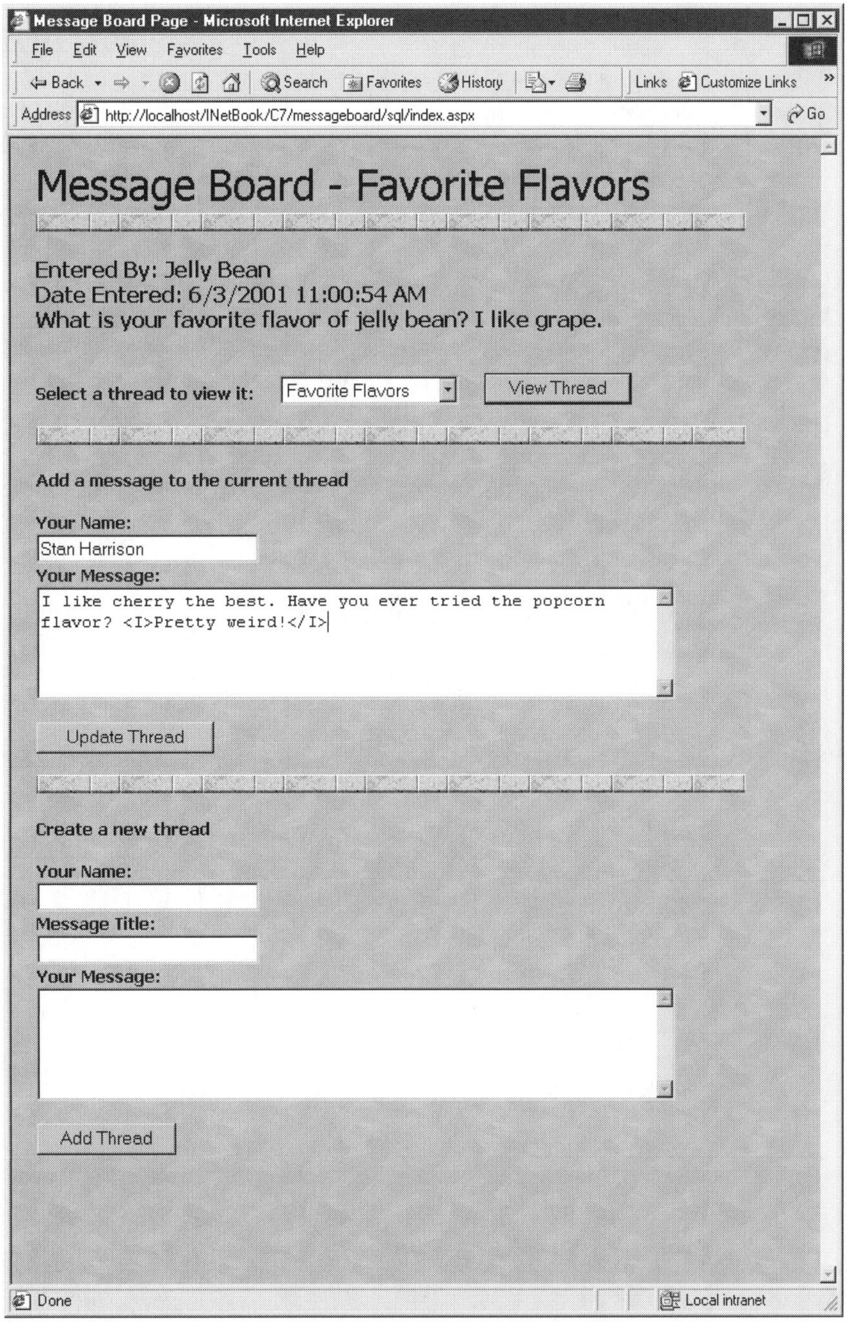

Figure 7-8 *Message Board page after new thread has been added*

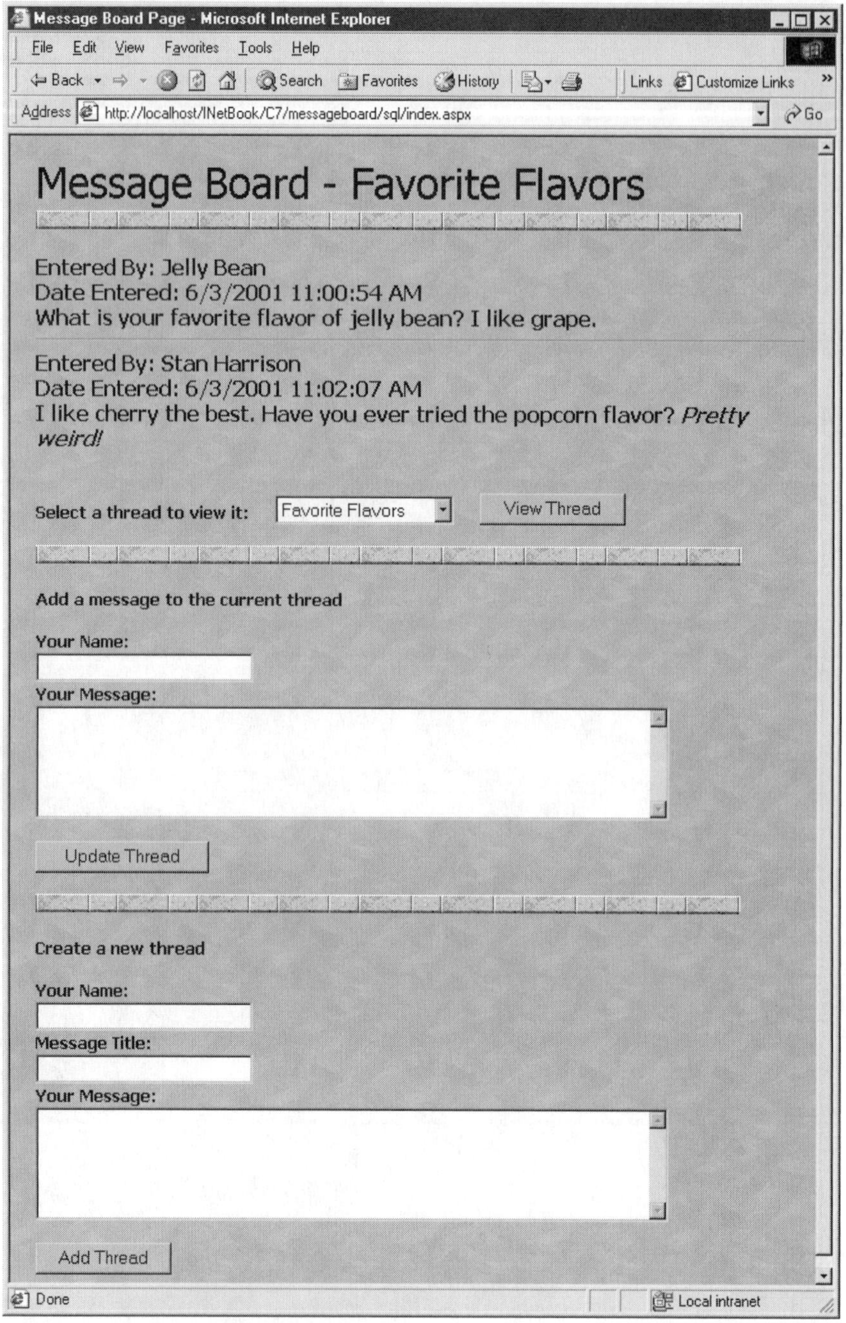

Figure 7-9 *Message Board after thread has been updated*

Message Board Database Component

C7MessageBoard.sql

The database required for use with the Message Board tool includes a single table. In this section, we will review the contents of that table.

Messages Field Specifications

Messages.txt

The field specifications for the fields in the Messages table are displayed in Table 7-2.

The Messages table stores the contents of the messages as they are displayed on the Message Board page. The MessageID field is the primary key in the table. It is automatically populated when a new record is added to the table.

The MessageTitle field stores the title of the message as it is displayed in the DropDownList and the title Label on the Message Board page. The MessageText field stores the contents of the message thread.

Message Board ASP.NET Code

The Message Board tool is composed of a single ASP.NET page. In this section, we will review the controls and code on that page.

Message Board ASP.NET Page

Index.aspx

The code on the Message Board page allows the visitor to view existing threads, to add messages to threads, and to create new message threads. At the top of the page,

Field Name	Field Type	Notes
MessageID	int	Primary Key, Identity Column
MessageTitle	varchar	Length = 50
MessageText	text	

Table 7-2 *Messages Field Specifications*

you will find three compiler directives that set up the run environment and import needed data libraries:

```
<%@ Page Language=VB Debug=true %>
<%@ Import Namespace="System.Data" %>
<%@ Import Namespace="System.Data.OLEDB" %>
```

Within the body of the page, we first define a Label control to display the title of the current thread:

```
<asp:Label
    id="lblTitle"
    Font-Size="25pt"
    Font-Name="Tahoma"
    Text="The Message Board"
    runat="server"
/>
```

Another Label control is defined beneath that. It displays the text of the current thread:

```
<asp:Label
    id="lblMessage"
    Font-Size="12pt"
    Font-Name="Tahoma"
    Font-Bold="True"
    runat="server"
/>
```

Next, we define a DropDownList that displays the names of the messages but also passes their IDs:

```
<asp:dropdownlist
    id="ddlMessages"
    runat=server
    DataTextField="MessageTitle"
    DataValueField="MessageID">
</asp:dropdownlist>
```

That is followed by a Button control that, when clicked, displays the message selected by the visitor:

```
<asp:button
    id="butViewThread"
    text="View Thread"
    Type="Submit"
    OnClick="ViewThread_Click"
    runat="server"
/>
```

In the next section of the page, we define a TextBox for the visitor to enter their name when updating an existing thread:

```
<asp:TextBox
    id="txtUpdateName"
    Columns="25"
    MaxLength="50"
    runat=server
/>
```

That is followed by another TextBox control, implemented as an HTML TextArea tag, where the visitor enters the text of their message being added to the current thread:

```
<asp:TextBox
    id="txtUpdateMessage"
    Columns="60"
    Rows="5"
    runat=server
    TextMode="MultiLine"
/>
```

The other control in this section is a Button that submits the visitor's request to add their message to the current thread:

```
<asp:button
    id="butUpdateThread"
    text="Update Thread"
    Type="Submit"
```

```
    OnClick="UpdateThread_Click"
    runat="server"
/>
```

The next section of the form allows the visitor to add a new thread. Therefore, we need a TextBox control for the visitor's name:

```
<asp:TextBox
    id="txtAddName"
    Columns="25"
    MaxLength="50"
    runat=server
/>
```

A second TextBox control is needed for the title of the thread:

```
<asp:TextBox
    id="txtAddTitle"
    Columns="25"
    MaxLength="50"
    runat=server
/>
```

And a third TextBox control allows the visitor to enter the text of their new thread:

```
<asp:TextBox
    id="txtAddMessage"
    Columns="60"
    Rows="5"
    runat=server
    TextMode="MultiLine"
/>
```

One other control on the page adds the new message thread when it is clicked

```
<asp:button
    id="butAddThread"
    text="Add Thread"
    Type="Submit"
    OnClick="AddThread_Click"
    runat="server"
/>
```

The code on the page is contained within four procedures. The first procedure fires when the page is loaded. It displays the first message in the Messages table and populates the DropDownList control.

```
Sub Page_Load(ByVal Sender as Object, ByVal E as EventArgs)
    If Not IsPostBack Then
        Dim DBConn as OleDbConnection
        Dim DBCommand As OleDbDataAdapter
        Dim DSPageData as New DataSet
        DBConn = New OleDbConnection("Provider=sqloledb;" _
            & "server=localhost;" _
            & "Initial Catalog=INETC7;" _
            & "User Id=sa;" _
            & "Password=yourpassword;")
        DBCommand = New OleDbDataAdapter _
            ("SELECT MessageID, MessageTitle, " _
            & "MessageText From Messages " _
            & "Where MessageID = (Select Min(MessageID) From " _
            & "Messages)", DBConn)
        DBCommand.Fill(DSPageData, _
            "CurrentMessage")
        Session("CurrentMessageID") = _
            DSPageData.Tables("CurrentMessage"). _
            Rows(0).Item("MessageID")
        lblTitle.Text = "Message Board - " _
            & DSPageData.Tables("CurrentMessage"). _
            Rows(0).Item("MessageTitle")
        lblMessage.Text = DSPageData.Tables("CurrentMessage"). _
            Rows(0).Item("MessageText")
        DBCommand = New OleDbDataAdapter _
            ("SELECT MessageID, MessageTitle " _
            & "from Messages " _
            & "Order By MessageTitle", DBConn)
        DBCommand.Fill(DSPageData, _
            "Messages")
        ddlMessages.DataSource = _
            DSPageData.Tables("Messages").DefaultView
        ddlMessages.DataBind()
    End If
End Sub
```

We only want this code to run when the page is first loaded

```
If Not IsPostBack Then
```

If this is the first run of the page, we need data objects:

```
Dim DBConn as OleDbConnection
Dim DBCommand As OleDbDataAdapter
Dim DSPageData as New DataSet
```

We start by connecting to the database:

```
DBConn = New OleDbConnection("Provider=sqloledb;" _
    & "server=localhost;" _
    & "Initial Catalog=INETC7;" _
    & "User Id=sa;" _
    & "Password=yourpassword;")
```

We then retrieve the first record in the Messages table. Note the use of a subquery to retrieve the lowest MessageID:

```
DBCommand = New OleDbDataAdapter _
    ("SELECT MessageID, MessageTitle, " _
    & "MessageText From Messages " _
    & "Where MessageID = (Select Min(MessageID) From " _
    & "Messages)", DBConn)
```

That record is placed in our DataSet object:

```
DBCommand.Fill(DSPageData, _
    "CurrentMessage")
    Session("CurrentMessageID") = _
    DSPageData.Tables("CurrentMessage"). _
    Rows(0).Item("MessageID")
```

We then store the ID of the message in a Session variable so that we will have it when we need to add to the current thread:

```
Session("CurrentMessageID") = _
    DSPageData.Tables("CurrentMessage"). _
    Rows(0).Item("MessageID")
```

We then place the title of the thread into the title Label control

```
lblTitle.Text = "Message Board - " _
    & DSPageData.Tables("CurrentMessage"). _
    Rows(0).Item("MessageTitle")
```

and the text of the thread into another Label control:

```
lblMessage.Text = DSPageData.Tables("CurrentMessage"). _
    Rows(0).Item("MessageText")
```

We then retrieve the titles and IDs of all the messages

```
DBCommand = New OleDbDataAdapter _
    ("SELECT MessageID, MessageTitle " _
    & "from Messages " _
    & "Order By MessageTitle", DBConn)
```

and place them into another table of our DataSet object

```
DBCommand.Fill(DSPageData, _
    "Messages")
```

which the DropDownList is bound to:

```
ddlMessages.DataSource = _
    DSPageData.Tables("Messages").DefaultView
ddlMessages.DataBind()
```

The next procedure fires when the visitor clicks the View Thread button. It displays the contents of the thread selected in the DropDownList.

```
Sub ViewThread_Click(Sender As Object, E As EventArgs)
    Dim DBConn as OleDbConnection
    Dim DBCommand As OleDbDataAdapter
    Dim DSPageData as New DataSet
    DBConn = New OleDbConnection("Provider=sqloledb;" _
        & "server=localhost;" _
        & "Initial Catalog=INETC7;" _
        & "User Id=sa;" _
        & "Password=yourpassword;")
    DBCommand = New OleDbDataAdapter _
        ("SELECT MessageID, MessageTitle, " _
        & "MessageText From Messages " _
        & "Where MessageID = " _
```

```
        & ddlMessages.SelectedItem.Value, DBConn)
    DBCommand.Fill(DSPageData, _
        "CurrentMessage")
    Session("CurrentMessageID") = _
        ddlMessages.SelectedItem.Value
    lblTitle.Text = "Message Board - " _
        & DSPageData.Tables("CurrentMessage"). _
        Rows(0).Item("MessageTitle")
    lblMessage.Text = DSPageData.Tables("CurrentMessage"). _
        Rows(0).Item("MessageText")
End Sub
```

Within this procedure, we need data variables:

```
Dim DBConn as OleDbConnection
Dim DBCommand As OleDbDataAdapter
Dim DSPageData as New DataSet
```

We also need to connect to our database:

```
DBConn = New OleDbConnection("Provider=sqloledb;" _
    & "server=localhost;" _
    & "Initial Catalog=INETC7;" _
    & "User Id=sa;" _
    & "Password=yourpassword;")
```

Then, we retrieve the contents of the message corresponding to the ID of the item selected in the DropDownList control:

```
DBCommand = New OleDbDataAdapter _
    ("SELECT MessageID, MessageTitle, " _
    & "MessageText From Messages " _
    & "Where MessageID = " _
    & ddlMessages.SelectedItem.Value, DBConn)
DBCommand.Fill(DSPageData, _
    "CurrentMessage")
```

The ID of the message is stored in a Session variable:

```
Session("CurrentMessageID") = _
    ddlMessages.SelectedItem.Value
```

The title of the message thread is placed into the first Label control:

```
lblTitle.Text = "Message Board - " _
    & DSPageData.Tables("CurrentMessage"). _
    Rows(0).Item("MessageTitle")
```

And the text of the message is placed into the other Label:

```
lblMessage.Text = DSPageData.Tables("CurrentMessage"). _
    Rows(0).Item("MessageText")
```

The next procedure fires when the Update Thread Button control is clicked. It adds the visitor's text to the current thread.

```
Sub UpdateThread_Click(Sender As Object, E As EventArgs)
    Dim DBConn as OleDbConnection
    Dim DBUpdate As New OleDbCommand
    DBConn = New OleDbConnection("Provider=sqloledb;" _
        & "server=localhost;" _
        & "Initial Catalog=INETC7;" _
        & "User Id=sa;" _
        & "Password=yourpassword;")
    DBUpdate.CommandText = "Update Messages set " _
        & "MessageText = Convert(varchar(5000), MessageText) " _
        & "+ '<hr>Entered By: " _
        & Replace(txtUpdateName.Text, "'", "''") _
        & "<br>Date Entered: " & Now() & "<br>" _
        & Replace(txtUpdateMessage.Text, "'", "''") _
        & "' Where MessageID = " _
        & Session("CurrentMessageID")
    DBUpdate.Connection = DBConn
    DBUpdate.Connection.Open
    DBUpdate.ExecuteNonQuery()
    lblMessage.Text = lblMessage.Text _
        & "<hr>Entered By: " _
        & txtUpdateName.Text _
        & "<br>Date Entered: " & Now() & "<br>" _
        & txtUpdateMessage.Text
    txtUpdateName.Text = ""
    txtUpdateMessage.Text = ""
End Sub
```

Here, too, we need data objects;

```
Dim DBConn as OleDbConnection
Dim DBUpdate As New OleDbCommand
```

And we need to connect to the database:

```
DBConn = New OleDbConnection("Provider=sqloledb;" _
    & "server=localhost;" _
    & "Initial Catalog=INETC7;" _
    & "User Id=sa;" _
    & "Password=yourpassword;")
```

We then update the current message based on the ID stored in our Session variable. Note that we concatenate to the existing message text. Note also that we mix text and HTML tags with the text entered by the visitor:

```
DBUpdate.CommandText = "Update Messages set " _
    & "MessageText = Convert(varchar(5000), MessageText) " _
    & "+ '<hr>Entered By: " _
    & Replace(txtUpdateName.Text, "'", "''") _
    & "<br>Date Entered: " & Now() & "<br>" _
    & Replace(txtUpdateMessage.Text, "'", "''") _
    & "' Where MessageID = " _
    & Session("CurrentMessageID")
```

The Command object will connect to the database through our Connection object:

```
DBUpdate.Connection = DBConn
DBUpdate.Connection.Open
```

We then update the current message

```
DBUpdate.ExecuteNonQuery()
```

and display the additional text back to the visitor through the message Label control:

```
lblMessage.Text = lblMessage.Text _
    & "<hr>Entered By: " _
    & txtUpdateName.Text _
    & "<br>Date Entered: " & Now() & "<br>" _
    & txtUpdateMessage.Text
```

We then clear the TextBox controls used by the visitor:

```
txtUpdateName.Text = ""
txtUpdateMessage.Text = ""
```

The other procedure on this page fires when the visitor clicks the Add Thread button. It adds the thread entered by the visitor to the database, updates the DropDownList, and displays the message added.

```
Sub AddThread_Click(Sender As Object, E As EventArgs)
    Dim DBConn as OleDbConnection
    Dim DBInsert As New OleDbCommand
    Dim DBCommand As OleDbDataAdapter
    Dim DSPageData as New DataSet
    DBConn = New OleDbConnection("Provider=sqloledb;" _
        & "server=localhost;" _
        & "Initial Catalog=INETC7;" _
        & "User Id=sa;" _
        & "Password=yourpassword;")
    DBInsert.CommandText = "Insert Into Messages " _
        & "(MessageTitle, MessageText) values (" _
        & "'" & Replace(txtAddTitle.Text, "'", "''") _
        & "', 'Entered By: " _
        & Replace(txtAddName.Text, "'", "''") _
        & "<br>Date Entered: " & Now() & "<br>" _
        & Replace(txtAddMessage.Text, "'", "''") & "')"
    DBInsert.Connection = DBConn
    DBInsert.Connection.Open
    DBInsert.ExecuteNonQuery()
    txtAddTitle.Text = ""
    txtAddName.Text = ""
    txtAddMessage.Text = ""
    DBCommand = New OleDbDataAdapter _
        ("SELECT MessageID, MessageTitle, " _
        & "MessageText From Messages " _
        & "Where MessageID = (Select Max(MessageID) From " _
        & "Messages)", DBConn)
    DBCommand.Fill(DSPageData, _
        "CurrentMessage")
    Session("CurrentMessageID") = _
        DSPageData.Tables("CurrentMessage"). _
```

```
            Rows(0).Item("MessageID")
        lblTitle.Text = "Message Board - " _
            & DSPageData.Tables("CurrentMessage"). _
            Rows(0).Item("MessageTitle")
        lblMessage.Text = DSPageData.Tables("CurrentMessage"). _
            Rows(0).Item("MessageText")
        DBCommand = New OleDbDataAdapter _
            ("SELECT MessageID, MessageTitle " _
            & "from Messages " _
            & "Order By MessageTitle", DBConn)
        DBCommand.Fill(DSPageData, _
            "Messages")
        ddlMessages.DataSource = _
            DSPageData.Tables("Messages").DefaultView
        ddlMessages.DataBind()
    End Sub
```

Within this procedure, we need data objects:

```
Dim DBConn as OleDbConnection
Dim DBInsert As New OleDbCommand
Dim DBCommand As OleDbDataAdapter
Dim DSPageData as New DataSet
```

We start by connecting to the database:

```
DBConn = New OleDbConnection("Provider=sqloledb;" _
    & "server=localhost;" _
    & "Initial Catalog=INETC7;" _
    & "User Id=sa;" _
    & "Password=yourpassword;")
```

We then insert the message entered by the visitor into the Messages table:

```
DBInsert.CommandText = "Insert Into Messages " _
    & "(MessageTitle, MessageText) values (" _
    & "'" & Replace(txtAddTitle.Text, "'", "''") _
    & "', 'Entered By: " _
    & Replace(txtAddName.Text, "'", "''") _
    & "<br>Date Entered: " & Now() & "<br>" _
    & Replace(txtAddMessage.Text, "'", "''") & "')"
DBInsert.Connection = DBConn
```

```
DBInsert.Connection.Open
DBInsert.ExecuteNonQuery()
```

Next, we clear out the TextBox controls that the visitor had placed text into:

```
txtAddTitle.Text = ""
txtAddName.Text = ""
txtAddMessage.Text = ""
```

We then select the message added from the database

```
DBCommand = New OleDbDataAdapter _
    ("SELECT MessageID, MessageTitle, " _
    & "MessageText From Messages " _
    & "Where MessageID = (Select Max(MessageID) From " _
    & "Messages)", DBConn)
DBCommand.Fill(DSPageData, _
    "CurrentMessage")
```

and store the ID of the message in our Session variable:

```
Session("CurrentMessageID") = _
    DSPageData.Tables("CurrentMessage"). _
    Rows(0).Item("MessageID")
```

We then place the title of the message in one Label control

```
lblTitle.Text = "Message Board - " _
    & DSPageData.Tables("CurrentMessage"). _
    Rows(0).Item("MessageTitle")
```

and the text of the message into another:

```
lblMessage.Text = DSPageData.Tables("CurrentMessage"). _
    Rows(0).Item("MessageText")
```

Then we need to retrieve the names and IDs of the messages so that we can repopulate the DropDownList control:

```
DBCommand = New OleDbDataAdapter _
    ("SELECT MessageID, MessageTitle " _
    & "from Messages " _
    & "Order By MessageTitle", DBConn)
```

Those are placed into our DataSet object:

```
DBCommand.Fill(DSPageData, _
    "Messages")
```

And we bind the DropDownList to that DataSet table:

```
ddlMessages.DataSource = _
    DSPageData.Tables("Messages").DefaultView
ddlMessages.DataBind()
```

Access Code Changes

C7MessageBoard.mdb

If you wish to use this solution with Access instead of SQL Server, you need to change the connect string from the one that points to the SQL Server database

```
DBConn = New OleDbConnection("Provider=sqloledb;" _
    & "server=localhost;" _
    & "Initial Catalog=INETC7;" _
    & "User Id=sa;" _
    & "Password=yourpassword;")
```

to one that points to your Access database:

```
DBConn = New OleDbConnection("PROVIDER=Microsoft.Jet.OLEDB.4.0;" _
    & "DATA SOURCE=" _
    & Server.MapPath("/INetBook/C7/MessageBoard/" _
    & "Access/C7MessageBoard.mdb;"))
```

The other change you need to make is to the update query. In SQL Server, we need the Convert function, and the "+" character is used for concatenation:

```
DBUpdate.CommandText = "Update Messages set " _
    & "MessageText = Convert(varchar(5000), MessageText) " _
    & "+ '<hr>Entered By: " _
    & Replace(txtUpdateName.Text, "'", "''") _
    & "<br>Date Entered: " & Now() & "<br>" _
    & Replace(txtUpdateMessage.Text, "'", "''") _
    & "' Where MessageID = " _
    & Session("CurrentMessageID")
```

In Access, we don't need the Convert function, and the "&" character is used to concatenate strings:

```
DBUpdate.CommandText = "Update Messages set " _
    & "MessageText = MessageText " _
    & "& '<hr>Entered By: " _
    & Replace(txtUpdateName.Text, "'", "''") _
    & "<br>Date Entered: " & Now() & "<br>" _
    & Replace(txtUpdateMessage.Text, "'", "''") _
    & "' Where MessageID = " _
    & Session("CurrentMessageID")
```

No other code changes should be needed.

CHAPTER

8

Tracking Visitors

The Usage Tracking site shows you how to track the date and time a visitor enters your site, the path that they explore through your site, and browser and platform information. The tool also provides ASP.NET pages that allow the web site administrator to view page hit and visitor information.

Sample Usage

The Usage Tracking site is divided into two parts. The first part of the site merely represents the site that you want to track visitors through. This site is made up of three pages. One of the pages is displayed in Figure 8-1.

Each of the sample pages records a hit to that page when it is visited. Information on the visitor is recorded once per visit.

The administration part of the site allows you to view information about the web site's activity. Figure 8-2 shows the entry page into this part of the application.

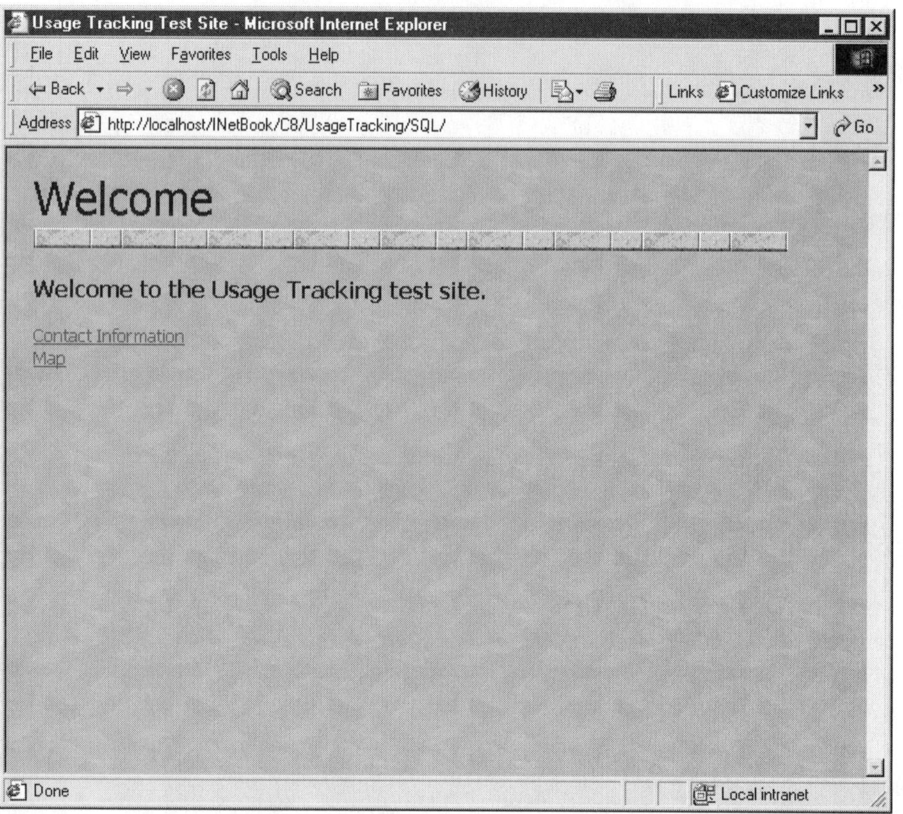

Figure 8-1 *Sample page that tracks visitors*

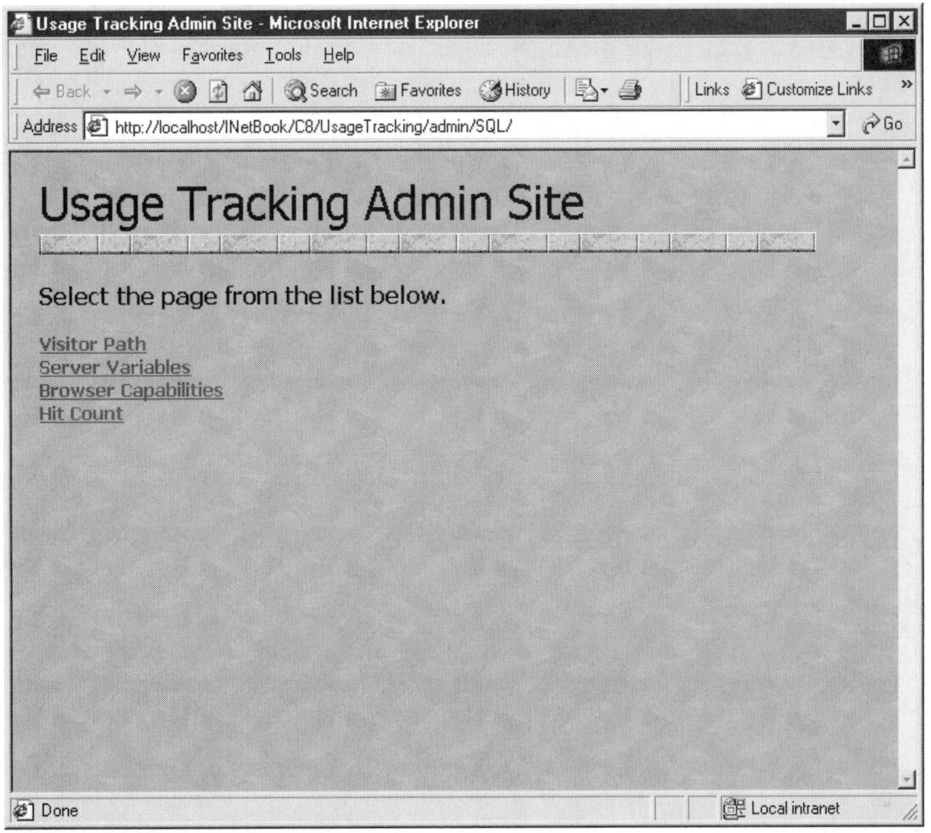

Figure 8-2 *Admin site Entry page*

From this page, you can link to the four pages that allow you to view and analyze the hit information. If you click the Visitor Path link, you are taken to the page displayed in Figure 8-3.

The Visitor Path page shows the activity of a single user through your site. At the top of the page, you see the date and time they entered the site, as well as the browser and platform that they were using. Then, in the DataGrid on the page, you can see the names of each of the pages that they visited and the order in which they were visited.

This type of information will help you learn the pattern of visitors at your site. You can see what page they entered through, what page they last viewed, and if they went back to a page.

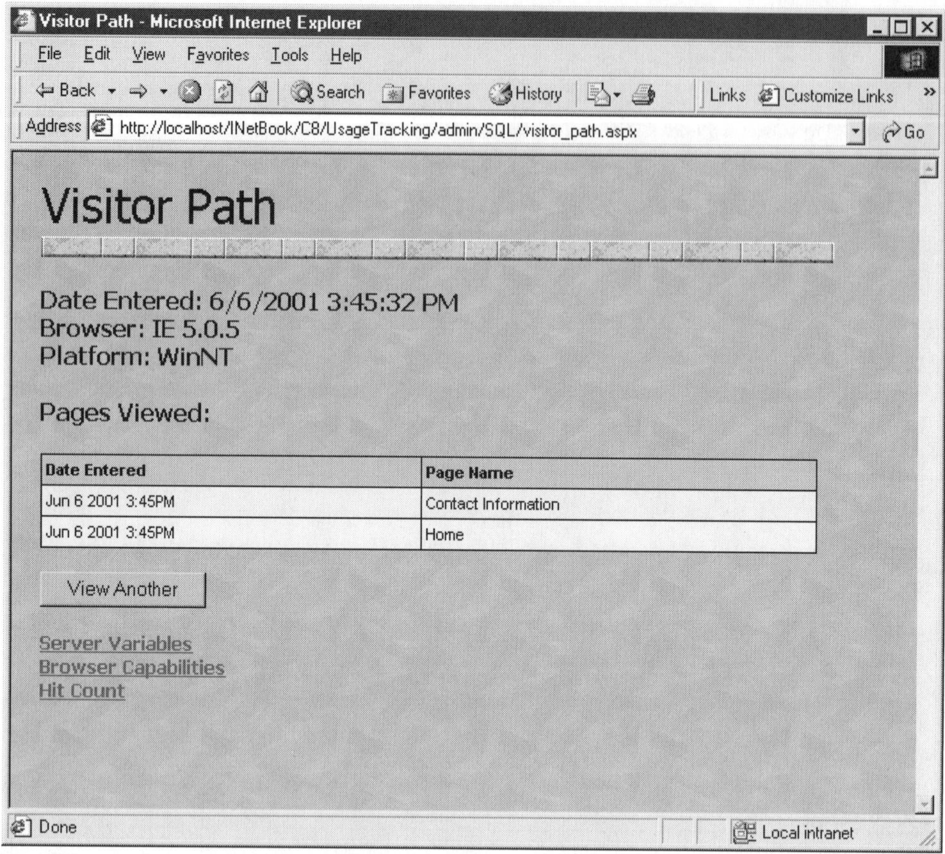

Figure 8-3 *Initial view of the Visitor Path page*

Note the View Another button. Click it to see another hit record like the one displayed in Figure 8-4.

This visitor entered the site through the Contact Information page. They then went to the Home page, followed by the Map page. That was where they left the site.

You can continue to browse through records one at a time in this fashion. Eventually when there are no more records to view, you will see a message stating this.

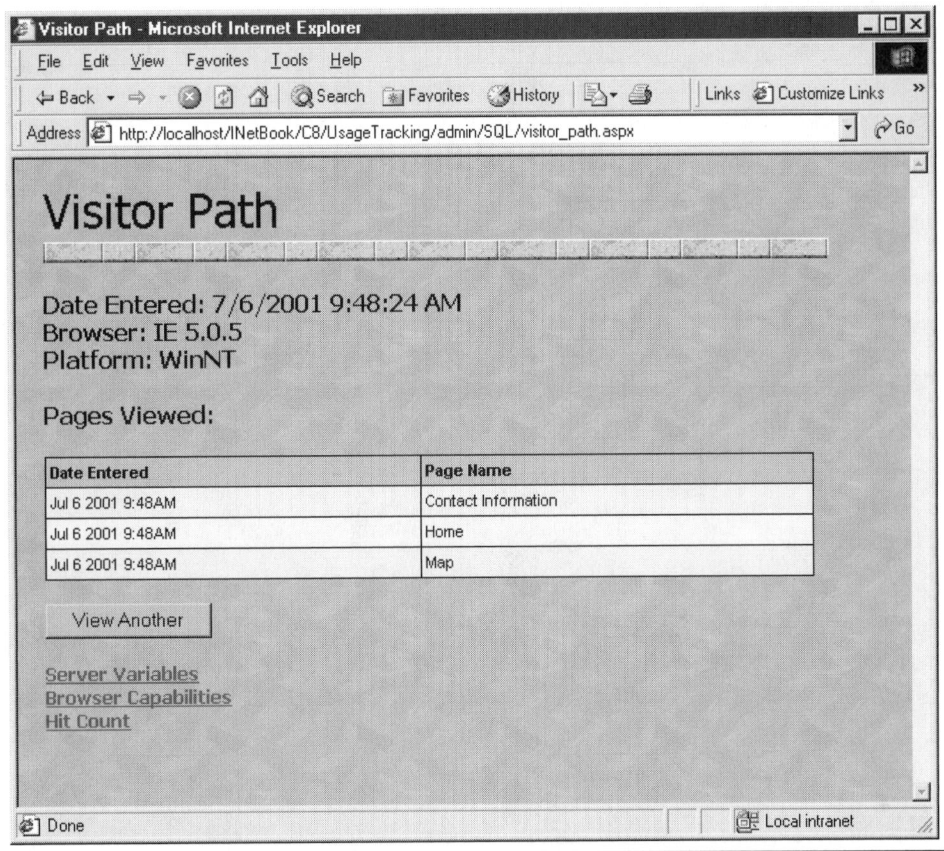

Figure 8-4 *Visitor Path page with a second record displayed*

From this page, you can link to the three other statistics pages. If you click the Server Variables page, you will be taken to the page displayed in Figure 8-5.

When the visitor first enters your site, we use code in the Global.asax file to record all the server variables that are passed into the page. This information includes things like the name of the server, the type of request, the filename being requested, and the IP address of the visitor.

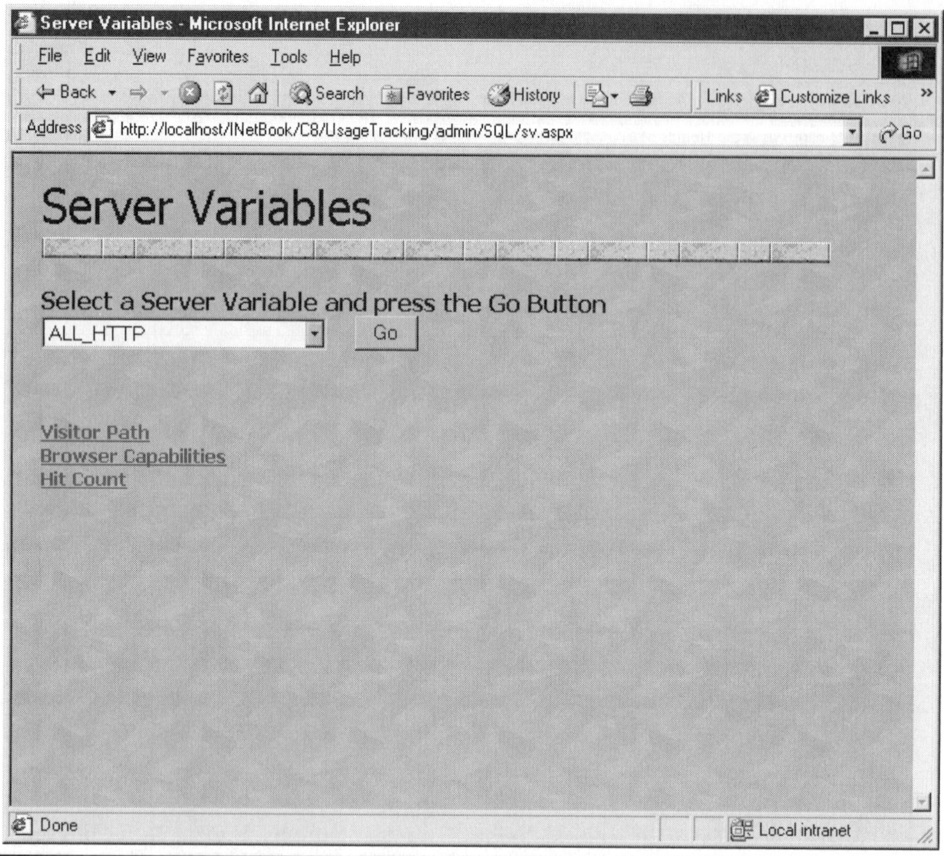

Figure 8-5 *Initial view of the Server Variables page*

The DropDownList on this page displays all the server variables that have been entered into the database table. You can select one of these to view the grouped values for that server variable. For example, take a look at Figure 8-6.

Here we have chosen to see the IP address of each of the visitors. This value is grouped in the DataGrid. Therefore, we can identify the IP addresses of the people who have visited the site the most.

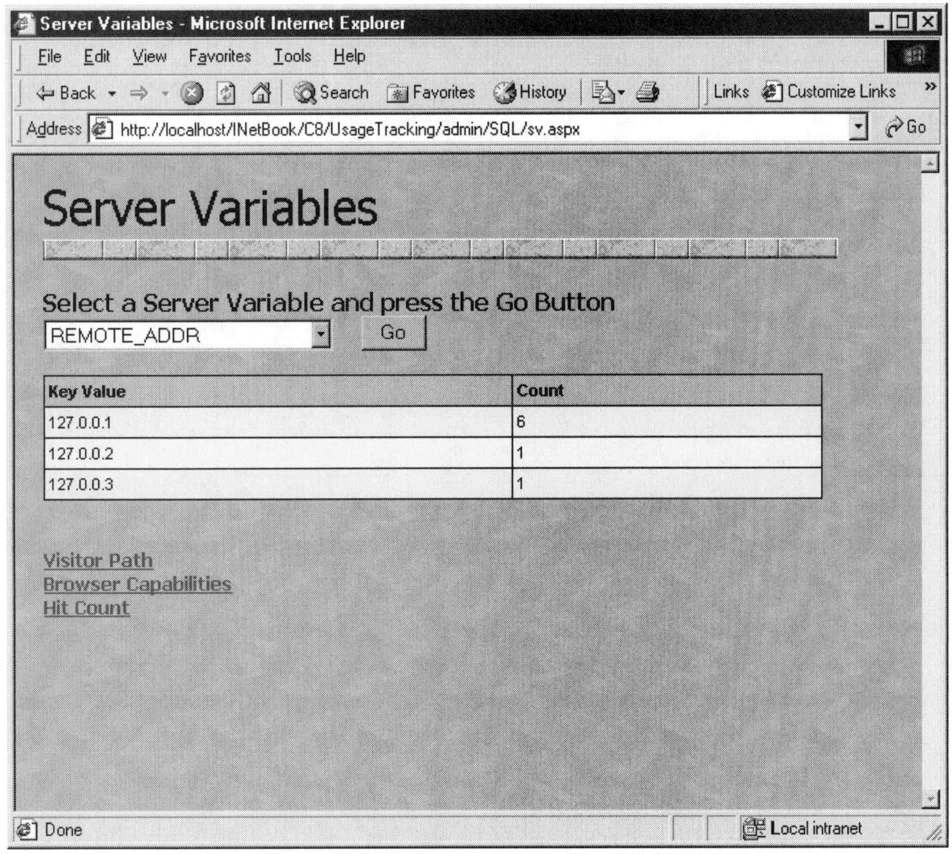

Figure 8-6 *Server Variable page displaying results*

The next page in the Admin site is the Browser Capabilities page. The initial view of this page is displayed in Figure 8-7.

Besides recording all the server variables when the visitor enters the site, we also store in the database information about their browser and platform. For example, we store whether they are from AOL, the name and version of their browser, and other such fields.

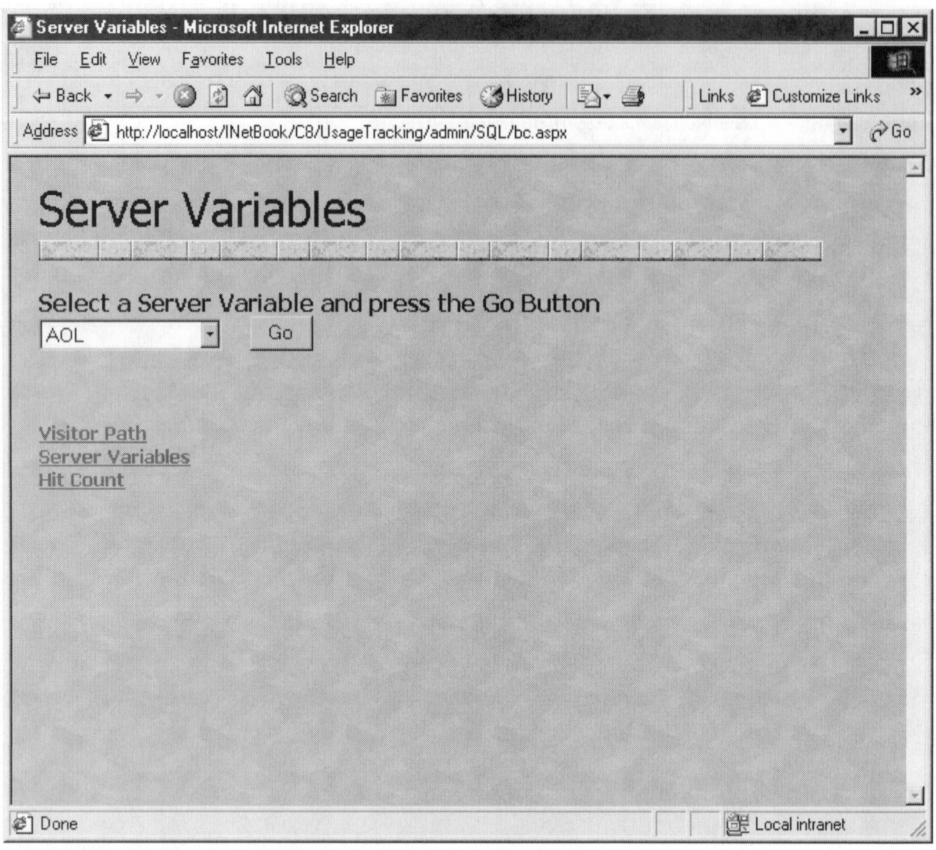

Figure 8-7 *Initial view of the Browser Capabilities page*

The DropDownList on this page displays each of those fields. When you select the field and click Go, you see the grouped values contained in that field as shown in Figure 8-8.

Here we have asked to see all the browsers that have been used to visit the site. The DataGrid therefore shows the number of each type recorded.

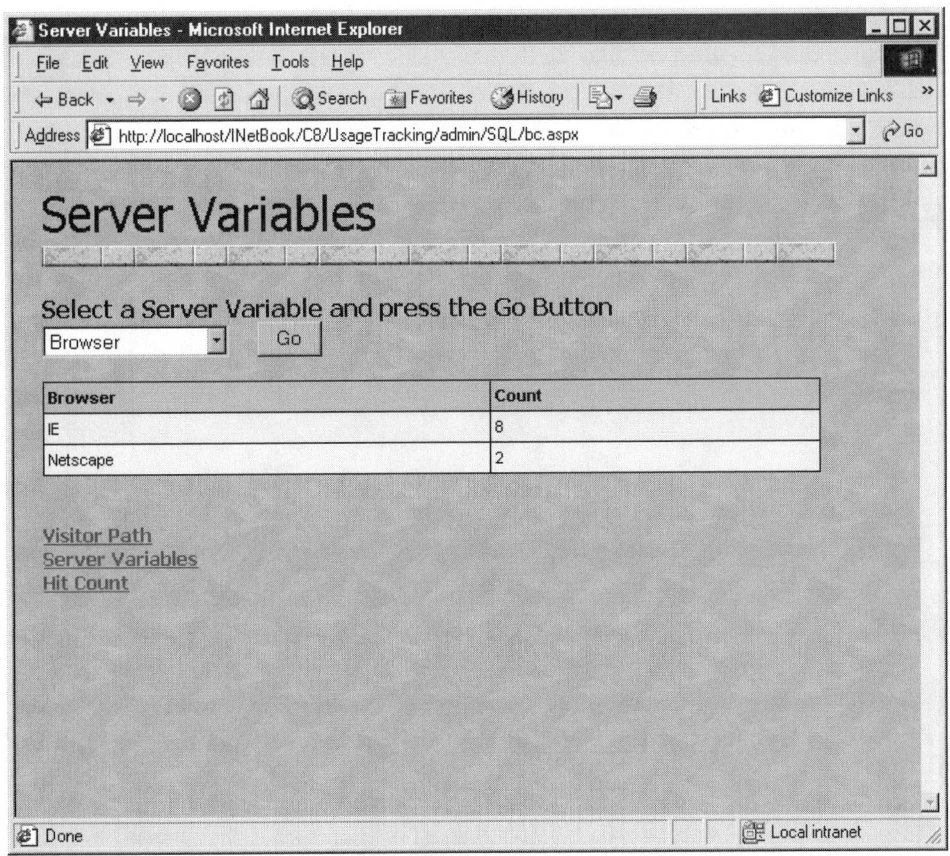

Figure 8-8 *Browser Capabilities page displaying the browsers used*

The last page in the Admin site is the Hit Count page. The initial view of that page is displayed in Figure 8-9.

The page shows the total number of times that each page in the site has been viewed. At the bottom of the page, you can specify dates that you want to view the hit counts for. But note that we use a validation control to make sure that only dates are entered. Once dates are correctly entered, you can click OK to see the hits for those dates, as displayed in Figure 8-10.

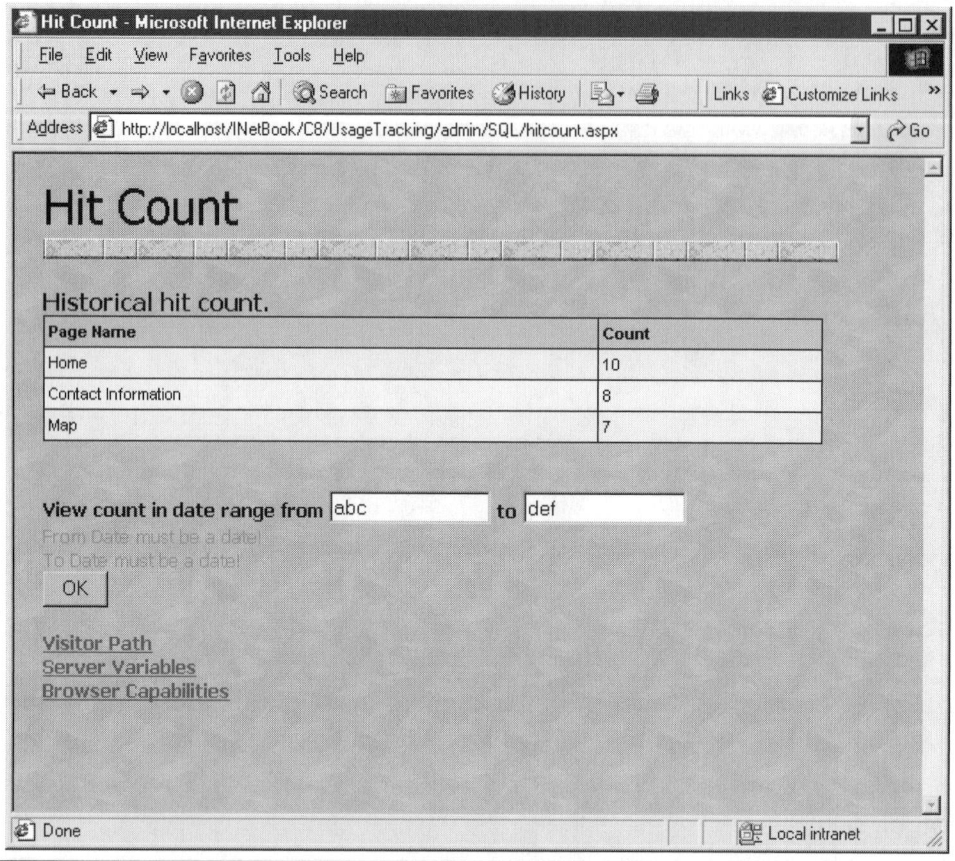

Figure 8-9 *Initial view of the Hit Count page*

Usage Tracking Database Component

C8UsageTracking.sql

The database required for the functionality of the Usage Tracking application includes three interrelated tables. In this section, we will review the relationships between the tables and the fields they contain.

Tables and Data Diagram

Figure 8-11 displays the relationships between the tables in the Usage Tracking database.

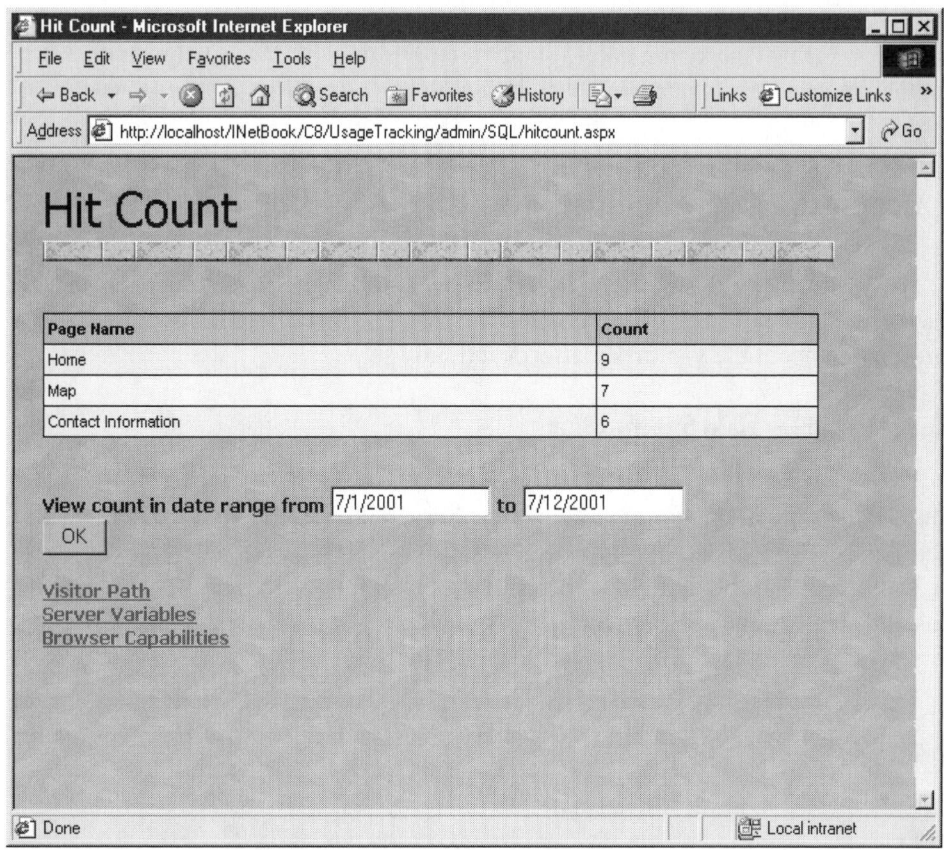

Figure 8-10 *Hit Count page limited by supplied date range*

The Visitors table is the top-level table in the database. It stores information about when the visitor entered the site and a variety of browser capabilities.

The ServerVariables table stores things such as the IP address of the remote user, the page requested, the server name, and other variables. Records in this table link to the Visitors table in a one-to-many relationship.

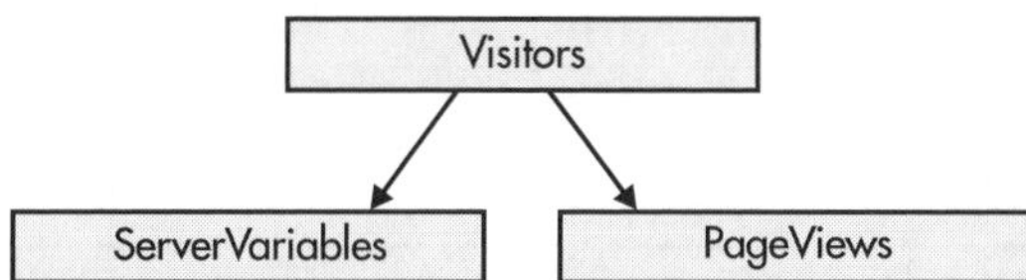

Figure 8-11 *Usage tracking data diagram*

Each time a visitor enters a page, a record is added to the PageViews table. The PageViews table is also in a one-to-many relationship with the Visitors table. Each visitor can visit many pages, but each hit recorded comes from a specific visitor.

Visitors Field Specifications

Visitors.txt

The field specifications for the fields in the Visitors table are displayed in Table 8-1.

The VisitorID field is the primary key in the table. The DateEntered field stores the date and time that the visitor entered the site. The rest of the fields store information about the visitor's platform and browser.

ServerVariables Field Specifications

ServerVariables.txt

The field specifications for the fields in the ServerVariables table are displayed in Table 8-2.

The ServerVariableID field is the primary key in this table. The VisitorID field links this table to the Visitors table. The KeyName field stores the name of the server variable, and the KeyValue field stores the value of the variable in that key.

Field Name	Field Type	Notes
VisitorID	int	Primary Key, Identity Column
DateEntered	datetime	
BackgroundSound	varchar	Length = 100
Beta	varchar	Length = 100
Browser	varchar	Length = 100
Cookies	varchar	Length = 100
Crawler	varchar	Length = 100
MajorVersion	varchar	Length = 100
MinorVersion	varchar	Length = 100
Platform	varchar	Length = 100
Win16	varchar	Length = 100
Win32	varchar	Length = 100

Table 8-1 *Visitors Field Specifications*

Field Name	Field Type	Notes
ServerVariableID	int	Primary Key, Identity Column
VisitorID	int	Foreign Key
KeyName	varchar	Length = 50
KeyValue	varchar	Length = 255

Table 8-2 *ServerVariables Field Specifications*

PageViews Field Specifications

PageViews.txt

The field specifications for the fields in the PageViews table are displayed in Table 8-3.

The PageViewID field is the primary key in this table. The VisitorID field links this table in a one-to-many relationship with the Visitors table. The PageName field stores the name of the page that the visitor is viewing. The DateEntered field stores the date and time that the visitor opened the page.

Usage Tracking ASP.NET Code

The Usage Tracking tool is stored in two directory structures. The first is the site that you are recording the activity for. This site includes a Global.asax file and three ASP.NET pages. The code on each of the ASP.NET pages is nearly identical, and only one of those pages is reviewed.

The other directory structure contains the Admin site and is made up of five ASP.NET pages. In this section, we will review the code and the controls on those pages.

Field Name	Field Type	Notes
PageViewID	int	Primary Key, Identity Column
VisitorID	int	Foreign Key
PageName	varchar	Length = 50
DateEntered	datetime	

Table 8-3 *PageViews Field Specifications*

Global.asax File

Global.asax

The Global.asax file has a procedure that runs when the visitor enters your site regardless of the page that they are using. The code records information about their browser and the server variables.

At the top of the page, we need to import two libraries so that we can extract and view data from the database:

```
<%@ Import Namespace="System.Data" %>
<%@ Import Namespace="System.Data.OLEDB" %>
```

The other code on the page fires when the session starts.

```
Sub Session_OnStart
    Dim BCaps As HttpBrowserCapabilities
    Dim DBConn as OleDbConnection
    Dim DBInsert As New OleDbCommand
    Dim DBCommand As OleDbDataAdapter
    Dim DSData as New DataSet
    Dim I As Integer
    Dim NameArray() As String
    Dim VisitorSV As NameValueCollection
    BCaps = Request.Browser
    DBConn = New OleDbConnection("Provider=sqloledb;" _
        & "server=localhost;" _
        & "Initial Catalog=INETC8;" _
        & "User Id=sa;" _
        & "Password=yourpassword;")
    DBInsert.CommandText = "Insert Into Visitors " _
        & "(DateEntered, AOL, BackgroundSounds, Beta, Browser, " _
        & "Cookies, Crawler, MajorVersion, MinorVersion, " _
        & "Platform, Win16, Win32) Values (GetDate(), " _
        & "'" & BCaps.AOL & "', " _
        & "'" & BCaps.BackgroundSounds & "', " _
        & "'" & BCaps.Beta & "', " _
        & "'" & BCaps.Browser & "', " _
        & "'" & BCaps.Cookies & "', " _
        & "'" & BCaps.Crawler & "', " _
        & "'" & BCaps.MajorVersion & "', " _
        & "'" & BCaps.MinorVersion & "', " _
        & "'" & BCaps.Platform & "', " _
        & "'" & BCaps.Win16 & "', " _
        & "'" & BCaps.Win32 & "')"
```

```
    DBInsert.Connection = DBConn
    DBInsert.Connection.Open
    DBInsert.ExecuteNonQuery()
    DBCommand = New OleDbDataAdapter _
        ("Select Max(VisitorID) as MaxID " _
        & "From Visitors", DBConn)
    DBCommand.Fill(DSData, _
        "CurrentID")
    Session("VisitorID") = DSData.Tables("CurrentID"). _
        Rows(0).Item("MaxID")
    VisitorSV = Request.ServerVariables
    NameArray = VisitorSV.AllKeys
    For I = 0 To UBound(NameArray)
        DBInsert.CommandText = "Insert Into ServerVariables " _
            & "(VisitorID, KeyName, KeyValue) values (" _
            & Session("VisitorID") & ", " _
            & "'" & NameArray(I) & "', " _
            & "'" _
            & Left(Replace(VisitorSV.Item(I), "'", "''"), 255) _
            & "')"
        DBInsert.ExecuteNonQuery()
    Next
End Sub
```

We start by declaring a variable that will store the visitor's browser capabilities:

```
Dim BCaps As HttpBrowserCapabilities
```

Within this procedure, we will also need data objects to add data to the database and retrieve data from it:

```
Dim DBConn as OleDbConnection
Dim DBInsert As New OleDbCommand
Dim DBCommand As OleDbDataAdapter
Dim DSData as New DataSet
```

We also need a variable for a loop

```
Dim I As Integer
```

and a string array that will store the key names of the server variables:

```
Dim NameArray() As String
```

We need one more object to store the server variable collection:

```
Dim VisitorSV As NameValueCollection
```

We then store the visitor's browser capabilities into a local variable:

```
BCaps = Request.Browser
```

Next, we connect to the database:

```
DBConn = New OleDbConnection("Provider=sqloledb;" _
    & "server=localhost;" _
    & "Initial Catalog=INETC8;" _
    & "User Id=sa;" _
    & "Password=yourpassword;")
```

We then insert a new record into the Visitors table. Note that we use the Browser Capabilities object to determine the values for most of the fields:

```
DBInsert.CommandText = "Insert Into Visitors " _
    & "(DateEntered, AOL, BackgroundSounds, Beta, Browser, " _
    & "Cookies, Crawler, MajorVersion, MinorVersion, " _
    & "Platform, Win16, Win32) Values (GetDate(), " _
    & "'" & BCaps.AOL & "', " _
    & "'" & BCaps.BackgroundSounds & "', " _
    & "'" & BCaps.Beta & "', " _
    & "'" & BCaps.Browser & "', " _
    & "'" & BCaps.Cookies & "', " _
    & "'" & BCaps.Crawler & "', " _
    & "'" & BCaps.MajorVersion & "', " _
    & "'" & BCaps.MinorVersion & "', " _
    & "'" & BCaps.Platform & "', " _
    & "'" & BCaps.Win16 & "', " _
    & "'" & BCaps.Win32 & "')"
```

The Command object will use our Connection object

```
DBInsert.Connection = DBConn
DBInsert.Connection.Open
```

so that it can add the record to the database:

```
DBInsert.ExecuteNonQuery()
```

Next, we need to retrieve the ID of the visitor that was just added to the database

```
DBCommand = New OleDbDataAdapter _
    ("Select Max(VisitorID) as MaxID " _
    & "From Visitors", DBConn)
```

and place it into our DataSet object:

```
DBCommand.Fill(DSData, _
    "CurrentID")
```

We then store that ID in a session variable so that we can access it from any of our other pages:

```
Session("VisitorID") = DSData.Tables("CurrentID"). _
    Rows(0).Item("MaxID")
```

Next, we need to store the server variables into our Collection object:

```
VisitorSV = Request.ServerVariables
```

We then retrieve the names of all of the server variables into one string array:

```
NameArray = VisitorSV.AllKeys
```

Now we can enter a loop so that we can process each element of the array:

```
For I = 0 To UBound(NameArray)
```

Within the loop, we add a record for each server variable name and value

```
DBInsert.CommandText = "Insert Into ServerVariables " _
    & "(VisitorID, KeyName, KeyValue) values (" _
    & Session("VisitorID") & ", " _
    & "'" & NameArray(I) & "', " _
    & "'" _
    & Left(Replace(VisitorSV.Item(I), "'", "''"), 255) _
    & "')"
DBInsert.ExecuteNonQuery()
```

before moving on to process the next record:

```
Next
```

Sample Site ASP.NET Page

Index.aspx, Contact_Information.aspx, Map.aspx

The other three files in the sample site simply contain a procedure that records a page hit. To do this, we need to import data libraries:

```
<%@ Import Namespace="System.Data" %>
<%@ Import Namespace="System.Data.OLEDB" %>
```

The one procedure in these pages fires when the page is loaded.

```
Sub Page_Load(ByVal Sender as Object, ByVal E as EventArgs)
    Dim DBConn as OleDbConnection
    Dim DBInsert As New OleDbCommand
    DBConn = New OleDbConnection("Provider=sqloledb;" _
        & "server=localhost;" _
        & "Initial Catalog=INETC8;" _
        & "User Id=sa;" _
        & "Password=yourpassword;")
    DBInsert.CommandText = "Insert Into PageViews " _
        & "(DateEntered, PageName, VisitorID) Values (" _
        & "GetDate(), 'Home', " & Session("VisitorID") & ")"
    DBInsert.Connection = DBConn
    DBInsert.Connection.Open
    DBInsert.ExecuteNonQuery()
End Sub
```

We will need data objects within this procedure:

```
Dim DBConn as OleDbConnection
Dim DBInsert As New OleDbCommand
```

We then connect to the database

```
DBConn = New OleDbConnection("Provider=sqloledb;" _
    & "server=localhost;" _
    & "Initial Catalog=INETC8;" _
    & "User Id=sa;" _
    & "Password=yourpassword;")
```

and insert a record in the PageViews table. Note that the name of the page being viewed is the Home page. You would change this for each page that you were tracking, giving it a unique name so that you could track it in the database:

```
DBInsert.CommandText = "Insert Into PageViews " _
    & "(DateEntered, PageName, VisitorID) Values (" _
    & "GetDate(), 'Home', " & Session("VisitorID") & ")"
DBInsert.Connection = DBConn
DBInsert.Connection.Open
```

That record is then inserted into the database:

```
DBInsert.ExecuteNonQuery()
```

Admin Menu ASP.NET Page

Index.aspx

The Admin Menu page contains no code. It provides links to the other pages in the Admin site. The page does contain two controls. The first control is used to display the title of the page:

```
<asp:Label
    id="lblTitle"
    Font-Size="25pt"
    Font-Name="Tahoma"
    Text="Usage Tracking Admin Site"
    runat="server"
/>
```

Another Label control that displays an instructional message to the administrator is declared

```
<asp:Label
    id="lblMessage"
    Font-Size="12pt"
    Font-Name="Tahoma"
    Font-Bold="True"
    Text="Select the page from the list below."
    runat="server"
/>
```

Visitor Path ASP.NET Page

Visitor_Path.aspx

The Visitor Path page displays information on a single visitor, including all the pages that they viewed. At the top of the page, we declare three compiler directives.

The first sets up the run environment, and the other two import the needed data libraries:

```
<%@ Page Language=VB Debug=true %>
<%@ Import Namespace="System.Data" %>
<%@ Import Namespace="System.Data.OLEDB" %>
```

Within the body of the page, we declare a Label control that displays the title of the page:

```
<asp:Label
    id="lblTitle"
    Font-Size="25pt"
    Font-Name="Tahoma"
    Text="Visitor Path"
    runat="server"
/>
```

A second Label is used to display the top-level information on the visitor record:

```
<asp:Label
    id="lblMessage"
    Font-Size="12pt"
    Font-Name="Tahoma"
    Font-Bold="True"
    runat="server"
/>
```

The next control we define on this page is a DataGrid that lists the pages visited by the visitor:

```
<asp:DataGrid
    id="dgPageViews"
    Width="90%"
    BackColor="beige"
    AlternatingItemStyle-BackColor="cornsilk"
    BorderColor="black"
    ShowFooter="false"
    CellPadding=3
    CellSpacing="0"
    Font-Name="Arial"
    Font-Size="8pt"
    ForeColor="Black"
```

```
    HeaderStyle-BackColor="burlywood"
    HeaderStyle-Font-Bold="True"
    runat="server">
</asp:DataGrid>
```

One other control on the page, a Button control, is defined. It allows the administrator to view another hit record when clicked

```
<asp:button
    id="butViewAnother"
    text="View Another"
    Type="Submit"
    OnClick="SubmitBtn_Click"
    runat="server"
/>
```

The code on the page runs within two procedures. The first procedure fires when the page is first loaded.

```
Sub Page_Load(ByVal Sender as Object, ByVal E as EventArgs)
    If Not IsPostBack Then
        Dim DBConn as OleDbConnection
        Dim DBCommand As OleDbDataAdapter
        Dim DSPageData as New DataSet
        DBConn = New OleDbConnection("Provider=sqloledb;" _
            & "server=localhost;" _
            & "Initial Catalog=INETC8;" _
            & "User Id=sa;" _
            & "Password=yourpassword;")
        DBCommand = New OleDbDataAdapter _
            ("Select VisitorID, DateEntered, Browser, " _
            & "Platform, MajorVersion, MinorVersion From " _
            & "Visitors Where VisitorID = " _
            & "(Select Max(VisitorID) From Visitors)" _
            , DBConn)
        DBCommand.Fill(DSPageData, _
            "VisitorRecord")
        Session("CurrentVisitorID") = _
            DSPageData.Tables("VisitorRecord"). _
            Rows(0).Item("VisitorID")
        lblMessage.Text = "Date Entered: " _
            & DSPageData.Tables("VisitorRecord"). _
            Rows(0).Item("DateEntered") _
```

```
                & "<br>Browser: " _
                & DSPageData.Tables("VisitorRecord"). _
                Rows(0).Item("Browser") & " " _
                & DSPageData.Tables("VisitorRecord"). _
                Rows(0).Item("MajorVersion") & "." _
                & DSPageData.Tables("VisitorRecord"). _
                Rows(0).Item("MinorVersion") _
                & "<br>Platform: " _
                & DSPageData.Tables("VisitorRecord"). _
                Rows(0).Item("Platform") _
                & "<br><br>Pages Viewed:<br><br>"
            DBCommand = New OleDbDataAdapter _
                ("Select Convert(varchar(25),DateEntered,100) " _
                & "as [Date Entered], " _
                & "PageName as [Page Name] From PageViews " _
                & "Where VisitorID = " & Session("CurrentVisitorID") _
                & " Order By DateEntered", DBConn)
            DBCommand.Fill(DSPageData, _
                "PageViews")
            dgPageViews.DataSource = _
                DSPageData.Tables("PageViews").DefaultView
            dgPageViews.DataBind()
        End If
End Sub
```

We want the code to run only when the page is first loaded

```
If Not IsPostBack Then
```

Within this procedure, we will need data objects:

```
Dim DBConn as OleDbConnection
Dim DBCommand As OleDbDataAdapter
Dim DSPageData as New DataSet
```

We start by connecting to the SQL Server database:

```
DBConn = New OleDbConnection("Provider=sqloledb;" _
    & "server=localhost;" _
    & "Initial Catalog=INETC8;" _
    & "User Id=sa;" _
    & "Password=yourpassword;")
```

We then retrieve information on the last visitor to the site. Note that we do this by retrieving the highest VisitorID through the subquery:

```
DBCommand = New OleDbDataAdapter _
    ("Select VisitorID, DateEntered, Browser, " _
    & "Platform, MajorVersion, MinorVersion From " _
    & "Visitors Where VisitorID = " _
    & "(Select Max(VisitorID) From Visitors)" _
    , DBConn)
```

That record is placed into our DataSet object:

```
DBCommand.Fill(DSPageData, _
    "VisitorRecord")
```

Next, we store the ID of this visitor record so that we will know which record to next retrieve

```
Session("CurrentVisitorID") = _
    DSPageData.Tables("VisitorRecord"). _
    Rows(0).Item("VisitorID")
```

We then place the top-level visitor information into our message Label control:

```
lblMessage.Text = "Date Entered: " _
    & DSPageData.Tables("VisitorRecord"). _
    Rows(0).Item("DateEntered") _
    & "<br>Browser: " _
    & DSPageData.Tables("VisitorRecord"). _
    Rows(0).Item("Browser") & " " _
    & DSPageData.Tables("VisitorRecord"). _
    Rows(0).Item("MajorVersion") & "." _
    & DSPageData.Tables("VisitorRecord"). _
    Rows(0).Item("MinorVersion") _
    & "<br>Platform: " _
    & DSPageData.Tables("VisitorRecord"). _
    Rows(0).Item("Platform") _
    & "<br><br>Pages Viewed:<br><br>"
```

Now we can retrieve all the pages viewed by this visitor from the PageViews table:

```
DBCommand = New OleDbDataAdapter _
    ("Select Convert(varchar(25),DateEntered,100) " _
```

```
    & "as [Date Entered], " _
    & "PageName as [Page Name] From PageViews " _
    & "Where VisitorID = " & Session("CurrentVisitorID") _
    & " Order By DateEntered", DBConn)
DBCommand.Fill(DSPageData, _
    "PageViews")
```

We then bind the DataGrid to the return from that table:

```
dgPageViews.DataSource = _
    DSPageData.Tables("PageViews").DefaultView
dgPageViews.DataBind()
```

The other procedure on the page fires when the button is clicked. It retrieves the next visitor record.

```
Sub SubmitBtn_Click(Sender As Object, E As EventArgs)
    Dim DBConn as OleDbConnection
    Dim DBCommand As OleDbDataAdapter
    Dim DSPageData as New DataSet
    DBConn = New OleDbConnection("Provider=sqloledb;" _
        & "server=localhost;" _
        & "Initial Catalog=INETC8;" _
        & "User Id=sa;" _
        & "Password=yourpassword;")
    DBCommand = New OleDbDataAdapter _
        ("Select VisitorID, DateEntered, Browser, " _
        & "Platform, MajorVersion, MinorVersion From " _
        & "Visitors Where VisitorID = " _
        & "(Select Max(VisitorID) From Visitors " _
        & "Where VisitorID < " _
        & Session("CurrentVisitorID") & ")", DBConn)
    DBCommand.Fill(DSPageData, _
        "VisitorRecord")
    If DSPageData.Tables("VisitorRecord").Rows.Count = 0 Then
        lblMessage.Text = "No more visits found."
    Else
        Session("CurrentVisitorID") = _
            DSPageData.Tables("VisitorRecord"). _
            Rows(0).Item("VisitorID")
        lblMessage.Text = "Date Entered: " _
            & DSPageData.Tables("VisitorRecord"). _
            Rows(0).Item("DateEntered") _
            & "<br>Browser: " _
```

```
            & DSPageData.Tables("VisitorRecord"). _
            Rows(0).Item("Browser") & " " _
            & DSPageData.Tables("VisitorRecord"). _
            Rows(0).Item("MajorVersion") & "." _
            & DSPageData.Tables("VisitorRecord"). _
            Rows(0).Item("MinorVersion") _
            & "<br>Platform: " _
            & DSPageData.Tables("VisitorRecord"). _
            Rows(0).Item("Platform") _
            & "<br><br>Pages Viewed:<br><br>"
        DBCommand = New OleDbDataAdapter _
            ("Select Convert(varchar(25),DateEntered,100) " _
            & "as [Date Entered], " _
            & "PageName as [Page Name] From PageViews " _
            & "Where VisitorID = " & Session("CurrentVisitorID") _
            & " Order By DateEntered", DBConn)
        DBCommand.Fill(DSPageData, _
            "PageViews")
        dgPageViews.DataSource = _
            DSPageData.Tables("PageViews").DefaultView
        dgPageViews.DataBind()
    End If
End Sub
```

Within this procedure, we need data objects:

```
Dim DBConn as OleDbConnection
Dim DBCommand As OleDbDataAdapter
Dim DSPageData as New DataSet
```

We start by connecting to the database:

```
DBConn = New OleDbConnection("Provider=sqloledb;" _
    & "server=localhost;" _
    & "Initial Catalog=INETC8;" _
    & "User Id=sa;" _
    & "Password=yourpassword;")
```

This time we retrieve the visitor record that occurred just prior to the last one we looked at:

```
DBCommand = New OleDbDataAdapter _
    ("Select VisitorID, DateEntered, Browser, " _
    & "Platform, MajorVersion, MinorVersion From " _
```

```
    & "Visitors Where VisitorID = " _
    & "(Select Max(VisitorID) From Visitors " _
    & "Where VisitorID < " _
    & Session("CurrentVisitorID") & ")", DBConn)
DBCommand.Fill(DSPageData, _
    "VisitorRecord")
```

We then make sure that we found a record:

```
If DSPageData.Tables("VisitorRecord").Rows.Count = 0 Then
```

If we didn't, we display this message to the Administrator:

```
lblMessage.Text = "No more visits found."
```

Otherwise, we store the ID of the visitor record retrieved

```
Session("CurrentVisitorID") = _
    DSPageData.Tables("VisitorRecord"). _
    Rows(0).Item("VisitorID")
```

and display the top-level data:

```
lblMessage.Text = "Date Entered: " _
    & DSPageData.Tables("VisitorRecord"). _
    Rows(0).Item("DateEntered") _
    & "<br>Browser: " _
    & DSPageData.Tables("VisitorRecord"). _
    Rows(0).Item("Browser") & " " _
    & DSPageData.Tables("VisitorRecord"). _
    Rows(0).Item("MajorVersion") & "." _
    & DSPageData.Tables("VisitorRecord"). _
    Rows(0).Item("MinorVersion") _
    & "<br>Platform: " _
    & DSPageData.Tables("VisitorRecord"). _
    Rows(0).Item("Platform") _
    & "<br><br>Pages Viewed:<br><br>"
```

We then retrieve the pages viewed by the visitor

```
DBCommand = New OleDbDataAdapter _
    ("Select Convert(varchar(25),DateEntered,100) " _
    & "as [Date Entered], " _
```

```
    & "PageName as [Page Name] From PageViews " _
    & "Where VisitorID = " & Session("CurrentVisitorID") _
    & " Order By DateEntered", DBConn)
```

placing them into our DataSet object:

```
DBCommand.Fill(DSPageData, _
    "PageViews")
```

And we bind our DataGrid to the DataSet object:

```
dgPageViews.DataSource = _
    DSPageData.Tables("PageViews").DefaultView
dgPageViews.DataBind()
```

Server Variables ASP.NET Page

SV.aspx

The Server Variables page allows the administrator of the site to view server variable keys and values grouped together so that their count can be seen.

At the top of the page, we declare three compiler directives. The first sets up the run environment, and the other two import the needed data libraries:

```
<%@ Page Language=VB Debug=true %>
<%@ Import Namespace="System.Data" %>
<%@ Import Namespace="System.Data.OLEDB" %>
```

Within the body of the page, we define a Label control that displays the title text for the page:

```
<asp:Label
    id="lblTitle"
    Font-Size="25pt"
    Font-Name="Tahoma"
    Text="Server Variables"
    runat="server"
/>
```

Another Label control that displays instructional text is defined

```
<asp:Label
    id="lblMessage"
    Font-Size="12pt"
```

```
    Font-Name="Tahoma"
    Font-Bold="True"
    Text="Select a Server Variable and press the Go Button"
    runat="server"
/>
```

Next, we define a DropDownList control. It will display a distinct list of all the server variables:

```
<asp:dropdownlist
    id="ddlSV"
    runat=server
    DataTextField="KeyName"
>
</asp:dropdownlist>
```

Next, we define a button that allows the visitor to view the results of the server variables:

```
<asp:button
    id="butGo"
    text="  Go  "
    Type="Submit"
    OnClick="SubmitBtn_Click"
    runat="server"
/>
```

One more control is defined on this page. A DataGrid that shows the grouped results of the server variable selected in the DropDownList is defined

```
<asp:DataGrid
    id="dgResults"
    Width="90%"
    BackColor="beige"
    AlternatingItemStyle-BackColor="cornsilk"
    BorderColor="black"
    ShowFooter="false"
    CellPadding=3
    CellSpacing="0"
    Font-Name="Arial"
    Font-Size="8pt"
    ForeColor="Black"
    HeaderStyle-BackColor="burlywood"
    HeaderStyle-Font-Bold="True"
```

```
    runat="server">
</asp:DataGrid>
```

The code on the page is contained within two procedures. The first code block fires when the page is loaded. It populates the DropDownList control.

```
Sub Page_Load(ByVal Sender as Object, ByVal E as EventArgs)
    If Not IsPostBack Then
        Dim DBConn as OleDbConnection
        Dim DBCommand As OleDbDataAdapter
        Dim DSPageData as New DataSet
        DBConn = New OleDbConnection("Provider=sqloledb;" _
            & "server=localhost;" _
            & "Initial Catalog=INETC8;" _
            & "User Id=sa;" _
            & "Password=yourpassword;")
        DBCommand = New OleDbDataAdapter _
            ("Select Distinct KeyName From ServerVariables " _
            & "Order By KeyName", DBConn)
        DBCommand.Fill(DSPageData, _
            "SVKeys")
        ddlSV.DataSource = _
            DSPageData.Tables("SVKeys").DefaultView
        ddlSV.DataBind()
    End If
End Sub
```

We want the code within this procedure to run only when the page is first loaded:

```
If Not IsPostBack Then
```

If that is the case, we need data objects:

```
Dim DBConn as OleDbConnection
Dim DBCommand As OleDbDataAdapter
Dim DSPageData as New DataSet
```

We start by connecting to the database:

```
DBConn = New OleDbConnection("Provider=sqloledb;" _
    & "server=localhost;" _
    & "Initial Catalog=INETC8;" _
    & "User Id=sa;" _
    & "Password=yourpassword;")
```

We then retrieve all the unique server variable names stored in the ServerVariables table:

```
DBCommand = New OleDbDataAdapter _
    ("Select Distinct KeyName From ServerVariables " _
    & "Order By KeyName", DBConn)
```

Those records are placed in our DataSet object:

```
DBCommand.Fill(DSPageData, _
    "SVKeys")
```

The DataGrid is bound to that object:

```
ddlSV.DataSource = _
    DSPageData.Tables("SVKeys").DefaultView
ddlSV.DataBind()
```

The other procedure fires when the administrator clicks the button. It populates the DataGrid according to the server variable selected in the DropDownList.

```
Sub SubmitBtn_Click(Sender As Object, E As EventArgs)
    Dim DBConn as OleDbConnection
    Dim DBCommand As OleDbDataAdapter
    Dim DSPageData as New DataSet
    DBConn = New OleDbConnection("Provider=sqloledb;" _
        & "server=localhost;" _
        & "Initial Catalog=INETC8;" _
        & "User Id=sa;" _
        & "Password=yourpassword;")
    DBCommand = New OleDbDataAdapter _
        ("Select KeyValue as [Key Value], " _
        & "Count(ServerVariableID) as [Count] " _
        & "From ServerVariables Where KeyName = '" _
        & ddlSV.SelectedItem.Text & "' Group By KeyValue " _
        & "Order By Count(ServerVariableID) DESC", DBConn)
    DBCommand.Fill(DSPageData, _
        "Results")
    dgResults.DataSource = _
        DSPageData.Tables("Results").DefaultView
    dgResults.DataBind()
End Sub
```

The data objects are declared

```
Dim DBConn as OleDbConnection
Dim DBCommand As OleDbDataAdapter
Dim DSPageData as New DataSet
```

And we connect to our database:

```
DBConn = New OleDbConnection("Provider=sqloledb;" _
    & "server=localhost;" _
    & "Initial Catalog=INETC8;" _
    & "User Id=sa;" _
    & "Password=yourpassword;")
```

We then group all the values for the key selected by the administrator and retrieve their count:

```
DBCommand = New OleDbDataAdapter _
    ("Select KeyValue as [Key Value], " _
    & "Count(ServerVariableID) as [Count] " _
    & "From ServerVariables Where KeyName = '" _
    & ddlSV.SelectedItem.Text & "' Group By KeyValue " _
    & "Order By Count(ServerVariableID) DESC", DBConn)
DBCommand.Fill(DSPageData, _
    "Results")
```

Our DataGrid is then bound to the records returned from that call:

```
dgResults.DataSource = _
    DSPageData.Tables("Results").DefaultView
dgResults.DataBind()
```

Browser Capabilities ASP.NET Page

BC.aspx

The Browser Capabilities page allows the administrator to view the number of visitors that have particular features as returned by the browser capabilities. At the top of the page, we define the three needed compiler directives:

```
<%@ Page Language=VB Debug=true %>
<%@ Import Namespace="System.Data" %>
<%@ Import Namespace="System.Data.OLEDB" %>
```

Within the body of the page, we define one Label control for the title of the page

```
<asp:Label
    id="lblTitle"
    Font-Size="25pt"
    Font-Name="Tahoma"
    Text="Server Variables"
    runat="server"
/>
```

and another that displays page instructions:

```
<asp:Label
    id="lblMessage"
    Font-Size="12pt"
    Font-Name="Tahoma"
    Font-Bold="True"
    Text="Select a Server Variable and press the Go Button"
    runat="server"
/>
```

Next, we define a DropDownList that allows the administrator to select a browser capability:

```
<asp:DropDownList
    id="ddlBC"
    runat=server>
    <asp:ListItem Value="AOL">AOL</asp:ListItem>
    <asp:ListItem Value="BackgroundSound">BG Sound</asp:ListItem>
    <asp:ListItem Value="Beta">Beta Browser</asp:ListItem>
    <asp:ListItem Value="Browser">Browser</asp:ListItem>
    <asp:ListItem Value="Cookies">Supports Cookies</asp:ListItem>
    <asp:ListItem Value="Crawler">Crawler</asp:ListItem>
    <asp:ListItem Value="Platform">Platform</asp:ListItem>
</asp:DropDownList>
```

That is followed by the Button control:

```
<asp:button
    id="butGo"
    text="  Go  "
    Type="Submit"
    OnClick="SubmitBtn_Click"
    runat="server"
/>
```

The other control on the page is a DataGrid, which displays the grouped values of the browser capability selected

```
<asp:DataGrid
    id="dgResults"
    Width="90%"
    BackColor="beige"
    AlternatingItemStyle-BackColor="cornsilk"
    BorderColor="black"
    ShowFooter="false"
    CellPadding=3
    CellSpacing="0"
    Font-Name="Arial"
    Font-Size="8pt"
    ForeColor="Black"
    HeaderStyle-BackColor="burlywood"
    HeaderStyle-Font-Bold="True"
    runat="server">
</asp:DataGrid>
```

The code on the page fires within a single event, which is when the button is clicked. The code populates the DataGrid according to the item selected in the DropDownList.

```
Sub SubmitBtn_Click(Sender As Object, E As EventArgs)
    Dim DBConn as OleDbConnection
    Dim DBCommand As OleDbDataAdapter
    Dim DSPageData as New DataSet
    DBConn = New OleDbConnection("Provider=sqloledb;" _
        & "server=localhost;" _
        & "Initial Catalog=INETC8;" _
        & "User Id=sa;" _
        & "Password=yourpassword;")
    DBCommand = New OleDbDataAdapter _
        ("Select " & ddlBC.SelectedItem.Value _
        & " as [" & ddlBC.SelectedItem.Text & "], " _
        & "Count(VisitorID) as [Count] " _
        & "From Visitors Group By " _
        & ddlBC.SelectedItem.Value _
        & " Order By Count(VisitorID) DESC", DBConn)
    DBCommand.Fill(DSPageData, _
        "Results")
    dgResults.DataSource = _
        DSPageData.Tables("Results").DefaultView
    dgResults.DataBind()
End Sub
```

The procedure needs data objects:

```
Dim DBConn as OleDbConnection
Dim DBCommand As OleDbDataAdapter
Dim DSPageData as New DataSet
```

We start by connecting to the database:

```
DBConn = New OleDbConnection("Provider=sqloledb;" _
    & "server=localhost;" _
    & "Initial Catalog=INETC8;" _
    & "User Id=sa;" _
    & "Password=yourpassword;")
```

We then retrieve the field selected by the visitor and group the values in that field. Note that we alias the field as it is displayed in the DropDownList to the administrator:

```
DBCommand = New OleDbDataAdapter _
    ("Select " & ddlBC.SelectedItem.Value _
    & " as [" & ddlBC.SelectedItem.Text & "], " _
    & "Count(VisitorID) as [Count] " _
    & "From Visitors Group By " _
    & ddlBC.SelectedItem.Value _
    & " Order By Count(VisitorID) DESC", DBConn)
```

Those records are placed in our DataSet object

```
DBCommand.Fill(DSPageData, _
    "Results")
```

which the DataGrid is bound to:

```
dgResults.DataSource = _
    DSPageData.Tables("Results").DefaultView
dgResults.DataBind()
```

Hit Count ASP.NET Page

HitCount.aspx

The Hit Count page allows the administrator to view the total number of page views historically or in a date range. At the top of the page, we define the same three compiler directives

```
<%@ Page Language=VB Debug=true %>
<%@ Import Namespace="System.Data" %>
<%@ Import Namespace="System.Data.OLEDB" %>
```

Within the body of the page, we define a Label control that displays the title of the page:

```
<asp:Label
    id="lblTitle"
    Font-Size="25pt"
    Font-Name="Tahoma"
    Text="Hit Count"
    runat="server"
/>
```

and another that initially displays descriptive text:

```
<asp:Label
    id="lblMessage"
    Font-Size="12pt"
    Font-Name="Tahoma"
    Font-Bold="True"
    Text="Historical hit count."
    runat="server"
/>
```

Next, we define the DataGrid that will display the page count:

```
<asp:DataGrid
    id="dgResults"
    Width="90%"
    BackColor="beige"
    AlternatingItemStyle-BackColor="cornsilk"
    BorderColor="black"
    ShowFooter="false"
    CellPadding=3
    CellSpacing="0"
    Font-Name="Arial"
    Font-Size="8pt"
    ForeColor="Black"
    HeaderStyle-BackColor="burlywood"
    HeaderStyle-Font-Bold="True"
    runat="server">
</asp:DataGrid>
```

That is followed by a TextBox, which is used to enter the start date to filter the hit records by

```
<asp:TextBox
    id="txtFromDate"
    Columns="15"
    MaxLength="30"
    runat=server
/>
```

and one for the end date:

```
<asp:TextBox
    id="txtToDate"
    Columns="15"
    MaxLength="30"
    runat=server
/>
```

We also need a Button control so that the records can be filtered

```
<asp:button
    id="butOK"
    text="  OK  "
    Type="Submit"
    OnClick="SubmitBtn_Click"
    runat="server"
/>
```

Additionally, we define two CompareValidator controls. The first makes sure that the value entered in the first TextBox control is a date:

```
<asp:CompareValidator
    id="cvFromDate"
    ControlToValidate="txtFromDate"
    Operator="DataTypeCheck"
    Type="Date"
    Display="Dynamic"
    Font-Size="10pt"
    runat="server">
    <br>From Date must be a date!
</asp:CompareValidator>
```

And another checks the second TextBox control to make sure it is a date:

```
<asp:CompareValidator
    id="cvToDate"
    ControlToValidate="txtToDate"
    Operator="DataTypeCheck"
    Type="Date"
    Display="Dynamic"
    Font-Size="10pt"
    runat="server">
    <br>To Date must be a date!
</asp:CompareValidator>
```

The code on the page fires in two events. The first fires when the page is loaded. It displays the page count for all the dates.

```
Sub Page_Load(ByVal Sender as Object, ByVal E as EventArgs)
    If Not IsPostBack Then
        Dim DBConn as OleDbConnection
        Dim DBCommand As OleDbDataAdapter
        Dim DSPageData as New DataSet
        DBConn = New OleDbConnection("Provider=sqloledb;" _
            & "server=localhost;" _
            & "Initial Catalog=INETC8;" _
            & "User Id=sa;" _
            & "Password=yourpassword;")
        DBCommand = New OleDbDataAdapter _
            ("Select PageName as [Page Name], " _
            & "Count(PageViewID) as [Count] From PageViews " _
            & "Group By PageName " _
            & "Order By Count(PageViewID) DESC", DBConn)
        DBCommand.Fill(DSPageData, _
            "PageViews")
        dgResults.DataSource = _
            DSPageData.Tables("PageViews").DefaultView
        dgResults.DataBind()
    End If
End Sub
```

We want this code to run only when the page is first loaded

```
If Not IsPostBack Then
```

If this is the first time it is loaded, we will need data variables:

```
Dim DBConn as OleDbConnection
Dim DBCommand As OleDbDataAdapter
Dim DSPageData as New DataSet
```

We start by connecting to the database:

```
DBConn = New OleDbConnection("Provider=sqloledb;" _
    & "server=localhost;" _
    & "Initial Catalog=INETC8;" _
    & "User Id=sa;" _
    & "Password=yourpassword;")
```

We then retrieve all the page names grouped and display their count:

```
DBCommand = New OleDbDataAdapter _
    ("Select PageName as [Page Name], " _
    & "Count(PageViewID) as [Count] From PageViews " _
    & "Group By PageName " _
    & "Order By Count(PageViewID) DESC", DBConn)
DBCommand.Fill(DSPageData, _
    "PageViews")
```

They are displayed in our DataGrid control:

```
dgResults.DataSource = _
    DSPageData.Tables("PageViews").DefaultView
dgResults.DataBind()
```

The other procedure fires when the administrator clicks the Button control. It displays the page-hit count for the date range entered.

```
Sub SubmitBtn_Click(Sender As Object, E As EventArgs)
        Dim DBConn as OleDbConnection
        Dim DBCommand As OleDbDataAdapter
        Dim DSPageData as New DataSet
        DBConn = New OleDbConnection("Provider=sqloledb;" _
            & "server=localhost;" _
            & "Initial Catalog=INETC8;" _
            & "User Id=sa;" _
            & "Password=yourpassword;")
        DBCommand = New OleDbDataAdapter _
```

```
            ("Select PageName as [Page Name], " _
            & "Count(PageViewID) as [Count] From PageViews " _
            & "Where DateEntered >= '" & txtFromDate.Text _
            & "' And DateEntered <= '" & txtToDate.Text _
            & "' Group By PageName " _
            & "Order By Count(PageViewID) DESC", DBConn)
        DBCommand.Fill(DSPageData, _
            "PageViews")
        dgResults.DataSource = _
            DSPageData.Tables("PageViews").DefaultView
        dgResults.DataBind()
        lblMessage.Text = ""
End Sub
```

This procedure requires data objects:

```
Dim DBConn as OleDbConnection
Dim DBCommand As OleDbDataAdapter
Dim DSPageData as New DataSet
```

So, we need to connect to the database:

```
DBConn = New OleDbConnection("Provider=sqloledb;" _
    & "server=localhost;" _
    & "Initial Catalog=INETC8;" _
    & "User Id=sa;" _
    & "Password=yourpassword;")
```

This time, we retrieve the names and count of the page hits only for those records that are within the date range entered by the visitor:

```
DBCommand = New OleDbDataAdapter _
    ("Select PageName as [Page Name], " _
    & "Count(PageViewID) as [Count] From PageViews " _
    & "Where DateEntered >= '" & txtFromDate.Text _
    & "' And DateEntered <= '" & txtToDate.Text _
    & "' Group By PageName " _
    & "Order By Count(PageViewID) DESC", DBConn)
```

Those records are placed in our DataSet object

```
DBCommand.Fill(DSPageData, _
    "PageViews")
```

and bound to our DataGrid:

```
dgResults.DataSource = _
    DSPageData.Tables("PageViews").DefaultView
dgResults.DataBind()
```

Finally, we clear the message Label, since this DataGrid does not display the historical page count:

```
lblMessage.Text = ""
```

Access Code Changes

C8UsageTracking.mdb

For this solution to work with Access instead of SQL Server, a few code changes were necessary. First, the connect string is changed on all the pages so that it uses the correct provider and points to the correct database:

```
DBConn = New OleDbConnection("PROVIDER=Microsoft.Jet.OLEDB.4.0;" _
    & "DATA SOURCE=" _
    & Server.MapPath("/INetBook/C8/UsageTracking/Admin/" _
    & "Access/C8UsageTracking.mdb;"))
```

On the Site pages, we used the SQL Server function GetDate() to return the current system date and time. In Access, the function Now() is used instead:

```
DBInsert.CommandText = "Insert Into PageViews " _
    & "(DateEntered, PageName, VisitorID) Values (" _
    & "Now, 'Map', " & Session("VisitorID") & ")"
```

In SQL Server, we used the Convert function to display the date in a more readable format. In Access, the Format function is substituted

```
DBCommand = New OleDbDataAdapter _
    ("Select Format(" _
    & "DateEntered, ""mmm, dd, yyyy hh:nn:ss"")" _
    & " as [Date Entered], " _
    & "PageName as [Page Name] From PageViews " _
    & "Where VisitorID = " & Session("CurrentVisitorID") _
    & " Order By DateEntered", DBConn)
```

The other change that is needed is in the where clause in the query on the Hit Count page. In SQL Server, dates are surrounded by the " ' " character. In Access, the "#"character is used:

```
DBCommand = New OleDbDataAdapter _
    ("Select PageName as [Page Name], " _
    & "Count(PageViewID) as [Count] From PageViews " _
    & "Where DateEntered >= #" & txtFromDate.Text _
    & "# And DateEntered <= #" & txtToDate.Text _
    & "# Group By PageName " _
    & "Order By Count(PageViewID) DESC", DBConn)
```

CHAPTER

9

Creating an Online Campus

Many companies need to present course or class content either to their employees or to their customers. For example, a company may need to train their employees on new equipment or safety procedures. Another company may need to offer courses to their customers because they are a school, or as a secondary way of increasing their main business activity. A store that sells plants may offer a course in taking care of those plants.

In this chapter, we will look at an application that enables you to bring your course material to your customers or your employees through your Web site. The Online Campus application allows students to enroll in courses. They can then review the course material, which is divided into sections, and they can take a quiz on each section.

Sample Usage

When the student first enters the application, they see the Log In page displayed in Figure 9-1.

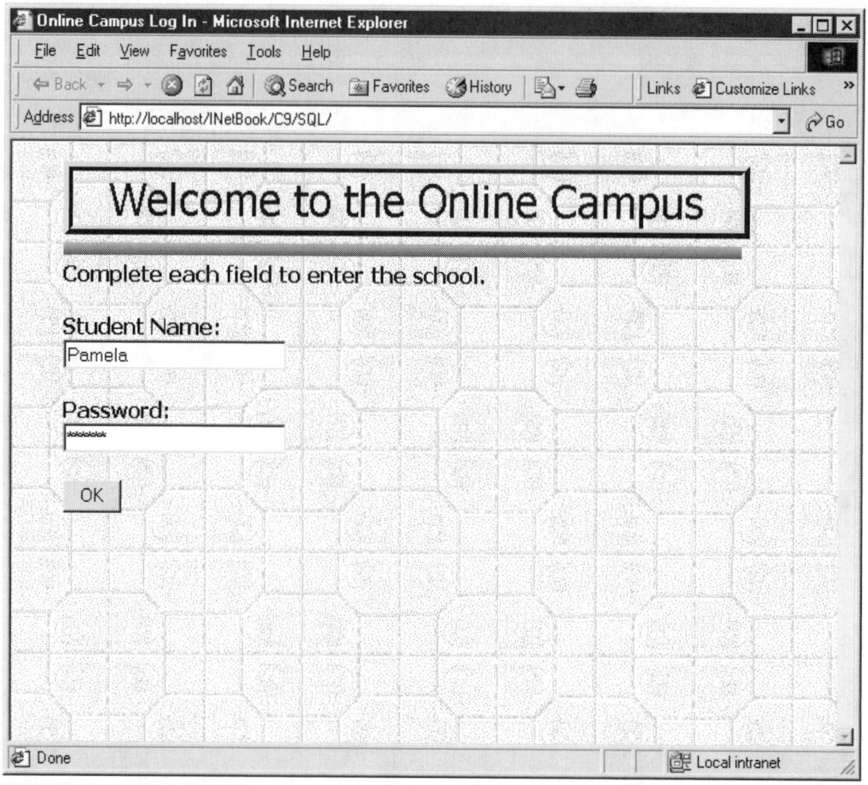

Figure 9-1 *Log In page*

From here the student enters their name and password. If what they enter is not a valid student name and password, the student receives an error message and can try again. If the student enters a correct name and password, they are taken to the Home Room page displayed in Figure 9-2.

The Home Room page allows the student to enter a course. But this student has not yet enrolled in a course, so all they can do is click the Enroll in a Course link. When they do that, they are taken to the Enroll page displayed in Figure 9-3.

In the body of the page, the student sees a list of all the courses available. When they select a course and click the OK button, they are enrolled in that course if they

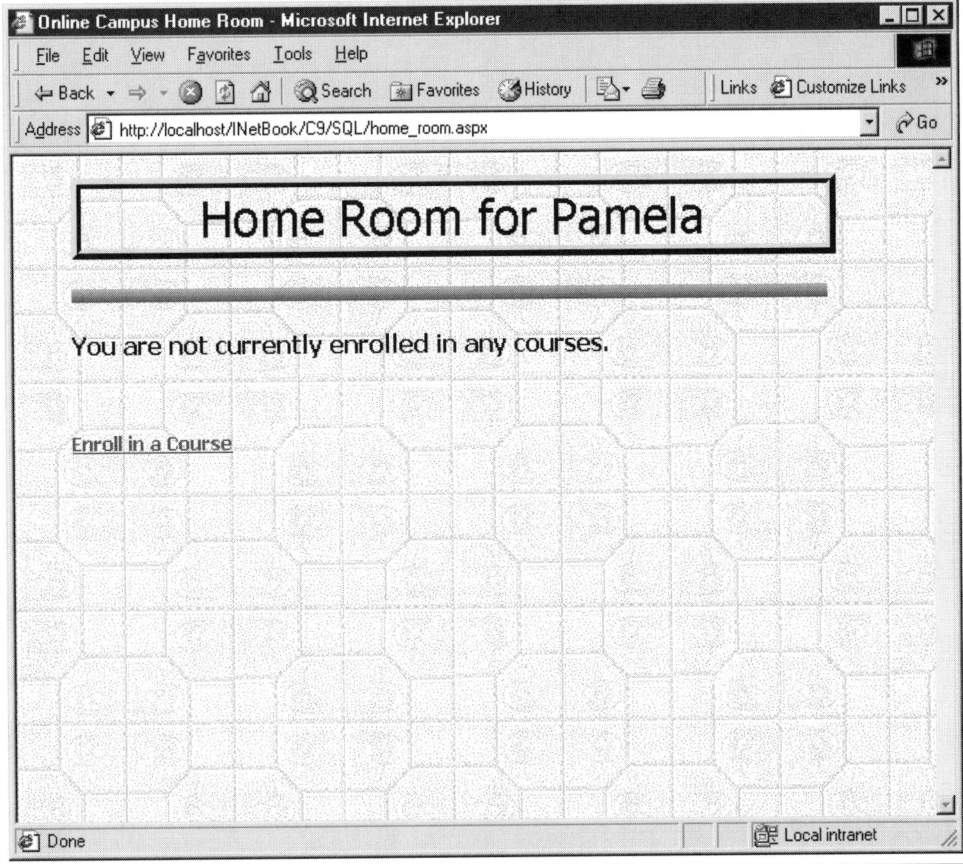

Figure 9-2 *Home Room page with no current courses*

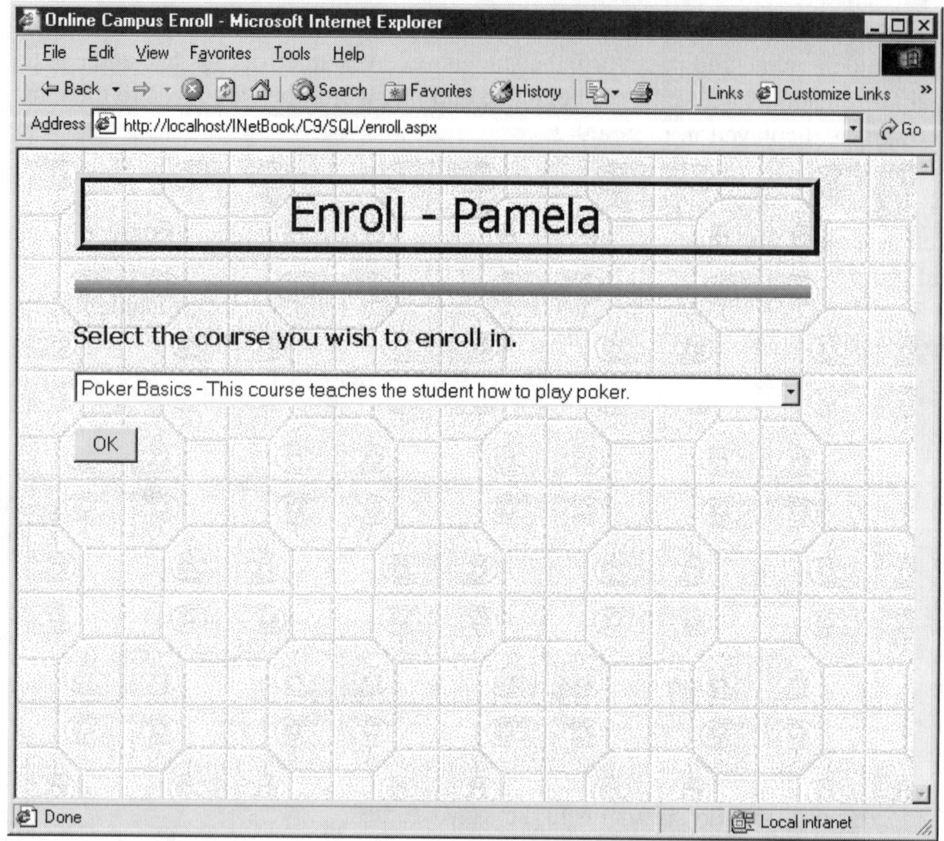

Figure 9-3 *Enroll page*

have not yet enrolled in that course. The student is then taken back to the Home Room page as shown in Figure 9-4.

Now the student sees the course they enrolled in on this page, as well as any other courses the student has already enrolled in. The student then would select the course

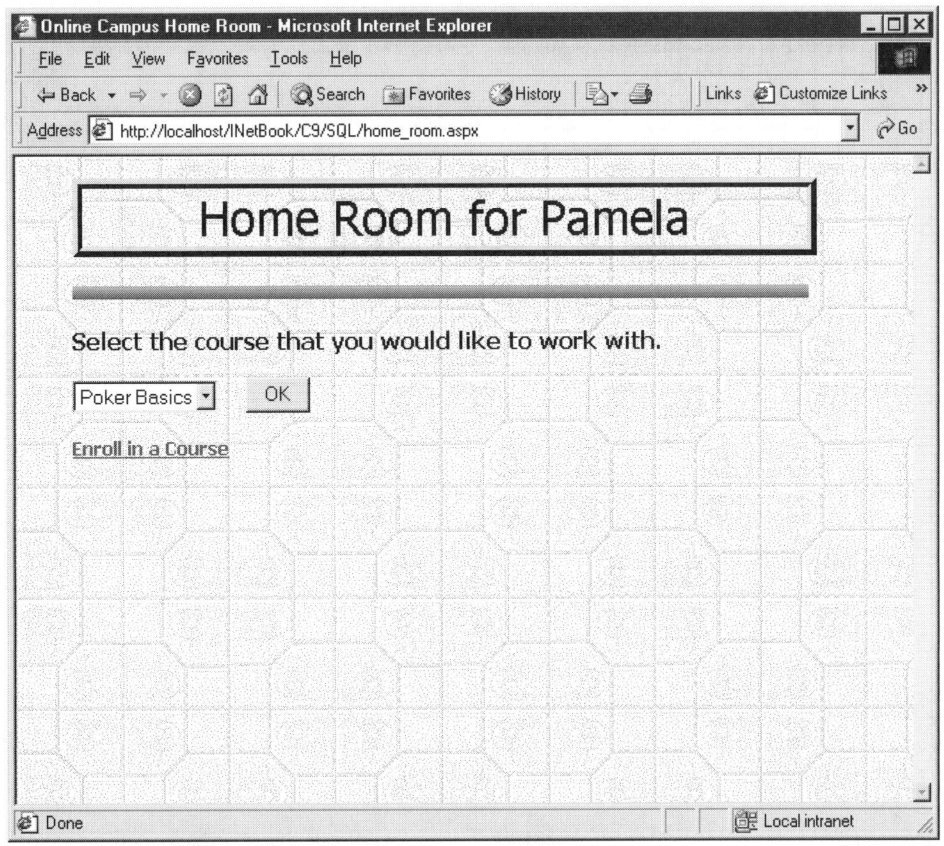

Figure 9-4 *Home Room page with course enrolled listed*

that they want to work with before clicking the OK button. The student is then sent to the Course page displayed in Figure 9-5.

The Course page allows the student to review section content or take a quiz. The student can also see the results of their quizzes, if any.

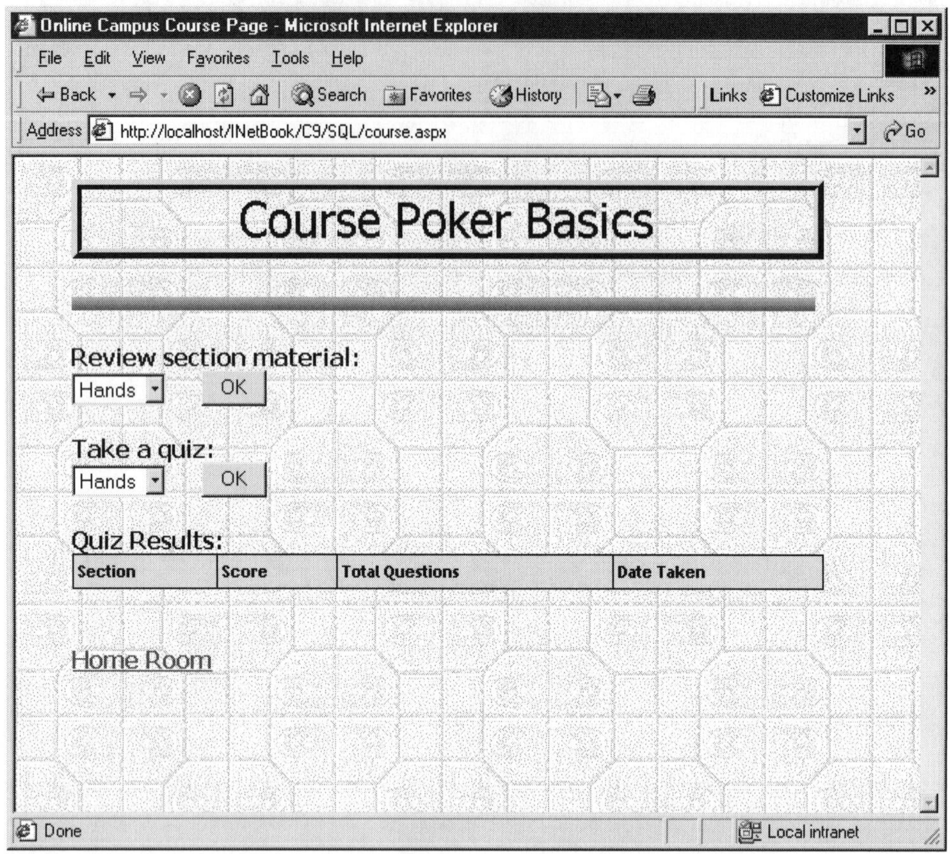

Figure 9-5 *Course page*

When the student selects course material, they are taken to the Course Content page displayed in Figure 9-6.

The first page of content for this particular section of the course is displayed to the student. Once the student is done with this page of content, they click the OK button to be taken to the next page of content, like the one displayed in Figure 9-7.

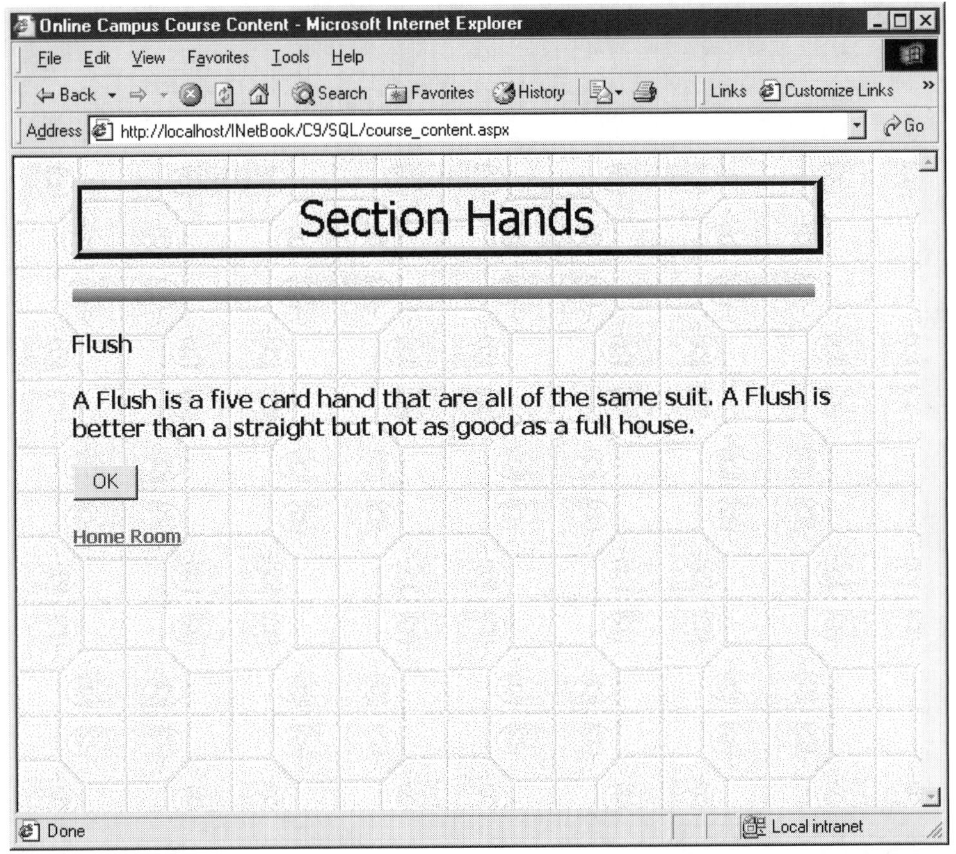

Figure 9-6 *Course Content page*

Each section must have at least one page of content. But it can have as many pages as you want. The student continues clicking the OK button to proceed. Eventually, they reach the end of the content for this section and are taken back to the Course page.

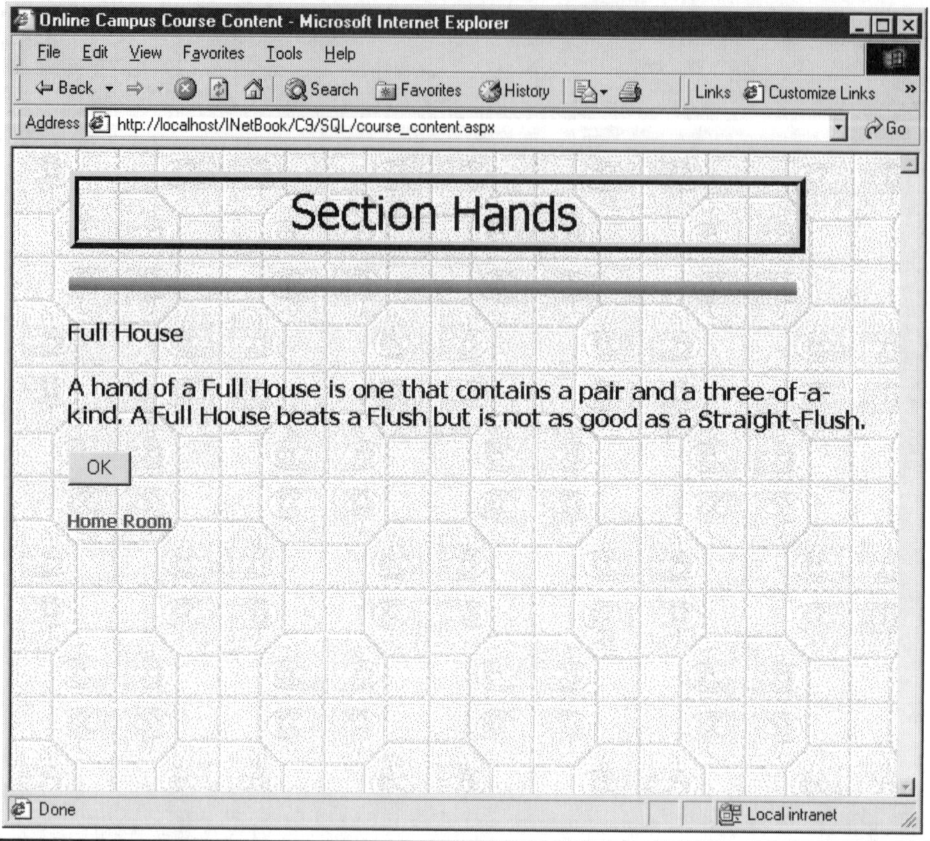

Figure 9-7 *More content on the Course Content page*

When the student selects a quiz from the Course page, they are taken to the Course Quiz page displayed in Figure 9-8.

The page displays all the questions for the section selected. Each section must have at least one question in it. But they can have as many questions as you want. Similarly, each question can have one or more answers.

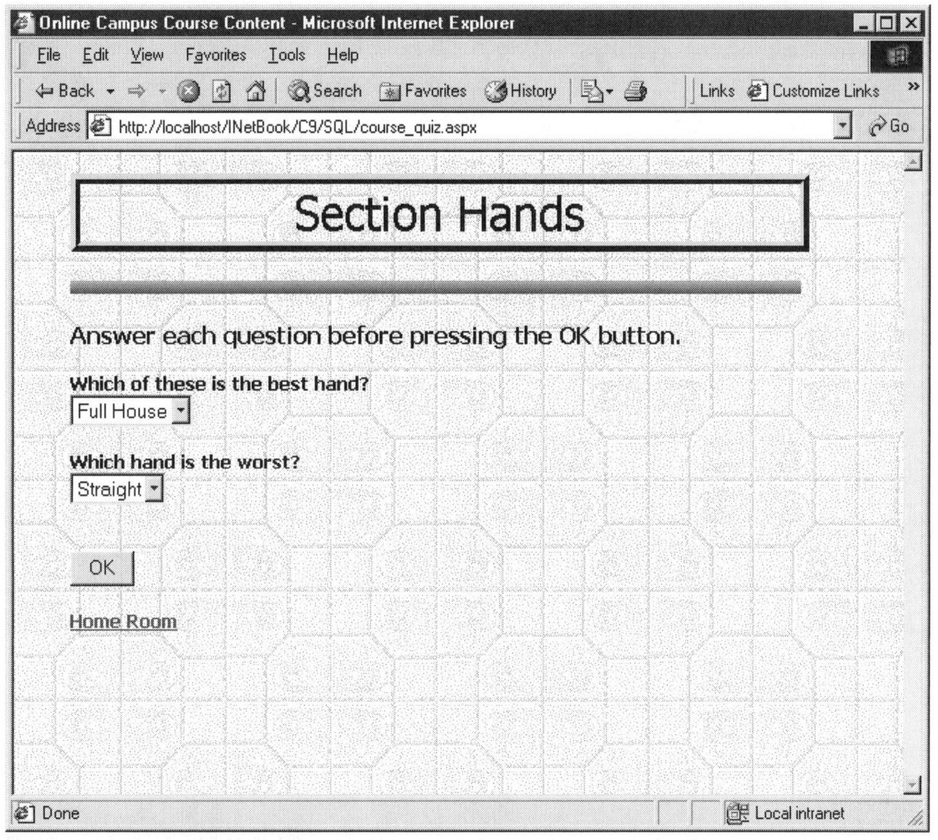

Figure 9-8 *Course Quiz page*

The student answers each question. When they click the OK button, their quiz is scored and they select the result of their quiz as is displayed in Figure 9-9.

Online Campus Database Component

C9OnlineCampus.sql

The database that is required to run the Online Campus application contains eight tables. These tables are related in a fairly complex fashion. In this section, we will review the relationships between the tables and the fields that they contain.

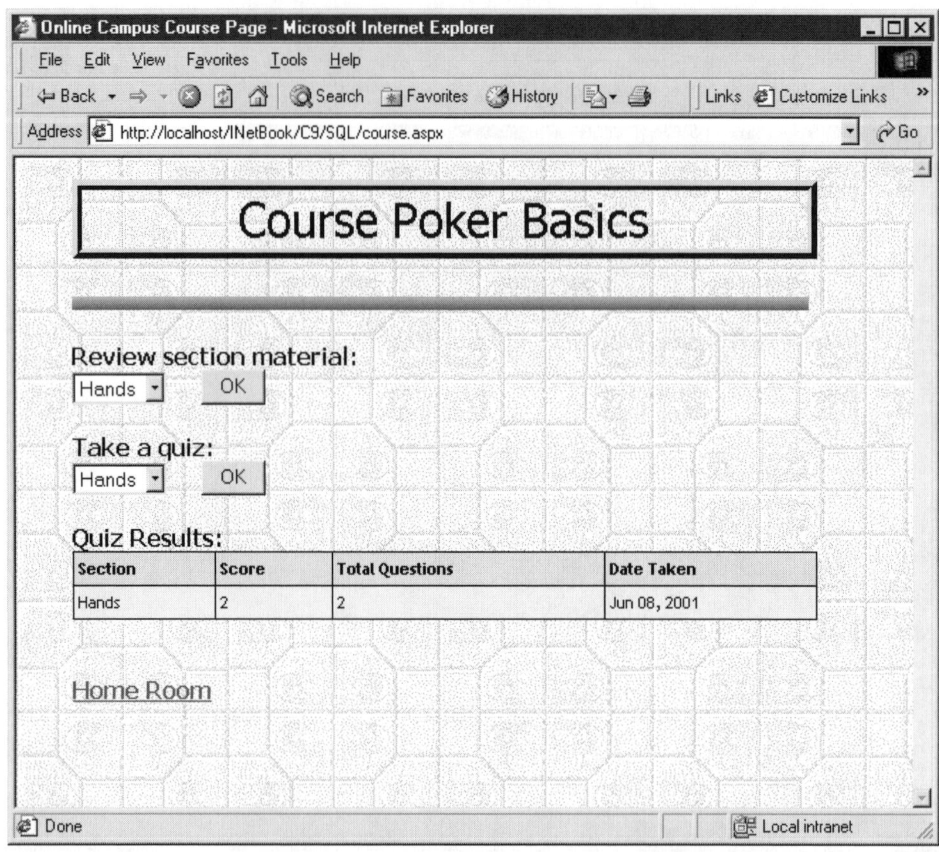

Figure 9-9 *Course page displaying quiz result*

Tables and Data Diagram

Figure 9-10 displays the relationships between the tables in the Online Campus database.

The database contains two top-level tables, Students and Courses. The Students table contains information about each student and the Courses table contains top-level information about each course. Each student can take many courses, and each course can have many students. That means that the two tables are in a

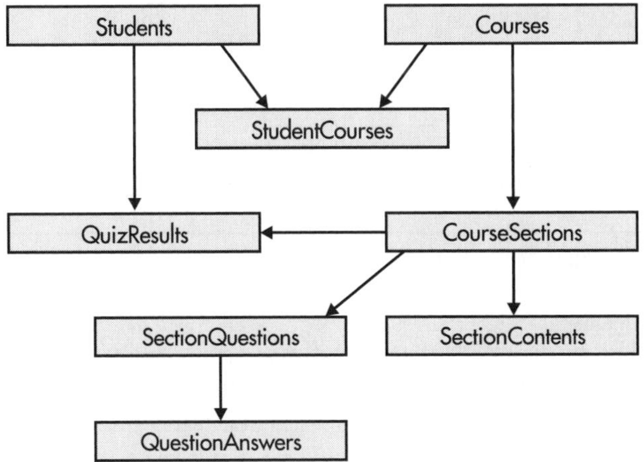

Figure 9-10 *Online Campus data diagram*

many-to-many relationship. The StudentsCourses table satisfies that relationship by linking to both tables in a one-to-many relationship.

Each course can have many sections. The section information for each course is stored in the CourseSections table. That table related to the Courses table in a one-to-many relationship.

The SectionQuestions table contains each of the questions used in a section. The SectionContents table contains the text content for each section. Both tables are in a one-to-many relationship with the CourseSections table, since each section can have many pages of content and many questions.

The QuestionAnswers table stores the possible answers to each question. It is in a one-to-many relationship with the SectionQuestions table, since each question can have many possible answers.

The QuizResults table stores the score of each quiz taken by the student. The table is in a one-to-many relationship with the Students table, since each student can take many quizzes. It is also in a one-to-many relationship with the CourseSections table, since many students can have taken each section's quiz.

Students Field Specifications

Students.txt

The field specifications for the fields in the Students table are displayed in Table 9-1.

Field Name	Field Type	Notes
StudentID	int	Primary Key, Identity Column
StudentName	varchar	Length = 100
Password	varchar	Length = 50
EmailAddress	varchar	Length = 50

Table 9-1 *Students Field Specifications*

The StudentID field is the primary key in this table. Since it is an identity column, it is automatically populated with a value when a new record is added to this table. The rest of the fields contain basic information about the student.

Courses Field Specifications

Courses.txt

The field specifications for the fields in the Courses table are displayed in Table 9-2.

The CourseID field is the primary key here. The other fields store basic information about the course as it appears in different DropDownList controls and Label controls.

StudentsCourses Field Specifications

StudentsCourses.txt

The field specifications for the fields in the StudentsCourses table are displayed in Table 9-3.

Field Name	Field Type	Notes
CourseID	int	Primary Key, Identity Column
CourseName	varchar	Length = 50
CourseDescription	varchar	Length = 255

Table 9-2 *Courses Field Specifications*

Field Name	Field Type	Notes
StudentCourseID	int	Primary Key, Identity Column
StudentID	int	Foreign Key
CourseID	int	Foreign Key
DateEnrolled	datetime	

Table 9-3 *StudentsCourses Field Specifications*

The StudentCourseID field is the primary key in the table. The StudentID field is a foreign key that links this table to the Students table. The CourseID field is another foreign key; it links this table to the Courses table.

CourseSections Field Specifications

CourseSections.txt

The field specifications for the fields in the CourseSections table are displayed in Table 9-4.

The CourseSectionID field is the primary key in this table, uniquely identifying each record. The CourseName links this table to the Courses table.

SectionContents Field Specifications

SectionContents.txt

The field specifications for the fields in the SectionContents table are displayed in Table 9-5.

Field Name	Field Type	Notes
CourseSectionID	int	Primary Key, Identity Column
CourseID	int	Foreign Key
SectionName	varchar	Length = 50

Table 9-4 *CourseSections Field Specifications*

Field Name	Field Type	Notes
SectionContentID	int	Primary Key, Identity Column
CourseSectionID	int	Foreign Key
SectionContentTitle	varchar	Length = 50
SectionContent	text	

Table 9-5 *SectionContents Field Specifications*

There are two keys in this table. The first is the primary key, SectionContentID. The other is a foreign key, CourseSectionID, which links this table to the CourseSections table. The other fields store the content for the topic.

SectionQuestions Field Specifications

SectionQuestions.txt

The field specifications for the fields in the SectionQuestions table are displayed in Table 9-6.

The SectionQuestionID field is the primary key in this table. The CourseSectionID field also links this table to the CourseSections table.

The QuestionText field contains the text of the question. The CorrectAnswer text needs to match exactly one of the choices that the student sees as an answer for this question so that the question is scored correctly.

QuestionAnswers Field Specifications

QuestionAnswers.txt

The field specifications for the fields in the QuestionAnswers table are displayed in Table 9-7.

Field Name	Field Type	Notes
SectionQuestionID	int	Primary Key, Identity Column
CourseSectionID	int	Foreign Key
QuestionText	varchar	Length = 255
CorrectAnswer	varchar	Length = 50

Table 9-6 *SectionQuestions Field Specifications*

Field Name	Field Type	Notes
QuestionAnswerID	int	Primary Key, Identity Column
SectionQuestionID	int	Foreign Key
AnswerText	varchar	Length = 50

Table 9-7 *QuestionAnswers Field Specifications*

In this table, the primary key is the QuestionAnswerID field. The SectionQuestionID field stores the ID of the question that the answer goes with. The AnswerText field stores the text of the answer as it is displayed on the Course Quiz page.

QuizResults Field Specifications

QuizResults.txt

The field specifications for the fields in the QuizResults table are displayed in Table 9-8.

The QuizResultID field is the primary key in this table. The StudentID field is a foreign key that links this table to the Students table. The other foreign key in this table is the CourseSectionID field, which links this table to the CourseSections table.

The Score field stores the number of questions the student answered correctly on the quiz. The TotalQuestions field stores the total number of questions on the quiz. And the DateTaken field stores the date and time that the student finished the quiz.

Field Name	Field Type	Notes
QuizResultID	int	Primary Key, Identity Column
StudentID	int	Foreign Key
CourseSectionID	int	Foreign Key
Score	int	
TotalQuestions	int	
DateTaken	datetime	

Table 9-8 *QuizResults Field Specifications*

Online Campus ASP.NET Code

The Online Campus application is made up of six ASP.NET pages. In this section of the chapter, we will review the code on those pages and the controls that they contain.

Log In ASP.NET Page

Index.aspx

The code on the Log In page checks the name and password entered by the student to see if they are valid.

At the top of the page we declare three compiler directives.

```
<%@ Page Language=VB Debug=true %>
<%@ Import Namespace="System.Data" %>
<%@ Import Namespace="System.Data.OLEDB" %>
```

The first tells the compiler the language we are using and that we want to be in debug mode. Remember to turn debug off when putting this application into production:

```
<%@ Page Language=VB Debug=true %>
```

The other two directives import data libraries:

```
<%@ Import Namespace="System.Data" %>
<%@ Import Namespace="System.Data.OLEDB" %>
```

Within the body of the page we declare one Label control that displays title text:

```
<asp:Label
    id="lblTitle"
    BorderWidth="7px"
    BorderStyle=7
    Width="90%"
    Font-Size="25pt"
    Font-Name="Tahoma"
    Text="<center>Welcome to the Online Campus</center>"
    runat="server"
/>
```

Another Label initially displays page instructions but also displays an error message if an invalid name or password is entered

```
<asp:Label
    id="lblMessage"
    Font-Size="12pt"
    Font-Name="Tahoma"
    Font-Bold="True"
    runat="server"
    Text="Complete each field to enter the school."
/>
```

Next, we define a TextBox for the student to enter their name:

```
<asp:TextBox
    id="txtStudentName"
    Columns="25"
    MaxLength="100"
    runat=server
/>
```

That field is required because of the RequiredFieldValidator linked to it:

```
<asp:RequiredFieldValidator
    id="rfvStudentName"
    ControlToValidate="txtStudentName"
    Display="Dynamic"
    Font-Name="Tahoma"
    Font-Size="10pt"
    runat=server>
    Student Name is Required!
</asp:RequiredFieldValidator>
```

We also need a TextBox control for the student's password

```
<asp:TextBox
    id="txtPassword"
    Columns="25"
    MaxLength="30"
    runat=server
    TextMode="Password"
/>
```

which is also a required field:

```
<asp:RequiredFieldValidator
    id="rfvPassword"
    ControlToValidate="txtPassword"
    Display="Dynamic"
    Font-Name="Verdana"
    Font-Size="10pt"
    runat=server>
    Password is Required!
</asp:RequiredFieldValidator>
```

The other control added to the page is a Button control:

```
<asp:button
    id="butOK"
    text="  OK  "
    Type="Submit"
    OnClick="SubmitBtn_Click"
    runat="server"
/>
```

When that button is clicked, the only code on the page fires.

```
Sub SubmitBtn_Click(Sender As Object, E As EventArgs)
    Dim DBConn as OleDbConnection
    Dim DBCommand As OleDbDataAdapter
    Dim DSLogin as New DataSet
    DBConn = New OleDbConnection("Provider=sqloledb;" _
        & "server=localhost;" _
        & "Initial Catalog=INETC9;" _
        & "User Id=sa;" _
        & "Password=yourpassword;")
    DBCommand = New OleDbDataAdapter _
        ("Select StudentID from " _
        & "Students Where " _
        & "StudentName = '" & txtStudentName.Text _
        & "' and Password = '" & txtPassword.Text _
        & "'", DBConn)
    DBCommand.Fill(DSLogin, _
        "StudentInfo")
    If DSLogin.Tables("StudentInfo"). _
        Rows.Count = 0 Then
        lblMessage.Text = "The student name and password " _
            & "were not found. Please try again."
```

```
    Else
        Session("StudentID") = DSLogin.Tables("StudentInfo"). _
            Rows(0).Item("StudentID")
        Session("StudentName") = txtStudentName.Text
        Response.Redirect("./home_room.aspx")
    End If
End Sub
```

The procedure validates the student's name and password. Therefore, we will need data objects:

```
Dim DBConn as OleDbConnection
Dim DBCommand As OleDbDataAdapter
Dim DSLogin as New DataSet
```

We start by connecting to the database:

```
DBConn = New OleDbConnection("Provider=sqloledb;" _
    & "server=localhost;" _
    & "Initial Catalog=INETC9;" _
    & "User Id=sa;" _
    & "Password=yourpassword;")
```

We then attempt to retrieve the ID of the student corresponding to the name and password they entered

```
DBCommand = New OleDbDataAdapter _
    ("Select StudentID from " _
    & "Students Where " _
    & "StudentName = '" & txtStudentName.Text _
    & "' and Password = '" & txtPassword.Text _
    & "'", DBConn)
DBCommand.Fill(DSLogin, _
    "StudentInfo")
```

We then check to see if a record was found

```
If DSLogin.Tables("StudentInfo"). _
    Rows.Count = 0 Then
```

If one wasn't, we display an error message to the student:

```
lblMessage.Text = "The student name and password " _
    & "were not found. Please try again."
```

Otherwise, we store the ID of the student into a Session variable so that it is available for other pages in the site:

```
Session("StudentID") = DSLogin.Tables("StudentInfo"). _
    Rows(0).Item("StudentID")
```

We also store the student's name

```
Session("StudentName") = txtStudentName.Text
```

and send the student to the Home Room page:

```
Response.Redirect("./home_room.aspx")
```

Home Room ASP.NET Page

Home_Room.aspx

The code on the Home Room page displays a list of all the courses that the student is enrolled in. Within the body of the page, we define a Label control that will display title text and the student's name:

```
<asp:Label
    id="lblTitle"
    BorderWidth="7px"
    BorderStyle=7
    Width="90%"
    Font-Size="25pt"
    Font-Name="Tahoma"
    runat="server"
/>
```

Another Label will display different text for whether the student has enrolled in any courses or not:

```
<asp:Label
    id="lblMessage"
    Font-Size="12pt"
    Font-Name="Tahoma"
    Font-Bold="True"
    runat="server"
/>
```

Next we define a DropDownList that will contain all the courses that the student is enrolled in:

```
<asp:dropdownlist
    id="ddlCoursesEnrolled"
    runat=server
    DataTextField="CourseName"
    DataValueField="CourseID">
</asp:dropdownlist>
```

The other control on the page is a Button that takes the visitor to the Courses page when clicked

```
<asp:button
    id="butOK"
    text="  OK  "
    Type="Submit"
    OnClick="SubmitBtn_Click"
    runat="server"
/>
```

The code on the page is contained within two code blocks. The first fires when the page is loaded.

```
Sub Page_Load(ByVal Sender as Object, ByVal E as EventArgs)
    If Len(Session("StudentID")) = 0 Then
        Response.Redirect("./index.aspx")
    End If
    If Not IsPostBack Then
        Dim DBConn as OleDbConnection
        Dim DBCommand As OleDbDataAdapter
        Dim DSPageData as New DataSet
        lblTitle.Text = "<center>Home Room for " _
            & Session("StudentName") & "</center>"
DBConn = New OleDbConnection("Provider=sqloledb;" _
    & "server=localhost;" _
    & "Initial Catalog=INETC9;" _
    & "User Id=sa;" _
    & "Password=yourpassword;")
DBCommand = New OleDbDataAdapter _
            ("Select Courses.CourseID, CourseName From Courses " _
```

```
            & "Inner Join StudentsCourses on " _
            & "Courses.CourseID = StudentsCourses.CourseID " _
            & "Where StudentID = " & Session("StudentID") _
            , DBConn)
        DBCommand.Fill(DSPageData, _
            "CoursesEnrolled")
        If DSPageData.Tables("CoursesEnrolled").Rows.Count = 0 Then
            lblMessage.Text = "You are not currently " _
                & "enrolled in any courses."
            ddlCoursesEnrolled.Visible = False
            butOK.Visible = False
        Else
            lblMessage.Text = "Select the course that you would " _
                & "like to work with."
            ddlCoursesEnrolled.DataSource = _
                DSPageData.Tables("CoursesEnrolled").DefaultView
            ddlCoursesEnrolled.DataBind()
        End If
    End If
End Sub
```

First, we check to see if the student has logged into the site:

```
If Len(Session("StudentID")) = 0 Then
```

If they haven't, they are sent to do so:

```
Response.Redirect("./index.aspx")
```

The rest of the code in this procedure should run only when the page is first loaded

```
If Not IsPostBack Then
```

We will need data objects:

```
Dim DBConn as OleDbConnection
Dim DBCommand As OleDbDataAdapter
Dim DSPageData as New DataSet
```

We start by placing fixed text and the student's name into the title Label of the page:

```
lblTitle.Text = "<center>Home Room for " _
    & Session("StudentName") & "</center>"
```

Next, we connect to the database:

```
DBConn = New OleDbConnection("Provider=sqloledb;" _
    & "server=localhost;" _
    & "Initial Catalog=INETC9;" _
    & "User Id=sa;" _
    & "Password=yourpassword;")
```

And we retrieve all the courses the student is enrolled in by linking the Courses table with the StudentsCourses table

```
DBCommand = New OleDbDataAdapter _
    ("Select Courses.CourseID, CourseName From Courses " _
    & "Inner Join StudentsCourses on " _
    & "Courses.CourseID = StudentsCourses.CourseID " _
    & "Where StudentID = " & Session("StudentID") _
    , DBConn)
```

into a DataSet object table called CoursesEnrolled:

```
DBCommand.Fill(DSPageData, _
    "CoursesEnrolled")
```

We then check to see if any records were returned

```
If DSPageData.Tables("CoursesEnrolled").Rows.Count = 0 Then
```

If none were returned, that means the visitor is not currently enrolled in any courses. So we display such a message:

```
lblMessage.Text = "You are not currently " _
    & "enrolled in any courses."
```

And we hide the DropDownList as well as the Button control:

```
ddlCoursesEnrolled.Visible = False
butOK.Visible = False
```

Otherwise, we display a different error message:

```
lblMessage.Text = "Select the course that you would " _
    & "like to work with."
```

And we bind the DropDownList to the DataSet object table:

```
ddlCoursesEnrolled.DataSource = _
    DSPageData.Tables("CoursesEnrolled").DefaultView
ddlCoursesEnrolled.DataBind()
```

The other procedure on the page fires when the student clicks the OK button.

```
Sub SubmitBtn_Click(Sender As Object, E As EventArgs)
    Session("CourseID") = ddlCoursesEnrolled.SelectedItem.Value
    Response.Redirect("./course.aspx")
End Sub
```

It stores the ID of the course selected by the student

```
Session("CourseID") = ddlCoursesEnrolled.SelectedItem.Value
```

and sends the student to the Course page:

```
Response.Redirect("./course.aspx")
```

Enroll ASP.NET Page

Enroll.aspx

The Enroll page displays a list of all the courses and allows the student to enroll in a course if they are not already enrolled in it. Within the body of the page, we define a Label control that will contain the name of the student and the title of the page:

```
<asp:Label
    id="lblTitle"
    BorderWidth="7px"
    BorderStyle=7
    Width="90%"
    Font-Size="25pt"
    Font-Name="Tahoma"
    runat="server"
/>
```

Another Label control that displays page instructions is defined

```
<asp:Label
    id="lblMessage"
    Font-Size="12pt"
    Font-Name="Tahoma"
```

```
        Font-Bold="True"
        runat="server"
        Text="Select the course you wish to enroll in."
/>
```

Next, we define a DropDownList, which will display all the courses

```
<asp:dropdownlist
    id="ddlCourses"
    runat=server
    DataTextField="CourseFullName"
    DataValueField="CourseID">
</asp:dropdownlist>
```

and a Button control that allows the student to enroll in a course:

```
<asp:button
    id="butOK"
    text="  OK  "
    Type="Submit"
    OnClick="SubmitBtn_Click"
    runat="server"
/>
```

The code on the page is contained within two procedures. The first procedure fires when the page is first loaded. It populates the DropDownList control.

```
Sub Page_Load(ByVal Sender as Object, ByVal E as EventArgs)
    If Len(Session("StudentID")) = 0 Then
        Response.Redirect("./index.aspx")
    End If
    If Not IsPostBack Then
        Dim DBConn as OleDbConnection
        Dim DBCommand As OleDbDataAdapter
        Dim DSPageData as New DataSet
        lblTitle.Text = "<center>Enroll - " _
            & Session("StudentName") & "</center>"
DBConn = New OleDbConnection("Provider=sqloledb;" _
    & "server=localhost;" _
    & "Initial Catalog=INETC9;" _
    & "User Id=sa;" _
    & "Password=yourpassword;")
DBCommand = New OleDbDataAdapter _
```

```
            ("Select CourseID, CourseName + ' - ' " _
            & " + CourseDescription as CourseFullName " _
            & "From Courses " _
            & "Order By CourseName", DBConn)
        DBCommand.Fill(DSPageData, _
            "Courses")
        ddlCourses.DataSource = _
            DSPageData.Tables("Courses").DefaultView
        ddlCourses.DataBind()
    End If
End Sub
```

The student should be at this page only if they have logged in:

```
If Len(Session("StudentID")) = 0 Then
```

If they haven't, they are sent to do so:

```
Response.Redirect("./index.aspx")
```

The rest of the code runs only when the page is first loaded, not when the form on the page is posted back:

```
If Not IsPostBack Then
```

If this is the first run, we need data objects:

```
Dim DBConn as OleDbConnection
Dim DBCommand As OleDbDataAdapter
Dim DSPageData as New DataSet
```

We start by placing fixed text and the student's name into the title Label control:

```
lblTitle.Text = "<center>Enroll - " _
    & Session("StudentName") & "</center>"
```

Then, we connect to the database:

```
DBConn = New OleDbConnection("Provider=sqloledb;" _
    & "server=localhost;" _
    & "Initial Catalog=INETC9;" _
    & "User Id=sa;" _
    & "Password=yourpassword;")
```

We then retrieve the course list

```
DBCommand = New OleDbDataAdapter _
    ("Select CourseID, CourseName + ' - ' " _
    & " + CourseDescription as CourseFullName " _
    & "From Courses " _
    & "Order By CourseName", DBConn)
DBCommand.Fill(DSPageData, _
    "Courses")
```

which is placed into the DropDownList control:

```
ddlCourses.DataSource = _
    DSPageData.Tables("Courses").DefaultView
ddlCourses.DataBind()
```

The other procedure on the page fires when the Button control is clicked. It enrolls the student in the course selected.

```
Sub SubmitBtn_Click(Sender As Object, E As EventArgs)
    Dim DBConn as OleDbConnection
    Dim DBCommand As OleDbDataAdapter
    Dim DSPageData as New DataSet
    Dim DBInsert As New OleDbCommand
    DBConn = New OleDbConnection("Provider=sqloledb;" _
        & "server=localhost;" _
        & "Initial Catalog=INETC9;" _
        & "User Id=sa;" _
        & "Password=yourpassword;")
    DBCommand = New OleDbDataAdapter _
        ("Select StudentCourseID from StudentsCourses " _
        & "Where StudentID = " & Session("StudentID") _
        & " and CourseID = " & ddlCourses.SelectedItem.Value _
        , DBConn)
    DBCommand.Fill(DSPageData, _
        "StudentCourse")
    If DSPageData.Tables("StudentCourse").Rows.Count = 0 Then
        DBInsert.CommandText = "Insert Into StudentsCourses " _
            & "(StudentID, CourseID, DateEnrolled) Values (" _
            & Session("StudentID") & ", " _
            & ddlCourses.SelectedItem.Value & ", " _
            & "GetDate())"
        DBInsert.Connection = DBConn
```

```
        DBInsert.Connection.Open
        DBInsert.ExecuteNonQuery()
    End If
    Response.Redirect("./home_room.aspx")
End Sub
```

The procedure requires data objects:

```
Dim DBConn as OleDbConnection
Dim DBCommand As OleDbDataAdapter
Dim DSPageData as New DataSet
Dim DBInsert As New OleDbCommand
```

We start by connecting to our SQL Server database:

```
DBConn = New OleDbConnection("Provider=sqloledb;" _
    & "server=localhost;" _
    & "Initial Catalog=INETC9;" _
    & "User Id=sa;" _
    & "Password=yourpassword;")
```

Next, we see if the student is already enrolled in this course:

```
DBCommand = New OleDbDataAdapter _
    ("Select StudentCourseID from StudentsCourses " _
    & "Where StudentID = " & Session("StudentID") _
    & " and CourseID = " & ddlCourses.SelectedItem.Value _
    , DBConn)
DBCommand.Fill(DSPageData, _
    "StudentCourse")
```

If they are, we will have a record in our DataSet object table. Otherwise, no records are returned

```
If DSPageData.Tables("StudentCourse").Rows.Count = 0 Then
```

And we enroll the student in the course:

```
DBInsert.CommandText = "Insert Into StudentsCourses " _
    & "(StudentID, CourseID, DateEnrolled) Values (" _
    & Session("StudentID") & ", " _
    & ddlCourses.SelectedItem.Value & ", " _
    & "GetDate())"
DBInsert.Connection = DBConn
DBInsert.Connection.Open
DBInsert.ExecuteNonQuery()
```

Finally, we send the student back to the Home Room page:

```
Response.Redirect("./home_room.aspx")
```

Course ASP.NET Page

Course.aspx

The code on the Course page allows the student to select a section that they wish to view the content of or to take a quiz for. The page also displays the results of all quizzes taken by this student in this course.

Within the body of the page, we define a Label control that will display the title of the course:

```
<asp:Label
    id="lblTitle"
    BorderWidth="7px"
    BorderStyle=7
    Width="90%"
    Font-Size="25pt"
    Font-Name="Tahoma"
    runat="server"
/>
```

Next, we define a DropDownList that the student can use to select a Section for which they wish to view content:

```
<asp:dropdownlist
    id="ddlSections1"
    runat=server
    DataTextField="SectionName"
    DataValueField="CourseSectionID">
</asp:dropdownlist>
```

That is followed by a Button control that takes the visitor to the Course Content page:

```
<asp:button
    id="butOKContent"
    text="  OK  "
    Type="Submit"
    OnClick="SubmitBtnContent_Click"
    runat="server"
/>
```

We also need a DropDownList so that the student can select a quiz they want to take

```
<asp:dropdownlist
    id="ddlSections2"
    runat=server
    DataTextField="SectionName"
    DataValueField="CourseSectionID">
</asp:dropdownlist>
```

and a Button to take them to that page:

```
<asp:button
    id="butOKQuiz"
    text="  OK  "
    Type="Submit"
    OnClick="SubmitBtnQuiz_Click"
    runat="server"
/>
```

One more control on the page, a DataGrid control, is defined to display the results of the quizzes taken by the student in this course:

```
<asp:DataGrid id="dgQuizResults" runat="server"
    Width="90%"
    BackColor="beige"
    AlternatingItemStyle-BackColor="cornsilk"
    BorderColor="black"
    CellPadding=3
    CellSpacing="0"
    Font-Name="Trebuchet MS"
    Font-Size="8pt"
    ForeColor="Black"
    HeaderStyle-BackColor="burlywood"
    HeaderStyle-Font-Bold="True"
/>
```

The code on the page is defined within three procedures. The first procedure fires when the student loads the page. It populates the DropDownList controls and the DataGrid control.

```
Sub Page_Load(ByVal Sender as Object, ByVal E as EventArgs)
    If Len(Session("StudentID")) = 0 Then
        Response.Redirect("./index.aspx")
```

```
End If
If Len(Session("CourseID")) = 0 Then
    Response.Redirect("./home_room.aspx")
End If
If Not IsPostBack Then
    Dim DBConn as OleDbConnection
    Dim DBCommand As OleDbDataAdapter
    Dim DSPageData as New DataSet
    DBConn = New OleDbConnection("Provider=sqloledb;" _
        & "server=localhost;" _
        & "Initial Catalog=INETC9;" _
        & "User Id=sa;" _
        & "Password=yourpassword;")
    DBCommand = New OleDbDataAdapter _
        ("Select CourseName from Courses Where " _
        & "CourseID = " & Session("CourseID") _
        , DBConn)
    DBCommand.Fill(DSPageData, _
        "CourseName")
    lblTitle.Text = "<center>Course " _
        & DSPageData.Tables("CourseName"). _
        Rows(0).Item("CourseName") _
        & "</center>"
    DBCommand = New OleDbDataAdapter _
        ("Select CourseSectionID, SectionName from " _
        & "CourseSections Where " _
        & "CourseID = " & Session("CourseID") _
        , DBConn)
    DBCommand.Fill(DSPageData, _
        "CourseSections")
    ddlSections1.DataSource = _
        DSPageData.Tables("CourseSections").DefaultView
    ddlSections1.DataBind()
    ddlSections2.DataSource = _
        DSPageData.Tables("CourseSections").DefaultView
    ddlSections2.DataBind()
    DBCommand = New OleDbDataAdapter _
        ("Select SectionName as [Section], Score, " _
        & "TotalQuestions as [Total Questions], " _
        & "Convert(varchar(12),DateTaken,107) " _
        & "as [Date Taken] From CourseSections " _
        & "Inner Join QuizResults On " _
        & "QuizResults.CourseSectionID = " _
        & "CourseSections.CourseSectionID Where StudentID = " _
```

```
            & Session("StudentID") & " And " _
            & "QuizResults.CourseSectionID In ((" _
            & "Select CourseSectionID from CourseSections where " _
            & "CourseID = " & Session("CourseID") & "))" _
            , DBConn)
        DBCommand.Fill(DSPageData, _
            "QuizResults")
        dgQuizResults.DataSource = _
            DSPageData.Tables("QuizResults").DefaultView
        dgQuizResults.DataBind()
    End If
End Sub
```

First, we make sure the student has logged in to the site:

```
If Len(Session("StudentID")) = 0 Then
```

If they haven't, they are sent to do so:

```
Response.Redirect("./index.aspx")
```

We also make sure that they selected a course before coming to this page:

```
If Len(Session("CourseID")) = 0 Then
```

If they haven't, they are taken to the Home Room page:

```
Response.Redirect("./home_room.aspx")
```

The rest of the code on the page should run only the first time the page is loaded

```
If Not IsPostBack Then
```

We need data objects:

```
Dim DBConn as OleDbConnection
Dim DBCommand As OleDbDataAdapter
Dim DSPageData as New DataSet
```

We start by connecting to the database:

```
DBConn = New OleDbConnection("Provider=sqloledb;" _
    & "server=localhost;" _
    & "Initial Catalog=INETC9;" _
```

```
    & "User Id=sa;" _
    & "Password=yourpassword;")
```

We then retrieve the name of the current course selected by the student

```
DBCommand = New OleDbDataAdapter _
    ("Select CourseName from Courses Where " _
    & "CourseID = " & Session("CourseID") _
    , DBConn)
```

and place it in a DataSet object table:

```
DBCommand.Fill(DSPageData, _
    "CourseName")
```

We then use the name of the course with fixed text for the title of the page:

```
lblTitle.Text = "<center>Course " _
    & DSPageData.Tables("CourseName"). _
    Rows(0).Item("CourseName") _
    & "</center>"
```

Next, we retrieve all the sections that are in the current course:

```
DBCommand = New OleDbDataAdapter _
    ("Select CourseSectionID, SectionName from " _
    & "CourseSections Where " _
    & "CourseID = " & Session("CourseID") _
    , DBConn)
DBCommand.Fill(DSPageData, _
    "CourseSections")
```

That section list is displayed in the first DropDownList control,

```
ddlSections1.DataSource = _
    DSPageData.Tables("CourseSections").DefaultView
ddlSections1.DataBind()
```

as well as in the second DropDownList control:

```
ddlSections2.DataSource = _
    DSPageData.Tables("CourseSections").DefaultView
ddlSections2.DataBind()
```

Next, we need to retrieve all the quiz results for the quizzes the student has taken in the current course. Note that we combine data from the CourseSections table and the QuizResults table. Also note the use of a subquery to limit the records returned to only those that are from sections in the current course:

```
DBCommand = New OleDbDataAdapter _
    ("Select SectionName as [Section], Score, " _
    & "TotalQuestions as [Total Questions], " _
    & "Convert(varchar(12),DateTaken,107) " _
    & "as [Date Taken] From CourseSections " _
    & "Inner Join QuizResults On " _
    & "QuizResults.CourseSectionID = " _
    & "CourseSections.CourseSectionID Where StudentID = " _
    & Session("StudentID") & " And " _
    & "QuizResults.CourseSectionID In ((" _
    & "Select CourseSectionID from CourseSections where " _
    & "CourseID = " & Session("CourseID") & "))" _
    , DBConn)
DBCommand.Fill(DSPageData, _
    "QuizResults")
```

Our DataGrid control is bound to the return of that query:

```
dgQuizResults.DataSource = _
    DSPageData.Tables("QuizResults").DefaultView
dgQuizResults.DataBind()
```

The next procedure fires when the content Button control is clicked.

```
Sub SubmitBtnContent_Click(Sender As Object, E As EventArgs)
    Session("CourseSectionID") = ddlSections1.SelectedItem.Value
    Response.Redirect("./course_content.aspx")
End Sub
```

We store the sections of the course selected by the student

```
Session("CourseSectionID") = ddlSections1.SelectedItem.Value
```

and send them to the Course Content page:

```
Response.Redirect("./course_content.aspx")
```

The last procedure on this page fires when the quiz Button control is clicked.

```
Sub SubmitBtnQuiz_Click(Sender As Object, E As EventArgs)
    Session("CourseSectionID") = ddlSections2.SelectedItem.Value
    Response.Redirect("./course_quiz.aspx")
End Sub
```

Again, we store the ID of the current section:

```
Session("CourseSectionID") = ddlSections2.SelectedItem.Value
```

But this time we send the student to the quiz page:

```
Response.Redirect("./course_quiz.aspx")
```

Course Content ASP.NET Page

Course_Content.aspx

The code on the Course Content page displays the content of the section one page at a time to the student. Within the body of the page, we define a Label that will display the name of the section

```
<asp:Label
    id="lblTitle"
    BorderWidth="7px"
    BorderStyle=7
    Width="90%"
    Font-Size="25pt"
    Font-Name="Tahoma"
    runat="server"
/>
```

and a second Label control that displays the section content:

```
<asp:Label
    id="lblMessage"
    Font-Size="12pt"
    Font-Name="Tahoma"
    Font-Bold="True"
    runat="server"
/>
```

The other control on the page is a Button that allows the student to move on to the next page of content:

```
<asp:button
    id="butOK"
    text="  OK  "
    Type="Submit"
    OnClick="SubmitBtn_Click"
    runat="server"
/>
```

The code on the page is contained within two procedures. The first procedure fires when the page is loaded. It makes sure the page was entered correctly and displays the first page of content for the section selected by the student.

```
Sub Page_Load(ByVal Sender as Object, ByVal E as EventArgs)
    If Len(Session("StudentID")) = 0 Then
        Response.Redirect("./index.aspx")
    End If
    If Len(Session("CourseSectionID")) = 0 Then
        Response.Redirect("./home_room.aspx")
    End If
    If Not IsPostBack Then
        Dim DBConn as OleDbConnection
        Dim DBCommand As OleDbDataAdapter
        Dim DSPageData as New DataSet
        DBConn = New OleDbConnection("Provider=sqloledb;" _
            & "server=localhost;" _
            & "Initial Catalog=INETC9;" _
            & "User Id=sa;" _
            & "Password=yourpassword;")
        DBCommand = New OleDbDataAdapter _
            ("Select SectionName from CourseSections Where " _
            & "CourseSectionID = " & Session("CourseSectionID") _
            , DBConn)
        DBCommand.Fill(DSPageData, _
            "SectionName")
        lblTitle.Text = "<center>Section " _
            & DSPageData.Tables("SectionName"). _
            Rows(0).Item("SectionName") _
            & "</center>"
        DBCommand = New OleDbDataAdapter _
```

```
            ("Select SectionContentID, SectionContentTitle, " _
            & "SectionContent from SectionContents Where " _
            & "SectionContentID = (Select Min(SectionContentID) " _
            & "From SectionContents Where CourseSectionID = " _
            & Session("CourseSectionID") & ")", DBConn)
        DBCommand.Fill(DSPageData, _
            "SectionContent")
        Session("CurrentSectionContentID") = _
            DSPageData.Tables("SectionContent"). _
            Rows(0).Item("SectionContentID")
        lblMessage.Text = DSPageData.Tables("SectionContent"). _
            Rows(0).Item("SectionContentTitle") _
            & "<br><br>" _
            & DSPageData.Tables("SectionContent"). _
            Rows(0).Item("SectionContent")
    End If
End Sub
```

We start by making sure the student has logged in, and if they haven't, we send them to do so:

```
If Len(Session("StudentID")) = 0 Then
    Response.Redirect("./index.aspx")
End If
```

Then we check to see if the student entered this page by first selecting a section:

```
If Len(Session("CourseSectionID")) = 0 Then
```

If not, they are sent back to the Home Room page:

```
Response.Redirect("./home_room.aspx")
```

The rest of the code fires only when the page is first loaded, not when the button is clicked

```
If Not IsPostBack Then
```

If that is the case, we need data objects:

```
Dim DBConn as OleDbConnection
Dim DBCommand As OleDbDataAdapter
Dim DSPageData as New DataSet
```

We start by connecting to the database:

```
DBConn = New OleDbConnection("Provider=sqloledb;" _
    & "server=localhost;" _
    & "Initial Catalog=INETC9;" _
    & "User Id=sa;" _
    & "Password=yourpassword;")
```

Next, we retrieve the title of the section

```
DBCommand = New OleDbDataAdapter _
    ("Select SectionName from CourseSections Where " _
    & "CourseSectionID = " & Session("CourseSectionID") _
    , DBConn)
DBCommand.Fill(DSPageData, _
    "SectionName")
```

and place it with fixed text into the title Label:

```
lblTitle.Text = "<center>Section " _
    & DSPageData.Tables("SectionName"). _
    Rows(0).Item("SectionName") _
    & "</center>"
```

Next, we need to retrieve the first content page for this section:

```
DBCommand = New OleDbDataAdapter _
    ("Select SectionContentID, SectionContentTitle, " _
    & "SectionContent from SectionContents Where " _
    & "SectionContentID = (Select Min(SectionContentID) " _
    & "From SectionContents Where CourseSectionID = " _
    & Session("CourseSectionID") & ")", DBConn)
DBCommand.Fill(DSPageData, _
    "SectionContent")
```

We store the ID of the content so that we can refer to it when we need to move on to the next page of content:

```
Session("CurrentSectionContentID") = _
    DSPageData.Tables("SectionContent"). _
    Rows(0).Item("SectionContentID")
```

And we place the content text into the other Label control:

```
lblMessage.Text = DSPageData.Tables("SectionContent"). _
    Rows(0).Item("SectionContentTitle") _
    & "<br><br>" _
    & DSPageData.Tables("SectionContent"). _
    Rows(0).Item("SectionContent")
```

The other procedure fires when the button on the page is clicked. It displays the next page of content.

```
Sub SubmitBtn_Click(Sender As Object, E As EventArgs)
    Dim DBConn as OleDbConnection
    Dim DBCommand As OleDbDataAdapter
    Dim DSPageData as New DataSet
    DBConn = New OleDbConnection("Provider=sqloledb;" _
        & "server=localhost;" _
        & "Initial Catalog=INETC9;" _
        & "User Id=sa;" _
        & "Password=yourpassword;")
    DBCommand = New OleDbDataAdapter _
        ("Select SectionContentID, SectionContentTitle, " _
        & "SectionContent from SectionContents Where " _
        & "SectionContentID = (Select Min(SectionContentID) " _
        & "From SectionContents Where SectionContentID > " _
        & Session("CurrentSectionContentID") _
        & " and CourseSectionID = " _
        & Session("CourseSectionID") & ")", DBConn)
    DBCommand.Fill(DSPageData, _
        "SectionContent")
    If DSPageData.Tables("SectionContent").Rows.Count = 0 Then
        Response.Redirect("./course.aspx")
    Else
        Session("CurrentSectionContentID") = _
            DSPageData.Tables("SectionContent"). _
            Rows(0).Item("SectionContentID")
        lblMessage.Text = DSPageData.Tables("SectionContent"). _
            Rows(0).Item("SectionContentTitle") _
            & "<br><br>" _
            & DSPageData.Tables("SectionContent"). _
            Rows(0).Item("SectionContent")
    End If
End Sub
```

We will need data objects:

```
Dim DBConn as OleDbConnection
Dim DBCommand As OleDbDataAdapter
Dim DSPageData as New DataSet
```

We start by connecting to the database:

```
DBConn = New OleDbConnection("Provider=sqloledb;" _
    & "server=localhost;" _
    & "Initial Catalog=INETC9;" _
    & "User Id=sa;" _
    & "Password=yourpassword;")
```

Next, we retrieve the next content page in terms of the ID of the last content page that we retrieved

```
DBCommand = New OleDbDataAdapter _
    ("Select SectionContentID, SectionContentTitle, " _
    & "SectionContent from SectionContents Where " _
    & "SectionContentID = (Select Min(SectionContentID) " _
    & "From SectionContents Where SectionContentID > " _
    & Session("CurrentSectionContentID") _
    & " and CourseSectionID = " _
    & Session("CourseSectionID") & ")", DBConn)
DBCommand.Fill(DSPageData, _
    "SectionContent")
```

We need to make sure that we are not done with the content of this section:

```
If DSPageData.Tables("SectionContent").Rows.Count = 0 Then
```

If we are, we send the student back to the course page:

```
Response.Redirect("./course.aspx")
```

Otherwise, we store the ID of the content record retrieved

```
Session("CurrentSectionContentID") = _
    DSPageData.Tables("SectionContent"). _
    Rows(0).Item("SectionContentID")
```

and display the text for that page:

```
lblMessage.Text = DSPageData.Tables("SectionContent"). _
    Rows(0).Item("SectionContentTitle") _
    & "<br><br>" _
    & DSPageData.Tables("SectionContent"). _
    Rows(0).Item("SectionContent")
```

Course Quiz ASP.NET Page

Course_Quiz.aspx

The code on the Course Quiz page displays the quiz for the section selected by the student. It also scores the quiz. The implementation of the page is made more complex because we don't know how many questions will be used from quiz to quiz. Therefore, we have to dynamically add controls to a Panel to allow for an unknown number of questions.

Within the body of the page, we define a Label control that will display the name of the section:

```
<asp:Label
    id="lblTitle"
    BorderWidth="7px"
    BorderStyle=7
    Width="90%"
    Font-Size="25pt"
    Font-Name="Tahoma"
    runat="server"
/>
```

A second Label control displays instructional text:

```
<asp:Label
    id="lblMessage"
    Font-Size="12pt"
    Font-Name="Tahoma"
    Font-Bold="True"
    Text="Answer each question before pressing the OK button."
    runat="server"
/>
```

Next, we define a Panel control where we will place the questions and answers dynamically when the page is loaded

```
<asp:Panel
    id="pnlQuestions"
```

```
    Width="90%"
    runat="server"
>
</asp:Panel>
```

One final control on the page is a Button control that, when clicked, submits the quiz for scoring:

```
<asp:button
    id="butOK"
    text="  OK  "
    Type="Submit"
    OnClick="SubmitBtn_Click"
    runat="server"
/>
```

The code on the page is contained within two procedures. The first procedure fires when the page is loaded. The procedure dynamically displays controls on the page for each question on the quiz.

```
Sub Page_Load(ByVal Sender as Object, ByVal E as EventArgs)
    If Len(Session("StudentID")) = 0 Then
        Response.Redirect("./index.aspx")
    End If
    If Len(Session("CourseSectionID")) = 0 Then
        Response.Redirect("./home_room.aspx")
    End If
    Dim DBConn as OleDbConnection
    Dim DBCommand As OleDbDataAdapter
    Dim DSPageData as New DataSet
    Dim I as Integer
    Dim J as Integer
    Dim TempID as String
    DBConn = New OleDbConnection("Provider=sqloledb;" _
        & "server=localhost;" _
        & "Initial Catalog=INETC9;" _
        & "User Id=sa;" _
        & "Password=yourpassword;")
    DBCommand = New OleDbDataAdapter _
        ("Select SectionName from CourseSections Where " _
        & "CourseSectionID = " & Session("CourseSectionID") _
        , DBConn)
```

```
    DBCommand.Fill(DSPageData, _
        "SectionName")
    lblTitle.Text = "<center>Section " _
        & DSPageData.Tables("SectionName"). _
        Rows(0).Item("SectionName") _
        & "</center>"
    DBCommand = New OleDbDataAdapter _
        ("Select SectionQuestionID, QuestionText " _
        & "From SectionQuestions Where CourseSectionID = " _
        & Session("CourseSectionID"), DBConn)
    DBCommand.Fill(DSPageData, _
        "QuizQuestions")
    For I = 0 to DSPageData.Tables("QuizQuestions"). _
        Rows.Count - 1
        Dim lcHTML = New LiteralControl
        lcHTML.Text = "<b>" _
        & DSPageData.Tables("QuizQuestions"). _
        Rows(I).Item("QuestionText") & "</b><br>"
        pnlQuestions.Controls.Add(lcHTML)
        Dim MyDDL = New DropDownList
        TempID = DSPageData.Tables("QuizQuestions"). _
        Rows(I).Item("SectionQuestionID")
        MyDDL.ID = "Q" & TempID
        DBCommand = New OleDbDataAdapter _
            ("Select AnswerText " _
            & "From QuestionAnswers Where SectionQuestionID = " _
            & TempID, DBConn)
        DBCommand.Fill(DSPageData, _
            TempID)
        For J = 0 to DSPageData.Tables(TempID). _
            Rows.Count - 1
            Dim MyItem = New ListItem
            MyItem.Text = DSPageData.Tables(TempID). _
            Rows(J).Item("AnswerText")
            MyDDL.Items.Add(MyItem)
        Next
        pnlQuestions.Controls.Add(MyDDL)
        Dim lcHTML2 = New LiteralControl
        lcHTML2.Text = "<br><br>"
        pnlQuestions.Controls.Add(lcHTML2)
    Next
End Sub
```

First, we make sure the student has logged in and send them to do so if they haven't

```
If Len(Session("StudentID")) = 0 Then
    Response.Redirect("./index.aspx")
End If
```

Then we make sure the student selected a section to take a quiz on:

```
If Len(Session("CourseSectionID")) = 0 Then
```

If they didn't, we send them to the Home Room page:

```
Response.Redirect("./home_room.aspx")
```

Otherwise, we can define needed data objects:

```
Dim DBConn as OleDbConnection
Dim DBCommand As OleDbDataAdapter
Dim DSPageData as New DataSet
```

We also need a couple of variables to allow us to iterate through loops

```
Dim I as Integer
Dim J as Integer
```

and a variable to store a temporary ID:

```
Dim TempID as String
```

Next, we connect to our database:

```
DBConn = New OleDbConnection("Provider=sqloledb;" _
    & "server=localhost;" _
    & "Initial Catalog=INETC9;" _
    & "User Id=sa;" _
    & "Password=yourpassword;")
```

We then retrieve the name of the section

```
DBCommand = New OleDbDataAdapter _
    ("Select SectionName from CourseSections Where " _
    & "CourseSectionID = " & Session("CourseSectionID") _
    , DBConn)
```

and place it in a DataSet object:

```
DBCommand.Fill(DSPageData, _
    "SectionName")
```

The text of the title Label is set to fixed text and the name of the section:

```
lblTitle.Text = "<center>Section " _
    & DSPageData.Tables("SectionName"). _
    Rows(0).Item("SectionName") _
    & "</center>"
```

Next, we retrieve all the questions on the quiz:

```
DBCommand = New OleDbDataAdapter _
    ("Select SectionQuestionID, QuestionText " _
    & "From SectionQuestions Where CourseSectionID = " _
    & Session("CourseSectionID"), DBConn)
DBCommand.Fill(DSPageData, _
    "QuizQuestions")
```

We then enter an outer loop that allows us to process each question on the quiz:

```
For I = 0 to DSPageData.Tables("QuizQuestions"). _
    Rows.Count - 1
```

We need a LiteralControl object so that we can place HTML text onto our Panel control:

```
Dim lcHTML = New LiteralControl
```

We place the text of the question, as well as HTML tags, into that object

```
lcHTML.Text = "<b>" _
    & DSPageData.Tables("QuizQuestions"). _
    Rows(I).Item("QuestionText") & "</b><br>"
```

and place it on the Panel control:

```
pnlQuestions.Controls.Add(lcHTML)
```

We also need to create a DropDownList that will contain the possible answers to the question:

```
Dim MyDDL = New DropDownList
```

We then store the ID of the question

```
TempID = DSPageData.Tables("QuizQuestions"). _
    Rows(I).Item("SectionQuestionID")
```

and use it with the letter “Q” to name the DropDownList:

```
MyDDL.ID = "Q" & TempID
```

Next, we retrieve all the answers for the current question:

```
DBCommand = New OleDbDataAdapter _
    ("Select AnswerText " _
    & "From QuestionAnswers Where SectionQuestionID = " _
    & TempID, DBConn)
DBCommand.Fill(DSPageData, _
    TempID)
```

Now we can enter our inner loop, which allows us to process each answer for the question:

```
For J = 0 to DSPageData.Tables(TempID). _
    Rows.Count - 1
```

Each answer needs to appear in the DropDownList control. So we need a ListItem object

```
Dim MyItem = New ListItem
```

which will contain the text of the answer:

```
MyItem.Text = DSPageData.Tables(TempID). _
    Rows(J).Item("AnswerText")
```

That object is appended to our DropDownList:

```
MyDDL.Items.Add(MyItem)
```

We then move on to process the next answer:

```
Next
```

After the inner loop is done, the DropDownList control can be added to the Panel control:

```
pnlQuestions.Controls.Add(MyDDL)
```

We then add some space between each question

```
Dim lcHTML2 = New LiteralControl
lcHTML2.Text = "<br><br>"
```

and move on to process the next question:

```
pnlQuestions.Controls.Add(lcHTML2)
```

The other procedure on this page fires when the Button control is clicked. It scores the quiz.

```
Sub SubmitBtn_Click(Sender As Object, E As EventArgs)
    Dim DBConn as OleDbConnection
    Dim DBInsert As New OleDbCommand
    Dim DBCommand As OleDbDataAdapter
    Dim DSPageData as New DataSet
    Dim MyControl as Control
    Dim MyDDL as DropDownList
    Dim TotalCorrect as Integer
    Dim TotalQuestions as Integer
    DBConn = New OleDbConnection("Provider=sqloledb;" _
        & "server=localhost;" _
        & "Initial Catalog=INETC9;" _
        & "User Id=sa;" _
        & "Password=yourpassword;")
    For Each MyControl in pnlQuestions.Controls
       If MyControl.GetType().FullName = _
            "System.Web.UI.WebControls.DropDownList" Then
            TotalQuestions = TotalQuestions + 1
            MyDDL = MyControl
            DBCommand = New OleDbDataAdapter _
                ("Select CorrectAnswer From SectionQuestions Where " _
                & "SectionQuestionID = " & Mid(MyDDL.ID, 2) _
                , DBConn)
            DBCommand.Fill(DSPageData, _
                "CorrectAnswer" & TotalQuestions)
            If MyDDL.SelectedItem.Text = _
                DSPageData.Tables _
                ("CorrectAnswer" & TotalQuestions). _
                Rows(I).Item("CorrectAnswer") Then
```

```
                TotalCorrect = TotalCorrect + 1
            End If
        End If
    Next
    DBInsert.CommandText = "Insert Into QuizResults (" _
        & "StudentID, CourseSectionID, DateTaken, " _
        & "Score, TotalQuestions) values (" _
        & Session("StudentID") & ", " & Session("CourseSectionID") _
        & ", GetDate(), " & TotalCorrect & ", " _
        & TotalQuestions & ")"
    DBInsert.Connection = DBConn
    DBInsert.Connection.Open
    DBInsert.ExecuteNonQuery()
    Response.Redirect("./course.aspx")
End Sub
```

Within this procedure, we will need data objects:

```
Dim DBConn as OleDbConnection
Dim DBInsert As New OleDbCommand
Dim DBCommand As OleDbDataAdapter
Dim DSPageData as New DataSet
```

We also need control objects that will allow us to iterate through all the controls on the Panel:

```
Dim MyControl as Control
Dim MyDDL as DropDownList
```

Two more variables are defined that will tally the number of questions on the quiz and the number correct:

```
Dim TotalCorrect as Integer
Dim TotalQuestions as Integer
```

We start by connecting to the database:

```
DBConn = New OleDbConnection("Provider=sqloledb;" _
    & "server=localhost;" _
    & "Initial Catalog=INETC9;" _
    & "User Id=sa;" _
    & "Password=yourpassword;")
```

We then enter a loop so that we can process each of the controls on the Panel control:

```
For Each MyControl in pnlQuestions.Controls
```

But we only want to process the DropDownList controls on the Panel. These are the controls that contain the answers to the questions. So, we check to see if the control is a DropDownList:

```
If MyControl.GetType().FullName = _
    "System.Web.UI.WebControls.DropDownList" Then
```

If it is, we increment our question counter:

```
TotalQuestions = TotalQuestions + 1
```

We then store the control in a DropDownList control

```
MyDDL = MyControl
```

and use its name to retrieve the correct answer to the question:

```
DBCommand = New OleDbDataAdapter _
    ("Select CorrectAnswer From SectionQuestions Where " _
    & "SectionQuestionID = " & Mid(MyDDL.ID, 2) _
    , DBConn)
DBCommand.Fill(DSPageData, _
    "CorrectAnswer" & TotalQuestions)
```

We then check to see if the answer selected matches the correct answer:

```
If MyDDL.SelectedItem.Text = _
    DSPageData.Tables _
 ("CorrectAnswer" & TotalQuestions). _
 Rows(I).Item("CorrectAnswer") Then
```

If so, we increment our correct answer counter:

```
TotalCorrect = TotalCorrect + 1
```

After the loop, we add the results of the quiz to the database:

```
DBInsert.CommandText = "Insert Into QuizResults (" _
    & "StudentID, CourseSectionID, DateTaken, " _
    & "Score, TotalQuestions) values (" _
    & Session("StudentID") & ", " & Session("CourseSectionID") _
    & ", GetDate(), " & TotalCorrect & ", " _
    & TotalQuestions & ")"
DBInsert.Connection = DBConn
DBInsert.Connection.Open
DBInsert.ExecuteNonQuery()
```

And we send the student back to the Course page:

```
Response.Redirect("./course.aspx")
```

Access Code Changes

C9OnlineCampus.mdb

For this solution to work with Access instead of SQL Server, a few code changes are necessary. First, the connect string is changed on all the pages so that it uses the correct provider and points to the correct database:

```
DBConn = New OleDbConnection("PROVIDER=Microsoft.Jet.OLEDB.4.0;" _
    & "DATA SOURCE=" _
    & Server.MapPath("/INetBook/C9/" _
    & "Access/C9OnlineCampus.mdb;"))
```

On the Course page, we have a query that uses the convert function to format a date. In Access, the format function is used

```
DBCommand = New OleDbDataAdapter _
    ("Select SectionName as [Section], Score, " _
    & "TotalQuestions as [Total Questions], " _
    & "Format(DateTaken,""mmm dd, yyyy"") " _
    & "as [Date Taken] From CourseSections " _
    & "Inner Join QuizResults On " _
    & "QuizResults.CourseSectionID = " _
    & "CourseSections.CourseSectionID Where StudentID = " _
    & Session("StudentID") & " And " _
    & "QuizResults.CourseSectionID In ((" _
    & "Select CourseSectionID from CourseSections where " _
    & "CourseID = " & Session("CourseID") & "))" _
    , DBConn)
```

In SQL Server, when we enrolled a student or added their quiz results to the database, we used the GetDate() function to return the current system date and time. In Access, we use the Now() function:

```
DBInsert.CommandText = "Insert Into StudentsCourses " _
    & "(StudentID, CourseID, DateEnrolled) Values (" _
    & Session("StudentID") & ", " _
    & ddlCourses.SelectedItem.Value & ", " _
    & "Now())"
```

No other code changes are needed.

CHAPTER

10

Adding Specialized Tools to a Company Site

In this chapter, we will look at three tools that would be used to accomplish a task for a specific type of company.

First, we will look at the Build an Object tool. This tool provides the mechanism for a company to create a wizard that the visitor can use to build some object such as a car, computer, or furniture set out of parts. As you will see when we look at this tool, it is adaptable for a variety of situations but will be presented for a specific task.

Then we will look at the Help Desk tool. In a variety of situations you may find that you need to take a visitor through a tree of questions to resolve a problem. The Help Desk tool performs such a task.

The last tool presented in this chapter is the Room Reservation tool. This tool would be used by a company to allow visitors to book a room of some kind or some other location for a period of time. The room's availability is checked against existing reservations, and the visitor is informed whether their reservation can be made.

Build an Object Tool

The Build an Object tool allows visitors to your site to build something complex out of step-by-step selections. This tool could be used on an e-commerce site for a visitor to piece together their wardrobe or to create a gift basket. Or maybe the tool could be used to provide content on an entertainment site. Maybe it would be used to allow visitors to select ingredient types and to come up with concoctions, or it could be used to piece together a band.

Whatever use is employed, the design is changed simply by asking different questions that come from the database and supplying different responses. For the presentation of this tool in this chapter, the tool is used to specify the parts for a computer.

Sample Usage

When the visitor first enters the tool, they see the first item that they can add to the object they are building. Such a page is displayed in Figure 10-1.

As you can see on this figure, we are building a computer. On the first page, you may want to provide some instructions beyond the first question to provide the visitor with an idea of how the tool works.

Here the visitor sees a list of monitors and selects the one that they want to go with their computer. Once they do that, they click Next to see the page displayed in Figure 10-2.

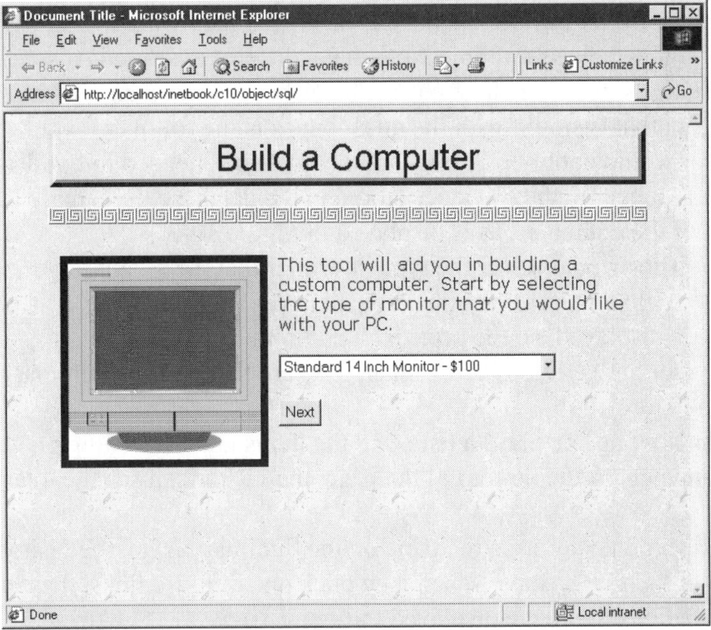

Figure 10-1 *Adding an item to the object*

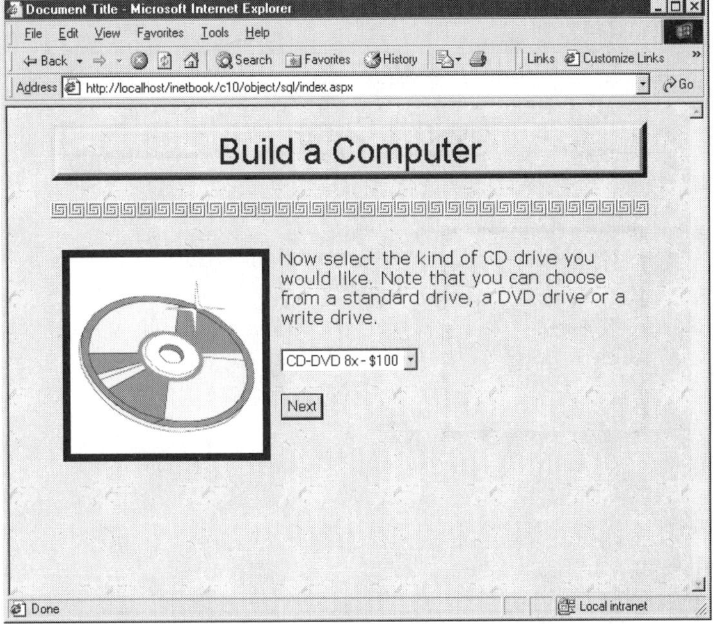

Figure 10-2 *Selecting a CD drive for the computer*

On this page, the visitor selects the CD drive that they want to add to the computer that they are assembling. Note that a different picture is displayed with this item even though it uses the same page. That is because the name of the picture is part of the data that is stored with the question, as is the rollover text of the picture.

The visitor would continue through all the questions needed to build a computer. The questions appear in the sequence stored in the database. Eventually, they get to the last part of the computer, as is displayed in Figure 10-3.

Here the visitor would select the type of printer that they want to go with the computer. Note that the price for the item is displayed. But whatever is placed in the database is displayed, so the price isn't automatically used.

Once the user has selected their printer, they are taken to the Summary page displayed in Figure 10-4.

The Summary page displays a list of all the items that the visitor has selected for their computer. At the bottom of the page, the visitor can see the total price for their purchase.

Using the second column in the table on the Summary page, the visitor can change any of their selections. When they click one of those links, they are taken to the Change Selection page displayed in Figure 10-5.

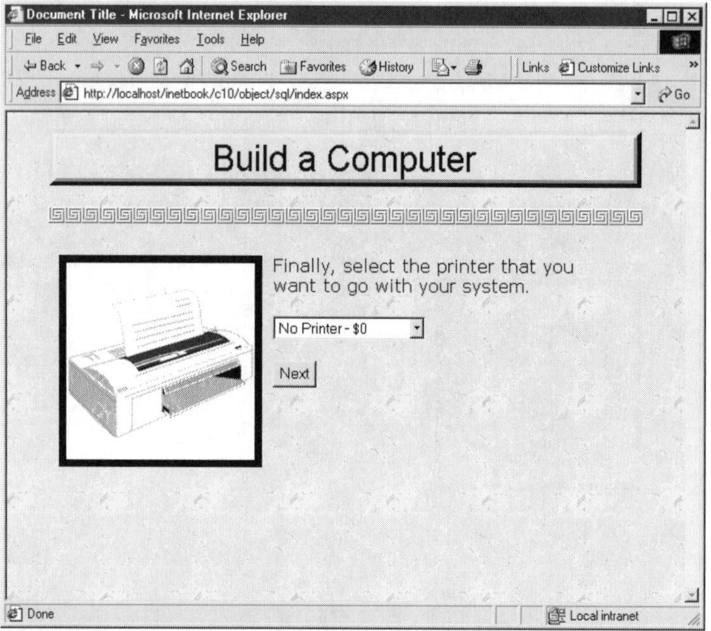

Figure 10-3 *Selecting a printer for the computer*

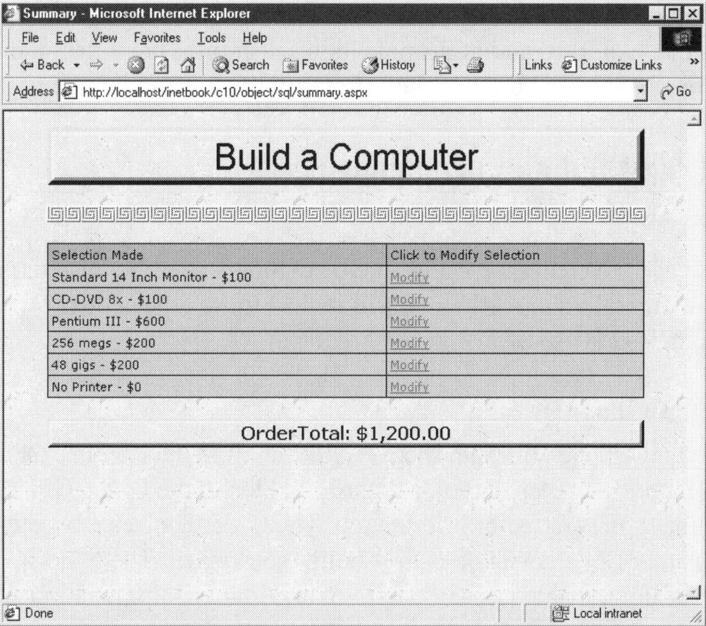

Figure 10-4 *Summary page*

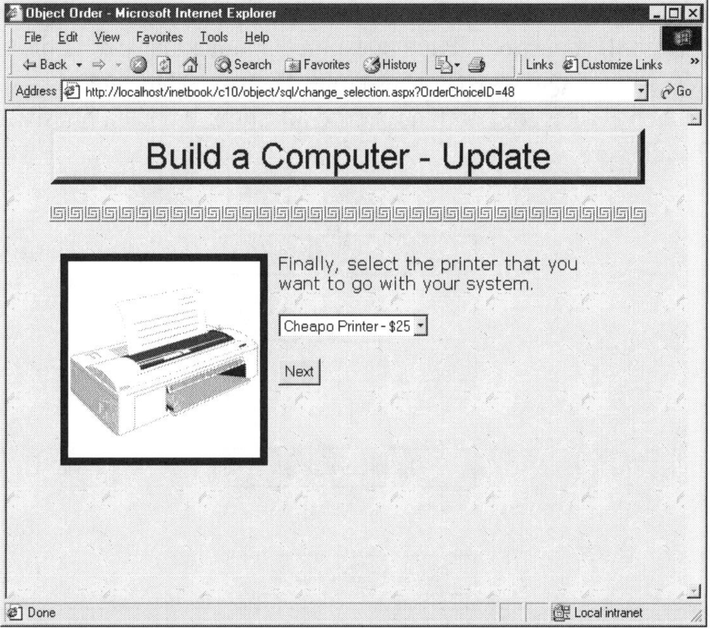

Figure 10-5 *Change Selection page*

Instead of having to go through the whole wizard again, the Change Selection page allows the visitor to modify a single item selection. They select the new item and click Next. When they do that, they are taken back to the Summary page.

Build an Object Database Component

C10Object.sql

The database used to create the Build an Object tool is made up of four tables that relate to each other. In this section we will review those tables, their relationships, and the specific fields used.

Tables and Data Diagram

Figure 10-6 shows the relationships between the tables in the Build an Object database.

When a visitor first enters a tool, a record is added to the ObjectOrders table. This table stores the top-level visitor information. The OrderChoices table stores each choice that is made by the visitor as they build their object. The ObjectOrders table and the OrderChoices table are in a one-to-many relationship. Each object put together can have many choices that make it up, but each choice made goes with a specific object.

The other two tables in the Build an Object database are the ObjectQuestions table and the QuestionChoices table. The ObjectQuestions table stores the top-level information about the questions. Each question can have many possible choices, which are stored in the QuestionChoices table. The two tables are in a one-to-many relationship. Each choice goes with a specific question, but each question can have many possible choices.

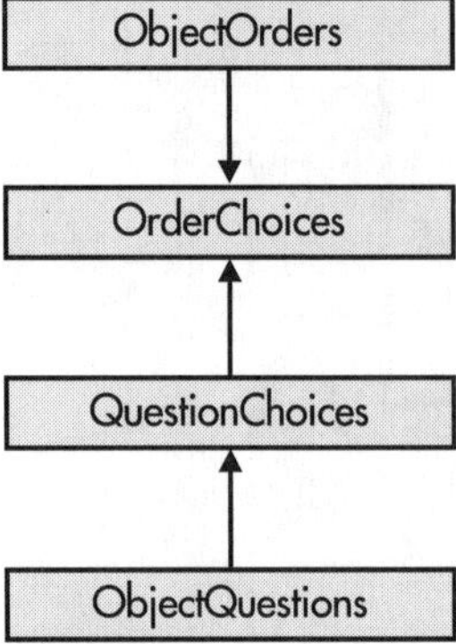

Figure 10-6 *Build an Object data diagram*

The other relationship in the database is between the QuestionChoices table and the OrderChoices table. They, too, relate in a one-to-many relationship. To allow the visitor to change one of their selections, we need to be able to return to a question according to the selection they made from the Summary page. This relationship allows us to do this.

ObjectOrders Field Specifications

ObjectOrders.txt

The field specifications for the fields in the ObjectOrders table are displayed in Table 10-1.

The ObjectOrderID field is the primary key in the table. The field is an identity column, so it is automatically populated when a new record is inserted.

The other field, DateEntered, stores the date and time that the record was added to the table.

OrderChoices Field Specifications

OrderChoices.txt

The field specifications for the fields in the OrderChoices table are displayed in Table 10-2.

The ObjectChoiceID field is the primary key in this table. The ObjectOrderID is a foreign key that links this table to the ObjectOrders table. The ChoiceID is also a foreign key and links this table to the QuestionChoices table.

The ChoiceText and ChoiceCost fields store the description and price of the choice that was made by the visitor when they made it.

ObjectQuestions Field Specifications

ObjectQuestions.txt

The field specifications for the fields in the ObjectQuestions table are displayed in Table 10-3.

Field Name	Field Type	Notes
ObjectOrderID	int	Primary Key, Identity Column
DateEntered	datetime	

Table 10-1 *ObjectOrders Field Specifications*

Field Name	Field Type	Notes
ObjectChoiceID	int	Primary Key, Identity Column
ObjectOrderID	int	Foreign Key
ChoiceID	int	Foreign Key
ChoiceText	varchar	Length = 100
ChoiceCost	money	

Table 10-2 *ObjectOrders Field Specifications*

The ObjectQuestionID field is the primary key in the table. The ObjectQuestionText field stores the text of the question as it appears on the Build Object and Change Selection pages.

The PicPath field stores the path to the picture that is to be used with the question. The PicAltText field stores the text that appears as the rollover for the graphic. The Sequence field stores the order that the questions should appear in. The first question must start with a 1, and each question must be incremented by 1 in the order that you want them to appear.

QuestionChoices Field Specifications

QuestionChoices.txt

The field specifications for the fields in the QuestionChoices table are displayed in Table 10-4.

The ChoiceID field is the primary key in this table. The ObjectQuestionID field is a foreign key that links this table to the ObjectQuestions table.

The ChoiceText field stores the text that the visitor sees for this item in the drop-down link on the Build Object and Change Selection pages. The ChoiceCost

Field Name	Field Type	Notes
ObjectQuestionID	int	Primary Key, Identity Column
ObjectQuestionText	varchar	Length = 255
PicPath	varchar	Length = 200
PicAltText	varchar	Length = 200
Sequence	int	

Table 10-3 *ObjectQuestions Field Specifications*

Field Name	Field Type	Notes
ChoiceID	int	Primary Key, Identity Column
ObjectQuestionID	int	Foreign Key
ChoiceText	varchar	Length = 100
ChoiceCost	money	

Table 10-4 *QuestionChoices Field Specifications*

field stores the amount of money that the item costs and is used for the object order total displayed on the Summary page.

Build an Object ASP.NET Code

The Build an Object tool is made up of three ASP.NET pages and a Global.asax configuration file. Since it uses the Global.asax configuration file, you need to install the tool as an ASP.NET Application through the Internet Services Manager.

In this section we will review the configuration file and the ASP.NET files.

Global.asax ASP.NET Page

Global.asax

The configuration file, Global.asax, provides us with a way to write code that runs when the application starts or ends or when a visitor's session starts or ends. For this case, we use the configuration file to store a title string.

```
<script language="VBScript" runat="Server">
Sub Application_OnStart
    Application("TitleText") = "Build a Computer"
End Sub
</script>
```

The string is stored in an application variable so that it is available to, and is used by, all the other pages in this tool. That string is the title text displayed at the top of each of the pages.

Build Object ASP.NET Page

Index.aspx

When the visitor navigates through their choices as they build their object, they are using the Build Object page. The Build Object page presents the questions, stores the choices made by visitors, and, when complete, directs the visitor to the summary page.

At the top of the page, you will see these compiler directives.

```
<%@ Page Language=VB EnableSessionState=true Debug=true %>
<%@ Import Namespace="System.Data" %>
<%@ Import Namespace="System.Data.OLEDB" %>
```

The first directive tells the compiler that we are writing our code in Visual Basic, that we are using sessions, and that we want debugging turned on. Note that you should turn debugging off if this page is used in production:

```
<%@ Page Language=VB EnableSessionState=true Debug=true %>
```

The other two directives tell the compiler that we need to import two namespaces. These namespaces allow us to access and manipulate the data in a SQL Server database or an Access database:

```
<%@ Import Namespace="System.Data" %>
<%@ Import Namespace="System.Data.OLEDB" %>
```

The objects in the body of the page are surrounded by Form tags so that we can process the page correctly:

```
<form runat="server">
</form>
```

Within the body of the page we need a label that displays the page title:

```
<asp:Label
    id="lblTitle"
    runat="server"
/>
```

We also need a label for the text of the current question:

```
<asp:Label
    id="lblQuestion"
    runat="server"
/>
```

Additionally, an image control is used to display the image that goes with each picture:

```
<asp:Image
    id="imgStepPicture"
    runat="server"
/>
```

A DropDownList control displays the choices for the question to the visitor:

```
<asp:dropdownlist
    id="ddlResponses"
    runat=server
    DataTextField="ChoiceText"
    DataValueField="ChoiceID">
</asp:dropdownlist>
```

Note that the visitor will see the text of the choice in the list,

```
DataTextField="ChoiceText"
```

but the ID of the choice is used internally to pass the item selected:

```
DataValueField="ChoiceID">
```

One other control on the form is a button:

```
<asp:button
    text="Next"
    Type="Submit"
    OnClick="SubmitBtn_Click"
    runat="server"
/>
```

Note that when the button is clicked, the SubmitBtn_Click procedure is called

```
OnClick="SubmitBtn_Click"
```

The code on the page is contained within two procedures. The first procedure fires when the page is opened

```
Sub Page_Load(ByVal Sender as Object, ByVal E as EventArgs)
    If Not IsPostBack then
        Dim DBConn as OleDbConnection
        Dim DBCommand As OleDbDataAdapter
```

```
Dim DSQuestion as DataSet
Dim DBInsert As New OleDbCommand
Session("CurrentSequenceNumber") = 1
DBConn = New OleDbConnection("Provider=sqloledb;" _
    & "server=localhost;" _
    & "Initial Catalog=INETC10;" _
    & "User Id=sa;" _
    & "Password=;")
DBInsert.CommandText = "Insert Into ObjectOrders " _
    & "(DateEntered) values ('" _
    & Now() & "')"
DBInsert.Connection = DBConn
DBInsert.Connection.Open
DBInsert.ExecuteNonQuery()
DSQuestion = New DataSet()
DBCommand = New OleDbDataAdapter _
    ("Select Max(ObjectOrderID) as MaxID " _
        & "From ObjectOrders",DBConn)
DBCommand.Fill(DSQuestion, _
    "CurrentID")
Session("ObjectOrderID") = _
    DSQuestion.Tables("CurrentID").Rows(0).Item("MaxID")
DBCommand = New OleDbDataAdapter _
    ("Select ObjectQuestionID, " _
        & "ObjectQuestionText, PicPath, " _
        & "PicAltText from ObjectQuestions " _
        & "Where Sequence = " _
        & Session("CurrentSequenceNumber"),DBConn)
DBCommand.Fill(DSQuestion, _
    "CurrentQuestion")
DBCommand = New OleDbDataAdapter _
    ("Select ChoiceID, ChoiceText " _
        & "From QuestionChoices " _
        & "Where ObjectQuestionID = " _
        & DSQuestion.Tables("CurrentQuestion"). _
        Rows(0).Item("ObjectQuestionID") _
        ,DBConn)
DBCommand.Fill(DSQuestion, _
    "CurrentResponses")
lblTitle.BorderWidth = New Unit("7px")
lblTitle.BorderStyle = 9
lblTitle.Width = New Unit("90%")
lblTitle.Font.Size = New FontUnit("25pt")
lblTitle.Font.Name = "Arial"
lblTitle.Text = Application("TitleText")
```

```
        imgStepPicture.AlternateText = _
            DSQuestion.Tables("CurrentQuestion").Rows(0).Item("PicAltText")
        imgStepPicture.ImageUrl = _
            DSQuestion.Tables("CurrentQuestion").Rows(0).Item("PicPath")
        imgStepPicture.BorderWidth = New Unit("7px")
        lblQuestion.Font.Size = New FontUnit("12pt")
        lblQuestion.Font.Name = "Verdana"
        lblQuestion.Text = _

SQuestion.Tables("CurrentQuestion").Rows(0).Item("ObjectQuestionText")
        ddlResponses.DataSource = _
            DSQuestion.Tables("CurrentResponses").DefaultView
        ddlResponses.DataBind()
    End If
End Sub
```

The code in this procedure is initialization code; it only needs to be run once. Therefore, we check to see if this is the first viewing of the page by making sure that the page has not been posted back:

```
If Not IsPostBack then
```

If it hasn't been, we need to run our initialization code. We will need a Connection object,

```
Dim DBConn as OleDbConnection
```

a Data Adapter object,

```
Dim DBCommand As OleDbDataAdapter
```

a DateSet object,

```
Dim DSQuestion as DataSet
```

and a Command object:

```
Dim DBInsert As New OleDbCommand
```

We need a Session variable that we can check from call to call of this page to store the sequence number of the current question. This variable does that, and we initialize it to 1:

```
Session("CurrentSequenceNumber") = 1
```

Next, we connect to our SQL Server database:

```
DBConn = New OleDbConnection("Provider=sqloledb;" _
    & "server=localhost;" _
    & "Initial Catalog=INETC10;" _
    & "User Id=sa;" _
    & "Password=;")
```

We need to add a new record to the ObjectOrders table that is used as the top-level record for this visitor. That query is placed into our Command object:

```
DBInsert.CommandText = "Insert Into ObjectOrders " _
    & "(DateEntered) values ('" _
    & Now() & "')"
```

The connection used in the Command object is also set,

```
DBInsert.Connection = DBConn
DBInsert.Connection.Open
```

and we run the query:

```
DBInsert.ExecuteNonQuery()
```

Next, we need to initialize our DataSet object

```
DSQuestion = New DataSet()
```

and set the SQL in our Data Adapter object so that it will retrieve the ID of the record we just inserted

```
DBCommand = New OleDbDataAdapter _
    ("Select Max(ObjectOrderID) as MaxID " _
    & "From ObjectOrders",DBConn)
```

We then retrieve that value in our DataSet object into a DataSet table called CurrentID:

```
DBCommand.Fill(DSQuestion, _
    "CurrentID")
```

That value is then placed into a Session variable so that we can track the visitor as they use the tool:

```
Session("ObjectOrderID") = _
    DSQuestion.Tables("CurrentID").Rows(0).Item("MaxID")
```

Next, we set our Data Adapter object up to retrieve the data for the first question:

```
DBCommand = New OleDbDataAdapter _
    ("Select ObjectQuestionID, " _
    & "ObjectQuestionText, PicPath, " _
    & "PicAltText from ObjectQuestions " _
    & "Where Sequence = " _
    & Session("CurrentSequenceNumber"),DBConn)
```

We place that data into our DataSet object in a DataSet Table called CurrentQuestion:

```
DBCommand.Fill(DSQuestion, _
    "CurrentQuestion")
```

Next, we set up our Data Adapter object so that it will retrieve choices for the current question:

```
DBCommand = New OleDbDataAdapter _
    ("Select ChoiceID, ChoiceText " _
    & "From QuestionChoices " _
    & "Where ObjectQuestionID = " _
    & DSQuestion.Tables("CurrentQuestion"). _
    Rows(0).Item("ObjectQuestionID") _
    ,DBConn)
```

And place the data retrieved from that object into a table of our DataSet object:

```
DBCommand.Fill(DSQuestion, _
    "CurrentResponses")
```

Now that all the data has been retrieved from the database, we can set up the content on the page. First, we set the style for the title label:

```
lblTitle.BorderWidth = New Unit("7px")
lblTitle.BorderStyle = 9
lblTitle.Width = New Unit("90%")
lblTitle.Font.Size = New FontUnit("25pt")
lblTitle.Font.Name = "Arial"
```

And place the text into it that comes from our Application variable defined in the Global.asax file:

```
lblTitle.Text = Application("TitleText")
```

The AlternateText property of the Image control is set to the PicAltText field for the current question record:

```
imgStepPicture.AlternateText = _
    DSQuestion.Tables("CurrentQuestion").Rows(0).Item("PicAltText")
```

We also set the path to the picture from the database:

```
imgStepPicture.ImageUrl = _
    DSQuestion.Tables("CurrentQuestion").Rows(0).Item("PicPath")
```

Then we give the Image control a border

```
imgStepPicture.BorderWidth = New Unit("7px")
```

and set the look of the label used to display the text of the question

```
lblQuestion.Font.Size = New FontUnit("12pt")
lblQuestion.Font.Name = "Verdana"
```

the text of which comes from the database:

```
lblQuestion.Text = _
DSQuestion.Tables("CurrentQuestion").Rows(0).Item("ObjectQuestionText")
```

Finally, we bind the DropDownList to the CurrentResponses table in our DataSet object:

```
ddlResponses.DataSource = _
    DSQuestion.Tables("CurrentResponses").DefaultView
ddlResponses.DataBind()
```

The other procedure on this page is called SubmitBtn_Click. It fires when the visitor clicks Next.

```
Sub SubmitBtn_Click(Sender As Object, E As EventArgs)
    Session("CurrentSequenceNumber") = _
        Session("CurrentSequenceNumber") + 1
```

```
Dim DBConn as OleDbConnection
Dim DBCommand As OleDbDataAdapter
Dim DSQuestion as DataSet
Dim DBInsert As New OleDbCommand
DBConn = New OleDbConnection("Provider=sqloledb;" _
           & "server=localhost;" _
           & "Initial Catalog=INETC10;" _
           & "User Id=sa;" _
           & "Password=;")
DSQuestion = New DataSet()
DBCommand = New OleDbDataAdapter _
    ("Select ChoiceText, ChoiceCost " _
    & "From QuestionChoices Where " _
    & "ChoiceID = " _
    & ddlResponses.SelectedItem.Value,DBConn)
DBCommand.Fill(DSQuestion, _
    "ChoiceInfo")
DBInsert.CommandText = "Insert Into OrderChoices " _
        & "(ObjectOrderID, ChoiceID, ChoiceText, ChoiceCost) " _
        & "values (" _
        & Session("ObjectOrderID") & ", " _
        & ddlResponses.SelectedItem.Value & ", '" _
        & DSQuestion.Tables("ChoiceInfo").Rows(0).Item("ChoiceText") _
        & "', " _
        & DSQuestion.Tables("ChoiceInfo").Rows(0).Item("ChoiceCost") _
        & ")"
DBInsert.Connection = DBConn
DBInsert.Connection.Open
DBInsert.ExecuteNonQuery()
DBCommand = New OleDbDataAdapter _
    ("Select ObjectQuestionID, " _
        & "ObjectQuestionText, PicPath, " _
        & "PicAltText from ObjectQuestions " _
        & "Where Sequence = " _
        & Session("CurrentSequenceNumber"),DBConn)
DBCommand.Fill(DSQuestion, _
    "CurrentQuestion")
If DSQuestion.Tables("CurrentQuestion").Rows.Count = 0 Then
    Response.Redirect("./summary.aspx")
End If
DBCommand = New OleDbDataAdapter _
```

```
        ("Select ChoiceID, ChoiceText " _
            & "From QuestionChoices " _
            & "Where ObjectQuestionID = " _

            &
SQuestion.Tables("CurrentQuestion").Rows(0).Item("ObjectQuestionID") _
            ,DBConn)
    DBCommand.Fill(DSQuestion, _
        "CurrentResponses")
    imgStepPicture.AlternateText = _
        DSQuestion.Tables("CurrentQuestion").Rows(0).Item("PicAltText")
    imgStepPicture.ImageUrl = _
        DSQuestion.Tables("CurrentQuestion").Rows(0).Item("PicPath")
    lblQuestion.Text = _
        DSQuestion.Tables("CurrentQuestion").Rows(0).Item("ObjectQuestionText")
    ddlResponses.DataSource = _
        DSQuestion.Tables("CurrentResponses").DefaultView
    ddlResponses.DataBind()
End Sub
```

One of the things we need to do is increment our sequence counter so that we can display the next question from the database.

```
Session("CurrentSequenceNumber") = _
    Session("CurrentSequenceNumber") + 1
```

Within the procedure we will need Connection, Data Adapter, DataSet, and Command objects to retrieve and manipulate the database data:

```
Dim DBConn as OleDbConnection
Dim DBCommand As OleDbDataAdapter
Dim DSQuestion as DataSet
Dim DBInsert As New OleDbCommand
```

We then connect to our SQL Server database

```
DBConn = New OleDbConnection("Provider=sqloledb;" _
    & "server=localhost;" _
    & "Initial Catalog=INETC10;" _
    & "User Id=sa;" _
    & "Password=;")
```

and initialize our DataSet object:

```
DSQuestion = New DataSet()
```

We need to retrieve the cost and the text of the choice made by the visitor that was returned through the DropDownList control:

```
DBCommand = New OleDbDataAdapter _
    ("Select ChoiceText, ChoiceCost " _
    & "From QuestionChoices Where " _
    & "ChoiceID = " _
    & ddlResponses.SelectedItem.Value,DBConn)
```

That data is placed in our DataSet object

```
DBCommand.Fill(DSQuestion, _
    "ChoiceInfo")
```

and is then used in the SQL text of an Insert statement, which adds the choice made by the visitor into the OrderChoices table:

```
DBInsert.CommandText = "Insert Into OrderChoices " _
    & "(ObjectOrderID, ChoiceID, ChoiceText, ChoiceCost) " _
    & "values (" _
    & Session("ObjectOrderID") & ", " _
    & ddlResponses.SelectedItem.Value & ", '" _
    & DSQuestion.Tables("ChoiceInfo").Rows(0).Item("ChoiceText") _
    & "', " _
    & DSQuestion.Tables("ChoiceInfo").Rows(0).Item("ChoiceCost") _
    & ")"
```

We then open the connection for the Command object

```
DBInsert.Connection = DBConn
DBInsert.Connection.Open
```

and execute the Insert statement:

```
DBInsert.ExecuteNonQuery()
```

Now that the visitor's choice has been added to the database, we need to retrieve the next question

```
DBCommand = New OleDbDataAdapter _
    ("Select ObjectQuestionID, " _
    & "ObjectQuestionText, PicPath, " _
```

```
    & "PicAltText from ObjectQuestions " _
    & "Where Sequence = " _
    & Session("CurrentSequenceNumber"),DBConn)
```

and place it into the DataSet object:

```
DBCommand.Fill(DSQuestion, _
    "CurrentQuestion")
```

But we need to make sure that there is another question:

```
If DSQuestion.Tables("CurrentQuestion").Rows.Count = 0 Then
```

If there isn't another question, we send the visitor to the Summary page:

```
Response.Redirect("./summary.aspx")
```

Otherwise, we need to retrieve the choices for the current question

```
DBCommand = New OleDbDataAdapter _
    ("Select ChoiceID, ChoiceText " _
    & "From QuestionChoices " _
    & "Where ObjectQuestionID = " _
    & DSQuestion.Tables("CurrentQuestion").Rows(0).Item("ObjectQuestionID") _
    ,DBConn)
DBCommand.Fill(DSQuestion, _
    "CurrentResponses")
```

and update the Image control for the new question,

```
imgStepPicture.AlternateText = _
    DSQuestion.Tables("CurrentQuestion").Rows(0).Item("PicAltText")
imgStepPicture.ImageUrl = _
    DSQuestion.Tables("CurrentQuestion").Rows(0).Item("PicPath")
```

as well as the question label:

```
lblQuestion.Text = _
    DSQuestion.Tables("CurrentQuestion").Rows(0).Item("ObjectQuestionText")
```

We also need to place the choices into the DropDownList control:

```
ddlResponses.DataSource = _
    DSQuestion.Tables("CurrentResponses").DefaultView
ddlResponses.DataBind()
```

Summary ASP.NET Page

Summary.aspx

The Summary page displays the choices made by the visitor during their session, shows the cost total for their object, and allows them to link to the Change Selection page to modify their selections.

At the top of the page, you will find some compiler directives:

```
<%@ Page Language=VB EnableSessionState=true Debug=true %>
<%@ Import Namespace="System.Data" %>
<%@ Import Namespace="System.Data.OLEDB" %>
```

The first one tells the compiler the language used, that we are using sessions, and that we want debugging on:

```
<%@ Page Language=VB EnableSessionState=true Debug=true %>
```

The other two allow us to connect to our database:

```
<%@ Import Namespace="System.Data" %>
<%@ Import Namespace="System.Data.OLEDB" %>
```

Within the body of the page we have a Label control for the page title:

```
<asp:Label
    id="lblTitle"
    runat="server"
/>
```

We also have a DataGrid control that displays the choices made by the visitor:

```
<asp:DataGrid
    id="dgSummaryInfo"
    AutoGenerateColumns="false"
    Width="90%"
    BackColor="#ccccff"
    BorderColor="black"
    ShowFooter="false"
    CellPadding=3
```

```
    CellSpacing="0"
    Font-Name="Verdana"
    Font-Size="8pt"
    HeaderStyle-BackColor="#aaaadd"
    OnItemCommand="Click_Grid"
    runat="server">
    <columns>
        <asp:BoundColumn
            HeaderText="Selection Made"
            DataField="ChoiceText"
        />
        <asp:BoundColumn
            HeaderText="Click to Modify Selection"
            DataField="OrderChoiceID"
            Visible="False"
        />
        <asp:ButtonColumn
            HeaderText="Click to Modify Selection"
            ButtonType="LinkButton"
            Text="Modify" CommandName="cmdModifyItem"
        />
    </columns>
</asp:DataGrid>
```

The first property in that declaration sets the name of the DataGrid:

```
id="dgSummaryInfo"
```

Then we turn off the automatic column generation feature, since we will define our own columns:

```
AutoGenerateColumns="false"
```

We then set up the look and size of the grid and its parts:

```
Width="90%"
BackColor="#ccccff"
BorderColor="black"
ShowFooter="false"
CellPadding=3
CellSpacing="0"
```

```
Font-Name="Verdana"
Font-Size="8pt"
HeaderStyle-BackColor="#aaaadd"
```

When the visitor clicks one of the links in the grid, the Click_Grid procedure will run

```
OnItemCommand="Click_Grid"
```

Next, we need to create the columns for our DataGrid:

```
<columns>
```

The first column is a bound column, which means that it is tied to a DataSet field:

```
<asp:BoundColumn
    HeaderText="Selection Made"
```

That field is the ChoiceText:

```
DataField="ChoiceText"
```

The second column is also a bound column:

```
<asp:BoundColumn
    HeaderText="Click to Modify Selection"
```

It is tied to the ID of the choice

```
DataField="OrderChoiceID"
```

and is not displayed to the visitor. As you will see further down, it is used in code:

```
Visible="False"
```

The third column is a button column:

```
<asp:ButtonColumn
    HeaderText="Click to Modify Selection"
That is displayed as a link:
ButtonType="LinkButton"
Text="Modify" CommandName="cmdModifyItem"
```

The code on the page is contained within two procedures. The first procedure fires whenever the page is loaded.

```
Sub Page_Load(ByVal Sender as Object, ByVal E as EventArgs)
    If Len(Session("ObjectOrderID")) = 0 Then
        Response.Redirect("./index.aspx")
    End If
    Dim DBConn as OleDbConnection
    Dim DBCommand As OleDbDataAdapter
    Dim DSSummaryData as New DataSet
    DBConn = New OleDbConnection("Provider=sqloledb;" _
        & "server=localhost;" _
        & "Initial Catalog=INETC10;" _
        & "User Id=sa;" _
        & "Password=;")
    DBCommand = New OleDbDataAdapter _
         ("Select ChoiceText, OrderChoiceID " _
         & "from OrderChoices " _
         & "Where ObjectOrderID = " _
         & Session("ObjectOrderID"),DBConn)
    DBCommand.Fill(DSSummaryData, _
        "GridInfo")
    DBCommand = New OleDbDataAdapter _
         ("Select Sum(ChoiceCost) as TheTotal " _
         & "from OrderChoices " _
         & "Where ObjectOrderID = " _
         & Session("ObjectOrderID"),DBConn)
    DBCommand.Fill(DSSummaryData, _
        "OrderTotal")
    dgSummaryInfo.DataSource = _
        DSSummaryData.Tables("GridInfo").DefaultView
    dgSummaryInfo.DataBind()
    lblTitle.BorderWidth = New Unit("7px")
    lblTitle.BorderStyle = 9
    lblTitle.Width = New Unit("90%")
    lblTitle.Font.Size = New FontUnit("25pt")
    lblTitle.Font.Name = "Arial"
    lblTitle.Text = Application("TitleText")
    lblTotal.Width = New Unit("90%")
    lblTotal.BorderWidth = New Unit("4px")
    lblTotal.BorderStyle = 9
    lblTotal.Font.Size = New FontUnit("12pt")
    lblTotal.Font.Bold = True
    lblTotal.Font.Name = "Verdana"
```

```
    lblTotal.Text = "OrderTotal: " _
        & FormatCurrency( _
        DSSummaryData.Tables("OrderTotal").Rows(0).Item("TheTotal"))
End Sub
```

The page should only be entered if the visitor has made their choices first:

```
If Len(Session("ObjectOrderID")) = 0 Then
```

If they haven't, we send them back to the Build Object page:

```
Response.Redirect("./index.aspx")
```

Otherwise, we declare data objects that will be needed in code:

```
Dim DBConn as OleDbConnection
Dim DBCommand As OleDbDataAdapter
Dim DSSummaryData as New DataSet
```

We then connect to our SQL Server database

```
DBConn = New OleDbConnection("Provider=sqloledb;" _
    & "server=localhost;" _
    & "Initial Catalog=INETC10;" _
    & "User Id=sa;" _
    & "Password=;")
```

and set up our Data Adapter object to retrieve all the choices made by the visitor:

```
DBCommand = New OleDbDataAdapter _
    ("Select ChoiceText, OrderChoiceID " _
    & "from OrderChoices " _
    & "Where ObjectOrderID = " _
    & Session("ObjectOrderID"),DBConn)
Those choices are placed into a table of our DataSet object:
DBCommand.Fill(DSSummaryData, _
    "GridInfo")
```

We also need to retrieve the total cost of building the object:

```
DBCommand = New OleDbDataAdapter _
    ("Select Sum(ChoiceCost) as TheTotal " _
    & "from OrderChoices " _
    & "Where ObjectOrderID = " _
    & Session("ObjectOrderID"),DBConn)
```

It, too, is placed into the DataSet object:

```
DBCommand.Fill(DSSummaryData, _
    "OrderTotal")
```

We then bind the DataGrid object to the GridInfo table of our DataSet object:

```
dgSummaryInfo.DataSource = _
    DSSummaryData.Tables("GridInfo").DefaultView
dgSummaryInfo.DataBind()
```

Next, we set up the appearance of the title label

```
lblTitle.BorderWidth = New Unit("7px")
lblTitle.BorderStyle = 9
lblTitle.Width = New Unit("90%")
lblTitle.Font.Size = New FontUnit("25pt")
lblTitle.Font.Name = "Arial"
```

and place the title text into it:

```
lblTitle.Text = Application("TitleText")
```

We also need to set up the appearance of the total label

```
lblTotal.Width = New Unit("90%")
lblTotal.BorderWidth = New Unit("4px")
lblTotal.BorderStyle = 9
lblTotal.Font.Size = New FontUnit("12pt")
lblTotal.Font.Bold = True
lblTotal.Font.Name = "Verdana"
```

which is set to the total cost text:

```
lblTotal.Text = "OrderTotal: " _
    & FormatCurrency( _
    DSSummaryData.Tables("OrderTotal").Rows(0).Item("TheTotal"))
```

The other procedure on the page fires when one of the items in the DataGrid is clicked.

```
Sub Click_Grid(ByVal Sender as Object, ByVal E as DataGridCommandEventArgs)
    Response.Redirect("./change_selection.aspx?OrderChoiceID=" _
        & E.Item.Cells(1).Text)
End Sub
```

Here's where the value of the second column in the DataGrid, the invisible one, is used. It is used to pass the ID of the specific choice clicked to the Change Selection page:

```
Response.Redirect("./change_selection.aspx?OrderChoiceID=" _
    & E.Item.Cells(1).Text)
```

Change Selection ASP.NET Page

Change_Selection.aspx

The Change Selection page is called when the visitor clicks one of the items in the DataGrid on the Summary page. It is used to modify the choice clicked by the visitor.

At the top of the page, you will find Compiler directives indicating the code environment and the namespaces imported:

```
<%@ Page Language=VB EnableSessionState=true Debug=true %>
<%@ Import Namespace="System.Data" %>
<%@ Import Namespace="System.Data.OLEDB" %>
```

The controls on the page are made up of a label for the title

```
<asp:Label
    id="lblTitle"
    runat="server"
/>
```

and a label for the text of the question that is being modified:

```
<asp:Label id="lblQuestion" runat="server"/>
```

We also need an Image control for the picture that goes with the question

```
<asp:Image id="imgStepPicture" runat="server"/>
```

as well as a DropDownList that will display the choices for the question,

```
<asp:dropdownlist
    id="ddlResponses"
    runat=server
    DataTextField="ChoiceText"
    DataValueField="ChoiceID">
</asp:dropdownlist><p></p>
```

and a button that will call the SubmitBtn_Click procedure when it is clicked

```
<asp:button
    text="Next"
    Type="Submit"
    OnClick="SubmitBtn_Click"
    runat="server"
/>
```

The code on the page consists of two procedures. The first fires when the page is loaded.

```
Sub Page_Load(ByVal Sender as Object, ByVal E as EventArgs)
    If Not IsPostBack then
        If Len(Page.Request.QueryString("OrderChoiceID")) = 0 Then
            Response.Redirect("./index.aspx")
        End If
        Session("CurrentOrderChoiceID") = _
            Page.Request.QueryString("OrderChoiceID")
        Dim DBConn as OleDbConnection
        Dim DBCommand As OleDbDataAdapter
        Dim DSQuestion as DataSet
        DBConn = New OleDbConnection("Provider=sqloledb;" _
            & "server=localhost;" _
            & "Initial Catalog=INETC10;" _
            & "User Id=sa;" _
            & "Password=;")
        DSQuestion = New DataSet()
        DBCommand = New OleDbDataAdapter _
            ("Select ChoiceID from OrderChoices " _
            & "Where OrderChoiceID = " _
            & Session("CurrentOrderChoiceID"),DBConn)
        DBCommand.Fill(DSQuestion, _
            "CurrentChoiceID")
        DBCommand = New OleDbDataAdapter _
            ("Select ObjectQuestionID from QuestionChoices " _
            & "Where ChoiceID = " _
            & DSQuestion.Tables("CurrentChoiceID").Rows(0).Item("ChoiceID") _
            ,DBConn)
        DBCommand.Fill(DSQuestion, _
            "CurrentQuestionID")
        DBCommand = New OleDbDataAdapter _
            ("Select ObjectQuestionID, " _
                & "ObjectQuestionText, PicPath, " _
                & "PicAltText from ObjectQuestions " _
                & "Where ObjectQuestionID = " _
```

```
                & DSQuestion.Tables("CurrentQuestionID"). _
                Rows(0).Item("ObjectQuestionID") _
                ,DBConn)
        DBCommand.Fill(DSQuestion, _
            "CurrentQuestion")
        DBCommand = New OleDbDataAdapter _
            ("Select ChoiceID, ChoiceText " _
                & "From QuestionChoices " _
                & "Where ObjectQuestionID = " _
                & DSQuestion.Tables("CurrentQuestion"). _
                Rows(0).Item("ObjectQuestionID") _
                ,DBConn)
        DBCommand.Fill(DSQuestion, _
            "CurrentResponses")
        lblTitle.BorderWidth = New Unit("7px")
        lblTitle.BorderStyle = 9
        lblTitle.Width = New Unit("90%")
        lblTitle.Font.Size = New FontUnit("25pt")
        lblTitle.Font.Name = "Arial"
        lblTitle.Text = Application("TitleText") _
            & " - Update"
        imgStepPicture.AlternateText = _
            DSQuestion.Tables("CurrentQuestion").Rows(0).Item("PicAltText")
        imgStepPicture.ImageUrl = _
            DSQuestion.Tables("CurrentQuestion").Rows(0).Item("PicPath")
        imgStepPicture.BorderWidth = New Unit("7px")
        lblQuestion.Font.Size = New FontUnit("12pt")
        lblQuestion.Font.Name = "Verdana"
        lblQuestion.Text = _

DSQuestion.Tables("CurrentQuestion").Rows(0).Item("ObjectQuestionText")
        ddlResponses.DataSource = _
            DSQuestion.Tables("CurrentResponses").DefaultView
        ddlResponses.DataBind()
    End If
End Sub
```

The procedure sets up the initial text and appearance of the page. So it runs only if the page has not been posted

```
If Not IsPostBack then
```

It should also run only if an OrderChoiceID was passed into it from the Summary page:

```
If Len(Page.Request.QueryString("OrderChoiceID")) = 0 Then
```

If it wasn't, we send the visitor back to the Build Object page:

```
Response.Redirect("./index.aspx")
```

Otherwise, we store the ID of the choice passed to the page into a Session variable so that it will be available when the page is posted

```
Session("CurrentOrderChoiceID") = _
    Page.Request.QueryString("OrderChoiceID")
```

We then declare some data variables

```
Dim DBConn as OleDbConnection
Dim DBCommand As OleDbDataAdapter
Dim DSQuestion as DataSet
```

and open a connection to our SQL Server database:

```
DBConn = New OleDbConnection("Provider=sqloledb;" _
    & "server=localhost;" _
    & "Initial Catalog=INETC10;" _
    & "User Id=sa;" _
    & "Password=;")
```

Next, we instantiate our DataSet object:

```
DSQuestion = New DataSet()
```

Passed into the page is the ID of the option selected and clicked by the visitor on the summary page. But we need to retrieve the ID of that specific choice

```
DBCommand = New OleDbDataAdapter _
    ("Select ChoiceID from OrderChoices " _
    & "Where OrderChoiceID = " _
    & Session("CurrentOrderChoiceID"),DBConn)
DBCommand.Fill(DSQuestion, _
    "CurrentChoiceID")
```

which is then used to retrieve the ID of the question that the choice goes with

```
DBCommand = New OleDbDataAdapter _
    ("Select ObjectQuestionID from QuestionChoices " _
    & "Where ChoiceID = " _
    & DSQuestion.Tables("CurrentChoiceID").Rows(0).Item("ChoiceID") _
```

```
    ,DBConn)
DBCommand.Fill(DSQuestion, _
    "CurrentQuestionID")
```

and that value is used to retrieve the data for the question that is to be used on this page:

```
DBCommand = New OleDbDataAdapter _
    ("Select ObjectQuestionID, " _
    & "ObjectQuestionText, PicPath, " _
    & "PicAltText from ObjectQuestions " _
    & "Where ObjectQuestionID = " _
    & DSQuestion.Tables("CurrentQuestionID"). _
    Rows(0).Item("ObjectQuestionID") _
    ,DBConn)
DBCommand.Fill(DSQuestion, _
    "CurrentQuestion")
```

It is also used to retrieve the choices for that question:

```
DBCommand = New OleDbDataAdapter _
    ("Select ChoiceID, ChoiceText " _
    & "From QuestionChoices " _
    & "Where ObjectQuestionID = " _
    & DSQuestion.Tables("CurrentQuestion"). _
    Rows(0).Item("ObjectQuestionID") _
    ,DBConn)
DBCommand.Fill(DSQuestion, _
    "CurrentResponses")
```

Now that we have all the data we need, we can set up the appearance of the title label

```
lblTitle.BorderWidth = New Unit("7px")
lblTitle.BorderStyle = 9
lblTitle.Width = New Unit("90%")
lblTitle.Font.Size = New FontUnit("25pt")
lblTitle.Font.Name = "Arial"
```

and set its text:

```
lblTitle.Text = Application("TitleText") _
    & " - Update"
```

We then set up the data used for the Image control

```
imgStepPicture.AlternateText = _
    DSQuestion.Tables("CurrentQuestion").Rows(0).Item("PicAltText")
imgStepPicture.ImageUrl = _
    DSQuestion.Tables("CurrentQuestion").Rows(0).Item("PicPath")
imgStepPicture.BorderWidth = New Unit("7px")
```

as well as the appearance and text for the question label:

```
lblQuestion.Font.Size = New FontUnit("12pt")
lblQuestion.Font.Name = "Verdana"
lblQuestion.Text = _
    DSQuestion.Tables("CurrentQuestion").Rows(0).Item("ObjectQuestionText")
```

We also need to bind the DropDownList to the DataSet table CurrentResponses:

```
ddlResponses.DataSource = _
    DSQuestion.Tables("CurrentResponses").DefaultView
ddlResponses.DataBind()
```

The other procedure on this page fires when the Next button is clicked.

```
Sub SubmitBtn_Click(Sender As Object, E As EventArgs)
    Dim DBConn as OleDbConnection
    Dim DBCommand As OleDbDataAdapter
    Dim DSQuestion as DataSet
    Dim DBUpdate As New OleDbCommand
    DBConn = New OleDbConnection("Provider=sqloledb;" _
           & "server=localhost;" _
           & "Initial Catalog=INETC10;" _
           & "User Id=sa;" _
           & "Password=;")
    DSQuestion = New DataSet()
    DBCommand = New OleDbDataAdapter _
        ("Select ChoiceText, ChoiceCost " _
        & "From QuestionChoices Where " _
        & "ChoiceID = " _
        & ddlResponses.SelectedItem.Value,DBConn)
    DBCommand.Fill(DSQuestion, _
        "ChoiceInfo")
    DBUpdate.CommandText = "Update OrderChoices set " _
        & "ChoiceID = " _
        & ddlResponses.SelectedItem.Value & ", " _
```

```
        & "ChoiceText = '" _
        & DSQuestion.Tables("ChoiceInfo").Rows(0).Item("ChoiceText") _
        & "', " & "ChoiceCost = " _
        & DSQuestion.Tables("ChoiceInfo").Rows(0).Item("ChoiceCost") _
        & " Where OrderChoiceID = " _
        & Session("CurrentOrderChoiceID")
    DBUpdate.Connection = DBConn
    DBUpdate.Connection.Open
    DBUpdate.ExecuteNonQuery()
    Response.Redirect("./summary.aspx")
End Sub
```

Within this procedure, we need to update the choice made by the visitor. So we will need some Data objects:

```
Dim DBConn as OleDbConnection
Dim DBCommand As OleDbDataAdapter
Dim DSQuestion as DataSet
Dim DBUpdate As New OleDbCommand
```

We connect to our SQL Server database

```
DBConn = New OleDbConnection("Provider=sqloledb;" _
    & "server=localhost;" _
    & "Initial Catalog=INETC10;" _
    & "User Id=sa;" _
    & "Password=;")
```

and instantiate the DataSet object:

```
DSQuestion = New DataSet()
```

We need to retrieve the cost and text for the choice selected by the visitor:

```
DBCommand = New OleDbDataAdapter _
    ("Select ChoiceText, ChoiceCost " _
    & "From QuestionChoices Where " _
    & "ChoiceID = " _
    & ddlResponses.SelectedItem.Value,DBConn)
```

That data is placed into a table in our DataSet object:

```
DBCommand.Fill(DSQuestion, _
    "ChoiceInfo")
```

That same data is used in a SQL Update statement that modifies the selection made by the visitor

```
DBUpdate.CommandText = "Update OrderChoices set " _
    & "ChoiceID = " _
    & ddlResponses.SelectedItem.Value & ", " _
    & "ChoiceText = '" _
    & DSQuestion.Tables("ChoiceInfo").Rows(0).Item("ChoiceText") _
    & "', " & "ChoiceCost = " _
    & DSQuestion.Tables("ChoiceInfo").Rows(0).Item("ChoiceCost") _
    & " Where OrderChoiceID = " _
    & Session("CurrentOrderChoiceID")
DBUpdate.Connection = DBConn
DBUpdate.Connection.Open
DBUpdate.ExecuteNonQuery()
```

before we send the visitor back to the Summary page:

```
Response.Redirect("./summary.aspx")
```

Access Code Changes

C10Object.mdb

The only code change that was needed to get this solution to work with Access instead of SQL Server was to change the connect string:

```
DBConn = New OleDbConnection("Provider=sqloledb;" _
    & "server=localhost;" _
    & "Initial Catalog=INETC10;" _
    & "User Id=sa;" _
    & "Password=;")
```

This was done so that it uses the proper provider and points to the correct database:

```
DBConn = New OleDbConnection("PROVIDER=Microsoft.Jet.OLEDB.4.0;" _
    & "DATA SOURCE=" _
    & Server.MapPath("/INetBook/C10/Object/Access/C10Object.mdb;"))
```

Note that you will need to modify the path to the location of the database on your server.

Help Desk Tool

The Help Desk tool takes the visitor through a series of questions that eventually lead to an answer to their question. The structure of the tool is such that the number of questions asked the visitor can vary according to the answer to each question. The visitor starts with a top-level question that, depending on their selection, leads to another question or an answer. Those other questions can then lead to even more questions. Eventually the visitor chooses a response to a question that leads to an answer that hopefully resolves the visitor's problem.

The tool can be implemented for a variety of help wizard purposes. It is implemented in the next section as a simple tool to diagnose the visitor's problem with their VCR.

Sample Usage

When the visitor first enters the VCR implementation of the Help Desk tool, they see the page displayed in Figure 10-7.

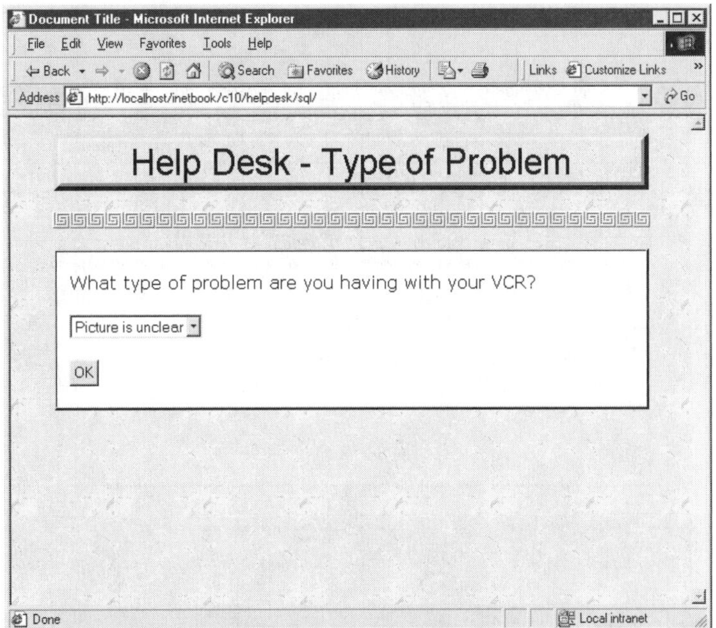

Figure 10-7 *First Help Desk screen of the VCR implementation of the tool*

Whether the tool is being used for VCR help, as in this example, or for some other purpose, you will want the tool to start with a top-level question. As you will see when we look at the database, this top-level record has a special value in one of the fields so that it always comes up first.

The visitor selects the best response for their situation and clicks OK. When they do that, they may see another question, like the one displayed in Figure 10-8.

Note the structure of the page. The top of the page displays a title based on the question being asked. The question being asked is a direct response to the last answer given by the visitor. Within a Panel control, the visitor sees the text of the question, the possible choices, and a Button control.

The visitor continues to answer questions until finally the choice they made leads to a resolution, like the one proposed in Figure 10-9.

Help Desk Database Component

C10HelpDesk.sql

The database used to create the Help Desk tool is made up of a single table that relates to itself. In this section we will review that table, its relationship, and its fields.

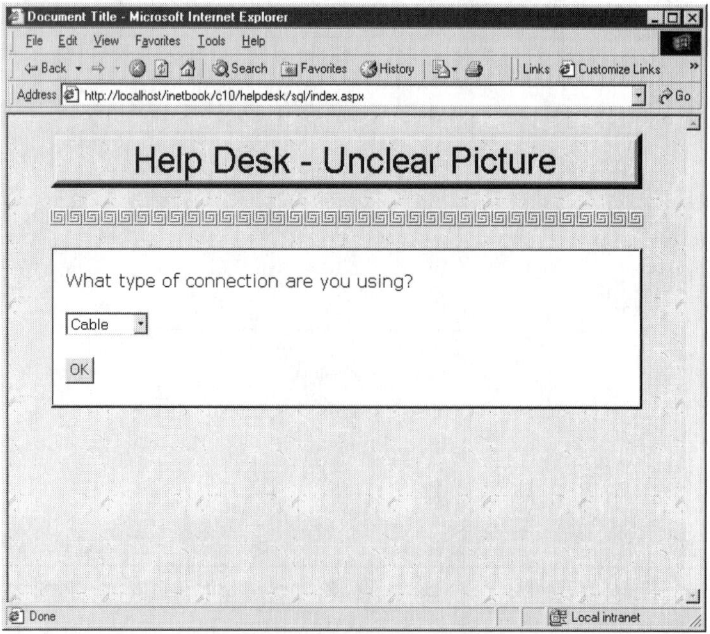

Figure 10-8 *Additional question from the Help Desk tool*

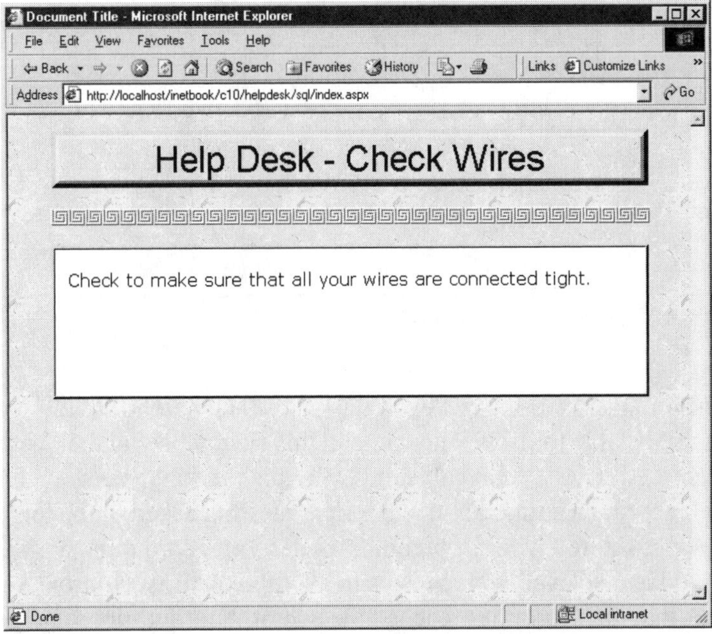

Figure 10-9 *Answer to a series of help desk questions*

Table and Data Diagram

Figure 10-10 shows the relationship that the single table has with itself.

Each question displayed in the help desk can have many possible choices that can go with it. These choices relate back to the original question asked. Therefore, the HelpDesk table is in a one-to-many relationship with itself.

HelpDesk Field Specifications

HelpDesk.txt

The field specifications for the fields in the HelpDesk table are displayed in Table 10-5.

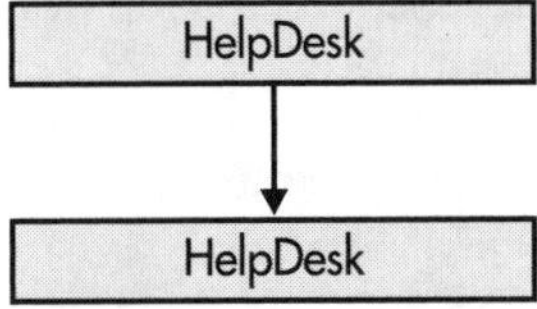

Figure 10-10 *Help Desk data diagram*

Field Name	Field Type	Notes
QuestionID	int	Primary Key, Identity Column
ParentID	int	Foreign Key
QorA	varchar	Length = 1
TitleText	varchar	Length = 20
TheMessage	varchar	Length = 225
TheChoice	varchar	Length = 50

Table 10-5 *HelpDesk Field Specifications*

The QuestionID is the primary key in this table. The ParentID field is a foreign key that links this table to itself. The value in this field tells you the question that this record is a choice for. A special value of "0" in this field indicates that this record is the top-level record, meaning that it is the first question asked in the tool.

The QorA field stored with the record is a question record or an answer record. A question record is displayed with choices in a DropDownList control. An answer record means that the visitor has reached the end of their questions and just an answer is displayed.

The TitleText field stores the text that appears along with the words "Help Desk" in the title label. The TheMessage field stores the text of the question or answer depending on what type of record this is. The choice field stores the text that is displayed for this record when it is displayed as a choice for its parent record in the DropDownList control.

Help Desk ASP.NET Code

The Help Desk tool is composed of a single ASP.NET page. The page displays both questions and answers. In this section, we will review the code on that page.

Help Desk ASP.NET Page

Index.aspx

The code on the Help Desk page connects to the database to guide the visitor through their choices until an answer is reached. At the top of the page, you will find three compiler directives.

```
<%@ Page Language=VB EnableSessionState=true Debug=true %>
<%@ Import Namespace="System.Data" %>
<%@ Import Namespace="System.Data.OLEDB" %>
```

The first directive tells the compiler what language our code is in, to enable session state, and that the debugging is on. Remember to Debug parameter in production:

```
<%@ Page Language=VB EnableSessionState=true Debug=true %>
```

The other two directives import the necessary namespaces so that we can access data in our SQL Server or Access database:

```
<%@ Import Namespace="System.Data" %>
<%@ Import Namespace="System.Data.OLEDB" %>
```

The body of the page is surrounded by a Server Form tag so that our code will run properly:

```
<form runat="server">
```

Within the body of the page a label is used to display the title of the page:

```
<asp:Label
    id="lblTitle"
    runat="server"
/>
```

The other controls on the page are placed on a Panel control:

```
<asp:Panel id="Panel1" runat="server"
    BackColor="ivory"
    Width="90%"
    BorderWidth="3px"
    BorderStyle=7
    HorizontalAlign="Left">
```

A Panel control is useful for graphically grouping together objects. It is also useful because when you make a panel invisible, all the child controls on the panel become invisible. By using such a technique, you can easily display a series of controls in one view of a page and a different set in another view of a page, as is done with tab-type controls.

The first control within the panel is a label that will display the text of the question or answer:

```
<asp:Label
    id="lblQuestion"
    runat="server"
/>
```

That is followed by a DropDownList control:

```
<asp:dropdownlist
    id="ddlAnswers"
    runat=server
    DataTextField="TheChoice"
    DataValueField="QuestionID">
</asp:dropdownlist>
```

Note that the visitor will see TheChoice field in the DropDownList:

```
DataTextField="TheChoice"
```

But in code we will receive the ID of the question:

```
DataValueField="QuestionID">
```

The other control on the panel is a Button control:

```
<asp:button
    id="butOK"
    text="OK"
    Type="Submit"
    OnClick="SubmitBtn_Click"
    runat="server"
/>
```

Note that when the button is clicked, the procedure indicated in this property is called

```
OnClick="SubmitBtn_Click"
```

Also note that the DropDownList and Button controls are only displayed when a question appears on the form.

The code on the page appears within two procedures. The first procedure fires when the page is opened.

```
Sub Page_Load(ByVal Sender as Object, ByVal E as EventArgs)
    If Not IsPostBack then
        Dim DBConn as OleDbConnection
        Dim DBCommand As OleDbDataAdapter
        Dim DSHelpDeskData as DataSet
        DBConn = New OleDbConnection("Provider=sqloledb;" _
```

```
        & "server=localhost;" _
        & "Initial Catalog=INETC10;" _
        & "User Id=sa;" _
        & "Password=yourpassword;")
    DSHelpDeskData = New DataSet()
    DBCommand = New OleDbDataAdapter _
        ("Select QuestionID, TitleText, TheMessage " _
        & "From HelpDesk Where ParentID = 0",DBConn)
    DBCommand.Fill(DSHelpDeskData, _
        "Question")
    DBCommand = New OleDbDataAdapter _
        ("Select QuestionID, TheChoice " _
        & "From HelpDesk " _
        & "Where ParentID = " _
            & DSHelpDeskData.Tables("Question"). _
            Rows(0).Item("QuestionID") _
            ,DBConn)
    DBCommand.Fill(DSHelpDeskData, _
        "Choices")
    lblTitle.BorderWidth = New Unit("7px")
    lblTitle.BorderStyle = 9
    lblTitle.Width = New Unit("90%")
    lblTitle.Font.Size = New FontUnit("25pt")
    lblTitle.Font.Name = "Arial"
    lblTitle.Text = "Help Desk - " _
        & DSHelpDeskData.Tables("Question"). _
            Rows(0).Item("TitleText")
    lblQuestion.Font.Size = New FontUnit("12pt")
    lblQuestion.Font.Name = "Verdana"
    lblQuestion.Text = _
        DSHelpDeskData.Tables("Question"). _
            Rows(0).Item("TheMessage")
    ddlAnswers.DataSource = _
        DSHelpDeskData.Tables("Choices").DefaultView
    ddlAnswers.DataBind()
  End If
End Sub
```

The code in this procedure sets up the appearance of some controls and displays the top-level question. So we only want it to run the first time the page is loaded. The first line of code makes sure that this is the first viewing of the page:

```
If Not IsPostBack then
```

If it is, we will need a Connection object,

```
Dim DBConn as OleDbConnection
```

a Data Adapter object,

```
Dim DBCommand As OleDbDataAdapter
```

and a DataSet object:

```
Dim DSHelpDeskData as DataSet
```

First, we need to connect to our SQL Server database:

```
DBConn = New OleDbConnection("Provider=sqloledb;" _
    & "server=localhost;" _
    & "Initial Catalog=INETC10;" _
    & "User Id=sa;" _
    & "Password=yourpassword;")
```

We then need to instantiate our DataSet object:

```
DSHelpDeskData = New DataSet()
```

We need to retrieve the data for the first question that is displayed in the help desk. Remember that the special value of 0 in the ParentID field means that this is the top-level record. So that is the record we retrieve

```
DBCommand = New OleDbDataAdapter _
    ("Select QuestionID, TitleText, TheMessage " _
    & "From HelpDesk Where ParentID = 0",DBConn)
```

and place into our DataSet object, in a DataSet table called Question:

```
DBCommand.Fill(DSHelpDeskData, _
    "Question")
```

We also need to retrieve the possible choices that go with this question

```
DBCommand = New OleDbDataAdapter _
    ("Select QuestionID, TheChoice " _
    & "From HelpDesk " _
```

```
    & "Where ParentID = " _
    & DSHelpDeskData.Tables("Question"). _
    Rows(0).Item("QuestionID") _
    ,DBConn)
```

and place them into our DataSet object in a table called Choices:

```
DBCommand.Fill(DSHelpDeskData, _
    "Choices")
```

Next, we set up the appearance of the Title label:

```
lblTitle.BorderWidth = New Unit("7px")
lblTitle.BorderStyle = 9
lblTitle.Width = New Unit("90%")
lblTitle.Font.Size = New FontUnit("25pt")
lblTitle.Font.Name = "Arial"
```

We then place the text "Help Desk", as well as the title text for this question from the database, into the Title label:

```
lblTitle.Text = "Help Desk - " _
    & DSHelpDeskData.Tables("Question"). _
    Rows(0).Item("TitleText")
```

We also set up the appearance of the Question label:

```
lblQuestion.Font.Size = New FontUnit("12pt")
lblQuestion.Font.Name = "Verdana"
```

We then place into the Text property of that label the text of the current question:

```
lblQuestion.Text = _
    DSHelpDeskData.Tables("Question"). _
    Rows(0).Item("TheMessage")
```

Finally, we need to bind the DropDownList to the Choices table of the DataSet object:

```
ddlAnswers.DataSource = _
    DSHelpDeskData.Tables("Choices").DefaultView
    ddlAnswers.DataBind()
```

The other procedure on the page fires when the OK button is clicked. It displays the text of the next question according to the choice made by the visitor, or it displays the answer for the choice if it doesn't lead to another question.

```
Sub SubmitBtn_Click(Sender As Object, E As EventArgs)
    Dim DBConn as OleDbConnection
    Dim DBCommand As OleDbDataAdapter
    Dim DSHelpDeskData as DataSet
    DBConn = New OleDbConnection("Provider=sqloledb;" _
        & "server=localhost;" _
        & "Initial Catalog=INETC10;" _
        & "User Id=sa;" _
        & "Password=yourpassword;")
    DSHelpDeskData = New DataSet()
    DBCommand = New OleDbDataAdapter _
        ("Select QorA, TitleText, TheMessage " _
        & "From HelpDesk Where QuestionID = " _
        & ddlAnswers.SelectedItem.Value,DBConn)
    DBCommand.Fill(DSHelpDeskData, _
        "Question")
    lblTitle.Text = "Help Desk - " _
        & DSHelpDeskData.Tables("Question"). _
            Rows(0).Item("TitleText")
    lblQuestion.Text = _
        DSHelpDeskData.Tables("Question"). _
            Rows(0).Item("TheMessage")
    If DSHelpDeskData.Tables("Question"). _
                Rows(0).Item("QorA") = "Q" Then
        DBCommand = New OleDbDataAdapter _
            ("Select QuestionID, TheChoice " _
            & "From HelpDesk " _
            & "Where ParentID = " _
            & ddlAnswers.SelectedItem.Value,DBConn)
        DBCommand.Fill(DSHelpDeskData, _
            "Choices")
        ddlAnswers.DataSource = _
            DSHelpDeskData.Tables("Choices").DefaultView
        ddlAnswers.DataBind()
    Else
        ddlAnswers.Visible = False
        butOK.Visible = False
    End If
End Sub
```

The procedure requires data objects so that we can retrieve information from our SQL Server database:

```
Dim DBConn as OleDbConnection
Dim DBCommand As OleDbDataAdapter
Dim DSHelpDeskData as DataSet
```

First, we connect to the database. Note that you would need to change the connect string to point to your server, database, and user information:

```
DBConn = New OleDbConnection("Provider=sqloledb;" _
    & "server=localhost;" _
    & "Initial Catalog=INETC10;" _
    & "User Id=sa;" _
    & "Password=yourpassword;")
```

We then instantiate our DataSet object

```
DSHelpDeskData = New DataSet()
```

and retrieve the next question or answer into it according to the choice made in the DropDownList by the visitor:

```
DBCommand = New OleDbDataAdapter _
    ("Select QorA, TitleText, TheMessage " _
    & "From HelpDesk Where QuestionID = " _
    & ddlAnswers.SelectedItem.Value,DBConn)
DBCommand.Fill(DSHelpDeskData, _
    "Question")
```

Regardless of whether the record is a question or an answer, we need to display the title in the title label

```
lblTitle.Text = "Help Desk - " _
    & DSHelpDeskData.Tables("Question"). _
    Rows(0).Item("TitleText")
```

and its text in the Question label:

```
lblQuestion.Text = _
    DSHelpDeskData.Tables("Question"). _
    Rows(0).Item("TheMessage")
```

But we need to take different actions on the other controls depending on whether this is a question or an answer. If this is a question

```
If DSHelpDeskData.Tables("Question"). _
    Rows(0).Item("QorA") = "Q" Then
```

we need to retrieve its choices into our DataSet object

```
DBCommand = New OleDbDataAdapter _
    ("Select QuestionID, TheChoice " _
    & "From HelpDesk " _
    & "Where ParentID = " _
    & ddlAnswers.SelectedItem.Value,DBConn)
DBCommand.Fill(DSHelpDeskData, _
    "Choices")
```

and then bind those choices into our DropDownList:

```
ddlAnswers.DataSource = _
    DSHelpDeskData.Tables("Choices").DefaultView
ddlAnswers.DataBind()
```

If the record is an answer record, the code will flow here:

```
Else
```

In that case, we don't need to display the DropDownList

```
ddlAnswers.Visible = False
```

or the OK button:

```
butOK.Visible = False
```

Access Code Changes

C10HelpDesk.mdb

The only code change that is needed to get this solution to work with Access instead of SQL Server is to change the connect string

```
DBConn = New OleDbConnection("Provider=sqloledb;" _
    & "server=localhost;" _
    & "Initial Catalog=INETC10;" _
    & "User Id=sa;" _
    & "Password=yourpassword;")
```

so that it uses the proper provider and points to the correct database:

```
DBConn = New OleDbConnection("PROVIDER=Microsoft.Jet.OLEDB.4.0;" _
    & "DATA SOURCE=" _
    & Server.MapPath("/INetBook/C10/HelpDesk/Access/C10HelpDesk.mdb;"))
```

Note that you will need to modify the path to the location of the database on your server.

Room Reservation Tool

The Room Reservation tool allows the visitor to book a room during the period of time that they specify. They select a room, providing dates and personal information. If their reservation does not conflict with existing reservations, it is made.

As you review this tool, note the use of Panel objects to toggle between views of the page. Since the tool is implemented as a single page, panels are used to distinguish what the visitor sees during the reservation process. Also note the complex query used to determine whether a reservation conflicts with an existing one.

Sample Usage

Figure 10-11 shows the page with the panel visible that allows the visitor to enter their information for their reservation.

Note the use of validation controls on the input panel. All of the TextBox controls are required, and the two date controls must have a date placed into them. The visitor can not proceed with their reservation until they place valid data into each field.

Once they do that, the validation messages go away, as you can see in Figure 10-12.

Now the visitor can proceed by clicking the Check Availability Button control. When they do that, they will see the message displayed in Figure 10-13 if their reservation can be placed.

If the reservation could not be made, the same panel is displayed but the visitor sees a different message, letting them know that the reservation did not succeed.

Room Reservation Database Component

C10Room.sql

The database used with the Room Reservation tool contains two tables. In this section we will review the relationship between the tables and the fields that they contain.

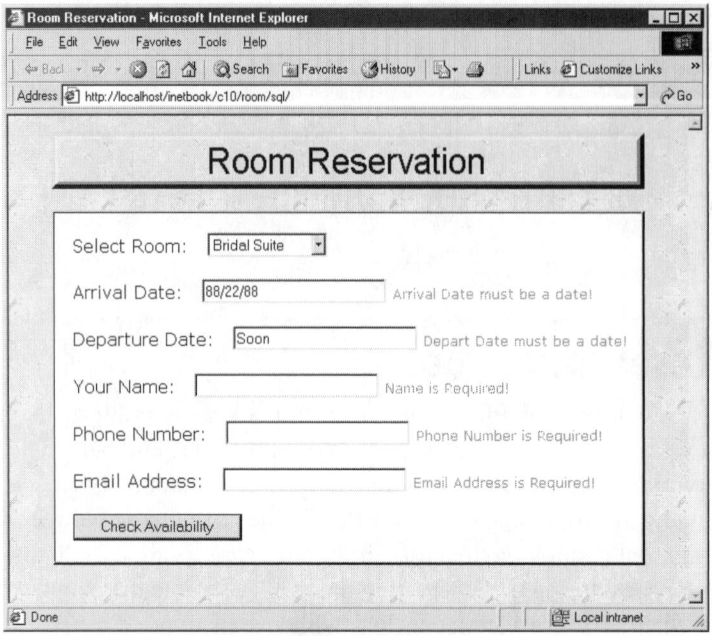

Figure 10-11 *Invalid room reservation data*

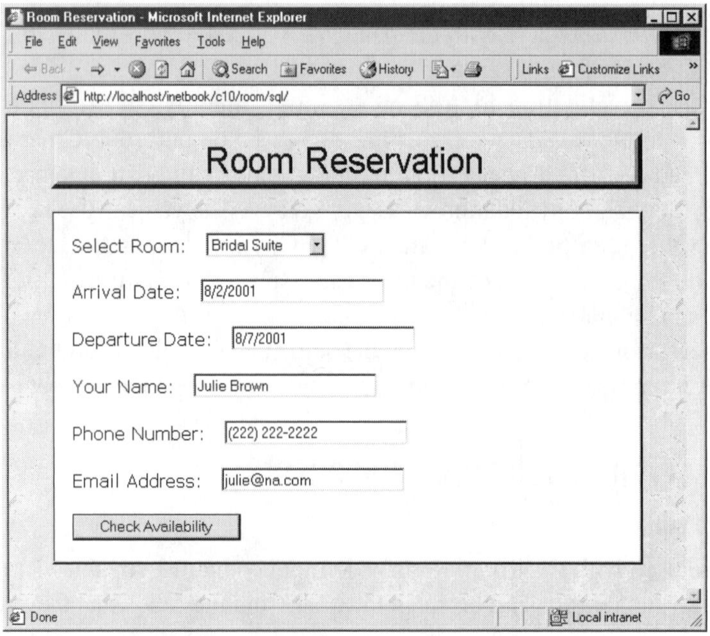

Figure 10-12 *Valid data on the input panel*

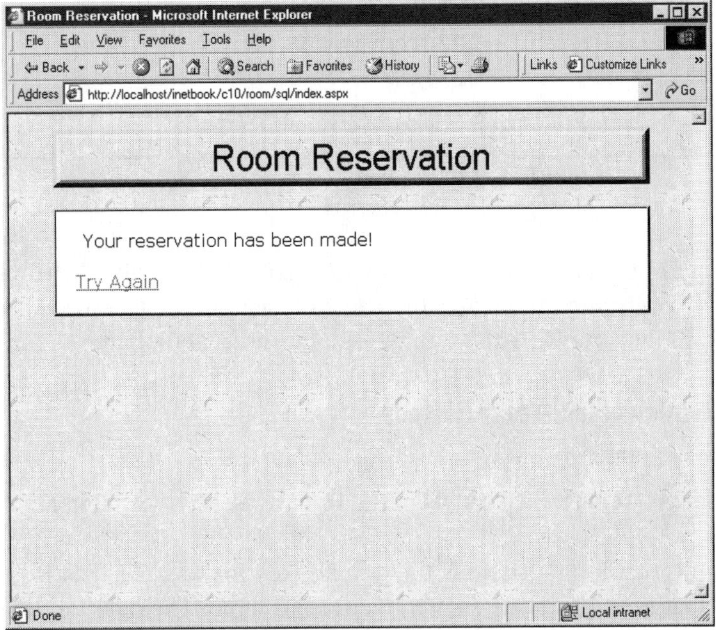

Figure 10-13 *Successful reservation message*

Table and Data Diagram

Figure 10-14 shows the relationship between the tables used in the Room Reservation tool.

The Rooms table stores the top-level information about a room. The RoomReservations table stores the data about each reservation made. The two tables relate in a one-to-many relationship. Each room can have many reservations, but each reservation goes with a single room.

Rooms Field Specifications

Rooms.txt

The field specifications for the fields in the Rooms table are displayed in Table 10-6.

Field Name	Field Type	Notes
RoomID	int	Primary Key, Identity Column
RoomName	varchar	Length = 50

Table 10-6 *Rooms Field Specifications*

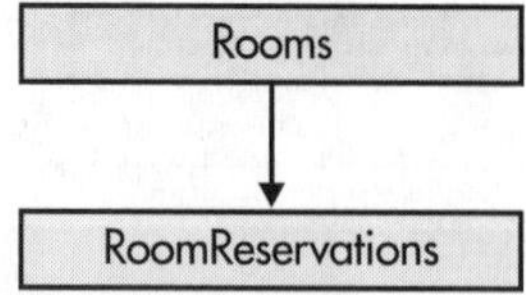

Figure 10-14 *Room Reservation data diagram*

The RoomID field is the primary key in this table. It uniquely identifies each record. The RoomName field stores the name of each room. That field is displayed to the visitor in the DropDownList on the Room Reservation page.

RoomReservations Field Specifications

RoomReservations.txt

The field specifications for the fields in the RoomReservations table are displayed in Table 10-7.

The RoomReservationID field is the primary key in the table. The RoomID is a foreign key that links this table back to the Rooms table. The date fields store when the reservation starts and ends. The other fields store personal information about the visitor making the reservation.

Room Reservation ASP.NET Code

The Room Reservation tool is implemented through a single ASP.NET page that uses two panels. In this section, we will review the code on that page.

Field Name	Field Type	Notes
RoomReservationID	int	Primary Key, Identity Column
RoomID	int	Primary Key, Identity Column
ArrivalDate	datetime	
DepartureDate	datetime	
CustomersName	varchar	Length = 50
PhoneNumber	varchar	Length = 50
EmailAddress	varchar	Length = 50

Table 10-7 *RoomReservations Field Specifications*

Room Reservation ASP.NET Page

Index.aspx

The code on the Room Reservation page initializes the input form and then checks to see if the reservation is possible. To accomplish its tasks, the following compiler directives are placed at the top of the page.

```
<%@ Page Language=VB Debug=true %>
<%@ Import Namespace="System.Data" %>
<%@ Import Namespace="System.Data.OLEDB" %>
```

The first directive tells the compiler the language we are using and that we want to be in debug mode, since we are working with our code and want to see more complete error messages.

```
<%@ Page Language=VB Debug=true %>
```

The other directives import the data libraries needed so that we can access, manipulate, and display the data component used in this tool:

```
<%@ Import Namespace="System.Data" %>
<%@ Import Namespace="System.Data.OLEDB" %>
```

The contents of the page are placed on an ASP.NET form:

```
<form runat="server">
```

At the top of the page, a Label control is used to display the title of the page. Note that the control is visible with both panels:

```
<asp:Label
    id="lblTitle"
    BorderWidth="7px"
    BorderStyle=9
    Width="90%"
    Font-Size="25pt"
    Font-Name="Arial"
    Text="Room Reservation"
    runat="server"
/>
```

The page contains two panels. The first panel is visible when the page is first opened and when a new reservation is attempted. It is the panel that contains the input form:

```
<asp:Panel
    id="pnlMakeReservation"
    runat="server"
    Font-Size="12pt"
    Font-Name="verdana"
    BackColor="ivory"
    Width="90%"
    BorderWidth="3px"
    BorderStyle=7
    HorizontalAlign="Left"
>
```

Within that panel we start with a DropDownList that displays the name of the room to the visitor but makes the ID of the room available to us in code:

```
<asp:dropdownlist
    id="ddlRoomID"
    runat=server
    DataTextField="RoomName"
    DataValueField="RoomID">
</asp:dropdownlist>
```

The next control is the panel in the TextBox control for the arrival date:

```
<asp:TextBox
    id="txtArrivalDate"
    Columns="25"
    MaxLength="30"
    runat=server
/>
```

That control has a RequiredFieldValidator control associated with it, making the arrival date a required field:

```
<asp:RequiredFieldValidator
    id="rfvArrivalDate"
    ControlToValidate="txtArrivalDate"
    Display="Dynamic"
    Font-Size="10pt"
```

```
    runat=server>
    Arrival Date is Required!
</asp:RequiredFieldValidator>
```

Also associated with the arrival date TextBox control is the CompareValidator control, which makes sure that the value entered into the TextBox is a date:

```
<asp:CompareValidator
    id="cvArrivalDate"
    ControlToValidate="txtArrivalDate"
    Operator="DataTypeCheck"
    Type="Date"
    Display="Dynamic"
    Font-Size="10pt"
    runat="server">
    Arrival Date must be a date!
</asp:CompareValidator>
```

This is done by setting the ControlToValidate property to the TextBox

```
ControlToValidate="txtArrivalDate"
```

and setting the Operator property to DataTypeCheck

```
Operator="DataTypeCheck"
```

and the Type property to Date:

```
Type="Date"
```

The next control on the page is the TextBox for the Departure date:

```
<asp:TextBox
    id="txtDepartureDate"
    Columns="25"
    MaxLength="30"
    runat=server
/>
```

That TextBox also has a RequiredFieldValidator associated with it:

```
<asp:RequiredFieldValidator
    id="rfvDepartureDate"
    ControlToValidate="txtDepartureDate"
```

```
    Display="Dynamic"
    Font-Size="10pt"
    runat=server>
    Departure Date is Required!
</asp:RequiredFieldValidator>
```

We also make sure that the visitor enters a valid date:

```
<asp:CompareValidator
    id="cvDepartureDate"
    ControlToValidate="txtDepartureDate"
    Operator="DataTypeCheck"
    Type="Date"
    Display="Dynamic"
    Font-Size="10pt"
    runat="server">
    Departure Date must be a date!
</asp:CompareValidator>
```

The next TextBox control is for the visitor's name:

```
<asp:TextBox
    id="txtName"
    Columns="25"
    MaxLength="50"
    runat=server
/>
```

It, too, is required

```
<asp:RequiredFieldValidator
    id="rfvName"
    ControlToValidate="txtName"
    Display="Dynamic"
    Font-Size="10pt"
    runat=server>
    Name is Required!
</asp:RequiredFieldValidator>
```

Note that the Display property for the validation controls is set to Dynamic:

```
Display="Dynamic"
```

This means that the format of the page will not plan for the presence of the validation text.

The next TextBox control is for the visitor's phone number

```
<asp:TextBox
    id="txtPhoneNumber"
    Columns="25"
    MaxLength="50"
    runat=server
/>
```

which is also required

```
<asp:RequiredFieldValidator
    id="rfvPhoneNumber"
    ControlToValidate="txtPhoneNumber"
    Display="Dynamic"
    Font-Size="10pt"
    runat=server>
    Phone Number is Required!
</asp:RequiredFieldValidator>
```

and the e-mail address TextBox control is set up similarly:

```
<asp:TextBox
    id="txtEmailAddress"
    Columns="25"
    MaxLength="50"
    runat=server
/>
<asp:RequiredFieldValidator id="rfvEmailAddress"
    ControlToValidate="txtEmailAddress"
    Display="Dynamic"
    Font-Size="10pt"
    runat=server>
    Email Address is Required!
</asp:RequiredFieldValidator>
```

One more control appears on the input panel. This is the Button control:

```
<asp:button
    id="butOK"
    text="Check Availability"
```

```
    Type="Submit"
    OnClick="SubmitBtn_Click"
    runat="server"
/>
```

Note that a procedure will run when the button is clicked

```
OnClick="SubmitBtn_Click"
```

The other panel on the page is used to display the results of the visitor's room reservation request. The panel is made visible after the visitor submits their request by clicking the Button control:

```
<asp:Panel
    id="pnlReservationResponse"
    runat="server"
    Font-Size="12pt"
    Font-Name="verdana"
    BackColor="ivory"
    Width="90%"
    BorderWidth="3px"
    BorderStyle=7
    HorizontalAlign="Left"
>
```

Contained on this panel is a single Label control that displays the results to the visitor:

```
<asp:Label
    id="lblResult"
    runat="server"
/>
```

The code on the page is divided into two procedures. The first procedure runs when the page is first loaded or when the visitor wants to try another reservation. The code in the procedure sets up the input panel.

```
Sub Page_Load(ByVal Sender as Object, ByVal E as EventArgs)
    If Not IsPostBack then
        Dim DBConn as OleDbConnection
        Dim DBCommand As OleDbDataAdapter
        Dim DSRoomData as New DataSet
        DBConn = New OleDbConnection("Provider=sqloledb;" _
            & "server=localhost;" _
```

```
            & "Initial Catalog=INETC10;" _
            & "User Id=sa;" _
            & "Password=yourpassword;")
        DBCommand = New OleDbDataAdapter _
            ("Select RoomID, RoomName " _
            & "From Rooms " _
            & "Order By RoomName",DBConn)
        DBCommand.Fill(DSRoomData, _
            "Rooms")
        ddlRoomID.DataSource = _
            DSRoomData.Tables("Rooms").DefaultView
        ddlRoomID.DataBind()
        pnlMakeReservation.Visible = True
        pnlReservationResponse.Visible = False
    End If
End Sub
```

We don't want this code to run after the button is clicked, so we check that:

```
If Not IsPostBack then
```

If it wasn't, we need to run our code. To set up the input form, we will need data objects:

```
Dim DBConn as OleDbConnection
Dim DBCommand As OleDbDataAdapter
Dim DSRoomData as New DataSet
```

We then connect to our SQL Server database. Remember that you will need to change the connect string to point to your database and user information:

```
DBConn = New OleDbConnection("Provider=sqloledb;" _
    & "server=localhost;" _
    & "Initial Catalog=INETC10;" _
    & "User Id=sa;" _
    & "Password=yourpassword;")
```

We then place SQL into our Data Adapter object that will retrieve all the names and IDs of the rooms for our DropDownList:

```
DBCommand = New OleDbDataAdapter _
    ("Select RoomID, RoomName " _
    & "From Rooms " _
    & "Order By RoomName",DBConn)
```

That data is placed into our DataSet object

```
DBCommand.Fill(DSRoomData, _
    "Rooms")
```

which is then bound to our DropDownList:

```
ddlRoomID.DataSource = _
    DSRoomData.Tables("Rooms").DefaultView
ddlRoomID.DataBind()
```

Finally, we make sure that the input panel is visible

```
pnlMakeReservation.Visible = True
```

and that the result panel isn't

```
pnlReservationResponse.Visible = False
```

The other procedure on this page fires when the visitor clicks the Button control. It checks to see if the reservation can be made, enters it into the database if it can, and informs the visitor of the results of their attempt.

```
Sub SubmitBtn_Click(Sender As Object, E As EventArgs)
    Dim DBConn as OleDbConnection
    Dim DBCommand As OleDbDataAdapter
    Dim DSRoomAvailable as New DataSet
    Dim DBInsert As New OleDbCommand
    DBConn = New OleDbConnection("Provider=sqloledb;" _
        & "server=localhost;" _
        & "Initial Catalog=INETC10;" _
        & "User Id=sa;" _
        & "Password=yourpassword;")
    DBCommand = New OleDbDataAdapter _
        ("Select Count(RoomReservationID) as TheCount " _
        & "From RoomReservations WHERE (RoomID = " _
        & ddlRoomID.SelectedItem.Value _
        & ") AND " _
        & "('" & txtArrivalDate.text & "' BETWEEN ArrivalDate " _
        & "AND DepartureDate) OR (RoomID = " _
        & ddlRoomID.SelectedItem.Value _
        & ") " _
        & "AND ('" & txtDepartureDate.text _
```

```
        & "' BETWEEN ArrivalDate AND DepartureDate) " _
        & "OR (RoomID = " _
        & ddlRoomID.SelectedItem.Value _
        & ") AND " _
        & "(ArrivalDate BETWEEN '" _
        & txtArrivalDate.text & "' AND '" _
        & txtDepartureDate.text & "') " _
        & "OR (RoomID = " _
        & ddlRoomID.SelectedItem.Value _
        & ") AND " _
        & "(DepartureDate BETWEEN '" _
        & txtArrivalDate.text & "' AND '" _
        & txtDepartureDate.text & "')", DBConn)
    DBCommand.Fill(DSRoomAvailable, _
        "RoomCount")
    If DSRoomAvailable.Tables("RoomCount"). _
        Rows(0).Item("TheCount") = 0 Then
        DBInsert.CommandText = "Insert Into RoomReservations " _
            & "(RoomID, ArrivalDate, DepartureDate, CustomersName, " _
            & "PhoneNumber, EmailAddress) values (" _
            & ddlRoomID.SelectedItem.Value & ", " _
            & "'" & txtArrivalDate.text & "', " _
            & "'" & txtDepartureDate.text & "', " _
            & "'" & txtName.text & "', " _
            & "'" & txtPhoneNumber.text & "', " _
            & "'" & txtEmailAddress.text & "')"
        DBInsert.Connection = DBConn
        DBInsert.Connection.Open
        DBInsert.ExecuteNonQuery()
        lblResult.Text = "Your reservation has been made!"
    Else
        lblResult.Text = "Oops! The room is not available at that time."
    End If
    pnlMakeReservation.Visible = False
    pnlReservationResponse.Visible = True
End Sub
```

We will need data objects in this procedure:

```
Dim DBConn as OleDbConnection
Dim DBCommand As OleDbDataAdapter
Dim DSRoomAvailable as New DataSet
Dim DBInsert As New OleDbCommand
```

First, we connect to our database:

```
DBConn = New OleDbConnection("Provider=sqloledb;" _
    & "server=localhost;" _
    & "Initial Catalog=INETC10;" _
    & "User Id=sa;" _
    & "Password=yourpassword;")
```

Then we write a complex query to see if the reservation is made. The query is complex because we have to check for four possible conflicting reservations against the room selected by the visitor. One condition is when the reservation being attempted contains a conflicting reservation within it. The second condition occurs when the reservation being attempted falls within another reservation. The third type of conflict occurs when the start date of the reservation falls within an existing reservation. And the fourth conflict type occurs when the end date falls within an existing reservation.

The query uses the Or operator to look for any records that meet any of these four conditions. The number of conflicting records is returned

```
DBCommand = New OleDbDataAdapter _
    ("Select Count(RoomReservationID) as TheCount " _
    & "From RoomReservations WHERE (RoomID = " _
    & ddlRoomID.SelectedItem.Value _
    & ") AND " _
    & "('" & txtArrivalDate.text & "' BETWEEN ArrivalDate " _
    & "AND DepartureDate) OR (RoomID = " _
    & ddlRoomID.SelectedItem.Value _
    & ") " _
    & "AND ('" & txtDepartureDate.text _
    & "' BETWEEN ArrivalDate AND DepartureDate) " _
    & "OR (RoomID = " _
    & ddlRoomID.SelectedItem.Value _
    & ") AND " _
    & "(ArrivalDate BETWEEN '" _
    & txtArrivalDate.text & "' AND '" _
    & txtDepartureDate.text & "') " _
    & "OR (RoomID = " _
    & ddlRoomID.SelectedItem.Value _
    & ") AND " _
    & "(DepartureDate BETWEEN '" _
    & txtArrivalDate.text & "' AND '" _
    & txtDepartureDate.text & "')", DBConn)
```

The result of that query is placed into our DataSet object:

```
DBCommand.Fill(DSRoomAvailable, _
    "RoomCount")
```

If the query returns a 0, that means the room reservation can be made

```
If DSRoomAvailable.Tables("RoomCount"). _
    Rows(0).Item("TheCount") = 0 Then
```

In that case, we can add the reservation to the system:

```
DBInsert.CommandText = "Insert Into RoomReservations " _
    & "(RoomID, ArrivalDate, DepartureDate, CustomersName, " _
    & "PhoneNumber, EmailAddress) values (" _
    & ddlRoomID.SelectedItem.Value & ", " _
    & "'" & txtArrivalDate.text & "', " _
    & "'" & txtDepartureDate.text & "', " _
    & "'" & txtName.text & "', " _
    & "'" & txtPhoneNumber.text & "', " _
    & "'" & txtEmailAddress.text & "')"
```

We then point the Command object to our database

```
DBInsert.Connection = DBConn
DBInsert.Connection.Open
```

and run it:

```
DBInsert.ExecuteNonQuery()
```

We also inform the visitor that their reservation succeeded

```
lblResult.Text = "Your reservation has been made!"
```

Otherwise, we tell the visitor that the reservation could not be made

```
lblResult.Text = "Oops! The room is not available at that time."
```

Regardless of whether the reservation was made or not, we don't want the input panel displayed

```
pnlMakeReservation.Visible = False
```

but we do want the results panel to be displayed

```
pnlReservationResponse.Visible = True
```

Access Code Changes

C10Room.mdb

Two changes are needed to get this solution to work with Access instead of SQL Server. The first is to change the connect string

```
DBConn = New OleDbConnection("Provider=sqloledb;" _
    & "server=localhost;" _
    & "Initial Catalog=INETC10;" _
    & "User Id=sa;" _
    & "Password=yourpassword;")
```

so that it uses the proper provider and points to the correct database:

```
DBConn = New OleDbConnection("PROVIDER=Microsoft.Jet.OLEDB.4.0;" _
    & "DATA SOURCE=" _
    & Server.MapPath("/INetBook/C10/Room/Access/C10Room.mdb;"))
```

Note that you will need to modify the path to the location of the database on your server.

The other change has to do with the Where clause in our SQL statement that looks for conflicting reservations. In SQL Server, dates in the Where clause are surrounded by the ' character:

```
DBCommand = New OleDbDataAdapter _
    ("Select Count(RoomReservationID) as TheCount " _
    & "From RoomReservations WHERE (RoomID = " _
    & ddlRoomID.SelectedItem.Value _
    & ") AND " _
    & "('" & txtArrivalDate.text & "' BETWEEN ArrivalDate " _
    & "AND DepartureDate) OR (RoomID = " _
    & ddlRoomID.SelectedItem.Value _
    & ") " _
    & "AND ('" & txtDepartureDate.text _
    & "' BETWEEN ArrivalDate AND DepartureDate) " _
    & "OR (RoomID = " _
    & ddlRoomID.SelectedItem.Value _
    & ") AND " _
```

```
    & "(ArrivalDate BETWEEN '" _
    & txtArrivalDate.text & "' AND '" _
    & txtDepartureDate.text & "') " _
    & "OR (RoomID = " _
    & ddlRoomID.SelectedItem.Value _
    & ") AND " _
    & "(DepartureDate BETWEEN '" _
    & txtArrivalDate.text & "' AND '" _
    & txtDepartureDate.text & "')", DBConn)
```

In Access, the # character is used instead, as you can see here:

```
DBCommand = New OleDbDataAdapter _
    ("Select Count(RoomReservationID) as TheCount " _
    & "From RoomReservations WHERE (RoomID = " _
    & ddlRoomID.SelectedItem.Value _
    & ") AND " _
    & "(#" & txtArrivalDate.text & "# BETWEEN ArrivalDate " _
    & "AND DepartureDate) OR (RoomID = " _
    & ddlRoomID.SelectedItem.Value _
    & ") " _
    & "AND (#" & txtDepartureDate.text _
    & "# BETWEEN ArrivalDate AND DepartureDate) " _
    & "OR (RoomID = " _
    & ddlRoomID.SelectedItem.Value _
    & ") AND " _
    & "(ArrivalDate BETWEEN #" _
    & txtArrivalDate.text & "# AND #" _
    & txtDepartureDate.text & "#) " _
    & "OR (RoomID = " _
    & ddlRoomID.SelectedItem.Value _
    & ") AND " _
    & "(DepartureDate BETWEEN #" _
    & txtArrivalDate.text & "# AND #" _
    & txtDepartureDate.text & "#)", DBConn)
```

No other changes are necessary.

CHAPTER

11

Implementing a Real Estate Site

One popular use of the Internet is to convey home listings to potential buyers. Whether the listings are offered by a real estate agent, a local newspaper, or a Web site dedicated to hosting listings, the elements of providing the information are about the same.

The visitor to the site needs to search through the listings using standard fields such as number of bedrooms, price, or square feet. Or the visitor to the site may want to go straight to a listing to read further information about it. In this chapter, we will look at a series of pages that allow the visitor to search, browse, and view home listings.

Searching and Viewing Home Listings

Before reviewing the code, the site as viewed by the visitor will be presented. When the visitor first enters the tool, they see the page displayed in Figure 11-1.

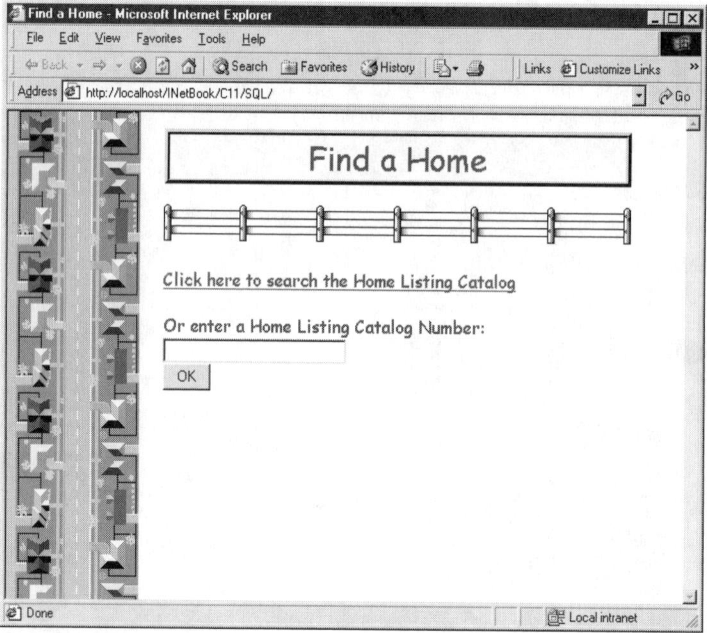

Figure 11-1 *Real Estate Site entry page*

One of the things the visitor can do from the entry page is go to the Search page. They do this by clicking the link on the page. The Search page is displayed in Figure 11-2.

The visitor uses the Search page to limit the home listings displayed. They can limit that list by the price of the home, either above a limit or below. They can also limit the search to the number of baths, the number of bedrooms, or a specific part of town. Additionally, the visitor uses this form to specify how records returned are sorted.

In this case, the visitor has chosen not to limit the listings by any parameter. So when they click OK, they are taken to the Search Results page displaying all the home listings in the catalog, as is shown in Figure 11-3.

At the top of the Search Results page, the visitor sees the number of records that matched their search. They also see the basic information about each of the matching listings. But the visitor doesn't have to view all the properties. Take a look at the Search page displayed in Figure 11-4.

Now the visitor is requesting to see only those listings that are priced between $100,000 and $300,000, that have at least two bathrooms and three bedrooms, and that are in the part of town called The Hills.

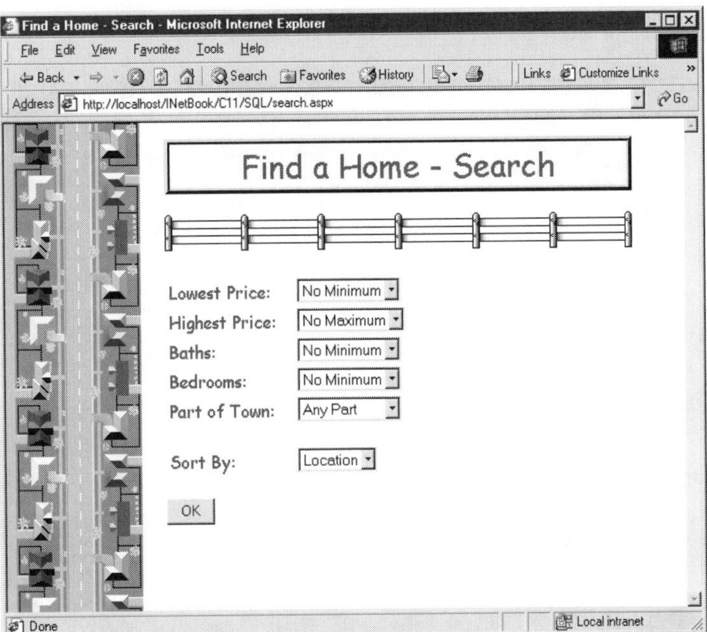

Figure 11-2 *Search page, unfiltered*

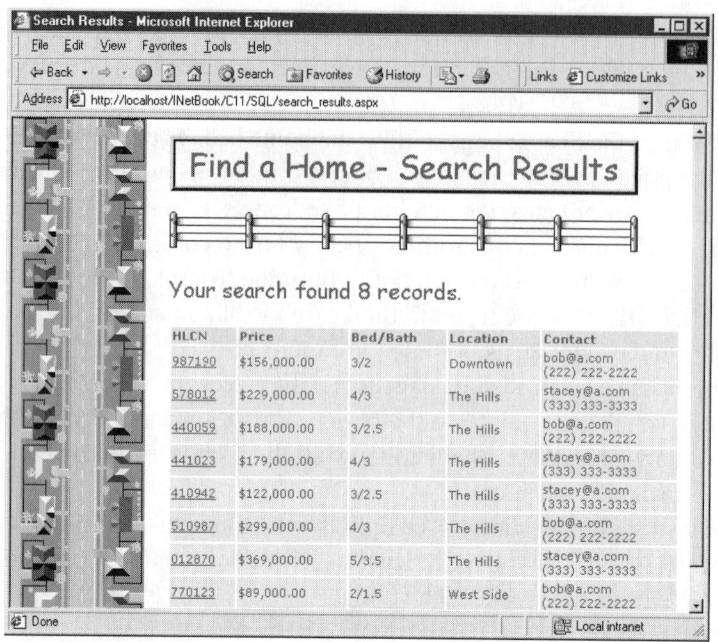

Figure 11-3 *Search Results page without a filter*

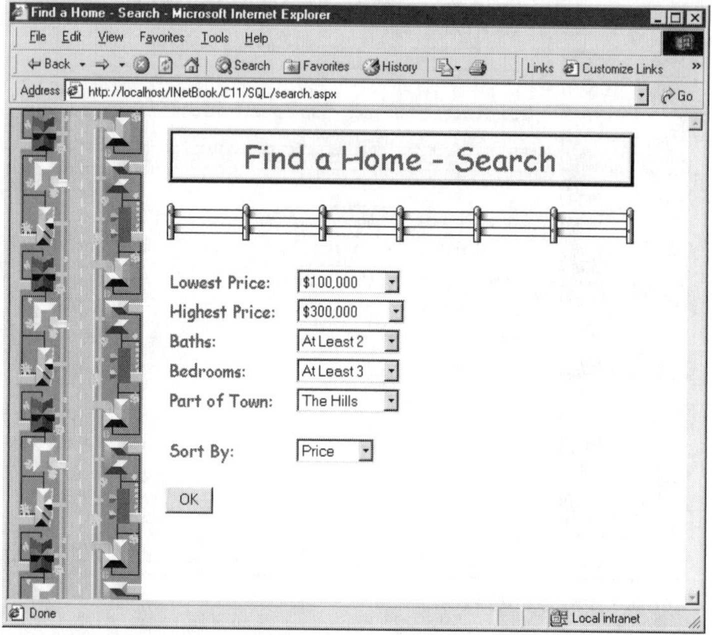

Figure 11-4 *Search page with filter*

When the visitor clicks OK, they see the filtered matching records displayed in Figure 11-5.

Now instead of the eight listings, the visitor sees only the five that match their search. Also notice that the records displayed are sorted by the price of the home.

Note the link in the HLCN column. If the visitor clicks the link, they are taken to the full listing for the home, as is displayed in Figure 11-6.

At the top of the Listing page, the visitor can see the Home Listing Catalog Number, HLCN. This number is important because they can enter the number to go straight to the listing from the Home page. Take a look at Figure 11-7.

The visitor enters the number into the TextBox on this page. Note, though, that the visitor has entered an incorrect number format. As you will see when we look at the code, the visitor must enter the complete six-digit HLCN before the OK button will work.

Back on the Listing page, the visitor sees all the information available about the home for sale. They can even see pictures of the home. In Figure 11-6, two pictures are displayed with the property. But take a look at Figure 11-8.

The tool is set up so that a listing can have no pictures or it can have as many pictures as are desired. In code, a DataList control is used to display the pictures four to a row.

Figure 11-5 *Filtered Search Results page*

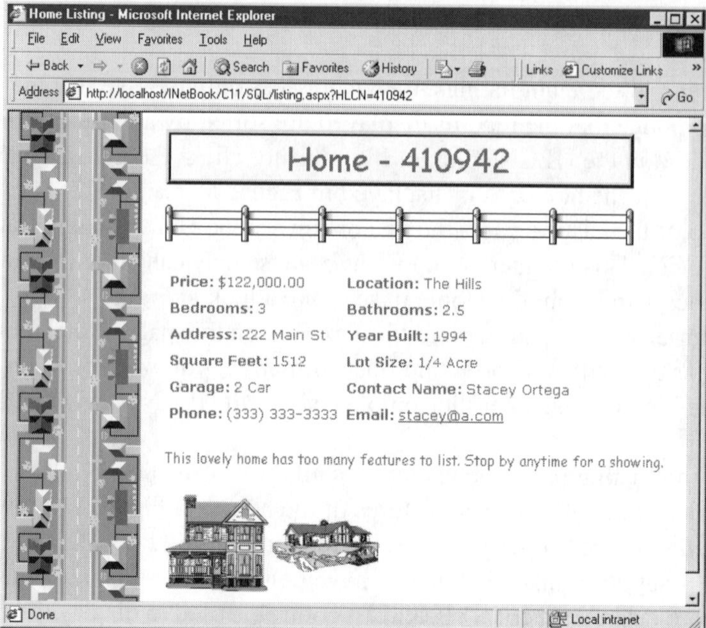

Figure 11-6 *Listing page*

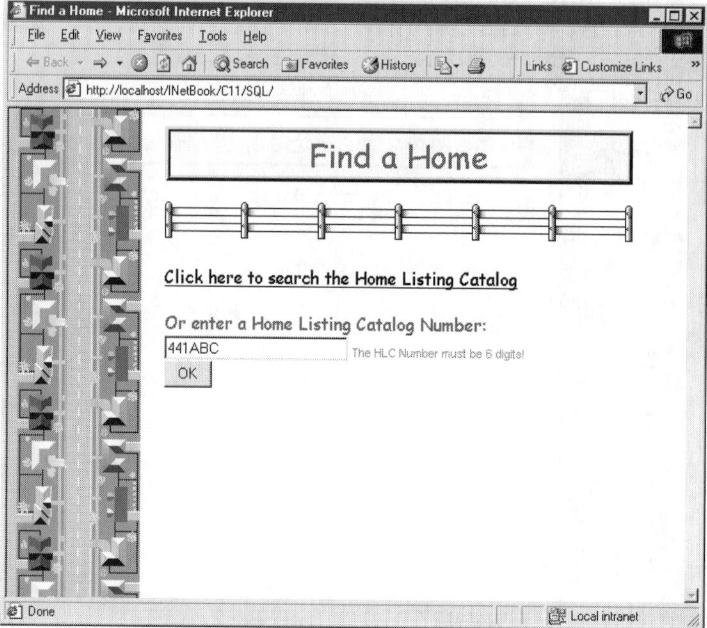

Figure 11-7 *Home page with incorrect HLCN format*

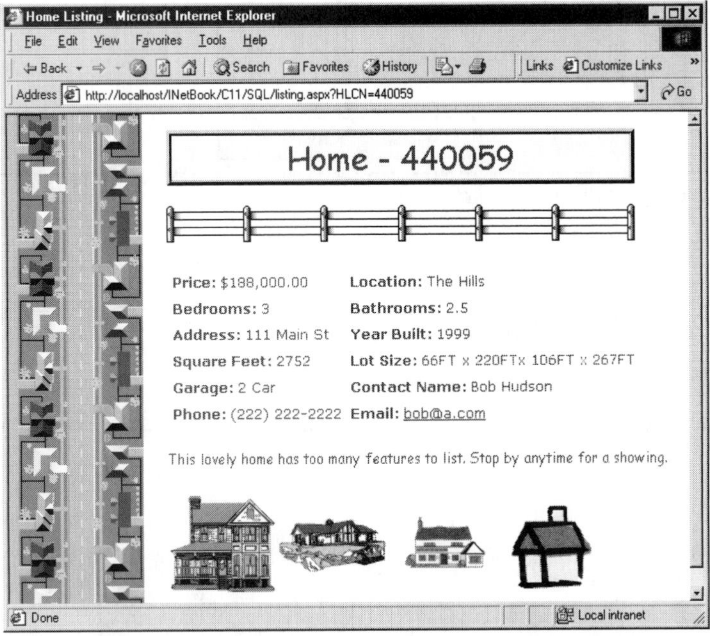

Figure 11-8 *Listing page with four pictures of home*

Real Estate Site Database Component

C11.sql

The database required to run the Real Estate tool is made up of two tables. In this section, we will review the relationship between the tables, their purpose, and the fields that they contain.

Tables and Data Diagram

Figure 11-9 shows the relationship between the tables in the Real Estate Site database.

The Listings table is the top-level table in the database. It contains all the text information about the home and the contact information for the home. The ListingPictures table stores pictures of the homes listed in the tool.

The two tables relate together in a one-to-many relationship. Each of the listings can have many picture records. But each picture record goes with a specific listing.

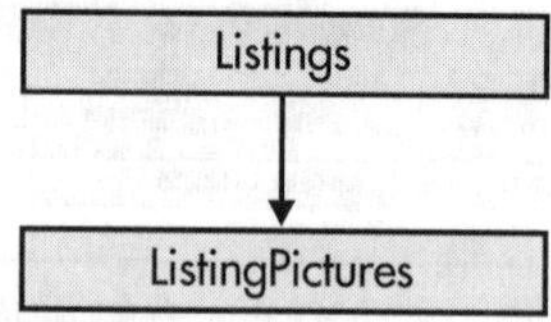

Figure 11-9 *Real estate site data diagram*

Listings Field Specifications

Listings.txt

The field specifications for the fields in the Listings table are displayed in Table 11-1.

Field Names	Field Type	Notes
ListingID	int	Primary Key, Identity Column
HLCN	varchar	Length = 6
HousePrice	money	
Bathrooms	float	
Bedrooms	int	
HomeLocation	varchar	Length = 50
ContactName	varchar	Length = 50
EmailContact	varchar	Length = 50
PhoneContact	varchar	Length = 50
Address	varchar	Length = 100
SquareFeet	varchar	Length = 50
YearBuilt	varchar	Length = 50
LotSize	varchar	Length = 50
Garage	varchar	Length = 50
Notes	varchar	Length = 255

Table 11-1 *Listings Field Specifications*

The ListingID field is the primary key in this table. Since it is an identity column, it is automatically populated when a new record is added. The HLCN is the Home Listing Catalog number. This number allows the user to quickly and easily access the listing for a specific home.

The rest of the fields store information about the home listing.

ListingPictures Field Specifications

ListingPictures.txt

The field specifications for the fields in the ListingPictures table are displayed in Table 11-2.

The ImageID field is the primary key in the table. The ListingID field is a foreign key that links this table to the Listings table.

The ImagePath field stores the address to the graphic that should be used with this listing. This could be a relative path:

```
./home.gif
```

Or a fully referenced path:

```
http://www.whatever.com/pics/home.gif
```

The other field in the table, ImageAlt, stores the text that appears in the AltText property of the image tag on the Web page. The text is visible when the visitor hovers their mouse over the picture.

Field Name	Field Type	Identity Column
ImageID	int	Primary Key, Identity Column
ListingID	int	Foreign Key
ImagePath	varchar	Length = 100
ImageAlt	varchar	Length = 100

Table 11-2 *ListingPictures Field Specifications*

Real Estate Site ASP.NET Code

The Real Estate site is made up of four ASP.NET pages. The pages employ a variety of controls to accomplish their functionality, including a DataGrid control and a Repeater control.

In this section, we will review the controls used and the code added to the four pages.

Home ASP.NET Page

Index.aspx

The Home page allows the user to connect to the Search page or to go directly to a listing. At the top of the page, you will find a single compiler directive line:

```
<%@ Page Language=VB EnableSessionState=true Debug=true %>
```

This directive tells the compiler that the language that the code is in is Visual Basic. It also tells the compiler that we will be using sessions and that debugging should be turned on. Remember to turn debugging off when you move this tool into production.

The body of the page contains an ASP.NET form tag so that our controls will be correctly processed

```
<Form runat="server">
```

Within the body of the page, we use a Label control to display some title text for the page:

```
<asp:Label
    id="lblTitle"
    BorderWidth="5px"
    BorderStyle=7
    BackColor="lightyellow"
    Width="439"
    Font-Size="22pt"
    Font-Name="Comic Sans MS"
    Text="<center>Find a Home</center>"
    runat="server"
/>
```

The next control on the page is a TextBox:

```
<asp:TextBox
    id="txtHLCN"
    Columns="25"
    MaxLength="8"
    runat=server
/>
```

This control allows the visitor to place an HLCN directly into it to go to the Listing page. The HLCN field must be exactly six characters and it must be a number. A RegularExpressionValidator control is used to make sure that that rule is followed

```
<asp:RegularExpressionValidator id="revHLCN"
    ControlToValidate="txtHLCN"
    ValidationExpression="^\d{6}$"
    Display="Dynamic"
    Font-Name="Arial"
    Font-Size="11"
    runat=server>
    The HLC Number must be 6 digits!
</asp:RegularExpressionValidator>
```

The control will check the txtHLCN TextBox

```
ControlToValidate="txtHLCN"
```

and make sure that it contains exactly six digits:

```
ValidationExpression="^\d{6}$"
```

The error message will be displayed dynamically, meaning that space is not allocated ahead of time for it:

```
    Display="Dynamic"
```

The text that appears if the rule is violated is this:

```
The HLC Number must be 6 digits!
```

The other control on the form is the Button control:

```
<asp:button
    id="butOK"
    text="  OK  "
    Type="Submit"
    OnClick="SubmitBtn_Click"
    runat="server"
/>
```

The procedure noted in the OnClick parameter will fire when the button is clicked with the form having been validated

```
OnClick="SubmitBtn_Click"
```

The only code on the page fires when the Button control is clicked

```
Sub SubmitBtn_Click(Sender As Object, E As EventArgs)
    Response.Redirect("./listing.aspx?HLCN=" _
        & txtHLCN.text)
End Sub
```

The code directs the visitor to the Listing page, passing to it the HLCN entered by the visitor:

```
Response.Redirect("./listing.aspx?HLCN=" _
    & txtHLCN.text)
```

Search ASP.NET Page

Search.aspx

The code on the Search page displays DropDownList controls that allow the visitor to filter and sort the Home Listings. Then, based on those selections, a SQL statement that is used on the Search Results page is prepared.

At the top of the page, a single compiler directive is declared

```
<%@ Page Language=VB EnableSessionState=true Debug=true %>
```

The directive tells the compiler the language we will be using, that we will be using sessions, and that we want debugging on.

The controls on the page are contained within an ASP.NET Web form:

```
<Form runat="server">
```

The first control on the page is a Label control that is used to display title text:

```
<asp:Label
    id="lblTitle"
    BorderWidth="5px"
    BorderStyle=7
    BackColor="lightyellow"
    Width="439"
    Font-Size="22pt"
    Font-Name="Comic Sans MS"
    Text="<center>Find a Home - Search</center>"
    runat="server"
/>
```

The next control on the page is a DropDownList control:

```
<asp:DropDownList
    id="ddlLowestPrice"
    runat=server>
    <asp:ListItem Value="0" Selected="True">No Minimum</asp:ListItem>
    <asp:ListItem Value="25000">$25,000</asp:ListItem>
    <asp:ListItem Value="50000">$50,000</asp:ListItem>
    <asp:ListItem Value="100000">$100,000</asp:ListItem>
    <asp:ListItem Value="200000">$200,000</asp:ListItem>
    <asp:ListItem Value="300000">$300,000</asp:ListItem>
    <asp:ListItem Value="500000">$500,000</asp:ListItem>
</asp:DropDownList>
```

The list of items in the control is a fixed list, meaning that it doesn't come from the database. Note that the first list item will be selected by default:

```
<asp:ListItem Value="0" Selected="True">No Minimum</asp:ListItem>
```

This list allows the visitor to specify a minimum value that the house should cost to be included in their search result. The next control does just the opposite:

```
<asp:DropDownList
    id="ddlHighestPrice"
    runat=server>
```

```
    <asp:ListItem Value="100000000" Selected="True">No Maximum</asp:ListItem>
    <asp:ListItem Value="50000">$50,000</asp:ListItem>
    <asp:ListItem Value="100000">$100,000</asp:ListItem>
    <asp:ListItem Value="200000">$200,000</asp:ListItem>
    <asp:ListItem Value="300000">$300,000</asp:ListItem>
    <asp:ListItem Value="500000">$500,000</asp:ListItem>
    <asp:ListItem Value="1000000">$1,000,000</asp:ListItem>
</asp:DropDownList>
```

It allows the visitor to specify the most that the house can cost to be included in the search results.

A third DropDownList allows the visitor to specify the minimum number of bathrooms that the house must have

```
<asp:DropDownList
    id="ddlBaths"
    runat=server>
    <asp:ListItem Value="0" Selected="True">No Minimum</asp:ListItem>
    <asp:ListItem Value="1">At Least 1</asp:ListItem>
    <asp:ListItem Value="1.5">At Least 1.5</asp:ListItem>
    <asp:ListItem Value="2">At Least 2</asp:ListItem>
    <asp:ListItem Value="2.5">At Least 2.5</asp:ListItem>
    <asp:ListItem Value="3">At Least 3</asp:ListItem>
    <asp:ListItem Value="4">At Least 4</asp:ListItem>
</asp:DropDownList>
```

Note that the values selected by the visitor will be used to build a SQL statement that selects just the records that match the criteria. So if the visitor were to choose the item text "At Least 1," the SQL statement would have a Where clause that included this:

```
BathRooms >= 1
```

The next DropDownList provides the mechanism for the visitor to limit the search results by the number of bedrooms:

```
<asp:DropDownList
    id="ddlBeds"
    runat=server>
    <asp:ListItem Value="0" Selected="True">No Minimum</asp:ListItem>
    <asp:ListItem Value="2">At Least 2</asp:ListItem>
    <asp:ListItem Value="3">At Least 3</asp:ListItem>
    <asp:ListItem Value="4">At Least 4</asp:ListItem>
    <asp:ListItem Value="5">At Least 5</asp:ListItem>
</asp:DropDownList>
```

Note that the default selected item in each DropDownList shouldn't limit the records at all. Therefore, if the visitor were to specify no search criteria, they should see all the records.

The other DropDownList that is used to limit the records returned is based on the location of the home listing:

```
<asp:DropDownList
    id="ddlPartOfTown"
    runat=server>
    <asp:ListItem Value="" Selected="True">Any Part</asp:ListItem>
    <asp:ListItem Value="West Side">West Side</asp:ListItem>
    <asp:ListItem Value="The Hills">The Hills</asp:ListItem>
    <asp:ListItem Value="North Peaks">North Peaks</asp:ListItem>
    <asp:ListItem Value="Downtown">Downtown</asp:ListItem>
</asp:DropDownList>
```

One other DropDownList appears on the page. It allows the visitor to select how they would like the matching records sorted

```
<asp:DropDownList
    id="ddlSort"
    runat=server>
    <asp:ListItem Value="HousePrice" Selected="True">Price</asp:ListItem>
    <asp:ListItem Value="HomeLocation">Location</asp:ListItem>
</asp:DropDownList>
```

The value selected by the visitor will be used directly in the Order By clause of a SQL statement.

The only other control on the form is the Button control that submits the form for processing when it is clicked

```
<asp:button
    id="butOK"
    text="  OK  "
    Type="Submit"
    OnClick="SubmitBtn_Click"
    runat="server"
/>
```

The only procedure on the page fires when the OK button is clicked

```
Sub SubmitBtn_Click(Sender As Object, E As EventArgs)
    Session("SearchSQL") = "Select HLCN, HousePrice, " _
```

```
        & "Convert(varchar(5),BedRooms) + '/' " _
        & "+ Convert(varchar(5),BathRooms) as BedBath, " _
        & "HomeLocation, " _
        & "EmailContact + '<br>' + PhoneContact " _
        & "as ContactInfo From Listings Where " _
        & "HousePrice >= " _
        & ddlLowestPrice.SelectedItem.Value _
        & " and HousePrice <= " _
        & ddlHighestPrice.SelectedItem.Value _
        & " and BathRooms >= " _
        & ddlBaths.SelectedItem.Value _
        & " and BedRooms >= " _
        & ddlBeds.SelectedItem.Value _
        & " and HomeLocation Like '%" _
        & ddlPartOfTown.SelectedItem.Value  & "%'" _
        & " Order By " _
        & ddlSort.SelectedItem.Value
    Response.Redirect("./search_results.aspx")
End Sub
```

The procedure builds and stores into a Session variable a SQL statement based on the criteria selected by the visitor on the page. The first page of the SQL statement specifies the fields we want returned

```
Session("SearchSQL") = "Select HLCN, HousePrice, " _
```

Note that the Bedrooms and Bathrooms fields are returned as a single field separated by a /, which is how they are displayed on the Search Results page:

```
& "Convert(varchar(5),BedRooms) + '/' "_
& "+ Convert(varchar(5),BathRooms) as BedBath, " _
& "HomeLocation, " _
```

Also note that the contact information is returned as a single field separated by a line break HTML tag:

```
& "EmailContact + '<br>' + PhoneContact " _
& "as ContactInfo From Listings Where " _
```

We then use each value selected by the visitor in the DropDownList controls within the Where clause of the SQL statement:

```
& "HousePrice >= " _
& ddlLowestPrice.SelectedItem.Value _
& " and HousePrice <= " _
& ddlHighestPrice.SelectedItem.Value _
& " and BathRooms >= " _
& ddlBaths.SelectedItem.Value _
& " and BedRooms >= " _
& ddlBeds.SelectedItem.Value _
```

Note here that the location selected by the visitor is used with the Like operator so that it can appear anywhere within the location field:

```
& " and HomeLocation Like '%" _
& ddlPartOfTown.SelectedItem.Value  & "%'" _
```

The field selected in the Sort DropDownList is then used within the Order By portion of the SQL statement:

```
& " Order By " _
& ddlSort.SelectedItem.Value
```

Finally, we direct the visitor to the Search Results page, where they will see the records returned by the SQL statement we just built

```
Response.Redirect("./search_results.aspx")
```

Search Results ASP.NET Page

Search_Results.aspx

The Search Results page shows the records that match the visitor's search criteria in a Repeater control.

At the top of the page, we define three compiler directives:

```
<%@ Page Language=VB EnableSessionState=true Debug=true %>
<%@ Import Namespace="System.Data" %>
<%@ Import Namespace="System.Data.OLEDB" %>
```

The first specifies how the page should run

```
<%@ Page Language=VB EnableSessionState=true Debug=true %>
```

The other two direct the compiler to import data libraries that we will need to connect to and to display database information on this page:

```
<%@ Import Namespace="System.Data" %>
<%@ Import Namespace="System.Data.OLEDB" %>
```

The first control on the page is a Label control that displays title text for the page:

```
<asp:Label
    id="lblTitle"
    BorderWidth="5px"
    BorderStyle=7
    BackColor="lightyellow"
    Width="439"
    Font-Size="22pt"
    Font-Name="Comic Sans MS"
    Text="<center>Find a Home - Search Results</center>"
    runat="server"
/>
```

Another Label control is used on the page. It will display the number of matching records to the visitor when the page is opened

```
<asp:Label
    id="lblCount"
    Font-Size="15pt"
    Font-Name="Comic Sans MS"
    runat="server"
/>
```

The other control on the page is the Repeater control, which will display the contents of the matching records through the use of four templates.

```
<asp:Repeater
    id="repSearchResults"
    runat="server"
    >
    < HeaderTemplate>
        <Table width="100%" style="font: 8pt verdana">
        <tr style="Background-Color:DFECD8">
        <td><b>HLCN</b></td>
        <td><b>Price</b></td>
        <td><b>Bed/Bath</b></td>
```

```
        <td><b>Location</b></td>
        <td><b>Contact</b></td>
        </tr>
    </ HeaderTemplate>
    < ItemTemplate>
        <tr style="Background-Color:FFECD9">
        <td>
            <%# "<a HREF=""./listing.aspx?HLCN=" _
            & DataBinder.Eval(Container.DataItem, "HLCN") & """>" _
            & DataBinder.Eval(Container.DataItem, "HLCN") & "</a>" %>
        </td>
        <td>
            <%# FormatCurrency(DataBinder. _
            Eval(Container.DataItem, "HousePrice")) %>
        </td>
        <td>
            <%# DataBinder.Eval(Container.DataItem, "BedBath") %>
        </td>
        <td>
            <%# DataBinder.Eval(Container.DataItem, "HomeLocation") %>
        </td>
        <td>
            <%# DataBinder.Eval(Container.DataItem, "ContactInfo") %>
        </td>
        </tr>
    </itemtemplate>
    < AlternatingItemTemplate>
        <tr style="Background-Color:FFECA8">
        <td>
            <%# "<a HREF=""./listing.aspx?HLCN=" _
            & DataBinder.Eval(Container.DataItem, "HLCN") & """>" _
            & DataBinder.Eval(Container.DataItem, "HLCN") _
            & "</a>" %>
        </td>
        <td>
            <%# FormatCurrency(DataBinder. _
            Eval(Container.DataItem, "HousePrice")) %>
        </td>
        <td>
            <%# DataBinder.Eval(Container.DataItem, "BedBath") %>
        </td>
        <td>
            <%# DataBinder.Eval(Container.DataItem, "HomeLocation") %>
```

```
        </td>
        <td>
            <%# DataBinder.Eval(Container.DataItem, "ContactInfo") %>
        </td>
        </tr>
    </AlternatingItemTemplate>
    < footertemplate>
        <tr style="Background-Color:DFECD8">
        <td><b>HLCN</b></td>
        <td><b>Price</b></td>
        <td><b>Bed/Bath</b></td>
        <td><b>Location</b></td>
        <td><b>Contact</b></td>
        </tr>
        </table>
    </footertemplate>
</asp:Repeater>
```

The Repeater control allows us to display information that repeats into the format we specify within our templates that are embedded within the control. In this case, the records will be displayed within the tags of an HTML table.

The first template is the HeaderTemplate. This is what you want to appear before any of the records are displayed.

```
< HeaderTemplate>
```

In this case, we open a Table tag:

```
<Table width="100%" style="font: 8pt verdana">
```

And in the first row of the table, we will display column headers in bold text:

```
    <tr style="Background-Color:DFECD8">
    <td><b>HLCN</b></td>
    <td><b>Price</b></td>
    <td><b>Bed/Bath</b></td>
    <td><b>Location</b></td>
    <td><b>Contact</b></td>
    </tr>
</headertemplate>
```

The next Template is the ItemTemplate. This represents the format that we want to use for the records that are displayed within the Repeater control when the page is opened. This template will actually be used for every other record, since we are using another item template defined through the AlternatingItemTemplate:

```
< ItemTemplate>
```

Each record is placed within its own row in the HTML record:

```
<tr style="Background-Color:FFECD9">
```

In the first cell of the table, we bind the HLCN field with a link to the Listing page:

```
<td>
    <%# "<a HREF="" ./listing.aspx?HLCN=" _
    & DataBinder.Eval(Container.DataItem, "HLCN") & """>" _
    & DataBinder.Eval(Container.DataItem, "HLCN") & "</a>" %>
</td>
```

In the next cell of the table, we bind the price of the house:

```
<td>
    <%# FormatCurrency(DataBinder. _
    Eval(Container.DataItem, "HousePrice")) %>
</td>
```

After that comes the number of bedrooms and baths:

```
<td>
    <%# DataBinder.Eval(Container.DataItem, "BedBath") %>
</td>
```

Following that, the location of the home is bound

```
<td>
    <%# DataBinder.Eval(Container.DataItem, "HomeLocation") %>
</td>
```

Bound to the last column in the HTML table will be the contact information for the listing:

```
<td>
    <%# DataBinder.Eval(Container.DataItem, "ContactInfo") %>
</td>
```

We then close the row and template:

```
    </tr>
</itemtemplate>
```

You can actually specify two templates in the Repeater control that are used for displaying records. If you do that, each template is used on every other record displayed. So the ItemTemplate would be used on the first, third, fifth, etc., records. And the AlternatingItemTemplate would be used on the second, fourth, sixth, etc.:

```
< AlternatingItemTemplate>
```

The data using this template also will be in an HTML Row tag. In this case, a different background color is used

```
<tr style="Background-Color:FFECA8">
```

In the first cell of the table, we display the HLCN field:

```
<td>
    <%# "<a HREF=""./listing.aspx?HLCN=" _
    & DataBinder.Eval(Container.DataItem, "HLCN") & """>" _
    & DataBinder.Eval(Container.DataItem, "HLCN") _
    & "</a>" %>
</td>
```

The next cell has the price of the house bound, formatted as currency:

```
<td>
    <%# FormatCurrency(DataBinder. _
    Eval(Container.DataItem, "HousePrice")) %>
</td>
```

The next cell will contain the BedBath field:

```
<td>
    <%# DataBinder.Eval(Container.DataItem, "BedBath") %>
</td>
```

That is followed by the location of the home:

```
<td>
    <%# DataBinder.Eval(Container.DataItem, "HomeLocation") %>
</td>
```

The contact information is in the last cell of the row:

```
<td>
    <%# DataBinder.Eval(Container.DataItem, "ContactInfo") %>
</td>
</tr>
</AlternatingItemTemplate>
```

The last template used in the Repeater control is the FooterTemplate. The FooterTemplate is displayed after all the records in the Repeater control:

```
< FooterTemplate>
```

Before closing the HTML table, we display one more row:

```
<tr style="Background-Color:DFECD8">
```

This row will contain the column headers, just like the first row. That way, if the table contains numerous records, the visitor will be able to see the column headers at the bottom of the table:

```
<td><b>HLCN</b></td>
    <td><b>Price</b></td>
    <td><b>Bed/Bath</b></td>
    <td><b>Location</b></td>
    <td><b>Contact</b></td>
</tr>
</table>
</FooterTemplate>
```

The code on the page fires when the page is loaded.

```
Sub Page_Load(ByVal Sender as Object, ByVal E as EventArgs)
    Dim DBConn as OleDbConnection
    Dim DBCommand As OleDbDataAdapter
    Dim DSHomeData as New DataSet
    DBConn = New OleDbConnection("Provider=sqloledb;" _
        & "server=localhost;" _
        & "Initial Catalog=INETC11;" _
        & "User Id=sa;" _
        & "Password=yourpassword;")
    DBCommand = New OleDbDataAdapter _
        (Session("SearchSQL"),DBConn)
    DBCommand.Fill(DSHomeData, _
        "SearchResults")
```

```
    repSearchResults.DataSource = _
        DSHomeData.Tables("SearchResults").DefaultView
    repSearchResults.DataBind()
    If DSHomeData.Tables("SearchResults").Rows.Count = 1 Then
        lblCount.Text = "Your search found 1" _
            & " record."
      Else
        lblCount.Text = "Your search found " _
            & DSHomeData.Tables("SearchResults").Rows.Count _
            & " records."
    End If
End Sub
```

We will need a Connection object to connect to our SQL Server database:

```
Dim DBConn as OleDbConnection
```

We will also need a Data Adapter object and a DataSet object:

```
Dim DBCommand As OleDbDataAdapter
Dim DSHomeData as New DataSet
```

We then connect to our SQL Server database. Note that you will need to change the connect string to the location of your database and your user information:

```
DBConn = New OleDbConnection("Provider=sqloledb;" _
    & "server=localhost;" _
    & "Initial Catalog=INETC11;" _
    & "User Id=sa;" _
    & "Password=yourpassword;")
```

The SQL text of the command object comes from the query statement we built on the Search page:

```
DBCommand = New OleDbDataAdapter _
    (Session("SearchSQL"),DBConn)
```

We then execute that SQL statement and place the records returned into our DataSet object in a table called SearchResults:

```
DBCommand.Fill(DSHomeData, _
    "SearchResults")
```

We then bind the Repeater control to our DataSet object:

```
repSearchResults.DataSource = _
    DSHomeData.Tables("SearchResults").DefaultView
repSearchResults.DataBind()
```

Last, we need to place text in the count label that shows the number of records that were returned in the search. The text reads a little differently if one record was returned

```
If DSHomeData.Tables("SearchResults").Rows.Count = 1 Then
    lblCount.Text = "Your search found 1" _
    & " record."
```

versus any other number of records returned

```
Else
    lblCount.Text = "Your search found " _
        & DSHomeData.Tables("SearchResults").Rows.Count _
        & " records."
End If
```

Listing ASP.NET Page

Listing.aspx

The Listing page displays all the text and pictures for the Home Listing Catalog Number passed into the page. The page uses three compiler directives.

```
<%@ Page Language=VB EnableSessionState=true Debug=true %>
<%@ Import Namespace="System.Data" %>
<%@ Import Namespace="System.Data.OLEDB" %>
```

The first specifies how we want the code on the page to run

```
<%@ Page Language=VB EnableSessionState=true Debug=true %>
```

The other two are required so that we can display database data on the page:

```
<%@ Import Namespace="System.Data" %>
<%@ Import Namespace="System.Data.OLEDB" %>
```

Within the page, a Label control is used to display title text for the page:

```
<asp:Label
    id="lblTitle"
    BorderWidth="5px"
    BorderStyle=7
    BackColor="lightyellow"
    Width="439"
    Font-Size="22pt"
    Font-Name="Comic Sans MS"
    runat="server"
/>
```

The code next defines another Label that will display all the text information about the listing, which will be concatenated from separate field values in our code:

```
<asp:Label
    id="lblHomeInfoBlob"
    Font-Size="10pt"
    Font-Name="Comic Sans MS"
    runat="server"
/>
```

One other control appears on the page, a DataList control:

```
<asp:DataList id="dlPics" runat="server"
    RepeatColumns="4">
    < ItemTemplate>
        <%# "<img SRC=""" & _
        DataBinder.Eval(Container.DataItem, "ImagePath") _
        & """ ALT=""" & DataBinder. _
        Eval(Container.DataItem, "ImageAlt")  & """>" %>
    </itemtemplate>
</asp:DataList>
```

The DataList control is used to display the pictures that go with the listing. They will be displayed four across

```
RepeatColumns="4">
```

A single template is used

```
< ItemTemplate>
```

Within the template, the path to the image is bound within an HTML Image tag, with the ALT property also being bound through the DataList:

```
    <%# "<img SRC=""" & _
    DataBinder.Eval(Container.DataItem, "ImagePath") _
    & """ ALT=""" & DataBinder. _
    Eval(Container.DataItem, "ImageAlt")  & """>" %>
</itemtemplate>
```

The code on the page fires when the page is first opened.

```
Sub Page_Load(ByVal Sender as Object, ByVal E as EventArgs)
    If Len(Page.Request.QueryString("HLCN")) = 0 Then
        Response.Redirect("./index.aspx")
    End If
    Dim DBConn as OleDbConnection
    Dim DBCommand As OleDbDataAdapter
    Dim DSHomeData as New DataSet
    DBConn = New OleDbConnection("Provider=sqloledb;" _
        & "server=localhost;" _
        & "Initial Catalog=INETC11;" _
        & "User Id=sa;" _
        & "Password=yourpassword;")
    DBCommand = New OleDbDataAdapter _
        ("Select * from Listings Where HLCN = '" _
        & Page.Request.QueryString("HLCN") & "'",DBConn)
    DBCommand.Fill(DSHomeData, _
        "Listing")
    If DSHomeData.Tables("Listing").Rows.Count = 0 Then
        lblHomeInfoBlob.Text = "The listing you entered " _
            & "was not found. The listing may have been " _
            & "sold or removed.<br>" _
            & "<a HREF=""./index.aspx"">Home</a>"
      Else
        lblHomeInfoBlob.Text = _
            "<TABLE CellPadding=""3"" style=""font: 10pt verdana"">" _
            & "<tr><td><b>Price: </b>" _
            & FormatCurrency(DSHomeData.Tables("Listing"). _
            Rows(0).Item("HousePrice")) _
            & "</td><td><b>Location: </b>" _
            & DSHomeData.Tables("Listing"). _
            Rows(0).Item("HomeLocation") _
            & "</td></tr>" _
            & "<tr><td><b>Bedrooms: </b>" _
```

```
            & DSHomeData.Tables("Listing"). _
            Rows(0).Item("Bedrooms") _
            & "</td><td><b>Bathrooms: </b>" _
            & DSHomeData.Tables("Listing"). _
            Rows(0).Item("Bathrooms") _
            & "</td></tr>" _
            & "<tr><td><b>Address: </b>" _
            & DSHomeData.Tables("Listing"). _
            Rows(0).Item("Address") _
            & "</td><td><b>Year Built: </b>" _
            & DSHomeData.Tables("Listing"). _
            Rows(0).Item("YearBuilt") _
            & "</td></tr>" _
            & "<tr><td><b>Square Feet: </b>" _
            & DSHomeData.Tables("Listing"). _
            Rows(0).Item("SquareFeet") _
            & "</td><td><b>Lot Size: </b>" _
            & DSHomeData.Tables("Listing"). _
            Rows(0).Item("LotSize") _
            & "</td></tr>" _
            & "<tr><td><b>Garage: </b>" _
            & DSHomeData.Tables("Listing"). _
            Rows(0).Item("Garage") _
            & "</td><td><b>Contact Name: </b>" _
            & DSHomeData.Tables("Listing"). _
            Rows(0).Item("ContactName") _
            & "</td></tr>" _
            & "<tr><td><b>Phone: </b>" _
            & DSHomeData.Tables("Listing"). _
            Rows(0).Item("PhoneContact") _
            & "</td><td><b>Email: </b>" _
            & "<a HREF=""mailto:" _
            & DSHomeData.Tables("Listing"). _
            Rows(0).Item("EmailContact") _
            & """>" _
            & DSHomeData.Tables("Listing"). _
            Rows(0).Item("EmailContact") _
            & "</a>" _
            & "</td></tr>" _
            & "</table><br>" _
            & DSHomeData.Tables("Listing"). _
            Rows(0).Item("Notes")
        DBCommand = New OleDbDataAdapter _
            ("Select ImagePath, ImageAlt " _
```

```
            & "From ListingPictures Where " _
            & "ListingID = " _
            & DSHomeData.Tables("Listing"). _
            Rows(0).Item("ListingID") _
            ,DBConn)
        DBCommand.Fill(DSHomeData, _
            "ListingPics")
        dlPics.DataSource = _
            DSHomeData.Tables("ListingPics").DefaultView
        dlPics.DataBind()
    End If
    lblTitle.Text = "<center>Home - " _
        & Page.Request.QueryString("HLCN") _
        & "</center>"
End Sub
```

The code on the page should only run if an HLCN was passed into the page:

```
If Len(Page.Request.QueryString("HLCN")) = 0 Then
```

If it wasn't, we send the visitor back to the Home page:

```
Response.Redirect("./index.aspx")
```

Otherwise, we declare the data variables we will need within our code:

```
Dim DBConn as OleDbConnection
Dim DBCommand As OleDbDataAdapter
Dim DSHomeData as New DataSet
```

We then connect to our database

```
DBConn = New OleDbConnection("Provider=sqloledb;" _
    & "server=localhost;" _
    & "Initial Catalog=INETC11;" _
    & "User Id=sa;" _
    & "Password=yourpassword;")
```

and set up our Data Adapter object to retrieve data on the listing requested

```
DBCommand = New OleDbDataAdapter _
    ("Select * from Listings Where HLCN = '" _
    & Page.Request.QueryString("HLCN") & "'",DBConn)
```

which is placed in our DataSet object in a DataSet table called Listing:

```
DBCommand.Fill(DSHomeData, _
    "Listing")
```

Next, we check to see if the HLCN passed into this page resulted in a record found in the database:

```
If DSHomeData.Tables("Listing").Rows.Count = 0 Then
```

If one wasn't, we display information to the visitor letting them know that the record they requested was not found

```
lblHomeInfoBlob.Text = "The listing you entered " _
    & "was not found. The listing may have been " _
    & "sold or removed.<br>" _
    & "<a HREF="" ./index.aspx"">Home</a>"
```

Otherwise, we build an HTML table that contains all the listing information for the home that the visitor requested to see

```
lblHomeInfoBlob.Text = _
    "<TABLE CellPadding=""3"" style=""font: 10pt verdana"">" _
```

Placed into the first row of the table are the price of the home and the location of the home:

```
& "<tr><td><b>Price: </b>" _
& FormatCurrency(DSHomeData.Tables("Listing"). _
Rows(0).Item("HousePrice")) _
& "</td><td><b>Location: </b>" _
& DSHomeData.Tables("Listing"). _
Rows(0).Item("HomeLocation") _
& "</td></tr>" _
```

In the next row of the HTML table, we place the number of bedrooms and the number of bathrooms:

```
& "<tr><td><b>Bedrooms: </b>" _
& DSHomeData.Tables("Listing"). _
Rows(0).Item("Bedrooms") _
& "</td><td><b>Bathrooms: </b>" _
& DSHomeData.Tables("Listing"). _
Rows(0).Item("Bathrooms") _
& "</td></tr>" _
```

Within the third row of the hidden HTML table, the visitor will see the address and the year the home was built

```
& "<tr><td><b>Address: </b>" _
& DSHomeData.Tables("Listing"). _
Rows(0).Item("Address") _
& "</td><td><b>Year Built: </b>" _
& DSHomeData.Tables("Listing"). _
Rows(0).Item("YearBuilt") _
& "</td></tr>" _
```

The next row of the table displays the number of square feet and the size of the lot that the home is on:

```
& "<tr><td><b>Square Feet: </b>" _
& DSHomeData.Tables("Listing"). _
Rows(0).Item("SquareFeet") _
& "</td><td><b>Lot Size: </b>" _
& DSHomeData.Tables("Listing"). _
Rows(0).Item("LotSize") _
& "</td></tr>" _
```

That is followed by the garage and contact name information:

```
& "<tr><td><b>Garage: </b>" _
& DSHomeData.Tables("Listing"). _
Rows(0).Item("Garage") _
& "</td><td><b>Contact Name: </b>" _
& DSHomeData.Tables("Listing"). _
Rows(0).Item("ContactName") _
& "</td></tr>" _
```

In the last row of the table, the visitor will find the rest of the contact information:

```
& "<tr><td><b>Phone: </b>" _
& DSHomeData.Tables("Listing"). _
Rows(0).Item("PhoneContact") _
& "</td><td><b>Email: </b>" _
& "<a HREF=""mailto:" _
& DSHomeData.Tables("Listing"). _
Rows(0).Item("EmailContact") _
& """>" _
& DSHomeData.Tables("Listing"). _
Rows(0).Item("EmailContact") _
& "</a>" _
& "</td></tr>" _
& "</table><br>" _
```

After the table, we need to display the notes that go with the home listing:

```
& DSHomeData.Tables("Listing"). _
Rows(0).Item("Notes")
```

Next, we need to retrieve the data for the pictures that go with the listing:

```
DBCommand = New OleDbDataAdapter _
    ("Select ImagePath, ImageAlt " _
    & "From ListingPictures Where " _
    & "ListingID = " _
    & DSHomeData.Tables("Listing"). _
    Rows(0).Item("ListingID") _
    ,DBConn)
```

That data is placed in our DataSet object

```
DBCommand.Fill(DSHomeData, _
    "ListingPics")
```

which is then bound to our DataList control:

```
dlPics.DataSource = _
    DSHomeData.Tables("ListingPics").DefaultView
dlPics.DataBind()
```

Regardless of whether the listing was found or not, we display the HLCN passed into the page in the title label:

```
lblTitle.Text = "<center>Home - " _
    & Page.Request.QueryString("HLCN") _
    & "</center>"
```

Access Code Changes

C11.mdb

For those who wish to use the Access database instead of a SQL Server database, a couple of code changes are necessary. First, the connect string for each of the database connection statements needs to change:

```
DBConn = New OleDbConnection("PROVIDER=Microsoft.Jet.OLEDB.4.0;" _
    & "DATA SOURCE=" _
    & Server.MapPath("/INetBook/C11/Access/C11.mdb;"))
```

You will need to change the path to the location where you put the Access database on your server.

The other change you will need to make is with the SQL statement that is built and stored on the Search page. The SQL statement uses the Convert function to allow us to combine textual and numeric data into a textual return value:

```
Session("SearchSQL") = "Select HLCN, HousePrice, " _
    & "Convert(varchar(5),BedRooms) + '/' " _
    & "+ Convert(varchar(5),BathRooms) as BedBath, " _
    & "HomeLocation, " _
    & "EmailContact + '<br>' + PhoneContact " _
    & "as ContactInfo From Listings Where " _
    & "HousePrice >= " _
    & ddlLowestPrice.SelectedItem.Value _
    & " and HousePrice <= " _
    & ddlHighestPrice.SelectedItem.Value _
    & " and BathRooms >= " _
    & ddlBaths.SelectedItem.Value _
    & " and BedRooms >= " _
    & ddlBeds.SelectedItem.Value _
    & " and HomeLocation Like '%" _
    & ddlPartOfTown.SelectedItem.Value  & "%'" _
    & " Order By " _
    & ddlSort.SelectedItem.Value
```

Access does not have a function called Convert. In this situation, no function call is needed. Access does the conversion automatically for you. So the function call is simply removed

```
Session("SearchSQL") = "Select HLCN, HousePrice, " _
    & "BedRooms & '/' " _
    & "& BathRooms as BedBath, " _
    & "HomeLocation, " _
    & "EmailContact + '<br>' + PhoneContact " _
    & "as ContactInfo From Listings Where " _
    & "HousePrice >= " _
```

```
& ddlLowestPrice.SelectedItem.Value _
& " and HousePrice <= " _
& ddlHighestPrice.SelectedItem.Value _
& " and BathRooms >= " _
& ddlBaths.SelectedItem.Value _
& " and BedRooms >= " _
& ddlBeds.SelectedItem.Value _
& " and HomeLocation Like '%" _
& ddlPartOfTown.SelectedItem.Value  & "%'" _
& " Order By " _
& ddlSort.SelectedItem.Value
```

No other code changes are required.

CHAPTER

12

Customizing the Visitor Experience

To add to the value of sites, and to increase the chances that a visitor will return, many sites allow visitors to customize the way they see the site. This personalization of the site comes in many forms. Many sites allow visitors to specify types of products that they prefer. Some sites display information that pertains to pages the visitor came to in the past. In this chapter, we will look at tools that allow your visitor to customize the way they experience your site.

First, we will look at the Bookmarks tool. This tool is useful with large sites that contain many pages. The tool allows the visitor to bookmark a page, which can then be accessed from their very own Bookmarks page.

That tool will accomplish its task through cookies. But for a variety of reasons, cookies don't always work. Therefore, the next tool we will look at is a Log In tool. This tool provides the functionality needed to identify a visitor by having them enter their name and password. The tool also provides an optional mechanism for visitors to register with the site.

Then at the end of this chapter, we will build on the Log In tool with the Preferences tool. This tool will show you how you can customize a page according to the visitor's preferences.

Bookmarks Tool

The Bookmarks tool is helpful if you have a large site or if you have content that is buried in pages of navigation. The tool allows the visitor to add a bookmark to pages within your site that they want to go back to. They can then go to their own Bookmarks page that contains a list of all the pages that they have bookmarked as well as links to those pages.

Sample Usage

The tool is implemented through a sample site that contains a Home page and two other content pages. When the visitor first enters this sample site, they see the Home page displayed in Figure 12-1.

From the Home page, the visitor can link to any other page of the site as well as the bookmark pages. Remember that this tool would be more useful for sites with many more pages than are displayed here.

If the visitor were to click the Bookmarks page now, they would see the page displayed in Figure 12-2.

Since this is the first visit for the visitor, they don't see any pages bookmarked here. They first need to add bookmarks to their favorite pages.

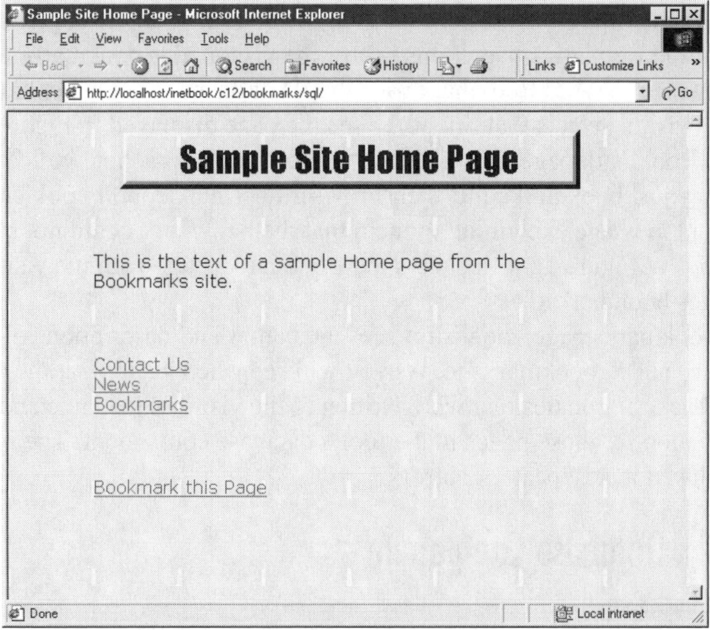

Figure 12-1 *Home page from sample implementation site*

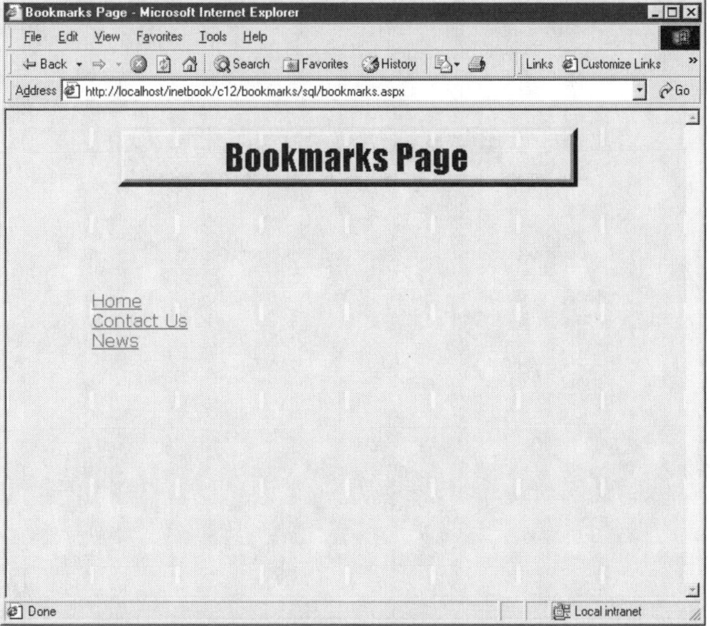

Figure 12-2 *Bookmarks page without any bookmarks*

At the bottom of the Home page, as well as the bottom of all the pages of the site, is a link to the Add Bookmark page. This is how the visitor adds bookmarks to pages. The link passes to the Add Bookmark page the ID of the page being bookmarked.

When the visitor selects that link, they see the page displayed in Figure 12-3.

The Add Bookmark page adds a cookie to the visitor's machine indicating the page that they just bookmarked. If their browser does not support cookies, they will see a different message explaining to them that the bookmark could not be added.

Take a look at Figure 12-4. It shows the Bookmarks page with the visitor's favorite pages bookmarked.

On the Bookmarks page, the visitor sees the names and descriptions of the pages that they have added bookmarks to. As you will see when we look at the code, the page reads back the cookies that were written to the visitor's machine and looks up page information for those pages in the tool's database component. The information is then displayed in a Repeater control.

Bookmarks Database Component

C12Bookmarks.sql

The database used in the Bookmarks tool contains a single table. That table stores data about the pages in the site. In this section, we will review the database.

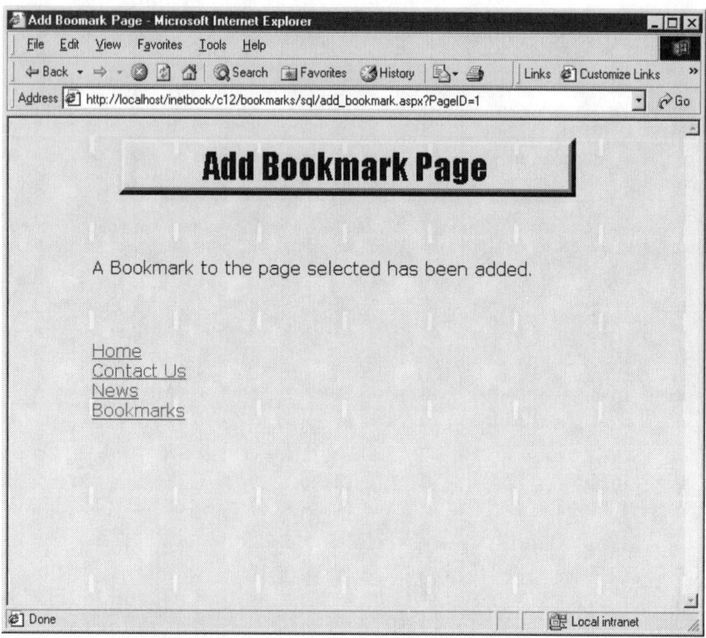

Figure 12-3 *Add Bookmark page*

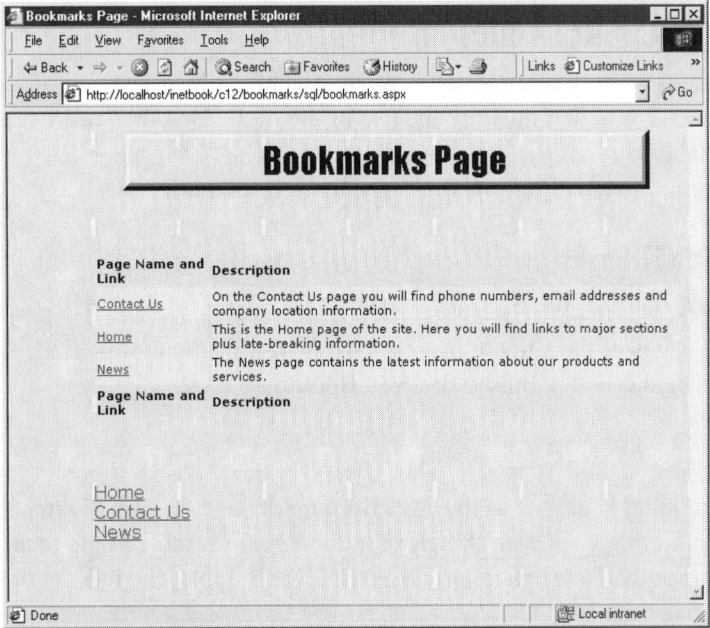

Figure 12-4 *Bookmarks page*

PageInfo Field Specifications

PageInfo.txt

The field specifications for the fields in the PageInfo table are displayed in Table 12-1.

The PageID is the primary key for this table. Since it is an identity column, it is automatically populated when a new record is added to this table.

The PageName field stores the name of the page as it is displayed in the Repeater control. The PageLocation field stores the Web address of the page in this record. This is where the visitor goes when they click the link in the Repeater control. The other field, PageDescription, stores the description of the page.

Field Name	Field Type	Notes
PageID	int	Primary Key, Identity Column
PageName	varchar	Length = 50
PageLocation	varchar	Length = 100
PageDescription	varchar	Length = 255

Table 12-1 *PageInfo Field Specifications*

Bookmarks ASP.NET Code

The Bookmarks page is made up of five pages. Three of the pages are just content pages that are used to demonstrate the use of the tool. The other two pages contain the functionality.

In this section, we will review the code in the Bookmarks tool.

Content ASP.NET Pages

Index.aspx, Contact_Us.aspx, News.aspx

The content pages of the site are just here to show how the tool is used. The only HTML of relevance is the link to the Add Bookmark page:

```
<a HREF="./add_bookmark.aspx?PageID=1">Bookmark this Page</a>
```

Note the ID that is passed to the Add Bookmark page, 1. This ID must match the ID of the record that goes with this page in the PageInfo table in the database. Therefore, since the News page has an ID of 3 in the table, the link on that page would look like this:

```
<a HREF="./add_bookmark.aspx?PageID=3">Bookmark this Page</a>
```

Add Bookmark ASP.NET Page

Add_Bookmark.aspx

The code on the Add Bookmark page validates that a parameter was passed into the page and that the visitor's browser supports cookies. It then adds a cookie to the visitor's computer.

At the top of the page, you will find this compiler directive:

```
<%@ Page Language=VB Debug=true %>
```

The directive tells the compiler that we are using Visual Basic as our default language and that we want debugging on. Remember to turn this off on your production machines.

Within the page, a Label control is used to display the title of the page:

```
<asp:Label
    id="lblTitle"
    BorderWidth="7px"
    BorderStyle=9
    Width="90%"
    Font-Size="25pt"
```

```
    Font-Name="Impact"
    Text="Add Bookmark Page"
    runat="server"
/>
```

A second label control displays a message with regard to the results of adding a cookie to the visitor's computer:

```
<asp:Label
    id="lblMessage"
    Font-Size="12pt"
    Font-Name="Verdana"
    runat="server"
/>
```

No other controls are needed on this page.

The only code block on the page fires when the page is loaded.

```
Sub Page_Load(ByVal Sender as Object, ByVal E as EventArgs)
    Dim BCaps As HttpBrowserCapabilities
    BCaps = Request.Browser
    If Len(Request.QueryString("PageID")) = 0 Then
        lblMessage.Text = "No Bookmark added. " _
            & "You need to select a page to add a " _
            & "bookmark to."
    ElseIf BCaps.Cookies = False Then
        lblMessage.Text = "No Bookmark added. " _
            & "Your browser does not support cookies!"
    Else
        Response.Cookies("Bookmark" _
            & Request.QueryString("PageID")).Expires = "5/1/2010"
        Response.Cookies("Bookmark" _
            & Request.QueryString("PageID")).Value = _
            Request.QueryString("PageID")
        lblMessage.Text = "A Bookmark to the page selected " _
            & "has been added."
    End If
End Sub
```

We need to determine if the visitor's browser supports cookies. Therefore, we will need a BrowserCapabilities object:

```
Dim BCaps As HttpBrowserCapabilities
```

That object is set to the visitor's browser specifications:

```
BCaps = Request.Browser
```

Next, we make sure a PageID was passed into this page:

```
If Len(Request.QueryString("PageID")) = 0 Then
```

If one wasn't, we display an error message to the visitor:

```
lblMessage.Text = "No Bookmark added. " _
    & "You need to select a page to add a " _
    & "bookmark to."
```

We also need to make sure that the visitor's browser supports cookies:

```
ElseIf BCaps.Cookies = False Then
```

If it doesn't, a different error message will be displayed

```
lblMessage.Text = "No Bookmark added. " _
    & "Your browser does not support cookies!"
```

Otherwise, the code flows here,

```
Else
```

and we can add a cookie to the visitor's computer. We set the cookie up so that it will expire in the distant future,

```
Response.Cookies("Bookmark" _
    & Request.QueryString("PageID")).Expires = "5/1/2010"
```

and we give it a value based on the PageID passed into this page:

```
Response.Cookies("Bookmark" _
    & Request.QueryString("PageID")).Value = _
    Request.QueryString("PageID")
```

Last, we display a success message to the visitor:

```
lblMessage.Text = "A Bookmark to the page selected " _
    & "has been added."
```

Bookmarks ASP.NET Page

Bookmarks.aspx

The code on the Bookmarks page displays, through a Repeater control, a list of all the pages bookmarked by the visitor. The code requires these compiler directives.

```
<%@ Page Language=VB Debug=true %>
<%@ Import Namespace="System.Data" %>
<%@ Import Namespace="System.Data.OLEDB" %>
```

The first sets up the environment the code runs in:

```
<%@ Page Language=VB Debug=true %>
```

The other two directives import data libraries into the page:

```
<%@ Import Namespace="System.Data" %>
<%@ Import Namespace="System.Data.OLEDB" %>
```

Within the body of the page, a Label control is used to display the title of the page:

```
<asp:Label
    id="lblTitle"
    BorderWidth="7px"
    BorderStyle=9
    Width="90%"
    Font-Size="25pt"
    Font-Name="Impact"
    Text="Bookmarks Page"
    runat="server"
/>
```

A Repeater control that will display the list of bookmarks is also defined.

```
<asp:Repeater
    id="repBookmarks"
    runat="server"
    >
    <headertemplate>
        <Table width="100%" style="font: 8pt verdana">
        <tr style="Background-Color:DFECD8">
        <td><b>Page Name and Link</b></td>
        <td><b>Description</b></td>
        </tr>
```

```
    </headertemplate>
    <itemtemplate>
        <tr style="Background-Color:FFECD9">
        <td>
            <%# "<a HREF=""" & DataBinder. _
                Eval(Container.DataItem, "PageLocation") _
                & """>" & DataBinder.Eval(Container.DataItem, _
                "PageName") & "</a>" %>
        </td>
        <td>
            <%# DataBinder.Eval(Container.DataItem,
"PageDescription") %>
        </td>
        </tr>
    </itemtemplate>
    <AlternatingItemTemplate>
        <tr style="Background-Color:FFECA8">
        <td>
            <%# "<a HREF=""" & DataBinder. _
                Eval(Container.DataItem, "PageLocation") _
                & """>" & DataBinder.Eval(Container.DataItem, _
                "PageName") & "</a>" %>
        </td>
        <td>
            <%# DataBinder.Eval(Container.DataItem,
            "PageDescription") %>
        </td>
        </tr>
    </AlternatingItemTemplate>
    <footertemplate>
        <tr style="Background-Color:DFECD8">
        <td><b>Page Name and Link</b></td>
        <td><b>Description</b></td>
        </tr>
        </table>
    </footertemplate>
</asp:Repeater>
```

The control is called repBookmarks:

```
<asp:Repeater
    id="repBookmarks"
    runat="server"
    >
```

The control defines four templates used to display information. The first is the header template. It is displayed before any data:

```
<headertemplate>
```

The data in the repeater will be displayed within an HTML table. So such a table is defined in the header section with the first row set to display the column headers:

```
    <Table width="100%" style="font: 8pt verdana">
    <tr style="Background-Color:DFECD8">
    <td><b>Page Name and Link</b></td>
    <td><b>Description</b></td>
    </tr>
</headertemplate>
```

The next template displays data in the odd numbered rows such as first, third, and fifth:

```
<itemtemplate>
```

Each record is placed within a row of the table:

```
<tr style="Background-Color:FFECD9">
```

Placed within the first cell are the name of the page and a link to the page:

```
<td>
    <%# "<a HREF=""" & DataBinder. _
    Eval(Container.DataItem, "PageLocation") _
    & """>" & DataBinder.Eval(Container.DataItem, _
    "PageName") & "</a>" %>
</td>
```

In the other cell is the description of the page:

```
<td>
    <%# DataBinder.Eval(Container.DataItem, "PageDescription") %>
</td>
</tr>
</itemtemplate>
```

The third template displays records in the even numbered rows like second, fourth, and sixth

```
<AlternatingItemTemplate>
    <tr style="Background-Color:FFECA8">
```

The cells are set up the same way, with the name and link in the first

```
<td>
    <%# "<a HREF=""" & DataBinder. _
    Eval(Container.DataItem, "PageLocation") _
    & """>" & DataBinder.Eval(Container.DataItem, _
    "PageName") & "</a>" %>
</td>
```

and the description of the page in the second:

```
<td>
    <%# DataBinder.Eval(Container.DataItem, "PageDescription") %>
</td>
</tr>
</AlternatingItemTemplate>
```

The fourth template appears at the bottom of the repeater after all the data is written

```
<footertemplate>
```

It rewrites the column heads and closes the HTML table:

```
<tr style="Background-Color:DFECD8">
<td><b>Page Name and Link</b></td>
<td><b>Description</b></td>
</tr>
</table>
</footertemplate>
</asp:Repeater>
```

The code on the page runs when the page is loaded

```
Sub Page_Load(ByVal Sender as Object, ByVal E as EventArgs)
    Dim DBConn as OleDbConnection
    Dim DBCommand As OleDbDataAdapter
    Dim DSBookmarks as New DataSet
    Dim TheQuery as String
    Dim MyCookieCollection as HTTPCookieCollection
    Dim i as integer
    MyCookieCollection = Request.Cookies
```

```
    For i = 0 to MyCookieCollection.Count - 1
        If Left(MyCookieCollection.Item(i).Name,8) _
            = "Bookmark" Then
            TheQuery = TheQuery & "PageID = " _
                & MyCookieCollection.Item(i).Value _
                & " or "
           End If
    Next
    If Len(TheQuery) > 0 Then
          TheQuery = Left(TheQuery, Len(TheQuery) - 3)
       TheQuery = "Select PageName, PageLocation, " _
               & "PageDescription From PageInfo Where " _
               & TheQuery & " Order By PageName"
        DBConn = New OleDbConnection("Provider=sqloledb;" _
            & "server=localhost;" _
            & "Initial Catalog=INETC12;" _
            & "User Id=sa;" _
            & "Password=yourpassword;")
        DBCommand = New OleDbDataAdapter _
            (TheQuery,DBConn)
        DBCommand.Fill(DSBookMarks, _
            "ThePageInfo")
        repBookmarks.DataSource = _
            DSBookmarks.Tables("ThePageInfo").DefaultView
        repBookmarks.DataBind()
       End If
End Sub
```

Within the procedure, we will need a Connection object,

```
Dim DBConn as OleDbConnection
```

as well as Data Adapter and DataSet objects for processing the database requests:

```
Dim DBCommand As OleDbDataAdapter
Dim DSBookmarks as New DataSet
```

We also need a string to store a temporary query as it is being built,

```
Dim TheQuery as String
```

a variable to store the visitor's cookie collection,

```
Dim MyCookieCollection as HTTPCookieCollection
```

and a variable used to iterate through a loop:

```
Dim i as integer
```

We then retrieve the visitor's cookie collection

```
MyCookieCollection = Request.Cookies
```

and enter a loop so that we can process each cookie:

```
For i = 0 to MyCookieCollection.Count - 1
```

When we stored the bookmarks as cookies on the visitor's machine, the name of each cookie started with Bookmark. We want to include only the values for those bookmarks. So we check the name here:

```
If Left(MyCookieCollection.Item(i).Name,8) _
    = "Bookmark" Then
```

If it is one of our bookmark cookies, we add it to our query string. The way the string will work is that each of the pages bookmarked will become part of the Where clause of a query that returns records that match any of the IDs in the visitor's cookies:

```
TheQuery = TheQuery & "PageID = " _
    & MyCookieCollection.Item(i).Value _
    & " or "
```

We then move on to process the next cookie:

```
Next
```

After the loop, we check to see if the visitor has any bookmarks. If they do, the code flows within the If statement,

```
If Len(TheQuery) > 0 Then
```

and we chop off the trailing Or in the Where clause we just built

```
TheQuery = Left(TheQuery, Len(TheQuery) - 3)
```

Next we add the Select and Order clauses to the temporary string:

```
TheQuery = "Select PageName, PageLocation, " _
    & "PageDescription From PageInfo Where " _
    & TheQuery & " Order By PageName"
```

We can now connect to the database

```
DBConn = New OleDbConnection("Provider=sqloledb;" _
    & "server=localhost;" _
    & "Initial Catalog=INETC12;" _
    & "User Id=sa;" _
    & "Password=yourpassword;")
```

and retrieve the matching PageInfo records

```
DBCommand = New OleDbDataAdapter _
    (TheQuery,DBConn)
```

into our DataSet object

```
DBCommand.Fill(DSBookMarks, _
    "ThePageInfo")
```

which is then bound to our Repeater control:

```
repBookmarks.DataSource = _
    DSBookmarks.Tables("ThePageInfo").DefaultView
repBookmarks.DataBind()
```

Access Code Changes

C12Bookmarks.mdb

The only code change needed to get this solution to work with Access instead of SQL Server is to change the connect string on the Bookmarks page

```
DBConn = New OleDbConnection("Provider=sqloledb;" _
    & "server=localhost;" _
    & "Initial Catalog=INETC12;" _
    & "User Id=sa;" _
    & "Password=yourpassword;")
```

so that it uses the proper provider and points to the correct database:

```
DBConn = New OleDbConnection("PROVIDER=Microsoft.Jet.OLEDB.4.0;" _
    & "DATA SOURCE=" _
    & Server.MapPath("/INetBook/C12/Bookmarks/" _
    & "Access/C12Bookmarks.mdb;"))
```

Note that you will need to modify the path to the location of the database on your server.

Log In Tool

The Log In tool provides the mechanism for you to have visitors enter your site by providing a user name and password. That pair is validated against the database, and if it exists, the user is allowed access to the site.

Through configuration of the tool, you determine how many attempts the visitor can have before the login completely fails. You also determine whether the visitor can register themselves through a New User page.

Once the visitor has successfully entered your site, you have them identified and can customize your site to suit their needs. This approach is often preferable to storing cookies on the visitor's computer, since the visitor may have cookies turned off in their browser. Also, they may be using a browser that does not support cookies. Or they may be connecting from a machine other than the one that the cookies are stored on.

Sample Usage

When the visitor first enters the site, they see the page displayed in Figure 12-5.

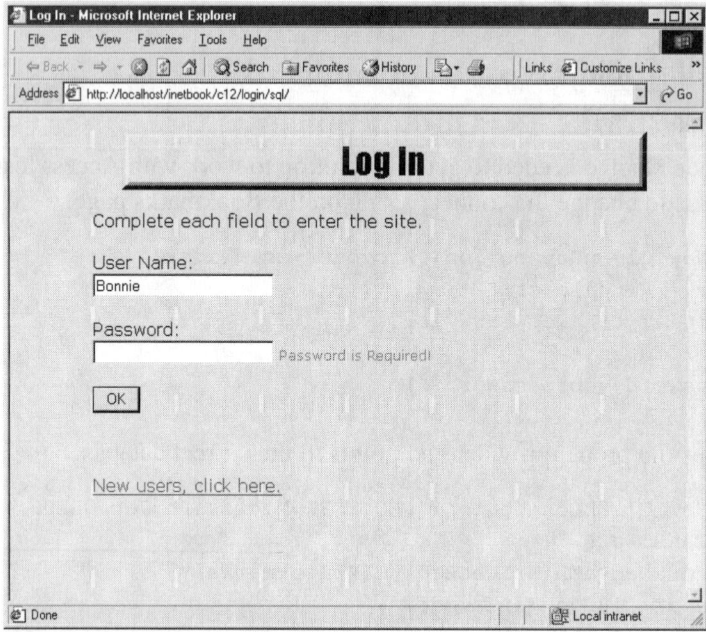

Figure 12-5 *Initial view of the Log In page*

The visitor must supply their user name and password on this page. Note that RequiredFieldValidator controls are used to make sure that the visitor enters something in each. As you can see, if they do not supply a value for each field, they see an error message.

Once they supply a value for each field, they can click the OK button and the form on the page is submitted. If the visitor enters an invalid user name / password pair, they see the message displayed in Figure 12-6.

Through a configuration file, you control how many times the visitor can attempt to log in before complete failure. Once that value is reached, they are taken to the Failed Log In page displayed in Figure 12-7.

Once the visitor enters this page, any attempts to log in will result in a failure until they launch a new session.

If the visitor enters a correct user name / password pair, they are taken to the Success Log In page displayed in Figure 12-8.

This page and any other pages that are accessed after a successful login check to make sure that a special session variable is present. If it is not, the visitor should be sent back to the Log In page. This prevents a visitor from going directly to a content page without first logging in.

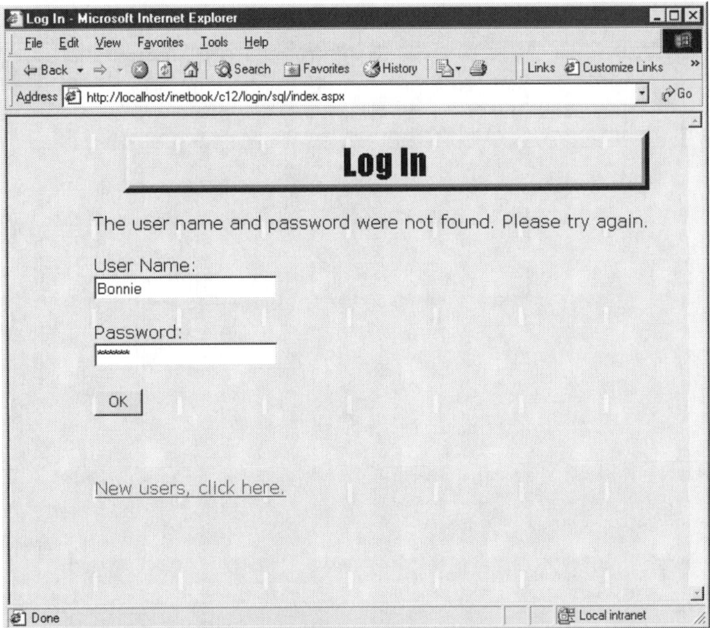

Figure 12-6 *Invalid login attempt message*

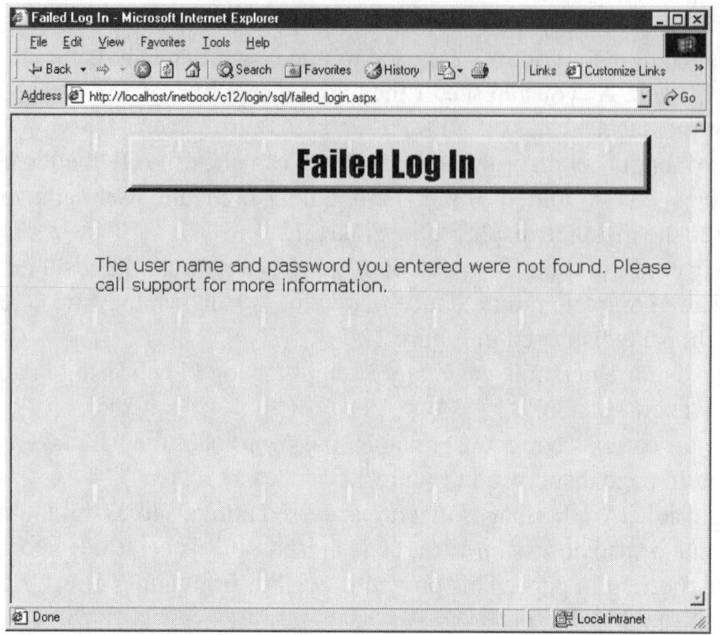

Figure 12-7 *Failed Log In page*

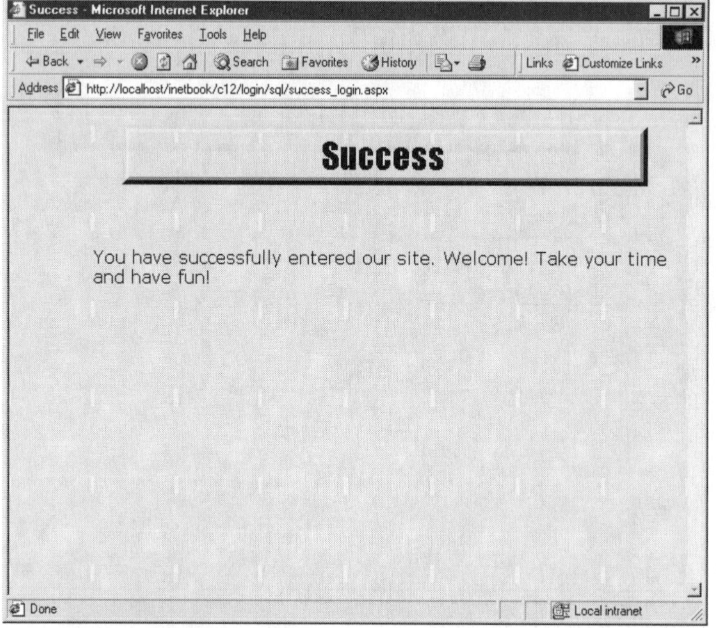

Figure 12-8 *Success Log In page*

Back on the Log In page displayed in Figure 12-5, there is a link to the New User page. This link appears only if the configuration file is set for it to display. In other words, you can control whether the visitor can register themselves by changing an Application variable. In this case, it is set on so that the visitor can click the link, which takes them to the page displayed in Figure 12-9.

The visitor must enter each field before proceeding. They also must enter the same password twice or the page will not be processed. Once the page has been successfully set, the visitor clicks OK. One more check is made, as you can see in Figure 12-10.

In the code, we make sure that the user name entered by the visitor is not in use by another visitor. If it is, they are asked to supply another user name. Otherwise, the visitor is added to the database and is taken to the Success Log In page.

Log In Database Component

C12LogIn.sql

The database used in the Log In tool contains a single table. That table stores data about the visitors to the site. In this section, we will review the database.

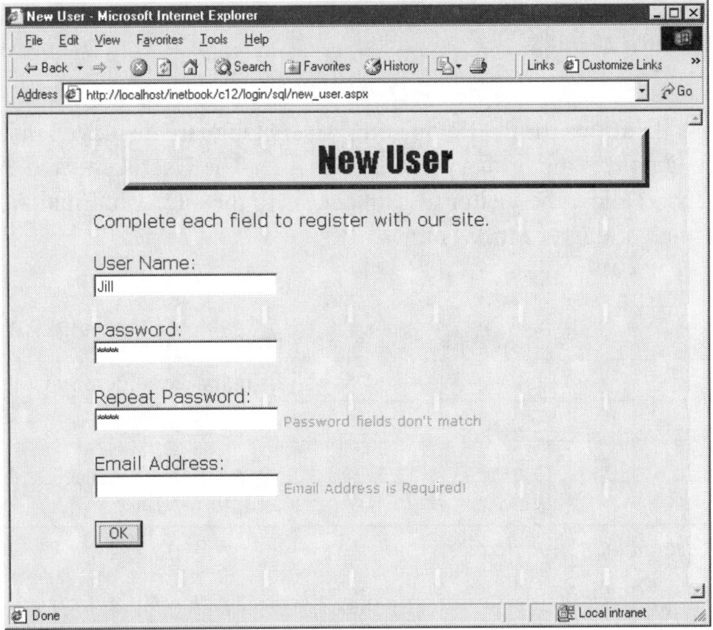

Figure 12-9 *Initial view of the New User page*

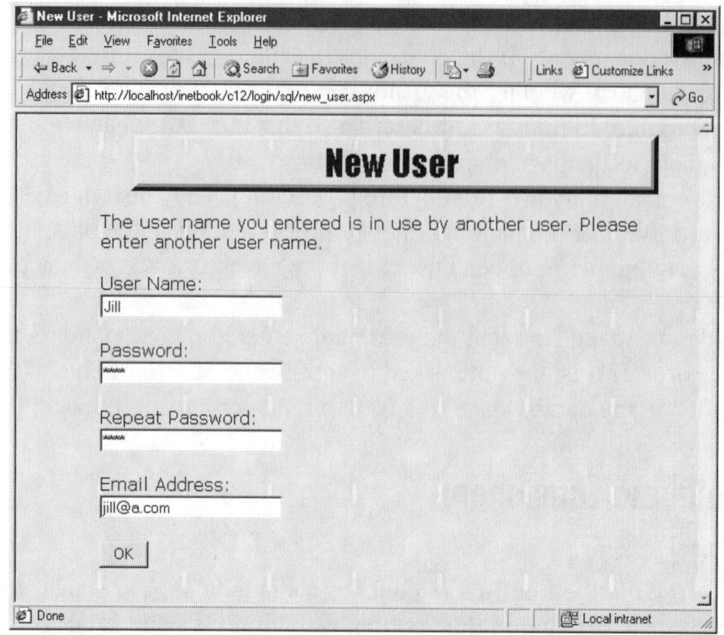

Figure 12-10 *User name in user error message*

Users Field Specifications

Users.txt

The field specifications for the fields in the Users table are displayed in Table 12-2.

The UserID field is the primary key in the table. The UserName and Password fields are used to allow the visitor to gain access to the site. The EmailAddress field stores the e-mail address of the visitor.

Field Name	Field Type	Notes
UserID	int	Primary Key, Identity Column
UserName	varchar	Length = 50
Password	varchar	Length = 50
EmailAddress	varchar	Length = 50

Table 12-2 *Users Field Specifications*

Log In ASP.NET Code

The Log In site is made up of ASP.NET pages as well as a Global.asax configuration file. Since it uses a Global.asax file, the directory that the tool is placed in is marked as an application through the Internet Services Manager.

In this section, we will review the configuration and ASP.NET pages.

Global.asax Configuration File

Global.asax

The code in the configuration file fires during two events. The first fires when the application first launches.

```
Sub Application_OnStart
    Application("AllowAdd") = True
    Application("MaxTries") = 3
End Sub
```

The first entry in the configuration file determines whether the visitor can register themselves. If it is set to true

```
Application("AllowAdd") = True
```

the visitor can enter and register themselves through the New User page. If it is set to false, the visitor can not enter the New User page.

The other setting determines how many times the visitor can attempt a login before being sent to the Failed Log In page:

```
Application("MaxTries") = 3
```

The other event that has code in the configuration file fires when the visitor first enters the site.

```
Sub Session_OnStart
    Session("NumTries") = 0
End Sub
```

It initializes the number of login attempts:

```
Session("NumTries") = 0
```

Log In ASP.NET Page

Index.aspx

The code on the Log In page validates the visitor's login attempt. At the top of the page, three compiler directives are declared.

```
<%@ Page Language=VB Debug=true %>
<%@ Import Namespace="System.Data" %>
<%@ Import Namespace="System.Data.OLEDB" %>
```

The first directive sets up the programming environment:

```
<%@ Page Language=VB Debug=true %>
```

The other two are needed to allow us to connect to the database:

```
<%@ Import Namespace="System.Data" %>
<%@ Import Namespace="System.Data.OLEDB" %>
```

Within the body of the page, a Label control is declared that is used for the title text displayed on the page:

```
<asp:Label
    id="lblTitle"
    BorderWidth="7px"
    BorderStyle=9
    Width="90%"
    Font-Size="25pt"
    Font-Name="Impact"
    Text="Log In"
    runat="server"
/>
```

Another label control displays a message to the visitor about the status of their login attempt:

```
<asp:Label
    id="lblMessage"
    Font-Size="12pt"
    Font-Name="Verdana"
    runat="server"
    Text="Complete each field to enter the site."
/>
```

Next, a TextBox control is defined that allows the visitor to enter their user name:

```
<asp:TextBox
    id="txtUserName"
    Columns="25"
    MaxLength="30"
    runat=server
/>
```

That TextBox must have a value inserted because of the RequiredFieldValidator control that is linked to it:

```
<asp:RequiredFieldValidator
    id="rfvUserName"
    ControlToValidate="txtUserName"
    Display="Dynamic"
    Font-Name="Verdana"
    Font-Size="10pt"
    runat=server>
    User Name is Required!
</asp:RequiredFieldValidator>
```

The other TextBox control on the page is for the visitor's password:

```
<asp:TextBox
    id="txtPassword"
    Columns="25"
    MaxLength="30"
    runat=server
    TextMode="Password"
/>
```

Note that the TextMode property is used so that "*" characters will appear when the visitor types into this field:

```
TextMode="Password"
```

The password is also a required field:

```
<asp:RequiredFieldValidator
    id="rfvPassword"
    ControlToValidate="txtPassword"
    Display="Dynamic"
```

```
    Font-Name="Verdana"
    Font-Size="10pt"
    runat=server>
    Password is Required!
</asp:RequiredFieldValidator>
```

Another control on the page is the OK button:

```
<asp:button
    id="butOK"
    text="   OK   "
    Type="Submit"
    OnClick="SubmitBtn_Click"
    runat="server"
/>
```

At the bottom of the page, a Label control is used to display the link to the New User page:

```
<asp:Label
    id="lblNewUser"
    Font-Size="12pt"
    Font-Name="Verdana"
    runat="server"
/>
```

The link is placed in a label so that we can control what is displayed though code, since the New User page is not always used.

The code on the page appears in two events. The first fires when the page is loaded.

```
Sub Page_Load(ByVal Sender as Object, ByVal E as EventArgs)
      If Application("AllowAdd") = True Then
        lblNewUser.Text = "<a HREF=""./new_user.aspx""" _
            & ">New users, click here.</a>"
      End If
      If Session("NumTries") > Application("MaxTries") Then
        Response.Redirect("./failed_login.aspx")
   End If
End Sub
```

First, we check to see if the visitor is allowed to register themselves in this implementation of the tool:

```
If Application("AllowAdd") = True Then
```

If so, we place a link to the New User page in a label:

```
lblNewUser.Text = "<a HREF=""./new_user.aspx""" _
   & ">New users, click here.</a>"
```

Next, we make sure that the visitor is not returning to this page after complete login failure:

```
If Session("NumTries") > Application("MaxTries") Then
```

If so, they are sent to the Failed Log In page:

```
Response.Redirect("./failed_login.aspx")
```

The other code on the page fires when the OK button is clicked. The procedure validates a login attempt.

```
Sub SubmitBtn_Click(Sender As Object, E As EventArgs)
    Dim DBConn as OleDbConnection
    Dim DBCommand As OleDbDataAdapter
    Dim DSLogin as New DataSet
    DBConn = New OleDbConnection("Provider=sqloledb;" _
        & "server=localhost;" _
        & "Initial Catalog=INETC12;" _
        & "User Id=sa;" _
        & "Password=yourpassword;")
    DBCommand = New OleDbDataAdapter _
        ("Select UserID from Users Where " _
        & "UserName = '" & txtUserName.Text _
        & "' and Password = '" & txtPassword.Text _
        & "'", DBConn)
    DBCommand.Fill(DSLogin, _
        "UserInfo")
    If DSLogin.Tables("UserInfo"). _
        Rows.Count = 0 Then
        Session("NumTries") = Session("NumTries") + 1
        If Session("NumTries") >= _
            Application("MaxTries") Then
            Response.Redirect("./failed_login.aspx")
        Else
            lblMessage.Text = "The user name and password " _
                & "were not found. Please try again."
```

```
            End If
        Else
            Session("UserID") = DSLogin.Tables("UserInfo"). _
                Rows(0).Item("UserID")
            Response.Redirect("./success_login.aspx")
        End If
End Sub
```

We will need data objects to connect to the database and manipulate the data:

```
Dim DBConn as OleDbConnection
Dim DBCommand As OleDbDataAdapter
Dim DSLogin as New DataSet
```

First, we connect to the database:

```
DBConn = New OleDbConnection("Provider=sqloledb;" _
    & "server=localhost;" _
    & "Initial Catalog=INETC12;" _
    & "User Id=sa;" _
    & "Password=yourpassword;")
```

And then we look for a matching user name and password pair entered by the visitor into the TextBox controls:

```
DBCommand = New OleDbDataAdapter _
    ("Select UserID from Users Where " _
    & "UserName = '" & txtUserName.Text _
    & "' and Password = '" & txtPassword.Text _
    & "'", DBConn)
```

The return of that call is placed into our DataSet object in a DataSet table called UserInfo:

```
DBCommand.Fill(DSLogin, _
    "UserInfo")
```

We then check to see if any records were returned

```
If DSLogin.Tables("UserInfo"). _
    Rows.Count = 0 Then
```

If none were, it means that the user name / password pair was not found. So we add 1 to the login attempts session variable:

```
Session("NumTries") = Session("NumTries") + 1
```

Then we check to see if the visitor has exceeded the number of allowable tries:

```
If Session("NumTries") >= _
    Application("MaxTries") Then
```

If so, they are sent to the Failed Log In page:

```
Response.Redirect("./failed_login.aspx")
```

Otherwise, we place an error message into our message variable:

```
lblMessage.Text = "The user name and password " _
    & "were not found. Please try again."
```

If the code flows here, it means that the visitor entered a valid login:

```
Else
```

In that case, we store their UserID in a session variable

```
Session("UserID") = DSLogin.Tables("UserInfo"). _
    Rows(0).Item("UserID")
```

and direct them to the Success Log In page.

```
Response.Redirect("./success_login.aspx")
```

Failed Log In ASP.NET Page

Failed_LogIn.aspx

No code appears on the Failed Log In page. It merely displays a message to the visitor letting them know that they were not allowed access to the database. You may want to place contact information on this page providing some way for the visitor to resolve their problem.

Success Log In ASP.NET Page

Success_LogIn.aspx

The Success Log In page is accessed after the visitor appropriately enters the site. The page demonstrates the code you would want to include on any content page that should not be accessed without first logging in.

The code on the page fires when the page is loaded

```
Sub Page_Load(ByVal Sender as Object, ByVal E as EventArgs)
    If Len(Session("UserID")) = 0 Then
        Response.Redirect("./index.aspx")
    End If
    lblMessage.Text = "You have successfully entered " _
        & "our site. Welcome! Take your time and have fun!"
End Sub
```

We check to see if a value has been placed into the UserID session variable:

```
If Len(Session("UserID")) = 0 Then
```

If no such value has been placed, that means the visitor has not logged in. In that case, we send the visitor to the Log In page:

```
Response.Redirect("./index.aspx")
```

Otherwise, we simply display a message on this page:

```
lblMessage.Text = "You have successfully entered " _
    & "our site. Welcome! Take your time and have fun!"
```

New User ASP.NET Page

New_User.aspx

The code on the New User page provides the mechanism for the visitor to register themselves in the database.

At the top of the page, three compiler directives are defined.

```
<%@ Page Language=VB Debug=true %>
<%@ Import Namespace="System.Data" %>
<%@ Import Namespace="System.Data.OLEDB" %>
```

The first tells the compiler the language we are using and that we are in debug mode:

```
<%@ Page Language=VB Debug=true %>
```

The other two are used to import data libraries into this page:

```
<%@ Import Namespace="System.Data" %>
<%@ Import Namespace="System.Data.OLEDB" %>
```

Numerous controls are defined within the body of the page. The first is a Label control that displays title text:

```
<asp:Label
    id="lblTitle"
    BorderWidth="7px"
    BorderStyle=9
    Width="90%"
    Font-Size="25pt"
    Font-Name="Impact"
    Text="New User"
    runat="server"
/>
```

Another Label control is displayed next. It is used to display a message with regard to the status of the add request:

```
<asp:Label
    id="lblMessage"
    Font-Size="12pt"
    Font-Name="Verdana"
    runat="server"
    Text="Complete each field to register with our site."
/>
```

Next, we declare a TextBox control for the user name field:

```
<asp:TextBox
    id="txtUserName"
    Columns="25"
    MaxLength="30"
    runat=server
/>
```

That control must have a value because of the RequiredFieldValidator:

```
<asp:RequiredFieldValidator
    id="rfvUserName"
    ControlToValidate="txtUserName"
    Display="Dynamic"
    Font-Name="Verdana"
    Font-Size="10pt"
    runat=server>
    User Name is Required!
</asp:RequiredFieldValidator>
```

Note that the control validates the txtUserName control

```
ControlToValidate="txtUserName"
```

and that it will display this error message:

```
User Name is Required!
```

The next control is a TextBox for the password field

```
<asp:TextBox
    id="txtPassword"
    Columns="25"
    MaxLength="30"
    runat=server
    TextMode="Password"
/>
```

which is also required

```
<asp:RequiredFieldValidator
    id="rfvPassword"
    ControlToValidate="txtPassword"
    Display="Dynamic"
    Font-Name="Verdana"
    Font-Size="10pt"
    runat=server>
    Password is Required!
</asp:RequiredFieldValidator>
```

Usually when you ask a user to enter a new password, you have them enter it twice to make sure that they enter it correctly. So we next define another TextBox control for the second password:

```
<asp:TextBox
    id="txtPassword2"
    Columns="25"
    MaxLength="30"
    runat=server
    TextMode="Password"
/>
```

It is required

```
<asp:RequiredFieldValidator
    id="rfvPassword2"
    ControlToValidate="txtPassword2"
    Display="Dynamic"
    Font-Name="Verdana"
    Font-Size="10pt"
    runat=server>
    Password is Required!
</asp:RequiredFieldValidator>
```

And through the use of a CompareValidator, we make sure that both passwords entered are the same:

```
<asp:CompareValidator id="cvPassword"
    ControlToValidate="txtPassword"
    ControlToCompare="txtPassword2"
    Display="Dynamic"
    Font-Name="Verdana"
    Font-Size="10pt"
    runat=server>
    Password fields don't match
</asp:CompareValidator>
```

The other TextBox on the page is for the e-mail address field:

```
<asp:TextBox
    id="txtEmailAddress"
    Columns="25"
    MaxLength="30"
    runat=server
/>
```

It too is a required field:

```
<asp:RequiredFieldValidator
    id="rfvEmailAddress"
    ControlToValidate="txtEmailAddress"
    Display="Dynamic"
    Font-Name="Verdana"
```

```
    Font-Size="10pt"
    runat=server>
    Email Address is Required!
</asp:RequiredFieldValidator>
```

The other control on the page is a button control:

```
<asp:button
    id="butOK"
    text="  OK  "
    Type="Submit"
    OnClick="SubmitBtn_Click"
    runat="server"
/>
```

When clicked, it fires this procedure:

```
OnClick="SubmitBtn_Click"
```

And that procedure is the only procedure on the page. It attempts to add the visitor's information to the database.

```
Sub SubmitBtn_Click(Sender As Object, E As EventArgs)
    Dim DBConn as OleDbConnection
    Dim DBCommand As OleDbDataAdapter
    Dim DSLogin as New DataSet
    Dim DBInsert As New OleDbCommand
    DBConn = New OleDbConnection("Provider=sqloledb;" _
        & "server=localhost;" _
        & "Initial Catalog=INETC12;" _
        & "User Id=sa;" _
        & "Password=yourpassword;")
    DBCommand = New OleDbDataAdapter _
        ("Select Count(UserID) as TheCount " _
        & "from Users Where " _
        & "UserName = '" & txtUserName.Text _
        & "'", DBConn)
    DBCommand.Fill(DSLogin, _
        "TheCount")
    If DSLogin.Tables("TheCount"). _
            Rows(0).Item("TheCount")  = 0 Then
        DBInsert.CommandText = "Insert Into Users " _
            & "(UserName, Password, EmailAddress) " _
```

```
            & "values (" _
            & "'" & txtUserName.text & "', " _
            & "'" & txtPassword.text & "', " _
            & "'" & txtEmailAddress.text & "')"
        DBInsert.Connection = DBConn
        DBInsert.Connection.Open
        DBInsert.ExecuteNonQuery()
        DBCommand = New OleDbDataAdapter _
            ("Select UserID from Users Where " _
            & "UserName = '" & txtUserName.Text _
            & "' and Password = '" & txtPassword.Text _
            & "'", DBConn)
        DBCommand.Fill(DSLogin, _
            "UserInfo")
        Session("UserID") = DSLogin.Tables("UserInfo"). _
            Rows(0).Item("UserID")
        Response.Redirect("./success_login.aspx")
       Else
           lblMessage.Text = "The user name you entered is in " _
            & "use by another user. Please enter " _
            & "another user name."
       End If
End Sub
```

The page requires four data object variables:

```
Dim DBConn as OleDbConnection
Dim DBCommand As OleDbDataAdapter
Dim DSLogin as New DataSet
Dim DBInsert As New OleDbCommand
```

First, we connect to the database:

```
DBConn = New OleDbConnection("Provider=sqloledb;" _
    & "server=localhost;" _
    & "Initial Catalog=INETC12;" _
    & "User Id=sa;" _
    & "Password=yourpassword;")
```

Then we check to see if the user name supplied by the visitor is in use:

```
DBCommand = New OleDbDataAdapter _
    ("Select Count(UserID) as TheCount " _
```

```
    & "from Users Where " _
    & "UserName = '" & txtUserName.Text _
    & "'", DBConn)
DBCommand.Fill(DSLogin, _
    "TheCount")
```

If the user name was not found, the count will be zero:

```
If DSLogin.Tables("TheCount"). _
    Rows(0).Item("TheCount")  = 0 Then
```

In that case, we can add the visitor's information to the database:

```
DBInsert.CommandText = "Insert Into Users " _
    & "(UserName, Password, EmailAddress) " _
    & "values (" _
    & "'" & txtUserName.text & "', " _
    & "'" & txtPassword.text & "', " _
    & "'" & txtEmailAddress.text & "')"
DBInsert.Connection = DBConn
DBInsert.Connection.Open
DBInsert.ExecuteNonQuery()
```

We then need to retrieve the ID of the visitor just added

```
DBCommand = New OleDbDataAdapter _
    ("Select UserID from Users Where " _
    & "UserName = '" & txtUserName.Text _
    & "' and Password = '" & txtPassword.Text _
    & "'", DBConn)
```

into our DataSet object

```
DBCommand.Fill(DSLogin, _
    "UserInfo")
```

which is then stored in a session variable so that the value will be available to other pages:

```
Session("UserID") = DSLogin.Tables("UserInfo"). _
    Rows(0).Item("UserID")
```

Finally, the visitor is sent to the Success Log In page:

```
Response.Redirect("./success_login.aspx")
```

If the code flows here, the user name entered is in use. We tell the visitor this and give them the opportunity to enter another user name:

```
lblMessage.Text = "The user name you entered is in " _
    & "use by another user. Please enter " _
    & "another user name."
```

Access Code Changes

C12LogIn.mdb

The only code change needed to get this solution to work with Access instead of SQL Server is to change the connect string

```
DBConn = New OleDbConnection("Provider=sqloledb;" _
    & "server=localhost;" _
    & "Initial Catalog=INETC12;" _
    & "User Id=sa;" _
    & "Password=yourpassword;")
```

so that it uses the proper provider and points to the correct database:

```
DBConn = New OleDbConnection("PROVIDER=Microsoft.Jet.OLEDB.4.0;" _
    & "DATA SOURCE=" _
    & Server.MapPath("/INetBook/C12/LogIn/" _
    & "Access/C12Login.mdb;"))
```

Note that you will need to modify the path to the location of the database on your server.

Preferences Tool

Change_Preferences.aspx, Demo.aspx, C12Preferences.sql, Users.txt, C12Preferences.mdb

The Preferences tool is based on the Log In tool. It includes all the pages discussed in the preceding section but adds two new pages. These pages allow the visitor to specify font and color preferences, which are then used to display content in the way the visitor wants on a demo page.

Sample Usage

The first of the two pages is the Change Preferences page, which is displayed in Figure 12-11.

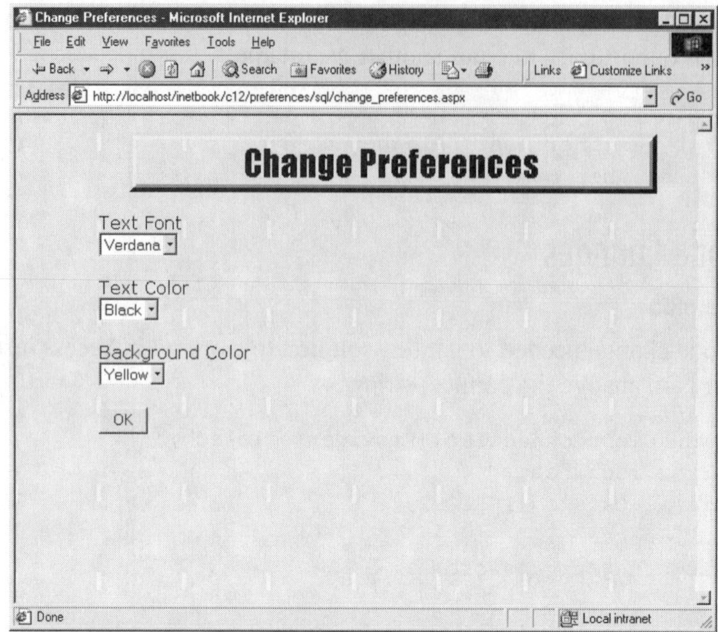

Figure 12-11 *Change Preferences page*

From this page, the visitor selects the color and font that they want to use within customizable pages. Once the visitor selects their style, they click OK and are taken to the Demo page displayed in Figure 12-12.

The Demo page displays text and the page in the style selected by the visitor. Those style selections are stored in the database so that they can be reused on other pages without the visitor's specifying them again.

PreferencesDatabase Component

C12Preferences.sql

The database used with the Preferences tool is based on the Log In database. It uses the same one table but adds new fields to it. In this section, we will review those changes.

Users Field Specifications

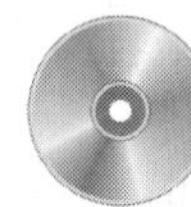

Users.txt

The field specifications for the fields in the Users table are displayed in Table 12-3.

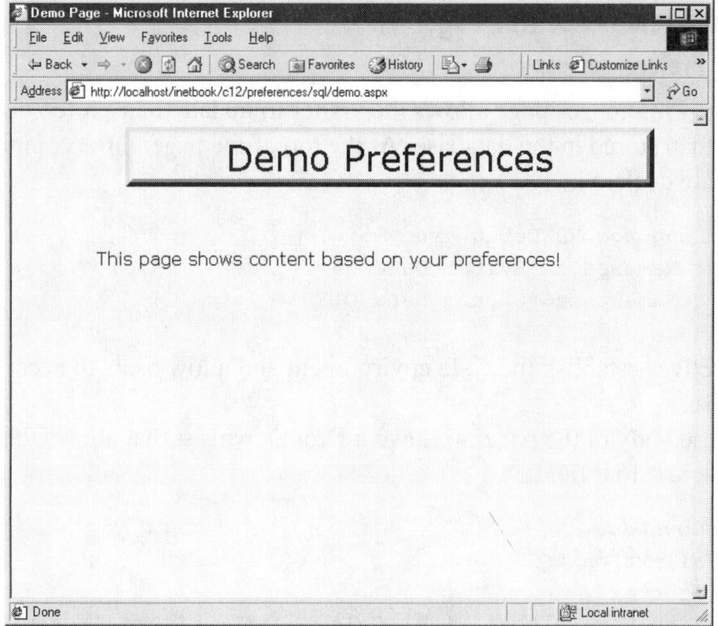

Figure 12-12 *Demo page*

The new fields in the table are the TextFont, TextColor, and BGColor fields. These fields store the preferences selected by the visitor on the Change Preferences page.

Preferences ASP.NET Code

The additional code in the Preferences tool is contained within two ASP.NET pages. In this section, we will review those changes.

Field Name	Field Type	Notes
UserID	int	Length = 50
UserName	varchar	Length = 50
Password	varchar	Length = 50
EmailAddress	varchar	Length = 50
TextFont	varchar	Length = 50
TextColor	varchar	Length = 50
BGColor	varchar	Length = 50

Table 12-3 *Users Field Specifications*

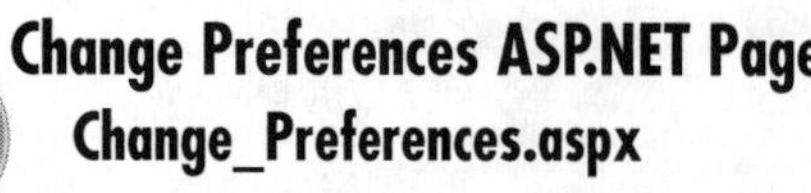

Change Preferences ASP.NET Page

Change_Preferences.aspx

The Change Preferences page allows the visitor to update their preferences, which are then stored in the database. At the top of the page, three compiler directives are declared.

```
<%@ Page Language=VB Debug=true %>
<%@ Import Namespace="System.Data" %>
<%@ Import Namespace="System.Data.OLEDB" %>
```

These directives establish the code environment and allow users to access our database.

Within the body of the page, we have a DropDownList that allows the visitor to select the text font field:

```
<asp:DropDownList
    id="ddlTextFont"
    runat=server>
    <asp:ListItem Value="Arial" Selected="True">Arial</asp:ListItem>
    <asp:ListItem Value="Impact">Impact</asp:ListItem>
    <asp:ListItem Value="Verdana">Verdana</asp:ListItem>
</asp:DropDownList>
```

The next DropDownList allows the visitor to select the color for the text:

```
<asp:DropDownList
    id="ddlTextColor"
    runat=server>
    <asp:ListItem Value="Black" Selected="True">Black</asp:ListItem>
    <asp:ListItem Value="Red">Red</asp:ListItem>
    <asp:ListItem Value="White">White</asp:ListItem>
</asp:DropDownList>
```

The third DropDownList allows the visitor to select their background color:

```
<asp:DropDownList
    id="ddlBGColor"
    runat=server>
    <asp:ListItem Value="Black" Selected="True">Black</asp:ListItem>
    <asp:ListItem Value="Yellow">Yellow</asp:ListItem>
    <asp:ListItem Value="White">White</asp:ListItem>
</asp:DropDownList>
```

The other control on the page is the OK button, which submits the form for processing:

```
<asp:button
    id="butOK"
    text="   OK   "
    Type="Submit"
    OnClick="SubmitBtn_Click"
    runat="server"
/>
```

The code on the page runs within two procedures. The first fires when the page is loaded

```
Sub Page_Load(ByVal Sender as Object, ByVal E as EventArgs)
    If Len(Session("UserID")) = 0 Then
        Response.Redirect("./index.aspx")
    End If
End Sub
```

It verifies that the visitor has logged in:

```
If Len(Session("UserID")) = 0 Then
```

If they haven't, they are sent to the Log In page:

```
Response.Redirect("./index.aspx")
```

The other procedure fires when the OK button is clicked.

```
Sub SubmitBtn_Click(Sender As Object, E As EventArgs)
    Dim DBConn as OleDbConnection
    Dim DBUpdate As New OleDbCommand
    DBConn = New OleDbConnection("Provider=sqloledb;" _
        & "server=localhost;" _
        & "Initial Catalog=INETC12;" _
        & "User Id=sa;" _
        & "Password=yourpassword;")
    DBUpdate.CommandText = "Update Users set " _
        & "TextFont = '" _
        & ddlTextFont.SelectedItem.Value & "', " _
        & "TextColor = '" _
        & ddlTextColor.SelectedItem.Value & "', " _
```

```
        & "BGColor = '" _
        & ddlBGCOlor.SelectedItem.Value & "' " _
        & "Where UserID = " & Session("UserID")
    DBUpdate.Connection = DBConn
    DBUpdate.Connection.Open
    DBUpdate.ExecuteNonQuery()
    Response.Redirect("./demo.aspx")
End Sub
```

We will need a Connection object and a Command object so that we can update the visitor's preferences:

```
Dim DBConn as OleDbConnection
Dim DBUpdate As New OleDbCommand
```

We start by connecting to the database:

```
DBConn = New OleDbConnection("Provider=sqloledb;" _
    & "server=localhost;" _
    & "Initial Catalog=INETC12;" _
    & "User Id=sa;" _
    & "Password=yourpassword;")
```

Our SQL statement will update the visitor's profile based on the preferences they selected:

```
DBUpdate.CommandText = "Update Users set " _
    & "TextFont = '" _
    & ddlTextFont.SelectedItem.Value & "', "_
    & "TextColor = '" _
    & ddlTextColor.SelectedItem.Value & "', "_
    & "BGColor = '" _
    & ddlBGCOlor.SelectedItem.Value & "' " _
    & "Where UserID = " & Session("UserID")
```

The Command object will use our Connection object:

```
DBUpdate.Connection = DBConn
DBUpdate.Connection.Open
```

We then run our SQL statement

```
DBUpdate.ExecuteNonQuery()
```

and send the visitor to the demo page:

```
Response.Redirect("./demo.aspx")
```

Demo ASP.NET Page

Demo.aspx

The Demo page shows you how can load the visitor's preferences into variables and then use them to change the design of the page. The page uses the same three compiler directives as the last page, which sets up the programming environment and allows users to connect to the database:

```
<%@ Page Language=VB Debug=true %>
<%@ Import Namespace="System.Data" %>
<%@ Import Namespace="System.Data.OLEDB" %>
```

Within the body of the page, two Label controls are defined that will have their font and color set according to the visitor's preferences:

```
<asp:Label
    id="lblTitle"
    BorderWidth="7px"
    BorderStyle=9
    Width="90%"
    Font-Size="25pt"
    Text="Demo Preferences"
    runat="server"
/>
<asp:Label
    id="lblMessage"
    Font-Size="12pt"
    runat="server"
/>
```

Three variables are declared with Private scope outside any procedure:

```
Private TheTextFont as String
Private TheTextColor as String
Private TheBGColor
```

This means that the variables will be accessible from any procedure within the page or directly within the body of the page. The variables will locally store the visitor's preferences.

The only procedure on the page fires when the page is loaded.

```
Sub Page_Load(ByVal Sender as Object, ByVal E as EventArgs)
    If Len(Session("UserID")) = 0 Then
        Response.Redirect("./index.aspx")
    End If
    Dim DBConn as OleDbConnection
    Dim DBCommand As OleDbDataAdapter
    Dim DSPrefs as New DataSet
    Dim MyColor as new System.Drawing.Color
    DBConn = New OleDbConnection("Provider=sqloledb;" _
        & "server=localhost;" _
        & "Initial Catalog=INETC12;" _
        & "User Id=sa;" _
        & "Password=yourpassword;")
    DBCommand = New OleDbDataAdapter _
        ("Select TextFont, TextColor, BGColor " _
        & "From Users Where " _
        & "UserID = " & Session("UserID"), DBConn)
    DBCommand.Fill(DSPrefs, _
        "Prefs")
    TheTextFont = DSPrefs.Tables("Prefs"). _
                Rows(0).Item("TextFont")
    TheTextColor = DSPrefs.Tables("Prefs"). _
                Rows(0).Item("TextColor")
    TheBGColor = DSPrefs.Tables("Prefs"). _
                Rows(0).Item("BGColor")
    lblMessage.Text = "This page shows content based " _
       & "on your preferences!"
    lblMessage.Font.Name = TheTextFont
    lblMessage.ForeColor= MyColor.FromName(TheTextColor)
    lblTitle.Font.Name = TheTextFont
    lblTitle.ForeColor= MyColor.FromName(TheTextColor)
End Sub
```

We start by making sure that the visitor has logged into our site:

```
If Len(Session("UserID")) = 0 Then
```

If they haven't, they are sent to the Log In page:

```
Response.Redirect("./index.aspx")
```

Otherwise, we can declare the database object we will need in code:

```
Dim DBConn as OleDbConnection
Dim DBCommand As OleDbDataAdapter
Dim DSPrefs as New DataSet
```

We also need a Color object. This object will be used to set the color of the Label controls in code. Unfortunately, in code, we can't set their color simply by supplying the color name:

```
Dim MyColor as new System.Drawing.Color
```

We start by connecting to our database:

```
DBConn = New OleDbConnection("Provider=sqloledb;" _
    & "server=localhost;" _
    & "Initial Catalog=INETC12;" _
    & "User Id=sa;" _
    & "Password=yourpassword;")
```

Our SQL statement is set to retrieve the visitor's preferences:

```
DBCommand = New OleDbDataAdapter _
    ("Select TextFont, TextColor, BGColor " _
    & "From Users Where " _
    & "UserID = " & Session("UserID"), DBConn)
```

The results of that query are placed in our DataSet object:

```
DBCommand.Fill(DSPrefs, _
    "Prefs")
```

The values retrieved from the database are then stored in our page-wide variables:

```
TheTextFont = DSPrefs.Tables("Prefs"). _
    Rows(0).Item("TextFont")
TheTextColor = DSPrefs.Tables("Prefs"). _
    Rows(0).Item("TextColor")
TheBGColor = DSPrefs.Tables("Prefs"). _
    Rows(0).Item("BGColor")
```

We then place some text in our message variable

```
lblMessage.Text = "This page shows content based " _
    & "on your preferences!"
```

and set the name of the font according to the visitor's preference:

```
lblMessage.Font.Name = TheTextFont
```

We then use our Color object to retrieve the correct font color by calling the FromName method:

```
lblMessage.ForeColor= MyColor.FromName(TheTextColor)
```

The same is done with the Title Label control:

```
lblTitle.Font.Name = TheTextFont
lblTitle.ForeColor= MyColor.FromName(TheTextColor)
```

Another method of using the visitor's preferences is to place them directly into the body of the page, as is done here:

```
BGColor="<% Response.Write(TheBGColor) %>"
```

Access Code Changes

C12Preferences.mdb

The only code change needed to get this solution to work with Access instead of SQL Server is to change the connect string

```
DBConn = New OleDbConnection("Provider=sqloledb;" _
    & "server=localhost;" _
    & "Initial Catalog=INETC12;" _
    & "User Id=sa;" _
    & "Password=yourpassword;")
```

so that it uses the proper provider and points to the correct database:

```
DBConn = New OleDbConnection("PROVIDER=Microsoft.Jet.OLEDB.4.0;" _
    & "DATA SOURCE=" _
    & Server.MapPath("/INetBook/C12/Preferences/" _
    & "Access/C12Preferences.mdb;"))
```

Note that you will need to modify the path to the location of the database on your server.

CHAPTER

13

Creating a Web Log Site

The Internet has become so vast and so very cluttered with poor-quality sites that to find a real gem is a rare event. When you do find that gem, you may feel compelled to share your luck with others. A Web Log site provides an excellent mechanism for conveying that information.

A Web Log is a site where members share links that they find on the Internet with each other. They do this in the form of posts that they make to the Web log. When a member finds a great site, they post a description of the site to other members, as well as to visitors to the site. The description usually contains a link to that site. The members can then go to a Comments page to discuss the link that was posted.

In this chapter, we will create a Web Log site that allows members to post Web log entries and comments. The site allows members to log in and nonmembers to register and become members.

As you review this site, pay attention to the Calendar control that allows the member or visitor to easily view postings from another day. Think about how this control would be useful in your site's navigational needs.

Sample Usage

When the member first comes to the Web Log site, they see the page displayed in Figure 13-1.

When the page opens, the member sees all the posts that have been made during the current date. At the top of the page, they see the total number of those posts. Then, a Repeater control is used to display each of the postings.

Each posting is made up of the title and the text of the posting. After that, the name of the member who made the posting is displayed along with a link to their e-mail address. Following that is the date that the item was posted.

Note the calendar at the bottom of the page. The member can use this calendar to view the postings from another date. For example, if the visitor clicks the number 28, they see the posting displayed in Figure 13-2.

Notice that the date the visitor clicked is in a different color on the calendar. Also note that we have placed the date in the message label at the top of the page.

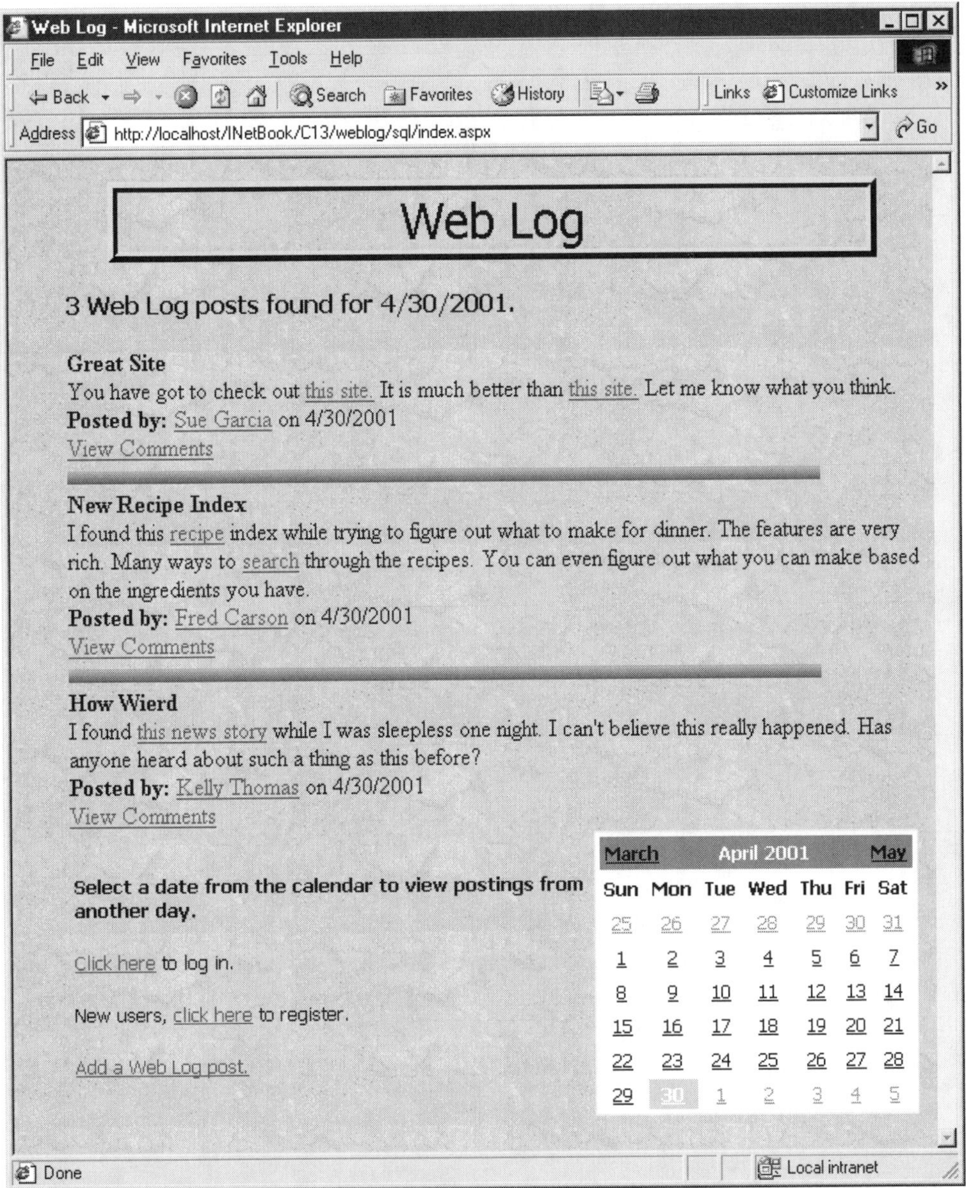

Figure 13-1 *Web Log page displaying default view*

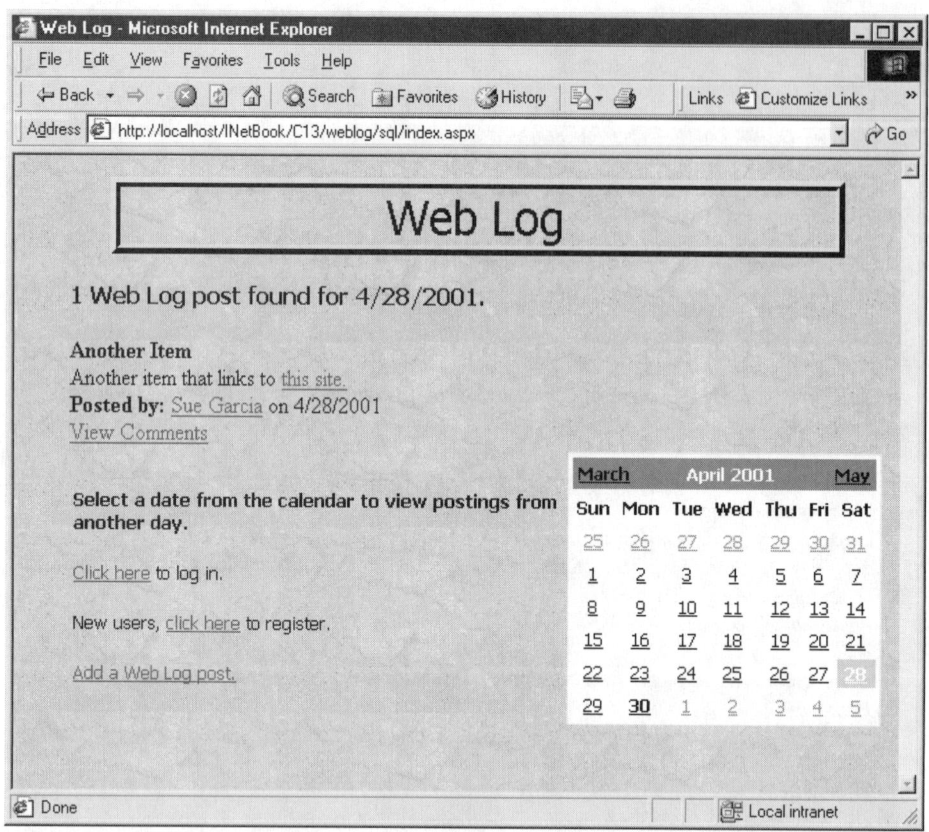

Figure 13-2 *Web Log page for a selected date*

Many of the features of the site can be accessed only if the visitor is a member and has logged into the site. To become a new member, the visitor uses the link at the bottom of the Web Log page.

Figure 13-3 shows that Register page.

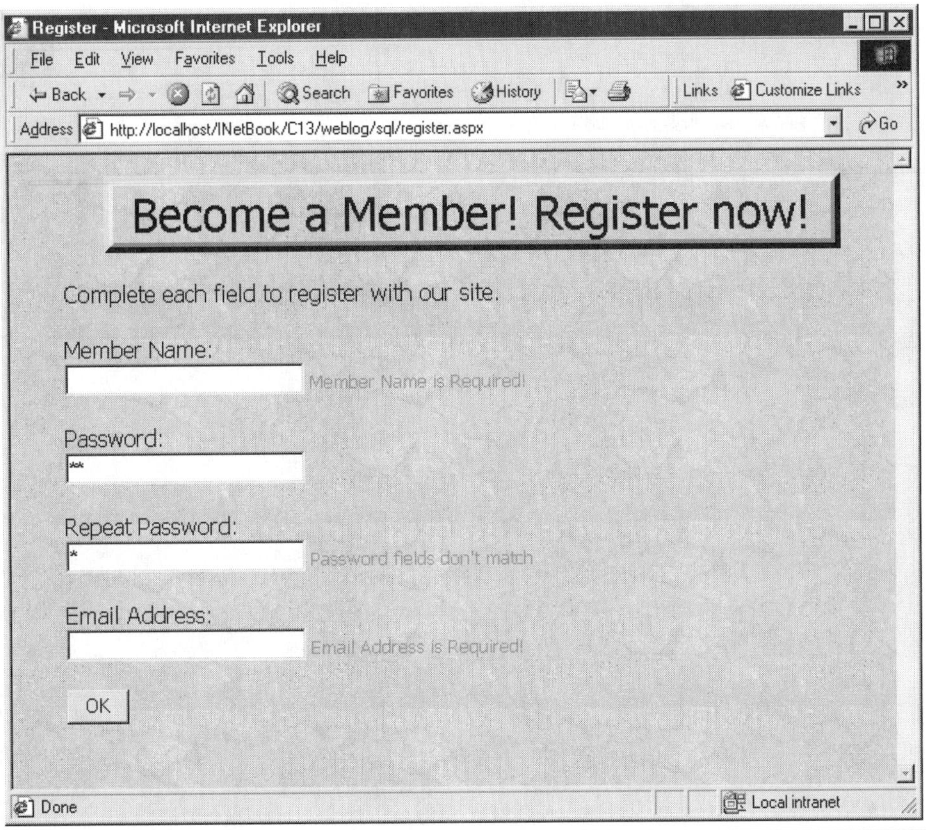

Figure 13-3 *Register page*

To register with the Web Log site, the visitor must enter values into each of the fields on that page. Validation controls are used to make sure that they enter something into each field and that the password fields match.

Another validation is performed, as you can see in Figure 13-4.

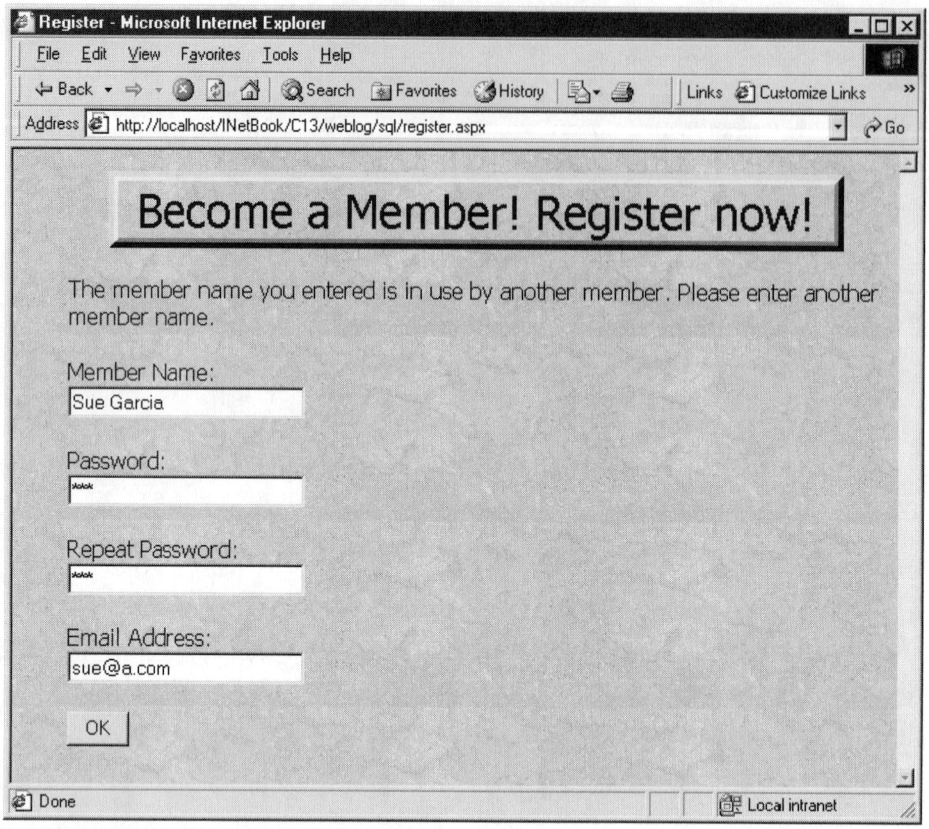

Figure 13-4 *Register page with error message*

The visitor can not use a member name that is already in use. If they enter a name that is already in use, they are asked to supply another name.

Once the member supplies validated registration information, their account is added and they are logged into the site. If they return to the site at another date, they can log back in by going to the Log In page through the link at the bottom of the Web Log page. That page is displayed in Figure 13-5.

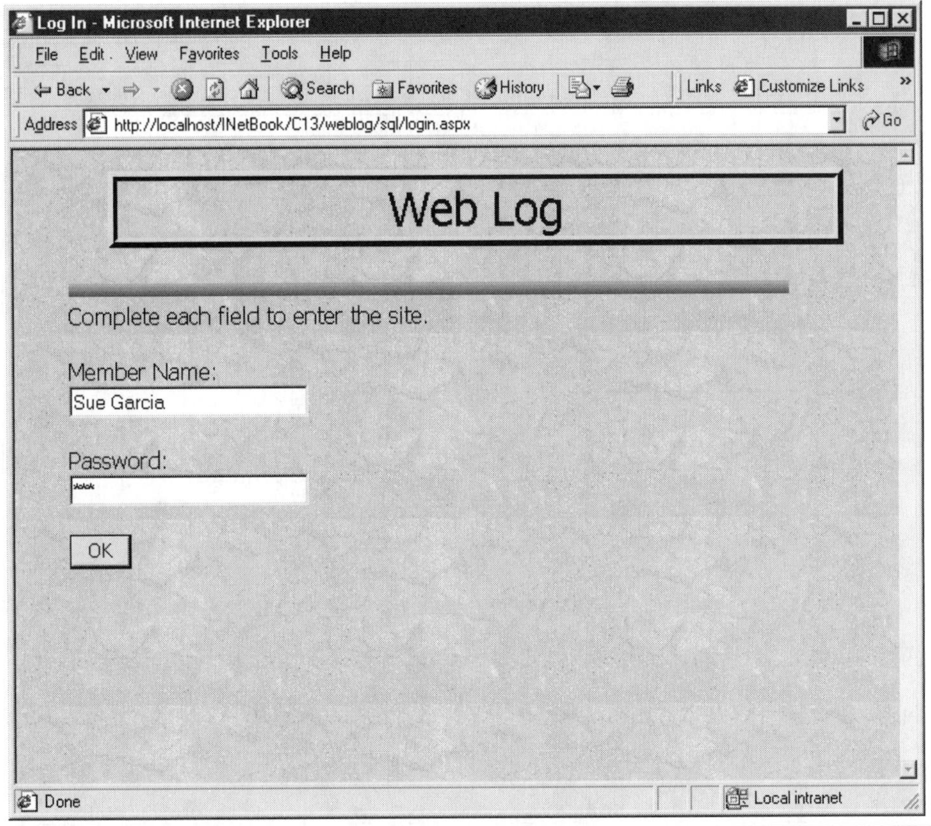

Figure 13-5 *Log In page*

The member must enter a valid member name and password to proceed. Once the member is logged in, they can add a post or a comment. If they attempt to go to either of those areas without first logging in, they are returned to the Log In page.

Back on the Web Log page, the visitor can select a link at the bottom of the page to add a post. When they do that, they see a page like the one displayed in Figure 13-6.

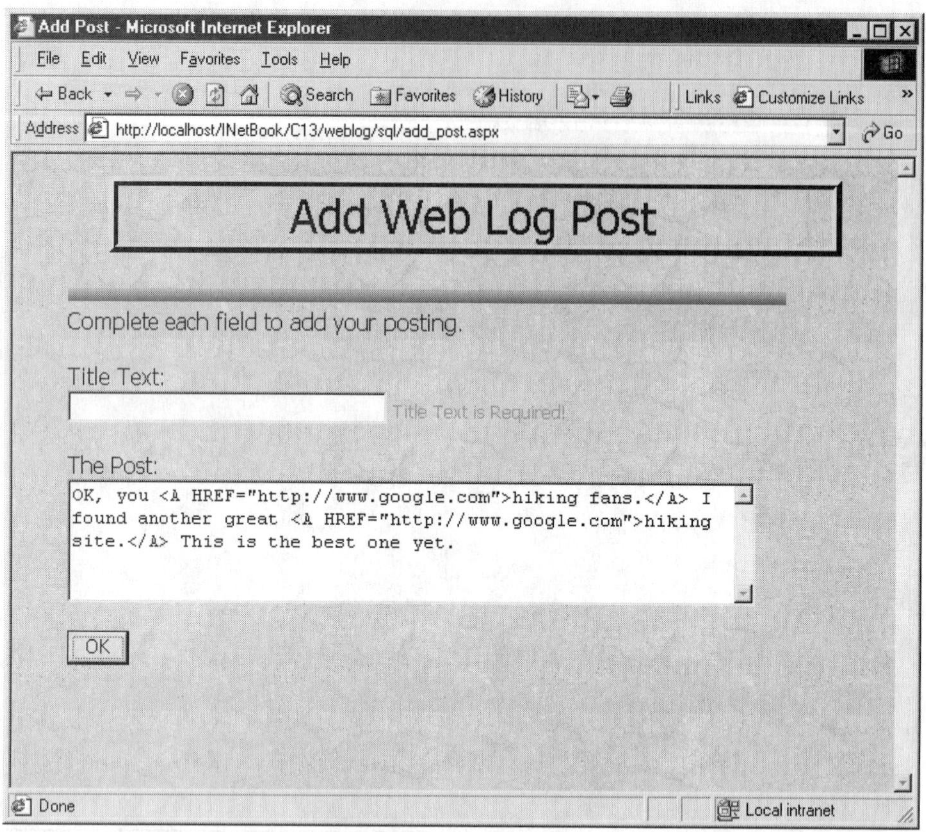

Figure 13-6 *Add Web Log Post page*

To add a posting, the visitor must put text in all the fields. Note that validation controls are used to make sure that they do this.

The Web log posting is then added to the database for the current date. The visitor is then taken back to the Web Log page, where they can see their new posting, as displayed in Figure 13-7.

Note that at the bottom of each listing is a link that says "View Comments." When the member clicks that link, they are taken to the page displayed in Figure 13-8.

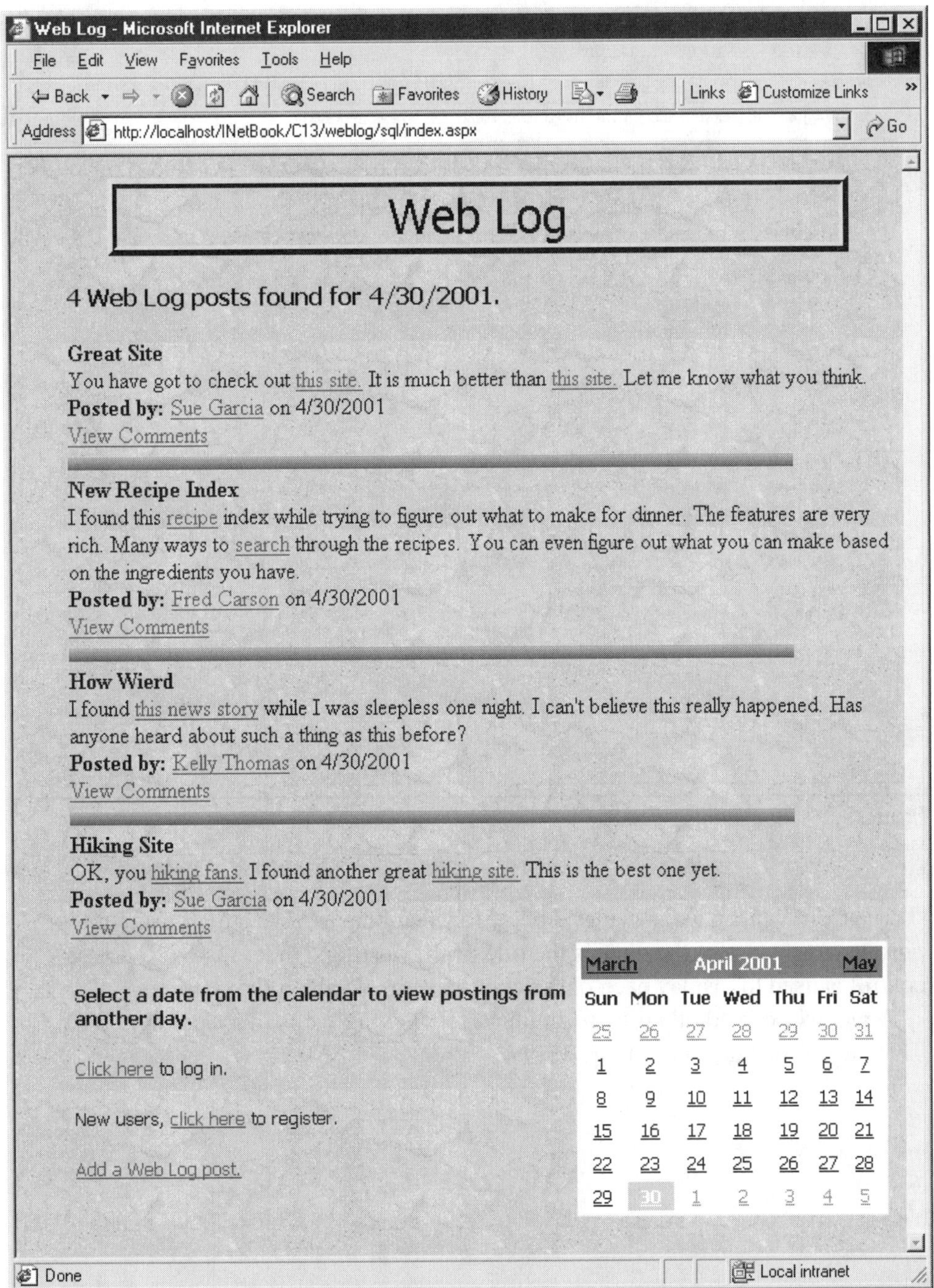

Figure 13-7 *Web Log page displaying new posting just added*

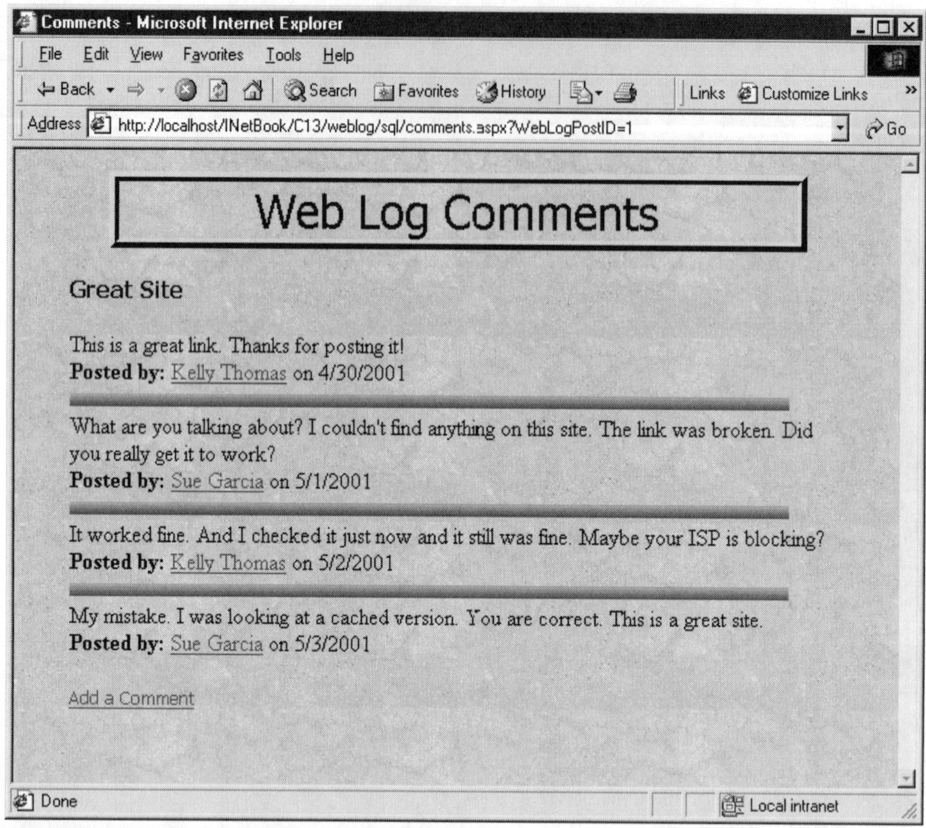

Figure 13-8 *Comments page*

The Comments page provides a place for members to have a dialog about the posting. At the top of the page is the title of the posting. Under that, a Repeater control is used to display each of the comments made about the posting.

A member can add their own comment by clicking the Add a Comment link. That page is displayed in Figure 13-9.

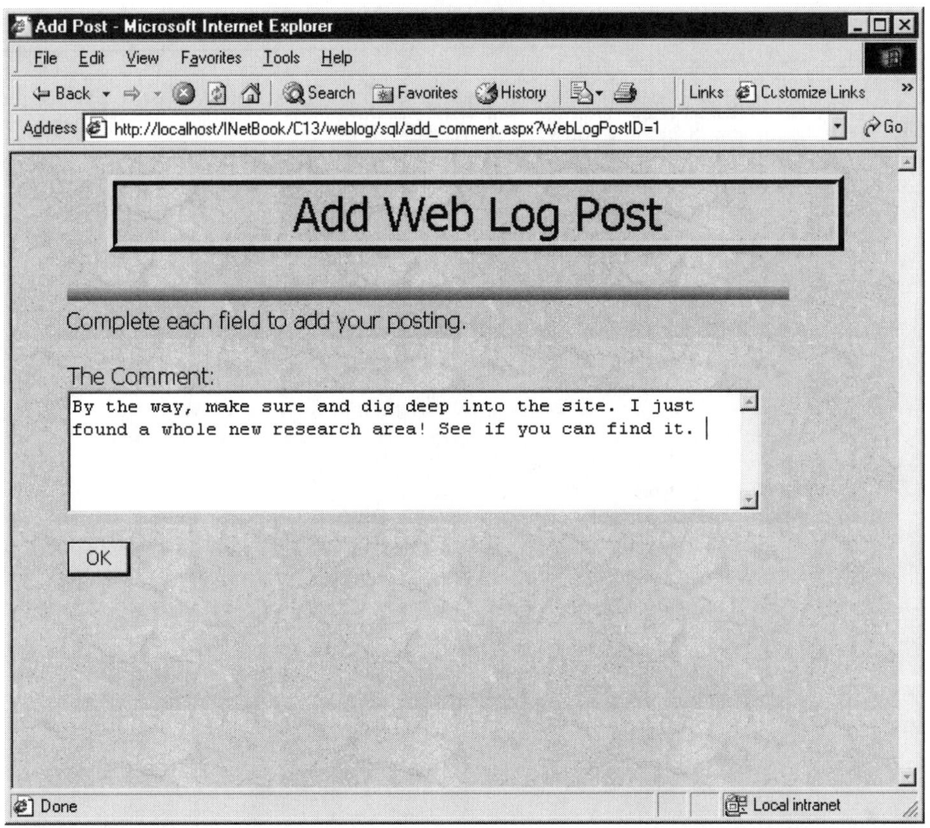

Figure 13-9 *Add a Comment page*

The member simply places their comment into the TextBox control. The code then adds their comment along with a date stamp as well as the member's ID to the database. The member is then taken back to the Comments page, where they can see the comment just added, as displayed in Figure 13-10.

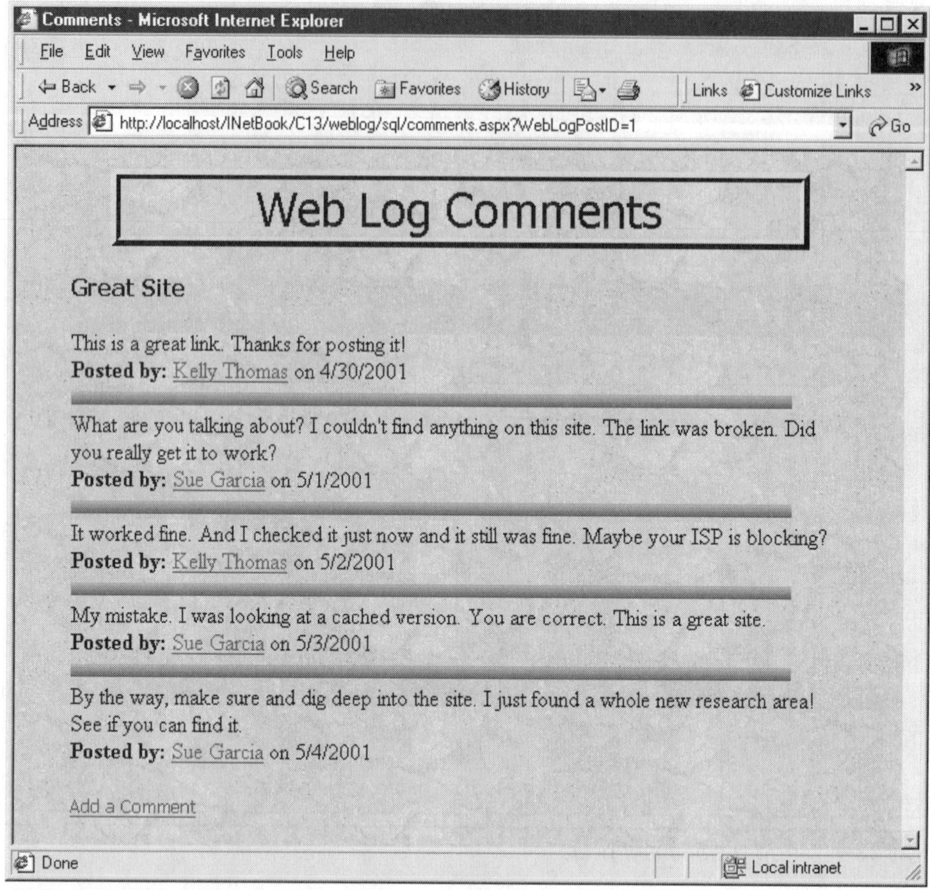

Figure 13-10 *Comments page with new comment added*

Web Log Database Component

C13WebLog.sql

The database required to run the Web Log site is made up of three interrelated tables. In this section, we will look at the relationships between the tables and the fields that make up the tables.

Tables and Data Diagram

Figure 13-11 shows the relationship between the tables in the Web Log database.

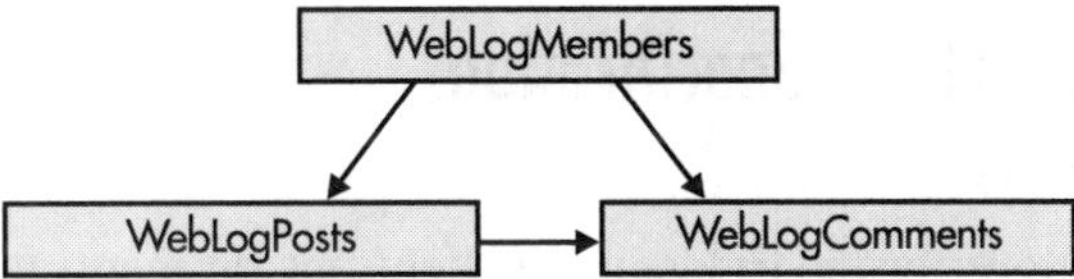

Figure 13-11 *Web Log data diagram*

The WebLogPosts table contains the postings themselves. The table is in a relationship with the WebLogMembers. Each posting was placed by a particular member, so the two tables are in a one-to-many relationship.

The WebLogMembers and the WebLogComments tables are also in a one-to-many relationship. The WebLogComments table contains the discussions made about each of the postings.

Each comment relates to a particular Web log posting. Therefore, those two tables are also in a one-to-many relationship.

WebLogPosts Field Specifications

WebLogPosts.txt

The field specifications for the fields in the WebLogPosts table are displayed in Table 13-1.

The WebLogPostID field is the primary key in the table. Since it is an identity column, it is populated with a unique value when a new record is added.

The TitleText field stores the title of the posting and is displayed at the top of the posting on the Web Log page. The ThePost field stores the text of the posting itself.

The WebLogMemberID is a foreign key that links this table to the WebLogMembers table. It stores the ID of the member who posted the item.

The DatePosted field stores the date that the item was posted by the member.

Field Name	Field Type	Notes
WebLogPostID	int	Primary Key
TitleText	varchar	Length = 100
ThePost	text	
WebLogMemberID	int	Foreign Key
DatePosted	datetime	

Table 13-1 *WebLogPosts Field Specifications*

WebLogComments Field Specifications

WebLogComments.txt

The field specifications for the fields in the WebLogComments table are displayed in Table 13-2.

The WebLogCommentID field is the primary key in this table. The table also contains two foreign keys. The WebLogPostID field links this table with the WebLogPosts table. It stores the ID of the posting that this comment goes with. The WebLogMemberID field links this table to the WebLogMembers table. It stores the ID of the member who placed the comment.

The CommentText field stores the text of the comment. And the DatePosted field stores the date that the comment was placed.

WebLogMembers Field Specifications

WebLogMembers.txt

The field specifications for the fields in the WebLogMembers table are displayed in Table 13-3.

The WebLogMemberID field is the primary key in this table. The other fields store data about the member.

Field Name	Field Type	Notes
WebLogCommentID	int	Primary Key
WebLogPostID	int	Foreign Key
WebLogMemberID	int	Foreign Key
CommentText	text	
DatePosted	datetime	

Table 13-2 *WebLogComments Field Specifications*

Field Name	Field Type	Notes
WebLogMemberID	int	Primary Key
MemberName	varchar	Length = 100
Password	varchar	Length = 50
EmailAddress	varchar	Length = 50

Table 13-3 *WebLogMembers Field Specifications*

Web Log ASP.NET Code

The Web Log site is made up of six ASP.NET pages. These pages employ controls like the Calendar, Repeater, TextBox, and validation controls to accomplish their tasks.

In this section, we will review those six pages that make up the tool.

Web Log ASP.NET Page

Index.aspx

The Web Log page displays the posts made by members and allows the member to view the postings for other dates through a Calendar control. The page also provides links to most of the other pages.

At the top of the page, three compiler directives are defined.

```
<%@ Page Language=VB Debug=true %>
<%@ Import Namespace="System.Data" %>
<%@ Import Namespace="System.Data.OLEDB" %>
```

The first directive tells the compiler that the language we are using is VB and that we are in debug mode. Note that you should turn off debug mode when placing this page in production:

```
<%@ Page Language=VB Debug=true %>
```

The other directives tell the compiler to import data libraries into our page:

```
<%@ Import Namespace="System.Data" %>
<%@ Import Namespace="System.Data.OLEDB" %>
```

Within the body of the page, a Label control is used to display some title text:

```
<asp:Label
    id="lblTitle"
    BorderWidth="7px"
    BorderStyle=7
    Width="90%"
    Font-Size="25pt"
    Font-Name="Tahoma"
    Text="Web Log"
    runat="server"
/>
```

Under that, another label is defined that displays a text message on the page:

```
<asp:Label
    id="lblMessage"
    Font-Size="12pt"
    Font-Name="Tahoma"
    Font-Bold="True"
    runat="server"
/>
```

Next, we define a Repeater control that will be used to display the Web log records.

```
<asp:Repeater
    id="repPosts"
    runat="server"
    >
    <itemtemplate>
        <b><%# DataBinder.Eval(Container.DataItem, _
        "TitleText") %></b>
        <br>
        <%# DataBinder.Eval(Container.DataItem, "ThePost") %>
        <br>
        <b>Posted by: </b>
```

```
        <a HREF="mailto:<%# DataBinder.Eval _
        (Container.DataItem, "EmailAddress") %>">
        <%# DataBinder.Eval(Container.DataItem, "MemberName") %></a>
        <%# "on " & DataBinder.Eval(Container.DataItem, "DatePosted")
%>
        <br>
        <a HREF="./comments.aspx?WebLogPostID=
        <%# DataBinder.Eval(Container.DataItem, "WebLogPostID") %>">
        View Comments</a>
    </itemtemplate>
    <separatortemplate>
        <br>
        <img SRC="./bar7.gif">
        <br>
    </separatortemplate>
</asp:Repeater>
```

First, we state the name of the control so that we can reference it in code:

```
id="repPosts"
```

And we tell the compiler that it is a server-side control:

```
runat="server"
```

Within the control, we define two templates. The first template describes the format that should be used to display each record:

```
<itemtemplate>
```

First, we want the title of the posting:

```
<b><%# DataBinder.Eval(Container.DataItem, _
"TitleText") %></b>
<br>
```

On the next line, we want the text of the posting:

```
<%# DataBinder.Eval(Container.DataItem, "ThePost") %>
<br>
```

That is followed by the name of the member who placed the posting, which is linked to their e-mail address:

```
<b>Posted by: </b>
<a HREF="mailto:<%# DataBinder.Eval _
(Container.DataItem, "EmailAddress") %>">
<%# DataBinder.Eval(Container.DataItem, "MemberName") %></a>
```

That is followed by the date the item was posted

```
<%# "on " & DataBinder.Eval(Container.DataItem, "DatePosted") %>
<br>
```

On the last line, we place a link to the Comments page that contains the ID of this posting:

```
<a HREF="./comments.aspx?WebLogPostID=
    <%# DataBinder.Eval(Container.DataItem, "WebLogPostID") %>">
    View Comments</a>
</itemtemplate>
```

The other template defined describes what is displayed between each record in the Repeater control:

```
<separatortemplate>
```

We simply place a graphical line to separate each record:

```
    <br>
    <img SRC="./bar7.gif">
    <br>
</separatortemplate>
```

The other control defined on this page is the Calendar control:

```
<asp:Calendar
    id="calDateToUse"
    runat="server"
    BackColor="ivory"
    CellPadding="3"
    CellSpacing="3"
    DayNameFormat="Short"
    FirstDayOfWeek="Default"
```

```
    NextPrevFormat="FullMonth"
    SelectionMode="Day"
    ShowDayHeader="True"
    ShowGridLines="False"
    ShowNextPrevMonth="True"
    ShowTitle="True"
    TitleFormat="MonthYear"
    TodayDayStyle-Font-Bold="True"
    DayHeaderStyle-Font-Bold="True"
    OtherMonthDayStyle-ForeColor="gray"
    TitleStyle-BackColor="#3366ff"
    TitleStyle-ForeColor="white"
    TitleStyle-Font-Bold="True"
    SelectedDayStyle-BackColor="#ffcc66"
    SelectedDayStyle-Font-Bold="True"
    Font-Name="Tahoma"
    Font-Size="12"
    OnSelectionChanged="calSelectChange"
/>
```

We state its name as it will be referenced in code:

```
id="calDateToUse"
```

This property displays the weekday names in the short format. Thus Monday is displayed as "Mon":

```
DayNameFormat="Short"
```

The next property defines that the first day of the week on the calendar should be whatever is the default:

```
FirstDayOfWeek="Default"
```

This property controls what is displayed in the links for the next month and the previous month. Here we elect to have the fill text of the name of the month displayed

```
NextPrevFormat="FullMonth"
```

With the SelectionMode property set to this value, the member can select only a single date as opposed to a range of dates:

```
SelectionMode="Day"
```

Here, we state that we want the title to contain the text of the current month and year:

```
TitleFormat="MonthYear"
```

And this event will be called when the member clicks one of the dates:

```
OnSelectionChanged="calSelectChange"
```

The code on the page is contained within two events. The first fires when the page is loaded.

```
Sub Page_Load(ByVal Sender as Object, ByVal E as EventArgs)
    If Not IsPostBack() Then
        Dim DBConn as OleDbConnection
        Dim DBCommand As OleDbDataAdapter
        Dim DSPosts as New DataSet
        DBConn = New OleDbConnection("Provider=sqloledb;" _
            & "server=localhost;" _
            & "Initial Catalog=INETC13;" _
            & "User Id=sa;" _
            & "Password=yourpassword;")
        DBCommand = New OleDbDataAdapter _
            ("Select WebLogPostID, TitleText, ThePost, " _
            & "DatePosted, MemberName, EmailAddress " _
            & "from WebLogPosts " _
            & "Left Join WebLogMembers On " _
            & "WebLogPosts.WebLogMemberID = " _
            & "WebLogMembers.WebLogMemberID Where " _
            & "DatePosted = '" & Today() & "'" _
            ,DBConn)
        DBCommand.Fill(DSPosts, _
            "ThePosts")
        repPosts.DataSource = _
            DSPosts.Tables("ThePosts").DefaultView
        repPosts.DataBind()
        calDateToUse.SelectedDate = Today()
        If DSPosts.Tables("ThePosts").Rows.Count = 1 Then
            lblMessage.Text = "1 Web Log post found for " _
                & Today() & "."
        Else
            lblMessage.Text = DSPosts.Tables("ThePosts").Rows.Count _
                & " Web Log posts found for " _
                & Today() & "."
```

```
        End If
    End If
End Sub
```

We want the code on the page to run only the first time the page is loaded

```
If Not IsPostBack() Then
```

If that is the case, we need data objects to connect to and retrieve data from our SQL Server database:

```
Dim DBConn as OleDbConnection
Dim DBCommand As OleDbDataAdapter
Dim DSPosts as New DataSet
```

We start by connecting to our database. Note that you will need to change the connect string to point to your own database and your own user information:

```
DBConn = New OleDbConnection("Provider=sqloledb;" _
    & "server=localhost;" _
    & "Initial Catalog=INETC13;" _
    & "User Id=sa;" _
    & "Password=yourpassword;")
```

We then place SQL text into our Data Adapter object so that it will retrieve all the posts for the current date. Note that we are using a join to retrieve data also from the WebLogMembers table. Also note that the function Today() is used to retrieve the current system date:

```
DBCommand = New OleDbDataAdapter _
    ("Select WebLogPostID, TitleText, ThePost, " _
    & "DatePosted, MemberName, EmailAddress " _
    & "from WebLogPosts " _
    & "Left Join WebLogMembers On " _
    & "WebLogPosts.WebLogMemberID = " _
    & "WebLogMembers.WebLogMemberID Where " _
    & "DatePosted = '" & Today() & "'" _
    ,DBConn)
```

The result of that query is placed into our DataSet object

```
DBCommand.Fill(DSPosts, _
    "ThePosts")
```

which the Repeater control is bound to:

```
repPosts.DataSource = _
    DSPosts.Tables("ThePosts").DefaultView
repPosts.DataBind()
```

We then set the selected date in the Calendar control to the current date:

```
calDateToUse.SelectedDate = Today()
```

Next, we check to see if the number of posts found was one:

```
If DSPosts.Tables("ThePosts").Rows.Count = 1 Then
```

If so, we place this text in the message label:

```
lblMessage.Text = "1 Web Log post found for " _
    & Today() & "."
```

Otherwise, the plural "posts" is used

```
lblMessage.Text = DSPosts.Tables("ThePosts").Rows.Count _
    & " Web Log posts found for " _
    & Today() & "."
```

The other procedure on this page fires when the date on the calendar changes by the member clicking it.

```
Sub calSelectChange(ByVal Sender as Object, ByVal E as EventArgs)
    Dim DBConn as OleDbConnection
    Dim DBCommand As OleDbDataAdapter
    Dim DSPosts as New DataSet
    DBConn = New OleDbConnection("Provider=sqloledb;" _
        & "server=localhost;" _
        & "Initial Catalog=INETC13;" _
        & "User Id=sa;" _
        & "Password=yourpassword;")
    DBCommand = New OleDbDataAdapter _
        ("Select WebLogPostID, TitleText, ThePost, " _
        & "DatePosted, MemberName, EmailAddress " _
        & "from WebLogPosts " _
        & "Left Join WebLogMembers On " _
        & "WebLogPosts.WebLogMemberID = " _
```

```
        & "WebLogMembers.WebLogMemberID Where " _
        & "DatePosted = '" _
        & calDateToUse.SelectedDate & "'" _
        ,DBConn)
    DBCommand.Fill(DSPosts, _
        "ThePosts")
    repPosts.DataSource = _
        DSPosts.Tables("ThePosts").DefaultView
    repPosts.DataBind()
    If DSPosts.Tables("ThePosts").Rows.Count = 1 Then
        lblMessage.Text = "1 Web Log post found for " _
            & calDateToUse.SelectedDate & "."
    Else
        lblMessage.Text = DSPosts.Tables("ThePosts").Rows.Count _
            & " Web Log posts found for " _
            & calDateToUse.SelectedDate & "."
    End If
End Sub
```

The procedure requires data objects so that we can connect to and retrieve data from the database:

```
Dim DBConn as OleDbConnection
Dim DBCommand As OleDbDataAdapter
Dim DSPosts as New DataSet
```

First, we connect to our database:

```
DBConn = New OleDbConnection("Provider=sqloledb;" _
    & "server=localhost;" _
    & "Initial Catalog=INETC13;" _
    & "User Id=sa;" _
    & "Password=yourpassword;")
```

We then retrieve all the posts corresponding to the date selected in the Calendar control by the member:

```
DBCommand = New OleDbDataAdapter _
    ("Select WebLogPostID, TitleText, ThePost, " _
    & "DatePosted, MemberName, EmailAddress " _
    & "from WebLogPosts " _
    & "Left Join WebLogMembers On " _
    & "WebLogPosts.WebLogMemberID = " _
```

```
    & "WebLogMembers.WebLogMemberID Where " _
    & "DatePosted = '" _
    & calDateToUse.SelectedDate & "'" _
    ,DBConn)
```

That data is placed into our DataSet object:

```
DBCommand.Fill(DSPosts, _
    "ThePosts")
```

And our Repeater control is bound to it:

```
repPosts.DataSource = _
    DSPosts.Tables("ThePosts").DefaultView
repPosts.DataBind()
```

We then check to see if the number of posts found is one:

```
If DSPosts.Tables("ThePosts").Rows.Count = 1 Then
```

If so, we use the singular, "post":

```
lblMessage.Text = "1 Web Log post found for " _
    & calDateToUse.SelectedDate & "."
```

Otherwise, the plural, "posts", is used

```
lblMessage.Text = DSPosts.Tables("ThePosts").Rows.Count _
    & " Web Log posts found for " _
    & calDateToUse.SelectedDate & "."
```

Comments ASP.NET Page

Comments.aspx

The code on the Comments page displays all the comments that go with the posting for which the ID was passed into the page.

The page defines three directives:

```
<%@ Page Language=VB Debug=true %>
<%@ Import Namespace="System.Data" %>
<%@ Import Namespace="System.Data.OLEDB" %>
```

The first defines the programming environment:

```
<%@ Page Language=VB Debug=true %>
```

The other two are required for the data access:

```
<%@ Import Namespace="System.Data" %>
<%@ Import Namespace="System.Data.OLEDB" %>
```

Within the body of the page, a Label control is defined to display some title text:

```
<asp:Label
    id="lblTitle"
    BorderWidth="7px"
    BorderStyle=7
    Width="90%"
    Font-Size="25pt"
    Font-Name="Tahoma"
    Text="Web Log Comments"
    runat="server"
/>
```

Another label is defined that will be used to display the title of the posting:

```
<asp:Label
    id="lblMessage"
    Font-Size="12pt"
    Font-Name="Tahoma"
    Font-Bold="True"
    runat="server"
/>
```

A Repeater control is next defined. It will display all the comments for the posting:

```
<asp:Repeater
    id="repComments"
    runat="server"
    >
    <itemtemplate>
        <%# DataBinder.Eval(Container.DataItem, "CommentText") %>
        <br>
```

```
        <b>Posted by: </b>
        <a HREF="mailto:
        <%# DataBinder.Eval(Container.DataItem, "EmailAddress") %>">
        <%# DataBinder.Eval(Container.DataItem, "MemberName") %></a>
        <%# "on " &
        DataBinder.Eval(Container.DataItem, "DatePosted") %>
    </itemtemplate>
    <separatortemplate>
        <br>
        <img SRC="./bar7.gif">
        <br>
    </separatortemplate>
</asp:Repeater>
```

The Repeater control uses two templates. The first defines the format of the records displayed in the control:

```
<itemtemplate>
```

We start by displaying the text of the comment:

```
<%# DataBinder.Eval(Container.DataItem, "CommentText") %>
<br>
```

That is followed by the member's name and e-mail address

```
<b>Posted by: </b>
<a HREF="mailto:
<%# DataBinder.Eval(Container.DataItem, "EmailAddress") %>">
<%# DataBinder.Eval(Container.DataItem, "MemberName") %></a>
```

and when the member entered the comment:

```
    <%# "on " &
    DataBinder.Eval(Container.DataItem, "DatePosted") %>
</itemtemplate>
```

The other template defines the format between each record:

```
<separatortemplate>
```

Here, we merely place an image bar:

```
    <br>
    <img SRC="./bar7.gif">
    <br>
</separatortemplate>
```

At the bottom of the page, we provide a link that allows the member to add their own comment. The link needs to pass to the Comments page the ID of the post that it goes with:

```
<a HREF="./add_comment.aspx?WebLogPostID=
<%# Request.QueryString("WebLogPostID") %>">Add a Comment</a>
```

The code on the page appears within a single procedure. That procedure runs when the page is loaded.

```
Sub Page_Load(ByVal Sender as Object, ByVal E as EventArgs)
    If Len(Request.QueryString("WebLogPostID")) = 0 Then
        lblMessage.Text = "This page can only be entered " _
            & "by clicking on the ""View Comments"" link " _
            & "on the Web Log Posts page."
    Else
        Dim DBConn as OleDbConnection
        Dim DBCommand As OleDbDataAdapter
        Dim DSPostInfo as New DataSet
        DBConn = New OleDbConnection("Provider=sqloledb;" _
            & "server=localhost;" _
            & "Initial Catalog=INETC13;" _
            & "User Id=sa;" _
            & "Password=yourpassword;")
        DBCommand = New OleDbDataAdapter _
            ("Select TitleText " _
            & "from WebLogPosts " _
            & "Where WebLogPostID = " _
            & Request.QueryString("WebLogPostID") _
            ,DBConn)
        DBCommand.Fill(DSPostInfo, _
            "TheTitle")
        DBCommand = New OleDbDataAdapter _
```

```
                ("Select CommentText, DatePosted, " _
                & "MemberName, EmailAddress " _
                & "from WebLogComments " _
                & "Left Join WebLogMembers On " _
                & "WebLogComments.WebLogMemberID = " _
                & "WebLogMembers.WebLogMemberID Where " _
                & "WebLogPostID = " _
                & Request.QueryString("WebLogPostID") _
                & " Order By DatePosted" _
                ,DBConn)
            DBCommand.Fill(DSPostInfo, _
                "TheComments")
            repComments.DataSource = _
                DSPostInfo.Tables("TheComments").DefaultView
            Page.DataBind()
            lblMessage.Text = DSPostInfo.Tables("TheTitle"). _
                    Rows(0).Item("TitleText")
    End If
End Sub
```

The code on the page should run only if a Web log ID was passed into the page:

```
If Len(Request.QueryString("WebLogPostID")) = 0 Then
```

If one wasn't, we display this message to the member:

```
lblMessage.Text = "This page can only be entered " _
    & "by clicking on the ""View Comments"" link " _
    & "on the Web Log Posts page."
```

Otherwise, we declare the needed data objects

```
Dim DBConn as OleDbConnection
Dim DBCommand As OleDbDataAdapter
Dim DSPostInfo as New DataSet
```

and connect to our database:

```
DBConn = New OleDbConnection("Provider=sqloledb;" _
    & "server=localhost;" _
    & "Initial Catalog=INETC13;" _
    & "User Id=sa;" _
    & "Password=yourpassword;")
```

In our Data Adapter object, we place SQL text that will retrieve the title of the Web log posting:

```
DBCommand = New OleDbDataAdapter _
    ("Select TitleText " _
    & "from WebLogPosts " _
    & "Where WebLogPostID = " _
    & Request.QueryString("WebLogPostID") _
    ,DBConn)
```

The title returned by that call is placed into our DataSet object:

```
DBCommand.Fill(DSPostInfo, _
    "TheTitle")
```

We also need to retrieve all the comments that go with the posting:

```
DBCommand = New OleDbDataAdapter _
    ("Select CommentText, DatePosted, " _
    & "MemberName, EmailAddress " _
    & "from WebLogComments " _
    & "Left Join WebLogMembers On " _
    & "WebLogComments.WebLogMemberID = " _
    & "WebLogMembers.WebLogMemberID Where " _
    & "WebLogPostID = " _
    & Request.QueryString("WebLogPostID") _
    & " Order By DatePosted" _
    ,DBConn)
```

And we place them, too, into our DataSet object:

```
DBCommand.Fill(DSPostInfo, _
    "TheComments")
```

That DataSet table is bound to our Repeater control:

```
repComments.DataSource = _
    DSPostInfo.Tables("TheComments").DefaultView
```

We then bind the whole page, which will bind the repeater control as well as the link at the bottom of the page to the Add a Comment page:

```
Page.DataBind()
```

Into the message label, we place the title of the Web log post:

```
lblMessage.Text = DSPostInfo.Tables("TheTitle"). _
    Rows(0).Item("TitleText")
```

Log In ASP.NET Page

LogIn.aspx

The code on the Log In page validates the member's attempt to log in to the site. The page requires the same three compiler directives:

```
<%@ Page Language=VB Debug=true %>
<%@ Import Namespace="System.Data" %>
<%@ Import Namespace="System.Data.OLEDB" %>
```

Within the body of the page, a Label control that will display title text is defined

```
<asp:Label
    id="lblTitle"
    BorderWidth="7px"
    BorderStyle=7
    Width="90%"
    Font-Size="25pt"
    Font-Name="Tahoma"
    Text="Web Log"
    runat="server"
/>
```

We also define a message label that will display instructions as well as an error message:

```
<asp:Label
    id="lblMessage"
    Font-Size="12pt"
    Font-Name="Tahoma"
    runat="server"
    Text="Complete each field to enter the site."
/>
```

The next control on the page is a TextBox control where the member can enter their name:

```
<asp:TextBox
    id="txtMemberName"
    Columns="25"
```

```
    MaxLength="30"
    runat=server
/>
```

After that, a RequiredFieldValidator control is defined to make sure that the member places their name in the field:

```
<asp:RequiredFieldValidator
    id="rfvMemberName"
    ControlToValidate="txtMemberName"
    Display="Dynamic"
    Font-Name="Tahoma"
    Font-Size="10pt"
    runat=server>
    Member Name is Required!
</asp:RequiredFieldValidator>
```

Another TextBox that provides the place for the visitor to enter their password is defined

```
<asp:TextBox
    id="txtPassword"
    Columns="25"
    MaxLength="30"
    runat=server
    TextMode="Password"
/>
```

Note the TextMode property is set to "Password," which will display the "*" character as the member types in their password:

```
TextMode="Password"
```

Another RequiredFieldValidator control requires the visitor to enter their password before the page can be posted

```
<asp:RequiredFieldValidator
    id="rfvPassword"
    ControlToValidate="txtPassword"
    Display="Dynamic"
    Font-Name="Verdana"
    Font-Size="10pt"
    runat=server>
    Password is Required!
</asp:RequiredFieldValidator>
```

The only other control on the page is a Button control:

```
<asp:button
    id="butOK"
    text="  OK  "
    Type="Submit"
    OnClick="SubmitBtn_Click"
    runat="server"
/>
```

When clicked, the button fires the only code on the page.

```
Sub SubmitBtn_Click(Sender As Object, E As EventArgs)
    Dim DBConn as OleDbConnection
    Dim DBCommand As OleDbDataAdapter
    Dim DSLogin as New DataSet
    DBConn = New OleDbConnection("Provider=sqloledb;" _
        & "server=localhost;" _
        & "Initial Catalog=INETC13;" _
        & "User Id=sa;" _
        & "Password=yourpassword;")
    DBCommand = New OleDbDataAdapter _
        ("Select WebLogMemberID from " _
        & "WebLogMembers Where " _
        & "MemberName = '" & txtMemberName.Text _
        & "' and Password = '" & txtPassword.Text _
        & "'", DBConn)
    DBCommand.Fill(DSLogin, _
        "MemberInfo")
    If DSLogin.Tables("MemberInfo"). _
        Rows.Count = 0 Then
        lblMessage.Text = "The member name and password " _
            & "were not found. Please try again."
    Else
        Session("WebLogMemberID") = DSLogin.Tables("MemberInfo"). _
            Rows(0).Item("WebLogMemberID")
        Response.Redirect("./index.aspx")
    End If
End Sub
```

The procedure requires a data object so that we can validate the member's login:

```
Dim DBConn as OleDbConnection
Dim DBCommand As OleDbDataAdapter
Dim DSLogin as New DataSet
```

We start by connecting to the database:

```
DBConn = New OleDbConnection("Provider=sqloledb;" _
    & "server=localhost;" _
    & "Initial Catalog=INETC13;" _
    & "User Id=sa;" _
    & "Password=yourpassword;")
```

Next, we place text into our Data Adapter object that looks for the member name and password supplied by the member:

```
DBCommand = New OleDbDataAdapter _
    ("Select WebLogMemberID from " _
    & "WebLogMembers Where " _
    & "MemberName = '" & txtMemberName.Text _
    & "' and Password = '" & txtPassword.Text _
    & "'", DBConn)
```

The data returned from that call is placed into our DataSet object:

```
DBCommand.Fill(DSLogin, _
    "MemberInfo")
```

We then check to see if a record was found

```
If DSLogin.Tables("MemberInfo"). _
    Rows.Count = 0 Then
```

If one wasn't, it means the login attempt was not valid:

```
lblMessage.Text = "The member name and password " _
    & "were not found. Please try again."
```

Otherwise, it was and we store the ID of the member into a Session variable

```
Session("WebLogMemberID") = DSLogin.Tables("MemberInfo"). _
    Rows(0).Item("WebLogMemberID")
```

and send the visitor back to the Web Log page:

```
Response.Redirect("./index.aspx")
```

Add Post ASP.NET Page

Add_Post.aspx

The code on the Add Post page allows a logged-in member to post their own Web log item. At the top of the page, we define three compiler directives that import data libraries into our code and set up the programming environment:

```
<%@ Page Language=VB Debug=true %>
<%@ Import Namespace="System.Data" %>
<%@ Import Namespace="System.Data.OLEDB" %>
```

Within the body of the page, a label that will display title text on the page is defined

```
<asp:Label
    id="lblTitle"
    BorderWidth="7px"
    BorderStyle=7
    Width="90%"
    Font-Size="25pt"
    Font-Name="Tahoma"
    Text="Add Web Log Post"
    runat="server"
/>
```

Another label displays the instructions for the page:

```
<asp:Label
    id="lblMessage"
    Font-Size="12pt"
    Font-Name="Tahoma"
    runat="server"
    Text="Complete each field to add your posting."
/>
```

After that, a TextBox control, which is used by the member to enter the title of the Web log posting, is defined

```
<asp:TextBox
    id="txtTitleText"
    Columns="35"
    MaxLength="60"
    runat=server
/>
```

The title field must contain a value:

```
<asp:RequiredFieldValidator
    id="rfvTitleText"
    ControlToValidate="txtTitleText"
    Display="Dynamic"
    Font-Name="Tahoma"
    Font-Size="10pt"
    runat=server>
    Title Text is Required!
</asp:RequiredFieldValidator>
```

Another TextBox control that allows the visitor to enter the text of the Web log post is defined

```
<asp:TextBox
    id="txtThePost"
    Columns="60"
    Rows="5"
    runat=server
    TextMode="MultiLine"
/>
```

Note the value placed into the TextMode property, which makes the TextBox appear with more than one row

```
TextMode="MultiLine"
```

and allows the Rows property to be used

```
Rows="5"
```

That field, too, is required

```
<asp:RequiredFieldValidator
    id="rfvThePost"
    ControlToValidate="txtThePost"
    Display="Dynamic"
    Font-Name="Verdana"
    Font-Size="10pt"
    runat=server>
    <br>The Post field is Required!
</asp:RequiredFieldValidator>
```

The only other control on the page is a button control:

```
<asp:button
    id="butOK"
    text="  OK  "
    Type="Submit"
    OnClick="SubmitBtn_Click"
    runat="server"
/>
```

The OnClick property defines the name of the procedure that is called when the button is clicked

```
OnClick="SubmitBtn_Click"
```

The code on the page is contained within two procedures. The first fires when the page is loaded.

```
Sub Page_Load(ByVal Sender as Object, ByVal E as EventArgs)
    If Len(Session("WebLogMemberID")) = 0 Then
        Response.Redirect("./login.aspx")
    End If
End Sub
```

The code makes sure that the member has logged in before coming to this page:

```
If Len(Session("WebLogMemberID")) = 0 Then
```

If they haven't, they are taken to the Log In page:

```
Response.Redirect("./login.aspx")
```

The other procedure runs when the Button control is clicked.

```
Sub SubmitBtn_Click(Sender As Object, E As EventArgs)
    Dim DBConn as OleDbConnection
    Dim DBCommand As OleDbDataAdapter
    Dim DBInsert As New OleDbCommand
    DBConn = New OleDbConnection("Provider=sqloledb;" _
        & "server=localhost;" _
        & "Initial Catalog=INETC13;" _
        & "User Id=sa;" _
        & "Password=yourpassword;")
    DBInsert.CommandText = "Insert Into WebLogPosts " _
```

```
        & "(TitleText, ThePost, WebLogMemberID, DatePosted) " _
        & "values (" _
        & "'" & Replace(txtTitleText.text, "'", "''") & "', " _
        & "'" & Replace(txtThePost.text, "'", "''") & "', " _
        & Session("WebLogMemberID") & ", " _
        & "'" & Today() & "')"
    DBInsert.Connection = DBConn
    DBInsert.Connection.Open
    DBInsert.ExecuteNonQuery()
    Response.Redirect("./index.aspx")
End Sub
```

The procedure requires data objects that allow us to connect to and insert data into our database:

```
Dim DBConn as OleDbConnection
Dim DBCommand As OleDbDataAdapter
Dim DBInsert As New OleDbCommand
```

We start in this procedure by connecting to our database:

```
DBConn = New OleDbConnection("Provider=sqloledb;" _
    & "server=localhost;" _
    & "Initial Catalog=INETC13;" _
    & "User Id=sa;" _
    & "Password=yourpassword;")
```

Then we place text into our Command object that will add the post entered by the member into the database. Note that we supply the ID of the member and today's date through the Today() function:

```
DBInsert.CommandText = "Insert Into WebLogPosts " _
    & "(TitleText, ThePost, WebLogMemberID, DatePosted) " _
    & "values (" _
    & "'" & Replace(txtTitleText.text, "'", "''") & "', " _
    & "'" & Replace(txtThePost.text, "'", "''") & "', " _
    & Session("WebLogMemberID") & ", " _
    & "'" & Today() & "')"
```

We then connect the Command object to the database through our Connection object

```
DBInsert.Connection = DBConn
DBInsert.Connection.Open
```

and run our Insert statement:

```
DBInsert.ExecuteNonQuery()
```

We next send the member back to the Web Log page:

```
Response.Redirect("./index.aspx")
```

Add Comment ASP.NET Page

Add_Comment.aspx

The Add Comment page allows the logged-in member to add a comment regarding one of the Web log posts. The page contains the three compiler directives defined at the top of the page:

```
<%@ Page Language=VB Debug=true %>
<%@ Import Namespace="System.Data" %>
<%@ Import Namespace="System.Data.OLEDB" %>
```

The first control on the page is a label that displays the title of the page:

```
<asp:Label
    id="lblTitle"
    BorderWidth="7px"
    BorderStyle=7
    Width="90%"
    Font-Size="25pt"
    Font-Name="Tahoma"
    Text="Add Web Log Post"
    runat="server"
/>
```

The next label is used to display page instructions:

```
<asp:Label
    id="lblMessage"
    Font-Size="12pt"
    Font-Name="Tahoma"
    runat="server"
    Text="Complete each field to add your posting."
/>
```

The next control in the body of the page provides the member with the space to enter their comment:

```
<asp:TextBox
    id="txtCommentText"
    Columns="60"
    Rows="5"
    runat=server
    TextMode="MultiLine"
/>
```

That field is required because a RequiredFieldValidator control is linked to it:

```
<asp:RequiredFieldValidator
    id="rfvCommentText"
    ControlToValidate="txtCommentText"
    Display="Dynamic"
    Font-Name="Verdana"
    Font-Size="10pt"
    runat=server>
    <br>The Post field is Required!
</asp:RequiredFieldValidator>
```

One more control on the page is a button that submits the contents of the form when the visitor is done with their comment:

```
<asp:button
    id="butOK"
    text="   OK   "
    Type="Submit"
    OnClick="SubmitBtn_Click"
    runat="server"
/>
```

Passed into the page is the ID of the Web log post that the comment goes with. We need that value when the contents of the page are submitted. Therefore, a Private variable is defined to store that value:

```
Private CurrentWebLogPostID as String
```

Two procedures are defined on this page. The first runs when the page is loaded.

```
Sub Page_Load(ByVal Sender as Object, ByVal E as EventArgs)
    If Len(Session("WebLogMemberID")) = 0 Then
        Response.Redirect("./login.aspx")
    End If
    If Len(Request.QueryString("WebLogPostID")) = 0 Then
        Response.Redirect("./index.aspx")
    End If
    CurrentWebLogPostID = Request.QueryString("WebLogPostID")
End Sub
```

We start by making sure that the member has logged in:

```
If Len(Session("WebLogMemberID")) = 0 Then
```

If they haven't, they are sent to do so:

```
Response.Redirect("./login.aspx")
```

Also, for the page to run correctly, the ID of the Web log posting that the comment goes with needs to be passed in:

```
If Len(Request.QueryString("WebLogPostID")) = 0 Then
```

If it wasn't, we send the visitor back to the Web Log page:

```
Response.Redirect("./index.aspx")
```

Otherwise, we store the ID passed in, into our Private variable:

```
CurrentWebLogPostID = Request.QueryString("WebLogPostID")
```

The other procedure fires when the OK button is clicked.

```
Sub SubmitBtn_Click(Sender As Object, E As EventArgs)
    Dim DBConn as OleDbConnection
    Dim DBCommand As OleDbDataAdapter
    Dim DBInsert As New OleDbCommand
    DBConn = New OleDbConnection("Provider=sqloledb;" _
        & "server=localhost;" _
        & "Initial Catalog=INETC13;" _
        & "User Id=sa;" _
        & "Password=yourpassword;")
```

```
    DBInsert.CommandText = "Insert Into WebLogComments " _
        & "(WebLogPostID, WebLogMemberID, CommentText, DatePosted) " _
        & "values (" _
        & CurrentWebLogPostID & ", " _
        & Session("WebLogMemberID") & ", " _
        & "'" & Replace(txtCommentText.text, "'", "''") & "', " _
        & "'" & Today() & "')"
    DBInsert.Connection = DBConn
    DBInsert.Connection.Open
    DBInsert.ExecuteNonQuery()
    Response.Redirect("./comments.aspx?WebLogPostID=" _
        & CurrentWebLogPostID)
End Sub
```

The procedure will need data objects:

```
Dim DBConn as OleDbConnection
Dim DBCommand As OleDbDataAdapter
Dim DBInsert As New OleDbCommand
```

We start by connecting to the database:

```
DBConn = New OleDbConnection("Provider=sqloledb;" _
    & "server=localhost;" _
    & "Initial Catalog=INETC13;" _
    & "User Id=sa;" _
    & "Password=yourpassword;")
```

And we place the text of an insert statement into our Command object:

```
DBInsert.CommandText = "Insert Into WebLogComments " _
    & "(WebLogPostID, WebLogMemberID, CommentText, DatePosted) " _
    & "values (" _
    & CurrentWebLogPostID & ", " _
    & Session("WebLogMemberID") & ", " _
    & "'" & Replace(txtCommentText.text, "'", "''") & "', " _
    & "'" & Today() & "')"
```

The comment is then added to the database:

```
DBInsert.Connection = DBConn
DBInsert.Connection.Open
DBInsert.ExecuteNonQuery()
```

And we send the member back to the Comments page:

```
Response.Redirect("./comments.aspx?WebLogPostID=" _
    & CurrentWebLogPostID)
```

Register ASP.NET Page

Register.aspx

The code on the Register page allows a visitor to become a member. The page defines the same three compiler directives:

```
<%@ Page Language=VB Debug=true %>
<%@ Import Namespace="System.Data" %>
<%@ Import Namespace="System.Data.OLEDB" %>
```

On the body of the page, a Label control that displays the title of the page is defined

```
<asp:Label
    id="lblTitle"
    BorderWidth="7px"
    BorderStyle=9
    Width="90%"
    Font-Size="25pt"
    Font-Name="Tahoma"
    Text="Become a Member! Register now!"
    runat="server"
/>
```

The next control is another label that displays the page instructions and any error messages when the page is submitted

```
<asp:Label
    id="lblMessage"
    Font-Size="12pt"
    Font-Name="Tahoma"
    runat="server"
    Text="Complete each field to register with our site."
/>
```

Next, a TextBox control is defined for the new member's name:

```
<asp:TextBox
    id="txtMemberName"
    Columns="25"
```

```
    MaxLength="30"
    runat=server
/>
```

That field is required through this RequiredFieldValidator control:

```
<asp:RequiredFieldValidator
    id="rfvMemberName"
    ControlToValidate="txtMemberName"
    Display="Dynamic"
    Font-Name="Tahoma"
    Font-Size="10pt"
    runat=server>
    Member Name is Required!
</asp:RequiredFieldValidator>
```

The next control is a TextBox for the new member's password:

```
<asp:TextBox
    id="txtPassword"
    Columns="25"
    MaxLength="30"
    runat=server
    TextMode="Password"
/>
```

That field is also required

```
<asp:RequiredFieldValidator
    id="rfvPassword"
    ControlToValidate="txtPassword"
    Display="Dynamic"
    Font-Name="Tahoma"
    Font-Size="10pt"
    runat=server>
    Password is Required!
</asp:RequiredFieldValidator>
```

A second password field is declared next. This is used to make sure the member enters the password they meant to enter, since they can't see what they type:

```
<asp:TextBox
    id="txtPassword2"
    Columns="25"
```

```
    MaxLength="30"
    runat=server
    TextMode="Password"
/>
```

The new member must enter this field:

```
<asp:RequiredFieldValidator
    id="rfvPassword2"
    ControlToValidate="txtPassword2"
    Display="Dynamic"
    Font-Name="Tahoma"
    Font-Size="10pt"
    runat=server>
    Password is Required!
</asp:RequiredFieldValidator>
```

And this password field must match the other one:

```
<asp:CompareValidator id="cvPassword"
    ControlToValidate="txtPassword"
    ControlToCompare="txtPassword2"
    Display="Dynamic"
    Font-Name="Tahoma"
    Font-Size="10pt"
    runat=server>
    Password fields don't match
</asp:CompareValidator>
```

One more TextBox control allows the new member to enter their e-mail address:

```
<asp:TextBox
    id="txtEmailAddress"
    Columns="25"
    MaxLength="30"
    runat=server
/>
```

That field is also required

```
<asp:RequiredFieldValidator
    id="rfvEmailAddress"
    ControlToValidate="txtEmailAddress"
```

```
    Display="Dynamic"
    Font-Name="Tahoma"
    Font-Size="10pt"
    runat=server>
    Email Address is Required!
</asp:RequiredFieldValidator>
```

The other control on the page is the Button control:

```
<asp:button
    id="butOK"
    text="  OK  "
    Type="Submit"
    OnClick="SubmitBtn_Click"
    runat="server"
/>
```

The only procedure on the page fires when the button is clicked

```
Sub SubmitBtn_Click(Sender As Object, E As EventArgs)
    Dim DBConn as OleDbConnection
    Dim DBCommand As OleDbDataAdapter
    Dim DSLogin as New DataSet
    Dim DBInsert As New OleDbCommand
    DBConn = New OleDbConnection("Provider=sqloledb;" _
        & "server=localhost;" _
        & "Initial Catalog=INETC13;" _
        & "User Id=sa;" _
        & "Password=yourpassword;")
    DBCommand = New OleDbDataAdapter _
        ("Select Count(WebLogMemberID) as TheCount " _
        & "from WebLogMembers Where " _
        & "MemberName = '" & txtMemberName.Text _
        & "'", DBConn)
    DBCommand.Fill(DSLogin, _
        "TheCount")
    If DSLogin.Tables("TheCount"). _
            Rows(0).Item("TheCount") = 0 Then
        DBInsert.CommandText = "Insert Into WebLogMembers " _
            & "(MemberName, Password, EmailAddress) " _
            & "values (" _
            & "'" & Replace(txtMemberName.text, "'", "''") & "', " _
            & "'" & Replace(txtPassword.text, "'", "''") & "', " _
```

```
            & "'" & Replace(txtEmailAddress.text, "'", "''") & "')"
        DBInsert.Connection = DBConn
        DBInsert.Connection.Open
        DBInsert.ExecuteNonQuery()
        DBCommand = New OleDbDataAdapter _
            ("Select webLogMemberID from WebLogMembers Where " _
            & "MemberName = '" & txtMemberName.Text _
            & "' and Password = '" & txtPassword.Text _
            & "'", DBConn)
        DBCommand.Fill(DSLogin, _
            "MemberInfo")
        Session("WebLogMemberID") = DSLogin.Tables("MemberInfo"). _
            Rows(0).Item("WebLogMemberID")
        Response.Redirect("./index.aspx")
       Else
        lblMessage.Text = "The member name you entered is in " _
            & "use by another member. Please enter " _
            & "another member name."
       End If
End Sub
```

The page requires data objects:

```
Dim DBConn as OleDbConnection
Dim DBCommand As OleDbDataAdapter
Dim DSLogin as New DataSet
Dim DBInsert As New OleDbCommand
```

We start by connecting to the database:

```
DBConn = New OleDbConnection("Provider=sqloledb;" _
    & "server=localhost;" _
    & "Initial Catalog=INETC13;" _
    & "User Id=sa;" _
    & "Password=yourpassword;")
```

We then place a query into our Data Adapter object that will check to see if the member name entered is already in use

```
DBCommand = New OleDbDataAdapter _
    ("Select Count(WebLogMemberID) as TheCount " _
    & "from WebLogMembers Where " _
```

```
    & "MemberName = '" & txtMemberName.Text _
    & "'", DBConn)
```

We place the return of that call into our DataSet object:

```
DBCommand.Fill(DSLogin, _
    "TheCount")
```

We then check to see if any matching records were found

```
If DSLogin.Tables("TheCount"). _
    Rows(0).Item("TheCount")  = 0 Then
```

If no record was found, it means the member name is available. In that case, we add the new member's information into the database. Note the use of the Replace function so that our query won't throw an error if the "'" character is used

```
DBInsert.CommandText = "Insert Into WebLogMembers " _
    & "(MemberName, Password, EmailAddress) " _
    & "values (" _
    & "'" & Replace(txtMemberName.text, "'", "''") & "', " _
    & "'" & Replace(txtPassword.text, "'", "''") & "', " _
    & "'" & Replace(txtEmailAddress.text, "'", "''") & "')"
DBInsert.Connection = DBConn
DBInsert.Connection.Open
DBInsert.ExecuteNonQuery()
```

We then need to log the visitor into the Web Log site. Therefore, we need to retrieve their ID

```
DBCommand = New OleDbDataAdapter _
    ("Select webLogMemberID from WebLogMembers Where " _
    & "MemberName = '" & txtMemberName.Text _
    & "' and Password = '" & txtPassword.Text _
    & "'", DBConn)
DBCommand.Fill(DSLogin, _
    "MemberInfo")
```

place it into a Session variable

```
Session("WebLogMemberID") = DSLogin.Tables("MemberInfo"). _
    Rows(0).Item("WebLogMemberID")
```

and redirect the member to the Web Log page:

```
Response.Redirect("./index.aspx")
```

If the member name was in use, the code flows here. We provide the new member with an error message and give them the opportunity to try again:

```
lblMessage.Text = "The member name you entered is in " _
    & "use by another member. Please enter "_
    & "another member name."
```

Access Code Changes

C13WebLog.mdb

If you wish to use the Access database instead of a SQL Server database, a couple of code changes are necessary. First, the connect string for each of the database connection statements needs to change to something like this so that the correct provider is used

```
DBConn = New OleDbConnection("PROVIDER=Microsoft.Jet.OLEDB.4.0;" _
    & "DATA SOURCE=" _
    & Server.MapPath("/INetBook/C13/WebLog/" _
    & "Access/C13WebLog.mdb;"))
```

You will need to change the path to the location where you put the Access database on your server.

The other change that is needed for this site to run with Access is to change the query on the Web Log page. In the Where clause, the date field is surrounded by the "'" character:

```
DBCommand = New OleDbDataAdapter _
    ("Select WebLogPostID, TitleText, ThePost, " _
    & "DatePosted, MemberName, EmailAddress " _
    & "from WebLogPosts " _
    & "Left Join WebLogMembers On " _
    & "WebLogPosts.WebLogMemberID = " _
    & "WebLogMembers.WebLogMemberID Where " _
    & "DatePosted = '" & Today() & "'" _
    ,DBConn)
```

That needs to be changed so the "#" character is used instead:

```
DBCommand = New OleDbDataAdapter _
    ("Select WebLogPostID, TitleText, ThePost, " _
    & "DatePosted, MemberName, EmailAddress " _
    & "from WebLogPosts " _
    & "Left Join WebLogMembers On " _
    & "WebLogPosts.WebLogMemberID = " _
    & "WebLogMembers.WebLogMemberID Where " _
    & "DatePosted = #" & Today() & "#" _
    ,DBConn)
```

CHAPTER

14

Enhancing a Site with Interactive Features

As a Web developer, you need to always be thinking about how to bring new features to your web site. You should consider what your visitors are looking for, what might be fun to them, and most importantly, what would bring them back to your site. In this chapter, we will look at four tools that can be useful within a variety of different types of web sites that may help draw more visitors to your site.

First, we will look at the Chat tool. The Chat tool allows visitors to your site to engage in live text conversations with other visitors at your site.

Then we will look at the Raw Query tool. This tool allows the visitor to enter their own raw SQL text. In code, we run the query and display the results to the visitor.

The third tool we will look at is the Tip of the Day tool. This tool displays a random tip that changes daily based on tips in a database table.

And then we will review the Link List tool. The Link List tool allows visitors to post links to other sites that appear on the Link List page.

Chat Tool

The Chat tool allows visitors who are currently connected to your site to engage in a live text conversation with each other. The chatters can send messages to everyone in the chat or they can whisper messages to a specific person.

As you review this tool, note the use of an ArrayList object that has application scope. It is used to maintain an active list of the current chatters.

Sample Usage

When the visitor to the Chat site first enters it, they see the page displayed in Figure 14-1.

Here you can see that the chatter tried to sign in without first entering a Chat Name. Since the field is required, they were not allowed access to the site.

One other sign-in requirement is displayed in Figure 14-2.

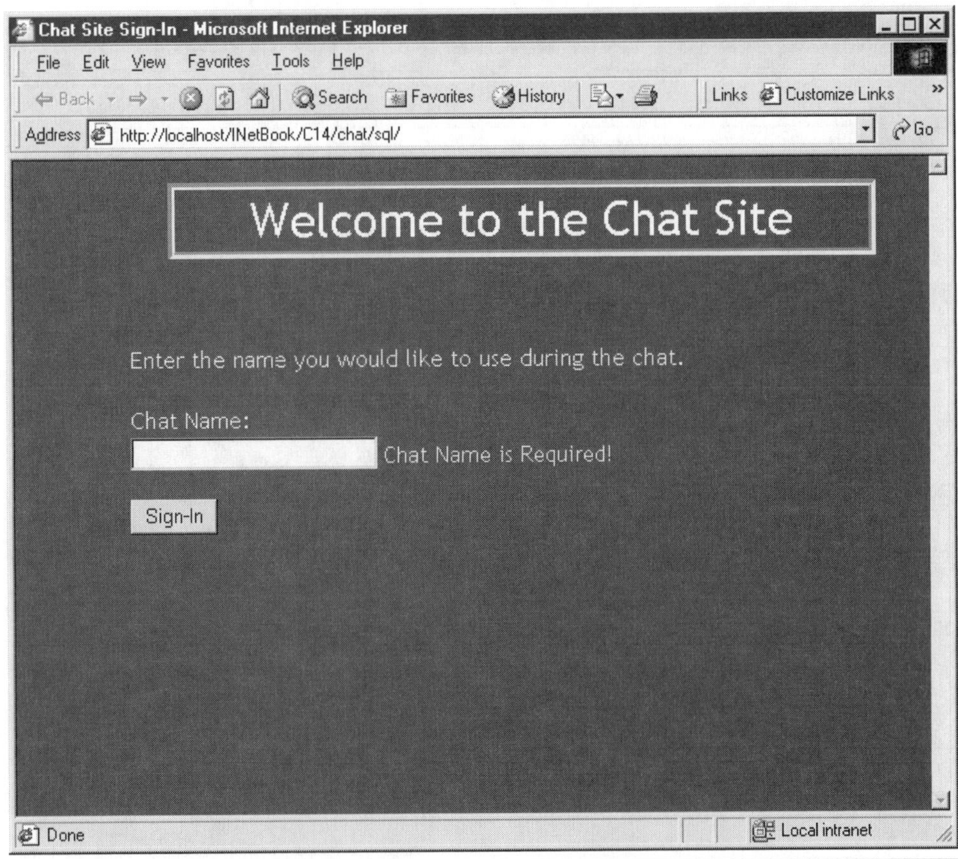

Figure 14-1 *Chat Sign-In page*

The chatter can not enter the tool by using a chat name that is in use by someone else. The names are stored in an ArrayList object in code. We look in that object to make sure the name is not in use.

Once the visitor does enter an unused name, they are taken to the Chat page displayed in Figure 14-3.

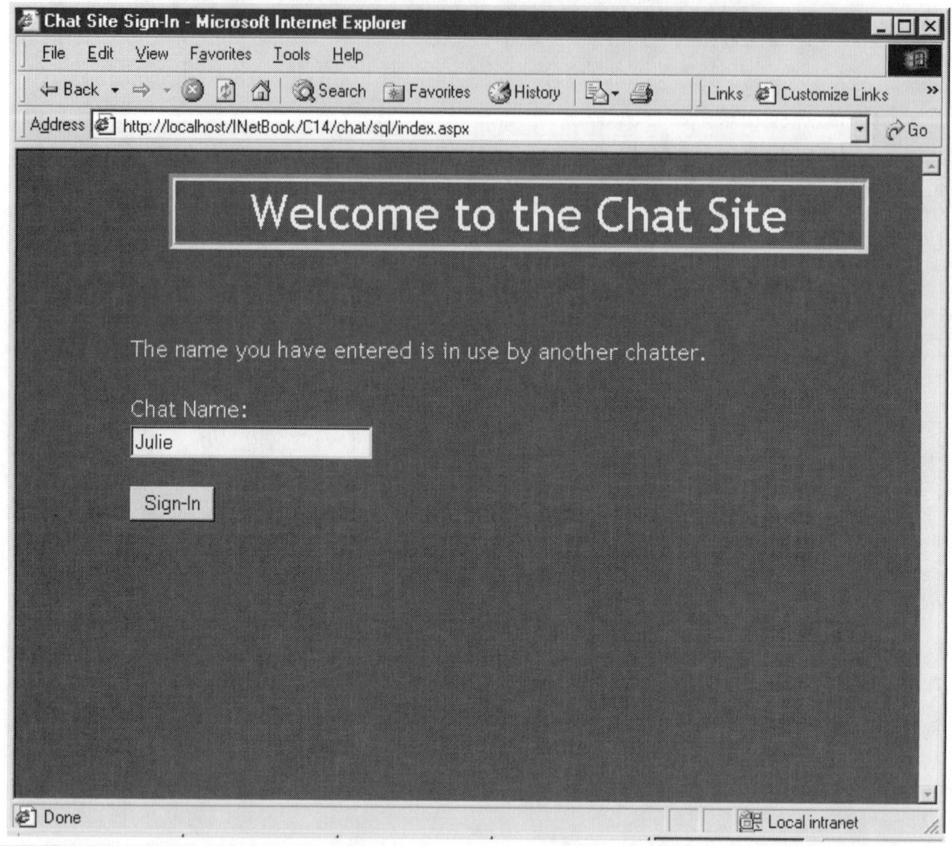

Figure 14-2 *Sign-In page with the chat name entered in use*

The Chat page is made up of two frames. The body frame displays messages to the visitor. And the bottom frame provides the place for the chatter to send their own message.

Here the chatter sees a message from the server that lets everyone know that they have just entered the chat. The visitor's chat session always starts like this. In fact, everyone connected with the chat sees this server message.

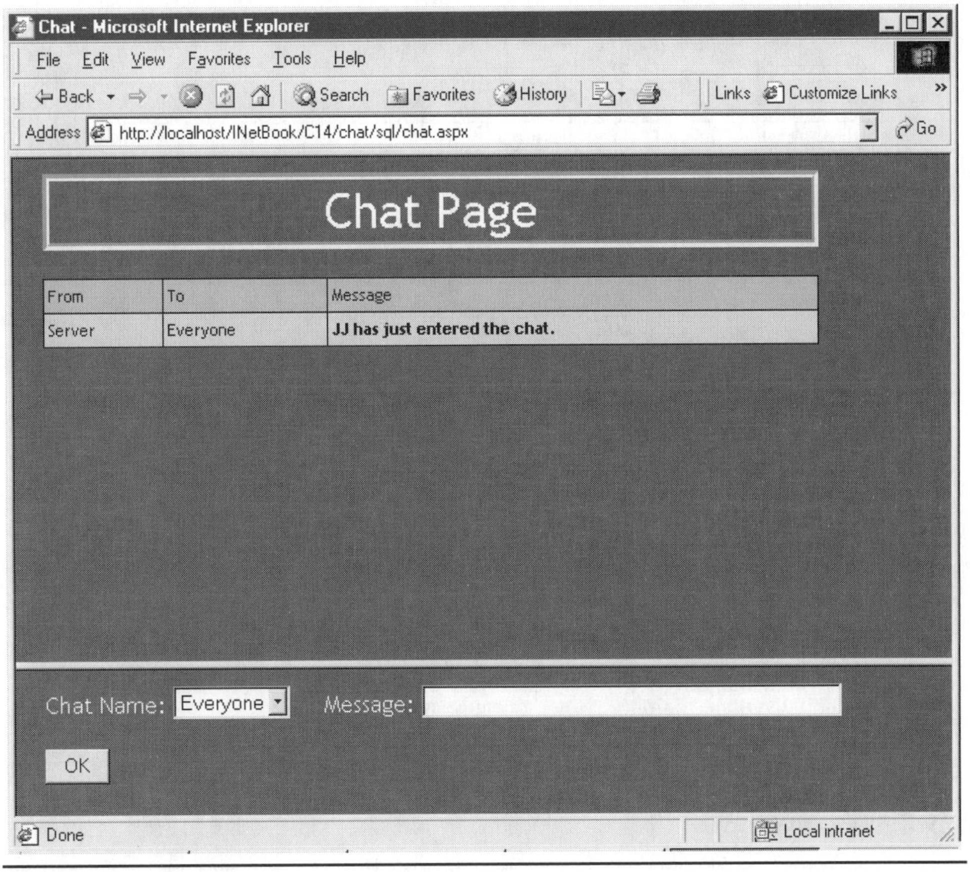

Figure 14-3 *Chat page*

The chatter can then send a message like that displayed in Figure 14-4.

The chatter first selects to whom the message should be delivered to through the Chat Name TextBox control. All the chatters are displayed in this list, including the special name "Everyone." The chatter then enters the text of the message and clicks OK. Since the message was sent to everyone, all the chatters will see this message.

But the message can be whispered to a specific person. Take a look at Figure 14-5.

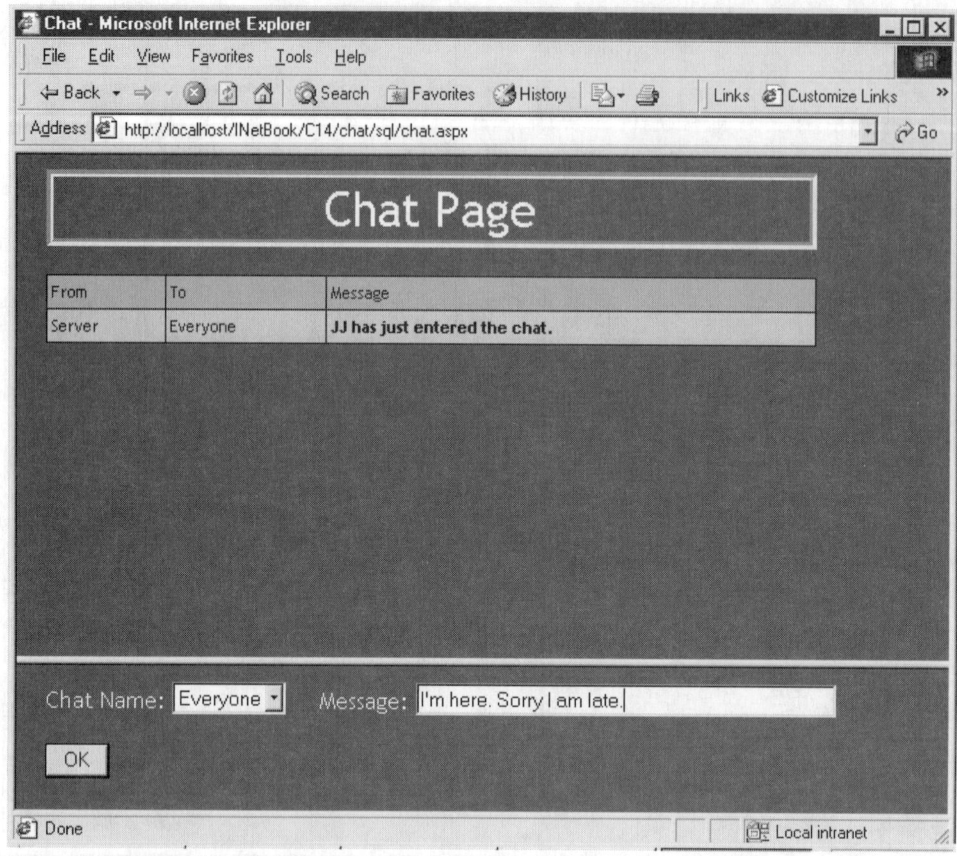

Figure 14-4 *Message sent to Everyone*

This figure shows the chat page for Julie, who has been in the chat for awhile before JJ entered, and who has been chatting with Ben. Julie wants to send a message just to JJ. So she selects JJ from the Chat Name TextBox control and enters

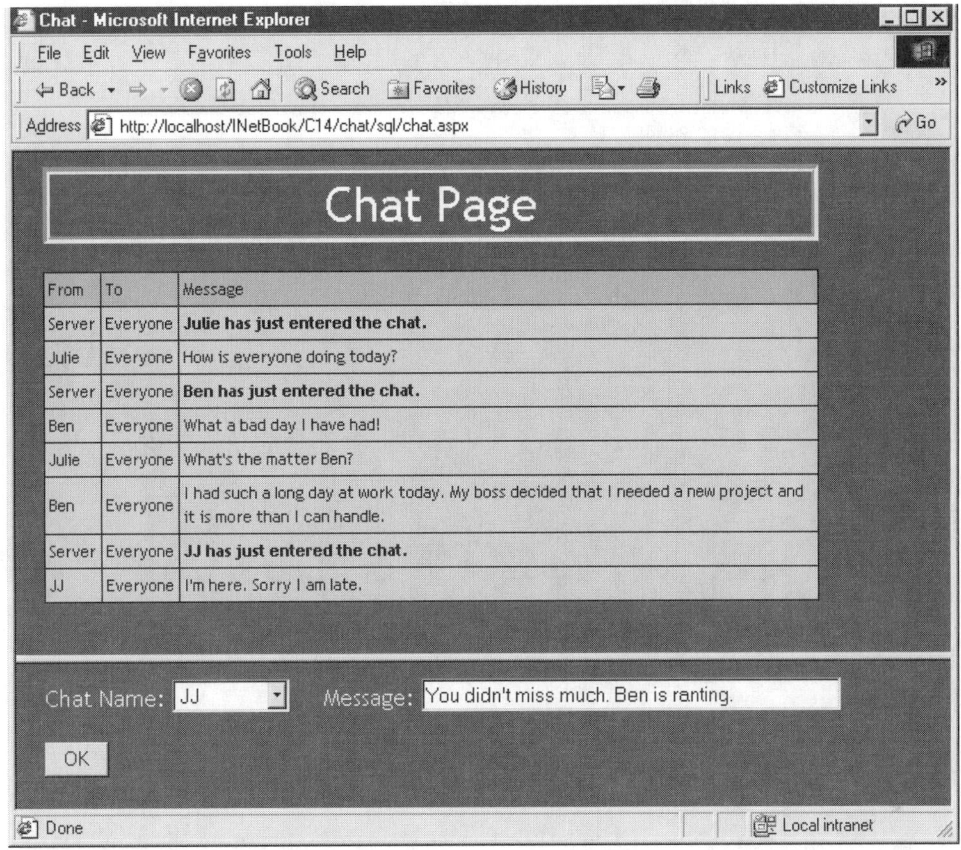

Figure 14-5 *Sending a whisper message*

her message. When she submits the message, JJ sees the message as shown in Figure 14-6.

But since the message was for JJ, Ben does not see it, as you can see in Figure 14-7.

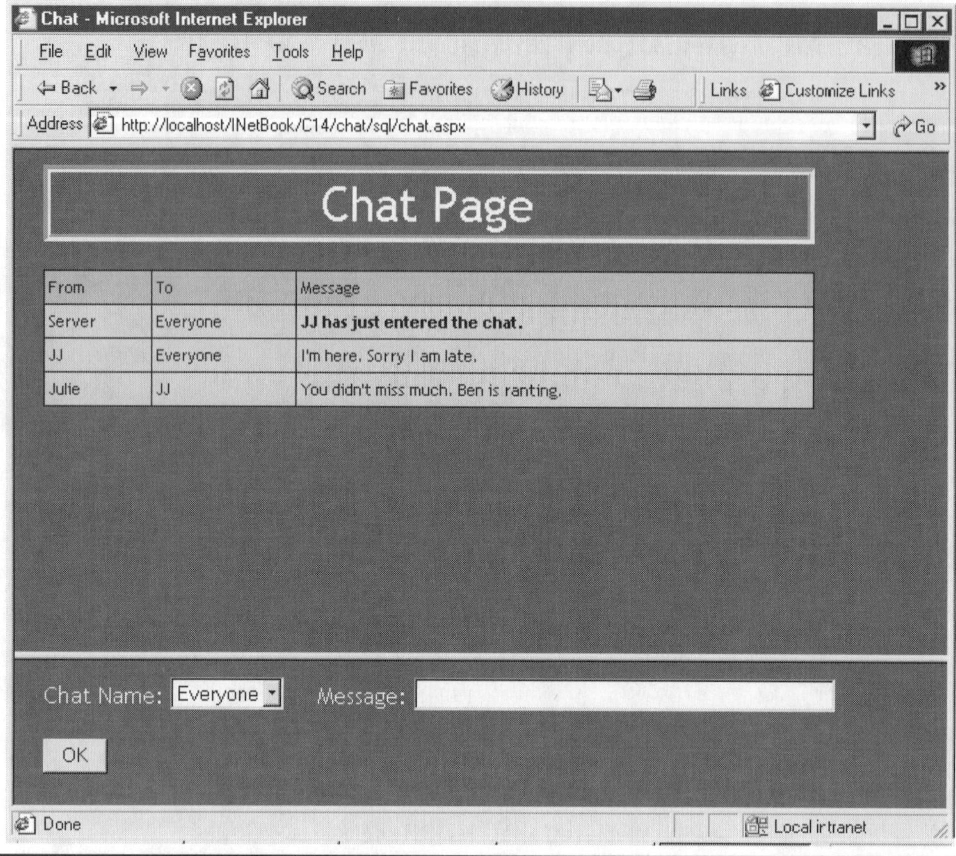

Figure 14-6 *Whisper displayed on the Chat page*

Chat Tool Database Component

C14Chat.sql

The Chat tool relies on a single database table to accomplish its functionality. The table stores the chat messages as the chatters enter them. In this section, we will review that table.

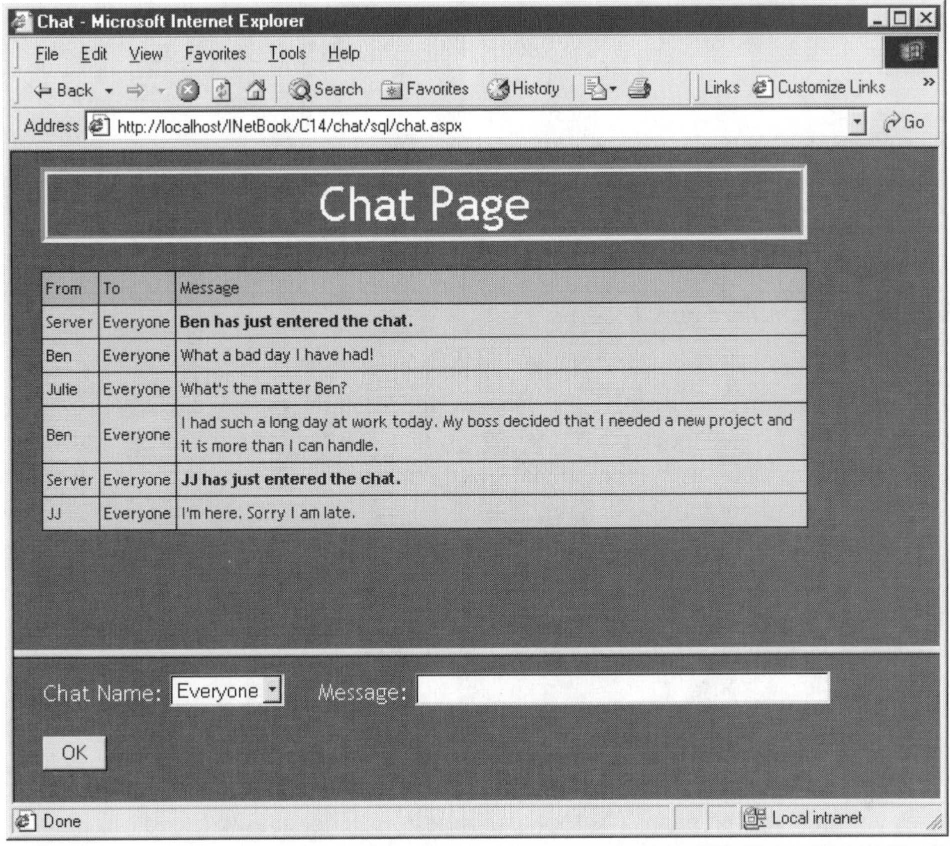

Figure 14-7 *Whisper not displayed to a chatter it was not addressed to*

Chats Field Specifications

Chats.txt

The field specifications for the fields in the Chats table are displayed in Table 14-1.

The ChatID field is the primary key in the table. It is an identity column, AutoNumber in Access, so when a new record is added to the table, it is set to an incremented unique value.

Field Name	Field Type	Notes
ChatID	int	Primary Key, Identity Column
WhenEntered	datetime	
EnteredBy	varchar	Length = 50
EnteredTo	varchar	Length = 50
TheMessage	varchar	Length = 50

Table 14-1 *Chats Field Specifications*

The WhenEntered field stores the date and time that the message was sent. The EnteredBy field stores the name of the person that sent the message. A special value of Server in this field means that the message was sent by the server and states that a chatter has entered or left.

The EnteredTo field stores the name of the chatter for whom the message is directed. A special value of Everyone in this field means that the message is for all the chatters.

The TheMessage field stores the text of the message.

Chat Tool ASP.NET Code

The Chat tool is made up of the Sign-In page, the main Chat page, and the frame pages within that Chat page. The tool also relies on a Global.asax file to run correctly. That means that the tool has been set as an Application through the Internet Services Manager.

In this section, we will review the files that make up the tool.

Global.asax File

Global.asax

The code in the Global.asax file initiates an ArrayList object and has some code that runs when the chatter's session ends.

At the very top of the page, you will find this object tag:

```
<object id="ChatNames"
    runat="server"
    class="System.Collections.ArrayList"
scope="Application" />
```

The object tag creates an object named ChatNames:

```
<object id="ChatNames"
```

That runs on the server:

```
runat="server"
```

The object is defined as an instance of the ArrayList class:

```
class="System.Collections.ArrayList"
```

It will be visible to all the pages through all the sessions in our tool:

```
scope="Application" />
```

The object is an ArrayList. An ArrayList is like an array. It provides a way for us to store a group of items. We can add items to the array, and we can remove items from the array. As you will see on another page, we can even search the array.

In this case, the array stores the list of all the chatter's names. That list is used to make sure the visitor does not enter a name that is in use. It is also used to populate the DropDownList control on the Chat Footer page.

The next two lines of code in the Global.asax file import data objects so that they can be used within this file:

```
<%@ Import Namespace="System.Data" %>
<%@ Import Namespace="System.Data.OLEDB" %>
```

Next, we define an event that fires when the application first starts

```
Sub Application_OnStart
      ChatNames.Add ("Everyone")
End Sub
```

The code adds the name Everyone to our chat list. This prevents a chatter from using that name and makes the special name available in the DropDownList on the Chat Footer page.

The next code block fires when the chatter's session expires, meaning that they have left the chat.

```
Sub Session_OnEnd
    Dim DBConn as OleDbConnection
```

```
    Dim DBInsert As New OleDbCommand
    DBConn = New OleDbConnection("Provider=sqloledb;" _
        & "server=localhost;" _
        & "Initial Catalog=INETC14;" _
        & "User Id=sa;" _
        & "Password=yourpassword;")
    DBInsert.CommandText = "Insert Into Chats " _
        & "(WhenEntered, EnteredBy, EnteredTo, TheMessage) " _
        & "values (" _
        & "'" & Now() & "', " _
        & "'Server', " _
        & "'Everyone', " _
        & "'<b>" & Session("ChatName") & " has just " _
        & "left the chat.</b>')"
    DBInsert.Connection = DBConn
    DBInsert.Connection.Open
    DBInsert.ExecuteNonQuery()
      ChatNames.Remove (Session("ChatName"))
End Sub
```

In that case, we will need data objects:

```
Dim DBConn as OleDbConnection
Dim DBInsert As New OleDbCommand
```

First, we connect to our database:

```
DBConn = New OleDbConnection("Provider=sqloledb;" _
    & "server=localhost;" _
    & "Initial Catalog=INETC14;" _
    & "User Id=sa;" _
    & "Password=yourpassword;")
```

We then place SQL text that sends a message to all chatters that tells them who has left the chat into a Command object:

```
DBInsert.CommandText = "Insert Into Chats " _
    & "(WhenEntered, EnteredBy, EnteredTo, TheMessage) " _
    & "values (" _
    & "'" & Now() & "', " _
    & "'Server', " _
    & "'Everyone', " _
    & "'<b>" & Session("ChatName") & " has just " _
    & "left the chat.</b>')"
```

We then run our query:

```
DBInsert.Connection = DBConn
DBInsert.Connection.Open
DBInsert.ExecuteNonQuery()
```

We need to do one more thing. We need to remove the chatter from our ArrayList. This allows someone else to use the chatter's name. It also removes the chatter's name from the DropDownList in the Chat Footer page.

```
ChatNames.Remove (Session("ChatName"))
```

Sign-In ASP.NET Pages

Index.aspx

The Sign-In page provides the mechanism for the visitor to become part of the chat. The page requires the visitor to enter a chat name and makes sure another chatter isn't using that name.

The page includes three compiler directives.

```
<%@ Page Language=VB Debug=true %>
<%@ Import Namespace="System.Data" %>
<%@ Import Namespace="System.Data.OLEDB" %>
```

The first tells the compiler that we will be using Visual Basic as our programming language. It also tells the compiler that we want to be in debug mode. Remember to turn debug mode off in production uses of this tool.

```
<%@ Page Language=VB Debug=true %>
```

The other two directives import data libraries into our page so that we can instantiate data objects that work with our SQL Server or Access databases:

```
<%@ Import Namespace="System.Data" %>
<%@ Import Namespace="System.Data.OLEDB" %>
```

Within the body of the page, we declare a Label control that displays the title text on the page:

```
<asp:Label
    id="lblTitle"
    BorderWidth="5px"
    BorderStyle=6
    Width="90%"
```

```
    Font-Size="25pt"
    Font-Name="Trebuchet MS"
    Text="Welcome to the Chat Site"
    runat="server"
/>
```

Another label is used to display instructions or an error message to the visitor:

```
<asp:Label
    id="lblMessage"
    Font-Size="12pt"
    Font-Name="Trebuchet MS"
    runat="server"
/>
```

Beneath that, a TextBox control is defined. This allows the visitor to enter their chat name:

```
<asp:TextBox
    id="txtChatName"
    Columns="25"
    MaxLength="30"
    runat=server
/>
```

Two requirements are made against that TextBox control that must be met for the page to be able to be submitted. First, the field is required. The visitor must enter something into it:

```
<asp:RequiredFieldValidator
    id="rfvMemberName"
    ControlToValidate="txtChatName"
    Display="Dynamic"
    Font-Name="Trebuchet MS"
    ForeColor="Yellow"
    Font-Size="11pt"
    runat=server>
    Chat Name is Required!
</asp:RequiredFieldValidator>
```

We also require, through a RegularExpressionValidator control, that the name entered by the visitor does not contain the " ' " character:

```
<asp:RegularExpressionValidator id="revMemberName"
    ControlToValidate="txtChatName"
    ValidationExpression="[^']*"
    Display="Dynamic"
    Font-Name="Trebuchet MS"
    ForeColor="Yellow"
    Font-Size="11pt"
    runat=server>
    The chat name must not include the ' character!
</asp:RegularExpressionValidator>
```

The control will validate our TextBox:

```
ControlToValidate="txtChatName"
```

The validation expression says that the visitor can enter any character except the " ' " character, as many times as they like:

```
ValidationExpression="[^']*"
```

The page does not reserve room for the error message unless it needs to be displayed

```
    Display="Dynamic"
```

And the text of the error message is contained within the opening and closing tags:

```
The chat name must not include the ' character!
```

One other control on the page is a button:

```
<asp:button
    id="butSignIn"
    text="Sign-In"
    Type="Submit"
    OnClick="SubmitBtn_Click"
    runat="server"
/>
```

It fires the event named here when the visitor clicks the button:

```
OnClick="SubmitBtn_Click"
```

The code on the page is contained within two procedures. The first fires when the page is loaded.

```
Sub Page_Load(ByVal Sender as Object, ByVal E as EventArgs)
    lblMessage.Text = "Enter the name you would " _
        & "like to use during the chat."
End Sub
```

It places instructions into our message label:

```
lblMessage.Text = "Enter the name you would " _
    & "like to use during the chat."
```

The other procedure fires when the button is clicked.

```
Sub SubmitBtn_Click(Sender As Object, E As EventArgs)
    If ChatNames.BinarySearch _
        (txtChatName.Text, New CaseInsensitiveComparer) >= 0 Then
        lblMessage.Text = "The name you have entered " _
            & "is in use by another chatter."
    Else
        Dim DBConn as OleDbConnection
        Dim DBCommand As OleDbDataAdapter
        Dim DSStartingPoint as New DataSet
        Dim DBInsert As New OleDbCommand
        ChatNames.Add(txtChatName.Text)
        Session("ChatName") = txtChatName.Text
        DBConn = New OleDbConnection("Provider=sqloledb;" _
            & "server=localhost;" _
            & "Initial Catalog=INETC14;" _
            & "User Id=sa;" _
            & "Password=yourpassword;")
        DBInsert.CommandText = "Insert Into Chats " _
            & "(WhenEntered, EnteredBy, EnteredTo, TheMessage) " _
            & "values (" _
            & "'" & Now() & "', " _
            & "'Server', " _
            & "'Everyone', " _
            & "'<b>" & Session("ChatName") & " has just " _
            & "entered the chat.</b>')"
        DBInsert.Connection = DBConn
        DBInsert.Connection.Open
        DBInsert.ExecuteNonQuery()
```

```
        DBCommand = New OleDbDataAdapter _
            ("Select Max(ChatID) as MaxID " _
            & "from Chats " _
            ,DBConn)
        DBCommand.Fill(DSStartingPoint, _
            "StartingPoint")
        Session("StartingPoint") =
DSStartingPoint.Tables("StartingPoint"). _
            Rows(0).Item("MaxID")
        Response.Redirect("./chat.aspx")
    End If
End Sub
```

The procedure first needs to check to see if the name entered by the visitor is already in use by another visitor. This is done by calling the BinarySearch method of the ArrayList object. The procedure in this case is called with two parameters. The first parameter is the text we are searching the list for. The second parameter indicates that we want the search for the text to be case-insensitive. In other words, Bob would match with BOB.

The method returns the position in the array that the item was found. A negative number is returned if the text was not found as one of the items in the array. Therefore, a number of 0 or greater means that the name was found:

```
If ChatNames.BinarySearch _
    (txtChatName.Text, New CaseInsensitiveComparer) >= 0 Then
```

In that case, we place an error message into the Text property of our Label control:

```
lblMessage.Text = "The name you have entered " _
    & "is in use by another chatter."
```

Otherwise, the name entered is valid. We will need data objects:

```
Dim DBConn as OleDbConnection
Dim DBCommand As OleDbDataAdapter
Dim DSStartingPoint as New DataSet
Dim DBInsert As New OleDbCommand
```

We start by adding the name entered by the visitor into our Public ArrayList object:

```
ChatNames.Add(txtChatName.Text)
```

That prevents another visitor from signing in with that same name.

We also need to store the name entered by the chatter into a session variable, which is then used on the Chat Footer page when a new message is sent:

```
Session("ChatName") = txtChatName.Text
```

Since someone has joined the chat, we need to add a new record to the Chats table indicating that fact. Therefore, we connect to the database:

```
DBConn = New OleDbConnection("Provider=sqloledb;" _
    & "server=localhost;" _
    & "Initial Catalog=INETC14;" _
    & "User Id=sa;" _
    & "Password=yourpassword;")
```

And we place SQL text into our command object to add a message from the server to the Chats table to everyone; this message tells everyone who has entered the chat:

```
DBInsert.CommandText = "Insert Into Chats " _
    & "(WhenEntered, EnteredBy, EnteredTo, TheMessage) " _
    & "values (" _
    & "'" & Now() & "', " _
    & "'Server', " _
    & "'Everyone', " _
    & "'<b>" &  Session("ChatName") & " has just " _
    & "entered the chat.</b>')"
```

The Command object uses our Connection object:

```
DBInsert.Connection = DBConn
DBInsert.Connection.Open
```

The record is then added to the table:

```
DBInsert.ExecuteNonQuery()
```

Next, we need to retrieve the point in the Chats table where the chatter has entered the chat. We can do this by looking for the ID of the record we just added to the Chats table:

```
DBCommand = New OleDbDataAdapter _
    ("Select Max(ChatID) as MaxID " _
    & "from Chats " _
    ,DBConn)
```

The return of that query is placed into our DataSet object:

```
DBCommand.Fill(DSStartingPoint, _
    "StartingPoint")
```

And the ID is stored in a Session variable so that it can be used on the Chat Body page:

```
Session("StartingPoint") = DSStartingPoint.Tables("StartingPoint"). _
    Rows(0).Item("MaxID")
```

We then send the chatter to the Chat page:

```
Response.Redirect("./chat.aspx")
```

Chat ASP.NET Pages

Chat.aspx

The Chat page defines the frames on the page. It also has a block of code that runs when the page is loaded.

```
Sub Page_Load(ByVal Sender as Object, ByVal E as EventArgs)
    If Len(Session("ChatName")) = 0 Then
        Response.Redirect("./index.aspx")
    End If
End Sub
```

The code checks to see if the chatter has signed in:

```
If Len(Session("ChatName")) = 0 Then
```

If they haven't, they are sent to the Sign-In page. This prevents someone from viewing the chat without first signing in:

```
Response.Redirect("./index.aspx")
```

Chat Body ASP.NET Pages

Body_Chat.aspx

The Chat Body page displays all the chat messages to the chatter that were to everyone or that were whispered by them or to them since they entered the chat.

The page declares three compiler directives:

```
<%@ Page Language=VB Debug=true %>
<%@ Import Namespace="System.Data" %>
<%@ Import Namespace="System.Data.OLEDB" %>
```

The first sets up compiler environment options:

```
<%@ Page Language=VB Debug=true %>
```

The other two are required, since the code on the page uses data objects:

```
<%@ Import Namespace="System.Data" %>
<%@ Import Namespace="System.Data.OLEDB" %>
```

The page contains an important HTML Meta tag called refresh:

```
<META HTTP-EQUIV="REFRESH" CONTENT="15;URL=body_chat.aspx">
```

This tag is how the chatter sees new messages. It updates the contents of the page every 15 seconds.

Within the body of the page, a Label control is defined for the title of the page:

```
<asp:Label
    id="lblTitle"
    BorderWidth="5px"
    BorderStyle=6
    Width="90%"
    Font-Size="25pt"
    Font-Name="Trebuchet MS"
    Text="<center>Chat Page</center>"
    runat="server"
/>
```

One other control is defined on the page, a DataGrid. This control displays all the chat messages in the form of an HTML table:

```
<asp:DataGrid
    id="dgChats"
    runat="server"
    Width="90%"
    BackColor="#ccccff"
    BorderColor="black"
    CellPadding=3
    CellSpacing="0"
    Font-Name="Trebuchet MS"
    Font-Size="8pt"
    ForeColor="Black"
    HeaderStyle-BackColor="#aaaadd"
/>
```

The code on the page is contained within a single event. That event fires when the page is loaded.

```
Sub Page_Load(ByVal Sender as Object, ByVal E as EventArgs)
    Dim DBConn as OleDbConnection
    Dim DBCommand As OleDbDataAdapter
    Dim DSChats as New DataSet
    DBConn = New OleDbConnection("Provider=sqloledb;" _
        & "server=localhost;" _
        & "Initial Catalog=INETC14;" _
        & "User Id=sa;" _
        & "Password=yourpassword;")
    DBCommand = New OleDbDataAdapter _
        ("Select EnteredBy as [From], " _
        & "EnteredTo as [To], " _
        & "TheMessage as [Message] from Chats " _
        & "Where ChatID >= " & Session("StartingPoint") _
        & " and (EnteredTo = 'Everyone' or EnteredTo = '" _
        & Session("ChatName") & "' or EnteredBy = '" _
        & Session("ChatName") & "') Order By " _
        & "WhenEntered",DBConn)
    DBCommand.Fill(DSChats, _
        "TheChats")
    dgChats.DataSource = _
        DSChats.Tables("TheChats").DefaultView
    dgChats.DataBind
End Sub
```

The code requires data objects, which are defined here:

```
Dim DBConn as OleDbConnection
Dim DBCommand As OleDbDataAdapter
Dim DSChats as New DataSet
```

We then connect to our SQL Server database:

```
DBConn = New OleDbConnection("Provider=sqloledb;" _
    & "server=localhost;" _
    & "Initial Catalog=INETC14;" _
    & "User Id=sa;" _
    & "Password=yourpassword;")
```

And then we retrieve all the chat messages from the Chats table

```
DBCommand = New OleDbDataAdapter _
    ("Select EnteredBy as [From], " _
```

```
    & "EnteredTo as [To], " _
    & "TheMessage as [Message] from Chats " _
```

that have been entered since the chatter entered the chat

```
& "Where ChatID >= " & Session("StartingPoint") _
```

that are sent out to everyone

```
& " and (EnteredTo = 'Everyone' or EnteredTo = '" _
```

or that are sent to this chatter

```
& Session("ChatName") & "' or EnteredBy = '" _
```

or that have been sent out by this chatter. The records are sorted by the date and time that they were entered

```
& Session("ChatName") & "') Order By " _
& "WhenEntered",DBConn)
```

The results of that query are placed into our DataSet object:

```
DBCommand.Fill(DSChats, _
    "TheChats")
```

The DataGrid control is then bound to our DataSet object:

```
dgChats.DataSource = _
    DSChats.Tables("TheChats").DefaultView
dgChats.DataBind
```

Chat Footer ASP.NET Pages

Body_Footer.aspx

The Chat Footer page displays a list of all the chatters and allows the chatter to send out a message. The page declares the same compiler directives:

```
<%@ Page Language=VB Debug=true %>
<%@ Import Namespace="System.Data" %>
<%@ Import Namespace="System.Data.OLEDB" %>
```

Within the body of the page, we declare a DropDownList that will contain the names of the chatters

```
<asp:DropDownList
    id="ddlTo"
    runat="server"
/>
```

and also a TextBox control that the chatter will use to enter their message:

```
<asp:TextBox
    id="txtMessage"
    Columns="45"
    MaxLength="255"
    runat=server
/>
```

A value must be placed into that TextBox because of the RequiredFieldValidator linked to the TextBox control:

```
<asp:RequiredFieldValidator
    id="rfvMessage"
    ControlToValidate="txtMessage"
    Display="Dynamic"
    Font-Name="Trebuchet MS"
    ForeColor="Yellow"
    Font-Size="10pt"
    runat=server>
    Message is Required!
</asp:RequiredFieldValidator>
```

The only other control on the page is a Button control:

```
<asp:button
    id="butOK"
    text="  OK  "
    Type="Submit"
    OnClick="SubmitBtn_Click"
    runat="server"
/>
```

The code on the page fires in two procedures. The first fires whenever the page is loaded

```
Sub Page_Load(ByVal Sender as Object, ByVal E as EventArgs)
    If Not IsPostBack Then
        ddlTo.DataSource = ChatNames
        ddlTo.DataBind
    End If
End Sub
```

We want this code to run only when the page is first loaded; during subsequent calls, the code runs in a different location:

```
If Not IsPostBack Then
```

The code simply binds the DropDownList to our ArrayList, which has the effect of displaying all the chat names in the DropDownList:

```
ddlTo.DataSource = ChatNames
ddlTo.DataBind
```

The other procedure on the page fires when the OK button is clicked.

```
Sub SubmitBtn_Click(Sender As Object, E As EventArgs)
    Dim DBConn as OleDbConnection
    Dim DBCommand As OleDbDataAdapter
    Dim DBInsert As New OleDbCommand
    DBConn = New OleDbConnection("Provider=sqloledb;" _
        & "server=localhost;" _
        & "Initial Catalog=INETC14;" _
        & "User Id=sa;" _
        & "Password=yourpassword;")
    DBInsert.CommandText = "Insert Into Chats " _
        & "(WhenEntered, EnteredBy, EnteredTo, TheMessage) " _
        & "values (" _
        & "'" & Now() & "', " _
        & "'" & Session("ChatName") & "', " _
        & "'" & ddlTo.SelectedItem.Value & "', " _
        & "'" & Replace(txtMessage.Text, "'", "''") & "')"
    DBInsert.Connection = DBConn
    DBInsert.Connection.Open
```

```
    DBInsert.ExecuteNonQuery()
    txtMessage.Text = ""
    ddlTo.DataSource = ChatNames
    ddlTo.DataBind
End Sub
```

The procedure requires Data objects to be instantiated

```
Dim DBConn as OleDbConnection
Dim DBCommand As OleDbDataAdapter
Dim DBInsert As New OleDbCommand
```

We start by connecting to the database:

```
DBConn = New OleDbConnection("Provider=sqloledb;" _
    & "server=localhost;" _
    & "Initial Catalog=INETC14;" _
    & "User Id=sa;" _
    & "Password=yourpassword;")
```

We then insert the message entered by the chatter into the Chats table

```
DBInsert.CommandText = "Insert Into Chats " _
    & "(WhenEntered, EnteredBy, EnteredTo, TheMessage) " _
    & "values (" _
    & "'" & Now() & "', " _
    & "'" & Session("ChatName") & "', " _
    & "'" & ddlTo.SelectedItem.Value & "', " _
    & "'" & Replace(txtMessage.Text, "'", "''") & "')"
DBInsert.Connection = DBConn
DBInsert.Connection.Open
DBInsert.ExecuteNonQuery()
```

and clear the message TextBox control Text property:

```
txtMessage.Text = ""
```

We then rebind the DropDownList control to the ArrayList so that the chatter will see any new names in the list for those who have just entered the chat:

```
ddlTo.DataSource = ChatNames
ddlTo.DataBind
```

Access Code Changes

C14Chat.mdb

The only code change needed for this tool to work with Access instead of SQL Server is to change the connect strings from this

```
DBConn = New OleDbConnection("Provider=sqloledb;" _
    & "server=localhost;" _
    & "Initial Catalog=INETC14;" _
    & "User Id=sa;" _
    & "Password=yourpassword;")
```

to a string that uses the correct provider and database location:

```
DBConn = New OleDbConnection("PROVIDER=Microsoft.Jet.OLEDB.4.0;" _
    & "DATA SOURCE=" _
    & Server.MapPath("/INetBook/C14/Chat/" _
    & "Access/C14Chat.mdb;"))
```

Raw QueryTool

Index.aspx

The Raw Query tool provides a way for visitors to enter their own ad hoc queries. The results of their queries are displayed in a Data Grid. You can use the tool against whatever database you want. To demonstrate the features of the tool, the Web Log database from Chapter 13 is employed.

Sample Usage

The Raw Query tool is made up of two panels that are displayed on a single page. Figure 14-8 shows the first panel.

The Query panel is made up of a TextBox control and a Button control. The visitor enters the query into the TextBox and clicks the button. Note, though, that validation rules are in place to make sure that the visitor enters the word "Select" and the word "From" into their query.

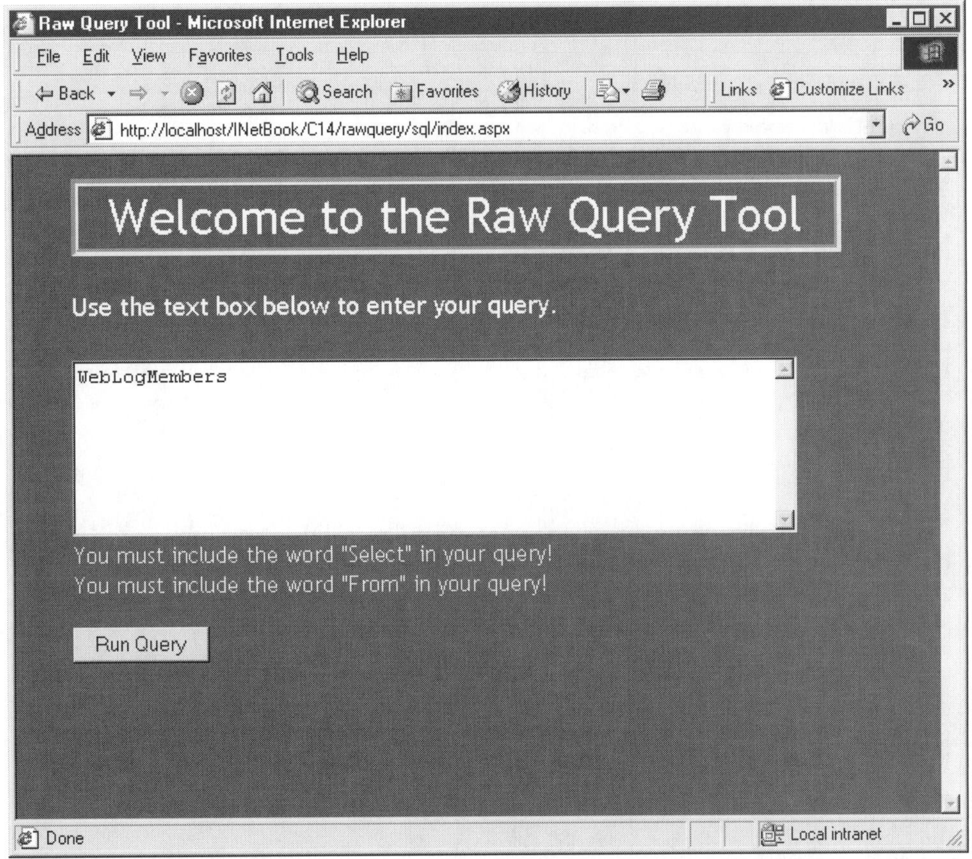

Figure 14-8 *Query Panel*

Once they enter those words, the error messages go away, as you can see in Figure 14-9.

The visitor can now click the Run Query button to see the results displayed in Figure 14-10.

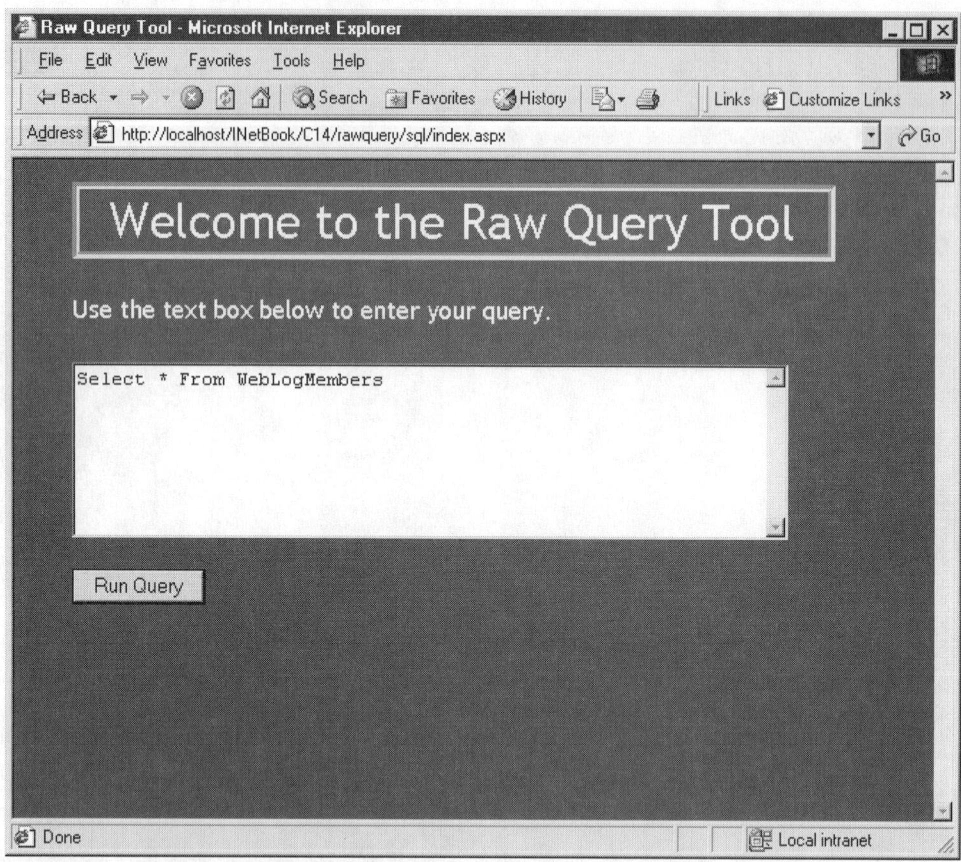

Figure 14-9 *Simple query expression*

The Results panel displays all the fields and all the records that were found for the visitor's query through a bound DataGrid.

But the query doesn't have to be so simple. Take a look at Figure 14-11.

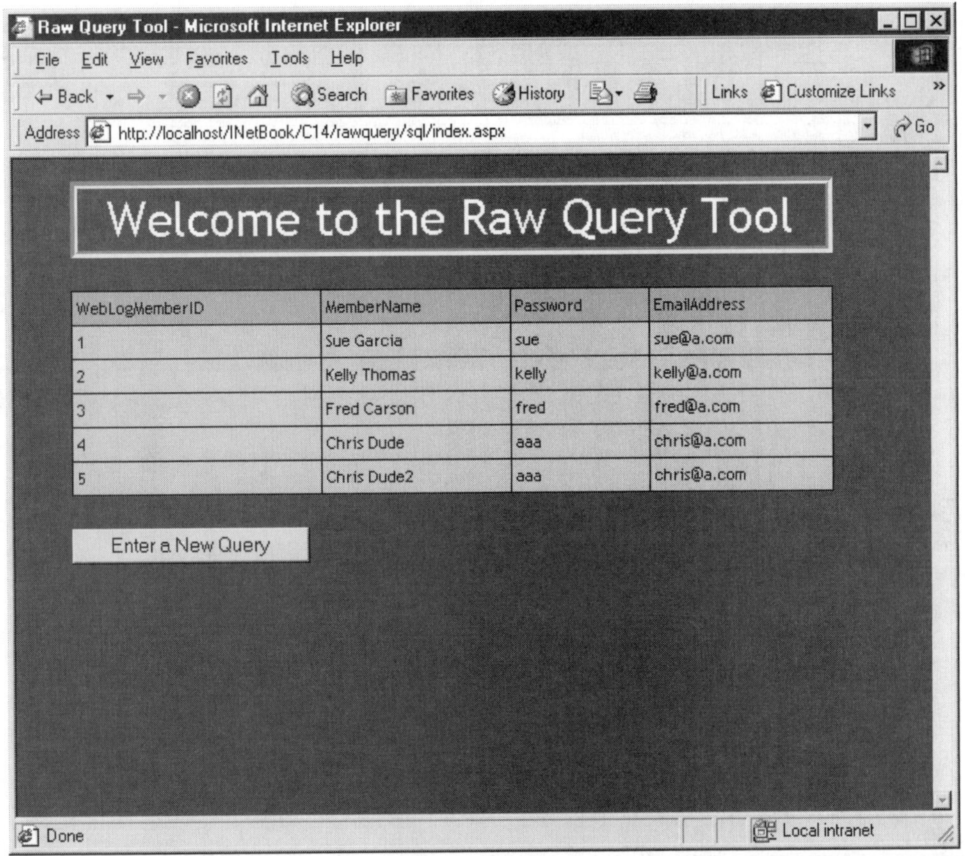

Figure 14-10 *Results panel*

Here the visitor has entered an aggregate query. They are asking for the name of each member who has made a posting to be listed with the number of postings made by that member. The results of that query are displayed in Figure 14-12.

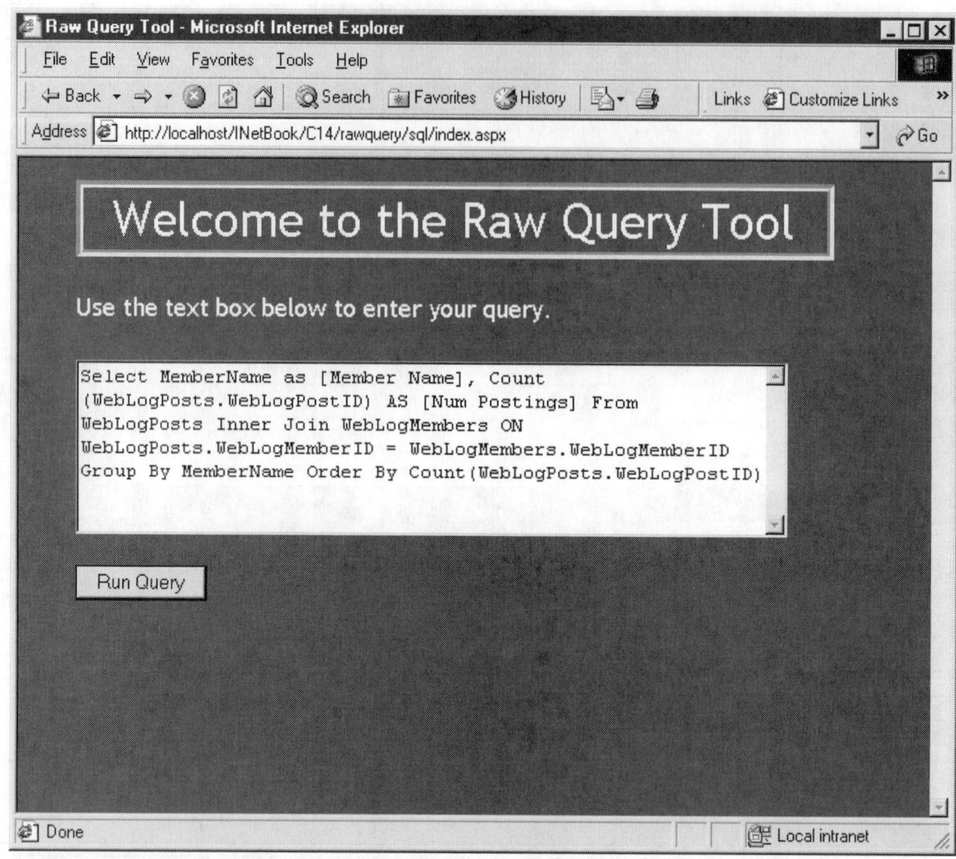

Figure 14-11 *Complex query displayed on the Query panel*

Raw Query ASP.NET Code

The Raw Query tool does not have a database component of its own. Instead, it connects to an existing database to display its results. The tool is made up of a single ASP.NET page. In this section, we will review that page.

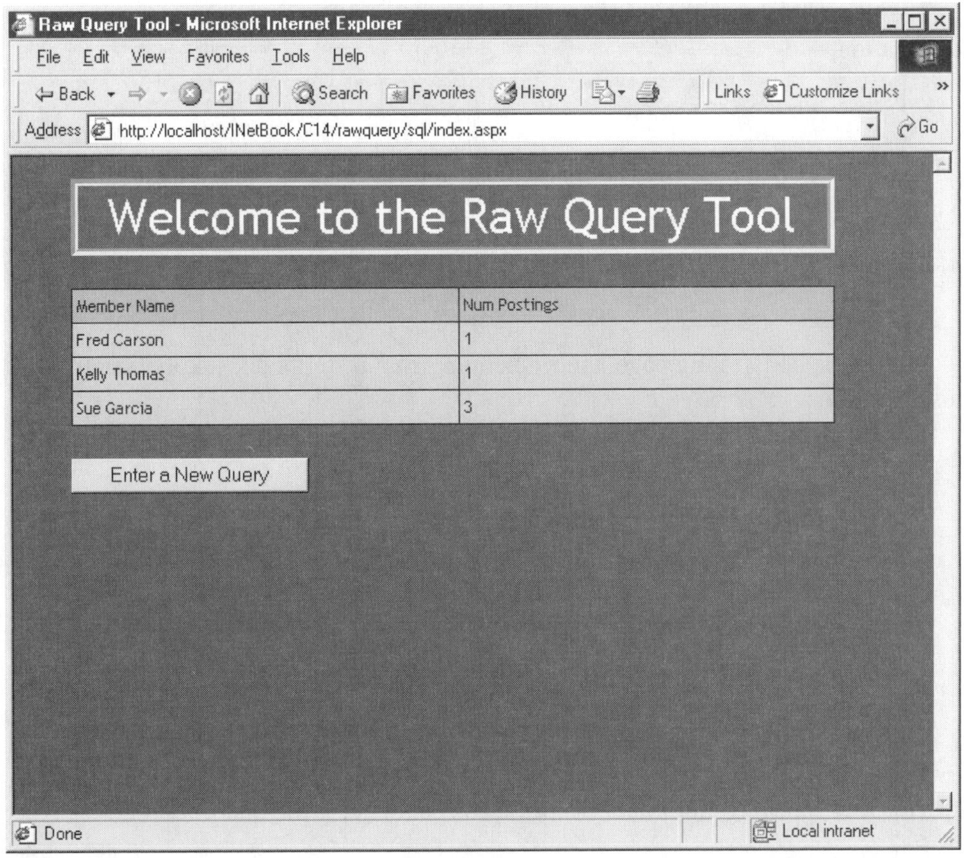

Figure 14-12 *Results of the complex query*

Raw Query ASP.NET Page

Index.aspx

The code on the Raw Query page runs the query entered by the visitor and displays its results. At the top of the page, three compiler directives are defined.

```
<%@ Page Language=VB Debug=true %>
<%@ Import Namespace="System.Data" %>
<%@ Import Namespace="System.Data.OLEDB" %>
```

The first tells the compiler that we are using Visual Basic and that we are in debug mode:

```
<%@ Page Language=VB Debug=true %>
```

The other two are required so that we can connect to, and retrieve data from, a database:

```
<%@ Import Namespace="System.Data" %>
<%@ Import Namespace="System.Data.OLEDB" %>
```

Within the body of the page, the first control that is defined is a Label control that displays title text:

```
<asp:Label
    id="lblTitle"
    BorderWidth="5px"
    BorderStyle=6
    Width="90%"
    Font-Size="25pt"
    Font-Name="Trebuchet MS"
    Text="<center>Welcome to the Raw Query Tool</center>"
    runat="server"
/>
```

The next control is our Panel control. This panel is for the query:

```
<asp:Panel
    id="pnlQuery"
    runat="server"
    Font-Size="13pt"
    Font-Name="Trebuchet MS"
    HorizontalAlign="Left"
>
```

Within the Panel, a TextBox allows the visitor to enter their query:

```
<asp:TextBox
    id="txtQuery"
    Columns="60"
    Rows="7"
    runat=server
    TextMode="MultiLine"
/>
```

The TextBox has three validation controls linked to it. The first makes sure that some text is entered into the Query TextBox:

```
<asp:RequiredFieldValidator
    id="rfvQuery"
    ControlToValidate="txtQuery"
    Display="Dynamic"
    Font-Name="Trebuchet MS"
    ForeColor="Yellow"
    Font-Size="11pt"
    runat=server>
    <br>A query must be entered!
</asp:RequiredFieldValidator>
```

The next control makes sure that the query entered by the visitor contains the word "From":

```
<asp:RegularExpressionValidator id="revSelect"
    ControlToValidate="txtQuery"
    ValidationExpression=".*(Select\b|select\b|SELECT\b).*"
    Display="Dynamic"
    Font-Name="Trebuchet MS"
    ForeColor="Yellow"
    Font-Size="11pt"
    runat=server>
    <br>You must include the word "Select" in your query!
</asp:RegularExpressionValidator>
```

Note the syntax of the validation expression. The text must contain the word "Select", "select", or "SELECT". The "|" denotes an or. The "\b" means that the phrase must be a word instead of part of a word. So the visitor must enter "Select", not "Selection":

```
ValidationExpression=".*(Select\b|select\b|SELECT\b).*"
```

The next validator makes sure that the query contains a form of the word From:

```
<asp:RegularExpressionValidator id="revFrom"
    ControlToValidate="txtQuery"
    ValidationExpression=".*(From\b|from\b|FROM\b).*"
    Display="Dynamic"
    Font-Name="Trebuchet MS"
    ForeColor="Yellow"
    Font-Size="11pt"
```

```
    runat=server>
    <br>You must include the word "From" in your query!
</asp:RegularExpressionValidator>
```

The other control on this Panel is a button:

```
<asp:button
    id="butQuery"
    text="Run Query"
    Type="Submit"
    OnClick="SubmitQuery_Click"
    runat="server"
/>
```

The next Panel control displays the results of running the query:

```
<asp:Panel
    id="pnlResults"
    runat="server"
    Font-Size="12pt"
    Font-Name="Trebuchet MS"
    HorizontalAlign="Left"
>
```

Within that Panel, we define a DataGrid that displays the results of the query:

```
<asp:DataGrid id="dgQueryResult" runat="server"
    Width="90%"
    BackColor="#ccccff"
    BorderColor="black"
    CellPadding=3
    CellSpacing="0"
    Font-Name="Trebuchet MS"
    Font-Size="8pt"
    ForeColor="Black"
    HeaderStyle-BackColor="#aaaadd"
/>
```

We also define the second button on the page:

```
<asp:button
        id="butResults"
        text="Enter a New Query"
```

```
        Type="Submit"
        OnClick="SubmitResults_Click"
        runat="server"
/>
```

The code on the page runs in three different events. The first code block fires when the page is loaded

```
Sub Page_Load(ByVal Sender as Object, ByVal E as EventArgs)
    If Not IsPostBack Then
        pnlQuery.Visible = True
        pnlResults.Visible = False
    End If
End Sub
```

We want this code to run only the first time that the page is loaded

```
If Not IsPostBack Then
```

If that is the case, we display the Query panel

```
pnlQuery.Visible = True
```

and hide the Results panel:

```
pnlResults.Visible = False
```

The next code block fires when the Run Query button is clicked.

```
Sub SubmitQuery_Click(Sender As Object, E As EventArgs)
    Dim DBConn as OleDbConnection
    Dim DBCommand As OleDbDataAdapter
    Dim DSResult as New DataSet
    DBConn = New OleDbConnection("Provider=sqloledb;" _
        & "server=localhost;" _
        & "Initial Catalog=INETC13;" _
        & "User Id=sa;" _
        & "Password=yourpassword;")
    DBCommand = New OleDbDataAdapter _
        (txtQuery.Text,DBConn)
    DBCommand.Fill(DSResult, _
        "TheStuff")
    dgQueryResult.DataSource = _
```

```
        DSResult.Tables("TheStuff").DefaultView
    dgQueryResult.DataBind
    pnlQuery.Visible = False
    pnlResults.Visible = True
End Sub
```

The procedure requires that we have data objects:

```
Dim DBConn as OleDbConnection
Dim DBCommand As OleDbDataAdapter
Dim DSResult as New DataSet
```

Remember that this solution does not have its own database. So here we connect to the Web Log database from Chapter 13:

```
DBConn = New OleDbConnection("Provider=sqloledb;" _
    & "server=localhost;" _
    & "Initial Catalog=INETC13;" _
    & "User Id=sa;" _
    & "Password=yourpassword;")
```

The SQL text that we place into our Data Adapter object comes straight from what the visitor entered into the TextBox control:

```
DBCommand = New OleDbDataAdapter _
    (txtQuery.Text,DBConn)
```

We then place the results of that query into our DataSet object

```
DBCommand.Fill(DSResult, _
    "TheStuff")
```

and bind our grid to that object:

```
dgQueryResult.DataSource = _
    DSResult.Tables("TheStuff").DefaultView
dgQueryResult.DataBind
```

Finally, we hide the Query panel

```
pnlQuery.Visible = False
```

and display the Results panel:

```
pnlResults.Visible = True
```

The other procedure on the page fires when the Enter A New Query button is clicked.

```
Sub SubmitResults_Click(Sender As Object, E As EventArgs)
    pnlQuery.Visible = True
    pnlResults.Visible = False
End Sub
```

It simply shows the Query panel

```
pnlQuery.Visible = True
```

and hides the Results panel.

```
pnlResults.Visible = False
```

Access Code Changes

Since this tool doesn't contain its own database, you would change the connect string in the code to the connect string that would allow the code to link to your database regardless of the type. As for the SQL syntax, the visitor would have to enter the correct query for the underlying type of the database.

Tip of the Day Tool

The Tip of the Day tool displays a random tip record that changes on a daily basis. In this implementation of the tool, the tip is placed on a Tip page. But you would probably want to include the tip on some other page that had other content, such as a Home page or a Tech page.

As you review this tool, note the use of the Random object to obtain a random number for choosing a tip.

Sample Usage

Figure 14-13 shows the Tip of the Day page.

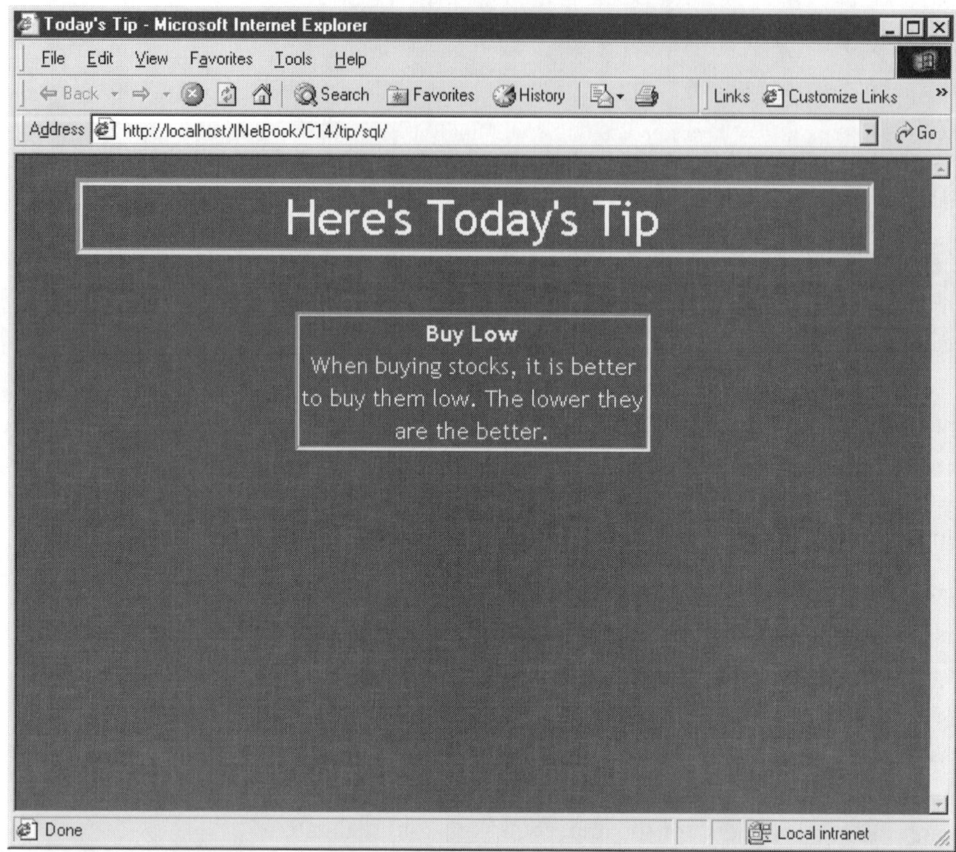

Figure 14-13 *Tip of the Day page*

The tip is made up of a title and the text of the tip. This tip will stay as the current tip with each viewing of the page until the date on the server changes. When it does, a new random tip is displayed or the current tip is randomly chosen again. Figure 14-14 shows a second tip displayed.

Tip of the Day Database Component

C14Tips.sql

The Tip of the Day tool requires a single database table to complete its functionality. The table stores the tip data. In this section, we will review the fields in that table.

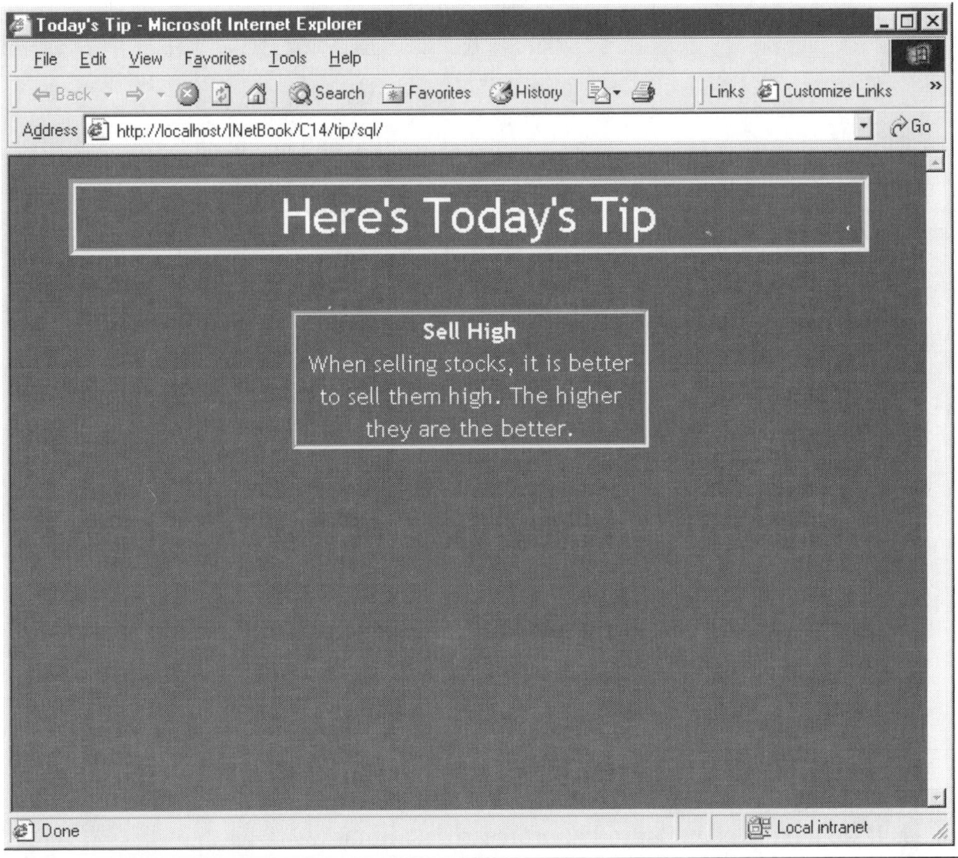

Figure 14-14 *Tip page after a new tip is displayed*

Tips Field Specifications

Tips.txt

The field specifications for the fields in the Tips table are displayed in Table 14-2.

The TipID field is the primary key in the table. The TipTitle field stores the title of the tip, and the TipText field stores the tip itself.

Tip of the Day ASP.NET Code

The code needed to implement the Tip of the Day tool is contained within a single ASP.NET page. Note that you would probably want to include this functionality within a more diverse page. In this section, we will review the code within this page.

Field Name	Field Type	Notes
TipID	int	Primary Key, Identity Column
TipTitle	varchar	Length = 50
TipText	varchar	Length = 255

Table 14-2 *Tips Field Specifications*

Tip of the Day ASP.NET Page

Index.aspx

The code in the Tip of the Day page displays the current tip and retrieves a random tip as the day changes.

The page requires these three compiler directives:

```
<%@ Page Language=VB Debug=true %>
<%@ Import Namespace="System.Data" %>
<%@ Import Namespace="System.Data.OLEDB" %>
```

First, we tell the compiler what language our code is in and that we want to be in debug mode:

```
<%@ Page Language=VB Debug=true %>
```

Then we tell the compiler to import these data libraries:

```
<%@ Import Namespace="System.Data" %>
<%@ Import Namespace="System.Data.OLEDB" %>
```

Within the body of the page, a Label control displays the title text:

```
<asp:Label
    id="lblTitle"
    BorderWidth="5px"
    BorderStyle=6
    Width="90%"
    Font-Size="25pt"
    Font-Name="Trebuchet MS"
    Text="<center>Here's Today's Tip</center>"
    runat="server"
/>
```

Another Label control will display the text of the tip:

```
<asp:Label
    id="lblMessage"
    BorderWidth="3px"
    BorderStyle=6
    Font-Size="12pt"
    Font-Name="Trebuchet MS"
    Width="40%"
    runat="server"
/>
```

The code on the page is contained within a single procedure that fires when the page is loaded.

```
Sub Page_Load(ByVal Sender as Object, ByVal E as EventArgs)
    Dim DBConn as OleDbConnection
    Dim DBCommand As OleDbDataAdapter
    Dim DSTip as New DataSet
    Dim MyRandom as New Random()
    Dim RowNumber as Long
    If Len(Application("TipDate")) = 0 Then
        Application("TipDate") = Today()
        DBConn = New OleDbConnection("Provider=sqloledb;" _
            & "server=localhost;" _
            & "Initial Catalog=INETC14;" _
            & "User Id=sa;" _
            & "Password=yourpassword;")
        DBCommand = New OleDbDataAdapter _
            ("Select TipTitle, TipText from " _
            & "Tips",DBConn)
        DBCommand.Fill(DSTip, _
            "Tips")
        RowNumber = MyRandom.Next _
            (0, DSTip.Tables("Tips").Rows.Count)
        Application("CurrentTip") = "<b>" _
            & DSTip.Tables("Tips").Rows(RowNumber).Item("TipTitle") _
            & "</b><br>" _
            & DSTip.Tables("Tips").Rows(RowNumber).Item("TipText")
    ElseIf Application("TipDate") <> Today() Then
        Application("TipDate") = Today()
        DBConn = New OleDbConnection("Provider=sqloledb;" _
            & "server=localhost;" _
```

```
            & "Initial Catalog=INETC14;" _
            & "User Id=sa;" _
            & "Password=yourpassword;")
        DBCommand = New OleDbDataAdapter _
            ("Select TipTitle, TipText from " _
            & "Tips",DBConn)
        DBCommand.Fill(DSTip, _
            "Tips")
        RowNumber = MyRandom.Next _
            (0, DSTip.Tables("Tips").Rows.Count)
        Application("CurrentTip") = "<b>" _
            & DSTip.Tables("Tips").Rows(RowNumber).Item("TipTitle") _
            & "</b><br>" _
            & DSTip.Tables("Tips").Rows(RowNumber).Item("TipText")
    End If
    lblMessage.Text = Application("CurrentTip")
End Sub
```

The code on the page will need data objects:

```
Dim DBConn as OleDbConnection
Dim DBCommand As OleDbDataAdapter
Dim DSTip as New DataSet
```

We also need a Random object, which is used to generate a random number:

```
Dim MyRandom as New Random()
```

This variable will store the random number that is generated and will be used to determine which tip to display:

```
Dim RowNumber as Long
```

First, we check to see if the application is just starting by seeing if a date is stored in this application variable:

```
If Len(Application("TipDate")) = 0 Then
```

If the application is just starting, we store today's date in that variable:

```
Application("TipDate") = Today()
```

And we need to grab a tip record. Therefore, we need to connect to the database

```
DBConn = New OleDbConnection("Provider=sqloledb;" _
    & "server=localhost;" _
    & "Initial Catalog=INETC14;" _
    & "User Id=sa;" _
    & "Password=yourpassword;")
```

and retrieve the tip records

```
DBCommand = New OleDbDataAdapter _
    ("Select TipTitle, TipText from " _
    & "Tips",DBConn)
```

and place them in our DataSet object:

```
DBCommand.Fill(DSTip, _
    "Tips")
```

We need to randomly choose one of the tip records. We do this by calling the Next method of the Random object. The first parameter is the lowest number we want to return—in this case a 0, which is the lowest row number in our DataSet object. The second parameter is one more than the top number we want to retrieve. So if there are 10 tip records, the range of random numbers will be 0 to 9. The random number generated is stored in our local variable:

```
RowNumber = MyRandom.Next _
    (0, DSTip.Tables("Tips").Rows.Count)
```

We then store the tip, based on that random number, in an Application variable:

```
Application("CurrentTip") = "<b>" _
    & DSTip.Tables("Tips").Rows(RowNumber).Item("TipTitle") _
    & "</b><br>" _
    & DSTip.Tables("Tips").Rows(RowNumber).Item("TipText")
```

The next condition we test for is whether the day is now different from when the tip was first displayed. This means we need to retrieve a new tip:

```
ElseIf Application("TipDate") <> Today() Then
```

First, though, we store the current date in our application variable:

```
Application("TipDate") = Today()
```

Then we connect to the database

```
DBConn = New OleDbConnection("Provider=sqloledb;" _
    & "server=localhost;" _
    & "Initial Catalog=INETC14;" _
    & "User Id=sa;" _
    & "Password=yourpassword;")
```

and retrieve the tips:

```
DBCommand = New OleDbDataAdapter _
    ("Select TipTitle, TipText from " _
    & "Tips",DBConn)
DBCommand.Fill(DSTip, _
    "Tips")
```

Once again, we generate a random number in the range of 0 to one less than the number of tip records:

```
RowNumber = MyRandom.Next _
    (0, DSTip.Tables("Tips").Rows.Count)
    Application("CurrentTip") = "<b>" _
    & DSTip.Tables("Tips").Rows(RowNumber).Item("TipTitle") _
    & "</b><br>" _
    & DSTip.Tables("Tips").Rows(RowNumber).Item("TipText")
```

If the day that the tip was first displayed is still today's date, we don't retrieve a new tip. Regardless of which of the conditions is the case, we display the tip in our Label control:

```
lblMessage.Text = Application("CurrentTip")
```

Link List Tool

A useful way that you can help visitors share information with other visitors, and in the process add content to your site, is to include link list functionality. The Link List tool allows visitors to view links submitted by other visitors and then add their own links.

Sample Usage

When the visitor first enters the Link List tool, they see the page displayed in Figure 14-15.

The Link List page contains all the links added by visitors to the site within a DataGrid control. The visitor can easily visit the links by clicking their name.

At the bottom of the page, the visitor can elect to add their own link by clicking the link. This takes the visitor to the Add Link page displayed in Figure 14-16.

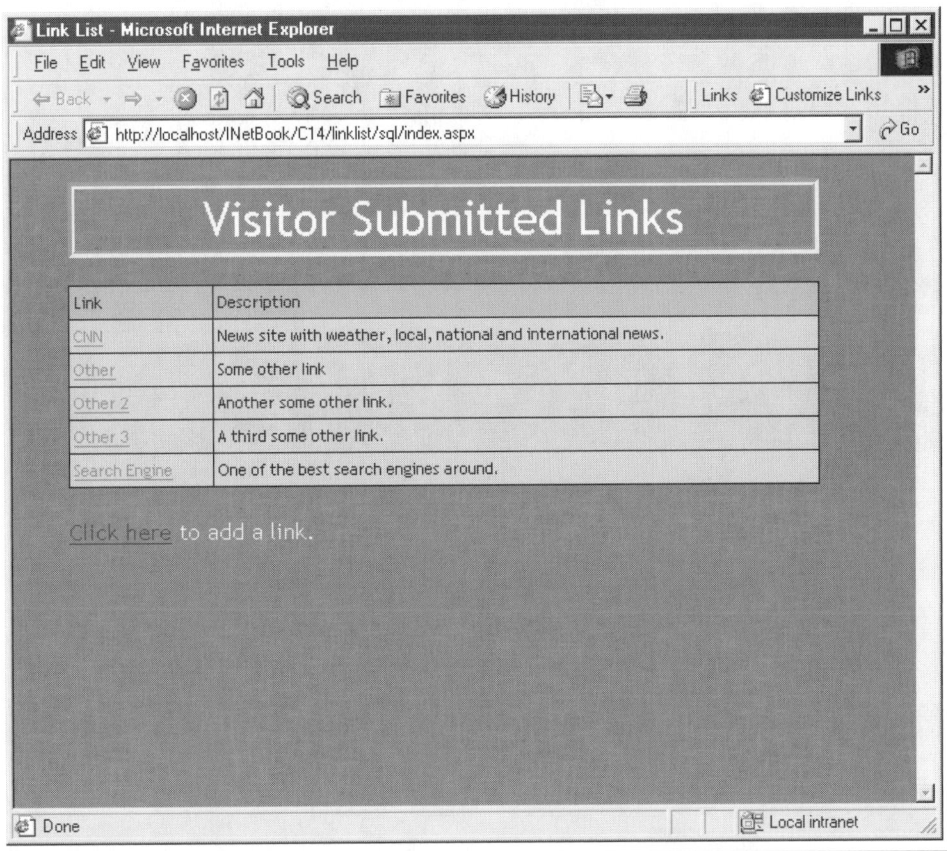

Figure 14-15 *Link List page*

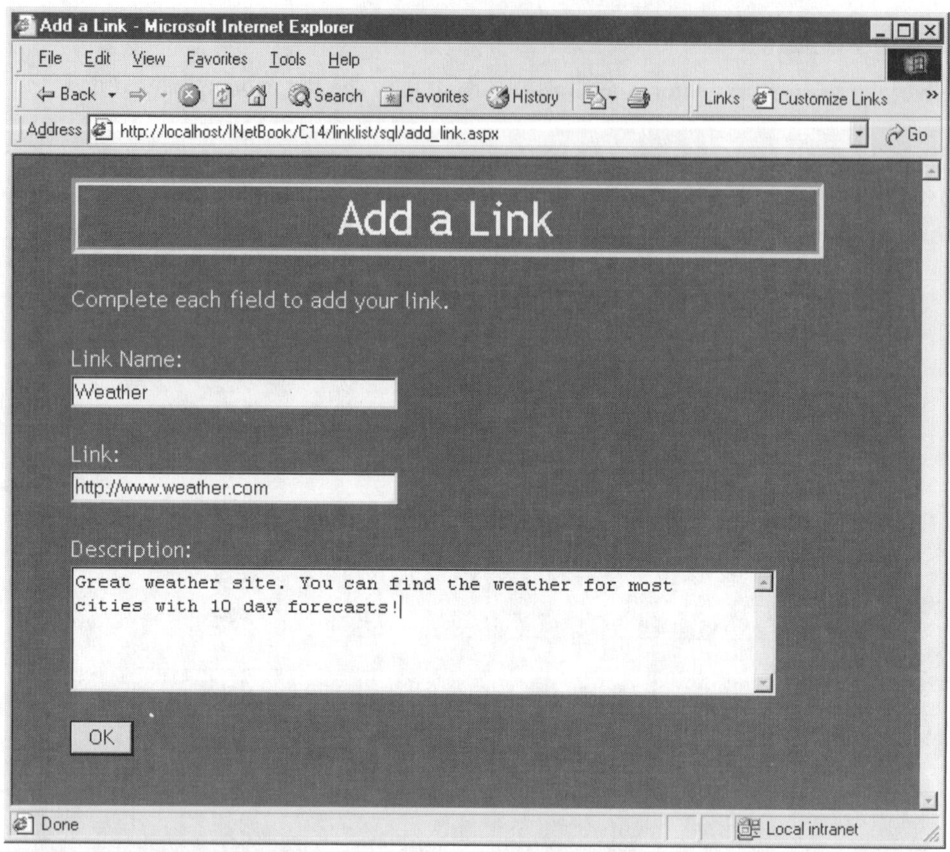

Figure 14-16 *Add a Link page*

The visitor must supply a name for the link, the location of the link, and a description of the link. If they do, they can click OK to have their link added. The visitor is then taken back to the Link List page, where their new link has been added, as you can see in Figure 14-17.

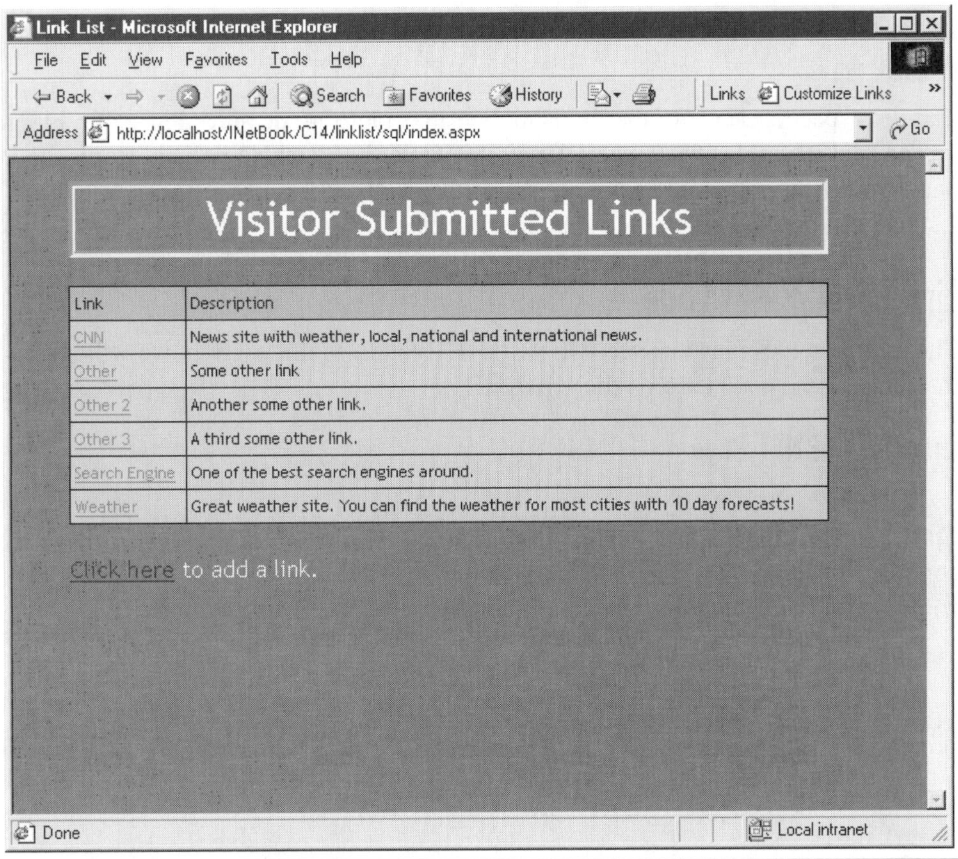

Figure 14-17 *Link List page with new link*

Link List Database Component

C14Links.sql

The Link List tool requires a single database table for its functionality. The table contains the link information. In this section, we will review the fields within that table.

Links Field Specifications

Links.txt

The field specifications for the fields in the Links table are displayed in Table 14-3.

The LinkID field is the primary key in the table. The LinkName field stores the name of the link. The LinkLink field stores the Web address of the Link. And the LinkDescription field stores the description of the link.

Link List ASP.NET Code

The Link List tool runs through two ASP.NET pages. In this section, we will review the controls and code used on those pages.

Link List ASP.NET Page

Index.aspx

The Link List page displays all the links in the Links table through a DataGrid control. At the top of the page, three compiler directives are defined. The directives configure the code environment and import data libraries into our code:

```
<%@ Page Language=VB Debug=true %>
<%@ Import Namespace="System.Data" %>
<%@ Import Namespace="System.Data.OLEDB" %>
```

Within the body of the page, a Label control displays title text:

```
<asp:Label
    id="lblTitle"
    BorderWidth="5px"
    BorderStyle=6
    Width="90%"
    Font-Size="25pt"
    Font-Name="Trebuchet MS"
    Text="<center>Visitor Submitted Links</center>"
    runat="server"
/>
```

Field Name	Field Type	Notes
LinkID	int	Primary Key, Identity Column
LinkName	varchar	Length = 100
LinkLink	varchar	Length = 100
LinkDescription	varchar	Length = 255

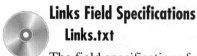

Table 14-3 *Links Field Specifications*

The page also contains a DataGrid control, which displays the Link List:

```
<asp:DataGrid
    id="dgLinks"
    AutoGenerateColumns="false"
    Width="90%"
    BackColor="#ccccff"
    BorderColor="black"
    ShowFooter="false"
    CellPadding=3
    CellSpacing="0"
    Font-Name="Trebuchet MS"
    Font-Size="8pt"
    ForeColor="Black"
    HeaderStyle-BackColor="#aaaadd"
    runat="server">
    <columns>
        <asp:HyperLinkColumn
            HeaderText="Link"
            DataNavigateUrlField="LinkLink"
            DataTextField="LinkName"
            Target="_self"
        />
        <asp:BoundColumn
            HeaderText="Description"
            DataField="LinkDescription"
        />
    </columns>
</asp:DataGrid>
```

Note that we are not using the automatic column generation:

```
AutoGenerateColumns="false"
```

Instead we define our own Column objects within the grid:

```
<columns>
```

The first column is defined as a hyperlink column:

```
<asp:HyperLinkColumn
```

The word “Link” is displayed for the column header:

```
HeaderText="Link"
```

When the visitor clicks the column, they are taken to the location matching this field:

```
DataNavigateUrlField="LinkLink"
```

But the name of the field is displayed in the column to the visitor:

```
DataTextField="LinkName"
```

When the visitor clicks the link, the site comes up within the same window that the list was in:

```
Target="_self"
```

The other column is a bound column

```
<asp:BoundColumn
    HeaderText="Description"
```

which will display the description of the link:

```
DataField="LinkDescription"
```

The only code on the page fires when the page is loaded.

```
Sub Page_Load(ByVal Sender as Object, ByVal E as EventArgs)
    Dim DBConn as OleDbConnection
    Dim DBCommand As OleDbDataAdapter
    Dim DSLinkData as New DataSet
    DBConn = New OleDbConnection("Provider=sqloledb;" _
        & "server=localhost;" _
        & "Initial Catalog=INETC14;" _
        & "User Id=sa;" _
        & "Password=yourpassword;")
    DBCommand = New OleDbDataAdapter _
         ("Select LinkLink, LinkName, LinkDescription " _
         & "From Links Order By LinkName", DBConn)
    DBCommand.Fill(DSLinkData, _
        "GridInfo")
    dgLinks.DataSource = _
        DSLinkData.Tables("GridInfo").DefaultView
    dgLinks.DataBind()
End Sub
```

The code requires that we declare data objects:

```
Dim DBConn as OleDbConnection
Dim DBCommand As OleDbDataAdapter
Dim DSLinkData as New DataSet
```

We start by connecting to our database

```
DBConn = New OleDbConnection("Provider=sqloledb;" _
    & "server=localhost;" _
    & "Initial Catalog=INETC14;" _
    & "User Id=sa;" _
    & "Password=yourpassword;")
```

select the link data

```
DBCommand = New OleDbDataAdapter _
    ("Select LinkLink, LinkName, LinkDescription " _
    & "From Links Order By LinkName", DBConn)
```

and place it into our DataSet object

```
DBCommand.Fill(DSLinkData, _
    "GridInfo")
```

which our DataGrid object is bound to:

```
dgLinks.DataSource = _
    DSLinkData.Tables("GridInfo").DefaultView
dgLinks.DataBind()
```

Add a Link ASP.NET Page

Add_Link.aspx

The Add a Link page allows the visitor to add their own link to the database. Within the body of the page, a Label control is defined for the title of the page:

```
<asp:Label
    id="lblTitle"
    BorderWidth="5px"
    BorderStyle=6
    Width="90%"
    Font-Size="25pt"
    Font-Name="Trebuchet MS"
    Text="<center>Add a Link</center>"
    runat="server"
/>
```

A second label displays instructions on the page:

```
<asp:Label
    id="lblMessage"
    Font-Size="12pt"
    Font-Name="Trebuchet MS"
    runat="server"
    Text="Complete each field to add your link."
/>
```

Next, you will find a TextBox control, which allows the visitor to enter the name of the link:

```
<asp:TextBox
    id="txtLinkName"
    Columns="35"
    MaxLength="100"
    runat=server
/>
```

The Link Name TextBox must contain a value, since this RequiredFieldValidator control is linked to it:

```
<asp:RequiredFieldValidator
    id="rfvLinkName"
    ControlToValidate="txtLinkName"
    Display="Dynamic"
    Font-Name="Trebuchet MS"
    Font-Size="10pt"
    ForeColor="Yellow"
    runat=server>
    Link Name is Required!
</asp:RequiredFieldValidator>
```

The next text box allows the visitor to enter the Web address for the link:

```
<asp:TextBox
    id="txtLinkLink"
    Columns="35"
    MaxLength="100"
    runat=server
/>
```

That field is also required

```
<asp:RequiredFieldValidator
    id="rfvLinkLink"
    ControlToValidate="txtLinkLink"
    Display="Dynamic"
    Font-Name="Trebuchet MS"
    Font-Size="10pt"
    ForeColor="Yellow"
    runat=server>
    Link is Required!
</asp:RequiredFieldValidator>
```

The other TextBox on the page allows the visitor to enter the description of the link being added

```
<asp:TextBox
    id="txtLinkDescription"
    Columns="60"
    Rows="5"
    runat=server
    TextMode="MultiLine"
/>
```

Because of this control, the visitor must enter a value in the description field:

```
<asp:RequiredFieldValidator
    id="rfvLinkDescription"
    ControlToValidate="txtLinkDescription"
    Display="Dynamic"
    Font-Name="Trebuchet MS"
    Font-Size="10pt"
    ForeColor="Yellow"
    runat=server>
    <br>The description is Required!
</asp:RequiredFieldValidator>
```

The only other control on the page is the Button control

```
<asp:button
    id="butOK"
    text="  OK  "
    Type="Submit"
    OnClick="SubmitBtn_Click"
    runat="server"
/>
```

which fires the only event on the page when the button is clicked

```
Sub SubmitBtn_Click(Sender As Object, E As EventArgs)
    Dim DBConn as OleDbConnection
    Dim DBCommand As OleDbDataAdapter
    Dim DBInsert As New OleDbCommand
    DBConn = New OleDbConnection("Provider=sqloledb;" _
        & "server=localhost;" _
        & "Initial Catalog=INETC14;" _
        & "User Id=sa;" _
        & "Password=yourpassword;")
    DBInsert.CommandText = "Insert Into Links " _
        & "(LinkName, LinkLink, LinkDescription) " _
        & "values (" _
        & "'" & Replace(txtLinkName.text, "'", "''") & "', " _
        & "'" & Replace(txtLinkLink.text, "'", "''") & "', " _
        & "'" & Replace(txtLinkDescription.text, "'", "''") & "')"
    DBInsert.Connection = DBConn
    DBInsert.Connection.Open
    DBInsert.ExecuteNonQuery()
    Response.Redirect("./index.aspx")
End Sub
```

The code requires that we declare data objects:

```
Dim DBConn as OleDbConnection
Dim DBCommand As OleDbDataAdapter
Dim DBInsert As New OleDbCommand
```

We start by connecting to our SQL Server database:

```
DBConn = New OleDbConnection("Provider=sqloledb;" _
    & "server=localhost;" _
    & "Initial Catalog=INETC14;" _
    & "User Id=sa;" _
    & "Password=yourpassword;")
```

We then place SQL text that will insert the new link into the database into our Command object:

```
DBInsert.CommandText = "Insert Into Links " _
    & "(LinkName, LinkLink, LinkDescription) " _
    & "values (" _
    & "'" & Replace(txtLinkName.text, "'", "''") & "', " _
```

```
    & "'" & Replace(txtLinkLink.text, "'", "''") & "', " _
    & "'" & Replace(txtLinkDescription.text, "'", "''") & "')"
```

The Command object will connect to our database through the Connection object:

```
DBInsert.Connection = DBConn
DBInsert.Connection.Open
```

We can then insert the new record

```
DBInsert.ExecuteNonQuery()
```

and send the visitor back to the Link List page:

```
Response.Redirect("./index.aspx")
```

Access Code Changes

C14Links.mdb

The only code change needed for this tool to work with Access instead of SQL Server is to change the connect strings from this

```
DBConn = New OleDbConnection("Provider=sqloledb;" _
    & "server=localhost;" _
    & "Initial Catalog=INETC14;" _
    & "User Id=sa;" _
    & "Password=yourpassword;")
```

to a string that uses the correct provider and database location:

```
DBConn = New OleDbConnection("PROVIDER=Microsoft.Jet.OLEDB.4.0;" _
    & "DATA SOURCE=" _
    & Server.MapPath("/INetBook/C14/LinkList/" _
    & "Access/C14Links.mdb;"))
```

No other code changes are necessary.

CHAPTER

15

Creating Human Resources Applications

Most companies have a similar need—the need to manage information related to working with employees. In this chapter, we will look at four solutions that allow you to manage aspects of employee information.

First, we will look at the Employee Leave Time tool. This tool allows employees to view the amount of sick time and vacation time that they have earned and used. They can even look at a future date to see how much leave time they will have then.

Then we will build on the Employee Leave Time tool with the Manager Leave Time tool. This tool allows a manager to accrue vacation or sick leave hours for all employees. It also allows managers to charge or add additional hours to an individual employee.

The third tool we will look at also builds on the first. It is the Employee of the Month tool. This simple one-page tool displays information about the current employee of the month.

Then, finally, we will look at the Job Board tool. The Job Board tool allows potential employees to view jobs that are available at your company.

Employee Leave Time Tool

The Employee Leave Time tool allows employees to sign into the company site. They then can view all the hours that they have earned and used with regard to their vacation time and sick time. The employee can also see summary information that depicts the number of hours of each type that they have left, as well as seeing how many hours they had or will have on some date other than the present.

Sample Usage

When the Employee first enters this site, they see the page displayed in Figure 15-1.

The employee uses this page to enter their short name and password. If the information does not match one of the employees, the employee is asked to sign in again. If the short name and password are found, the visitor is taken to the Leave Activity page displayed in Figure 15-2.

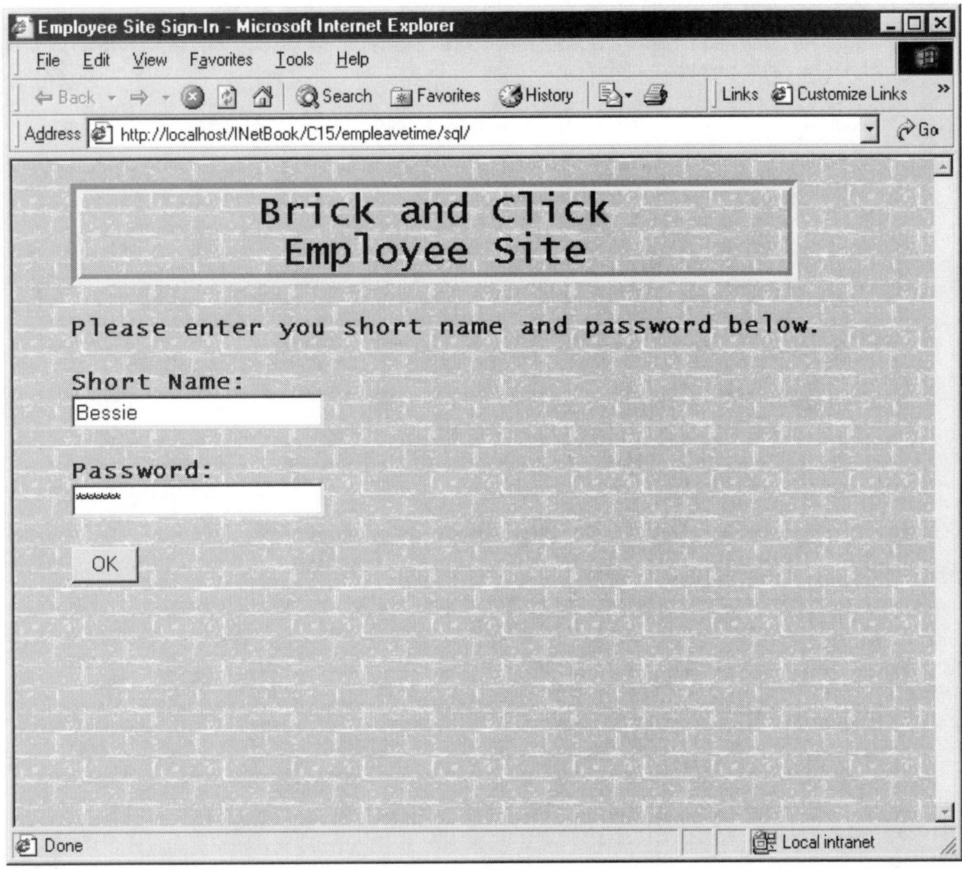

Figure 15-1 *Sign-In page*

The Leave Activity is divided into three panels. When the visitor first enters the page, they are presented with the Sick Leave panel. This panel shows all the dates that the employee earned and used their sick leave in a DataGrid. At the bottom of the page, the employee can click the buttons to view other panels on this page.

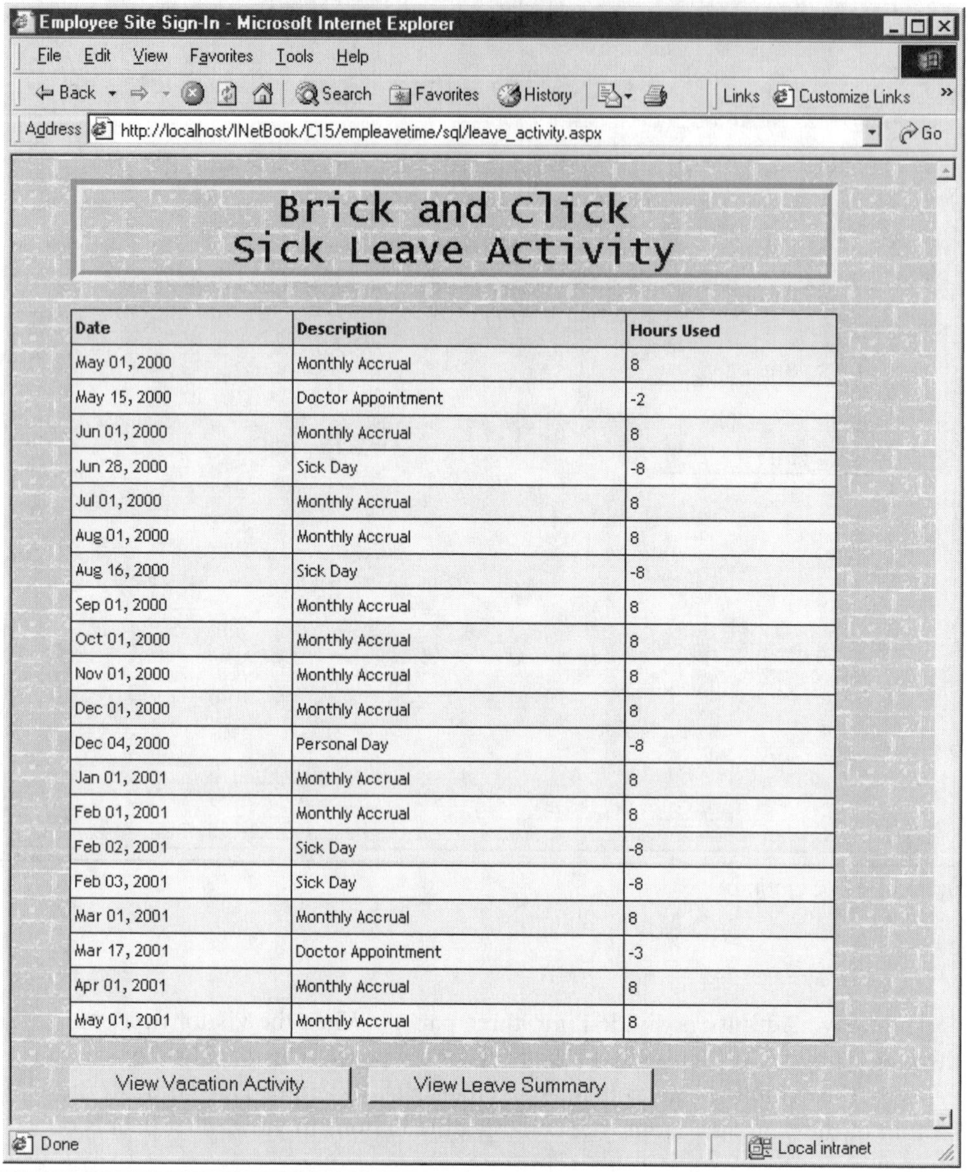

Brick and Click
Sick Leave Activity

Date	Description	Hours Used
May 01, 2000	Monthly Accrual	8
May 15, 2000	Doctor Appointment	-2
Jun 01, 2000	Monthly Accrual	8
Jun 28, 2000	Sick Day	-8
Jul 01, 2000	Monthly Accrual	8
Aug 01, 2000	Monthly Accrual	8
Aug 16, 2000	Sick Day	-8
Sep 01, 2000	Monthly Accrual	8
Oct 01, 2000	Monthly Accrual	8
Nov 01, 2000	Monthly Accrual	8
Dec 01, 2000	Monthly Accrual	8
Dec 04, 2000	Personal Day	-8
Jan 01, 2001	Monthly Accrual	8
Feb 01, 2001	Monthly Accrual	8
Feb 02, 2001	Sick Day	-8
Feb 03, 2001	Sick Day	-8
Mar 01, 2001	Monthly Accrual	8
Mar 17, 2001	Doctor Appointment	-3
Apr 01, 2001	Monthly Accrual	8
May 01, 2001	Monthly Accrual	8

View Vacation Activity | View Leave Summary

Figure 15-2 *Sick Leave panel of the Leave Activity page*

Figure 15-3 displays the Vacation Leave panel.

The Vacation Leave panel shows all the dates that the employee earned and used their vacation time. Note that the records in the DataGrid are displayed by date.

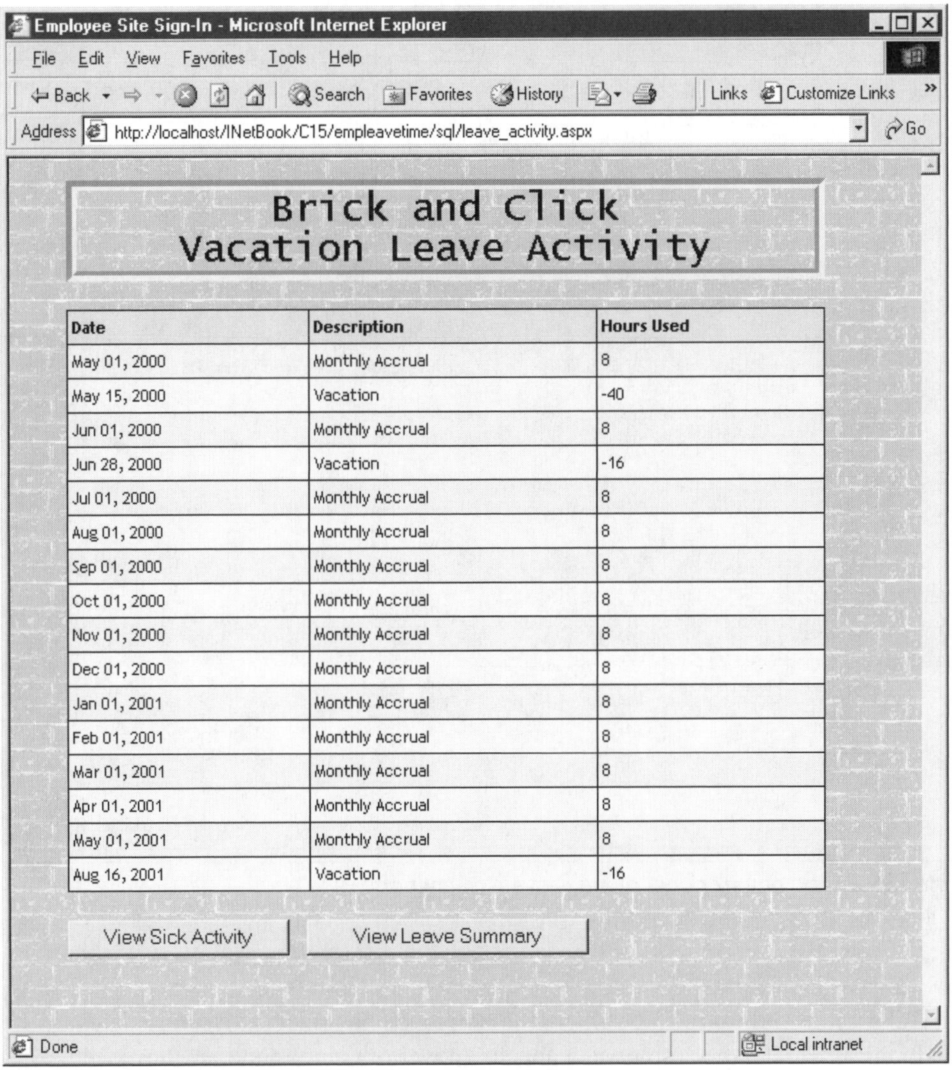

Brick and Click
Vacation Leave Activity

Date	Description	Hours Used
May 01, 2000	Monthly Accrual	8
May 15, 2000	Vacation	-40
Jun 01, 2000	Monthly Accrual	8
Jun 28, 2000	Vacation	-16
Jul 01, 2000	Monthly Accrual	8
Aug 01, 2000	Monthly Accrual	8
Sep 01, 2000	Monthly Accrual	8
Oct 01, 2000	Monthly Accrual	8
Nov 01, 2000	Monthly Accrual	8
Dec 01, 2000	Monthly Accrual	8
Jan 01, 2001	Monthly Accrual	8
Feb 01, 2001	Monthly Accrual	8
Mar 01, 2001	Monthly Accrual	8
Apr 01, 2001	Monthly Accrual	8
May 01, 2001	Monthly Accrual	8
Aug 16, 2001	Vacation	-16

Figure 15-3 *Vacation Leave panel of the Leave Activity page*

The other panel on this page is accessible by clicking the View Leave Summary button. That panel is displayed in Figure 15-4.

The employee sees through this panel the total number of sick and vacation hours that they have remaining. They can then use the calendar to select a date in the past to see how many hours they had at that time.

Figure 15-4 *Summary panel of the Leave Activity page*

Take a look at Figure 15-5, where the employee has selected a future date.

In this example, the employee wants to know how much time off they will have in December. That amount is reflected on this page when the employee selects a date in that month. As you will see when we look at the code, the prediction of the number of hours that the employee will have is based on monthly accrual fields.

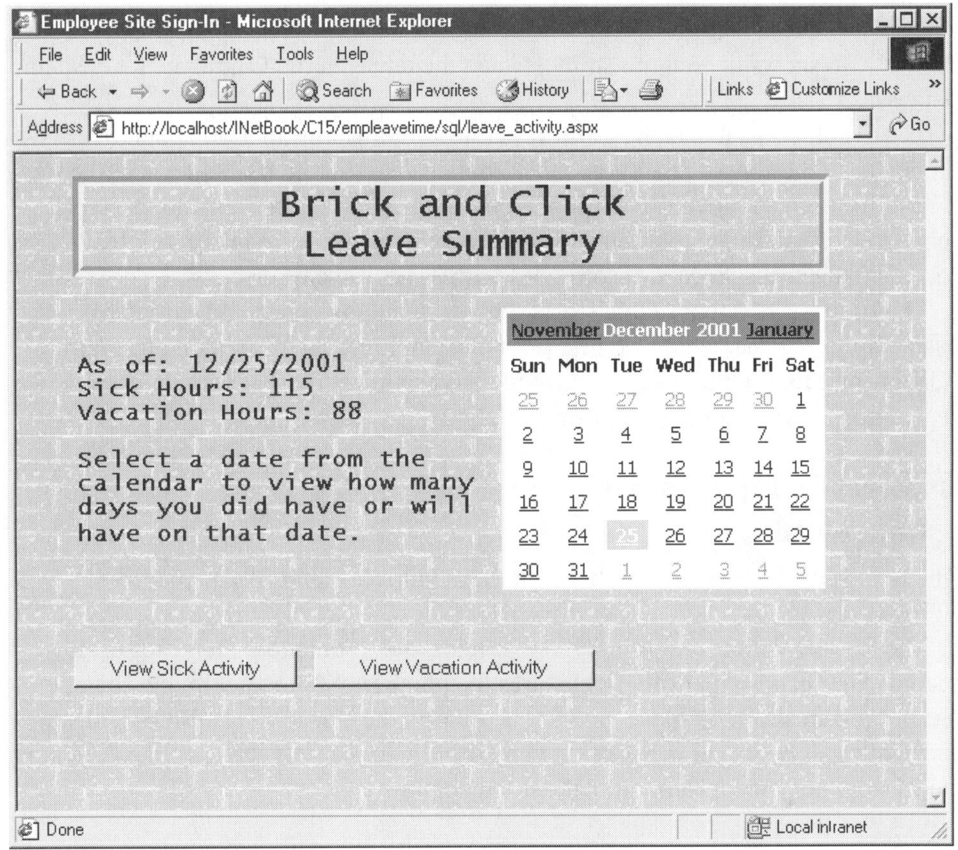

Figure 15-5 *Future date selected on the Summary panel*

Employee Leave Time Database Component

C15EmpLeaveTime.sql

The database required to run the Employee Leave Time application is made up of three interrelated tables. In this section, we will look at the relationships between the tables and the fields that make up those tables.

Tables and Data Diagram

Figure 15-6 shows the relationship between the tables in the Employee Leave Time database.

The Employees table is the top-level table. It stores information about the employees. The EmpSickActivity table contains the sick hours used and earned by and for each employee. The Employees table and the EmpSickActivity table relate in a one-to-many relationship. Each employee can have many sick leave records, but each sick leave record goes with a specific employee.

The EmpVacatActivity table stores the vacation hours used and earned by each employee. That table also relates to the Employees table in a one-to-many relationship. Each employee can have many vacation activity records, but each record goes with a specific employee.

Employees Field Specifications

Employees.txt

The field specifications for the fields in the Employees table are displayed in Table 15-1.

The EmpID field is the primary key in this table. It uniquely identifies each record. The SickAccrualRate field stores the number of hours per month that the employee earns for sick leave activity. Similarly, the VacatAccrualRate field stores the number of hours per month earned by the employee for vacation time. The other fields store personal information about the employee.

EmpSickActivity Field Specifications

EmpSickActivity.txt

The field specifications for the fields in the EmpSickActivity table are displayed in Table 15-2.

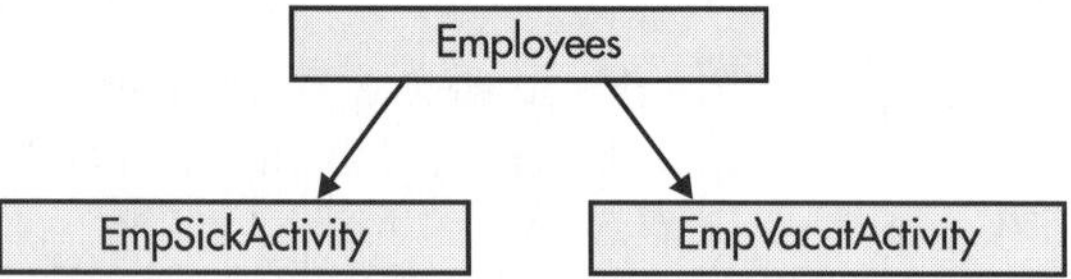

Figure 15-6 *Employee Leave Time data diagram*

Field Name	Field Type	Notes
EmpID	int	Primary Key, Identity Column
EmpLastName	varchar	Length = 50
EmpFirstName	varchar	Length = 50
ShortName	varchar	Length = 50
Password	varchar	Length = 50
EmailAddress	varchar	Length = 50
PhoneNumber	varchar	Length = 50
SickAccrualRate	int	
VacatAccrualRate	int	

Table 15-1 *Employees Field Specifications*

The EmpSickID is the primary key in this table. The EmpID field is a foreign key that links this table with the Employees table. The ActivityDate field stores the date that the sick leave use is for. The NumHours field stores the number of hours taken. And the TheNote field stores a description of the activity.

EmpVacatActivity Field Specifications

EmpVacatActivity.txt

The field specifications for the fields in the EmpVacatActivity table are displayed in Table 15-3.

Field Name	Field Type	Notes
EmpSickID	int	Primary Key, Identity Column
EmpID	int	Foreign Key
ActivityDate	datetime	
NumHours	float	
TheNote	varchar	Length = 255

Table 15-2 *EmpSickActivity Field Specifications*

Field Name	Field Type	Notes
EmpVacatID	int	Primary Key, Identity Column
EmpID	int	Foreign Key
ActivityDate	datetime	
NumHours	float	
TheNote	varchar	Length = 255

Table 15-3 *EmpVacatActivity Field Specifications*

The EmpVacatID field is the primary key in this table. The EmpID field links this table to the Employees table. The ActivityDate field stores the date that the vacation hours were earned or used on. The NumHours field stores the number of hours that were earned or used with this record. And the TheNote field stores a description of the activity.

Employee Leave Time ASP.NET Code

The Employee Leave Time application is made up of two pages. One allows the employee to sign in, and the other displays the activity data. The activity page is complex, since it is made up of three panels.

In this section, we will review the controls contained on the pages and the code used in the pages.

Sign-In ASP.NET Page

Index.aspx

The Sign-In page allows the visitor to enter their name and password so that they can access the rest of the site. At the top of the page, three compiler directives are defined.

```
<%@ Page Language=VB Debug=true %>
<%@ Import Namespace="System.Data" %>
<%@ Import Namespace="System.Data.OLEDB" %>
```

The first directive tells the compiler the language we will be using and that we want debugging on, which with some errors displays more detailed error information. Remember to turn this off when you run this code in a production environment:

```
<%@ Page Language=VB Debug=true %>
```

We also need to import into this page two libraries that will allow us to connect to our database and display its information:

```
<%@ Import Namespace="System.Data" %>
<%@ Import Namespace="System.Data.OLEDB" %>
```

The controls on the page are contained within an ASP.NET form tag:

```
<form runat="server">
```

The first control on the page is used to display the title of the page:

```
<asp:Label
    id="lblTitle"
    BorderWidth="7px"
    BorderStyle=6
    Width="90%"
    Font-Size="20pt"
    Font-Name="Lucida Console"
    Text="<center>Brick and Click<br>Employee Site</center>"
    runat="server"
/>
```

Next, another Label control is defined. It displays instructions or an error message to the employee:

```
<asp:Label
    id="lblMessage"
    Font-Size="12pt"
    Font-Bold="True"
    Font-Name="Lucida Console"
    runat="server"
/>
```

Next, we define a TextBox for the employee to enter their short name:

```
<asp:TextBox
    id="txtShortName"
    Columns="25"
    MaxLength="30"
    runat=server
/>
```

That field is required, since a RequiredFieldValidator control that links to it is defined

```
<asp:RequiredFieldValidator
    id="rfvShortName"
    ControlToValidate="txtShortName"
    Display="Dynamic"
    Font-Name="Lucida Console"
    Font-Size="10pt"
    runat=server>
    Short Name is Required!
</asp:RequiredFieldValidator>
```

Next, we define another TextBox control for the employee's password:

```
<asp:TextBox
    id="txtPassword"
    Columns="25"
    MaxLength="30"
    runat=server
    TextMode="Password"
/>
```

Note how the TextMode property is set:

```
TextMode="Password"
```

Setting it to this value means that the employee will see the "*" character as they type in their password into the TextBox control.

The password TextBox also has a RequiredFieldValidator linked to it:

```
<asp:RequiredFieldValidator
    id="rfvPassword"
    ControlToValidate="txtPassword"
    Display="Dynamic"
    Font-Name="Lucida Console"
    Font-Size="10pt"
    runat=server>
    Password is Required!
</asp:RequiredFieldValidator><br><br>
```

The other control on the page is a Button control that the employee clicks when they are signing in:

```
<asp:button
    id="butOK"
    text="  OK  "
    OnClick="SubmitBtn_Click"
    runat="server"
/>
```

The code on the page fires through two events. The first procedure runs when the visitor enters the page:

```
Sub Page_Load(ByVal Sender as Object, ByVal E as EventArgs)
    lblMessage.Text = "Please enter you short name " _
        & "and password below."
End Sub
```

It sets the text in the message label control to the instructions:

```
lblMessage.Text = "Please enter you short name " _
    & "and password below."
```

The other procedure fires when the employee submits the form by clicking the Button control:

```
Sub SubmitBtn_Click(Sender As Object, E As EventArgs)
    Dim DBConn as OleDbConnection
    Dim DBCommand As OleDbDataAdapter
    Dim DSSignIn as New DataSet
    DBConn = New OleDbConnection("Provider=sqloledb;" _
        & "server=localhost;" _
        & "Initial Catalog=INETC15;" _
        & "User Id=sa;" _
        & "Password=yourpassword;")
    DBCommand = New OleDbDataAdapter _
        ("Select EmpID from " _
        & "Employees Where " _
        & "ShortName = '" & txtShortName.Text _
        & "' and Password = '" & txtPassword.Text _
        & "'", DBConn)
    DBCommand.Fill(DSSignIn, _
        "EmpInfo")
    If DSSignIn.Tables("EmpInfo"). _
        Rows.Count = 0 Then
        lblMessage.Text = "The short name and password " _
```

```
            & "were not found.<br>Please try again."
    Else
        Session("EmpID") = DSSignIn.Tables("EmpInfo"). _
            Rows(0).Item("EmpID")
        Response.Redirect("./leave_activity.aspx")
    End If
End Sub
```

Within this procedure, we will need data objects so that we can connect to the database and retrieve information:

```
Dim DBConn as OleDbConnection
Dim DBCommand As OleDbDataAdapter
Dim DSSignIn as New DataSet
```

We start by connecting to our SQL Server database:

```
DBConn = New OleDbConnection("Provider=sqloledb;" _
    & "server=localhost;" _
    & "Initial Catalog=INETC15;" _
    & "User Id=sa;" _
    & "Password=yourpassword;")
```

We then place SQL text that looks for an employee record matching the short name and password entered by the employee into our Data Adapter object:

```
DBCommand = New OleDbDataAdapter _
    ("Select EmpID from " _
    & "Employees Where " _
    & "ShortName = '" & txtShortName.Text _
    & "' and Password = '" & txtPassword.Text _
    & "'", DBConn)
```

We then run that query and place the results into our DataSet object:

```
DBCommand.Fill(DSSignIn, _
    "EmpInfo")
```

We next check to see if any record was found with that name and password:

```
If DSSignIn.Tables("EmpInfo"). _
    Rows.Count = 0 Then
```

If one was not found, that means the employee entered an invalid short name or password. Therefore, we inform them of the problem through our message label:

```
lblMessage.Text = "The short name and password " _
    & "were not found.<br>Please try again."
```

Otherwise, the code flows here and we store the ID of the employee into a session variable so that we can retrieve it from any of the pages within this tool:

```
Session("EmpID") = DSSignIn.Tables("EmpInfo"). _
    Rows(0).Item("EmpID")
```

We then send the employee to the Leave Activity page:

```
Response.Redirect("./leave_activity.aspx")
```

Leave Activity ASP.NET Pages

Leave_Activity.aspx

The Leave Activity page is made up of three panels that display either the sick leave data, the vacation data, or the summary data. The employee clicks buttons on the page to view the different panels. Panel controls are used because they make it easy to have certain controls visible and invisible, since controls contained within a Panel control become visible and invisible along with the panel.

At the top of the page, you will find these compiler directives, which set up the language environment and import data libraries:

```
<%@ Page Language=VB Debug=true %>
<%@ Import Namespace="System.Data" %>
<%@ Import Namespace="System.Data.OLEDB" %>
```

The first control you will find in the body of the page is a Panel control for sick leave information:

```
<asp:Panel
    id="pnlSickActivity"
    runat="server"
>
```

Within that panel, the first control displays the title of this section:

```
<asp:Label
    id="lblTitle1"
    BorderWidth="7px"
    BorderStyle=6
    Width="90%"
    Font-Size="20pt"
```

```
    Font-Name="Lucida Console"
    Text="<center>Brick and Click<br>Sick Leave Activity</center>"
    runat="server"
/>
```

Next, a DataGrid control that will contain the sick leave activity from the database is defined:

```
<asp:DataGrid id="dgSickActivity" runat="server"
    Width="90%"
    BackColor="beige"
    AlternatingItemStyle-BackColor="cornsilk"
    BorderColor="black"
    CellPadding=3
    CellSpacing="0"
    Font-Name="Trebuchet MS"
    Font-Size="8pt"
    ForeColor="Black"
    HeaderStyle-BackColor="burlywood"
    HeaderStyle-Font-Bold="True"
/>
```

Two buttons are also contained within this panel. The first allows the employee to switch to the Vacation Leave panel:

```
<asp:button
    id="butViewVacat"
    text="View Vacation Activity"
    Type="Submit"
    OnClick="SubmitViewVacat_Click"
    runat="server"
/>
```

The other panel allows the employee to switch to the Summary panel:

```
<asp:button
    id="butViewSummary"
    text="View Leave Summary"
    Type="Submit"
    OnClick="SubmitViewSummary_Click"
    runat="server"
/>
```

That control is the last control on this panel:

```
</asp:Panel>
```

The next panel displays the vacation leave activity:

```
<asp:Panel
    id="pnlVacatActivity"
    runat="server"
>
```

The first control on that panel displays the title for this section:

```
<asp:Label
    id="lblTitle2"
    BorderWidth="7px"
    BorderStyle=6
    Width="90%"
    Font-Size="20pt"
    Font-Name="Lucida Console"
    Text="<center>Brick and Click<br>Vacation Leave Activity</center>"
    runat="server"
/>
```

The next control defined is a DataGrid control, which will show the employee all their vacation leave activity:

```
<asp:DataGrid id="dgVacatActivity" runat="server"
    Width="90%"
    BackColor="beige"
    AlternatingItemStyle-BackColor="cornsilk"
    BorderColor="black"
    CellPadding=3
    CellSpacing="0"
    Font-Name="Trebuchet MS"
    Font-Size="8pt"
    ForeColor="Black"
    HeaderStyle-BackColor="burlywood"
    HeaderStyle-Font-Bold="True"
/>
```

After that, a Button control is defined, which allows the employee to go to the Sick Leave panel:

```
<asp:button
    id="butViewSick"
    text="View Sick Activity"
    Type="Submit"
    OnClick="SubmitViewSick_Click"
    runat="server"
/>
```

One more button allows the employee to switch to the Summary panel:

```
<asp:button
    id="butViewSummary2"
    text="View Leave Summary"
    Type="Submit"
    OnClick="SubmitViewSummary_Click"
    runat="server"
/>
```

That is the last control on that panel:

```
</asp:Panel>
```

The third panel displays the summary information:

```
<asp:Panel
    id="pnlSummary"
    runat="server"
>
```

It contains a Label control for its title:

```
<asp:Label
    id="lblTitle3"
    BorderWidth="7px"
    BorderStyle=6
    Width="90%"
    Font-Size="20pt"
    Font-Name="Lucida Console"
    Text="<center>Brick and Click<br>Leave Summary</center>"
    runat="server"
/>
```

We then have another Label control that displays the summary text to the employee:

```
<asp:Label
    id="lblMessage"
    Font-Size="12pt"
    Font-Bold="True"
    Font-Name="Lucida Console"
    runat="server"
/>
```

After that, a Calendar control is defined that allows the employee to view their summary information based on a different date:

```
<asp:Calendar
    id="calDateToUse"
    runat="server"
    BackColor="ivory"
    CellPadding="3"
    CellSpacing="3"
    DayNameFormat="Short"
    FirstDayOfWeek="Default"
    NextPrevFormat="FullMonth"
    SelectionMode="Day"
    ShowDayHeader="True"
    ShowGridLines="False"
    ShowNextPrevMonth="True"
    ShowTitle="True"
    TitleFormat="MonthYear"
    TodayDayStyle-Font-Bold="True"
    DayHeaderStyle-Font-Bold="True"
    OtherMonthDayStyle-ForeColor="gray"
    TitleStyle-BackColor="#3366ff"
    TitleStyle-ForeColor="white"
    TitleStyle-Font-Bold="True"
    SelectedDayStyle-BackColor="#ffcc66"
    SelectedDayStyle-Font-Bold="True"
    Font-Name="Tahoma"
    Font-Size="12"
    OnSelectionChanged="calSelectChange"
/>
```

This event is called when the employee clicks a different date:

```
OnSelectionChanged="calSelectChange"
```

Two buttons are also found on this panel. The first toggles the employee back to the Sick Leave panel:

```
<asp:button
    id="butViewSick2"
    text="View Sick Activity"
    Type="Submit"
    OnClick="SubmitViewSick_Click"
    runat="server"
/>
```

The other displays the Vacation Leave panel when it is clicked

```
<asp:button
    id="butViewVacat2"
    text="View Vacation Activity"
    Type="Submit"
    OnClick="SubmitViewVacat_Click"
    runat="server"
/>
```

We then need to close this third Panel control:

```
</asp:Panel>
```

The code on the page is contained within five events. The first code block fires when the page is loaded.

```
Sub Page_Load(ByVal Sender as Object, ByVal E as EventArgs)
    If Len(Session("EmpID")) = 0 Then
        Response.Redirect("./index.aspx")
    End If
    If Not IsPostBack Then
        Dim DBConn as OleDbConnection
        Dim DBCommand As OleDbDataAdapter
        Dim DSPageData as New DataSet
        DBConn = New OleDbConnection("Provider=sqloledb;" _
            & "server=localhost;" _
            & "Initial Catalog=INETC15;" _
            & "User Id=sa;" _
            & "Password=yourpassword;")
        DBCommand = New OleDbDataAdapter _
            ("Select Convert(varchar(12),ActivityDate,107) as [Date], " _
```

```
            & "TheNote as [Description], " _
            & "NumHours as [Hours Used] " _
            & "From EmpSickActivity " _
            & "Where EmpID = " & Session("EmpID") _
            & " Order By ActivityDate", DBConn)
        DBCommand.Fill(DSPageData, _
            "SickActivity")
        dgSickActivity.DataSource = _
            DSPageData.Tables("SickActivity").DefaultView
        dgSickActivity.DataBind
        pnlSickActivity.Visible = True
        pnlVacatActivity.Visible = False
        pnlSummary.Visible = False
    End If
End Sub
```

The employee should come to this page only if they have signed in. We can check that by looking at the Session variable set on the Sign-In page:

```
If Len(Session("EmpID")) = 0 Then
```

If the variable isn't set, the employee is sent back to the Sign-In page:

```
Response.Redirect("./index.aspx")
```

The next section of the code should run only when the page is first loaded, which means the Sick Leave panel needs to be displayed

```
If Not IsPostBack Then
```

If that is the case, we need data objects:

```
Dim DBConn as OleDbConnection
Dim DBCommand As OleDbDataAdapter
Dim DSPageData as New DataSet
```

And we start by connecting to our SQL Server database:

```
DBConn = New OleDbConnection("Provider=sqloledb;" _
    & "server=localhost;" _
    & "Initial Catalog=INETC15;" _
    & "User Id=sa;" _
    & "Password=yourpassword;")
```

We then retrieve from the database all the sick leave records for the current employee. Note the use of the Convert function so that we see only the date portion of the date field instead of the time along with it. Also note that the fields are aliased with names that are easier to read, which is what the employee sees in the column headers of the data grid:

```
DBCommand = New OleDbDataAdapter _
    ("Select Convert(varchar(12),ActivityDate,107) as [Date], " _
    & "TheNote as [Description], " _
    & "NumHours as [Hours Used] " _
    & "From EmpSickActivity " _
    & "Where EmpID = " & Session("EmpID") _
    & " Order By ActivityDate", DBConn)
```

We then place the return of that query into our DataSet object:

```
DBCommand.Fill(DSPageData, _
    "SickActivity")
```

The Sick Activity DataGrid control is bound to that table in the DataSet object:

```
dgSickActivity.DataSource = _
    DSPageData.Tables("SickActivity").DefaultView
dgSickActivity.DataBind
```

We then show the employee the Sick Activity panel

```
pnlSickActivity.Visible = True
```

and hide the other two:

```
pnlVacatActivity.Visible = False
pnlSummary.Visible = False
```

The next procedure fires whenever either of the View Vacation Activity buttons is clicked.

```
Sub SubmitViewVacat_Click(Sender As Object, E As EventArgs)
    Dim DBConn as OleDbConnection
    Dim DBCommand As OleDbDataAdapter
    Dim DSPageData as New DataSet
    DBConn = New OleDbConnection("Provider=sqloledb;" _
        & "server=localhost;" _
```

```
        & "Initial Catalog=INETC15;" _
        & "User Id=sa;" _
        & "Password=yourpassword;")
    DBCommand = New OleDbDataAdapter _
        ("Select Convert(varchar(12),ActivityDate,107) as [Date], " _
        & "TheNote as [Description], " _
        & "NumHours as [Hours Used] " _
        & "From EmpVacatActivity " _
        & "Where EmpID = " & Session("EmpID") _
        & " Order By ActivityDate", DBConn)
    DBCommand.Fill(DSPageData, _
        "VacatActivity")
    dgVacatActivity.DataSource = _
        DSPageData.Tables("VacatActivity").DefaultView
    dgVacatActivity.DataBind
    pnlSickActivity.Visible = False
    pnlVacatActivity.Visible = True
    pnlSummary.Visible = False
End Sub
```

Within this procedure, we will need data objects:

```
Dim DBConn as OleDbConnection
Dim DBCommand As OleDbDataAdapter
Dim DSPageData as New DataSet
```

First, our connection object is set to point to our SQL Server database:

```
DBConn = New OleDbConnection("Provider=sqloledb;" _
    & "server=localhost;" _
    & "Initial Catalog=INETC15;" _
    & "User Id=sa;" _
    & "Password=yourpassword;")
```

We then retrieve all the vacation activity for the currently signed-in employee

```
DBCommand = New OleDbDataAdapter _
    ("Select Convert(varchar(12),ActivityDate,107) as [Date], " _
    & "TheNote as [Description], " _
    & "NumHours as [Hours Used] " _
    & "From EmpVacatActivity " _
    & "Where EmpID = " & Session("EmpID") _
    & " Order By ActivityDate", DBConn)
```

and place that data into our DataSet object:

```
DBCommand.Fill(DSPageData, _
    "VacatActivity")
```

The Vacation Activity DataGrid is bound to that DataSet table:

```
dgVacatActivity.DataSource = _
    DSPageData.Tables("VacatActivity").DefaultView
dgVacatActivity.DataBind
```

We then hide the Sick Activity panel

```
pnlSickActivity.Visible = False
```

show the vacation one

```
pnlVacatActivity.Visible = True
```

and hide the summary one:

```
pnlSummary.Visible = False
```

The third procedure fires when either of the View Sick Activity buttons is clicked. The code sets up the Sick Activity panel.

```
Sub SubmitViewSick_Click(Sender As Object, E As EventArgs)
    Dim DBConn as OleDbConnection
    Dim DBCommand As OleDbDataAdapter
    Dim DSPageData as New DataSet
    DBConn = New OleDbConnection("Provider=sqloledb;" _
        & "server=localhost;" _
        & "Initial Catalog=INETC15;" _
        & "User Id=sa;" _
        & "Password=yourpassword;")
    DBCommand = New OleDbDataAdapter _
        ("Select Convert(varchar(12),ActivityDate,107) as [Date], " _
        & "TheNote as [Description], " _
        & "NumHours as [Hours Used] " _
        & "From EmpSickActivity " _
        & "Where EmpID = " & Session("EmpID") _
        & " Order By ActivityDate", DBConn)
    DBCommand.Fill(DSPageData, _
```

```
        "SickActivity")
    dgSickActivity.DataSource = _
        DSPageData.Tables("SickActivity").DefaultView
    dgSickActivity.DataBind
    pnlSickActivity.Visible = True
    pnlVacatActivity.Visible = False
    pnlSummary.Visible = False
End Sub
```

The procedure requires data objects:

```
Dim DBConn as OleDbConnection
Dim DBCommand As OleDbDataAdapter
Dim DSPageData as New DataSet
```

We start by connecting to our database

```
DBConn = New OleDbConnection("Provider=sqloledb;" _
    & "server=localhost;" _
    & "Initial Catalog=INETC15;" _
    & "User Id=sa;" _
    & "Password=yourpassword;")
```

and retrieving all the sick leave activity for the signed-in employee

```
DBCommand = New OleDbDataAdapter _
    ("Select Convert(varchar(12),ActivityDate,107) as [Date], " _
    & "TheNote as [Description], " _
    & "NumHours as [Hours Used] " _
    & "From EmpSickActivity " _
    & "Where EmpID = " & Session("EmpID") _
    & " Order By ActivityDate", DBConn)
```

which is placed into a table called SickActivity in our DataSet object:

```
DBCommand.Fill(DSPageData, _
    "SickActivity")
```

The Sick Activity DataGrid is bound to the DataSet table we just created

```
dgSickActivity.DataSource = _
    DSPageData.Tables("SickActivity").DefaultView
dgSickActivity.DataBind
```

We then display the Sick Activity panel

```
pnlSickActivity.Visible = True
```

and hide the other two panels:

```
pnlVacatActivity.Visible = False
pnlSummary.Visible = False
```

The fourth procedure fires when the employee clicks either of the View Leave Summary buttons.

```
Sub SubmitViewSummary_Click(Sender As Object, E As EventArgs)
    Dim DBConn as OleDbConnection
    Dim DBCommand As OleDbDataAdapter
    Dim DSPageData as New DataSet
    DBConn = New OleDbConnection("Provider=sqloledb;" _
        & "server=localhost;" _
        & "Initial Catalog=INETC15;" _
        & "User Id=sa;" _
        & "Password=yourpassword;")
    DBCommand = New OleDbDataAdapter _
        ("Select Sum(NumHours) as SumSickHours " _
        & "From EmpSickActivity " _
        & "Where EmpID = " & Session("EmpID") _
        , DBConn)
    DBCommand.Fill(DSPageData, _
        "SumSick")
    DBCommand = New OleDbDataAdapter _
        ("Select Sum(NumHours) as SumVacatHours " _
        & "From EmpVacatActivity " _
        & "Where EmpID = " & Session("EmpID") _
        , DBConn)
    DBCommand.Fill(DSPageData, _
        "SumVacat")
    lblMessage.Text = "As of: " & Today() _
        & "<br>Sick Hours: " _
        & DSPageData.Tables("SumSick"). _
        Rows(0).Item("SumSickHours") _
        & "<br>Vacation Hours: " _
        & DSPageData.Tables("SumVacat"). _
        Rows(0).Item("SumVacatHours") _
        & "<br><br>Select a date from the calendar " _
```

```
        & "to view how many days you did have or " _
        & "will have on that date."
    calDateToUse.SelectedDate = Today()
    pnlSickActivity.Visible = False
    pnlVacatActivity.Visible = False
    pnlSummary.Visible = True
End Sub
```

The page requires data objects:

```
Dim DBConn as OleDbConnection
Dim DBCommand As OleDbDataAdapter
Dim DSPageData as New DataSet
```

We need to connect to our database:

```
DBConn = New OleDbConnection("Provider=sqloledb;" _
    & "server=localhost;" _
    & "Initial Catalog=INETC15;" _
    & "User Id=sa;" _
    & "Password=yourpassword;")
```

The first thing we retrieve from the database is the total sum of the number of sick hours used and earned by the signed-in employee:

```
DBCommand = New OleDbDataAdapter _
    ("Select Sum(NumHours) as SumSickHours " _
    & "From EmpSickActivity " _
    & "Where EmpID = " & Session("EmpID") _
    , DBConn)
```

That result is placed into a DataSet object table:

```
DBCommand.Fill(DSPageData, _
    "SumSick")
```

Next, we retrieve the sum of the vacation hours used and earned for the current employee:

```
DBCommand = New OleDbDataAdapter _
   ("Select Sum(NumHours) as SumVacatHours " _
   & "From EmpVacatActivity " _
   & "Where EmpID = " & Session("EmpID") _
   , DBConn)
```

That value is placed into another table within our DataSet objects:

```
DBCommand.Fill(DSPageData, _
    "SumVacat")
```

Those values, along with today's date, are placed with descriptive text into our message label on the Summary panel:

```
lblMessage.Text = "As of: " & Today() _
    & "<br>Sick Hours: " _
    & DSPageData.Tables("SumSick"). _
    Rows(0).Item("SumSickHours") _
    & "<br>Vacation Hours: " _
    & DSPageData.Tables("SumVacat"). _
    Rows(0).Item("SumVacatHours") _
    & "<br><br>Select a date from the calendar " _
    & "to view how many days you did have or " _
    & "will have on that date."
```

Today's date also will appear as the selected date on the Calendar control:

```
calDateToUse.SelectedDate = Today()
```

We then hide the Sick and Vacation panels

```
pnlSickActivity.Visible = False
pnlVacatActivity.Visible = False
```

but show the Summary panel:

```
pnlSummary.Visible = True
```

The last event fires when the employee selects a date on the calendar. When they do that, we need to show them the number of hours they had on that date or will have on that date.

```
Sub calSelectChange(ByVal Sender as Object, ByVal E as EventArgs)
    Dim DBConn as OleDbConnection
    Dim DBCommand As OleDbDataAdapter
    Dim DSPageData as New DataSet
    DBConn = New OleDbConnection("Provider=sqloledb;" _
        & "server=localhost;" _
        & "Initial Catalog=INETC15;" _
        & "User Id=sa;" _
```

```
        & "Password=yourpassword;")
    If calDateToUse.SelectedDate <= Today()
        DBCommand = New OleDbDataAdapter _
            ("Select Sum(NumHours) as SumSickHours " _
            & "From EmpSickActivity " _
            & "Where EmpID = " & Session("EmpID") _
            & " and ActivityDate <= '" _
            & calDateToUse.SelectedDate & "'" _
            , DBConn)
        DBCommand.Fill(DSPageData, _
            "SumSick")
        DBCommand = New OleDbDataAdapter _
            ("Select Sum(NumHours) as SumVacatHours " _
            & "From EmpVacatActivity " _
            & "Where EmpID = " & Session("EmpID") _
            & " and ActivityDate <= '" _
            & calDateToUse.SelectedDate & "'" _
            , DBConn)
        DBCommand.Fill(DSPageData, _
            "SumVacat")
        lblMessage.Text = "As of: " _
            & calDateToUse.SelectedDate _
            & "<br>Sick Hours: " _
            & DSPageData.Tables("SumSick"). _
            Rows(0).Item("SumSickHours") _
            & "<br>Vacation Hours: " _
            & DSPageData.Tables("SumVacat"). _
            Rows(0).Item("SumVacatHours") _
            & "<br><br>Select a date from the calendar " _
            & "to view how many days you did have or " _
            & "will have on that date."
    Else
        Dim TempSick as Single
        Dim TempVacat as Single
        Dim NumMonths as Long
        DBCommand = New OleDbDataAdapter _
            ("Select Sum(NumHours) as SumSickHours " _
            & "From EmpSickActivity " _
            & "Where EmpID = " & Session("EmpID") _
            , DBConn)
        DBCommand.Fill(DSPageData, _
            "SumSick")
        DBCommand = New OleDbDataAdapter _
            ("Select Sum(NumHours) as SumVacatHours " _
```

```
            & "From EmpVacatActivity " _
            & "Where EmpID = " & Session("EmpID") _
            , DBConn)
        DBCommand.Fill(DSPageData, _
            "SumVacat")
        DBCommand = New OleDbDataAdapter _
            ("Select SickAccrualRate, VacatAccrualRate " _
            & "From Employees Where EmpID = " _
            & Session("EmpID") _
            , DBConn)
        DBCommand.Fill(DSPageData, _
            "EmpInfo")
        NumMonths = DateDiff(DateInterval.Month, _
            Today(), calDateToUse.SelectedDate)
        TempSick = NumMonths * DSPageData.Tables("EmpInfo"). _
            Rows(0).Item("SickAccrualRate")
        TempSick = TempSick + DSPageData.Tables("SumSick"). _
            Rows(0).Item("SumSickHours")
        TempVacat = NumMonths * DSPageData.Tables("EmpInfo"). _
            Rows(0).Item("VacatAccrualRate")
        TempVacat = TempVacat + DSPageData.Tables("SumVacat"). _
            Rows(0).Item("SumVacatHours")
        lblMessage.Text = "As of: " _
            & calDateToUse.SelectedDate _
            & "<br>Sick Hours: " _
            & TempSick  _
            & "<br>Vacation Hours: " _
            & TempVacat _
            & "<br><br>Select a date from the calendar " _
            & "to view how many days you did have or " _
            & "will have on that date."
    End If
    pnlSickActivity.Visible = False
    pnlVacatActivity.Visible = False
    pnlSummary.Visible = True
End Sub
```

Within this procedure, we will need data objects:

```
Dim DBConn as OleDbConnection
Dim DBCommand As OleDbDataAdapter
Dim DSPageData as New DataSet
```

We start by connecting to the database:

```
DBConn = New OleDbConnection("Provider=sqloledb;" _
    & "server=localhost;" _
    & "Initial Catalog=INETC15;" _
    & "User Id=sa;" _
    & "Password=yourpassword;")
```

We then check to see if the date selected by the employee is either the present or a past date:

```
If calDateToUse.SelectedDate <= Today()
```

If the date is in the past, we retrieve the total number of sick hours that were earned and used as of that date

```
DBCommand = New OleDbDataAdapter _
    ("Select Sum(NumHours) as SumSickHours " _
    & "From EmpSickActivity " _
    & "Where EmpID = " & Session("EmpID") _
    & " and ActivityDate <= '" _
    & calDateToUse.SelectedDate & "'" _
    , DBConn)
```

which is placed into our DataSet object:

```
DBCommand.Fill(DSPageData, _
    "SumSick")
```

We also need to retrieve and place into our DataSet object the number of vacation hours earned and used as of that date:

```
DBCommand = New OleDbDataAdapter _
    ("Select Sum(NumHours) as SumVacatHours " _
    & "From EmpVacatActivity " _
    & "Where EmpID = " & Session("EmpID") _
    & " and ActivityDate <= '" _
    & calDateToUse.SelectedDate & "'" _
    , DBConn)
DBCommand.Fill(DSPageData, _
    "SumVacat")
```

Those hours retrieved, along with the date selected by the employee, are placed with descriptive text into our message label on the Summary panel:

```
lblMessage.Text = "As of: " _
    & calDateToUse.SelectedDate _
```

```
    & "<br>Sick Hours: " _
    & DSPageData.Tables("SumSick"). _
    Rows(0).Item("SumSickHours") _
    & "<br>Vacation Hours: " _
    & DSPageData.Tables("SumVacat"). _
    Rows(0).Item("SumVacatHours") _
    & "<br><br>Select a date from the calendar " _
    & "to view how many days you did have or " _
    & "will have on that date."
```

If the employee chose a date in the future on the Calendar object, the code flows here:

```
Else
```

In that case, we need a few variables to store temporary information as we calculate future values:

```
Dim TempSick as Single
Dim TempVacat as Single
Dim NumMonths as Long
```

We then retrieve the current total number of sick hours

```
DBCommand = New OleDbDataAdapter _
    ("Select Sum(NumHours) as SumSickHours " _
    & "From EmpSickActivity " _
    & "Where EmpID = " & Session("EmpID") _
    , DBConn)
```

and place it into our DataSet object:

```
DBCommand.Fill(DSPageData, _
    "SumSick")
```

We do the same for the vacation hours:

```
DBCommand = New OleDbDataAdapter _
    ("Select Sum(NumHours) as SumVacatHours " _
    & "From EmpVacatActivity " _
    & "Where EmpID = " & Session("EmpID") _
    , DBConn)
DBCommand.Fill(DSPageData, _
    "SumVacat")
```

We also need to retrieve the accrual rates for the employee, since we need to calculate the number of hours that the employee is projected to have in the future:

```
DBCommand = New OleDbDataAdapter _
    ("Select SickAccrualRate, VacatAccrualRate " _
    & "From Employees Where EmpID = " _
    & Session("EmpID") _
    , DBConn)
DBCommand.Fill(DSPageData, _
    "EmpInfo")
```

Next, we need to calculate the number of months between now and the date selected on the calendar by the employee:

```
NumMonths = DateDiff(DateInterval.Month, _
    Today(), calDateToUse.SelectedDate)
```

That value is used to determine how many sick hours the employee will have by the future date selected

```
TempSick = NumMonths * DSPageData.Tables("EmpInfo"). _
    Rows(0).Item("SickAccrualRate")
```

which is then added to their current amount:

```
TempSick = TempSick + DSPageData.Tables("SumSick"). _
    Rows(0).Item("SumSickHours")
```

The same calculation is performed for the vacation hours:

```
TempVacat = NumMonths * DSPageData.Tables("EmpInfo"). _
    Rows(0).Item("VacatAccrualRate")
TempVacat = TempVacat + DSPageData.Tables("SumVacat"). _
    Rows(0).Item("SumVacatHours")
```

Those values are placed in our label on the Summary panel along with the date selected by the employee and some descriptive text:

```
lblMessage.Text = "As of: " _
    & calDateToUse.SelectedDate _
    & "<br>Sick Hours: " _
    & TempSick _
    & "<br>Vacation Hours: " _
    & TempVacat _
```

```
    & "<br><br>Select a date from the calendar " _
    & "to view how many days you did have or " _
    & "will have on that date."
```

Regardless of whether the date selected was in the past or the future, we hide the Sick and Vacation panels

```
pnlSickActivity.Visible = False
pnlVacatActivity.Visible = False
```

and show the Summary panel:

```
pnlSummary.Visible = True
```

Access Code Changes

C15EmpLeaveTime.mdb

A few changes are needed for this solution to work with Access instead of SQL Server. First, the connection objects used throughout the code need to change from this

```
DBConn = New OleDbConnection("Provider=sqloledb;" _
    & "server=localhost;" _
    & "Initial Catalog=INETC15;" _
    & "User Id=sa;" _
    & "Password=yourpassword;")
```

to something like this that points to the location of your Access database:

```
DBConn = New OleDbConnection("PROVIDER=Microsoft.Jet.OLEDB.4.0;" _
    & "DATA SOURCE=" _
    & Server.MapPath("/INetBook/C15/EmpLeaveTime/" _
    & "Access/C15EmpLeaveTime.mdb;"))
```

Next, the Convert function used in this SQL statement

```
DBCommand = New OleDbDataAdapter _
    ("Select Convert(varchar(12),ActivityDate,107) as [Date], " _
    & "TheNote as [Description], " _
    & "NumHours as [Hours Used] " _
    & "From EmpSickActivity " _
    & "Where EmpID = " & Session("EmpID") _
    & " Order By ActivityDate", DBConn)
```

is a function native to SQL Server. In Access, the Format function is used instead:

```
DBCommand = New OleDbDataAdapter _
    ("Select Format(ActivityDate,""mmm dd, yyyy"") as [Date], " _
    & "TheNote as [Description], " _
    & "NumHours as [Hours Used] " _
    & "From EmpSickActivity " _
    & "Where EmpID = " & Session("EmpID") _
    & " Order By ActivityDate", DBConn)
```

The third change is in the Where clause of SQL statements. Dates in a SQL Server Where clause are surrounded by the " " " character:

```
DBCommand = New OleDbDataAdapter _
    ("Select Sum(NumHours) as SumSickHours " _
    & "From EmpSickActivity " _
    & "Where EmpID = " & Session("EmpID") _
    & " and ActivityDate <= '" _
    & calDateToUse.SelectedDate & "'" _
    , DBConn)
```

In Access, you need to use the "#" character:

```
DBCommand = New OleDbDataAdapter _
    ("Select Sum(NumHours) as SumSickHours " _
    & "From EmpSickActivity " _
    & "Where EmpID = " & Session("EmpID") _
    & " and ActivityDate <= #" _
    & calDateToUse.SelectedDate & "#" _
    , DBConn)
```

Manager Leave Time Tool

Index.aspx

The Manager Leave Time tool builds on the Employee Leave Time tool. A manager can use this tool to add and use sick and vacation hours for all employees or a specific employee.

Sample Usage

When the manager first enters this one-page tool, they see the default view of the page, as shown in Figure 15-7.

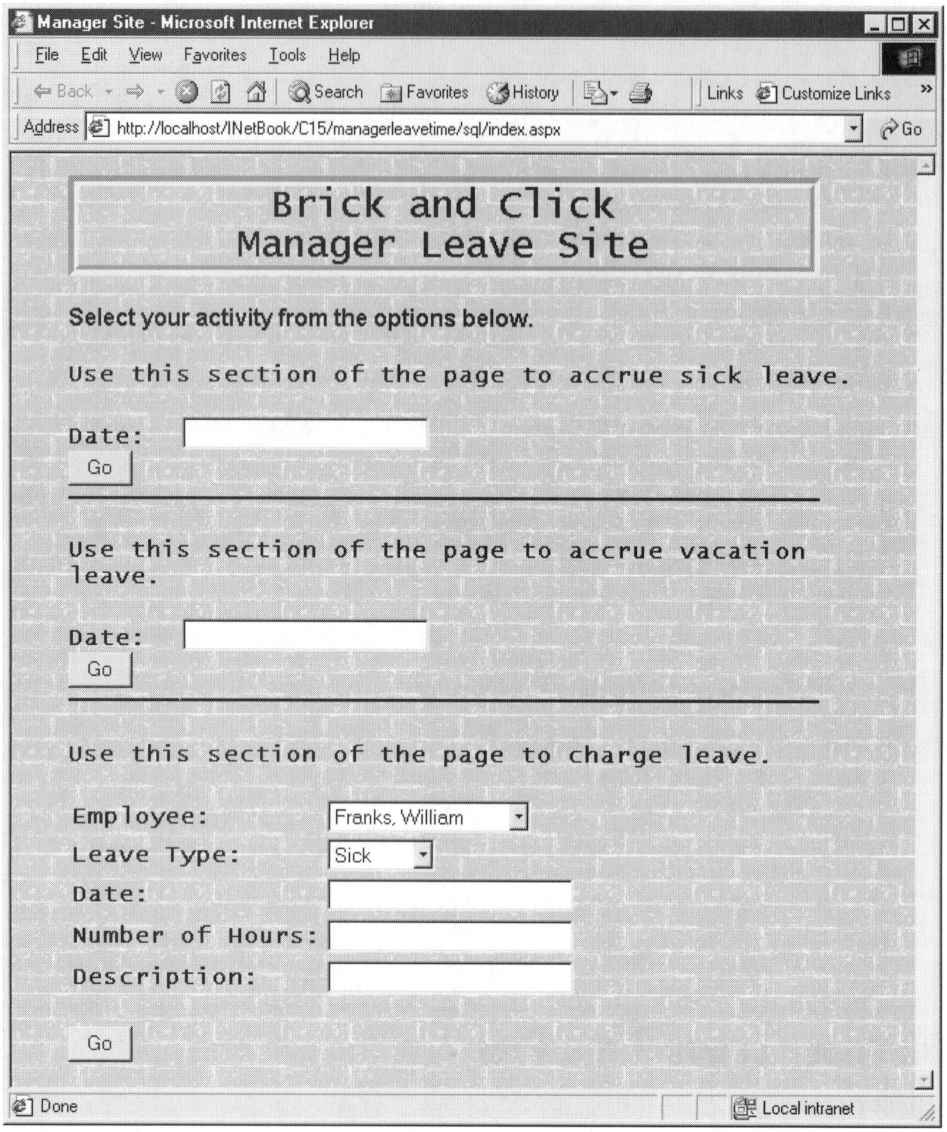

Figure 15-7 *Default view of Manager's page*

The page is divided into three parts. The top part of the page provides a way for the manager to add the monthly sick leave hours to all employees based on their accrual rate. When the manager does that, they see the message displayed in Figure 15-8.

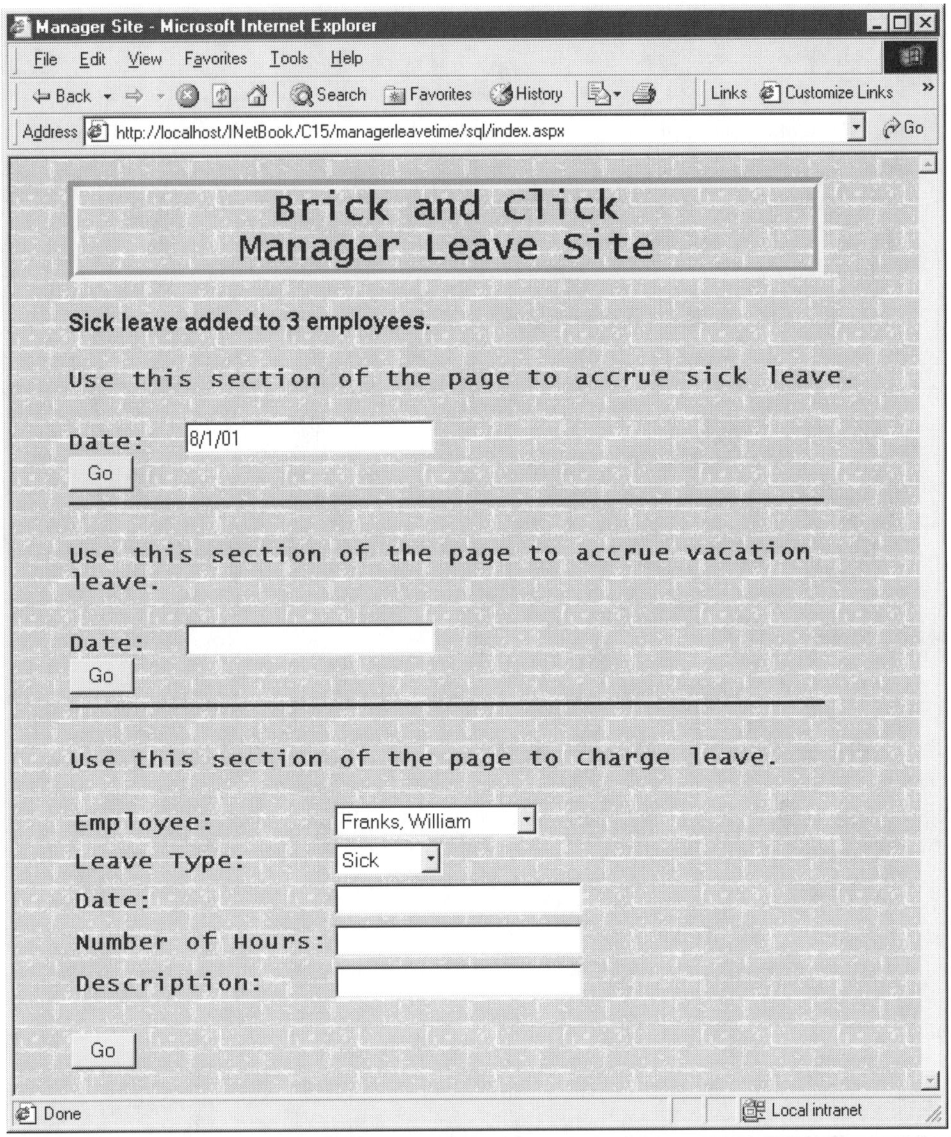

Figure 15-8 *View after adding sick leave records*

The manager receives feedback about the number of employee sick leave records that were processed.

In the middle of the page, the manager can add vacation hours for each employee. The manager enters the date for which the hours are effective and clicks the second Go button. When they do that, they see the page displayed in Figure 15-9.

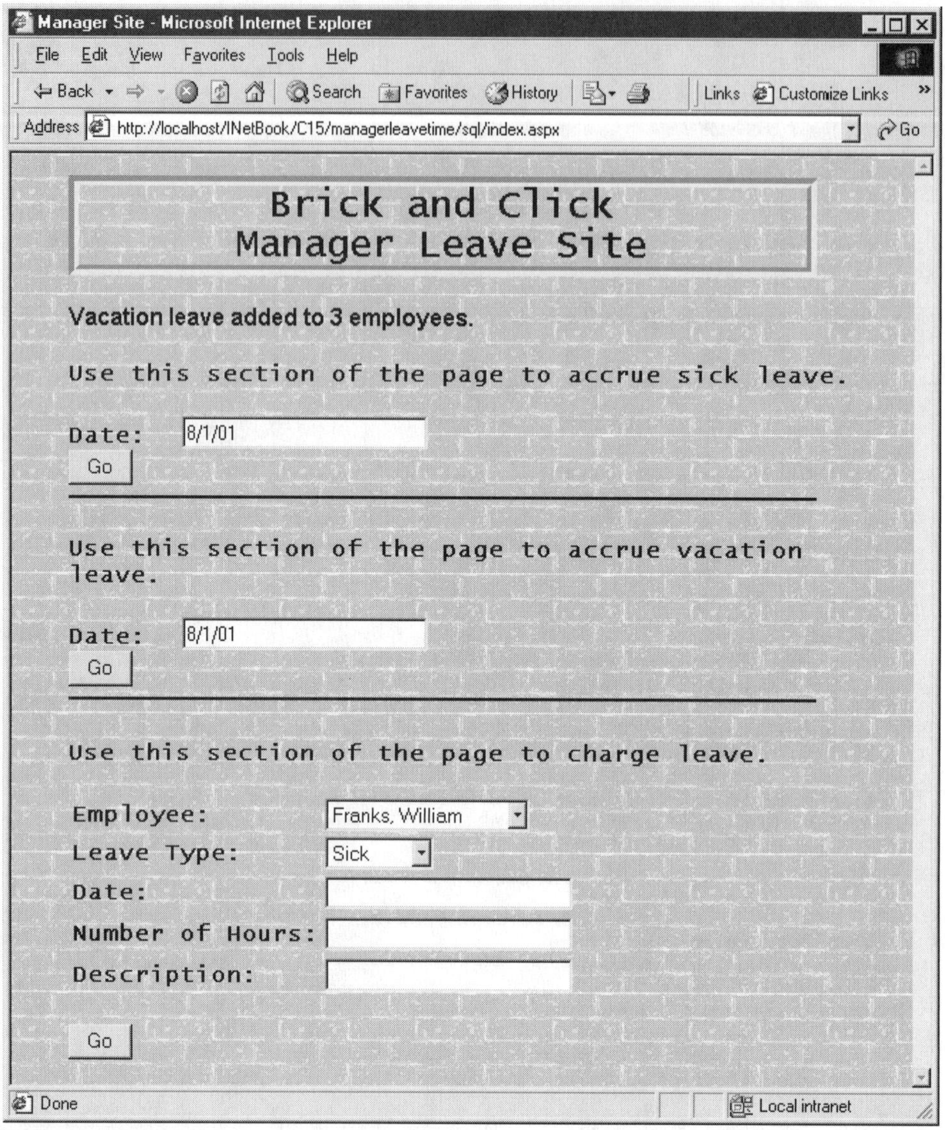

Figure 15-9 *Adding vacation leave records*

The manager receives the feedback that the records were added.

The bottom part of the form allows the manager to charge a specific employee with leave or to give an employee additional leave hours. Take a look at Figure 15-10.

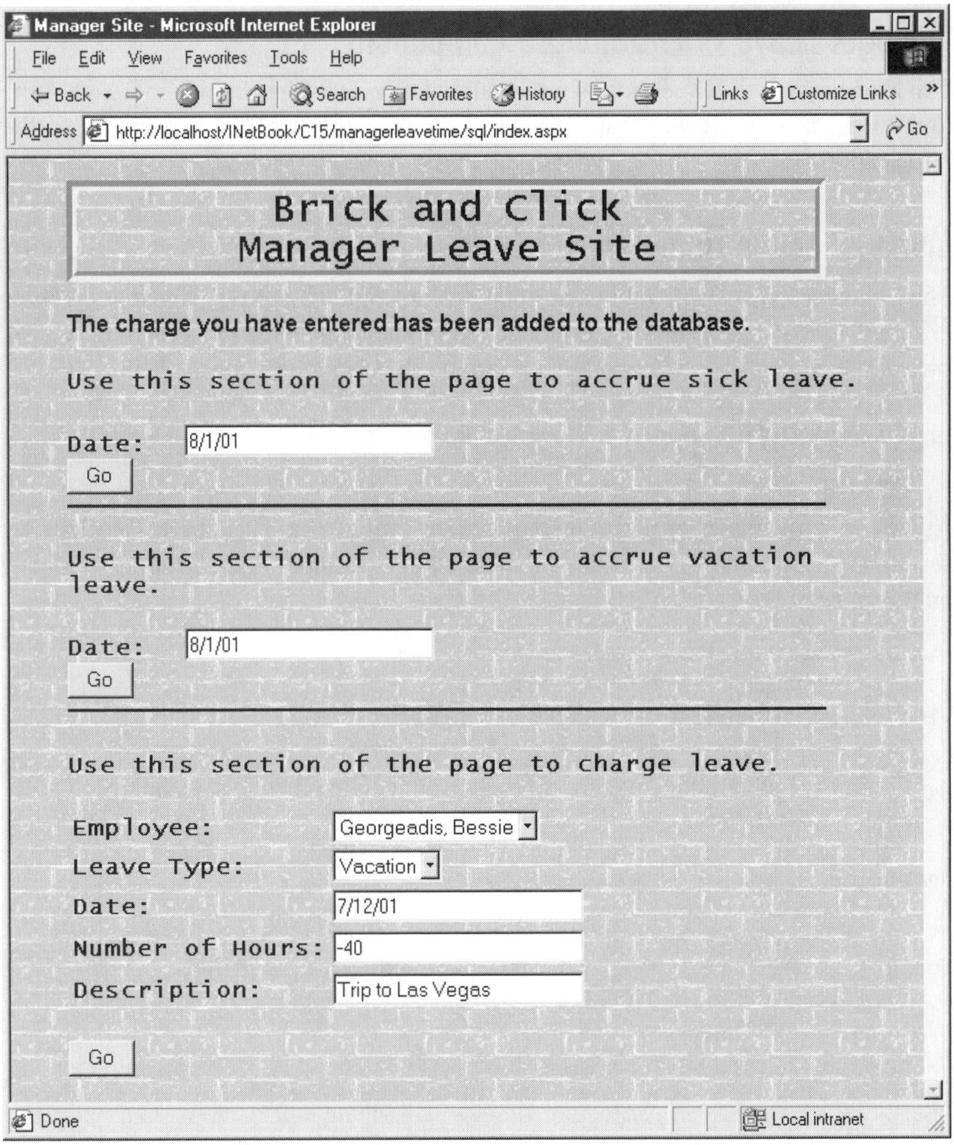

Figure 15-10 *Charging leave time to an employee*

Here an employee is being charged 40 hours of vacation time based on the date given. When the manager clicks the Go button, a record is added to either the sick leave or the vacation leave for the employee.

Manager Leave Time Database Component

The Manager Leave Time tool uses the same database as the Employee Leave Time tool. Please see a review of that database in the last section of this chapter for further information.

Manager Leave Time ASP.NET Code

The Manager Leave Time tool is composed of a single ASP.NET page that takes different actions based on the button clicked by the manager. In this section, we will review the controls contained on that page and the code it contains.

Manager ASP.NET Page

Index.aspx

At the top of the manager page, three compiler directives are declared. The first sets up the programming environment. The other two import data libraries needed on this page:

```
<%@ Page Language=VB Debug=true %>
<%@ Import Namespace="System.Data" %>
<%@ Import Namespace="System.Data.OLEDB" %>
```

Within the body of the page, the first control declared displays a label that contains some title text:

```
<asp:Label
    id="lblTitle"
    BorderWidth="7px"
    BorderStyle=6
    Width="90%"
    Font-Size="20pt"
    Font-Name="Lucida Console"
    Text="<center>Brick and Click<br>Manager Leave Site</center>"
    runat="server"
/>
```

The next label displays the status of the activity last chosen by the manager:

```
<asp:Label
    id="lblStatus"
    Font-Size="12pt"
    Font-Bold="True"
```

```
    Font-Name="Arial"
    Text="Select your activity from the options below."
    runat="server"
/>
```

Then in the sick leave section of the page, we have a TextBox control where the manager can enter the accrual date:

```
<asp:TextBox
    id="txtSickDate"
    Columns="25"
    MaxLength="30"
    runat=server
/>
```

That is followed by a button that the manager clicks when they want to add sick leave records:

```
<br><asp:button
    id="butSickLeave"
    text="  Go  "
    OnClick="SickLeave_Click"
    runat="server"
/>
```

In the vacation leave section of the page, we have another TextBox control for the accrual date

```
<asp:TextBox
    id="txtVacatDate"
    Columns="25"
    MaxLength="30"
    runat=server
/>
```

and a button to allow the manager to add vacation leave records:

```
<asp:button
    id="butVacatLeave"
    text="  Go  "
    OnClick="VacatLeave_Click"
    runat="server"
/>
```

The first control in the charge leave section of the page is a DropDownList control that provides a list of all the employees:

```
<asp:dropdownlist
    id="ddlEmpID"
    runat=server
    DataTextField="EmpName"
    DataValueField="EmpID">
</asp:dropdownlist>
```

Note that the manager sees the name of the employee:

```
DataTextField="EmpName"
```

But the ID of the employee is used in code:

```
DataValueField="EmpID"
```

The next control is another DropDownList control. It allows the manager to select whether the leave is sick leave or vacation leave:

```
<asp:dropdownlist
    id="ddlLeaveType"
    runat=server>
    <asp:ListItem Value="Sick">Sick</asp:ListItem>
    <asp:ListItem Value="Vacation">Vacation</asp:ListItem>
</asp:dropdownlist>
```

Those controls are followed by TextBox controls for the manager to enter the other charge leave fields. First, they enter the date that the charge is for:

```
<asp:TextBox
    id="txtDateUsed"
    Columns="25"
    MaxLength="30"
    runat=server
/>
```

Then the manager enters the number of hours being charged

```
<asp:TextBox
    id="txtNumHours"
    Columns="25"
```

```
    MaxLength="30"
    runat=server
/>
```

That is followed by the description of the charge:

```
<asp:TextBox
    id="txtDescription"
    Columns="25"
    MaxLength="255"
    runat=server
/>
```

Then the final button control, which when clicked processes the leave charge request, is defined on this page:

```
id="butChargeLeave"
    text="  Go  "
    OnClick="ChargeLeave_Click"
    runat="server"
/>
```

The code on the page is contained within four events. The first event fires when the page is loaded

```
Sub Page_Load(ByVal Sender as Object, ByVal E as EventArgs)
    If Not IsPostBack Then
        Dim DBConn as OleDbConnection
        Dim DBCommand As OleDbDataAdapter
        Dim DSPageData as New DataSet
        DBConn = New OleDbConnection("Provider=sqloledb;" _
            & "server=localhost;" _
            & "Initial Catalog=INETC15;" _
            & "User Id=sa;" _
            & "Password=yourpassword;")
        DBCommand = New OleDbDataAdapter _
            ("Select EmpLastName + ', ' + " _
            & "EmpFirstName as EmpName, EmpID " _
            & "From Employees Order By EmpLastName" _
            ,DBConn)
        DBCommand.Fill(DSPageData, _
            "EmpList")
        ddlEmpID.DataSource = _
```

```
            DSPageData.Tables("EmpList").DefaultView
        ddlEmpID.DataBind()
    End If
End Sub
```

We want this code to run only when the page is first loaded

```
If Not IsPostBack Then
```

Within this statement, we declare data objects so that we can retrieve data from the database:

```
Dim DBConn as OleDbConnection
Dim DBCommand As OleDbDataAdapter
Dim DSPageData as New DataSet
```

We start by connecting to our SQL Server database:

```
DBConn = New OleDbConnection("Provider=sqloledb;" _
    & "server=localhost;" _
    & "Initial Catalog=INETC15;" _
    & "User Id=sa;" _
    & "Password=yourpassword;")
```

And we place SQL text into our Data Adapter object to retrieve the name of the employee concatenated from their first and last names. Also, the ID of the employee is retrieved

```
DBCommand = New OleDbDataAdapter _
    ("Select EmpLastName + ', ' + " _
    & "EmpFirstName as EmpName, EmpID " _
    & "From Employees Order By EmpLastName" _
    ,DBConn)
```

That query is executed and the result placed in our DataSet object:

```
DBCommand.Fill(DSPageData, _
    "EmpList")
```

The employee DropDownList is bound to this DataSet:

```
ddlEmpID.DataSource = _
    DSPageData.Tables("EmpList").DefaultView
ddlEmpID.DataBind()
```

The next procedure fires when the Sick Leave button is clicked

```
Sub SickLeave_Click(Sender As Object, E As EventArgs)
```

We will need to retrieve data from, and insert data into, the database:

```
Dim DBConn as OleDbConnection
Dim DBCommand As OleDbDataAdapter
Dim DBInsert As New OleDbCommand
Dim DSEmpData as New DataSet
```

We also need a variable for a For block:

```
Dim I as Integer
```

We start by connecting to the database:

```
DBConn = New OleDbConnection("Provider=sqloledb;" _
    & "server=localhost;" _
    & "Initial Catalog=INETC15;" _
    & "User Id=sa;" _
    & "Password=yourpassword;")
```

We need to retrieve the ID of each employee, as well as their sick hour accrual rate:

```
DBCommand = New OleDbDataAdapter _
    ("Select EmpID, SickAccrualRate " _
    & "From Employees" _
    ,DBConn)
```

That data is placed into our DataSet object:

```
DBCommand.Fill(DSEmpData, _
    "EmpList")
```

Next, we initialize the connection of our Command object:

```
DBInsert.Connection = DBConn
DBInsert.Connection.Open
```

We then enter a loop so that we can process each of the employee records:

```
For I = 0 to DSEmpData.Tables("EmpList"). _
    Rows.Count - 1
```

We then add a record into the EmpSickActivity table for each of the employees based on their accrual rate

```
DBInsert.CommandText = "Insert Into " _
    & "EmpSickActivity (EmpID, ActivityDate, " _
    & "NumHours, TheNote) " _
    & "values (" _
    & DSEmpData.Tables("EmpList"). _
    Rows(I).Item("EmpID") & ", " _
    & "'" & txtSickDate.Text & "', " _
    & DSEmpData.Tables("EmpList"). _
    Rows(I).Item("SickAccrualRate") & ", " _
    & "'Monthly Accrual')"
DBInsert.ExecuteNonQuery()
```

before moving on to process the next record:

```
Next I
```

After the loop, we place text in our status label that tells the manager how many employee records were processed

```
lblStatus.Text = "Sick leave added to " _
    & DSEmpData.Tables("EmpList"). _
    Rows.Count & " employees."
```

The next procedure fires when the Vacation Leave button is clicked

```
Sub VacatLeave_Click(Sender As Object, E As EventArgs)
    Dim DBConn as OleDbConnection
    Dim DBCommand As OleDbDataAdapter
    Dim DBInsert As New OleDbCommand
    Dim DSEmpData as New DataSet
    Dim I as Integer
    DBConn = New OleDbConnection("Provider=sqloledb;" _
        & "server=localhost;" _
        & "Initial Catalog=INETC15;" _
        & "User Id=sa;" _
        & "Password=yourpassword;")
    DBCommand = New OleDbDataAdapter _
        ("Select EmpID, VacatAccrualRate " _
        & "From Employees" _
        ,DBConn)
    DBCommand.Fill(DSEmpData, _
        "EmpList")
```

```
    DBInsert.Connection = DBConn
    DBInsert.Connection.Open
    For I = 0 to DSEmpData.Tables("EmpList"). _
        Rows.Count - 1
        DBInsert.CommandText = "Insert Into " _
            & "EmpVacatActivity (EmpID, ActivityDate, " _
            & "NumHours, TheNote) " _
            & "values (" _
            & DSEmpData.Tables("EmpList"). _
            Rows(I).Item("EmpID") & ", " _
            & "'" & txtVacatDate.Text & "', " _
            & DSEmpData.Tables("EmpList"). _
            Rows(I).Item("VacatAccrualRate") & ", " _
            & "'Monthly Accrual')"
        DBInsert.ExecuteNonQuery()
    Next I
    lblStatus.Text = "Vacation leave added to " _
        & DSEmpData.Tables("EmpList"). _
        Rows.Count & " employees."
End Sub
```

Within this procedure, we need to accrue vacation hours for each employee. Therefore, we will need data objects

```
Dim DBConn as OleDbConnection
Dim DBCommand As OleDbDataAdapter
Dim DBInsert As New OleDbCommand
Dim DSEmpData as New DataSet
```

as well as a variable for a For block:

```
Dim I as Integer
```

We then connect up to our SQL Server database

```
DBConn = New OleDbConnection("Provider=sqloledb;" _
    & "server=localhost;" _
    & "Initial Catalog=INETC15;" _
    & "User Id=sa;" _
    & "Password=yourpassword;")
```

and retrieve a list of all the IDs of the employees with their vacation accrual rate:

```
DBCommand = New OleDbDataAdapter _
    ("Select EmpID, VacatAccrualRate " _
```

```
    & "From Employees" _
    ,DBConn)
```

Into our DataSet object:

```
DBCommand.Fill(DSEmpData, _
    "EmpList")
```

We then initialize the connection for our Command object

```
DBInsert.Connection = DBConn
DBInsert.Connection.Open
```

and enter a loop so that we can process each of the employee records:

```
For I = 0 to DSEmpData.Tables("EmpList"). _
    Rows.Count - 1
```

Within the loop, a record is added to the EmpVacatActivity table for each of the employees based on their accrual rate:

```
DBInsert.CommandText = "Insert Into " _
    & "EmpVacatActivity (EmpID, ActivityDate, " _
    & "NumHours, TheNote) " _
    & "values (" _
    & DSEmpData.Tables("EmpList"). _
    Rows(I).Item("EmpID") & ", " _
    & "'" & txtVacatDate.Text & "', " _
    & DSEmpData.Tables("EmpList"). _
    Rows(I).Item("VacatAccrualRate") & ", " _
    & "'Monthly Accrual')"
DBInsert.ExecuteNonQuery()
```

And then we move on to the next record:

```
Next I
```

After the loop, we display to the manager, through our status label, the number of employee records processed

```
lblStatus.Text = "Vacation leave added to " _
    & DSEmpData.Tables("EmpList"). _
    Rows.Count & " employees."
```

The last procedure fires when the Charge Leave button is clicked.

```
Sub ChargeLeave_Click(Sender As Object, E As EventArgs)
    Dim DBConn as OleDbConnection
    Dim DBInsert As New OleDbCommand
    DBConn = New OleDbConnection("Provider=sqloledb;" _
        & "server=localhost;" _
        & "Initial Catalog=INETC15;" _
        & "User Id=sa;" _
        & "Password=yourpassword;")
    DBInsert.Connection = DBConn
    DBInsert.Connection.Open
    If ddlLeaveType.SelectedItem.Text = "Sick" Then
        DBInsert.CommandText = "Insert Into " _
            & "EmpSickActivity (EmpID, ActivityDate, " _
            & "NumHours, TheNote) " _
            & "values (" _
            & ddlEmpID.SelectedItem.Value & ", " _
            & "'" & txtDateUsed.Text & "', " _
            & txtNumHours.Text & ", " _
            & "'" _
            & Replace(txtDescription.Text, "'", "''") _
            & "')"
    Else
        DBInsert.CommandText = "Insert Into " _
            & "EmpVacatActivity (EmpID, ActivityDate, " _
            & "NumHours, TheNote) " _
            & "values (" _
            & ddlEmpID.SelectedItem.Value & ", " _
            & "'" & txtDateUsed.Text & "', " _
            & txtNumHours.Text & ", " _
            & "'" _
            & Replace(txtDescription.Text, "'", "''") _
            & "')"
    End If
    DBInsert.ExecuteNonQuery()
    lblStatus.Text = "The charge you have entered has " _
        & "been added to the database."
End Sub
```

Within this procedure, we will need a Connection object and a Command object:

```
Dim DBConn as OleDbConnection
Dim DBInsert As New OleDbCommand
```

A connection to the database is established

```
DBConn = New OleDbConnection("Provider=sqloledb;" _
    & "server=localhost;" _
    & "Initial Catalog=INETC15;" _
    & "User Id=sa;" _
    & "Password=yourpassword;")
```

that will be used by our Command object:

```
DBInsert.Connection = DBConn
DBInsert.Connection.Open
```

We then check to see if the manager is charging sick leave to an employee:

```
If ddlLeaveType.SelectedItem.Text = "Sick" Then
```

If so, a record is added to the EmpSickActivity table based on the text entered by the manager on that section of the form:

```
DBInsert.CommandText = "Insert Into " _
    & "EmpSickActivity (EmpID, ActivityDate, " _
    & "NumHours, TheNote) " _
    & "values (" _
    & ddlEmpID.SelectedItem.Value & ", " _
    & "'" & txtDateUsed.Text & "', " _
    & txtNumHours.Text & ", " _
    & "'" _
    & Replace(txtDescription.Text, "'", "''") _
    & "')"
```

Otherwise, a record is added to the EmpVacatActivity table:

```
DBInsert.CommandText = "Insert Into " _
    & "EmpVacatActivity (EmpID, ActivityDate, " _
    & "NumHours, TheNote) " _
    & "values (" _
    & ddlEmpID.SelectedItem.Value & ", " _
    & "'" & txtDateUsed.Text & "', " _
    & txtNumHours.Text & ", " _
    & "'" _
    & Replace(txtDescription.Text, "'", "''") _
    & "')"
    End If
```

Regardless of which table is being added to, we execute the Command object

```
DBInsert.ExecuteNonQuery()
```

and inform the manager of the action taken

```
lblStatus.Text = "The charge you have entered has " _
    & "been added to the database."
```

Access Code Changes

The only code change that should be needed for this solution to work with Access is to change the connection object

```
DBConn = New OleDbConnection("Provider=sqloledb;" _
    & "server=localhost;" _
    & "Initial Catalog=INETC15;" _
    & "User Id=sa;" _
    & "Password=yourpassword;")
```

to something like this that points to the location of your Access database:

```
DBConn = New OleDbConnection("PROVIDER=Microsoft.Jet.OLEDB.4.0;" _
    & "DATA SOURCE=" _
    & Server.MapPath("/INetBook/C15/EmpLeaveTime/" _
    & "Access/C15EmpLeaveTime.mdb;"))
```

Employee of the Month Tool

Index.aspx

The Employee of the Month tool provides a simple way for you to give recognition to one of your company's employees. The page displays whichever employee is the current employee of the month.

Sample Usage

Figure 15-11 shows the Employee of the Month page.

The page displays a combination of fixed text and database information for the current employee of the month.

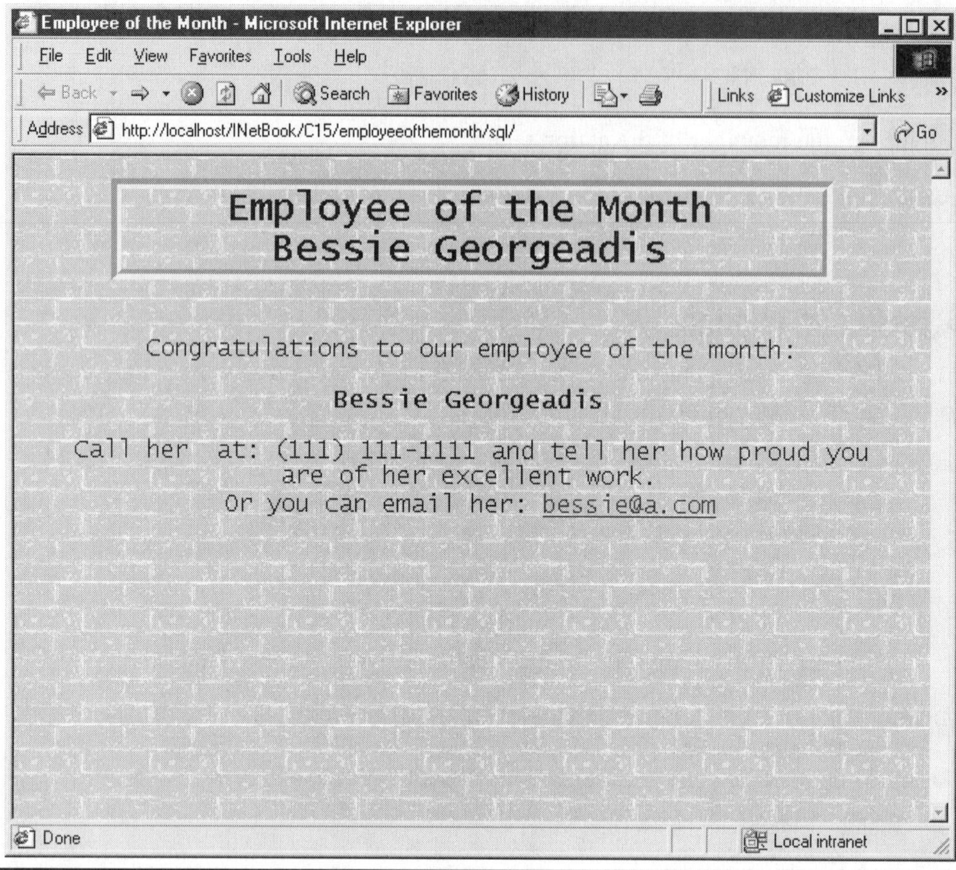

Figure 15-11 *Employee of the Month page*

Employee of the Month Database Component

The Employee of the Month database uses the same employee database discussed in the previous two sections of this chapter. It does make one change. It adds a new field of type bit to the Employees table called EmployeeOfTheMonth. The field needs to contain a value of one for the current employee of the month. In Access, the field was implemented as a Yes/No field.

Employee of the Month ASP.NET Code

The Employee of the Month tool is composed of a single ASP.NET page. In this section, we will review that page.

Employee of the Month ASP.NET Page

Index.aspx

The code on the Employee of the Month page displays information on the current recipient of the employee of the month award. At the top of the page, three compiler directives are written.

```
<%@ Page Language=VB Debug=true %>
<%@ Import Namespace="System.Data" %>
<%@ Import Namespace="System.Data.OLEDB" %>
```

The first directive tells the compiler the language we are using, VB, and that we are in debug mode:

```
<%@ Page Language=VB Debug=true %>
```

The other two are needed so that we can gain access to our database component:

```
<%@ Import Namespace="System.Data" %>
<%@ Import Namespace="System.Data.OLEDB" %>
```

Within the body of the page, we have two labels. The first displays the title text of the page:

```
<asp:Label
    id="lblTitle"
    BorderWidth="7px"
    BorderStyle=6
    Width="90%"
    Font-Size="20pt"
    Font-Name="Lucida Console"
    runat="server"
/>
```

The other label will display the information about the employee of the month:

```
<asp:Label
    id="lblMessage"
    Font-Size="13pt"
    Font-Name="Lucida Console"
    runat="server"
/>
```

The code on the page fires when the page is loaded.

```
Sub Page_Load(ByVal Sender as Object, ByVal E as EventArgs)
    Dim DBConn as OleDbConnection
    Dim DBCommand As OleDbDataAdapter
    Dim DSPageData as New DataSet
    DBConn = New OleDbConnection("Provider=sqloledb;" _
        & "server=localhost;" _
        & "Initial Catalog=INETC15;" _
        & "User Id=sa;" _
        & "Password=yourpassword;")
    DBCommand = New OleDbDataAdapter _
        ("Select EmpFirstName + ' ' + " _
        & "EmpLastName as EmpName, " _
        & "EmailAddress, PhoneNumber " _
        & "From Employees Where " _
        & "EmployeeOfTheMonth = 1", DBConn)
    DBCommand.Fill(DSPageData, _
        "EmpOfTheMonth")
    lblTitle.Text="<center>Employee of the Month<br>" _
        & DSPageData.Tables("EmpOfTheMonth"). _
        Rows(0).Item("EmpName") _
        & "</center>"
    lblMessage.Text = "<center>Congratulations to our " _
        & "employee of the month:<br><br><b>" _
        & DSPageData.Tables("EmpOfTheMonth"). _
        Rows(0).Item("EmpName") & "</b><br><br>" _
        & "Call her at: " _
        & DSPageData.Tables("EmpOfTheMonth"). _
        Rows(0).Item("PhoneNumber") _
        & " and tell her how proud you are of her " _
        & "excellent work.<br>Or you can email her: " _
        & "<a href=""mailto:" _
        & DSPageData.Tables("EmpOfTheMonth"). _
        Rows(0).Item("EmailAddress") _
        & """>" & DSPageData.Tables("EmpOfTheMonth"). _
        Rows(0).Item("EmailAddress") _
        & "</a>"
End Sub
```

Within the code block, we will need data objects:

```
Dim DBConn as OleDbConnection
Dim DBCommand As OleDbDataAdapter
Dim DSPageData as New DataSet
```

We start by connecting to our database:

```
DBConn = New OleDbConnection("Provider=sqloledb;" _
    & "server=localhost;" _
    & "Initial Catalog=INETC15;" _
    & "User Id=sa;" _
    & "Password=yourpassword;")
```

Next, we place SQL text that retrieves the needed information for the employee who is marked as the employee of the month into our Data Adapter object:

```
DBCommand = New OleDbDataAdapter _
    ("Select EmpFirstName + ' ' + " _
    & "EmpLastName as EmpName, " _
    & "EmailAddress, PhoneNumber " _
    & "From Employees Where " _
    & "EmployeeOfTheMonth = 1", DBConn)
```

The result of running that query is placed into our DataSet object:

```
DBCommand.Fill(DSPageData, _
    "EmpOfTheMonth")
```

The name of the employee is placed with some fixed text into our title label:

```
lblTitle.Text="<center>Employee of the Month<br>" _
    & DSPageData.Tables("EmpOfTheMonth"). _
    Rows(0).Item("EmpName") _
    & "</center>"
```

Similarly, we place the basic information about the employee with fixed text into the message label:

```
lblMessage.Text = "<center>Congratulations to our " _
    & "employee of the month:<br><br><b>" _
    & DSPageData.Tables("EmpOfTheMonth"). _
    Rows(0).Item("EmpName") & "</b><br><br>" _
    & "Call her at: " _
    & DSPageData.Tables("EmpOfTheMonth"). _
    Rows(0).Item("PhoneNumber") _
    & " and tell her how proud you are of her " _
    & "excellent work.<br>Or you can email her: " _
    & "<a href=""mailto:" _
    & DSPageData.Tables("EmpOfTheMonth"). _
    Rows(0).Item("EmailAddress") _
```

```
    & """>" & DSPageData.Tables("EmpOfTheMonth"). _
    Rows(0).Item("EmailAddress") _
    & "</a>"
```

Access Code Changes

We need to make two changes to our Employee of the Month tool to make it work with Access instead of SQL Server. The first change that should be needed for this solution to work with Access is to change the connection object

```
DBConn = New OleDbConnection("Provider=sqloledb;" _
    & "server=localhost;" _
    & "Initial Catalog=INETC15;" _
    & "User Id=sa;" _
    & "Password=yourpassword;")
```

to something like this that points to the location of your Access database:

```
DBConn = New OleDbConnection("PROVIDER=Microsoft.Jet.OLEDB.4.0;" _
    & "DATA SOURCE=" _
    & Server.MapPath("/INetBook/C15/EmpLeaveTime/" _
    & "Access/C15EmpLeaveTime.mdb;"))
```

Access does not correctly convert the value of one in this Where clause to True. So this needs to be changed

```
DBCommand = New OleDbDataAdapter _
    ("Select EmpFirstName + ' ' + " _
    & "EmpLastName as EmpName, " _
    & "EmailAddress, PhoneNumber " _
    & "From Employees Where " _
    & "EmployeeOfTheMonth = 1", DBConn)
```

to this:

```
DBCommand = New OleDbDataAdapter _
    ("Select EmpFirstName + ' ' + " _
    & "EmpLastName as EmpName, " _
    & "EmailAddress, PhoneNumber " _
    & "From Employees Where " _
    & "EmployeeOfTheMonth = True", DBConn)
```

Job Board Tool

When the visitor first enters the Job Board tool, they see the page displayed in Figure 15-12.

The Job Board page displays basic information about all the jobs available. The visitor can then click one of the job titles to see the Job Information page displayed in Figure 15-13.

The Job Information page displays all the data about the job. Here the visitor can find out if they are qualified for the job and who to contact if they are interested.

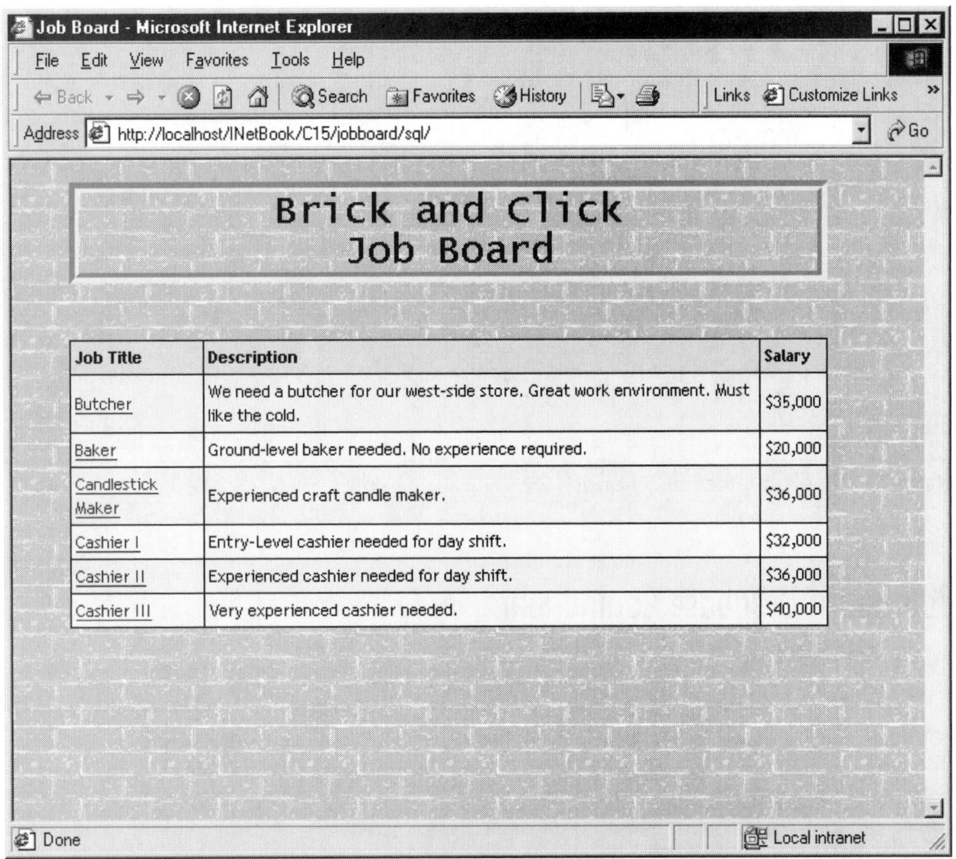

Figure 15-12 *Job Board page*

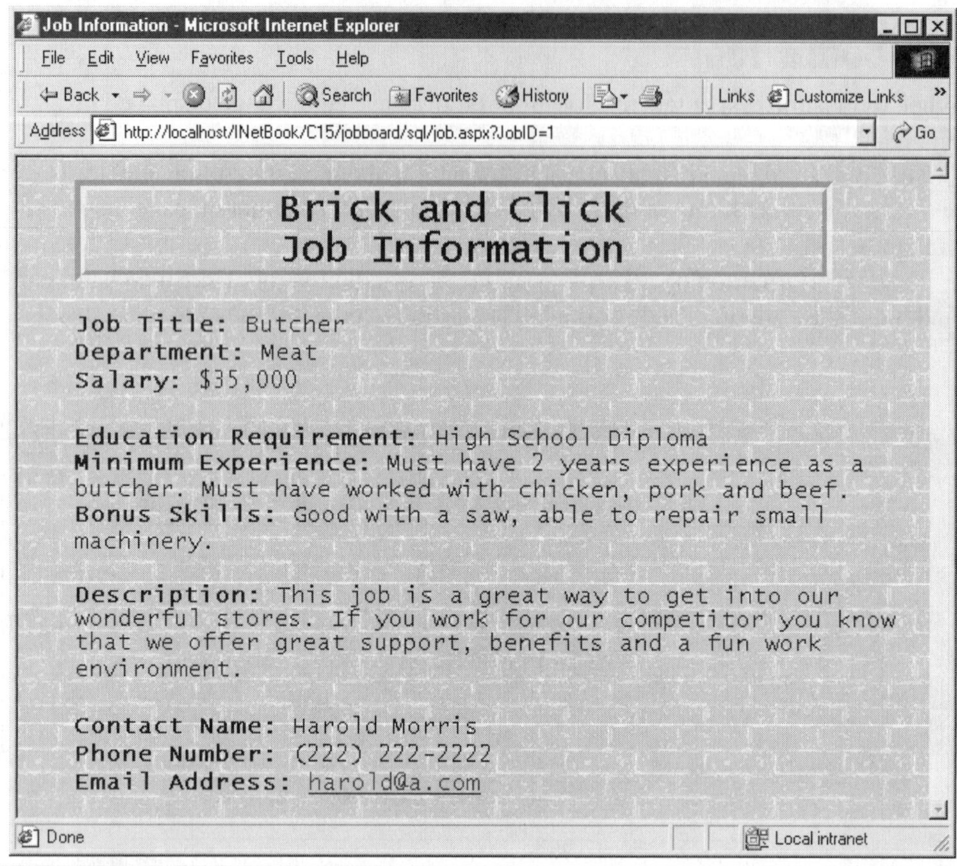

Figure 15-13 *Job Information page*

Job Board Database Component

C15JobBoard.sql

The Job Board tool requires one table for its functionality. That table contains all the job information. In this section, we will review the fields within that table.

Jobs Field Specifications

Jobs.txt

The field specifications for the fields in the Jobs table are displayed in Table 15-4.

The JobID field is the primary key for this table. Note the two different description fields, BriefDescription and LongDescription. The BriefDescription field is used on

Field Name	Field Type	Notes
JobID	int	Primary Key, Identity Column
JobTitle	varchar	Length = 50
BriefDescription	varchar	Length = 100
Department	varchar	Length =50
Salary	varchar	Length =50
EdReq	varchar	Length =255
MinExp	varchar	Length =255
BonusSkills	varchar	Length =255
LongDescription	text	
ContactName	varchar	Length =100
ContactPhoneNumber	varchar	Length =50
ContactEmailAddress	varchar	Length =50

Table 15-4 *Jobs Field Specifications*

the DataGrid on the Job Board page, while the LongDescription field is used on the Job Information page. The rest of the fields store other basic information about the job as it is displayed either on the Job Board page or the Job Information page.

Job Board ASP.NET Code

The Job Board tool is composed of two ASP.NET pages. In this section, we will review the code on the controls used on those pages.

Job Board ASP.NET Page

Index.aspx

The Job Board page displays all the jobs available to the visitor through a DataGrid control. At the top of the page, three compiler directives are defined that are required for the page's functionality:

```
<%@ Page Language=VB Debug=true %>
<%@ Import Namespace="System.Data" %>
<%@ Import Namespace="System.Data.OLEDB" %>
```

Within the body of the page, two controls are defined. The first one displays title text to the visitor:

```
<asp:Label
    id="lblTitle"
    BorderWidth="7px"
    BorderStyle=6
    Width="90%"
    Font-Size="20pt"
    Font-Name="Lucida Console"
    Text="<center>Brick and Click<br>Job Board</center>"
    runat="server"
/>
```

The other one displays the list of jobs to the visitor:

```
<asp:DataGrid id="dgJobList" runat="server"
    Width="90%"
    BackColor="beige"
    AlternatingItemStyle-BackColor="cornsilk"
    BorderColor="black"
    CellPadding=3
    CellSpacing="0"
    Font-Name="Trebuchet MS"
    Font-Size="8pt"
    ForeColor="Black"
    HeaderStyle-BackColor="burlywood"
    HeaderStyle-Font-Bold="True"
/>
```

All the code for the page is contained within a single event. That event fires when the page is loaded.

```
Sub Page_Load(ByVal Sender as Object, ByVal E as EventArgs)
    Dim DBConn as OleDbConnection
    Dim DBCommand As OleDbDataAdapter
    Dim DSPageData as New DataSet
    DBConn = New OleDbConnection("Provider=sqloledb;" _
        & "server=localhost;" _
        & "Initial Catalog=INETC15;" _
        & "User Id=sa;" _
        & "Password=yourpassword;")
    DBCommand = New OleDbDataAdapter _
```

```
        ("Select '<a href=""./job.aspx?JobID=' + " _
        & "convert(varchar(10), JobID) + '"">' + " _
        & "JobTitle + '</a>' as [Job Title], " _
        & "BriefDescription as [Description], " _
        & "Salary from Jobs", DBConn)
    DBCommand.Fill(DSPageData, _
        "JobList")
    dgJobList.DataSource = _
        DSPageData.Tables("JobList").DefaultView
    dgJobList.DataBind
End Sub
```

The page requires data objects so that we can retrieve and display the job listings to the visitor:

```
Dim DBConn as OleDbConnection
Dim DBCommand As OleDbDataAdapter
Dim DSPageData as New DataSet
```

We start by connecting to our database:

```
DBConn = New OleDbConnection("Provider=sqloledb;" _
    & "server=localhost;" _
    & "Initial Catalog=INETC15;" _
    & "User Id=sa;" _
    & "Password=yourpassword;")
```

We then retrieve the basic information about each job for the DataGrid. Note how the JobID field and the JobTitle field are combined with HTML to return a field that links to the Job Information page aliased as Job Title:

```
DBCommand = New OleDbDataAdapter _
    ("Select '<a href=""./job.aspx?JobID=' + " _
    & "convert(varchar(10), JobID) + '"">' + " _
    & "JobTitle + '</a>' as [Job Title], " _
    & "BriefDescription as [Description], " _
    & "Salary from Jobs", DBConn)
```

The results of running that query are placed into our DataSet object:

```
DBCommand.Fill(DSPageData, _
    "JobList")
```

Then we bind our DataGrid to that DataSet object, which will automatically display all the columns in the underlying table that it is bound to:

```
dgJobList.DataSource = _
    DSPageData.Tables("JobList").DefaultView
dgJobList.DataBind
```

Job Information ASP.NET Page

Job.aspx

The Job Information page displays all the information about the job through a series of Label controls. At the top of the page, you will find the same three compiler directives:

```
<%@ Page Language=VB Debug=true %>
<%@ Import Namespace="System.Data" %>
<%@ Import Namespace="System.Data.OLEDB" %>
```

Then in the body of the page, a Label control is defined for the title of the page:

```
<asp:Label
    id="lblTitle"
    BorderWidth="7px"
    BorderStyle=6
    Width="90%"
    Font-Size="20pt"
    Font-Name="Lucida Console"
    Text="<center>Brick and Click<br>Job Information</center>"
    runat="server"
/>
```

The rest of the page is made up of a series of Label controls that are identical to this one:

```
<asp:Label
    id="lblJobTitle"
    Font-Size="12pt"
    Font-Name="Lucida Console"
    runat="server"
/>
```

Placed into each of these labels is the data for the specific field that they are named for. So in this one, the title of the job is displayed.

The code on this page runs when the page is loaded.

```
Sub Page_Load(ByVal Sender as Object, ByVal E as EventArgs)
    If Len(Request.QueryString("JobID")) = 0 Then
        Response.Redirect("./index.aspx")
    End If
    Dim DBConn as OleDbConnection
    Dim DBCommand As OleDbDataAdapter
    Dim DSPageData as New DataSet
    DBConn = New OleDbConnection("Provider=sqloledb;" _
        & "server=localhost;" _
        & "Initial Catalog=INETC15;" _
        & "User Id=sa;" _
        & "Password=yourpassword;")
    DBCommand = New OleDbDataAdapter _
        ("Select * from Jobs Where " _
        & "JobID = " & Request.QueryString("JobID") _
        , DBConn)
    DBCommand.Fill(DSPageData, _
        "Job")
    lblJobTitle.Text="<b>Job Title:</b> " _
        & DSPageData.Tables("Job"). _
        Rows(0).Item("JobTitle")
    lblDepartment.Text="<b>Department:</b> " _
        & DSPageData.Tables("Job"). _
        Rows(0).Item("Department")
    lblSalary.Text="<b>Salary:</b> " _
        & DSPageData.Tables("Job"). _
        Rows(0).Item("Salary")
    lblEdReq.Text="<b>Education Requirement:</b> " _
        & DSPageData.Tables("Job"). _
        Rows(0).Item("EdReq")
    lblMinExp.Text="<b>Minimum Experience:</b> " _
        & DSPageData.Tables("Job"). _
        Rows(0).Item("MinExp")
    lblBonusSkills.Text="<b>Bonus Skills:</b> " _
        & DSPageData.Tables("Job"). _
        Rows(0).Item("BonusSkills")
    lblLongDescription.Text="<b>Description:</b> " _
        & DSPageData.Tables("Job"). _
        Rows(0).Item("LongDescription")
    lblContactName.Text="<b>Contact Name:</b> " _
        & DSPageData.Tables("Job"). _
        Rows(0).Item("ContactName")
    lblContactPhoneNumber.Text="<b>Phone Number:</b> " _
        & DSPageData.Tables("Job"). _
```

```
        Rows(0).Item("ContactPhoneNumber")
    lblContactEmailAddress.Text="<b>Email Address:</b> " _
        & "<a href=""mailto:" & DSPageData.Tables("Job"). _
        Rows(0).Item("ContactEmailAddress") _
        & """>" & DSPageData.Tables("Job"). _
        Rows(0).Item("ContactEmailAddress") & "</a>"
End Sub
```

We start by making sure that the page was entered with a JobID passed in:

```
If Len(Request.QueryString("JobID")) = 0 Then
```

If it wasn't, the visitor is sent back to the Job Board page:

```
Response.Redirect("./index.aspx")
```

Otherwise, we can declare the needed data objects

```
Dim DBConn as OleDbConnection
Dim DBCommand As OleDbDataAdapter
Dim DSPageData as New DataSet
```

and connect to our SQL Server database:

```
DBConn = New OleDbConnection("Provider=sqloledb;" _
    & "server=localhost;" _
    & "Initial Catalog=INETC15;" _
    & "User Id=sa;" _
    & "Password=yourpassword;")
```

Next, we retrieve all the information for the job based on the ID that was passed into this page:

```
DBCommand = New OleDbDataAdapter _
    ("Select * from Jobs Where " _
    & "JobID = " & Request.QueryString("JobID") _
    , DBConn)
DBCommand.Fill(DSPageData, _
    "Job")
```

Those fields retrieved are then placed into the corresponding label controls. First, the title of the job:

```
lblJobTitle.Text="<b>Job Title:</b> " _
    & DSPageData.Tables("Job"). _
    Rows(0).Item("JobTitle")
```

Then the department of the job:

```
lblDepartment.Text="<b>Department:</b> " _
    & DSPageData.Tables("Job"). _
    Rows(0).Item("Department")
```

That is followed by the salary information. Note that the field date is combined with text that names the field that will appear in bold:

```
lblSalary.Text="<b>Salary:</b> " _
    & DSPageData.Tables("Job"). _
    Rows(0).Item("Salary")
```

After that, the requirements and skills fields:

```
lblEdReq.Text="<b>Education Requirement:</b> " _
    & DSPageData.Tables("Job"). _
    Rows(0).Item("EdReq")
lblMinExp.Text="<b>Minimum Experience:</b> " _
    & DSPageData.Tables("Job"). _
    Rows(0).Item("MinExp")
lblBonusSkills.Text="<b>Bonus Skills:</b> " _
    & DSPageData.Tables("Job"). _
    Rows(0).Item("BonusSkills")
```

Next, the long description appears

```
lblLongDescription.Text="<b>Description:</b> " _
    & DSPageData.Tables("Job"). _
    Rows(0).Item("LongDescription")
```

followed by the contact information:

```
lblContactName.Text="<b>Contact Name:</b> " _
    & DSPageData.Tables("Job"). _
    Rows(0).Item("ContactName")
lblContactPhoneNumber.Text="<b>Phone Number:</b> " _
    & DSPageData.Tables("Job"). _
    Rows(0).Item("ContactPhoneNumber")
```

Note that the e-mail address field appears as a link to that e-mail address so that when the visitor clicks it, a new e-mail window opens:

```
lblContactEmailAddress.Text="<b>Email Address:</b> " _
    & "<a href=""mailto:" & DSPageData.Tables("Job"). _
    Rows(0).Item("ContactEmailAddress") _
    & """>" & DSPageData.Tables("Job"). _
    Rows(0).Item("ContactEmailAddress") & "</a>"
```

Access Code Changes

C15JobBoard.mdb

Two changes were needed for this tool to work with an Access database instead of a SQL Server database. First, we need to change the connect string from the SQL Server string

```
DBConn = New OleDbConnection("Provider=sqloledb;" _
    & "server=localhost;" _
    & "Initial Catalog=INETC15;" _
    & "User Id=sa;" _
    & "Password=yourpassword;")
```

to a string that refers to the location of the Access database:

```
DBConn = New OleDbConnection("PROVIDER=Microsoft.Jet.OLEDB.4.0;" _
    & "DATA SOURCE=" _
    & Server.MapPath("/INetBook/C15/JobBoard/" _
    & "Access/C15JobBoard.mdb;"))
```

The other change has to do with the query found on the Job Board page. In the SQL Server version, we needed to convert the int JobID field to a varchar field so that it could be concatenated with the JobTitle field. We also used the "+" character as the concatenation character:

```
DBCommand = New OleDbDataAdapter _
    ("Select '<a href=""./job.aspx?JobID=' + " _
    & "convert(varchar(10), JobID) + '"">' + " _
    & "JobTitle + '</a>' as [Job Title], " _
    & "BriefDescription as [Description], " _
    & "Salary from Jobs", DBConn)
```

In Access, there is no Convert function and no replacement is required. Also, the concatenation character in Access is the "&" character:

```
DBCommand = New OleDbDataAdapter _
    ("Select '<a href="".job.aspx?JobID=' & " _
    & "JobID & '"">' & " _
    & "JobTitle & '</a>' as [Job Title], " _
    & "BriefDescription as [Description], " _
    & "Salary from Jobs", DBConn)
```

No other code changes were needed.

CHAPTER

16

Increasing Site Traffic with Fun Functionality

For many sites in many situations, you may need to add functionality to your site that doesn't directly benefit the site owners. But indirectly, the increased traffic of adding fun tools to your site justifies adding ancillary functionality.

In this chapter, we will review three solutions that provide this traffic-improving quality to your site.

First, we will look at the Classifieds application. This tool allows visitors to browse or search through classifieds entered by other visitors to your site. The visitor can then add their own ad, or they can remove the classified ad.

Then we will look at the Birthday Card tool. This tool allows the visitor to send a message out to someone whose birthday it is. That person then clicks a link in their e-mail to receive their online birthday card.

The other tool we will look at is the simple one-page Movie Listing page. This tool lists movies and their show times at local theatres.

Classifieds Tool

The Classifieds tool allows visitors to browse through categories of classified ads or to search through the ads database. With this tool, the visitor can also add their own classified ad or remove an ad that they previously placed.

Sample Usage

When the visitor enters the Classifieds site, they see the page displayed in Figure 16-1.

From this page, the visitor can start looking at ads by entering a search phrase in the TextBox control. Here, the visitor has entered the text "like new." When they click OK, they will see the Ad List page displayed in Figure 16-2.

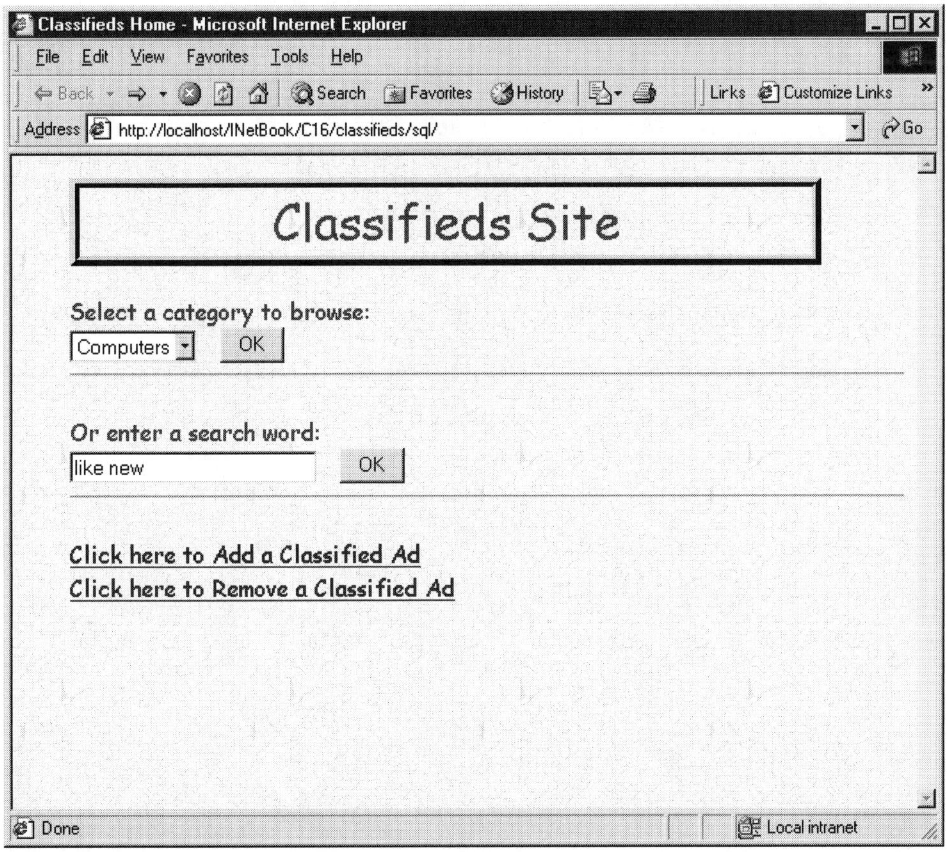

Figure 16-1 *Classifieds Home page*

At the top of the page, the visitor sees how many ads matched their search. The search text can be found anywhere in the title of the product or in the description of the product.

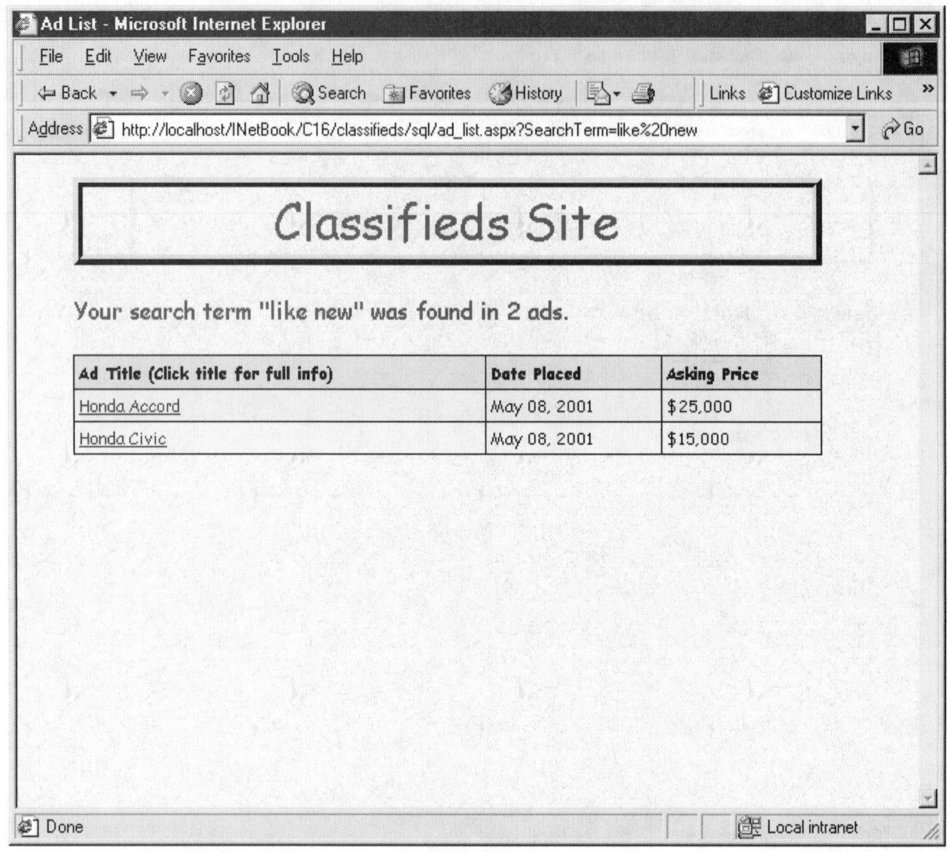

Figure 16-2 *Ad List page with search results*

Back on the Home page, the visitor can also elect to view all the products in a particular category. They do this by selecting the desired category and clicking OK. The results of doing this with the Electronics category are displayed in Figure 16-3.

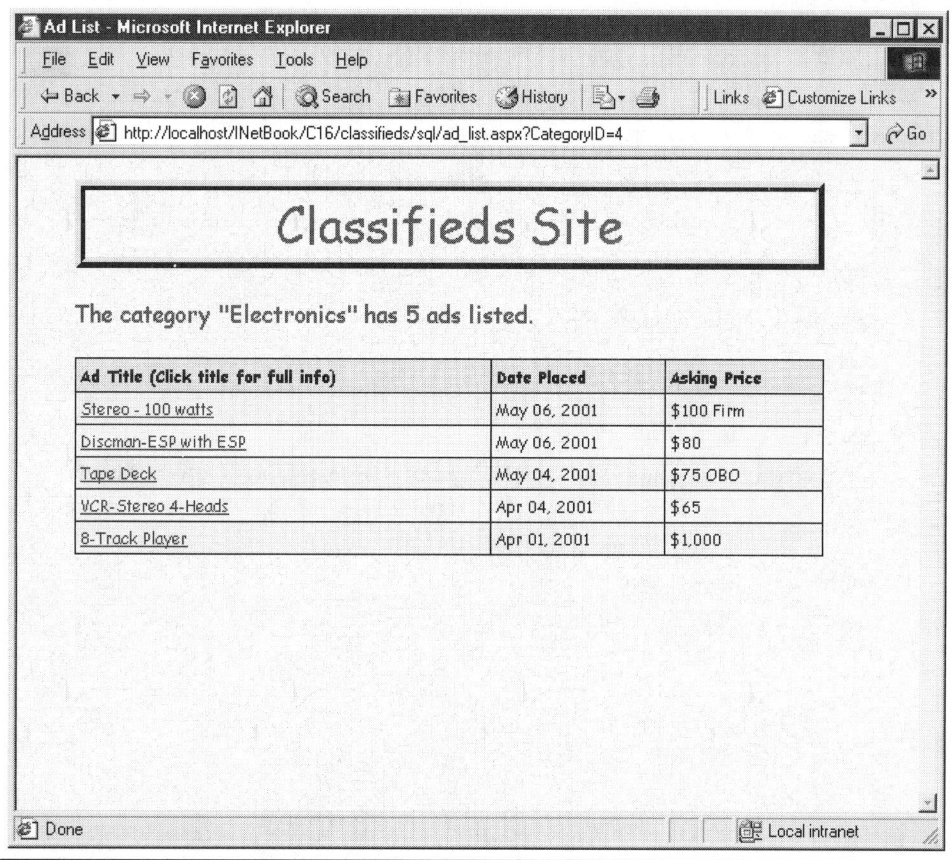

Figure 16-3 *Ad List displaying ads in a category*

Here, the visitor sees the number of ads in the category they selected. In the DataGrid, the visitor can view the basic information for the matching ads. If the visitor clicks the name of one of the ads, they see the full information for the ad as shown in Figure 16-4.

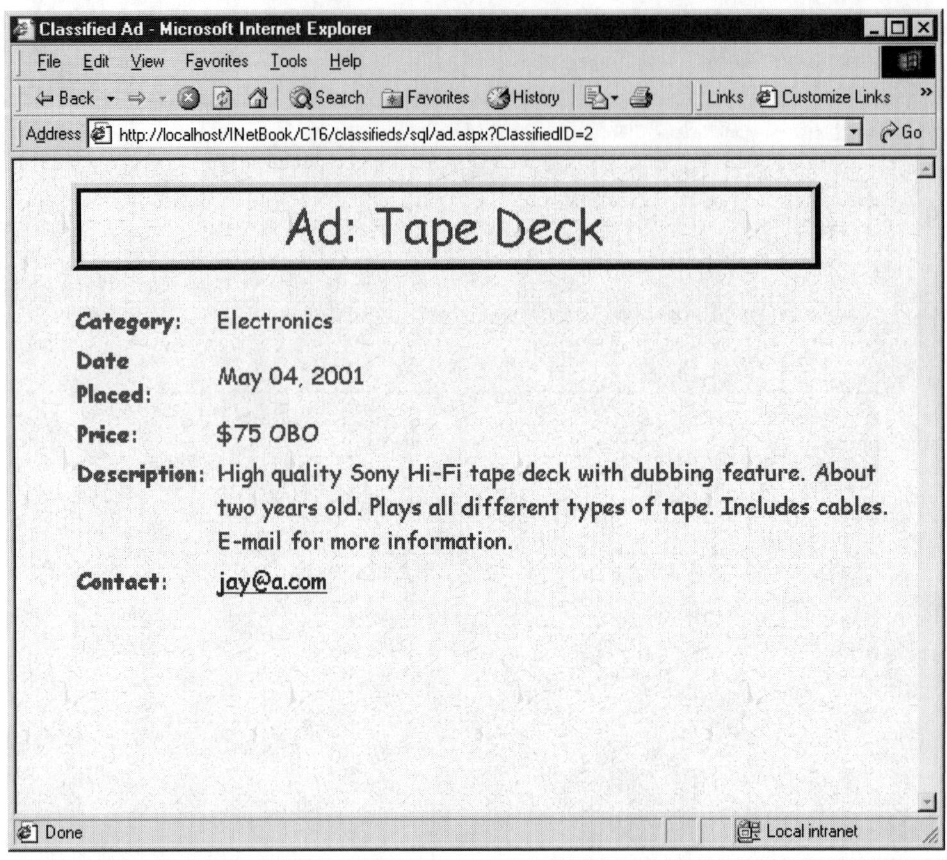

Figure 16-4 *Ad page*

Back on the Home page, the visitor can click a link to place their own advertisement. The resulting page is displayed in Figure 16-5.

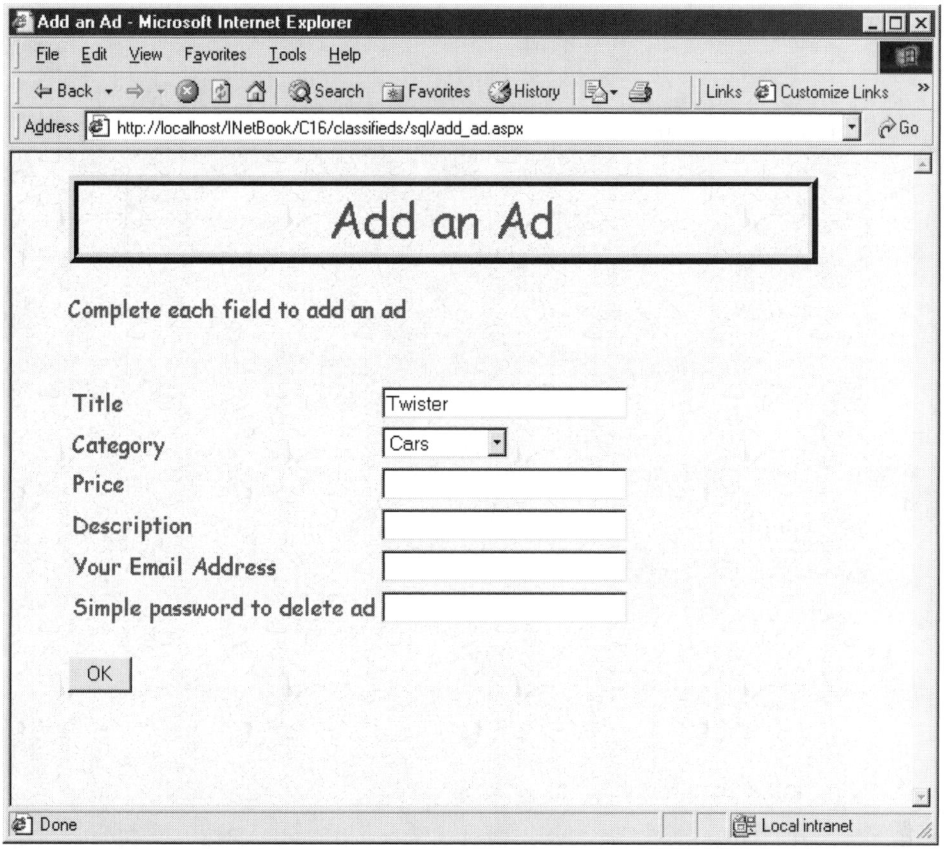

Figure 16-5 *Add an Ad page*

The visitor enters the information from their ad and clicks OK. All the fields must contain a value. If they don't, the visitor sees a message box with an error message like the one displayed in Figure 16-6.

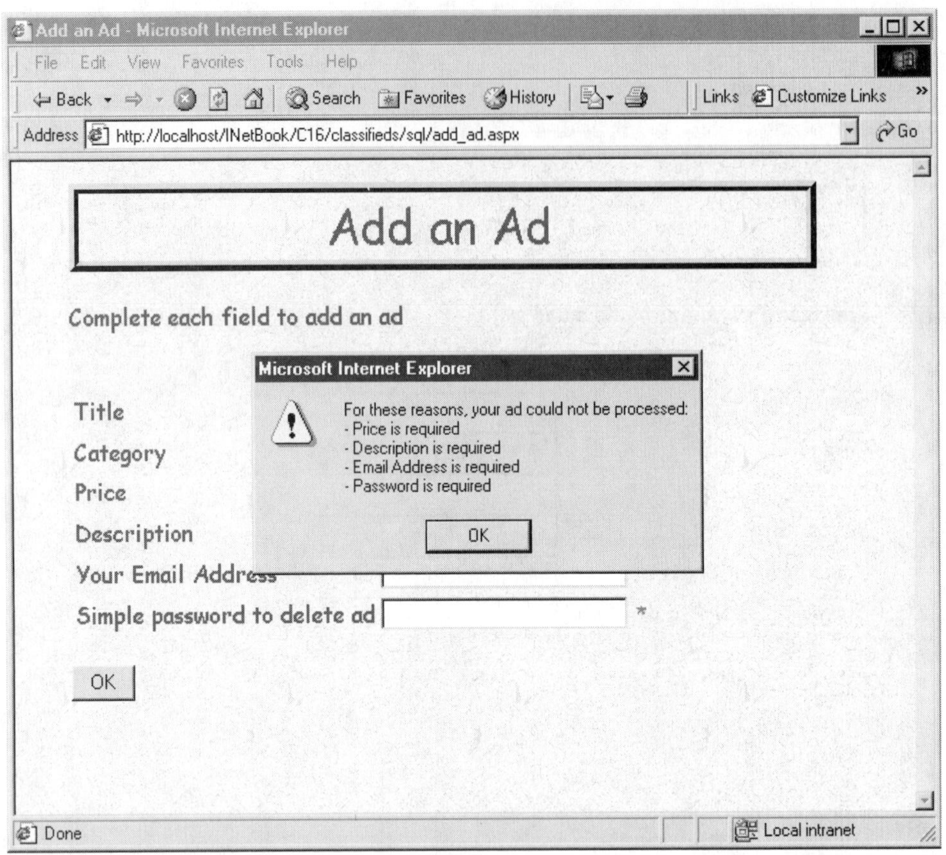

Figure 16-6 *Add an Ad error message*

The message box is produced through the use of a ValidationSummary control.

Once the visitor does supply a value for each of the fields on the Add an Ad page, they can click OK and the form will be processed. The visitor then sees a message like the one displayed in Figure 16-7.

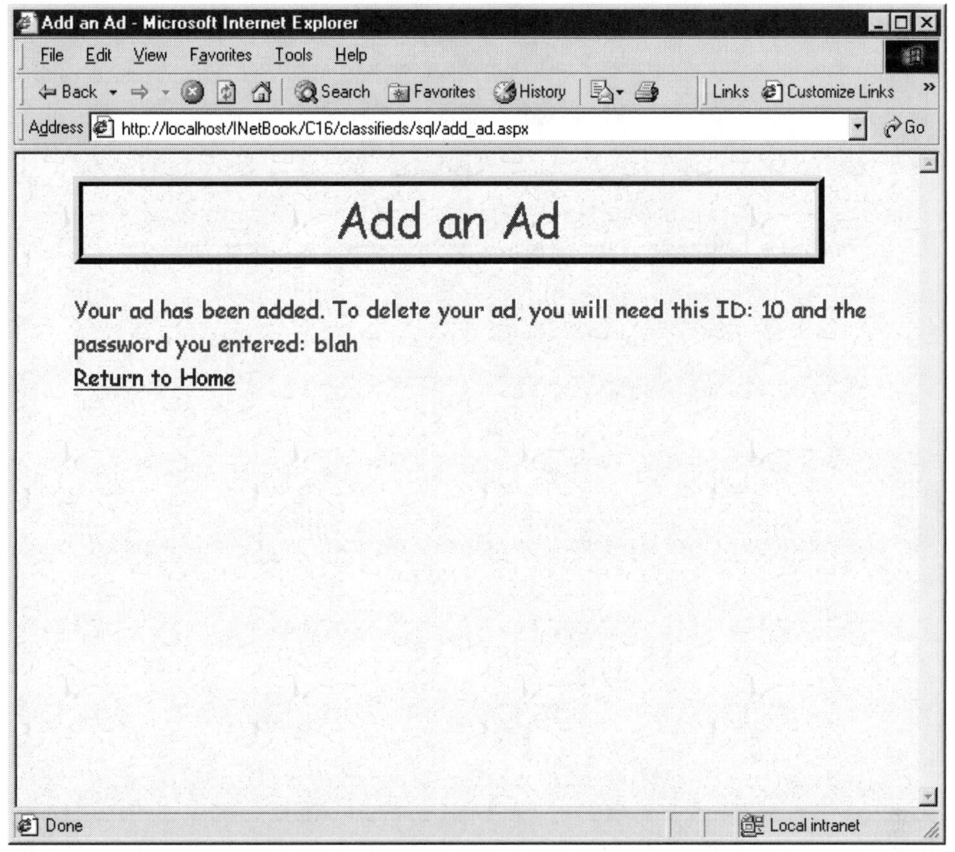

Figure 16-7 *Add an Ad success message*

The visitor is informed that to delete their ad, they will need the ID mentioned along with their password. When the visitor is ready to delete their ad, they go to the Remove Ad page through the Home page to see it as shown in Figure 16-8.

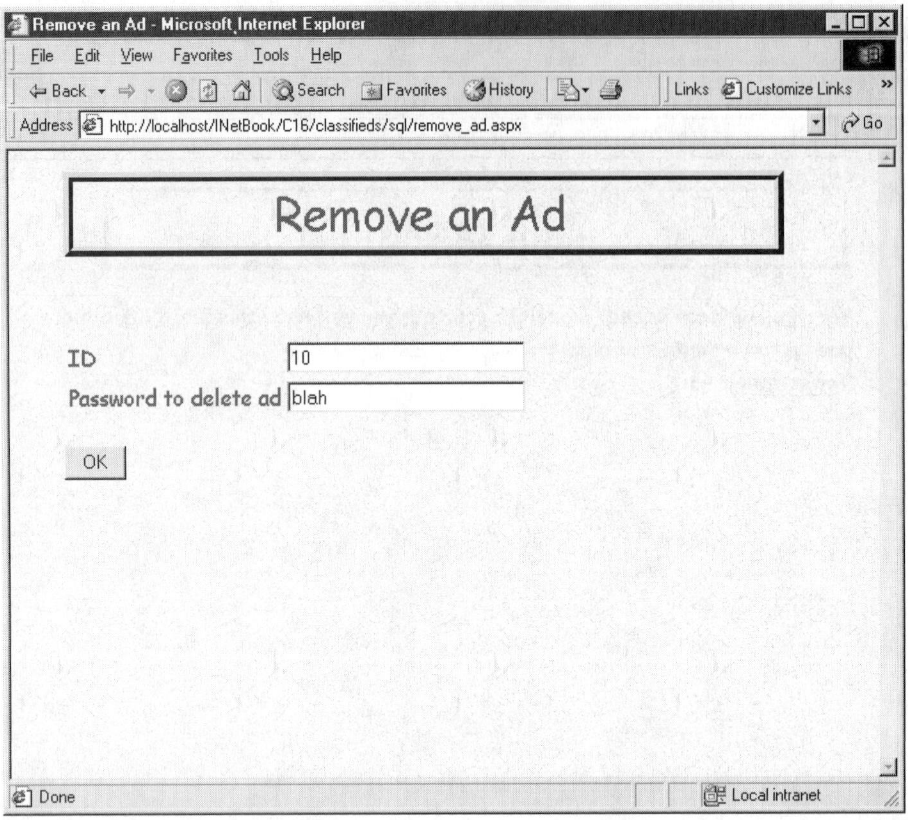

Figure 16-8 *Remove an Ad page*

As the visitor was informed, they must enter their ID and password. When they click OK, the record that matches the information, if any, is deleted.

Classifieds Database Component

C16Classifieds.sql

The back-end database required to run the Classifieds application contains two interrelated tables. In this section, we will review the relationship between the tables and the fields contained within them.

Tables and Data Diagram

Figure 16-9 shows the relationship between the tables in the Classifieds database.

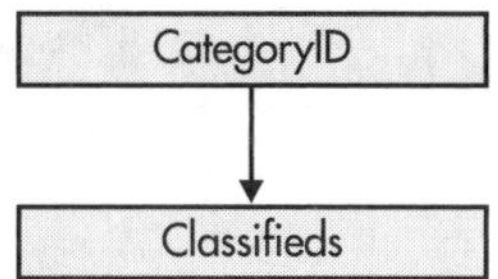

Figure 16-9 *Classifieds data diagram*

The Classifieds table contains all the information about the ads themselves. The Categories table stores the names of the categories that an ad can be in. The two tables relate in a one-to-many relationship. Each of the ads belongs to a single category, but each category can contain many different ads.

Categories Field Specifications

Categories.txt

The field specifications for the fields in the Categories table are displayed in Table 16-1.

The CategoryID field is the primary field in the table. The field is automatically populated with an incremented value when a new record is added, since it is an identity column. The other field, CategoryName, stores the name of the category.

Classifieds Field Specifications

Classifieds.txt

The field specifications for the fields in the Classifieds table are displayed in Table 16-2.

The ClassifiedID field is the primary key in this table. The CategoryID field is a foreign key that links this table to the Categories table. The rest of the fields store the particulars about the ad.

Field Name	Field Type	Notes
CategoryID	int	Primary Key, Identity Column
CategoryName	varchar	Length = 50

Table 16-1

Field Name	Field Type	Notes
ClassifiedID	int	Primary Key, Identity Column
CategoryID	int	Foreign Key
TitleText	varchar	Length = 50
DatePlaced	datetime	
Price	varchar	Length = 50
Description	varchar	Length = 255
EmailAddress	varchar	Length = 50
Password	varchar	Length = 50

Table 16-2 *Classifieds Field Specifications*

Classifieds ASP.NET Code

The Classifieds application is composed of five ASP.NET pages. In this section, we will review the controls and code that make up those pages.

Classifieds Home ASP.NET Page

Index.aspx

The Home page displays a list of categories to the visitor and links the visitor to some of the other pages in the site. At the top of the page, three compiler directives are defined.

```
<%@ Page Language=VB Debug=true %>
<%@ Import Namespace="System.Data" %>
<%@ Import Namespace="System.Data.OLEDB" %>
```

The first tells the compiler the language we will be using and that we are in debug mode. Remember to turn off debug mode when you move this solution to a production machine:

```
<%@ Page Language=VB EnableSessionState=true Debug=true %>
```

The other directives import libraries that are required so that we can retrieve and display data from the database:

```
<%@ Import Namespace="System.Data" %>
<%@ Import Namespace="System.Data.OLEDB" %>
```

Within the body of the page, we define a Label control that displays the title text on the page:

```
<asp:Label
    id="lblTitle"
    BorderWidth="7px"
    BorderStyle=7
    Width="90%"
    Font-Size="25pt"
    Font-Name="Comic Sans MS"
    Text="<center>Classifieds Site</center>"
    runat="server"
/>
```

The next control that we define is another label that is used to display instructions for this section of the page:

```
<asp:Label
    id="lblMessage1"
    Font-Size="12pt"
    Font-Name="Comic Sans MS"
    runat="server"
    Text="Select a category to browse:"
/>
```

The next control on the page is a DropDownList that displays the categories to the visitor:

```
<asp:dropdownlist
    id="ddlCategoryID"
    runat=server
    DataTextField="CategoryName"
    DataValueField="CategoryID">
</asp:dropdownlist>
```

Note that the visitor will see the name of the category:

```
DataTextField="CategoryName"
```

But through code, we can access the ID of the category:

```
DataValueField="CategoryID"
```

A button is defined next that is clicked by the visitor to search based on a category:

```
<asp:button
    id="butCategory"
    text="  OK  "
    Type="Submit"
    OnClick="SubmitCategory_Click"
    runat="server"
/>
```

Next, you will find another label that displays text for the search section of the page:

```
<asp:Label
    id="lblMessage2"
    Font-Size="12pt"
    Font-Name="Comic Sans MS"
    runat="server"
    Text="Or enter a search word:"
/>
```

After that, a TextBox is defined for putting in the search text:

```
<asp:TextBox
    id="txtSearchWord"
    Columns="25"
    MaxLength="50"
    runat=server
/>
```

And another button indicates that the visitor wants to search using their search text:

```
<asp:button
    id="butSearch"
    text="  OK  "
    Type="Submit"
    OnClick="SubmitSearch_Click"
    runat="server"
/>
```

The code on the page is contained within three procedures. The first code block runs when the page is loaded. The code populates the DropDownList control.

```
Sub Page_Load(ByVal Sender as Object, ByVal E as EventArgs)
    If Not IsPostBack Then
        Dim DBConn as OleDbConnection
        Dim DBCommand As OleDbDataAdapter
        Dim DSPageData as New DataSet
        DBConn = New OleDbConnection("Provider=sqloledb;" _
            & "server=localhost;" _
            & "Initial Catalog=INETC16;" _
            & "User Id=sa;" _
            & "Password=yourpassword;")
        DBCommand = New OleDbDataAdapter _
            ("Select * from Categories " _
            & "Order By CategoryName", DBConn)
        DBCommand.Fill(DSPageData, _
            "Categories")
        ddlCategoryID.DataSource = _
                DSPageData.Tables("Categories").DefaultView
        ddlCategoryID.DataBind()
    End If
End Sub
```

The code should run only when the page is loaded

```
If Not IsPostBack Then
```

If that is the case, we will need three data objects: one to connect to the database

```
Dim DBConn as OleDbConnection
```

another to run a query through

```
Dim DBCommand As OleDbDataAdapter
```

and a third for the results of that query:

```
Dim DSPageData as New DataSet
```

We start by connecting to our SQL Server database:

```
DBConn = New OleDbConnection("Provider=sqloledb;" _
    & "server=localhost;" _
```

```
    & "Initial Catalog=INETC16;" _
    & "User Id=sa;" _
    & "Password=yourpassword;")
```

We then place a query that will retrieve the names and IDs of the categories into our Data Adapter object:

```
DBCommand = New OleDbDataAdapter _
    ("Select * from Categories " _
    & "Order By CategoryName", DBConn)
```

The result of running that query is placed into our DataSet object:

```
DBCommand.Fill(DSPageData, _
    "Categories")
```

And our DropDownList is bound to that DataSet object:

```
ddlCategoryID.DataSource = _
    DSPageData.Tables("Categories").DefaultView
ddlCategoryID.DataBind()
```

The next event fires when the OK button in the category section of the page is clicked.

```
Sub SubmitCategory_Click(Sender As Object, E As EventArgs)
    Response.Redirect("./ad_list.aspx?CategoryID=" _
        & ddlCategoryID.SelectedItem.Value)
End Sub
```

The code sends the visitor to the Ad List page, passing to it the ID of the category selected by the visitor:

```
Response.Redirect("./ad_list.aspx?CategoryID=" _
    & ddlCategoryID.SelectedItem.Value)
```

The next procedure runs when the OK button is clicked on the Search section of the page.

```
Sub SubmitSearch_Click(Sender As Object, E As EventArgs)
    Response.Redirect("./ad_list.aspx?SearchTerm=" _
        & txtSearchWord.Text)
End Sub
```

The code also sends the visitor to the Ad List page. But this time we pass the search text to that page:

```
Response.Redirect("./ad_list.aspx?SearchTerm=" _
    & txtSearchWord.Text)
```

Ad List ASP.NET Page

Ad_List.aspx

The code on the Ad List page displays a list of all the matching ads to the visitor, regardless of whether the visitor is searching the ads or wants to display all the ads in a single category.

At the top of the page, compiler directives are declared that set up the run environment and import data libraries:

```
<%@ Page Language=VB Debug=true %>
<%@ Import Namespace="System.Data" %>
<%@ Import Namespace="System.Data.OLEDB" %>
```

Within the body of the page, a Label control is used to display the title of the page:

```
<asp:Label
    id="lblTitle"
    BorderWidth="7px"
    BorderStyle=7
    Width="90%"
    Font-Size="25pt"
    Font-Name="Comic Sans MS"
    Text="<center>Classifieds Site</center>"
    runat="server"
/>
```

Another label is defined to display the total number of matching ads to the visitor:

```
<asp:Label
    id="lblMessage"
    Font-Size="12pt"
    Font-Name="Comic Sans MS"
    runat="server"
/>
```

The only other control on the page is the DataGrid control used to display the matching records:

```
<asp:DataGrid
    id="dgAds"
    AutoGenerateColumns="false"
    Width="90%"
    BackColor="beige"
    AlternatingItemStyle-BackColor="cornsilk"
    BorderColor="black"
    ShowFooter="false"
    CellPadding=3
    CellSpacing="0"
    Font-Name="Comic Sans MS"
    Font-Size="8pt"
    ForeColor="Black"
    HeaderStyle-BackColor="burlywood"
    HeaderStyle-Font-Bold="True"
    runat="server">
    <columns>
        <asp:HyperLinkColumn
            HeaderText="Ad Title (Click title for full info)"
            DataNavigateUrlField="ClassifiedID"
            DataNavigateUrlFormatString="./ad.aspx?ClassifiedID={0}"
            DataTextField="TitleText"
            Target="_self"
        />
        <asp:BoundColumn
            HeaderText="Date Placed"
            DataField="TheDate"
        />
        <asp:BoundColumn
            HeaderText="Asking Price"
            DataField="Price"
        />
    </columns>
</asp:DataGrid>
```

Note that we are setting up the properties so that our own columns will be displayed instead of the automatic ones:

```
AutoGenerateColumns="false"
```

The first of our columns is a HyperLinkColumn:

```
<asp:HyperLinkColumn
    HeaderText="Ad Title (Click title for full info)"
```

Note that the linked field is set to the ID of the ad:

```
DataNavigateUrlField="ClassifiedID"
```

Here, we tell the compiler that that ID should be placed in the position of the {0} characters:

```
DataNavigateUrlFormatString="./ad.aspx?ClassifiedID={0}"
```

Therefore, if the ad had an ID of 10, clicking the link would send the visitor to this page:

```
./ad.aspx?ClassifiedID=10
```

Within the column in the DataGrid, the visitor sees the title of the ad:

```
DataTextField="TitleText"
```

And when they click the link, no new window will open:

```
Target="_self"
```

The next column is a BoundColumn that will display the date that the ad was placed

```
<asp:BoundColumn
    HeaderText="Date Placed"
    DataField="TheDate"
/>
```

And the third column displays the asking price:

```
<asp:BoundColumn
    HeaderText="Asking Price"
    DataField="Price"
/>
```

The code on the page fires in a single event when the page is loaded.

```
Sub Page_Load(ByVal Sender as Object, ByVal E as EventArgs)
    Dim DBConn as OleDbConnection
    Dim DBCommand As OleDbDataAdapter
    Dim DSPageData as New DataSet
    DBConn = New OleDbConnection("Provider=sqloledb;" _
        & "server=localhost;" _
        & "Initial Catalog=INETC16;" _
        & "User Id=sa;" _
        & "Password=yourpassword;")
    If Len(Request.QueryString("CategoryID")) Then
        DBCommand = New OleDbDataAdapter _
            ("Select CategoryName from Categories " _
            & "Where CategoryID = " _
            & Request.QueryString("CategoryID"), DBConn)
        DBCommand.Fill(DSPageData, _
            "CategoryName")
        DBCommand = New OleDbDataAdapter _
            ("Select ClassifiedID, TitleText, " _
            & "Convert(varchar(12),DatePlaced,107) " _
            & "as TheDate, Price from Classifieds " _
            & "Where CategoryID = " _
            & Request.QueryString("CategoryID") _
            & " Order By DatePlaced DESC" _
            , DBConn)
        DBCommand.Fill(DSPageData, _
            "Ads")
        lblMessage.Text = "The category """ _
            & DSPageData.Tables("CategoryName"). _
            Rows(0).Item("CategoryName") _
            & """ has " _
            & DSPageData.Tables("Ads").Rows.Count _
            & " ads listed."
        dgAds.DataSource = _
            DSPageData.Tables("Ads").DefaultView
        dgAds.DataBind
    ElseIf Len(Request.QueryString("SearchTerm")) Then
        DBCommand = New OleDbDataAdapter _
            ("Select ClassifiedID, TitleText, " _
            & "Convert(varchar(12),DatePlaced,107) " _
```

```
            & "as TheDate, Price from Classifieds " _
            & "Where TitleText Like '%" _
            & Replace(Request.QueryString("SearchTerm"), "'", "''") _
            & "%' or Description Like '%" _
            & Replace(Request.QueryString("SearchTerm"), "'", "''") _
            & "%' Order By DatePlaced DESC" _
            , DBConn)
        DBCommand.Fill(DSPageData, _
            "Ads")
        dgAds.DataSource = _
            DSPageData.Tables("Ads").DefaultView
        dgAds.DataBind
        lblMessage.Text = "Your search term """ _
            & Request.QueryString("SearchTerm") _
            & """ was found in " _
            & DSPageData.Tables("Ads").Rows.Count _
            & " ads."
    Else
        Response.Redirect("./index.aspx")
    End If
End Sub
```

Within the page, we will need data objects to connect to our database and display its information:

```
Dim DBConn as OleDbConnection
Dim DBCommand As OleDbDataAdapter
Dim DSPageData as New DataSet
```

We start by connecting to the database:

```
DBConn = New OleDbConnection("Provider=sqloledb;" _
    & "server=localhost;" _
    & "Initial Catalog=INETC16;" _
    & "User Id=sa;" _
    & "Password=yourpassword;")
```

And then we check to see if the visitor entered this page by selecting a category on the Home page:

```
If Len(Request.QueryString("CategoryID")) Then
```

If so, we retrieve the name of the category corresponding to that ID:

```
DBCommand = New OleDbDataAdapter _
    ("Select CategoryName from Categories " _
    & "Where CategoryID = " _
    & Request.QueryString("CategoryID"), DBConn)
```

And we place it into a table called CategoryName in our DataSet object:

```
DBCommand.Fill(DSPageData, _
    "CategoryName")
```

Next, we retrieve all the ads in the category selected by the visitor. Note the use of the SQL Server Convert function to extract just the date portion from the DatePlaced field:

```
DBCommand = New OleDbDataAdapter _
    ("Select ClassifiedID, TitleText, " _
    & "Convert(varchar(12),DatePlaced,107) " _
    & "as TheDate, Price from Classifieds " _
    & "Where CategoryID = " _
    & Request.QueryString("CategoryID") _
    & " Order By DatePlaced DESC" _
    , DBConn)
```

We then place the results of that query into another table in our DataSet object:

```
DBCommand.Fill(DSPageData, _
    "Ads")
```

We then display summary information in our message label to the visitor:

```
lblMessage.Text = "The category """ _
    & DSPageData.Tables("CategoryName"). _
    Rows(0).Item("CategoryName") _
    & """ has " _
    & DSPageData.Tables("Ads").Rows.Count _
    & " ads listed."
```

And we bind our DataGrid to our DataSet object:

```
dgAds.DataSource = _
    DSPageData.Tables("Ads").DefaultView
dgAds.DataBind
```

We next check to see if the visitor entered this page by entering in search text:

```
ElseIf Len(Request.QueryString("SearchTerm")) Then
```

If that is the case, we need to retrieve all the records that match the visitor's search term in the TitleText or Description fields

```
DBCommand = New OleDbDataAdapter _
    ("Select ClassifiedID, TitleText, " _
    & "Convert(varchar(12),DatePlaced,107) " _
    & "as TheDate, Price from Classifieds " _
    & "Where TitleText Like '%" _
    & Replace(Request.QueryString("SearchTerm"), "'", "''") _
    & "%' or Description Like '%" _
    & Replace(Request.QueryString("SearchTerm"), "'", "''") _
    & "%' Order By DatePlaced DESC" _
    , DBConn)
```

place that into the DataSet object

```
DBCommand.Fill(DSPageData, _
    "Ads")
```

and bind our DataGrid to that DataSet object table:

```
dgAds.DataSource = _
    DSPageData.Tables("Ads").DefaultView
dgAds.DataBind
```

Finally, we display summary information through the message label to the visitor:

```
lblMessage.Text = "Your search term """ _
    & Request.QueryString("SearchTerm") _
    & """ was found in " _
    & DSPageData.Tables("Ads").Rows.Count _
    & " ads."
```

If the code flows here, the visitor did not enter this page correctly:

```
Else
```

In that case, we send the visitor back to the Home page:

```
Response.Redirect("./index.aspx")
```

Ad ASP.NET Page

Ad.aspx

The Ad page displays the full contents of the Ad selected by the visitor. At the top of the page, we need the same three compiler directives:

```
<%@ Page Language=VB Debug=true %>
<%@ Import Namespace="System.Data" %>
<%@ Import Namespace="System.Data.OLEDB" %>
```

Within the body of the page, we have one label that will display the name of the ad in the form of a title:

```
<asp:Label
    id="lblTitle"
    BorderWidth="7px"
    BorderStyle=7
    Width="90%"
    Font-Size="25pt"
    Font-Name="Comic Sans MS"
    Text="<center>Classifieds Site</center>"
    runat="server"
/>
```

One other label that displays the rest of the ad information is defined

```
<asp:Label
    id="lblMessage"
    Font-Size="12pt"
    Font-Name="Comic Sans MS"
    runat="server"
/>
```

The code on the page is contained within a single event, which fires when the page is loaded

```
Sub Page_Load(ByVal Sender as Object, ByVal E as EventArgs)
    If Len(Request.QueryString("ClassifiedID")) = 0 Then
        Response.Redirect("./index.aspx")
    End If
    Dim DBConn as OleDbConnection
    Dim DBCommand As OleDbDataAdapter
    Dim DSPageData as New DataSet
```

```
    DBConn = New OleDbConnection("Provider=sqloledb;" _
        & "server=localhost;" _
        & "Initial Catalog=INETC16;" _
        & "User Id=sa;" _
        & "Password=yourpassword;")
    DBCommand = New OleDbDataAdapter _
        ("Select TitleText, " _
        & "Convert(varchar(12),DatePlaced,107) " _
        & "as TheDate, Price, Description, EmailAddress, " _
        & "CategoryName from Classifieds Left Join " _
        & "Categories On Classifieds.CategoryID = " _
        & "Categories.CategoryID Where ClassifiedID = " _
        & Request.QueryString("ClassifiedID"), DBConn)
    DBCommand.Fill(DSPageData, _
        "Ad")
    lblTitle.Text = "<center>Ad: " _
        & DSPageData.Tables("Ad").Rows(0).Item("TitleText") _
        & "</center>"
    lblMessage.Text = "<table><tr><td><b>Category:</b></td>" _
        & "<td>" _
        & DSPageData.Tables("Ad").Rows(0).Item("CategoryName") _
        & "</td></tr><tr><td><b>Date Placed:</b></td>" _
        & "<td>" _
        & DSPageData.Tables("Ad").Rows(0).Item("TheDate") _
        & "</td></tr><tr><td><b>Price:</b></td>" _
        & "<td>" _
        & DSPageData.Tables("Ad").Rows(0).Item("Price") _
        & "</td></tr><tr VAlign=""TOP"">" _
        & "<td><b>Description:</b></td>" _
        & "<td>" _
        & DSPageData.Tables("Ad").Rows(0).Item("Description") _
        & "</td></tr><tr><td><b>Contact:</b></td>" _
        & "<td><a href=""mailto:" _
        & DSPageData.Tables("Ad").Rows(0).Item("EmailAddress") _
        & """>" _
        & DSPageData.Tables("Ad").Rows(0).Item("EmailAddress") _
        & "</a></td></tr><table>"
End Sub
```

First, we make sure that an ID was passed into this page:

```
If Len(Request.QueryString("ClassifiedID")) = 0 Then
```

If one wasn't, the visitor entered this page incorrectly and they are sent back to the Home page:

```
Response.Redirect("./index.aspx")
```

Otherwise, we declare data objects

```
Dim DBConn as OleDbConnection
Dim DBCommand As OleDbDataAdapter
Dim DSPageData as New DataSet
```

and start by connecting to our database:

```
DBConn = New OleDbConnection("Provider=sqloledb;" _
    & "server=localhost;" _
    & "Initial Catalog=INETC16;" _
    & "User Id=sa;" _
    & "Password=yourpassword;")
```

We then retrieve the information for the ad selected by the visitor, which includes the category name joined to the Classifieds table:

```
DBCommand = New OleDbDataAdapter _
    ("Select TitleText, " _
    & "Convert(varchar(12),DatePlaced,107) " _
    & "as TheDate, Price, Description, EmailAddress, " _
    & "CategoryName from Classifieds Left Join " _
    & "Categories On Classifieds.CategoryID = " _
    & "Categories.CategoryID Where ClassifiedID = " _
    & Request.QueryString("ClassifiedID"), DBConn)
```

The return of that query is placed into our DataSet object:

```
DBCommand.Fill(DSPageData, _
    "Ad")
```

The title from the ad retrieved is then placed into our title label:

```
lblTitle.Text = "<center>Ad: " _
    & DSPageData.Tables("Ad").Rows(0).Item("TitleText") _
    & "</center>"
```

The rest of the fields are concatenated into the other label. The fields and their captions are aligned through an HTML table:

```
lblMessage.Text = "<table><tr><td><b>Category:</b></td>" _
    & "<td>" _
    & DSPageData.Tables("Ad").Rows(0).Item("CategoryName") _
    & "</td></tr><tr><td><b>Date Placed:</b></td>" _
    & "<td>" _
    & DSPageData.Tables("Ad").Rows(0).Item("TheDate") _
    & "</td></tr><tr><td><b>Price:</b></td>" _
    & "<td>" _
    & DSPageData.Tables("Ad").Rows(0).Item("Price") _
    & "</td></tr><tr VAlign=""TOP"">" _
    & "<td><b>Description:</b></td>" _
    & "<td>" _
    & DSPageData.Tables("Ad").Rows(0).Item("Description") _
    & "</td></tr><tr><td><b>Contact:</b></td>" _
    & "<td><a href=""mailto:" _
    & DSPageData.Tables("Ad").Rows(0).Item("EmailAddress") _
    & """>" _
    & DSPageData.Tables("Ad").Rows(0).Item("EmailAddress") _
    & "</a></td></tr><table>"
```

Add an Ad ASP.NET Page

Add_Ad.aspx

The Add Ad page allows the visitor to add their own ad to the database. At the top of the page, the compiler directives are defined

```
<%@ Page Language=VB EnableSessionState=true Debug=true %>
<%@ Import Namespace="System.Data" %>
<%@ Import Namespace="System.Data.OLEDB" %>
```

The first control on the page is a Label control that will display the title of the page:

```
<asp:Label
    id="lblTitle"
    BorderWidth="7px"
    BorderStyle=7
    Width="90%"
```

```
    Font-Size="25pt"
    Font-Name="Comic Sans MS"
    Text="<center>Add an Ad</center>"
    runat="server"
/>
```

Another label that displays instructions for the page or a success message after an ad has been added is defined

```
<asp:Label
    id="lblMessage"
    Font-Size="12pt"
    Font-Name="Comic Sans MS"
    runat="server"
/>
```

To easily toggle their visibility, the rest of the controls are placed on a Panel control:

```
<asp:Panel
    id="pnlForm"
    runat="server"
>
```

Back in Figure 16-6, you saw that the validation error messages were displayed to the visitor in a message box. This is done through this ValidationSummary control:

```
<asp:ValidationSummary ID="vsAllErros"
    DisplayMode="BulletList"
    ShowMessageBox="True"
    ShowSummary="False"
    runat="server"
    HeaderText="For these reasons, your ad could not be processed:"
    Font-Name="Comic Sans MS"
    Font-Size="12"
/>
```

If there are any validation errors on the page, they will be displayed as a bullet list

```
DisplayMode="BulletList"
```

in a message box

```
ShowMessageBox="True"
```

but not in a summary at the top of the page:

```
ShowSummary="False"
```

And before any error messages, this text appears

```
HeaderText="For these reasons, your ad could not be processed:"
```

Next on the page, we define a TextBox so that the visitor can enter the title of the ad:

```
<asp:TextBox
    id="txtTitleText"
    Columns="25"
    MaxLength="50"
    runat=server
/>
```

That field is required

```
<asp:RequiredFieldValidator
    id="rfvTitleText"
    ControlToValidate="txtTitleText"
```

This text will be displayed in the message box if the rule is violated

```
ErrorMessage="Title is required"
Display="Static"
runat=server>
```

And next to the TextBox, the visitor will see this character:

```
*
</asp:RequiredFieldValidator>
```

Next, we define a DropDownList that allows the visitor to select the category that the ad is to go in:

```
<asp:dropdownlist
    id="ddlCategoryID"
    runat=server
```

```
        DataTextField="CategoryName"
        DataValueField="CategoryID">
</asp:dropdownlist>
```

Next, we define a TextBox for the visitor to enter the price:

```
<asp:TextBox
    id="txtPrice"
    Columns="25"
    MaxLength="50"
    runat=server
/>
```

The visitor must enter a value into this field:

```
<asp:RequiredFieldValidator
    id="rfvPrice"
    ControlToValidate="txtPrice"
    ErrorMessage="Price is required"
    Display="Static"
    runat=server>
    *
</asp:RequiredFieldValidator>
```

The next TextBox control allows the visitor to enter a description of the product for which they are placing an ad:

```
<asp:TextBox
    id="txtDescription"
    Columns="25"
    MaxLength="255"
    runat=server
/>
```

This field is required because a RequiredFieldValidator is linked to that TextBox control:

```
<asp:RequiredFieldValidator
    id="rfvDescription"
    ControlToValidate="txtDescription"
    ErrorMessage="Description is required"
    Display="Static"
    runat=server>
```

```
    *
</asp:RequiredFieldValidator>
```

That is followed by the e-mail address

```
<asp:TextBox
    id="txtEmailAddress"
    Columns="25"
    MaxLength="50"
    runat=server
/>
```

which is also required

```
<asp:RequiredFieldValidator
    id="rfvEmailAddress"
    ControlToValidate="txtEmailAddress"
    ErrorMessage="Email Address is required"
    Display="Static"
    runat=server>
    *
</asp:RequiredFieldValidator>
```

One more TextBox control is defined for the password field:

```
<asp:TextBox
    id="txtPassword"
    Columns="25"
    MaxLength="50"
    runat=server
/>
```

That field, too, is required

```
<asp:RequiredFieldValidator
    id="rfvPassword"
    ControlToValidate="txtPassword"
    ErrorMessage="Password is required"
    Display="Static"
    runat=server>
    *
</asp:RequiredFieldValidator>
```

One more control on the page is a Button control that the visitor clicks when they want to submit the form:

```
<asp:button
    id="butAdd"
    text="  OK  "
    Type="Submit"
    OnClick="SubmitAdd_Click"
    runat="server"
/>
```

The code on the page is defined within two procedures. The first fires when the page is loaded.

```
Sub Page_Load(ByVal Sender as Object, ByVal E as EventArgs)
    If Not IsPostBack Then
        Dim DBConn as OleDbConnection
        Dim DBCommand As OleDbDataAdapter
        Dim DSPageData as New DataSet
        DBConn = New OleDbConnection("Provider=sqloledb;" _
            & "server=localhost;" _
            & "Initial Catalog=INETC16;" _
            & "User Id=sa;" _
            & "Password=yourpassword;")
        DBCommand = New OleDbDataAdapter _
            ("Select * from Categories " _
            & "Order By CategoryName", DBConn)
        DBCommand.Fill(DSPageData, _
            "Categories")
        ddlCategoryID.DataSource = _
                DSPageData.Tables("Categories").DefaultView
        ddlCategoryID.DataBind()
        pnlForm.Visible = True
        lblMessage.Text = "Complete each field to add an ad"
    End If
End Sub
```

The code in this procedure should fire only when the page is loaded

```
If Not IsPostBack Then
```

If that is the case, we need to populate the DropDownList. Therefore, we will need data objects:

```
Dim DBConn as OleDbConnection
Dim DBCommand As OleDbDataAdapter
Dim DSPageData as New DataSet
```

We start by connecting to the database:

```
DBConn = New OleDbConnection("Provider=sqloledb;" _
    & "server=localhost;" _
    & "Initial Catalog=INETC16;" _
    & "User Id=sa;" _
    & "Password=yourpassword;")
```

And then we retrieve all the categories

```
DBCommand = New OleDbDataAdapter _
    ("Select * from Categories " _
    & "Order By CategoryName", DBConn)
```

and place them into our DataSet object:

```
DBCommand.Fill(DSPageData, _
    "Categories")
```

Our DropDownList is bound then to that DataSet object table:

```
ddlCategoryID.DataSource = _
    DSPageData.Tables("Categories").DefaultView
ddlCategoryID.DataBind()
```

We then display the Panel control that contains the TextBox and DropDownList controls

```
pnlForm.Visible = True
```

and place instruction text into our message label:

```
lblMessage.Text = "Complete each field to add an ad"
```

The other procedure fires when the visitor clicks the OK button on the form. The code in this procedure needs to add the visitor's ad to the database and display a success message.

```
Sub SubmitAdd_Click(Sender As Object, E As EventArgs)
    Dim DBConn as OleDbConnection
    Dim DBInsert As New OleDbCommand
    Dim DBCommand As OleDbDataAdapter
    Dim DSNewID as New DataSet
    DBConn = New OleDbConnection("Provider=sqloledb;" _
                & "server=localhost;" _
                & "Initial Catalog=INETC16;" _
                & "User Id=sa;" _
                & "Password=yourpassword;")
    DBInsert.CommandText = "Insert Into Classifieds (" _
        & "CategoryID, TitleText, DatePlaced, Price, " _
        & "Description, EmailAddress, Password) values (" _
        & ddlCategoryID.SelectedItem.Value & ", " _
        & "'" & Replace(txtTitleText.Text, "'", "''") & "', " _
        & "'" & Today() & "', " _
        & "'" & Replace(txtPrice.Text, "'", "''") & "', " _
        & "'" & Replace(txtDescription.Text, "'", "''") & "', " _
        & "'" & Replace(txtEmailAddress.Text, "'", "''") & "', " _
        & "'" & Replace(txtPassword.Text, "'", "''") & "')"
    DBInsert.Connection = DBConn
    DBInsert.Connection.Open
    DBInsert.ExecuteNonQuery()
    DBCommand = New OleDbDataAdapter _
        ("Select Max(ClassifiedID) as TheID from Classifieds" _
        , DBConn)
    DBCommand.Fill(DSNewID, _
        "TheID")
    pnlForm.Visible = False
    lblMessage.Text = "Your ad has been added. " _
        & "To delete your ad, you will need this ID: " _
        & DSNewID.Tables("TheID").Rows(0).Item("TheID") _
        & " and the password you entered: " _
        & txtPassword.Text _
        & "<br><a href=""./index.aspx"">Return to Home</a>"
End Sub
```

To accomplish that, we will need data objects:

```
Dim DBConn as OleDbConnection
Dim DBInsert As New OleDbCommand
Dim DBCommand As OleDbDataAdapter
Dim DSNewID as New DataSet
```

We start by connecting to our database:

```
DBConn = New OleDbConnection("Provider=sqloledb;" _
    & "server=localhost;" _
    & "Initial Catalog=INETC16;" _
    & "User Id=sa;" _
    & "Password=yourpassword;")
```

We then place text into our command object that adds the visitor's ad into the database:

```
DBInsert.CommandText = "Insert Into Classifieds (" _
    & "CategoryID, TitleText, DatePlaced, Price, " _
    & "Description, EmailAddress, Password) values (" _
    & ddlCategoryID.SelectedItem.Value & ", " _
    & "'" & Replace(txtTitleText.Text, "'", "''") & "', " _
    & "'" & Today() & "', " _
    & "'" & Replace(txtPrice.Text, "'", "''") & "', " _
    & "'" & Replace(txtDescription.Text, "'", "''") & "', " _
    & "'" & Replace(txtEmailAddress.Text, "'", "''") & "', " _
    & "'" & Replace(txtPassword.Text, "'", "''") & "')"
```

The Command object will connect to the database through our connection object:

```
DBInsert.Connection = DBConn
DBInsert.Connection.Open
```

We then run our Insert query:

```
DBInsert.ExecuteNonQuery()
```

Next, we need to retrieve the ID of the ad we just added

```
DBCommand = New OleDbDataAdapter _
    ("Select Max(ClassifiedID) as TheID from Classifieds" _
    , DBConn)
```

which is placed into our DataSet object:

```
DBCommand.Fill(DSNewID, _
    "TheID")
```

We then hide the form on the page

```
pnlForm.Visible = False
```

and display the ID to the visitor along with the password they entered so that they will know how to remove their message once it has been added

```
lblMessage.Text = "Your ad has been added. " _
    & "To delete your ad, you will need this ID: " _
    & DSNewID.Tables("TheID").Rows(0).Item("TheID") _
    & " and the password you entered: " _
    & txtPassword.Text _
    & "<br><a href="" ./index.aspx"">Return to Home</a>"
```

Remove Ad ASP.NET Page

Remove_Ad.aspx

The remove page allows the visitor to remove an ad with the ID and the password that they supplied on the Add an Ad page. At the top of the page, we define our compiler directives:

```
<%@ Page Language=VB Debug=true %>
<%@ Import Namespace="System.Data" %>
<%@ Import Namespace="System.Data.OLEDB" %>
```

Within the body of the page, we have a Label control for the title of the page:

```
<asp:Label
    id="lblTitle"
    BorderWidth="7px"
    BorderStyle=7
    Width="90%"
    Font-Size="25pt"
    Font-Name="Comic Sans MS"
    Text="<center>Remove an Ad</center>"
    runat="server"
/>
```

Next, we define a ValidationSummary control so that the visitor will see any validation errors in a message box when they try to submit the form:

```
<asp:ValidationSummary
    ID="vsAllErrors"
    DisplayMode="BulletList"
    ShowMessageBox="True"
    ShowSummary="False"
    runat="server"
    HeaderText="For these reasons, your ad could not be processed:"
    Font-Name="Comic Sans MS"
    Font-Size="12"
/>
```

Next, we supply a TextBox control for the visitor to enter the ID of the ad they wish to delete

```
<asp:TextBox
    id="txtID"
    Columns="25"
    MaxLength="50"
    runat=server
/>
```

That field is required

```
<asp:RequiredFieldValidator
    id="rfvID"
    ControlToValidate="txtID"
    ErrorMessage="ID is required"
    Display="Dynamic"
    runat=server>
    *
</asp:RequiredFieldValidator>
```

And it must be an integer:

```
<asp:CompareValidator
    id="cvID"
    ControlToValidate="txtID"
    Operator="DataTypeCheck"
    Type="Integer"
```

```
    ErrorMessage="ID Must be a number"
    Display="Dynamic"
    runat="server">
    *
</asp:CompareValidator>
```

The other TextBox control on the page allows the visitor to enter the password that goes with the ad

```
<asp:TextBox
    id="txtPassword"
    Columns="25"
    MaxLength="50"
    runat=server
/>
```

which is also required

```
<asp:RequiredFieldValidator
   id="rfvPassword"
   ControlToValidate="txtPassword"
   ErrorMessage="Password is required"
   Display="Static"
   runat=server>
   *
</asp:RequiredFieldValidator>
```

The other control on the page is a button that submits the contents of the form:

```
<asp:button
    id="butRemove"
    text="  OK  "
    Type="Submit"
    OnClick="SubmitRemove_Click"
    runat="server"
/>
```

The only code on the page fires when that button is clicked.

```
Sub SubmitRemove_Click(Sender As Object, E As EventArgs)
    Dim DBConn as OleDbConnection
    Dim DBDelete As New OleDbCommand
    DBConn = New OleDbConnection("Provider=sqloledb;" _
```

```
        & "server=localhost;" _
        & "Initial Catalog=INETC16;" _
        & "User Id=sa;" _
        & "Password=yourpassword;")
    DBDelete.CommandText = "Delete From Classifieds Where " _
        & "ClassifiedID = " _
        & txtID.Text _
        & " and Password = '" _
        & Replace(txtPassword.Text, "'", "''") _
        & "'"
    DBDelete.Connection = DBConn
    DBDelete.Connection.Open
    DBDelete.ExecuteNonQuery()
    Response.Redirect("./index.aspx")
End Sub
```

It needs data objects so that we can delete the ad desired by the visitor:

```
Dim DBConn as OleDbConnection
Dim DBDelete As New OleDbCommand
```

We start by connecting to our database:

```
DBConn = New OleDbConnection("Provider=sqloledb;" _
    & "server=localhost;" _
    & "Initial Catalog=INETC16;" _
    & "User Id=sa;" _
    & "Password=yourpassword;")
```

And then we place a SQL Delete statement into our Command object:

```
DBDelete.CommandText = "Delete From Classifieds Where " _
    & "ClassifiedID = " _
    & txtID.Text _
    & " and Password = '" _
    & Replace(txtPassword.Text, "'", "''") _
    & "'"
```

Our Command object will connect to the database through our Connection object:

```
DBDelete.Connection = DBConn
DBDelete.Connection.Open
```

We then run our Delete statement

```
DBDelete.ExecuteNonQuery()
```

and send the visitor back to the Home page:

```
Response.Redirect("./index.aspx")
```

Access Code Changes

C16Classifieds.mdb

Two code changes are needed to get this application to work with an Access database instead of a SQL Server database. First, the connect strings on all the pages need to change from this

```
DBConn = New OleDbConnection("Provider=sqloledb;" _
    & "server=localhost;" _
    & "Initial Catalog=INETC16;" _
    & "User Id=sa;" _
    & "Password=yourpassword;")
```

to something that points to your Access database:

```
DBConn = New OleDbConnection("PROVIDER=Microsoft.Jet.OLEDB.4.0;" _
    & "DATA SOURCE=" _
    & Server.MapPath("/INetBook/C16/Classifieds/" _
    & "Access/C16Classifieds.mdb;"))
```

On the DataGrid on the Ad List page, we display only the date portion of a datetime field through the SQL Server Convert function:

```
DBCommand = New OleDbDataAdapter _
    ("Select ClassifiedID, TitleText, " _
    & "Convert(varchar(12),DatePlaced,107) " _
    & "as TheDate, Price from Classifieds " _
    & "Where CategoryID = " _
```

```
    & Request.QueryString("CategoryID") _
    & " Order By DatePlaced DESC" _
    , DBConn)
```

In Access, the Format function is used instead:

```
DBCommand = New OleDbDataAdapter _
    ("Select ClassifiedID, TitleText, " _
    & "Format(DatePlaced,""mmm dd, yyyy"") " _
    & "as TheDate, Price from Classifieds " _
    & "Where CategoryID = " _
    & Request.QueryString("CategoryID") _
    & " Order By DatePlaced DESC" _
    , DBConn)
```

No other code changes are required.

Birthday Card Tool

Another fun tool that you can add to your site is a Birthday Card tool. This tool allows visitors to come to your site, select a card, customize it, and submit it. The person who is having a birthday receives an e-mail message with a link to their card. They then can click the link to view their card.

As you review this tool, think about other implementations that you could make. For example, you could create a Post Card tool that sends a greeting to someone, a nice way of increasing traffic. Or you could create an Invitation tool. The visitor to your site would enter a list of recipients and customize the invitation. Then the recipients would return to your site to see the invitation.

Sample Usage

To send out a birthday card, the visitor enters the Create a Card page. That page is displayed in Figure 16-10.

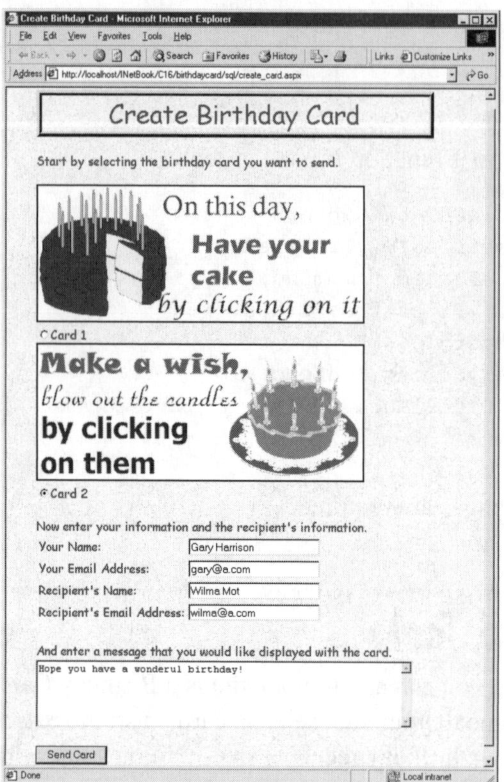

Figure 16-10 *Create a Card page*

The first step in creating a card is for the visitor to select the type of card. Here, they are presented with two cards. But you could include more yourself. Then the visitor enters in information about themselves and the recipient of the card. Also, the visitor enters a personal message that goes with the card.

When the visitor clicks the Send Card button, they see a message letting them know that their card has been sent. The recipient of the birthday card then receives an e-mail message like the one displayed in Figure 16-11.

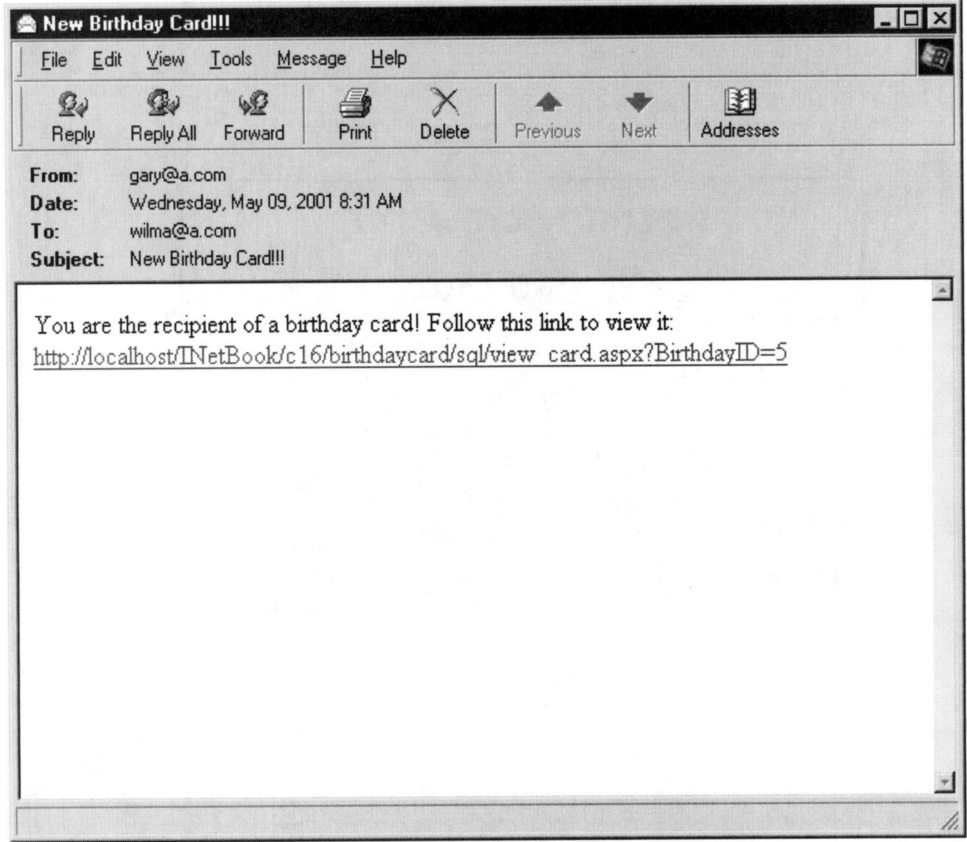

Figure 16-11 *E-mail sent from Create a Card page*

Note that the recipient can see who sent them the card from the e-mail address. The recipient would then click the link in the message to be taken to the first part of their card as displayed in Figure 16-12.

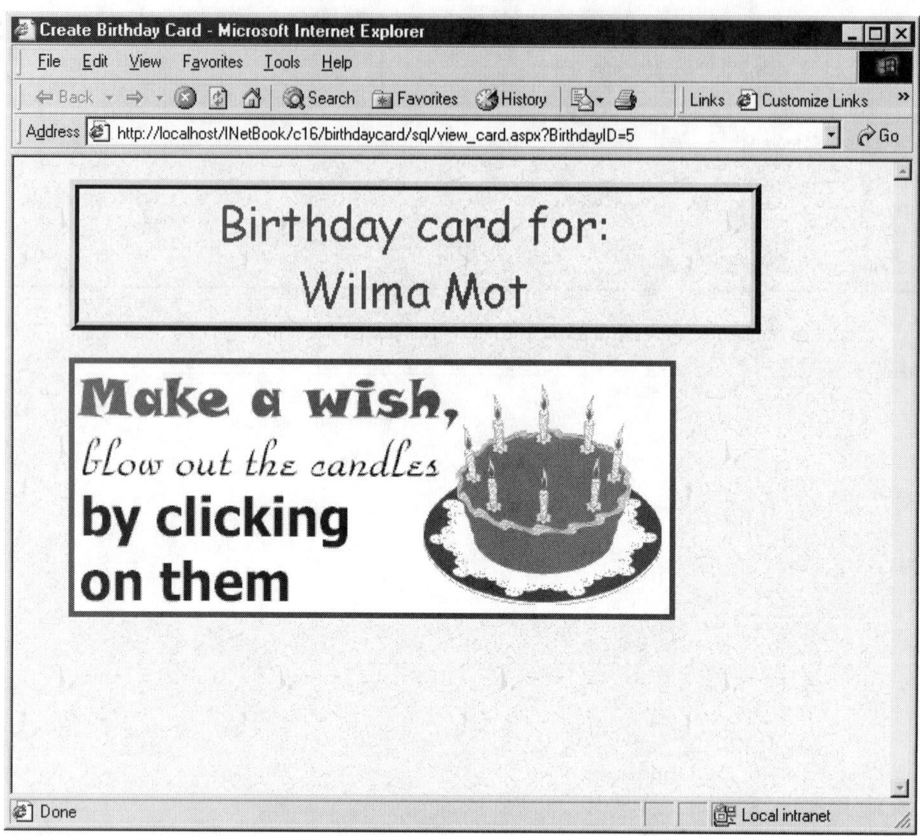

Figure 16-12 *First part of View Card page*

Each of the birthday cards is divided into two halves. The first half has a picture for the recipient of the card to click. When they do that, they see the second part of the card as it is displayed in Figure 16-13.

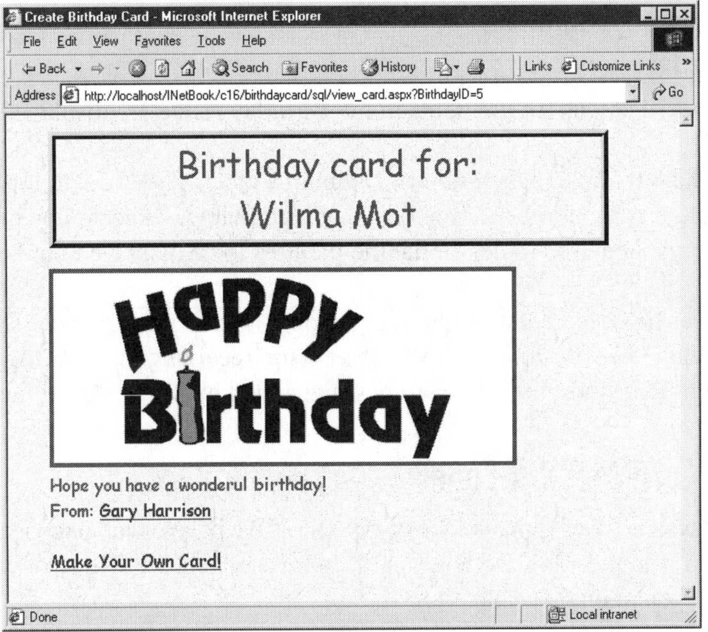

Figure 16-13 *Second part of the View Card page*

The second part of the page displays another image as well as the personal information entered by the sender of the birthday card.

Birthday Card Database Component

C16Birthdays.sql

The Birthday Card tool requires a back-end database to store the information entered by the sender of the card. In this section, we will review the one table in the database.

Birthdays Field Specifications

Birthdays.txt

The field specifications for the fields in the Birthdays table are displayed in Table 16-3.

The BirthdayID field is the primary key in this table. The CardNumber field stores the identifying number of the birthday card that was selected by the sender. This number is then used to determine the pictures to be displayed on the View Card page.

The sender fields store data about the person who is sending the card. The recipient fields store information about the person receiving the card. And the TheMessage field stores the personal message added by the sender of the card.

Birthday Card ASP.NET Code

The Birthday Card tool is made up of two ASP.NET pages. One page is used to create a card, and the other to view a card. In this section, we will review the code and controls found on those pages.

Create a Card ASP.NET Page

Create_Card.aspx

The Create a Card page allows the visitor to create and send an e-mail message out to the recipient of a card. At the top of the page, four compiler directives are defined.

Field Name	Field Type	Notes
BirthdayID	int	Primary Key, Identity Column
CardNumber	int	
SendersName	varchar	Length = 100
SendersEmail	varchar	Length = 100
RecipientsName	varchar	Length = 100
RecipientsEmail	varchar	Length = 100
TheMessage	text	

Table 16-3 *Birthdays Field Specifications*

```
<%@ Page Language=VB Debug=true %>
<%@ Import Namespace="System.Data" %>
<%@ Import Namespace="System.Data.OLEDB" %>
<%@ Import Namespace="System.Web.Mail" %>
```

The first directive tells the compiler that our code is in Visual Basic and that we are in debug mode:

```
<%@ Page Language=VB Debug=true %>
```

The next two directives import libraries that allow us to connect to the database and retrieve information into this page:

```
<%@ Import Namespace="System.Data" %>
<%@ Import Namespace="System.Data.OLEDB" %>
```

The other directive imports the library that allows creating and sending of an e-mail message:

```
<%@ Import Namespace="System.Web.Mail" %>
```

Within the body of the page, we declare a Label control that will display the title of the page:

```
<asp:Label
    id="lblTitle"
    BorderWidth="7px"
    BorderStyle=7
    Width="90%"
    Font-Size="25pt"
    Font-Name="Comic Sans MS"
    Text="<center>Create Birthday Card</center>"
    runat="server"
/>
```

Next, another label is defined to display instructions for the first part of the page:

```
<asp:Label
    id="lblMessage1"
    Font-Size="12pt"
    Font-Name="Comic Sans MS"
    runat="server"
    Text="Start by selecting the birthday card you want to send."
/>
```

The rest of the controls on the page are placed within a panel to make them easier to toggle their visibility:

```
<asp:Panel
    id="pnlMakeCard"
    runat="server"
>
```

Next, we display to the visitor the first part of each of the birthday card images along with a RadioButton control so that they can select the card:

```
<asp:RadioButton
    id="rdoCard1"
    Text="Card 1"
    Font-Size="12pt"
    Font-Name="Comic Sans MS"
    Checked="True"
    GroupName="rgCards"
    runat="server"
/>
```

That is followed by the image and the RadioButton control for the second birthday card. Note that both RadioButton controls share the same group name. This links them and prevents the visitor from selecting more than one:

```
<asp:RadioButton
    id="rdoCard2"
    Text="Card 2"
    Font-Size="12pt"
    Font-Name="Comic Sans MS"
    GroupName="rgCards"
    runat="server"
/>
```

That control is followed by another label that displays the header for the next section of the page:

```
<asp:Label
    id="lblMessage2"
    Font-Size="12pt"
    Font-Name="Comic Sans MS"
```

```
    runat="server"
    Text="Now enter your information and the recipient's
information."
/>
```

We follow that with four TextBox controls. The first is for the name of the sender of the birthday card:

```
<asp:TextBox
    id="txtSendersName"
    Columns="25"
    MaxLength="100"
    runat=server
/>
```

That is followed by the e-mail address of the sender:

```
<asp:TextBox
    id="txtSendersEmail"
    Columns="25"
    MaxLength="100"
    runat=server
/>
```

Next comes the TextBox control for the recipient's name

```
<asp:TextBox
    id="txtRecipientsName"
    Columns="25"
    MaxLength="100"
    runat=server
/>
```

and their e-mail address:

```
<asp:TextBox
    id="txtRecipientsEmail"
    Columns="25"
    MaxLength="100"
    runat=server
/>
```

One more TextBox control allows the visitor to enter their custom message, which is to be displayed with the e-card:

```
<asp:TextBox
    id="txtTheMessage"
    Columns="60"
    Rows="5"
    runat=server
    TextMode="MultiLine"
/>
```

The last control on the page is a button that allows the visitor to submit their request:

```
<asp:button
    id="butSendCard"
    text="Send Card"
    Type="Submit"
    OnClick="SubmitSendCard_Click"
    runat="server"
/>
```

The only code on the page fires when this button is clicked.

```
Sub SubmitSendCard_Click(Sender As Object, E As EventArgs)
    Dim DBConn as OleDbConnection
    Dim DBInsert As New OleDbCommand
    Dim DBCommand As OleDbDataAdapter
    Dim DSNewID as New DataSet
    Dim TempCardNumber as Integer
    Dim TheMessage as String
    Dim TheMailMessage as New MailMessage
    Dim TheMailConnection as New SmtpMail
    If rdoCard1.Checked Then
        TempCardNumber = 1
    Else
        TempCardNumber = 2
    End If
    DBConn = New OleDbConnection("Provider=sqloledb;" _
        & "server=localhost;" _
        & "Initial Catalog=INETC16;" _
        & "User Id=sa;" _
        & "Password=yourpassword;")
```

```
    DBInsert.CommandText = "Insert Into Birthdays " _
        & "(CardNumber, SendersName, SendersEmail, " _
        & "RecipientsName, RecipientsEmail, TheMessage) " _
        & "values (" _
        & TempCardNumber & ", " _
        & "'" & Replace(txtSendersName.Text, "'", "''") & "', " _
        & "'" & Replace(txtSendersEmail.Text, "'", "''") & "', " _
        & "'" & Replace(txtRecipientsName.Text, "'", "''") & "', " _
        & "'" & Replace(txtRecipientsEmail.Text, "'", "''") & "', " _
        & "'" & Replace(txtTheMessage.Text, "'", "''") & "')"
    DBInsert.Connection = DBConn
    DBInsert.Connection.Open
    DBInsert.ExecuteNonQuery()
    DBCommand = New OleDbDataAdapter _
        ("Select Max(BirthdayID) as TheID from Birthdays" _
        , DBConn)
    DBCommand.Fill(DSNewID, _
        "TheID")
    TheMessage = "You are the recipient of a birthday card! " _
        & "Follow this link to view it: " _
        & "http://localhost/INetBook/c16/" _
        & "birthdaycard/sql/view_card.aspx?BirthdayID=" _
        & DSNewID.Tables("TheID").Rows(0).Item("TheID")
    TheMailMessage.From = txtSendersEmail.Text
    TheMailMessage.To = txtRecipientsEmail.Text
    TheMailMessage.Subject = "New Birthday Card!!!"
    TheMailMessage.Body = TheMessage
    TheMailConnection.Send(TheMailMessage)
    pnlMakeCard.Visible = False
    lblMessage1.Text = "Your card has been sent."
End Sub
```

Within this procedure, we will need data objects so that we can add a record to the database and retrieve data from it:

```
Dim DBConn as OleDbConnection
Dim DBInsert As New OleDbCommand
Dim DBCommand As OleDbDataAdapter
Dim DSNewID as New DataSet
```

This variable will store the number of the card selected by the visitor:

```
Dim TempCardNumber as Integer
```

This variable will store the text of our e-mail message as we construct it:

```
Dim TheMessage as String
```

Two more objects are needed. One is an e-mail message object:

```
Dim TheMailMessage as New MailMessage
```

The other allows us to send out an e-mail message through our SMTP server:

```
Dim TheMailConnection as New SmtpMail
```

First, we check to see if the visitor selected the first birthday card:

```
If rdoCard1.Checked Then
```

If so, we set our temporary variable to 1:

```
TempCardNumber = 1
```

Otherwise, the other card was selected

```
TempCardNumber = 2
```

Next, we need to connect to the database:

```
DBConn = New OleDbConnection("Provider=sqloledb;" _
    & "server=localhost;" _
    & "Initial Catalog=INETC16;" _
    & "User Id=sa;" _
    & "Password=yourpassword;")
```

We then place a SQL Insert statement that adds a record into the Birthdays table based on the data entered by the recipient into our Command object:

```
DBInsert.CommandText = "Insert Into Birthdays " _
    & "(CardNumber, SendersName, SendersEmail, " _
    & "RecipientsName, RecipientsEmail, TheMessage) " _
    & "values (" _
    & TempCardNumber & ", " _
    & "'" & Replace(txtSendersName.Text, "'", "''") & "', " _
    & "'" & Replace(txtSendersEmail.Text, "'", "''") & "', " _
    & "'" & Replace(txtRecipientsName.Text, "'", "''") & "', " _
```

```
    & "'" & Replace(txtRecipientsEmail.Text, "'", "''") & "', " _
    & "'" & Replace(txtTheMessage.Text, "'", "''") & "')"
```

The Command object will connect to the database through our Connection object:

```
DBInsert.Connection = DBConn
DBInsert.Connection.Open
```

We then run our SQL statement:

```
DBInsert.ExecuteNonQuery()
```

Next, we need to retrieve the ID of the record that was just added

```
DBCommand = New OleDbDataAdapter _
    ("Select Max(BirthdayID) as TheID from Birthdays" _
    , DBConn)
```

That ID is placed into our DataSet object:

```
DBCommand.Fill(DSNewID, _
    "TheID")
```

We then create the text of our e-mail message using the ID of the record added so that it will be part of the link included in the message:

```
TheMessage = "You are the recipient of a birthday card! " _
    & "Follow this link to view it: " _
    & "http://localhost/INetBook/c16/" _
    & "birthdaycard/sql/view_card.aspx?BirthdayID=" _
    & DSNewID.Tables("TheID").Rows(0).Item("TheID")
```

Now we can set the properties of our e-mail message. First, we set who it is from

```
TheMailMessage.From = txtSendersEmail.Text
```

then who it is to

```
TheMailMessage.To = txtRecipientsEmail.Text
```

the subject of the message

```
TheMailMessage.Subject = "New Birthday Card!!!"
```

and the text of the message:

```
TheMailMessage.Body = TheMessage
```

After that, we can send the e-mail to the recipient:

```
TheMailConnection.Send(TheMailMessage)
```

Finally, we hide the panel that the form controls are on

```
pnlMakeCard.Visible = False
```

and display a success message to the visitor:

```
lblMessage1.Text = "Your card has been sent."
```

View Card ASP.NET Page

View_Card.aspx

The View Card page displays the contents of the card to the visitor. The contents are displayed in two parts by the use of Panel controls. At the top of the page, we have these compiler directives that set up the run environment and import data libraries:

```
<%@ Page Language=VB Debug=true %>
<%@ Import Namespace="System.Data" %>
<%@ Import Namespace="System.Data.OLEDB" %>
```

Within the body of the page, we have a title TextBox that will contain the name of the recipient:

```
<asp:Label
    id="lblTitle"
    BorderWidth="7px"
    BorderStyle=7
    Width="90%"
    Font-Size="25pt"
    Font-Name="Comic Sans MS"
    runat="server"
/>
```

That is followed by the definition of the first Panel control:

```
<asp:Panel
    id="pnlCard1"
    runat="server"
>
```

This panel contains a single control: an ImageButton control. This control allows us to display a picture that the visitor can click, and we can have code run when they do click it. As you will see, that code toggles which panel is made visible:

```
<asp:ImageButton
    id="imgButton"
    runat="server"
    BorderWidth="4px"
    OnClick="SubmitPart1_Click"
/>
```

After closing the first panel

```
</asp:Panel>
```

we start the second panel:

```
<asp:Panel
    id="pnlCard2"
    runat="server"
>
```

That panel contains an Image control for the second part of the birthday card

```
<asp:Image
    id="imgCard"
    runat="server"
    BorderWidth="4px"
/>
```

as well as a Label for the text of the birthday card:

```
<asp:Label
    id="lblMessage"
    Font-Size="12pt"
    Font-Name="Comic Sans MS"
    runat="server"
/>
```

The code on the page is contained within two events. The first runs when the page is loaded.

```
Sub Page_Load(ByVal Sender as Object, ByVal E as EventArgs)
    If Not IsPostBack Then
        If Len(Request.QueryString("BirthdayID")) = 0 Then
            Response.Redirect("create_card.aspx")
        End If
        Dim DBConn as OleDbConnection
        Dim DBCommand As OleDbDataAdapter
        Dim DSPageData as New DataSet
        DBConn = New OleDbConnection("Provider=sqloledb;" _
            & "server=localhost;" _
            & "Initial Catalog=INETC16;" _
            & "User Id=sa;" _
            & "Password=yourpassword;")
        DBCommand = New OleDbDataAdapter _
            ("Select CardNumber, SendersName, SendersEmail, " _
            & "RecipientsName, TheMessage From Birthdays " _
            & "Where BirthdayID = " _
            & Request.QueryString("BirthdayID"), DBConn)
        DBCommand.Fill(DSPageData, _
            "BDay")
        imgButton.ImageUrl="./bday" _
            & DSPageData.Tables("BDay").Rows(0).Item("CardNumber") _
            & "a.gif"
        imgCard.ImageUrl="./bday" _
            & DSPageData.Tables("BDay").Rows(0).Item("CardNumber") _
            & "b.gif"
        lblTitle.Text="<center>Birthday card for:<br>" _
            &
DSPageData.Tables("BDay").Rows(0).Item("RecipientsName") _
            & "</center>"
        lblMessage.Text = _
            DSPageData.Tables("BDay").Rows(0).Item("TheMessage") _
            & "<br>From: <a href=""mailto:" _
            & DSPageData.Tables("BDay").Rows(0).Item("SendersEmail")
_
            & """>" _
            & DSPageData.Tables("BDay").Rows(0).Item("SendersName") _
            & "</a><br><br><a href=""./create_card.aspx"">" _
            & "Make Your Own Card!</a>"
        pnlCard1.Visible = True
```

```
        pnlCard2.Visible = False
    End If
End Sub
```

The code in this procedure should run only when the page is loaded:

```
If Not IsPostBack Then
```

We start by making sure the page was entered with the ID of a birthday card:

```
If Len(Request.QueryString("BirthdayID")) = 0 Then
```

If it wasn't, we send the visitor to the Create a Card page:

```
Response.Redirect("create_card.aspx")
```

Otherwise, we declare some data objects

```
Dim DBConn as OleDbConnection
Dim DBCommand As OleDbDataAdapter
Dim DSPageData as New DataSet
```

and connect to our database:

```
DBConn = New OleDbConnection("Provider=sqloledb;" _
    & "server=localhost;" _
    & "Initial Catalog=INETC16;" _
    & "User Id=sa;" _
    & "Password=yourpassword;")
```

We then retrieve data from the Birthdays table based on the ID passed into this page:

```
DBCommand = New OleDbDataAdapter _
    ("Select CardNumber, SendersName, SendersEmail, " _
    & "RecipientsName, TheMessage From Birthdays " _
    & "Where BirthdayID = " _
    & Request.QueryString("BirthdayID"), DBConn)
```

That data is placed in our DataSet object:

```
DBCommand.Fill(DSPageData, _
    "BDay")
```

Next, we set the path to the first image of the birthday card according to the number of the card selected when it was created. Note that the name of the image comes from fixed text and the card number:

```
imgButton.ImageUrl="./bday" _
    & DSPageData.Tables("BDay").Rows(0).Item("CardNumber") _
    & "a.gif"
```

The second image is similarly set:

```
imgCard.ImageUrl="./bday" _
    & DSPageData.Tables("BDay").Rows(0).Item("CardNumber") _
    & "b.gif"
```

We then place the recipient's name into the title of the page:

```
lblTitle.Text="<center>Birthday card for:<br>" _
    & DSPageData.Tables("BDay").Rows(0).Item("RecipientsName") _
    & "</center>"
```

And the rest of the birthday card data is placed into the message label:

```
lblMessage.Text = _
    DSPageData.Tables("BDay").Rows(0).Item("TheMessage") _
    & "<br>From: <a href=""mailto:" _
    & DSPageData.Tables("BDay").Rows(0).Item("SendersEmail") _
    & """>" _
    & DSPageData.Tables("BDay").Rows(0).Item("SendersName") _
    & "</a><br><br><a href=""./create_card.aspx"">" _
    & "Make Your Own Card!</a>"
```

We then make the first panel visible

```
pnlCard1.Visible = True
```

and hide the other panel:

```
pnlCard2.Visible = False
```

The other code block fires when the recipient of the card clicks the first image:

```
Sub SubmitPart1_Click(Sender As Object, E As ImageClickEventArgs)
    pnlCard1.Visible = False
```

```
    pnlCard2.Visible = True
End Sub
```

The code hides the first panel

```
pnlCard1.Visible = False
```

and shows the second panel:

```
pnlCard2.Visible = True
```

Access Code Changes

C16Birthdays.mdb

The only code change that needs to be made if you wish to use Access instead of SQL Server is to change the connect string from pointing to SQL Server

```
DBConn = New OleDbConnection("Provider=sqloledb;" _
    & "server=localhost;" _
    & "Initial Catalog=INETC16;" _
    & "User Id=sa;" _
    & "Password=yourpassword;")
```

to pointing to your Access database:

```
DBConn = New OleDbConnection("PROVIDER=Microsoft.Jet.OLEDB.4.0;" _
    & "DATA SOURCE=" _
    & Server.MapPath("/INetBook/C16/birthdaycard/" _
    & "Access/C16Birthdays.mdb;"))
```

Movie Listing Tool

Another way that you can increase your traffic is by providing pages that are useful for people who live in your community. The tool presented in this section of the chapter is such a device. The visitor to this one-page tool selects the name of the local theatre and sees the movies playing there.

Sample Usage

When the visitor first enters this tool, they see the page displayed in Figure 16-14.

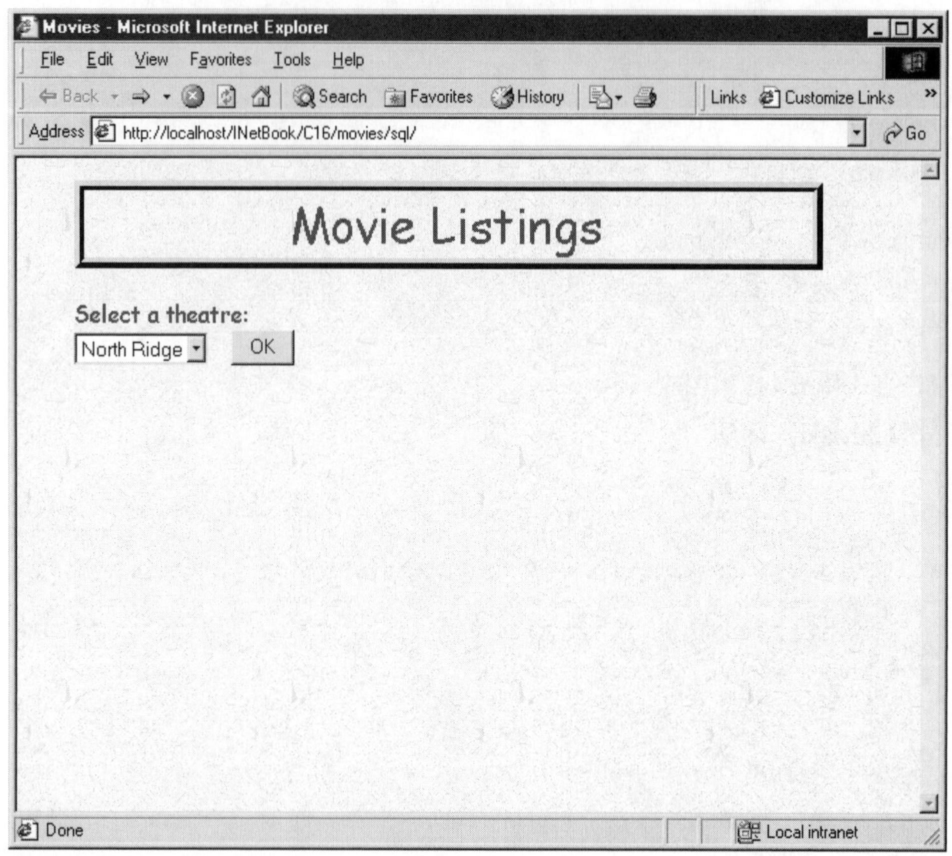

Figure 16-14 *Movie Listing page, initial view*

The visitor is presented with a list of theatres. When they click OK, they see all the movies that are playing at the theatre they selected. This view of the page is displayed in Figure 16-15.

Movie Listing Database Component

C16Movies.sql

The back-end database required to run the Movie Listing page contains two interrelated tables. In this section, we will review the relationship between the tables and the fields contained within them.

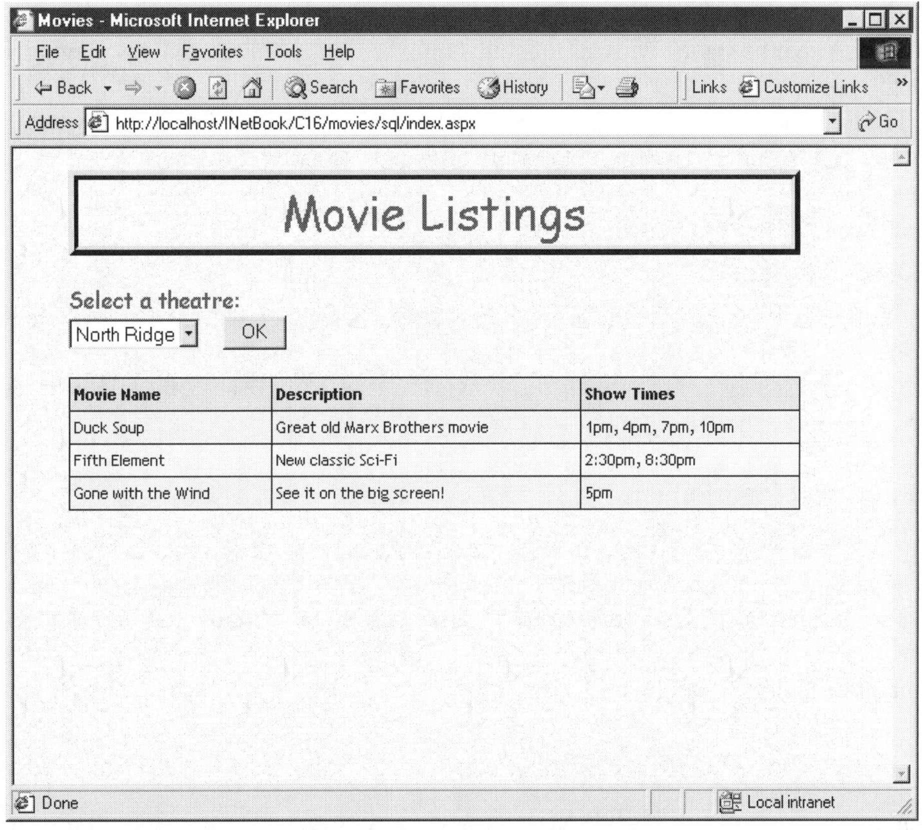

Figure 16-15 *Movie Listing page with movies displayed*

Tables and Data Diagram

Figure 16-16 shows the relationship between the tables in the Movie Listing database.

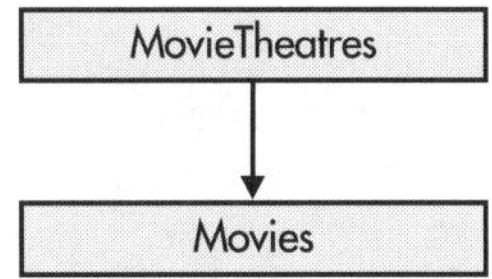

Figure 16-16 *Movie Listing Data Diagram*

The MovieTheatres table is the top level. It contains information about the theatres. The other table, Movies, contains information about the movies playing at the theatres.

The two tables relate in a one-to-many relationship. Each of the movies listed goes with a particular theatre, but each theatre can list many movies.

MovieTheatres Field Specifications

MovieTheatres.txt

The field specifications for the fields in the MovieTheatres table are displayed in Table 16-4.

The primary key in this table is the MovieTheatreID field. The other field stores the name of the theatre.

Movies Field Specifications

Movies.txt

The field specifications for the fields in the Movies table are displayed in Table 16-5.

The MovieID field is the primary key in the table. The MovieTheatreID field is a foreign key that links this table with the MovieTheatres table. The rest of the fields store information about the movie.

Movie Listing ASP.NET Code

Just one page is required for the Movie Listing tool. In this section, we will review the code and the controls on that page.

Movie Listing ASP.NET Page

Index.aspx

The Movie Listing page displays a list of all the theatres and movies playing at the theatre selected by the visitor. At the top of the page, three compiler directives are defined to set up the run environment and import needed data libraries:

```
<%@ Page Language=VB EnableSessionState=true Debug=true %>
<%@ Import Namespace="System.Data" %>
<%@ Import Namespace="System.Data.OLEDB" %>
```

Field Name	Field Type	Notes
MovieTheatreID	int	Primary Key, Identity Column
TheatreName	varchar	Length = 50

Table 16-5 *MovieTheatres Field Specifications*

Within the body of the page, a label is declared that contains title text for the page:

```
<asp:Label
    id="lblTitle"
    BorderWidth="7px"
    BorderStyle=7
    Width="90%"
    Font-Size="25pt"
    Font-Name="Comic Sans MS"
    Text="<center>Movie Listings</center>"
    runat="server"
/>
```

Another label is used to display instructions:

```
<asp:Label
    id="lblMessage1"
    Font-Size="12pt"
    Font-Name="Comic Sans MS"
    runat="server"
    Text="Select a theatre:"
/>
```

Field Name	Field Type	Notes
MovieID	int	Primary Key, Identity Column
MovieTheatreID	int	Foreign Key
MovieName	varchar	Length = 50
MovieDescription	varchar	Length = 255
ShowTimes	varchar	Length = 255

Table 16-4 *Movies Field Specifications*

A DropDownList control is used to display a list of the theatres to the visitor:

```
<asp:dropdownlist
    id="ddlMovieTheatreID"
    runat=server
    DataTextField="TheatreName"
    DataValueField="MovieTheatreID">
</asp:dropdownlist>
```

That is followed by a Button control:

```
<asp:button
    id="butSelectTheatre"
    text="   OK   "
    Type="Submit"
    OnClick="SubmitTheatre_Click"
    runat="server"
/>
```

And the other control on the page is the DataGrid that displays the movies to the visitor:

```
<asp:DataGrid id="dgMovies" runat="server"
    Width="90%"
    BackColor="beige"
    AlternatingItemStyle-BackColor="cornsilk"
    BorderColor="black"
    CellPadding=3
    CellSpacing="0"
    Font-Name="Trebuchet MS"
    Font-Size="8pt"
    ForeColor="Black"
    HeaderStyle-BackColor="burlywood"
    HeaderStyle-Font-Bold="True"
/>
```

The code on the page runs in two procedures. The first code block fires when the page is loaded

```
Sub Page_Load(ByVal Sender as Object, ByVal E as EventArgs)
    If Not IsPostBack Then
        Dim DBConn as OleDbConnection
```

```
        Dim DBCommand As OleDbDataAdapter
        Dim DSPageData as New DataSet
        DBConn = New OleDbConnection("Provider=sqloledb;" _
            & "server=localhost;" _
            & "Initial Catalog=INETC16;" _
            & "User Id=sa;" _
            & "Password=yourpassword;")
        DBCommand = New OleDbDataAdapter _
            ("Select * from MovieTheatres " _
            & "Order By TheatreName", DBConn)
        DBCommand.Fill(DSPageData, _
            "Theatres")
        ddlMovieTheatreID.DataSource = _
                DSPageData.Tables("Theatres").DefaultView
        ddlMovieTheatreID.DataBind()
    End If
End Sub
```

This code block sets up our DropDownList. Therefore, we want it to run only when the page is first loaded

```
If Not IsPostBack Then
```

If that is the case, we will need data objects:

```
Dim DBConn as OleDbConnection
Dim DBCommand As OleDbDataAdapter
Dim DSPageData as New DataSet
```

We start by connecting to our SQL Server database:

```
DBConn = New OleDbConnection("Provider=sqloledb;" _
    & "server=localhost;" _
    & "Initial Catalog=INETC16;" _
    & "User Id=sa;" _
    & "Password=yourpassword;")
```

And then we retrieve the list of theatres

```
DBCommand = New OleDbDataAdapter _
    ("Select * from MovieTheatres " _
    & "Order By TheatreName", DBConn)
```

into our DataSet object:

```
DBCommand.Fill(DSPageData, _
    "Theatres")
```

We then bind our DropDownList to that DataSet object:

```
ddlMovieTheatreID.DataSource = _
    DSPageData.Tables("Theatres").DefaultView
ddlMovieTheatreID.DataBind()
```

The other procedure runs when the button on the page is clicked. It populates the DataGrid with the movies corresponding to the theatre selected by the visitor.

```
Sub SubmitTheatre_Click(Sender As Object, E As EventArgs)
    Dim DBConn as OleDbConnection
    Dim DBCommand As OleDbDataAdapter
    Dim DSPageData as New DataSet
    DBConn = New OleDbConnection("Provider=sqloledb;" _
        & "server=localhost;" _
        & "Initial Catalog=INETC16;" _
        & "User Id=sa;" _
        & "Password=yourpassword;")
    DBCommand = New OleDbDataAdapter _
        ("Select MovieName as [Movie Name], " _
        & "MovieDescription as [Description], " _
        & "ShowTimes as [Show Times] from Movies " _
        & "Where MovieTheatreID = " _
        & ddlMovieTheatreID.SelectedItem.Value _
        & " Order By MovieName", DBConn)
    DBCommand.Fill(DSPageData, _
        "Movies")
    dgMovies.DataSource = _
        DSPageData.Tables("Movies").DefaultView
    dgMovies.DataBind
End Sub
```

The procedure requires data objects:

```
Dim DBConn as OleDbConnection
Dim DBCommand As OleDbDataAdapter
Dim DSPageData as New DataSet
```

We start by connecting to our database:

```
DBConn = New OleDbConnection("Provider=sqloledb;" _
   & "server=localhost;" _
   & "Initial Catalog=INETC16;" _
   & "User Id=sa;" _
   & "Password=yourpassword;")
```

We are going to let the DataGrid automatically create the columns according to the fields that we bind to it. Therefore, we need to alias the fields returned so that they are more readable when they are placed into the header row of the DataGrid:

```
DBCommand = New OleDbDataAdapter _
    ("Select MovieName as [Movie Name], " _
    & "MovieDescription as [Description], " _
    & "ShowTimes as [Show Times] from Movies " _
    & "Where MovieTheatreID = " _
    & ddlMovieTheatreID.SelectedItem.Value _
    & " Order By MovieName", DBConn)
```

We then place the return of that query into our DataSet object

```
DBCommand.Fill(DSPageData, _
    "Movies")
```

and bind our DataGrid to it:

```
dgMovies.DataSource = _
    DSPageData.Tables("Movies").DefaultView
dgMovies.DataBind
```

Access Code Changes

C16Movies.mdb

The only code change that needs to be made if you wish to use Access instead of SQL Server is to change the connect string from pointing to SQL Server

```
DBConn = New OleDbConnection("Provider=sqloledb;" _
    & "server=localhost;" _
    & "Initial Catalog=INETC16;" _
    & "User Id=sa;" _
    & "Password=yourpassword;")
```

to pointing to your Access database:

```
DBConn = New OleDbConnection("PROVIDER=Microsoft.Jet.OLEDB.4.0;" _
    & "DATA SOURCE=" _
    & Server.MapPath("/INetBook/C16/movies/" _
    & "Access/C16Movies.mdb;"))
```

Note that you will also need to change the path to the location where you placed the Access database.

CHAPTER

17

Implementing an Online Store

Most companies have a need to display their wares to their customers. They at least need to display a product catalog. But also, they likely need to allow customers to order their products.

In this chapter, we will look at the Online Store application. This site allows visitors to browse through items in the product catalog and place those items in a shopping cart. The visitor can then have their order processed by checking out.

Sample Usage

The Online Store application could be used to sell a variety of products. To demonstrate its use in this chapter, the tool is presented as a store that sells clothes.

When the visitor first enters the site, they see the home page displayed in Figure 17-1.

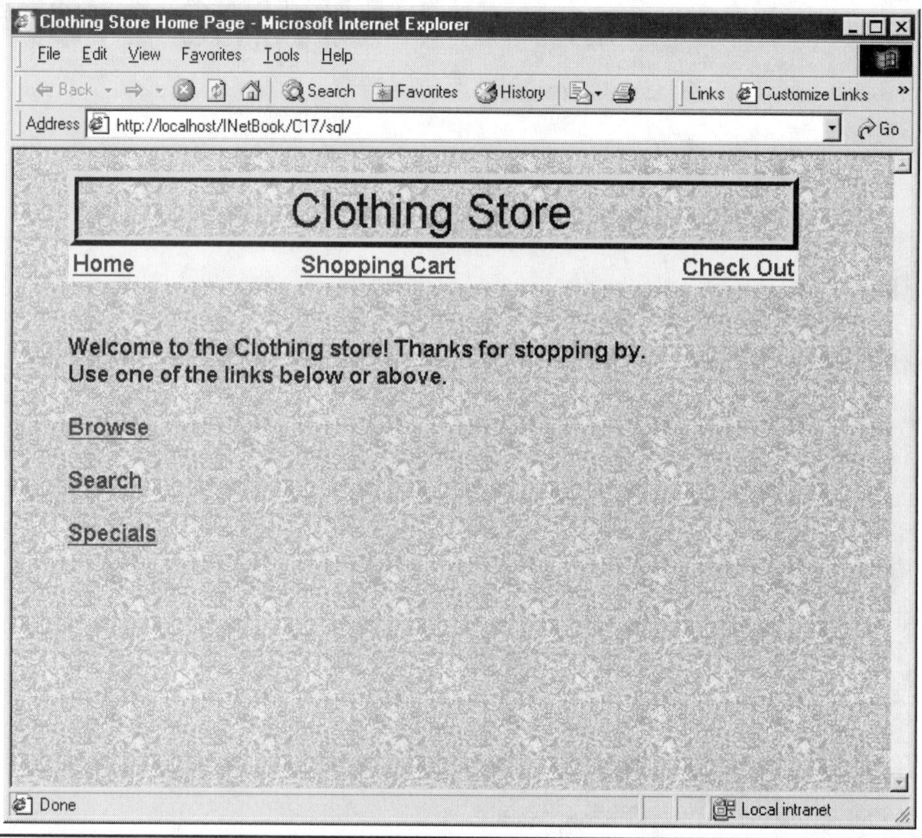

Figure 17-1 *Home page*

At the top of each of the pages within this site, the visitor can always navigate to this page, the Shopping Cart page, or the Check Out page.

From this page, the visitor decides how they want to view the products in the catalog. One way they can do that is by clicking the link to the Specials page. That page is displayed in Figure 17-2.

The Specials page uses a DataGrid control to display all the products that are marked as currently being on special.

Another way that the visitor can view the products in the catalog is by searching through it. The visitor does this by selecting the Search link displayed on the Home page. That Search page is displayed in Figure 17-3.

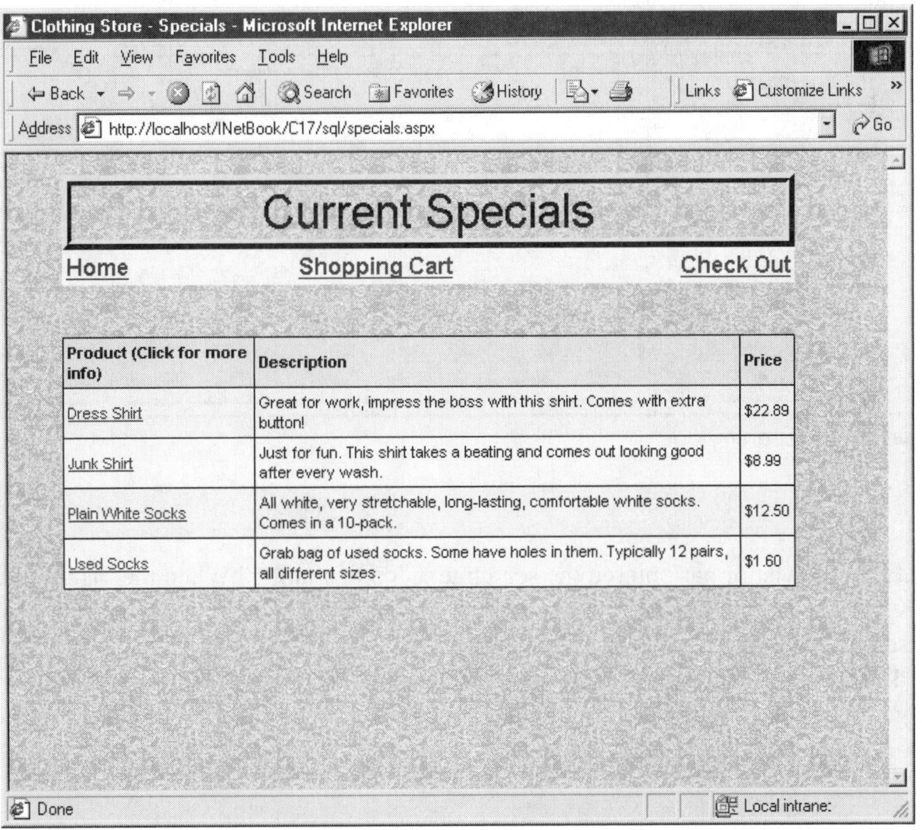

Figure 17-2 *Specials page*

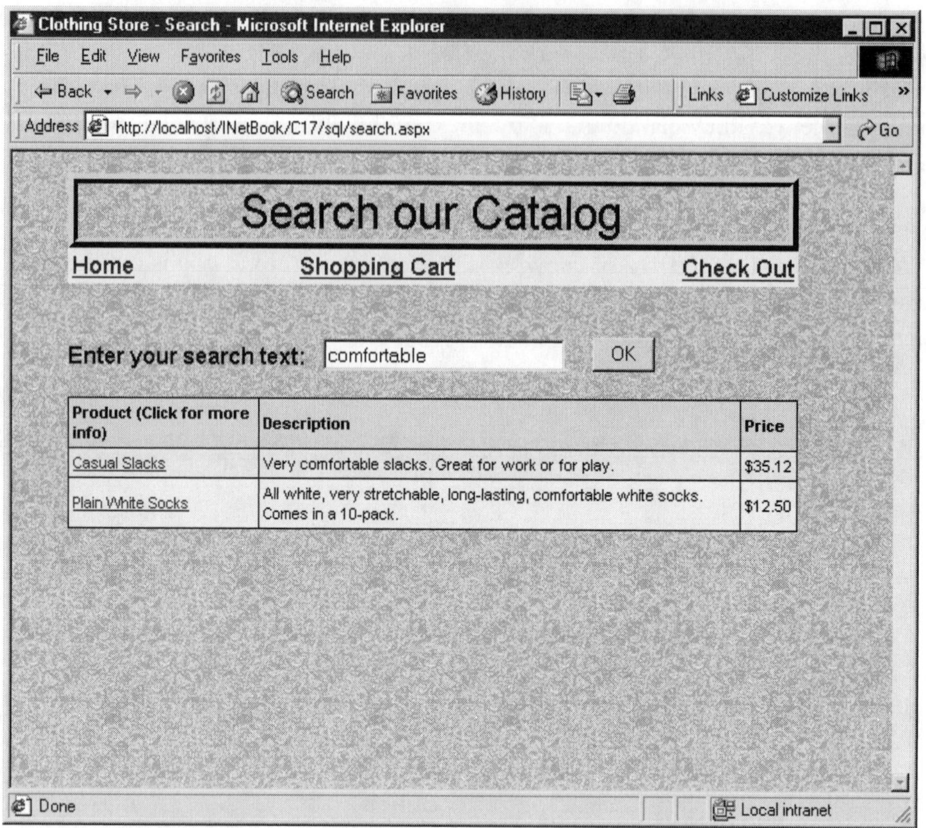

Figure 17-3 *Search page*

Here, the visitor has entered the search text "comfortable." When the visitor clicks OK, they see in the DataGrid control all the products for which the name or brief description contains the search text entered.

The third way that visitors can view products in the catalog is through the Browse page. When they select that from the Home page, they see the top-level view of the browse page displayed in Figure 17-4.

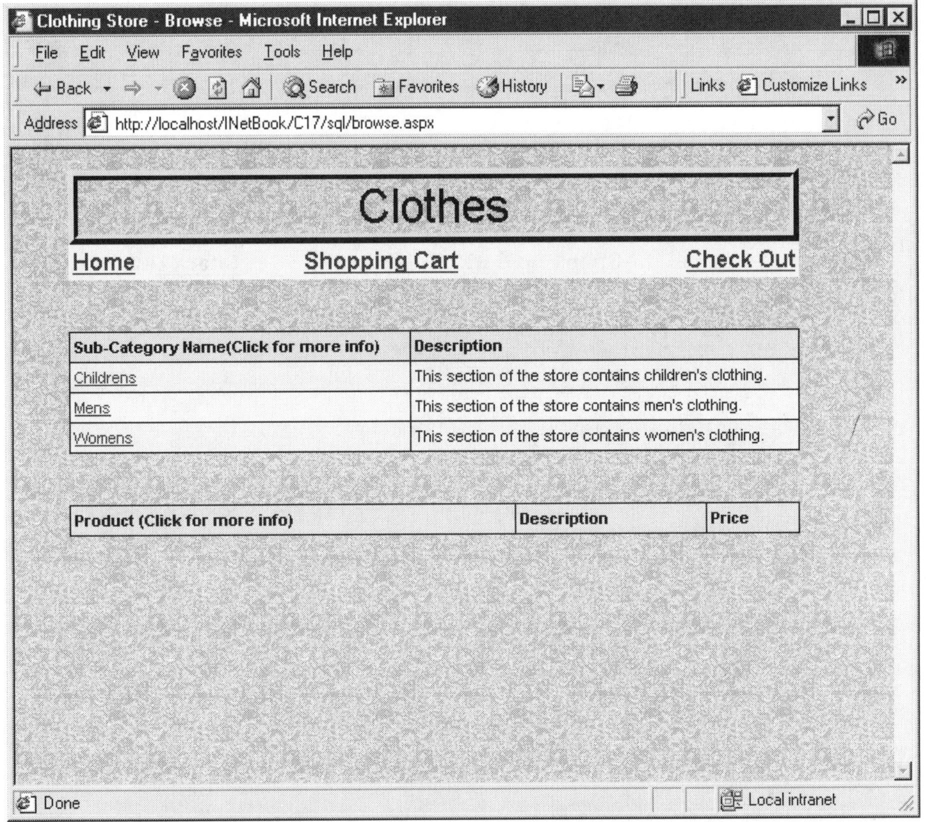

Figure 17-4 *Clothes category displayed on the Browse page*

The product catalog is made up of products that are listed in a category. The categories are a hierarchy of names that allow the visitor to drill deeper into a more specific category. Each category can have zero or more subcategories, and each category can have zero or more products listed in it.

When the visitor first enters the Browse page, they see the top-level category that you indicate in code. In this case, the category is called Clothes. It has three subcategories and no products.

But take a look at Figure 17-5.

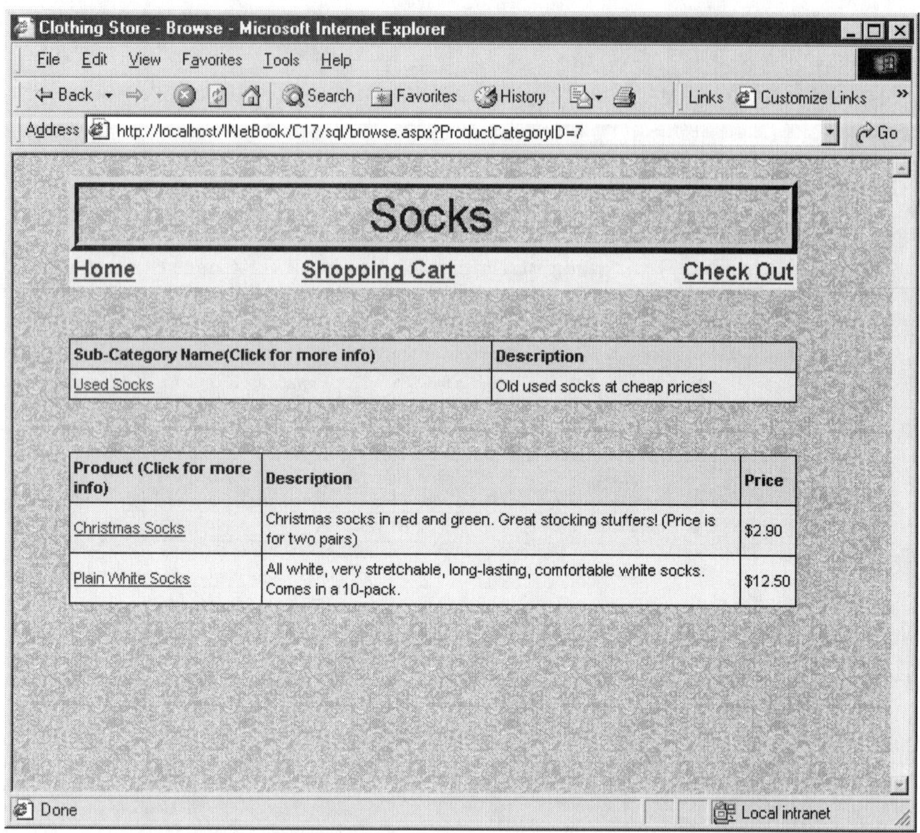

Figure 17-5 *Socks category displayed on the Browse page*

Here we see the Socks category. This product category has one subcategory and two products listed in it. But as you can see in Figure 17-6, we can also have a category with no subcategories but that does have products.

In this case, the Used Socks category is displayed. It contains a single product but no subcategories.

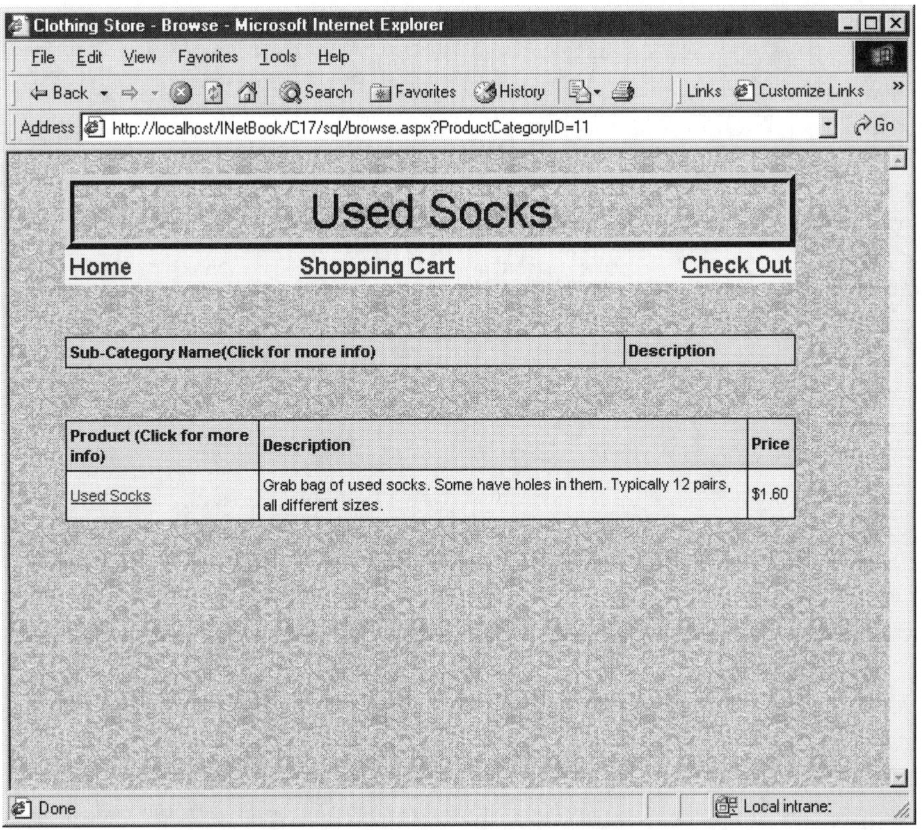

Figure 17-6 *Used Socks category displayed on the Browse page*

Regardless of whether the visitor views products through the Search page, the Specials page, or the Browse page, the products listed all have the same elements. The visitor sees the name of the product along with a brief description and the price for the product. The visitor can then click the name of the product to see its full listing as shown in Figure 17-7.

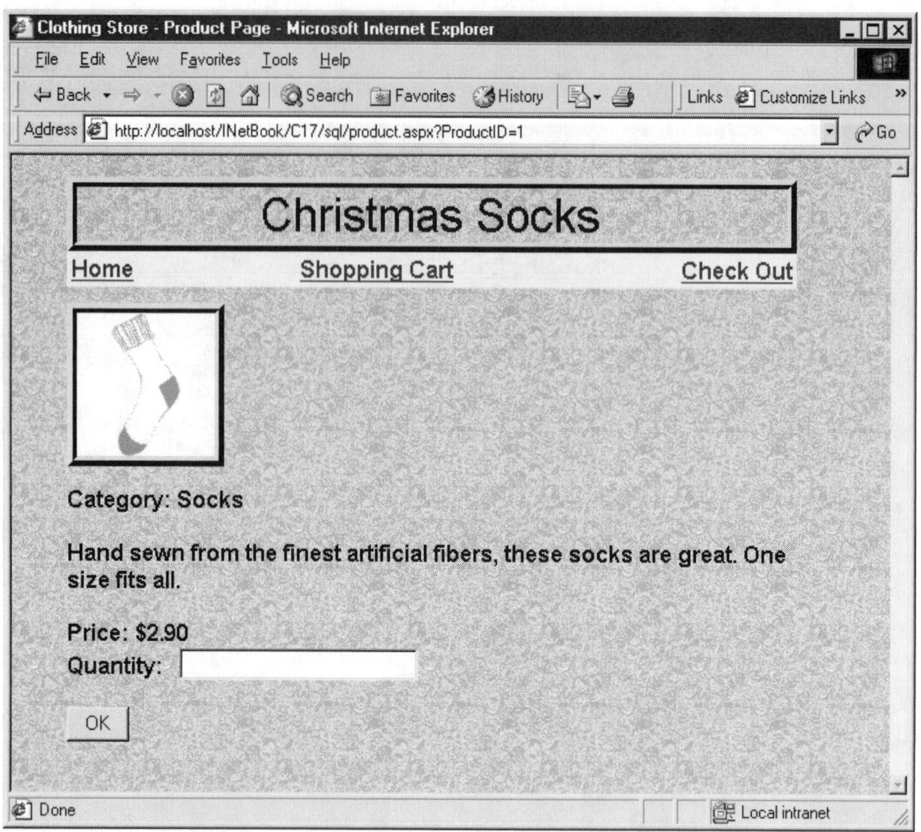

Figure 17-7 *Products page*

In addition to displaying further information about the product, the Products page also displays a small picture of the product. When it is clicked, the visitor sees the full-sized picture of the item.

If the visitor wants to order the item, they enter a value in the Quantity field and click OK. Note that validation rules are put into place to make sure that the visitor enters something in the quantity field and that the value falls within a specified range.

When they click OK, the item is added to their shopping cart and the visitor is taken to the Shopping Cart page displayed in Figure 17-8.

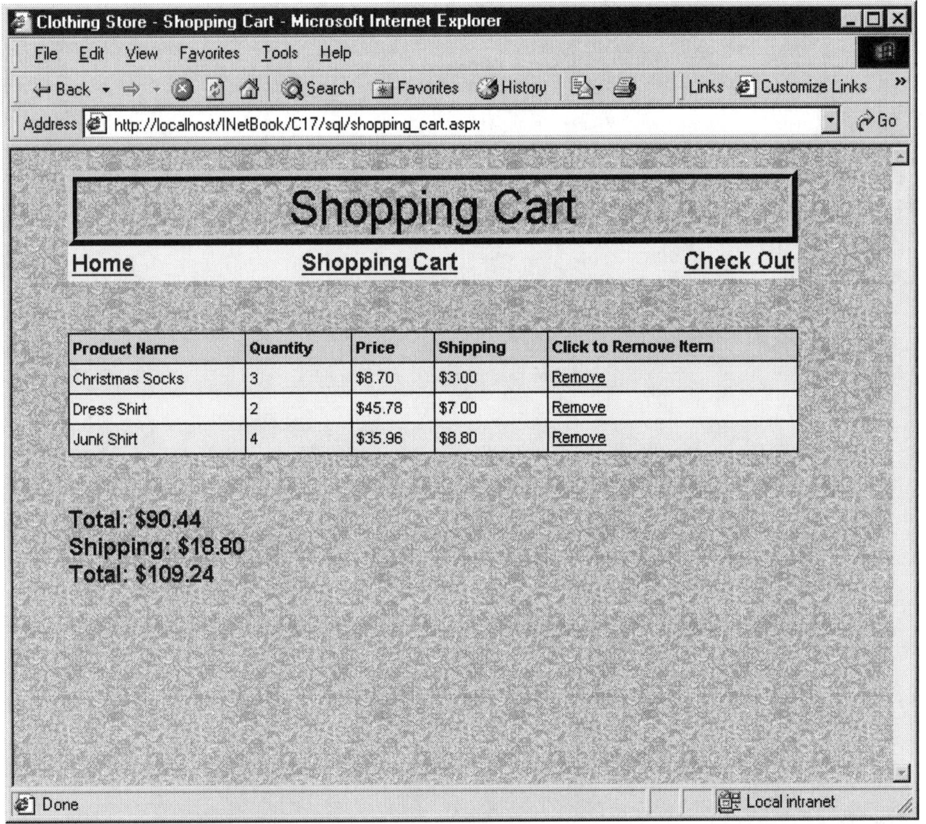

Figure 17-8 *Shopping Cart page*

The Shopping Cart page uses a DataGrid to show a list of all the items ordered by the visitor. At the bottom of the page, the visitor sees dollar totals for their order.

Within the DataGrid, a visitor can remove an item from their shopping cart by clicking the Remove link. Take a look at Figure 17-9. Here the visitor has removed the Dress Shirt product.

Note that the totals are updated to reflect the product having been removed from the shopping cart.

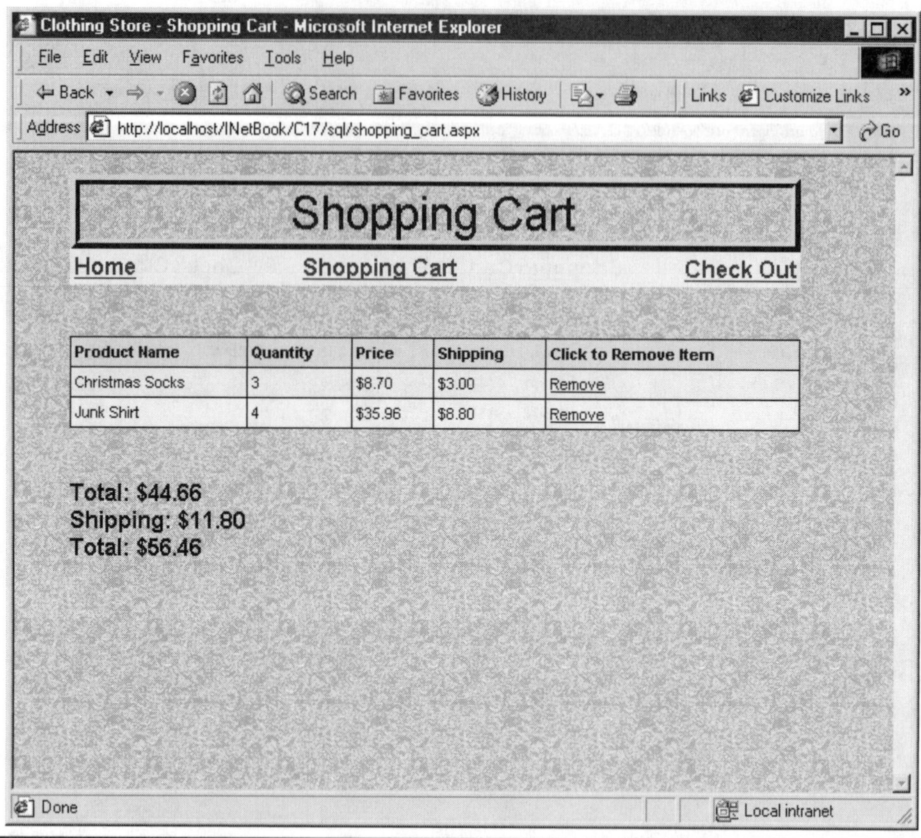

Figure 17-9 *Item removed from Shopping Cart*

When the visitor is ready to process their order, they click the Check Out link and are taken to the Check Out page displayed in Figure 17-10.

The Check Out page provides the place for the visitor to enter all their personal information. Each of the fields on this page is required. If the visitor leaves any blank, they see a message box that is generated through a ValidationSummary control.

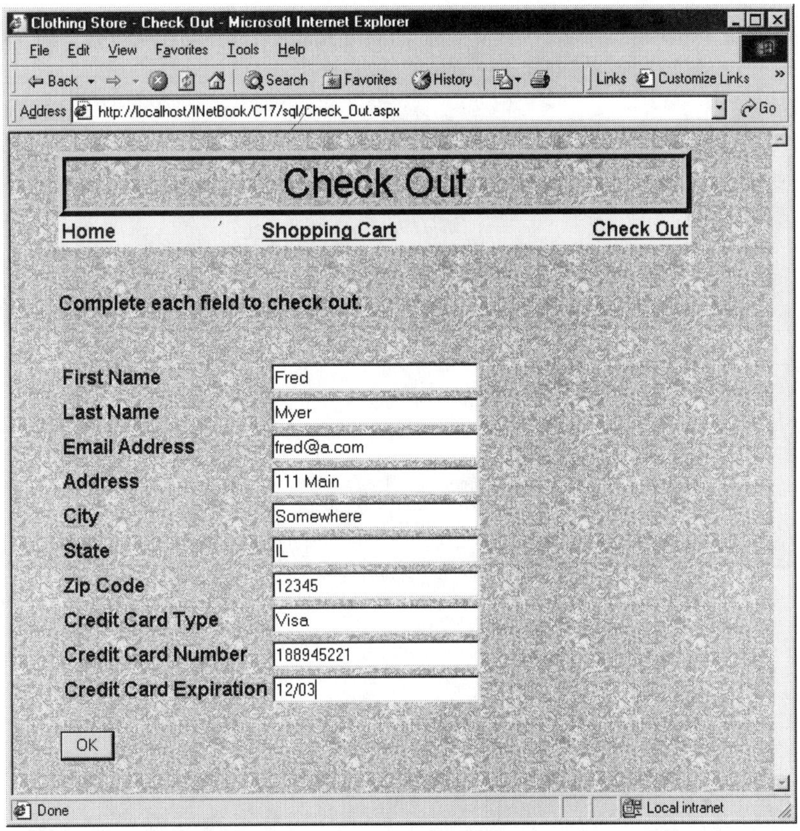

Figure 17-10 *Check Out page*

Once the visitor has completed the form, they can click OK and be presented with the message displayed in Figure 17-11.

At this point, the visitor's order is marked as placed and their session is ended.

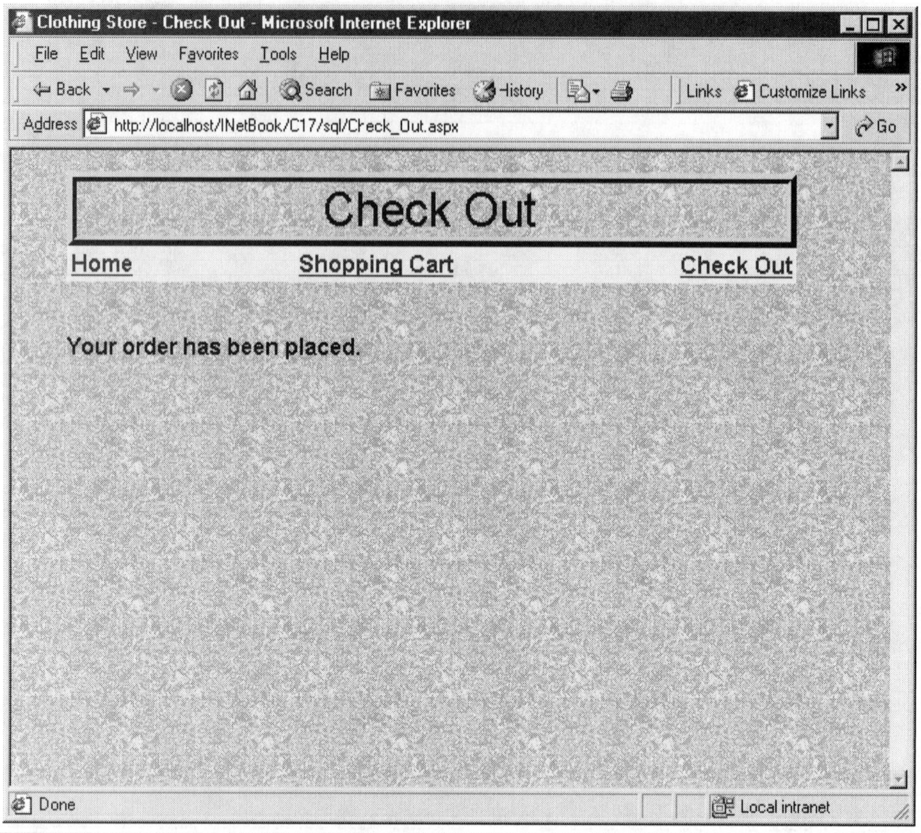

Figure 17-11 *Check Out page completed*

Online Store Database Component

C17.sql

The database required to run the Online Store application is made up of four interrelated tables. In this section, we will look at the relationships between the tables and the fields that make up the tables.

Tables and Data Diagram

Figure 17-12 shows the relationship between the tables in the Online Store database.

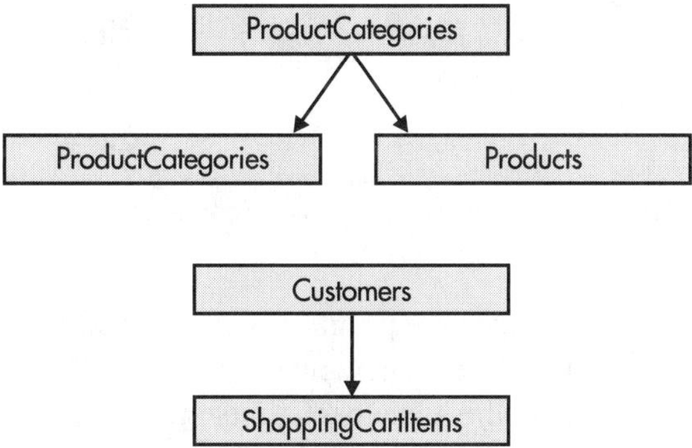

Figure 17-12 *Online Store Data Diagram*

The ProductCategories table stores the names of the categories that the visitor can browse through. Each category is a child category to another category. For example, the category of "Spring Jackets" would be a subcategory to "Jackets". Therefore, the ProductCategories table relates to itself in a one-to-many relationship.

The Products table stores the information on each of the products in the catalog. That table is in a one-to-many relationship with the ProductCategories table. Each product belongs to a specific category, but each category can have many sub-categories.

The other part of the database involves customers and the items that they order. The Customers table stores information about the customer. The ShoppingCartItems table stores the items placed into the shopping cart by each customer. The tables are in a one-to-many relationship. Each of the Customers can order many items, but each item goes with a specific customer order.

ProductCategories Field Specifications

ProductCategories.txt

The field specifications for the fields in the ProductCategories table are displayed in Table 17-1.

Field Name	Field Type	Notes
ProductCategoryID	int	Primary Key, Identity Column
ParentCategoryID	int	Foreign Key

Table 17-1 *ProductCategories Field Specifications*

Field Name	Field Type	Notes
CategoryName	varchar	Length = 50
CategoryDescription	varchar	Length = 255

Table 17-1 *ProductCategories Field Specifications* (continued)

The ProductCategoryID field is the primary key in this table. It is automatically populated with a unique value when a new record is added. The ParentCategoryID field is a foreign key that links this table back to itself.

The CategoryName and CategoryDescription fields store information about the category as it is displayed on the Browse page.

Products Field Specifications

Products.txt

The field specifications for the fields in the Products table are displayed in Table 17-2.

The ProductID field is the primary key in this table. The ProductCategoryID field is a foreign key that links this table to the ProductCategories table.

The PathToIcon field and the PathToFull field store the relative or full path to the image for the small and large pictures of each product.

The CurrentSpecial field has a value of 1 if the product should be included on the Specials page. In Access, a value of True indicates that the record should be included.

Field Name	Field Type	Notes
ProductID	int	Primary Key, Identity Column
ProductCategoryID	int	Foreign Key
ProductName	varchar	Length = 50
BriefDescription	varchar	Length = 100
LongDescription	text	
PathToIcon	varchar	Length = 100
PathToFull	varchar	Length = 100
Price	money	
ShippingCharge	money	
CurrentSpecial	bit	

Table 17-2 *Products Field Specifications*

The rest of the fields store information about the product.

Customers Field Specifications

Customers.txt

The field specifications for the fields in the Customers table are displayed in Table 17-3.

The CustomerID field is the primary key. The DateEntered field stores the date and time at which the visitor first put an item into their shopping cart. When a record is first created, the Status field contains the text "Shopping." When the visitor checks out, the text is changed to "Order Placed."

The rest of the fields contain information about the customer.

ShoppingCartItems Field Specifications

ShoppingCartItems.txt

The field specifications for the fields in the ShoppingCartItems table are displayed in Table 17-4.

Field Name	Field Type	Notes
CustomerID	int	Primary Key, Identity Column
DateEntered	datetime	
FirstName	varchar	Length = 50
LastName	varchar	Length = 50
EmailAddress	varchar	Length = 50
Address	varchar	Length = 100
City	varchar	Length = 100
State	varchar	Length = 2
ZipCode	varchar	Length = 50
CCType	varchar	Length = 50
CCNumber	varchar	Length = 50
CCExpiration	varchar	Length = 50
Status	varchar	Length = 50

Table 17-3 *Customers Field Specifications*

Field Name	Field Type	Notes
ShoppingCartItemID	int	Primary Key, Identity Column
CustomerID	int	Foreign Key
ProductName	varchar	Length = 50
Price	money	
Shipping	money	
Quantity	int	

Table 17-4 *ShoppingCartItems Field Specifications*

The ShoppingCartItemID field is the primary key. The CustomerID field links this table to the Customers table. The rest of the fields store information about the item placed into the shopping cart by the customer.

Online Store ASP.NET Code

The Online Store site is made up of seven ASP.NET pages. These pages use a variety of controls to accomplish their functionality.

In this section, we will review these seven pages that make up the tool.

Home ASP.NET Page

Index.aspx

The Home page does not have any code. It simply displays links and messages to the visitor. The page contains a single control, a Label, which displays the title of the page to the visitor:

```
<asp:Label
    id="lblTitle"
    BorderWidth="7px"
    BorderStyle=7
    Width="90%"
    Font-Size="25pt"
    Font-Name="Arial"
    Text="<center>Clothing Store</center>"
    runat="server"
/>
```

Specials ASP.NET Page

Specials.aspx

The Specials page displays a list of all the items that are marked as being currently on special. At the top of the page, three compiler directives are used.

```
<%@ Page Language=VB Debug=true %>
<%@ Import Namespace="System.Data" %>
<%@ Import Namespace="System.Data.OLEDB" %>
```

The first tells the compiler that we are using Visual Basic as our language and that we are in debug mode. Remember to turn that off when you use this tool in production:

```
<%@ Page Language=VB Debug=true %>
```

The other two directives tell the compiler to import to data libraries so that we can connect to, and display data from, our database:

```
<%@ Import Namespace="System.Data" %>
<%@ Import Namespace="System.Data.OLEDB" %>
```

Within the body of the page, a Label control is used to display the title of the page:

```
<asp:Label
    id="lblTitle"
    BorderWidth="7px"
    BorderStyle=7
    Width="90%"
    Font-Size="25pt"
    Font-Name="Arial"
    Text="<center>Current Specials</center>"
    runat="server"
/>
```

The next control is the DataGrid that displays all the product records that are marked as special:

```
<asp:DataGrid
    id="dgSpecials"
    AutoGenerateColumns="false"
    Width="90%"
    BackColor="beige"
```

```
    AlternatingItemStyle-BackColor="cornsilk"
    BorderColor="black"
    ShowFooter="false"
    CellPadding=3
    CellSpacing="0"
    Font-Name="Arial"
    Font-Size="8pt"
    ForeColor="Black"
    HeaderStyle-BackColor="burlywood"
    HeaderStyle-Font-Bold="True"
    runat="server">
    <columns>
        <asp:HyperLinkColumn
            HeaderText="Product (Click for more info)"
            DataNavigateUrlField="ProductID"

DataNavigateUrlFormatString="./product.aspx?ProductID={0}"
            DataTextField="ProductName"
            Target="_self"
        />
        <asp:BoundColumn
            HeaderText="Description"
            DataField="BriefDescription"
        />
        <asp:BoundColumn
            HeaderText="Price"
            DataField="Price"
            DataFormatString="{0:C}"
        />
    </columns>
</asp:DataGrid>
```

Note that we don't have the columns automatically generated

```
AutoGenerateColumns="false"
```

Instead, we add the columns ourselves within the DataGrid definition. The first column displays the name of the product. But when clicked, it sends the visitor to the Products page. Note that the ID of the product will replace the "{0}" text in the DataNavigateUrlFormatString property:

```
<asp:HyperLinkColumn
    HeaderText="Product (Click for more info)"
```

```
    DataNavigateUrlField="ProductID"
    DataNavigateUrlFormatString="./product.aspx?ProductID={0}"
    DataTextField="ProductName"
    Target="_self"
/>
```

The next column will display the description of the product:

```
<asp:BoundColumn
    HeaderText="Description"
    DataField="BriefDescription"
/>
```

The third column displays the price of the product. Note the DataFormatString property. The "0" indicates that we want to format the first field in this column. The "C" indicates that we want it formatted as currency:

```
<asp:BoundColumn
    HeaderText="Price"
    DataField="Price"
    DataFormatString="{0:C}"
/>
```

The code on the page runs when the page is loaded.

```
Sub Page_Load(ByVal Sender as Object, ByVal E as EventArgs)
    Dim DBConn as OleDbConnection
    Dim DBCommand As OleDbDataAdapter
    Dim DSPageData as New DataSet
    DBConn = New OleDbConnection("Provider=sqloledb;" _
        & "server=localhost;" _
        & "Initial Catalog=INETC17;" _
        & "User Id=sa;" _
        & "Password=yourpassword;")
    DBCommand = New OleDbDataAdapter _
        ("Select ProductID, ProductName, BriefDescription, " _
        & "Price From Products Where CurrentSpecial = 1 " _
        & "Order By ProductName", DBConn)
    DBCommand.Fill(DSPageData, _
        "Products")
    dgSpecials.DataSource = _
        DSPageData.Tables("Products").DefaultView
    dgSpecials.DataBind
End Sub
```

The code requires an OleDbConnection object so that we can connect to our SQL Server or Access database:

```
Dim DBConn as OleDbConnection
```

We also need a Data Adapter object to retrieve data from the database

```
Dim DBCommand As OleDbDataAdapter
```

and a DataSet object to place that data into:

```
Dim DSPageData as New DataSet
```

We start by connecting to our database:

```
DBConn = New OleDbConnection("Provider=sqloledb;" _
    & "server=localhost;" _
    & "Initial Catalog=INETC17;" _
    & "User Id=sa;" _
    & "Password=yourpassword;")
```

And we place SQL text into our Data Adapter object that will retrieve all the products on special:

```
DBCommand = New OleDbDataAdapter _
    ("Select ProductID, ProductName, BriefDescription, " _
    & "Price From Products Where CurrentSpecial = 1 " _
    & "Order By ProductName", DBConn)
```

The result of running that query is placed into a table called Products within our DataSet object:

```
DBCommand.Fill(DSPageData, _
    "Products")
```

We then bind our DataGrid to that DataSet table:

```
dgSpecials.DataSource = _
    DSPageData.Tables("Products").DefaultView
dgSpecials.DataBind
```

Search ASP.NET Page

Search.aspx

The Search page allows the visitor to enter search text, which is used to search for products that contain that text in the database. At the top of the page, you will find three compiler directives that are required for this page:

```
<%@ Page Language=VB Debug=true %>
<%@ Import Namespace="System.Data" %>
<%@ Import Namespace="System.Data.OLEDB" %>
```

Within the body of the page, a Label control that contains the title of the page is defined

```
<asp:Label
    id="lblTitle"
    BorderWidth="7px"
    BorderStyle=7
    Width="90%"
    Font-Size="25pt"
    Font-Name="Arial"
    Text="<center>Search our Catalog</center>"
    runat="server"
/>
```

The next control on the page is a TextBox that the visitor uses to enter their search text:

```
<asp:TextBox
    id="txtSearchText"
    Columns="25"
    MaxLength="30"
    runat=server
/>
```

That is followed by a Button control that the visitor clicks when they want to submit their search:

```
<asp:button
    id="butOK"
```

```
    text="  OK  "
    Type="Submit"
    OnClick="SubmitBtn_Click"
    runat="server"
/>
```

The other control on the page is a DataGrid that displays any products that match the visitor's search:

```
<asp:DataGrid
    id="dgProducts"
    AutoGenerateColumns="false"
    Width="90%"
    BackColor="beige"
    AlternatingItemStyle-BackColor="cornsilk"
    BorderColor="black"
    ShowFooter="false"
    CellPadding=3
    CellSpacing="0"
    Font-Name="Arial"
    Font-Size="8pt"
    ForeColor="Black"
    HeaderStyle-BackColor="burlywood"
    HeaderStyle-Font-Bold="True"
    runat="server">
    <columns>
        <asp:HyperLinkColumn
            HeaderText="Product (Click for more info)"
            DataNavigateUrlField="ProductID"

DataNavigateUrlFormatString="./product.aspx?ProductID={0}"
            DataTextField="ProductName"
            Target="_self"
        />
        <asp:BoundColumn
            HeaderText="Description"
            DataField="BriefDescription"
        />
        <asp:BoundColumn
            HeaderText="Price"
            DataField="Price"
            DataFormatString="{0:C}"
        />
    </columns>
</asp:DataGrid>
```

The code on the page runs only when the OK button is clicked.

```
Sub SubmitBtn_Click(Sender As Object, E As EventArgs)
    Dim DBConn as OleDbConnection
    Dim DBCommand As OleDbDataAdapter
    Dim DSPageData as New DataSet
    DBConn = New OleDbConnection("Provider=sqloledb;" _
        & "server=localhost;" _
        & "Initial Catalog=INETC17;" _
        & "User Id=sa;" _
        & "Password=yourpassword;")
    DBCommand = New OleDbDataAdapter _
        ("Select ProductID, ProductName, BriefDescription, " _
        & "Price From Products Where ProductName Like '%" _
        & txtSearchText.Text & "%' or BriefDescription " _
        & "Like '%" & txtSearchText.Text & "%' Order By " _
        & "ProductName", DBConn)
    DBCommand.Fill(DSPageData, _
        "Products")
    dgProducts.DataSource = _
        DSPageData.Tables("Products").DefaultView
    dgProducts.DataBind
End Sub
```

Within this procedure, we will need data objects:

```
Dim DBConn as OleDbConnection
Dim DBCommand As OleDbDataAdapter
Dim DSPageData as New DataSet
```

We start by connecting to our database:

```
DBConn = New OleDbConnection("Provider=sqloledb;" _
    & "server=localhost;" _
    & "Initial Catalog=INETC17;" _
    & "User Id=sa;" _
    & "Password=yourpassword;")
```

We then retrieve from the database all the products that contain the search text entered by the visitor in the name of the product or in its description:

```
DBCommand = New OleDbDataAdapter _
    ("Select ProductID, ProductName, BriefDescription, " _
```

```
    & "Price From Products Where ProductName Like '%" _
    & txtSearchText.Text & "%' or BriefDescription " _
    & "Like '%" & txtSearchText.Text & "%' Order By " _
    & "ProductName", DBConn)
```

The result of running that query is placed into our DataSet object:

```
DBCommand.Fill(DSPageData, _
    "Products")
```

We then bind our DataGrid to that DataSet object:

```
dgProducts.DataSource = _
    DSPageData.Tables("Products").DefaultView
dgProducts.DataBind
```

Browse ASP.NET Page

Browse.aspx

The Browse page allows the visitor to view categories within categories and products within categories. At the top of the page, we declare three compiler directives that set up the run environment and import needed data libraries:

```
<%@ Page Language=VB Debug=true %>
<%@ Import Namespace="System.Data" %>
<%@ Import Namespace="System.Data.OLEDB" %>
```

The first control on the page is a Label control used to display the name of the category the visitor is browsing

```
<asp:Label
    id="lblTitle"
    BorderWidth="7px"
    BorderStyle=7
    Width="90%"
    Font-Size="25pt"
    Font-Name="Arial"
runat="server"
/>
```

That is followed by a DataGrid that will display all the subcategories in the current category:

```
<asp:DataGrid
    id="dgCategories"
    AutoGenerateColumns="false"
    Width="90%"
    BackColor="beige"
    AlternatingItemStyle-BackColor="cornsilk"
    BorderColor="black"
    ShowFooter="false"
    CellPadding=3
    CellSpacing="0"
    Font-Name="Arial"
    Font-Size="8pt"
    ForeColor="Black"
    HeaderStyle-BackColor="burlywood"
    HeaderStyle-Font-Bold="True"
    runat="server">
    <columns>
        <asp:HyperLinkColumn
            HeaderText="Sub-Category Name(Click for more info)"
            DataNavigateUrlField="ProductCategoryID"

DataNavigateUrlFormatString="./browse.aspx?ProductCategoryID={0}"
            DataTextField="CategoryName"
            Target="_self"
        />
        <asp:BoundColumn
            HeaderText="Description"
            DataField="CategoryDescription"
        />
    </columns>
</asp:DataGrid>
```

The first column in that DataGrid displays the name of the category to the visitor. When they click the name, they are taken back to this same page, passing to it the ID of the subcategory selected

```
<asp:HyperLinkColumn
    HeaderText="Sub-Category Name(Click for more info)"
```

```
    DataNavigateUrlField="ProductCategoryID"
    DataNavigateUrlFormatString="./browse.aspx?ProductCategoryID={0}"
    DataTextField="CategoryName"
    Target="_self"
/>
```

The other column in this DataGrid displays the description of the category to the visitor:

```
<asp:BoundColumn
    HeaderText="Description"
    DataField="CategoryDescription"
/>
```

The other control on the page is a DataGrid that displays the matching products that is the same as those found on the Specials and Search pages:

```
<asp:DataGrid
    id="dgProducts"
    AutoGenerateColumns="false"
    Width="90%"
    BackColor="beige"
    AlternatingItemStyle-BackColor="cornsilk"
    BorderColor="black"
    ShowFooter="false"
    CellPadding=3
    CellSpacing="0"
    Font-Name="Arial"
    Font-Size="8pt"
    ForeColor="Black"
    HeaderStyle-BackColor="burlywood"
    HeaderStyle-Font-Bold="True"
    runat="server">
    <columns>
        <asp:HyperLinkColumn
            HeaderText="Product (Click for more info)"
            DataNavigateUrlField="ProductID"

DataNavigateUrlFormatString="./product.aspx?ProductID={0}"
            DataTextField="ProductName"
            Target="_self"
        />
        <asp:BoundColumn
```

```
            HeaderText="Description"
            DataField="BriefDescription"
        />
        <asp:BoundColumn
            HeaderText="Price"
            DataField="Price"
            DataFormatString="{0:C}"
        />
    </columns>
</asp:DataGrid>
```

The code on the page runs when the page is first loaded.

```
Sub Page_Load(ByVal Sender as Object, ByVal E as EventArgs)
    Dim DBConn as OleDbConnection
    Dim DBCommand As OleDbDataAdapter
    Dim DSPageData as New DataSet
    Dim CurrentCategoryID as Long
    If Len(Request.QueryString("ProductCategoryID")) = 0 Then
        CurrentCategoryID = 1
    Else
        CurrentCategoryID = Request.QueryString("ProductCategoryID")
    End If
    DBConn = New OleDbConnection("Provider=sqloledb;" _
        & "server=localhost;" _
        & "Initial Catalog=INETC17;" _
        & "User Id=sa;" _
        & "Password=yourpassword;")
    DBCommand = New OleDbDataAdapter _
        ("Select ProductID, ProductName, BriefDescription, " _
        & "Price From Products Where " _
        & "ProductCategoryID = " & CurrentCategoryID _
        & " Order By ProductName", DBConn)
    DBCommand.Fill(DSPageData, _
        "Products")
    dgProducts.DataSource = _
        DSPageData.Tables("Products").DefaultView
    dgProducts.DataBind
    DBCommand = New OleDbDataAdapter _
        ("Select ProductCategoryID, CategoryName, " _
        & "CategoryDescription From ProductCategories Where " _
        & "ParentCategoryID = " & CurrentCategoryID _
        & " Order By CategoryName", DBConn)
```

```
    DBCommand.Fill(DSPageData, _
        "Categories")
    dgCategories.DataSource = _
        DSPageData.Tables("Categories").DefaultView
    dgCategories.DataBind
    DBCommand = New OleDbDataAdapter _
        ("Select CategoryName " _
        & "From ProductCategories Where " _
        & "ProductCategoryID = " & CurrentCategoryID _
        , DBConn)
    DBCommand.Fill(DSPageData, _
        "CategoryName")
    lblTitle.Text = "<center>" _
        & DSPageData.Tables("CategoryName"). _
        Rows(0).Item("CategoryName") & "</center>"
End Sub
```

Within this code block, we need data objects:

```
Dim DBConn as OleDbConnection
Dim DBCommand As OleDbDataAdapter
Dim DSPageData as New DataSet
```

We also need a variable to store the ID of the current category:

```
Dim CurrentCategoryID as Long
```

When the visitor first starts to browse through the categories, no ID is passed into this page:

```
If Len(Request.QueryString("ProductCategoryID")) = 0 Then
```

In that case, we set it to 1, which is the ID of the Clothes category. Note that you would need to change this to the ID of the category you want as the top-level category:

```
CurrentCategoryID = 1
```

Otherwise, we use the category that was passed into this page when the visitor clicked a category name in the DataGrid control:

```
CurrentCategoryID = Request.QueryString("ProductCategoryID")
```

Then, we can connect to the database

```
DBConn = New OleDbConnection("Provider=sqloledb;" _
    & "server=localhost;" _
    & "Initial Catalog=INETC17;" _
    & "User Id=sa;" _
    & "Password=yourpassword;")
```

and retrieve all the products for the current category

```
DBCommand = New OleDbDataAdapter _
    ("Select ProductID, ProductName, BriefDescription, " _
    & "Price From Products Where " _
    & "ProductCategoryID = " & CurrentCategoryID _
    & " Order By ProductName", DBConn)
```

and place them into our DataSet object:

```
DBCommand.Fill(DSPageData, _
    "Products")
```

We then bind the products DataGrid to that DataSet table:

```
dgProducts.DataSource = _
    DSPageData.Tables("Products").DefaultView
dgProducts.DataBind
```

We also need to retrieve all the subcategories for the current category:

```
DBCommand = New OleDbDataAdapter _
    ("Select ProductCategoryID, CategoryName, " _
    & "CategoryDescription From ProductCategories Where " _
    & "ParentCategoryID = " & CurrentCategoryID _
    & " Order By CategoryName", DBConn)
```

We place them into another table of our DataSet object

```
DBCommand.Fill(DSPageData, _
   "Categories")
```

which the other DataGrid is bound to:

```
dgCategories.DataSource = _
    DSPageData.Tables("Categories").DefaultView
dgCategories.DataBind
```

One more thing we need to retrieve is the name of the current category

```
DBCommand = New OleDbDataAdapter _
    ("Select CategoryName " _
    & "From ProductCategories Where " _
    & "ProductCategoryID = " & CurrentCategoryID _
    , DBConn)
DBCommand.Fill(DSPageData, _
    "CategoryName")
```

so that we can place it in our title Label:

```
lblTitle.Text = "<center>" _
    & DSPageData.Tables("CategoryName"). _
    Rows(0).Item("CategoryName") & "</center>"
```

Products ASP.NET Page

Products.aspx

The Products page displays full information about a product to the visitor. The visitor can then place that product into their shopping cart.

At the top of the page, the same three compiler directives are defined

```
<%@ Page Language=VB Debug=true EnableSessionState=true %>
<%@ Import Namespace="System.Data" %>
<%@ Import Namespace="System.Data.OLEDB" %>
```

Within the body of the page, a Label is defined to display the name of the product as the title:

```
<asp:Label
    id="lblTitle"
    BorderWidth="7px"
    BorderStyle=7
    Width="90%"
    Font-Size="25pt"
```

```
    Font-Name="Arial"
    Text="<center>Current Specials</center>"
    runat="server"
/>
```

Next, a HyperLink control that is used to display the small picture of the product is defined. The control also links to the large picture of the product when it is clicked

```
<asp:HyperLink
    id="hypIcon"
    runat="server"
    Text="Click to view larger image"
    BorderWidth="7px"
    BorderStyle=7
/>
```

Next, we display the name of the category in a Label control:

```
<asp:Label
    id="lblCategoryName"
    Font-Bold="True"
    runat="server"
/>
```

That is followed by a label for the full description of the product

```
<asp:Label
    id="lblLongDescription"
    Font-Bold="True"
    Width="90%"
    runat="server"
/>
```

and a Label control for the price of the product:

```
<asp:Label
    id="lblPrice"
    Font-Bold="True"
    runat="server"
/>
```

The next control is a TextBox where the visitor enters the quantity of the product that they wish to order:

```
<asp:TextBox
    id="txtQuantity"
    Columns="25"
    MaxLength="30"
    runat=server
/>
```

Because of these validator controls, the quantity field is required

```
<asp:RequiredFieldValidator
    id="rfvQuantity"
    ControlToValidate="txtQuantity"
    Display="Dynamic"
    Font-Name="Verdana"
    Font-Bold="True"
    Font-Size="10pt"
    runat=server>
    The Quantity field is Required!
</asp:RequiredFieldValidator>
```

And it must be an Integer in the range of 1 to 30:

```
<asp:RangeValidator
    id="rngQuantity"
    ControlToValidate="txtQuantity"
    Type="Integer"
    MinimumValue=1
    MaximumValue=30
    Display="Dynamic"
    Font-Name="Verdana"
    Font-Bold="True"
    Font-Size="10pt"
    runat="server">
    The Quantity field must be from 1 to 30!
</asp:RangeValidator>
```

The only other control on the page is a Button that allows the visitor to order the item:

```
<asp:button
    id="butOK"
    text="  OK  "
    Type="Submit"
    OnClick="SubmitBtn_Click"
    runat="server"
/>
```

The page contains two code blocks. The first fires when the page is loaded

```
Sub Page_Load(ByVal Sender as Object, ByVal E as EventArgs)
    If Not IsPostBack Then
        Dim DBConn as OleDbConnection
        Dim DBCommand As OleDbDataAdapter
        Dim DSPageData as New DataSet
        If Len(Request.QueryString("ProductID")) = 0 Then
            Response.Redirect("./index.aspx")
        End If
        DBConn = New OleDbConnection("Provider=sqloledb;" _
            & "server=localhost;" _
            & "Initial Catalog=INETC17;" _
            & "User Id=sa;" _
            & "Password=yourpassword;")
        DBCommand = New OleDbDataAdapter _
            ("Select ProductName, LongDescription, " _
            & "PathToIcon, PathToFull, Price, CategoryName " _
            & "From Products Left Join ProductCategories On " _
            & "Products.ProductCategoryID = " _
            & "ProductCategories.ProductCategoryID Where " _
            & "ProductID = " & Request.QueryString("ProductID") _
            , DBConn)
        DBCommand.Fill(DSPageData, _
            "ProductData")
        lblTitle.Text = "<center>" _
            & DSPageData.Tables("ProductData"). _
            Rows(0).Item("ProductName") & "</center>"
        lblCategoryName.Text = "Category: " _
            & DSPageData.Tables("ProductData"). _
            Rows(0).Item("CategoryName")
        hypIcon.ImageUrl = DSPageData.Tables("ProductData"). _
            Rows(0).Item("PathToIcon")
        hypIcon.NavigateUrl = DSPageData.Tables("ProductData"). _
            Rows(0).Item("PathToFull")
```

```
        lblLongDescription.Text = DSPageData.Tables("ProductData"). _
            Rows(0).Item("LongDescription")
        lblPrice.Text = "Price: " _
            & FormatCurrency(DSPageData.Tables("ProductData"). _
            Rows(0).Item("Price"))
    End If
End Sub
```

We want this code to run only when the page is first loaded

```
If Not IsPostBack Then
```

If that is the case, we need data objects:

```
Dim DBConn as OleDbConnection
Dim DBCommand As OleDbDataAdapter
Dim DSPageData as New DataSet
```

But before we use them, we make sure that the ID of a product was passed into this page:

```
If Len(Request.QueryString("ProductID")) = 0 Then
```

If one wasn't, the visitor should not be at this page and we send them to the Home page:

```
Response.Redirect("./index.aspx")
```

Otherwise, we can connect to the database

```
DBConn = New OleDbConnection("Provider=sqloledb;" _
    & "server=localhost;" _
    & "Initial Catalog=INETC17;" _
    & "User Id=sa;" _
    & "Password=yourpassword;")
```

and retrieve all the information about the product, including the name of the category, which is joined to the Products table through the ProductCategories table:

```
DBCommand = New OleDbDataAdapter _
    ("Select ProductName, LongDescription, " _
    & "PathToIcon, PathToFull, Price, CategoryName " _
    & "From Products Left Join ProductCategories On " _
```

```
    & "Products.ProductCategoryID = " _
    & "ProductCategories.ProductCategoryID Where " _
    & "ProductID = " & Request.QueryString("ProductID") _
    , DBConn)
```

That data is placed into our DataSet object:

```
DBCommand.Fill(DSPageData, _
    "ProductData")
```

We then place the name of the product into our title Label control:

```
lblTitle.Text = "<center>" _
    & DSPageData.Tables("ProductData"). _
    Rows(0).Item("ProductName") & "</center>"
```

The category name is placed into another label:

```
lblCategoryName.Text = "Category: " _
    & DSPageData.Tables("ProductData"). _
    Rows(0).Item("CategoryName")
```

The HyperLink control has its image path set to the file that contains the small picture:

```
hypIcon.ImageUrl = DSPageData.Tables("ProductData"). _
    Rows(0).Item("PathToIcon")
```

And it will link to the big picture of the product:

```
hypIcon.NavigateUrl = DSPageData.Tables("ProductData"). _
    Rows(0).Item("PathToFull")
```

We also need to display the description of the product

```
lblLongDescription.Text = DSPageData.Tables("ProductData"). _
    Rows(0).Item("LongDescription")
```

and the price of the product, which is formatted as currency:

```
lblPrice.Text = "Price: " _
    & FormatCurrency(DSPageData.Tables("ProductData"). _
    Rows(0).Item("Price"))
```

The other procedure on the page fires when the form is submitted, which means that the visitor is ordering the product.

```
Sub SubmitBtn_Click(Sender As Object, E As EventArgs)
    Dim DBConn as OleDbConnection
    Dim DBInsert As New OleDbCommand
    Dim DBCommand As OleDbDataAdapter
    Dim DSPageData as New DataSet
    Dim CurrentQuantity as Integer
    Dim CurrentPrice as Single
    Dim CurrentShipping as Single
    Dim CurrentProductName as String
    DBConn = New OleDbConnection("Provider=sqloledb;" _
        & "server=localhost;" _
        & "Initial Catalog=INETC17;" _
        & "User Id=sa;" _
        & "Password=yourpassword;")
    DBInsert.Connection = DBConn
    DBInsert.Connection.Open
    If Len(Session("CustomerID")) = 0 Then
        DBInsert.CommandText = "Insert Into Customers " _
            & "(Status, DateEntered) values ('Shopping', '" _
            & Now() & "')"
        DBInsert.ExecuteNonQuery()
        DBCommand = New OleDbDataAdapter _
            ("Select Max(CustomerID) as MaxID " _
            & "From Customers", DBConn)
        DBCommand.Fill(DSPageData, _
            "CustomerID")
        Session("CustomerID") = DSPageData.Tables("CustomerID"). _
            Rows(0).Item("MaxID")
    End If
    DBCommand = New OleDbDataAdapter _
        ("Select ProductName, ShippingCharge, " _
        & "Price From Products Where " _
        & "ProductID = " & Request.QueryString("ProductID") _
        , DBConn)
    DBCommand.Fill(DSPageData, _
        "ProductData")
    CurrentQuantity = txtQuantity.Text
    CurrentPrice = CurrentQuantity * _
        DSPageData.Tables("ProductData"). _
        Rows(0).Item("Price")
    CurrentShipping = CurrentQuantity * _
        DSPageData.Tables("ProductData"). _
```

```
        Rows(0).Item("ShippingCharge")
    CurrentProductName = DSPageData.Tables("ProductData"). _
        Rows(0).Item("ProductName")
    DBInsert.CommandText = "Insert Into ShoppingCartItems " _
        & "(CustomerID, ProductName, Quantity, Price, Shipping) " _
        & "values (" _
        & Session("CustomerID") & ", " _
        & "'" & CurrentProductName & "', " _
        & CurrentQuantity & ", " _
        & CurrentPrice & ", " _
        & CurrentShipping & ")"
    DBInsert.ExecuteNonQuery()
    Response.Redirect("./shopping_cart.aspx")
End Sub
```

We will need data objects that allow us to retrieve and insert data into our database:

```
Dim DBConn as OleDbConnection
Dim DBInsert As New OleDbCommand
Dim DBCommand As OleDbDataAdapter
Dim DSPageData as New DataSet
```

We also declare a variable to store the quantity ordered

```
Dim CurrentQuantity as Integer
```

as well as the price

```
Dim CurrentPrice as Single
```

and shipping cost of the product ordered

```
Dim CurrentShipping as Single
Dim CurrentProductName as String
```

We start by connecting to the database:

```
DBConn = New OleDbConnection("Provider=sqloledb;" _
    & "server=localhost;" _
    & "Initial Catalog=INETC17;" _
    & "User Id=sa;" _
    & "Password=yourpassword;")
```

We set up our Command object so that it will use this database connection:

```
DBInsert.Connection = DBConn
DBInsert.Connection.Open
```

Next, we check to see if the visitor has already placed anything in their shopping cart:

```
If Len(Session("CustomerID")) = 0 Then
```

If not, we need to create a new customer record for them:

```
DBInsert.CommandText = "Insert Into Customers " _
    & "(Status, DateEntered) values ('Shopping', '" _
    & Now() & "')"
DBInsert.ExecuteNonQuery()
```

Next, we need to retrieve the ID for this new customer

```
DBCommand = New OleDbDataAdapter _
    ("Select Max(CustomerID) as MaxID " _
    & "From Customers", DBConn)
DBCommand.Fill(DSPageData, _
    "CustomerID")
```

and place it into a Session variable so that it will be available from other pages:

```
Session("CustomerID") = DSPageData.Tables("CustomerID"). _
    Rows(0).Item("MaxID")
```

After that, we need to retrieve information about the product ordered by the visitor:

```
DBCommand = New OleDbDataAdapter _
    ("Select ProductName, ShippingCharge, " _
    & "Price From Products Where " _
    & "ProductID = " & Request.QueryString("ProductID") _
    , DBConn)
DBCommand.Fill(DSPageData, _
    "ProductData")
```

We then store the quantity ordered into a local variable

```
CurrentQuantity = txtQuantity.Text
```

and use that value to calculate the total price for this item

```
CurrentPrice = CurrentQuantity * _
    DSPageData.Tables("ProductData"). _
    Rows(0).Item("Price")
```

as well as the total shipping charge for this item:

```
CurrentShipping = CurrentQuantity * _
    DSPageData.Tables("ProductData"). _
    Rows(0).Item("ShippingCharge")
```

We also store the name of the product in a local variable:

```
CurrentProductName = DSPageData.Tables("ProductData"). _
    Rows(0).Item("ProductName")
```

Those values are all used to add a new record to the ShoppingCartItems page for this customer:

```
DBInsert.CommandText = "Insert Into ShoppingCartItems " _
    & "(CustomerID, ProductName, Quantity, Price, Shipping) " _
    & "values (" _
    & Session("CustomerID") & ", " _
    & "'" & CurrentProductName & "', " _
    & CurrentQuantity & ", " _
    & CurrentPrice & ", " _
    & CurrentShipping & ")"
DBInsert.ExecuteNonQuery()
```

We can then send the visitor to the Shopping Cart page:

```
Response.Redirect("./shopping_cart.aspx")
```

Shopping Cart ASP.NET Page

Shopping_Cart.aspx

The code on the Shopping Cart page displays all the items ordered by the visitor. It also allows the visitor to remove items from their shopping cart. At the top of the page, we defined compiler directives that import the needed data libraries and that set up the run environment:

```
<%@ Page Language=VB Debug=true %>
<%@ Import Namespace="System.Data" %>
<%@ Import Namespace="System.Data.OLEDB" %>
```

Within the body of the page, we define a Label control that displays the title of the page:

```
<asp:Label
    id="lblTitle"
    BorderWidth="7px"
    BorderStyle=7
    Width="90%"
    Font-Size="25pt"
    Font-Name="Arial"
    Text="<center>Shopping Cart</center>"
    runat="server"
/>
```

Next, a DataGrid control is defined to display the items in the shopping cart:

```
<asp:DataGrid
    id="dgShoppingCart"
    AutoGenerateColumns="false"
    Width="90%"
    BackColor="beige"
    AlternatingItemStyle-BackColor="cornsilk"
    BorderColor="black"
    ShowFooter="false"
    CellPadding=3
    CellSpacing="0"
    Font-Name="Arial"
    Font-Size="8pt"
    ForeColor="Black"
    HeaderStyle-BackColor="burlywood"
    HeaderStyle-Font-Bold="True"
    OnItemCommand="Click_Grid"
    runat="server">
    <columns>
        <asp:BoundColumn
            HeaderText="Product Name"
            DataField="ProductName"
        />
        <asp:BoundColumn
            HeaderText="Quantity"
            DataField="Quantity"
```

```
        />
        <asp:BoundColumn
            HeaderText="Price"
            DataField="Price"
            DataFormatString="{0:C}"
        />
        <asp:BoundColumn
            HeaderText="Shipping"
            DataField="Shipping"
            DataFormatString="{0:C}"
        />
        <asp:BoundColumn
            DataField="ShoppingCartItemID"
            Visible="False"
        />
        <asp:ButtonColumn
            HeaderText="Click to Remove Item"
            ButtonType="LinkButton"
            Text="Remove"
            CommandName="cmdRemoveItem"
        />
    </columns>
</asp:DataGrid>
```

Note that when the visitor clicks a link in the DataGrid, this event will fire

```
OnItemCommand="Click_Grid"
```

The first column in our DataGrid displays the name of the product ordered

```
<asp:BoundColumn
    HeaderText="Product Name"
    DataField="ProductName"
/>
```

That is followed by the quantity ordered

```
<asp:BoundColumn
    HeaderText="Quantity"
    DataField="Quantity"
/>
```

Then comes the price of the product, which is formatted as currency

```
<asp:BoundColumn
    HeaderText="Price"
    DataField="Price"
    DataFormatString="{0:C}"
/>
```

as is the shipping charge:

```
<asp:BoundColumn
    HeaderText="Shipping"
    DataField="Shipping"
    DataFormatString="{0:C}"
/>
```

The next column is hidden. It contains the ID of the shopping cart item. It will be used when we remove an item from the shopping cart in our code:

```
<asp:BoundColumn
    DataField="ShoppingCartItemID"
    Visible="False"
/>
```

The last column is a Button column that displays a link with the text Remove in it. This is what the visitor clicks when they want to remove an item from the shopping cart:

```
<asp:ButtonColumn
    HeaderText="Click to Remove Item"
    ButtonType="LinkButton"
    Text="Remove"
    CommandName="cmdRemoveItem"
/>
```

After the DataGrid, three Label controls are defined. The first will display the product total:

```
<asp:Label
    id="lblPriceTotal"
    Font-Bold="True"
    Width="90%"
```

```
    runat="server"
/>
```

The second will display the shipping total:

```
<asp:Label
    id="lblShippingTotal"
    Font-Bold="True"
    Width="90%"
    runat="server"
/>
```

And the third will display the grand total for all the products and the shipping:

```
<asp:Label
    id="lblGrandTotal"
    Font-Bold="True"
    Width="90%"
    runat="server"
/>
```

The code on the page is divided into two events. This code block runs when the page is loaded.

```
Sub Page_Load(ByVal Sender as Object, ByVal E as EventArgs)
    If Len(Session("CustomerID")) <> 0 Then
        Dim DBConn as OleDbConnection
        Dim DBCommand As OleDbDataAdapter
        Dim DSPageData as New DataSet
        DBConn = New OleDbConnection("Provider=sqloledb;" _
            & "server=localhost;" _
            & "Initial Catalog=INETC17;" _
            & "User Id=sa;" _
            & "Password=yourpassword;")
        DBCommand = New OleDbDataAdapter _
            ("Select ShoppingCartItemID, ProductName, " _
            & "Quantity, Price, Shipping From " _
            & "ShoppingCartItems Where " _
            & "CustomerID = " & Session("CustomerID") _
            & " Order By ProductName" _
            , DBConn)
        DBCommand.Fill(DSPageData, _
            "ShoppingCart")
```

```
        If DSPageData.Tables("ShoppingCart").Rows.Count = 0 Then
            lblPriceTotal.Text = "You do not have any items " _
                & "in your shopping chart."
        Else
            dgShoppingCart.DataSource = _
                DSPageData.Tables("ShoppingCart").DefaultView
            dgShoppingCart.DataBind
            DBCommand = New OleDbDataAdapter _
                ("Select Sum(Price) as PriceSum, " _
                & "Sum(Shipping) as ShippingSum From " _
                & "ShoppingCartItems Where " _
                & "CustomerID = " & Session("CustomerID") _
                , DBConn)
            DBCommand.Fill(DSPageData, _
                "Totals")
            lblPriceTotal.Text = "Total: " _
                & FormatCurrency(DSPageData.Tables("Totals"). _
                Rows(0).Item("PriceSum"))
            lblShippingTotal.Text = "Shipping: " _
                & FormatCurrency(DSPageData.Tables("Totals"). _
                Rows(0).Item("ShippingSum"))
            lblGrandTotal.Text = "Total: " _
                & FormatCurrency(DSPageData.Tables("Totals"). _
                Rows(0).Item("PriceSum") + _
                DSPageData.Tables("Totals"). _
                Rows(0).Item("ShippingSum"))
        End If
    Else
        lblPriceTotal.Text = "You do not have any items " _
            & "in your shopping chart."
    End If
End Sub
```

We first check to see if the visitor has placed anything in their shopping cart yet:

```
If Len(Session("CustomerID")) <> 0 Then
```

If they have, we will need data objects:

```
Dim DBConn as OleDbConnection
Dim DBCommand As OleDbDataAdapter
Dim DSPageData as New DataSet
```

We start by connecting to the database:

```
DBConn = New OleDbConnection("Provider=sqloledb;" _
    & "server=localhost;" _
    & "Initial Catalog=INETC17;" _
    & "User Id=sa;" _
    & "Password=yourpassword;")
```

We retrieve the items ordered by the visitor

```
DBCommand = New OleDbDataAdapter _
    ("Select ShoppingCartItemID, ProductName, " _
    & "Quantity, Price, Shipping From " _
    & "ShoppingCartItems Where " _
    & "CustomerID = " & Session("CustomerID") _
    & " Order By ProductName" _
    , DBConn)
```

and place them into our DataSet object:

```
DBCommand.Fill(DSPageData, _
    "ShoppingCart")
```

Next, we need to make sure that the visitor still has something in their shopping cart. They could have added an item and then removed it:

```
If DSPageData.Tables("ShoppingCart").Rows.Count = 0 Then
```

If that is the case, we just display this message to the visitor:

```
lblPriceTotal.Text = "You do not have any items " _
    & "in your shopping chart."
```

Otherwise, we can bind our DataGrid to the DataSet object:

```
dgShoppingCart.DataSource = _
    DSPageData.Tables("ShoppingCart").DefaultView
dgShoppingCart.DataBind
```

Next, we need to retrieve the product totals

```
DBCommand = New OleDbDataAdapter _
    ("Select Sum(Price) as PriceSum, " _
```

```
    & "Sum(Shipping) as ShippingSum From " _
    & "ShoppingCartItems Where " _
    & "CustomerID = " & Session("CustomerID") _
    , DBConn)
```

into our DataSet object:

```
DBCommand.Fill(DSPageData, _
    "Totals")
```

We then place those totals into our three total Label controls:

```
lblPriceTotal.Text = "Total: " _
    & FormatCurrency(DSPageData.Tables("Totals"). _
    Rows(0).Item("PriceSum"))
lblShippingTotal.Text = "Shipping: " _
    & FormatCurrency(DSPageData.Tables("Totals"). _
    Rows(0).Item("ShippingSum"))
lblGrandTotal.Text = "Total: " _
    & FormatCurrency(DSPageData.Tables("Totals"). _
    Rows(0).Item("PriceSum") + _
    DSPageData.Tables("Totals"). _
    Rows(0).Item("ShippingSum"))
```

If the code flows here, it means that the visitor has not yet placed anything into their shopping cart:

```
Else
```

So we just display this message:

```
lblPriceTotal.Text = "You do not have any items " _
    & "in your shopping chart."
```

The other procedure fires when the visitor clicks one of the Remove links in the DataGrid control.

```
Sub Click_Grid(ByVal Sender as Object, ByVal E as
DataGridCommandEventArgs)
    Dim DBConn as OleDbConnection
    Dim DBDelete As New OleDbCommand
    Dim DBCommand As OleDbDataAdapter
    Dim DSPageData as New DataSet
```

```
DBConn = New OleDbConnection("Provider=sqloledb;" _
    & "server=localhost;" _
    & "Initial Catalog=INETC17;" _
    & "User Id=sa;" _
    & "Password=yourpassword;")
DBDelete.CommandText = "Delete from ShoppingCartItems " _
    & "Where ShoppingCartItemID = " _
    & E.Item.Cells(4).Text
DBDelete.Connection = DBConn
DBDelete.Connection.Open
DBDelete.ExecuteNonQuery()
DBCommand = New OleDbDataAdapter _
    ("Select ShoppingCartItemID, ProductName, " _
    & "Quantity, Price, Shipping From " _
    & "ShoppingCartItems Where " _
    & "CustomerID = " & Session("CustomerID") _
    & " Order By ProductName" _
    , DBConn)
DBCommand.Fill(DSPageData, _
    "ShoppingCart")
dgShoppingCart.DataSource = _
    DSPageData.Tables("ShoppingCart").DefaultView
dgShoppingCart.DataBind
if DSPageData.Tables("ShoppingCart").Rows.Count = 0 Then
    lblPriceTotal.Text = "You do not have any items " _
        & "in your shopping chart."
    lblShippingTotal.Text = ""
    lblGrandTotal.Text = ""
Else
    DBCommand = New OleDbDataAdapter _
        ("Select Sum(Price) as PriceSum, " _
        & "Sum(Shipping) as ShippingSum From " _
        & "ShoppingCartItems Where " _
        & "CustomerID = " & Session("CustomerID") _
        , DBConn)
    DBCommand.Fill(DSPageData, _
        "Totals")
    lblPriceTotal.Text = "Total: " _
        & FormatCurrency(DSPageData.Tables("Totals"). _
        Rows(0).Item("PriceSum"))
    lblShippingTotal.Text = "Shipping: " _
        & FormatCurrency(DSPageData.Tables("Totals"). _
        Rows(0).Item("ShippingSum"))
```

```
        lblGrandTotal.Text = "Total: " _
            & FormatCurrency(DSPageData.Tables("Totals"). _
            Rows(0).Item("PriceSum") + _
            DSPageData.Tables("Totals"). _
            Rows(0).Item("ShippingSum"))
    End If
End Sub
```

We will need data variables to retrieve and delete data from our database:

```
Dim DBConn as OleDbConnection
Dim DBDelete As New OleDbCommand
Dim DBCommand As OleDbDataAdapter
Dim DSPageData as New DataSet
```

We start by connecting to the database:

```
DBConn = New OleDbConnection("Provider=sqloledb;" _
    & "server=localhost;" _
    & "Initial Catalog=INETC17;" _
    & "User Id=sa;" _
    & "Password=yourpassword;")
```

We then place Delete SQL text into our command object to remove the record selected in the DataGrid by the visitor:

```
DBDelete.CommandText = "Delete from ShoppingCartItems " _
    & "Where ShoppingCartItemID = " _
    & E.Item.Cells(4).Text
```

The Command object will use our Connection object:

```
DBDelete.Connection = DBConn
DBDelete.Connection.Open
```

We then delete the offending record:

```
DBDelete.ExecuteNonQuery()
```

Next, we need to retrieve the remaining items in the visitor's shopping cart

```
DBCommand = New OleDbDataAdapter _
    ("Select ShoppingCartItemID, ProductName, " _
```

```
    & "Quantity, Price, Shipping From " _
    & "ShoppingCartItems Where " _
    & "CustomerID = " & Session("CustomerID") _
    & " Order By ProductName" _
    , DBConn)
```

and place them into our DataSet object

```
DBCommand.Fill(DSPageData, _
    "ShoppingCart")
```

which our DataGrid is bound to:

```
dgShoppingCart.DataSource = _
    DSPageData.Tables("ShoppingCart").DefaultView
dgShoppingCart.DataBind
```

We need to retrieve the totals. But the visitor may have deleted the last item in their shopping cart:

```
if DSPageData.Tables("ShoppingCart").Rows.Count = 0 Then
```

If that is the case, we simply display this message

```
lblPriceTotal.Text = "You do not have any items " _
    & "in your shopping chart."
```

and clear our other total labels:

```
lblShippingTotal.Text = ""
lblGrandTotal.Text = ""
```

Otherwise, we need to retrieve the new totals

```
DBCommand = New OleDbDataAdapter _
    ("Select Sum(Price) as PriceSum, " _
    & "Sum(Shipping) as ShippingSum From " _
    & "ShoppingCartItems Where " _
    & "CustomerID = " & Session("CustomerID") _
    , DBConn)
DBCommand.Fill(DSPageData, _
    "Totals")
```

and place them into our three total Label controls:

```
lblPriceTotal.Text = "Total: " _
    & FormatCurrency(DSPageData.Tables("Totals"). _
    Rows(0).Item("PriceSum"))
lblShippingTotal.Text = "Shipping: " _
    & FormatCurrency(DSPageData.Tables("Totals"). _
    Rows(0).Item("ShippingSum"))
lblGrandTotal.Text = "Total: " _
    & FormatCurrency(DSPageData.Tables("Totals"). _
    Rows(0).Item("PriceSum") + _
    DSPageData.Tables("Totals"). _
    Rows(0).Item("ShippingSum"))
```

Check Out ASP.NET Page

Check_Out.aspx

The Check Out page allows the visitor to submit their personal information and to mark the order as having been placed. At the top of the page, we have our three compiler directives:

```
<%@ Page Language=VB Debug=true %>
<%@ Import Namespace="System.Data" %>
<%@ Import Namespace="System.Data.OLEDB" %>
```

Within the body of the page, a label is used to display the title of the page:

```
<asp:Label
    id="lblTitle"
    BorderWidth="7px"
    BorderStyle=7
    Width="90%"
    Font-Size="25pt"
    Font-Name="Arial"
    Text="<center>Check Out</center>"
    runat="server"
/>
```

Another Label control initially displays instructions but also displays a success message when the form on the page is submitted

```
<asp:Label
    id="lblMessage"
```

```
    Font-Bold="True"
    Width="90%"
    Text="Complete each field to check out."
    runat="server"
/>
```

The rest of the controls on the page are placed on a Panel so that we can easily toggle their visibility:

```
<asp:Panel
    id="pnlForm"
    runat="server"
>
```

Next, a ValidationSummary control is defined. It is used to tell the visitor what fields they still need to complete when they attempt to submit the form. Note that the message is displayed as a message box:

```
<asp:ValidationSummary ID="vsAllErrors"
    DisplayMode="BulletList"
    ShowMessageBox="True"
    ShowSummary="False"
    runat="server"
    HeaderText="You need to enter a value in these fields:"
/>
```

The rest of the controls, except for one, are made up of a TextBox control for the visitor to enter a piece of information about themselves

```
<asp:TextBox
    id="txtFirstName"
    Columns="25"
    MaxLength="50"
    runat=server
/>
```

paired with a RequiredFieldValidator control to make sure that they enter a value into it:

```
<asp:RequiredFieldValidator
    id="rfvFirstName"
    ControlToValidate="txtFirstName"
    ErrorMessage="First Name"
```

```
    Display="Static"
    runat=server>
    *
</asp:RequiredFieldValidator>
```

The only other control on the page is a Button that submits the form for processing

```
<asp:button
    id="butAdd"
    text="  OK  "
    Type="Submit"
    OnClick="SubmitCheckOut_Click"
    runat="server"
/>
```

The code on the page fires in two events. The first fires when the page is loaded.

```
Sub Page_Load(ByVal Sender as Object, ByVal E as EventArgs)
    If Len(Session("CustomerID")) = 0 Then
        Response.Redirect("./shopping_cart.aspx")
    End If
End Sub
```

It simply makes sure that the visitor has ordered something:

```
If Len(Session("CustomerID")) = 0 Then
```

If they haven't, we send them to the Shopping Cart page, where they will see the message that nothing is in their shopping cart:

```
Response.Redirect("./shopping_cart.aspx")
```

The other code block fires when the OK button is clicked.

```
Sub SubmitCheckOut_Click(Sender As Object, E As EventArgs)
    Dim DBConn as OleDbConnection
    Dim DBUpdate As New OleDbCommand
    DBConn = New OleDbConnection("Provider=sqloledb;" _
        & "server=localhost;" _
        & "Initial Catalog=INETC17;" _
        & "User Id=sa;" _
        & "Password=yourpassword;")
    DBUpdate.CommandText = "Update Customers set " _
```

```
        & "Status = 'Order Placed', " _
        & "FirstName = '" _
        & Replace(txtFirstName.Text, "'", "''") & "', " _
        & "LastName = '" _
        & Replace(txtLastName.Text, "'", "''") & "', " _
        & "EmailAddress = '" _
        & Replace(txtEmailAddress.Text, "'", "''") & "', " _
        & "Address = '" _
        & Replace(txtAddress.Text, "'", "''") & "', " _
        & "City = '" _
        & Replace(txtCity.Text, "'", "''") & "', " _
        & "State = '" _
        & Replace(txtState.Text, "'", "''") & "', " _
        & "ZipCode = '" _
        & Replace(txtZipCode.Text, "'", "''") & "', " _
        & "CCType = '" _
        & Replace(txtCCType.Text, "'", "''") & "', " _
        & "CCNumber = '" _
        & Replace(txtCCNumber.Text, "'", "''") & "', " _
        & "CCExpiration = '" _
        & Replace(txtCCExpiration.Text, "'", "''") & "' " _
        & "Where CustomerID = " & Session("CustomerID")
    DBUpdate.Connection = DBConn
    DBUpdate.Connection.Open
    DBUpdate.ExecuteNonQuery()
    Session.Abandon
    pnlForm.Visible = False
    lblMessage.Text = "Your order has been placed."
End Sub
```

Within this procedure, we will need data objects so that we can update the customer's record:

```
Dim DBConn as OleDbConnection
Dim DBUpdate As New OleDbCommand
```

We start by connecting to the database:

```
DBConn = New OleDbConnection("Provider=sqloledb;" _
    & "server=localhost;" _
    & "Initial Catalog=INETC17;" _
    & "User Id=sa;" _
    & "Password=yourpassword;")
```

Then we update the customer's record with the information they entered in the TextBox controls on this page. Note that we also change the status of the customer:

```
DBUpdate.CommandText = "Update Customers set " _
    & "Status = 'Order Placed', " _
    & "FirstName = '" _
    & Replace(txtFirstName.Text, "'", "''") & "', " _
    & "LastName = '" _
    & Replace(txtLastName.Text, "'", "''") & "', " _
    & "EmailAddress = '" _
    & Replace(txtEmailAddress.Text, "'", "''") & "', " _
    & "Address = '" _
    & Replace(txtAddress.Text, "'", "''") & "', " _
    & "City = '" _
    & Replace(txtCity.Text, "'", "''") & "', " _
    & "State = '" _
    & Replace(txtState.Text, "'", "''") & "', " _
    & "ZipCode = '" _
    & Replace(txtZipCode.Text, "'", "''") & "', " _
    & "CCType = '" _
    & Replace(txtCCType.Text, "'", "''") & "', " _
    & "CCNumber = '" _
    & Replace(txtCCNumber.Text, "'", "''") & "', " _
    & "CCExpiration = '" _
    & Replace(txtCCExpiration.Text, "'", "''") & "' " _
    & "Where CustomerID = " & Session("CustomerID")
DBUpdate.Connection = DBConn
DBUpdate.Connection.Open
DBUpdate.ExecuteNonQuery()
```

We then end the visitor's session

```
Session.Abandon
```

hide the form on the page

```
pnlForm.Visible = False
```

and display a success message to the visitor:

```
lblMessage.Text = "Your order has been placed."
```

Access Code Changes

C17.mdb

Two changes need to be made if you wish to use this solution with an Access database instead of a SQL Server database. First, you need to change the connect string so that it uses the correct provider and so that it points to the correct database:

```
DBConn = New OleDbConnection("PROVIDER=Microsoft.Jet.OLEDB.4.0;" _
    & "DATA SOURCE=" _
    & Server.MapPath("/INetBook/C17/" _
    & "Access/C17.mdb;"))
```

The other change that needs to be made is to the query on the special page. In SQL Server, we looked for all the records that had a 1 in the CurrentSpecial field. But in Access, we need to change that to True:

```
DBCommand = New OleDbDataAdapter _
    ("Select ProductID, ProductName, BriefDescription, " _
    & "Price From Products Where CurrentSpecial = True " _
    & "Order By ProductName", DBConn)
```

No other code changes are needed.

CHAPTER 18

Creating an Online Auction

In the last chapter, we looked at a solution that allowed your visitors to shop through the items in your store and to order those items. The solution presented in this chapter also allows visitors to view your products. But the products in this case are sold through an auction.

Auctions provide an additional way for you and your company to sell your wares. Often they are used to sell products with a limited stock, items that have been refurbished, or items that are used. With this tool, visitors sign into the auction and can then place bids on any open auction items. Bids placed by visitors must be at least as much as the minimum bid and must be greater than all previous bids.

Allowing Customers to Bid for Products

When the visitor first enters the Auction site, they see the page displayed in Figure 18-1.

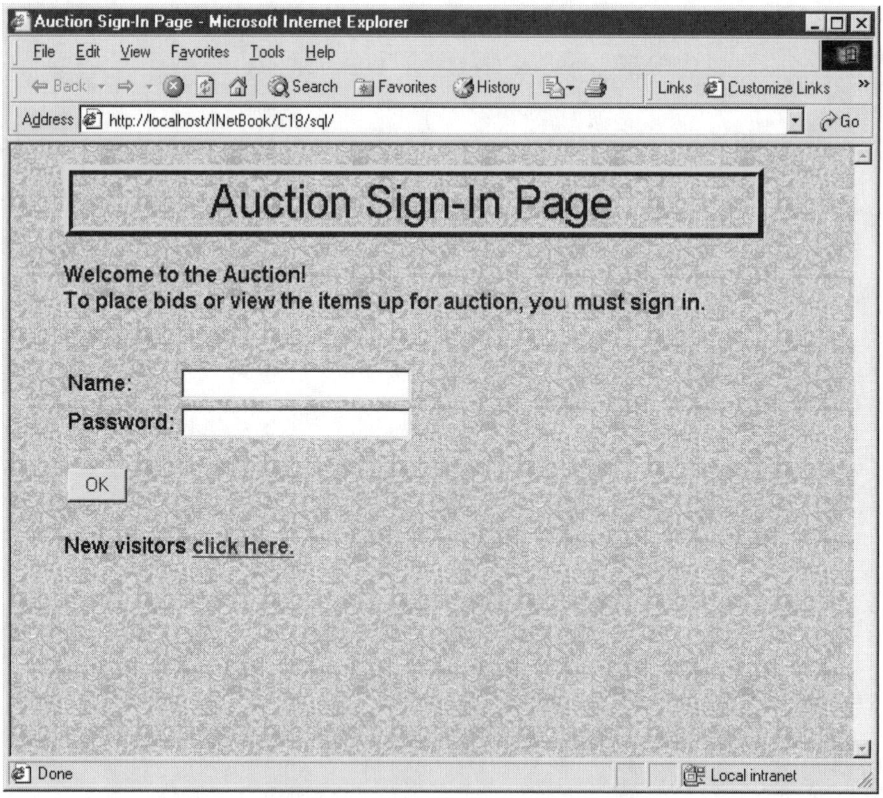

Figure 18-1 *Online Auction Sign-In page*

On this page, the visitor is welcomed to the site. If they are an existing auction participant, they can enter their name and password. Otherwise, the visitor needs to click the link to the New User page that is at the bottom of this page.

When they do that, they see the page displayed in Figure 18-2.

On this page, the visitor enters their personal information. Note that all the fields are required, and the password field must match in the two instances. Also, as you will see when we look at the code for this page, the visitor must enter a name that is not in use by another visitor.

Once the visitor has completed the information on the page correctly, or if they entered their name and password on the Sign-In page, they are taken to the Auction Items page displayed in Figure 18-3.

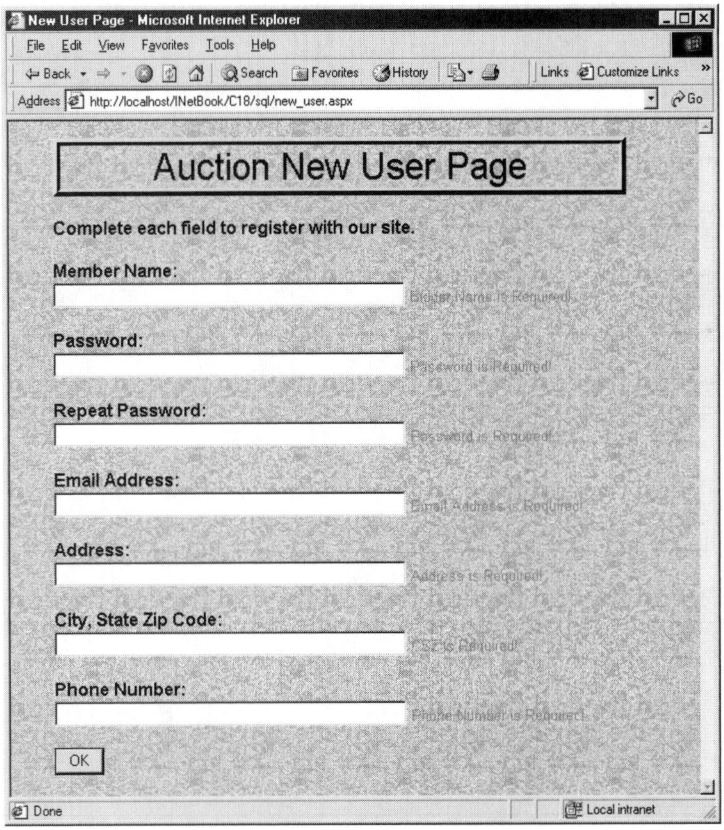
New User Page - Microsoft Internet Explorer
File Edit View Favorites Tools Help
Back Search Favorites History
Links Customize Links
Address http://localhost/INetBook/C18/sql/new_user.aspx
Go
Auction New User Page
Complete each field to register with our site.
Member Name:
Password:
Repeat Password:
Email Address:
Address:
City, State Zip Code:
Phone Number:
OK
Done
Local intranet

Figure 18-2 *New User page*

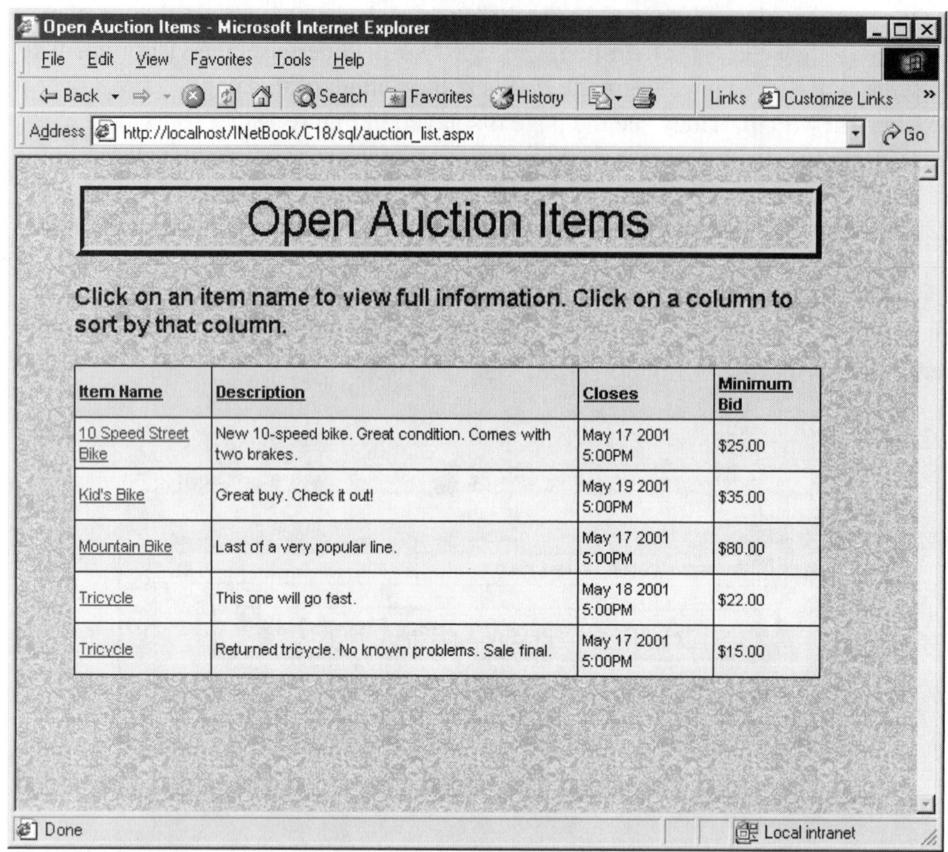

Figure 18-3 *Auction Items page*

The Auction Items page displays, through the use of a DataGrid, all the auction items that are not yet closed, according to their close date. Note that the visitor can sort the DataGrid by clicking one of the column headers. Take a look at Figure 18-4.

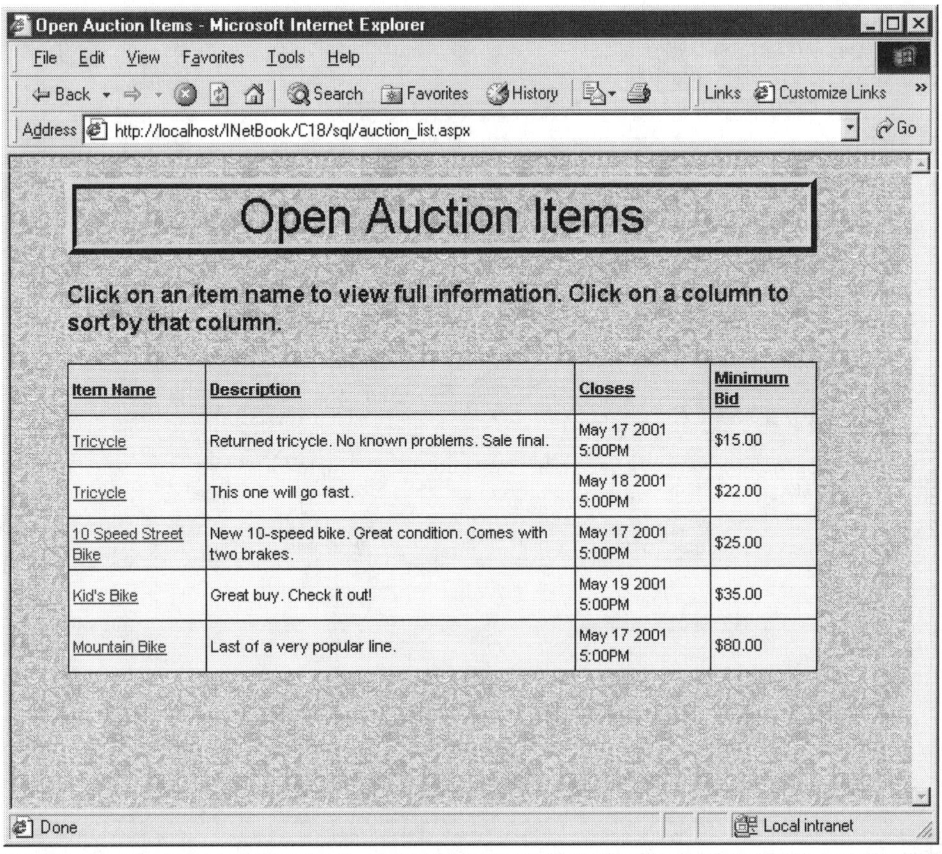

Figure 18-4 *Auction Items page sorted by minimum bid*

Here the visitor has clicked the Minimum Bid column. In code, we capture the name of the column clicked and then redisplay the grid with the items sorted by that field.

To view the complete information for an auction item, the visitor simply clicks its name in the DataGrid. They are then taken to an Auction Item page, like the one displayed in Figure 18-5.

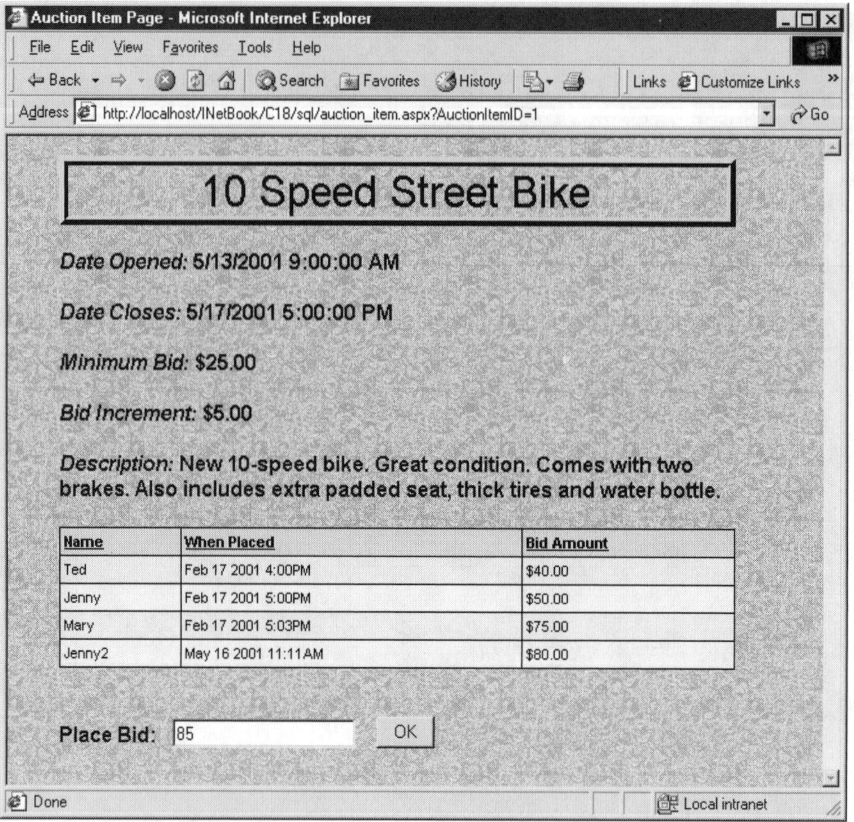

Figure 18-5 *Auction Item page*

The top part of the page displays all the information for the item. Then, in a DataGrid, the visitor sees the bidding history for this item. As with the DataGrid on the Auction Items page, the visitor can click any of the columns to sort the records in the DataGrid by that field.

At the bottom of the page the visitor can bid on this auction item. Through code, we show the minimum value for the next bid based on the highest bid plus the bid increment amount. If no bid has been made on the auction item, then the minimum bid amount is used.

The visitor can enter one of these values or any value greater than that. When they click OK, their bid is added to the DataGrid, as you can see in Figure 18-6.

Note that the next bid now reflects the new bid entered by the current visitor.

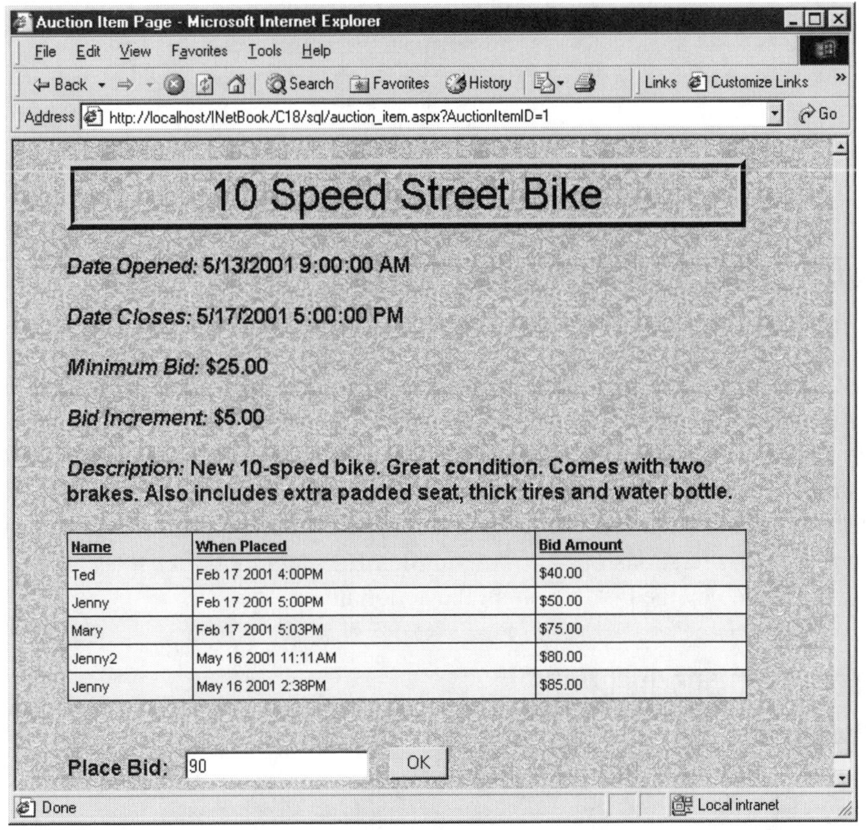

Figure 18-6 *Auction Item page with new bid added*

Online Auction Database Component

C18.sql

The database required to run the Online Auction site is made up of three interrelated tables. In this section, we will look at the relationships between the tables and the fields that make up the tables.

Tables and Data Diagram

Figure 18-7 shows the relationships between the tables in the Online Auction database.

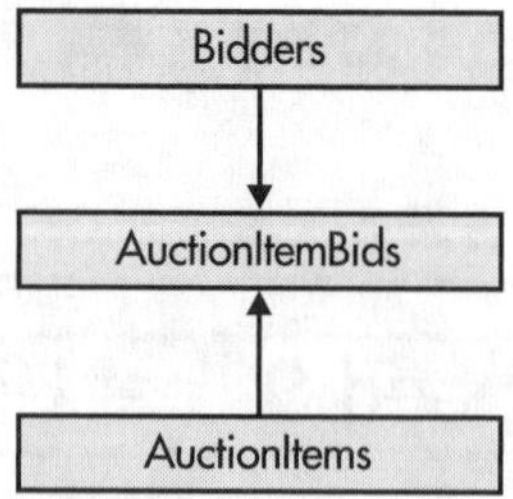

Figure 18-7 *Online Auction data diagram*

The Bidders table stores information about the visitors who place bids at the site. The AuctionItems table stores data about each of the items that is up for auction. Since each auction item can have many bids and each bidder can bid on many items, the two tables relate in a many-to-many relationship.

Because of that relationship, we need a connecting table that relates to these two in a one-to-many relationship. The AuctionItemBids table satisfies that role. It stores all the bids made by the bidders on all the action items.

Bidders Field Specifications

Bidders.txt

The field specifications for the fields in the Bidders table are displayed in Table 18-1.

Field Name	Field Type	Notes
BidderID	int	Primary Key, Identity Column
BidderName	varchar	Length = 100
Password	varchar	Length = 50
EmailAddress	varchar	Length = 100
Address	varchar	Length = 100
CSZ	varchar	Length = 100
PhoneNumber	varchar	Length = 100

Table 18-1 *Bidders Field Specifications*

The BidderID field is the primary key in this table. Since it is an identity column, it is automatically populated with a value when a new record is added.

The rest of the fields store personal information about the visitor that they enter on the New User page.

AuctionItems Field Specifications

AuctionItems.txt

The field specifications for the fields in the AuctionItems table are displayed in Table 18-2.

The AuctionItemID field is the primary key in this table. The MinimumBid field stores the lowest bid that will be accepted for the item. The BidIncrement field stores the dollar amount by which a bid must exceed the current highest bid for it to be acceptable.

The OpenDate stores the date that the item became available. The CloseDate stores the date and time when the auction closes. When this time passes, the item no longer appears on the Auction Items page.

The other fields store general information about the item up for auction.

Field Name	Field Type	Notes
AuctionItemID	int	Primary Key, Identity Column
ItemName	varchar	Length = 50
MinimumBid	money	
BidIncrement	money	
OpenDate	datetime	
CloseDate	datetime	
BriefDescription	varchar	Length = 100
FullDescription	text	

Table 18-2 *AuctionItems Field Specifications*

Field Name	Field Type	Notes
AuctionItemBidID	int	Primary Key, Identity Column
AuctionItemID	int	Foreign Key
BidderID	int	Foreign Key
BidAmount	money	
WhenPlaced	datetime	

Table 18-3 *AuctionItemBids Field Specifications*

AuctionItemBids Field Specifications

AuctionItemBids.txt

The field specifications for the fields in the AuctionItemBids table are displayed in Table 18-3.

The AuctionItemBids table links the other two tables. So, in addition to the primary key field, you will notice two foreign keys that link this table to the two other tables in the database.

The BidAmount field stores the dollar amount of the bid, and the WhenPlaced field stores the date and time that the bid was placed.

Online Auction ASP.NET Code

The Online Auction site is made up of four ASP.NET pages. These pages use a variety of controls to accomplish their functionality.

In this section, we will review the four pages that make up the tool. As you review this tool, pay close attention to the method employed to allow the visitor to sort the DataGrids and to prevent the visitor from entering an invalid bid.

Sign-In ASP.NET Page

Index.aspx

The Sign-In page allows an existing member of the auction site to return by entering their name and password. At the top of the page, three compiler directives are declared.

```
<%@ Page Language=VB Debug=true %>
<%@ Import Namespace="System.Data" %>
<%@ Import Namespace="System.Data.OLEDB" %>
```

The first directive tells the compiler that we are using Visual Basic and that we are in debug mode:

```
<%@ Page Language=VB Debug=true %>
```

Note that you should turn debugging off when you deploy this site in a production environment.

The next two directives tell the compiler that we need these libraries imported so that we can access data in our database:

```
<%@ Import Namespace="System.Data" %>
<%@ Import Namespace="System.Data.OLEDB" %>
```

Within the body of the page, we declare a Label control that displays the title of the page:

```
<asp:Label
    id="lblTitle"
    BorderWidth="7px"
    BorderStyle=7
    Width="90%"
    Font-Size="25pt"
    Font-Name="Arial"
    Text="<center>Auction Sign-In Page</center>"
    runat="server"
/>
```

Another label that will display instructions or an error message to the visitor is defined

```
<asp:Label
    id="lblMessage"
    Font-Bold="True"
    runat="server"
/>
```

The next control defined on the page is a TextBox control that allows the visitor to enter their name:

```
<asp:TextBox
    id="txtBidderName"
    Columns="25"
    MaxLength="100"
    runat=server
/>
```

That field is required because we link a RequiredFieldValidator to it:

```
<asp:RequiredFieldValidator
    id="rfvBidderName"
    ControlToValidate="txtBidderName"
    Display="Dynamic"
    Font-Name="Arial"
    Font-Size="10pt"
    runat=server>
    Name is Required!
</asp:RequiredFieldValidator>
```

The other TextBox control on the page allows the visitor to enter their password. Note the setting in the TextMode property, which displays this TextBox as a password TextBox:

```
<asp:TextBox
    id="txtPassword"
    Columns="25"
    MaxLength="50"
    TextMode="Password"
    runat=server
/>
```

This field is also required

```
<asp:RequiredFieldValidator
    id="rfvPassword"
    ControlToValidate="txtPassword"
    Display="Dynamic"
    Font-Name="Arial"
    Font-Size="10pt"
    runat=server>
```

```
    Password is Required!
</asp:RequiredFieldValidator>
```

The only other control on the page is a button that submits the data entered by the visitor when it is clicked

```
<asp:button
    id="butOK"
    text="  OK  "
    Type="Submit"
    OnClick="SubmitBtn_Click"
    runat="server"
/>
```

The code on this page is defined within two procedures. The first fires when the page loads.

```
Sub Page_Load(ByVal Sender as Object, ByVal E as EventArgs)
    If Not IsPostBack Then
        lblMessage.Text = "Welcome to the Auction!<br>" _
            & "To place bids or view the items up for auction, " _
            & "you must sign in."
    End If
End Sub
```

Within the procedure, we want the code to run only when the page is first loaded

```
If Not IsPostBack Then
```

If that is the case, we place instructional text into our message Label control:

```
lblMessage.Text = "Welcome to the Auction!<br>" _
    & "To place bids or view the items up for auction, " _
    & "you must sign in."
```

The other procedure fires when the OK button is clicked.

```
Sub SubmitBtn_Click(Sender As Object, E As EventArgs)
    Dim DBConn as OleDbConnection
    Dim DBCommand As OleDbDataAdapter
    Dim DSSignIn as New DataSet
    DBConn = New OleDbConnection("Provider=sqloledb;" _
        & "server=localhost;" _
```

```
        & "Initial Catalog=INETC18;" _
        & "User Id=sa;" _
        & "Password=yourpassword;")
    DBCommand = New OleDbDataAdapter _
        ("Select BidderID from " _
        & "Bidders Where " _
        & "BidderName = '" & txtBidderName.Text _
        & "' and Password = '" & txtPassword.Text _
        & "'", DBConn)
    DBCommand.Fill(DSSignIn, _
        "BidderInfo")
    If DSSignIn.Tables("BidderInfo"). _
        Rows.Count = 0 Then
        lblMessage.Text = "The name and password " _
            & "were not found. Please try again."
    Else
        Session("BidderID") = DSSignin.Tables("BidderInfo"). _
            Rows(0).Item("BidderID")
        Response.Redirect("./auction_list.aspx")
    End If
End Sub
```

Within this procedure, we will need a database connection object

```
Dim DBConn as OleDbConnection
```

as well as a Data Adapter object

```
Dim DBCommand As OleDbDataAdapter
```

and a DataSet object to retrieve data into:

```
Dim DSSignIn as New DataSet
```

We start by connecting to our SQL Server database:

```
DBConn = New OleDbConnection("Provider=sqloledb;" _
    & "server=localhost;" _
    & "Initial Catalog=INETC18;" _
    & "User Id=sa;" _
    & "Password=yourpassword;")
```

And we place SQL text that will retrieve the ID of the bidder corresponding to the name and password entered on this page into our Data Adapter object:

```
DBCommand = New OleDbDataAdapter _
    ("Select BidderID from " _
    & "Bidders Where " _
    & "BidderName = '" & txtBidderName.Text _
    & "' and Password = '" & txtPassword.Text _
    & "'", DBConn)
```

That data is retrieved into our DataSet object:

```
DBCommand.Fill(DSSignIn, _
    "BidderInfo")
```

We then check to see if a matching record was found by looking at the number of records returned

```
If DSSignIn.Tables("BidderInfo"). _
    Rows.Count = 0 Then
```

If no record was found, the visitor did not enter a valid name and password. So we display this message:

```
lblMessage.Text = "The name and password " _
    & "were not found. Please try again."
```

Otherwise, we store the ID of the visitor in a Session variable so that we can refer to it from other pages without requiring the visitor to sign in again:

```
Session("BidderID") = DSSignin.Tables("BidderInfo"). _
    Rows(0).Item("BidderID")
```

We then send the visitor to the Auction Items page:

```
Response.Redirect("./auction_list.aspx")
```

New User ASP.NET Page

New_User.aspx

The New User page allows visitors to your site to become bidders by entering their personal information. At the top of the page, we declare three compiler directives that import libraries and set up the programming environment:

```
<%@ Page Language=VB Debug=true %>
<%@ Import Namespace="System.Data" %>
<%@ Import Namespace="System.Data.OLEDB" %>
```

Within the body of the page, a Label that contains the title of the page is defined

```
<asp:Label
    id="lblTitle"
    BorderWidth="7px"
    BorderStyle=7
    Width="90%"
    Font-Size="25pt"
    Font-Name="Arial"
    Text="<center>Auction New User Page</center>"
    runat="server"
/>
```

Another Label control will display instructions or an error message on the page:

```
<asp:Label
    id="lblMessage"
    Font-Bold="True"
    runat="server"
    Text="Complete each field to register with our site."
/>
```

The next control on the page is a TextBox control that the visitor uses to place their name in:

```
<asp:TextBox
    id="txtBidderName"
    Columns="50"
    MaxLength="100"
    runat=server
/>
```

That field is required because this RequiredFieldValidator is linked to it:

```
<asp:RequiredFieldValidator
    id="rfvBidderName"
    ControlToValidate="txtBidderName"
    Display="Dynamic"
    Font-Name="Arial"
    Font-Size="10pt"
    runat=server>
    Bidder Name is Required!
</asp:RequiredFieldValidator>
```

The next control is another TextBox where the visitor enters their password:

```
<asp:TextBox
    id="txtPassword"
    Columns="50"
    MaxLength="50"
    runat=server
    TextMode="Password"
/>
```

That field, too, is required

```
<asp:RequiredFieldValidator
    id="rfvPassword"
    ControlToValidate="txtPassword"
    Display="Dynamic"
    Font-Name="Arial"
    Font-Size="10pt"
    runat=server>
    Password is Required!
</asp:RequiredFieldValidator>
```

We then ask the visitor to reenter their password to make sure that they entered it correctly, since they can't see the characters that they type in a password field:

```
<asp:TextBox
    id="txtPassword2"
    Columns="50"
    MaxLength="50"
    runat=server
    TextMode="Password"
/>
```

The visitor must enter a value in this field:

```
<asp:RequiredFieldValidator
    id="rfvPassword2"
    ControlToValidate="txtPassword2"
    Display="Dynamic"
    Font-Name="Arial"
    Font-Size="10pt"
    runat=server>
    Password is Required!
</asp:RequiredFieldValidator>
```

And the text they enter must match the text that they placed in the first password TextBox:

```
<asp:CompareValidator id="cvPassword"
    ControlToValidate="txtPassword"
    ControlToCompare="txtPassword2"
    Display="Dynamic"
    Font-Name="Arial"
    Font-Size="10pt"
    runat=server>
    Password fields don't match
</asp:CompareValidator>
```

Additionally, we ask the visitor for their e-mail address

```
<asp:TextBox
    id="txtEmailAddress"
    Columns="50"
    MaxLength="100"
    runat=server
/>
```

which is required

```
<asp:RequiredFieldValidator
    id="rfvEmailAddress"
    ControlToValidate="txtEmailAddress"
    Display="Dynamic"
    Font-Name="Arial"
    Font-Size="10pt"
    runat=server>
    Email Address is Required!
</asp:RequiredFieldValidator>
```

as is their physical address

```
<asp:TextBox
    id="txtAddress"
    Columns="50"
    MaxLength="100"
    runat=server
/>
<asp:RequiredFieldValidator
    id="rfvAddress"
```

```
    ControlToValidate="txtAddress"
    Display="Dynamic"
    Font-Name="Arial"
    Font-Size="10pt"
    runat=server>
    Address is Required!
</asp:RequiredFieldValidator>
```

their city, state, ZIP code

```
<asp:TextBox
    id="txtCSZ"
    Columns="50"
    MaxLength="100"
    runat=server
/>
<asp:RequiredFieldValidator
    id="rfvCSZ"
    ControlToValidate="txtCSZ"
    Display="Dynamic"
    Font-Name="Arial"
    Font-Size="10pt"
    runat=server>
    CSZ is Required!
</asp:RequiredFieldValidator>
```

and their phone number:

```
<asp:TextBox
    id="txtPhoneNumber"
    Columns="50"
    MaxLength="100"
    runat=server
/>
<asp:RequiredFieldValidator
    id="rfvPhoneNumber"
    ControlToValidate="txtPhoneNumber"
    Display="Dynamic"
    Font-Name="Arial"
    Font-Size="10pt"
    runat=server>
    Phone Number is Required!
</asp:RequiredFieldValidator>
```

The only other control on the page is a button that submits the form when it is clicked

```
<asp:button
    id="butOK"
    text="  OK  "
    Type="Submit"
    OnClick="SubmitBtn_Click"
    runat="server"
/>
```

The code that runs when that button is clicked is the only code on the page.

```
Sub SubmitBtn_Click(Sender As Object, E As EventArgs)
    Dim DBConn as OleDbConnection
    Dim DBCommand As OleDbDataAdapter
    Dim DSSignin as New DataSet
    Dim DBInsert As New OleDbCommand
    DBConn = New OleDbConnection("Provider=sqloledb;" _
        & "server=localhost;" _
        & "Initial Catalog=INETC18;" _
        & "User Id=sa;" _
        & "Password=yourpassword;")
    DBCommand = New OleDbDataAdapter _
        ("Select Count(BidderID) as TheCount " _
        & "from Bidders Where " _
        & "BidderName = '" & txtBidderName.Text _
        & "'", DBConn)
    DBCommand.Fill(DSSignIn, _
        "TheCount")
    If DSSignin.Tables("TheCount"). _
            Rows(0).Item("TheCount")  = 0 Then
        DBInsert.CommandText = "Insert Into Bidders " _
            & "(BidderName, Password, EmailAddress, Address, " _
            & "CSZ, PhoneNumber) " _
            & "values (" _
            & "'" & Replace(txtBidderName.text, "'", "''") & "', " _
            & "'" & Replace(txtPassword.text, "'", "''") & "', " _
            & "'" & Replace(txtEmailAddress.text, "'", "''") _
            & "', " _
            & "'" & Replace(txtAddress.text, "'", "''") & "', " _
            & "'" & Replace(txtCSZ.text, "'", "''") & "', " _
            & "'" & Replace(txtPhoneNumber.text, "'", "''") & "')"
```

```
        DBInsert.Connection = DBConn
        DBInsert.Connection.Open
        DBInsert.ExecuteNonQuery()
        DBCommand = New OleDbDataAdapter _
            ("Select BidderID from Bidders Where " _
            & "BidderName = '" & txtBidderName.Text _
            & "' and Password = '" & txtPassword.Text _
            & "'", DBConn)
        DBCommand.Fill(DSSignin, _
            "BidderInfo")
        Session("BidderID") = DSSignin.Tables("BidderInfo"). _
            Rows(0).Item("BidderID")
        Response.Redirect("./auction_list.aspx")
    Else
        lblMessage.Text = "The name you entered is in " _
            & "use by another member. Please enter " _
            & "another member name."
    End If
End Sub
```

Within the procedure, we will need data objects:

```
Dim DBConn as OleDbConnection
Dim DBCommand As OleDbDataAdapter
Dim DSSignin as New DataSet
Dim DBInsert As New OleDbCommand
```

We start by connecting to our database:

```
DBConn = New OleDbConnection("Provider=sqloledb;" _
    & "server=localhost;" _
    & "Initial Catalog=INETC18;" _
    & "User Id=sa;" _
    & "Password=yourpassword;")
```

We then need to check to see if the name entered by the visitor is in use by another visitor:

```
DBCommand = New OleDbDataAdapter _
    ("Select Count(BidderID) as TheCount " _
    & "from Bidders Where " _
    & "BidderName = '" & txtBidderName.Text _
    & "'", DBConn)
```

```
DBCommand.Fill(DSSignIn, _
    "TheCount")
```

If no records were returned, it means the visitor can use the name they entered

```
If DSSignin.Tables("TheCount"). _
   Rows(0).Item("TheCount") = 0 Then
```

Therefore, we add their information to the database

```
DBInsert.CommandText = "Insert Into Bidders " _
    & "(BidderName, Password, EmailAddress, Address, " _
    & "CSZ, PhoneNumber) " _
    & "values (" _
    & "'" & Replace(txtBidderName.text, "'", "''") & "', " _
    & "'" & Replace(txtPassword.text, "'", "''") & "', " _
    & "'" & Replace(txtEmailAddress.text, "'", "''") _
    & "', " _
    & "'" & Replace(txtAddress.text, "'", "''") & "', " _
    & "'" & Replace(txtCSZ.text, "'", "''") & "', " _
    & "'" & Replace(txtPhoneNumber.text, "'", "''") & "')"
DBInsert.Connection = DBConn
DBInsert.Connection.Open
DBInsert.ExecuteNonQuery()
```

and retrieve the ID that was used for the new record we just added

```
DBCommand = New OleDbDataAdapter _
    ("Select BidderID from Bidders Where " _
    & "BidderName = '" & txtBidderName.Text _
    & "' and Password = '" & txtPassword.Text _
    & "'", DBConn)
DBCommand.Fill(DSSignin, _
    "BidderInfo")
```

which we store in a Session variable so that we can refer to it from other pages in this site:

```
Session("BidderID") = DSSignin.Tables("BidderInfo"). _
    Rows(0).Item("BidderID")
```

We then send the visitor to the Auction Items page:

```
Response.Redirect("./auction_list.aspx")
```

If the code flows here, it means the visitor entered a name that is in use by another visitor:

```
Else
```

We inform them of the problem and don't allow them access to the rest of the site:

```
lblMessage.Text = "The name you entered is in " _
    & "use by another member. Please enter " _
    & "another member name."
```

Auction Items ASP.NET Page

Auction_List.aspx

The code on the Auction Items page displays a list of all the open auction items. It also allows the visitor to sort the items in the DataGrid by clicking a column head.

At the top of the page, we have the same three compiler directives:

```
<%@ Page Language=VB Debug=true %>
<%@ Import Namespace="System.Data" %>
<%@ Import Namespace="System.Data.OLEDB" %>
```

Within the body of the page, we have one Label control that displays the title of the page

```
<asp:Label
    id="lblTitle"
    BorderWidth="7px"
    BorderStyle=7
    Width="90%"
    Font-Size="25pt"
    Font-Name="Arial"
    Text="<center>Open Auction Items</center>"
    runat="server"
/>
```

and another that displays instructions for the page:

```
<asp:Label
    id="lblMessage"
    Font-Bold="True"
    Width="90%"
    runat="server"
    Text="Click on an item name to view full information.
```

```
    Click on a column to sort by that column."
/>
```

The only other control on the page is the DataGrid that displays the auction items:

```
<asp:DataGrid
    id="dgAuctionItems"
    Width="90%"
    BackColor="beige"
    AlternatingItemStyle-BackColor="cornsilk"
    BorderColor="black"
    ShowFooter="false"
    CellPadding=3
    CellSpacing="0"
    Font-Name="Arial"
    Font-Size="8pt"
    ForeColor="Black"
    HeaderStyle-BackColor="burlywood"
    HeaderStyle-Font-Bold="True"
    AllowSorting="true"
    OnSortCommand="Sort_Grid"
    runat="server">
</asp:DataGrid>
```

This property turns the column headers into links:

```
AllowSorting="true"
```

And this is the procedure that runs when the visitor clicks one of those column headers:

```
OnSortCommand="Sort_Grid"
```

The code on this page runs within two procedures. The first fires when the page is loaded.

```
Sub Page_Load(ByVal Sender as Object, ByVal E as EventArgs)
    If Len(Session("BidderID")) = 0 Then
        Response.Redirect("./index.aspx")
    End If
    Dim DBConn as OleDbConnection
    Dim DBCommand As OleDbDataAdapter
    Dim DSPageData as New DataSet
```

```
    DBConn = New OleDbConnection("Provider=sqloledb;" _
        & "server=localhost;" _
        & "Initial Catalog=INETC18;" _
        & "User Id=sa;" _
        & "Password=yourpassword;")
    DBCommand = New OleDbDataAdapter _
        ("Select '<a HREF="./auction_item.aspx?AuctionItemID=' " _
        & "+ Convert(varchar(50), AuctionItemID) + '"">' + " _
        & "ItemName + '</a>' as [Item Name], " _
        & "BriefDescription as [Description], " _
        & "Convert(varchar(30), CloseDate, 100) as [Closes], " _
        & "'$' + Convert(varchar(30), MinimumBid, 1) " _
        & "as [Minimum Bid] " _
        & "From AuctionItems Where CloseDate >= GetDate() " _
        & "Order By ItemName", DBConn)
    DBCommand.Fill(DSPageData, _
        "AuctionItems")
    dgAuctionItems.DataSource = _
        DSPageData.Tables("AuctionItems").DefaultView
    dgAuctionItems.DataBind
End Sub
```

The visitor can access this page only if they have signed in:

```
If Len(Session("BidderID")) = 0 Then
```

If they haven't, they are sent back to the Sign-In page:

```
Response.Redirect("./index.aspx")
```

Otherwise, we declare needed data objects:

```
Dim DBConn as OleDbConnection
Dim DBCommand As OleDbDataAdapter
Dim DSPageData as New DataSet
```

We start by connecting to our database:

```
DBConn = New OleDbConnection("Provider=sqloledb;" _
    & "server=localhost;" _
    & "Initial Catalog=INETC18;" _
    & "User Id=sa;" _
    & "Password=yourpassword;")
```

Next, we place SQL text into the Data Adapter object to retrieve the items for the DataGrid. Note that the first column will contain the name of the item but will link to the Auction Item page:

```
DBCommand = New OleDbDataAdapter _
    ("Select '<a href="" ./auction_item.aspx?AuctionItemID=' " _
    & "+ Convert(varchar(50), AuctionItemID) + '"">' + " _
    & "ItemName + '</a>' as [Item Name], " _
    & "BriefDescription as [Description], " _
```

The third column will display the date, which is formatted so that both the date and the time appear

```
& "Convert(varchar(30), CloseDate, 100) as [Closes], " _
```

The fourth column will display the minimum bid for the item formatted as currency:

```
& "'$' + Convert(varchar(30), MinimumBid, 1) " _
& "as [Minimum Bid] " _
```

Only the items that are still open are returned

```
& "From AuctionItems Where CloseDate >= GetDate() " _
& "Order By ItemName", DBConn)
```

We then place the return of that query into our DataSet object:

```
DBCommand.Fill(DSPageData, _
    "AuctionItems")
```

The DataGrid is then bound to the DataSet object:

```
dgAuctionItems.DataSource = _
    DSPageData.Tables("AuctionItems").DefaultView
dgAuctionItems.DataBind
```

The other procedure on the page fires when the visitor clicks one of the column headers.

```
Sub Sort_Grid(ByVal Sender as Object, _
    ByVal E as DataGridSortCommandEventArgs)
    Dim DBConn as OleDbConnection
    Dim DBCommand As OleDbDataAdapter
```

```
    Dim DSPageData as New DataSet
    Dim SortField as String
    If E.SortExpression.ToString() = "Item Name" Then
        SortField = "ItemName"
    ElseIf E.SortExpression.ToString() = "Description" Then
        SortField = "BriefDescription"
    ElseIf E.SortExpression.ToString() = "Closes" Then
        SortField = "CloseDate"
    Else
        SortField = "MinimumBid"
    End If
    DBConn = New OleDbConnection("Provider=sqloledb;" _
        & "server=localhost;" _
        & "Initial Catalog=INETC18;" _
        & "User Id=sa;" _
        & "Password=yourpassword;")
    DBCommand = New OleDbDataAdapter _
        ("Select '<a href="./auction_item.aspx?AuctionItemID=' " _
        & "+ Convert(varchar(50), AuctionItemID) + '"">' + " _
        & "ItemName + '</a>' as [Item Name], " _
        & "BriefDescription as [Description], " _
        & "Convert(varchar(30), CloseDate, 100) as [Closes], " _
        & "'$' + Convert(varchar(30), MinimumBid, 1) " _
        & "as [Minimum Bid] " _
        & "From AuctionItems Where CloseDate >= GetDate() " _
        & "Order By " & SortField, DBConn)
    DBCommand.Fill(DSPageData, _
        "AuctionItems")
    dgAuctionItems.DataSource = _
        DSPageData.Tables("AuctionItems").DefaultView
    dgAuctionItems.DataBind
End Sub
```

Within the procedure, we will need data objects

```
Dim DBConn as OleDbConnection
Dim DBCommand As OleDbDataAdapter
Dim DSPageData as New DataSet
```

as well as a string to store the name of the field that we need to sort by:

```
Dim SortField as String
```

The name of the field clicked by the visitor is returned through the SortExpression object. After checking the name of the field clicked, we store the corresponding field name from our table into the temporary string:

```
If E.SortExpression.ToString() = "Item Name" Then
    SortField = "ItemName"
ElseIf E.SortExpression.ToString() = "Description" Then
    SortField = "BriefDescription"
ElseIf E.SortExpression.ToString() = "Closes" Then
    SortField = "CloseDate"
Else
    SortField = "MinimumBid"
End If
```

We then connect to our database:

```
DBConn = New OleDbConnection("Provider=sqloledb;" _
    & "server=localhost;" _
    & "Initial Catalog=INETC18;" _
    & "User Id=sa;" _
    & "Password=yourpassword;")
```

And we retrieve the open auction items now sorted by the field clicked by the visitor:

```
DBCommand = New OleDbDataAdapter _
    ("Select '<a href=""./auction_item.aspx?AuctionItemID=' " _
    & "+ Convert(varchar(50), AuctionItemID) + '"">' + " _
    & "ItemName + '</a>' as [Item Name], " _
    & "BriefDescription as [Description], " _
    & "Convert(varchar(30), CloseDate, 100) as [Closes], " _
    & "'$' + Convert(varchar(30), MinimumBid, 1) " _
    & "as [Minimum Bid] " _
    & "From AuctionItems Where CloseDate >= GetDate() " _
    & "Order By " & SortField, DBConn)
DBCommand.Fill(DSPageData, _
    "AuctionItems")
```

We then bind our DataGrid to the DataSet object:

```
dgAuctionItems.DataSource = _
    DSPageData.Tables("AuctionItems").DefaultView
dgAuctionItems.DataBind
```

Auction Item ASP.NET Page

Auction_Item.aspx

The Auction Item page displays detailed information about the auction item selected by the visitor. It also allows the visitor to sort the bid data displayed in the DataGrid and lets the visitor add a bid to the item.

At the top of the page, we have the three compiler directives that import needed libraries and set up the code environment:

```
<%@ Page Language=VB Debug=true %>
<%@ Import Namespace="System.Data" %>
<%@ Import Namespace="System.Data.OLEDB" %>
```

Within the body of the page, a Label will display the name of the item:

```
<asp:Label
    id="lblTitle"
    BorderWidth="7px"
    BorderStyle=7
    Width="90%"
    Font-Size="25pt"
    Font-Name="Arial"
runat="server"
/>
```

Another Label will display the other information about the auction item:

```
<asp:Label
    id="lblFullInfo"
    Font-Bold="True"
    Width="90%"
    runat="server"
/>
```

The next control is a DataGrid that displays all the bids that go with this auction item:

```
<asp:DataGrid
    id="dgBids"
    Width="90%"
    BackColor="beige"
    AlternatingItemStyle-BackColor="cornsilk"
```

```
    BorderColor="black"
    ShowFooter="false"
    CellPadding=3
    CellSpacing="0"
    Font-Name="Arial"
    Font-Size="8pt"
    ForeColor="Black"
    HeaderStyle-BackColor="burlywood"
    HeaderStyle-Font-Bold="True"
    AllowSorting="true"
    OnSortCommand="Sort_Grid"
    runat="server">
</asp:DataGrid>
```

Note that sorting is turned on within this DataGrid.

We also declare a TextBox control for the visitor to enter their bid

```
<asp:TextBox
    id="txtBidAmount"
    Columns="20"
    MaxLength="50"
    runat=server
/>
```

as well as a button to submit their bid:

```
<asp:button
    id="butOK"
    text="  OK  "
    Type="Submit"
    OnClick="SubmitBtn_Click"
    runat="server"
/>
```

If the visitor tries to submit a bid, they must enter a bid value:

```
<asp:RequiredFieldValidator
    id="rfvBidAmount"
    ControlToValidate="txtBidAmount"
    Display="Dynamic"
    Font-Name="Arial"
    Font-Size="10pt"
    runat=server>
```

```
    Bid Amount is Required!
</asp:RequiredFieldValidator>
```

And in code, we will establish the minimum value that can be placed in that TextBox control:

```
<asp:RangeValidator
    id="rngBidAmount"
    ControlToValidate="txtBidAmount"
    Type="Currency"
    MaximumValue="1000000000"
    MinimumValue="0"
    Display="Dynamic"
    Font-Name="Arial"
    Font-Size="10pt"
    runat="server">
    The Bid amount you entered is not high enough!
</asp:RangeValidator>
```

The code on the page runs within three procedures. The first procedure fires when the page is loaded.

```
Sub Page_Load(ByVal Sender as Object, ByVal E as EventArgs)
    If Len(Session("BidderID")) = 0 Then
        Response.Redirect("./index.aspx")
    End If
    If Len(Request.QueryString("AuctionItemID")) = 0 Then
        Response.Redirect("./auction_list.aspx")
    End If
    If Not IsPostBack Then
        Dim DBConn as OleDbConnection
        Dim DBCommand As OleDbDataAdapter
        Dim DSPageData as New DataSet
        DBConn = New OleDbConnection("Provider=sqloledb;" _
            & "server=localhost;" _
            & "Initial Catalog=INETC18;" _
            & "User Id=sa;" _
            & "Password=yourpassword;")
        DBCommand = New OleDbDataAdapter _
            ("Select ItemName, MinimumBid, OpenDate, " _
            & "CloseDate, BidIncrement, FullDescription " _
            & "From AuctionItems Where AuctionItemID = " _
            & Request.QueryString("AuctionItemID"), DBConn)
```

```
DBCommand.Fill(DSPageData, _
    "AuctionItem")
lblTitle.Text = "<center>" _
    & DSPageData.Tables("AuctionItem"). _
    Rows(0).Item("ItemName") & "</center>"
lblFullInfo.Text = "<i>Date Opened: </i>" _
    & DSPageData.Tables("AuctionItem"). _
    Rows(0).Item("OpenDate") & "<br><br>" _
    & "<i>Date Closes: </i>" _
    & DSPageData.Tables("AuctionItem"). _
    Rows(0).Item("CloseDate") & "<br><br>" _
    & "<i>Minimum Bid: </i>" _
    & FormatCurrency(DSPageData.Tables("AuctionItem"). _
    Rows(0).Item("MinimumBid")) & "<br><br>" _
    & "<i>Bid Increment: </i>" _
    & FormatCurrency(DSPageData.Tables("AuctionItem"). _
    Rows(0).Item("BidIncrement")) & "<br><br>" _
    & "<i>Description: </i>" _
    & DSPageData.Tables("AuctionItem"). _
    Rows(0).Item("FullDescription") & "<br><br>"
DBCommand = New OleDbDataAdapter _
    ("Select BidderName as [Name], " _
    & "Convert(varchar(30), WhenPlaced, 100) " _
    & "as [When Placed], " _
    & "'$' + Convert(varchar(30), BidAmount, 1) " _
    & "as [Bid Amount] " _
    & "From AuctionItemBids " _
    & "Inner Join Bidders On AuctionItemBids.BidderID = " _
    & "Bidders.BidderID Where AuctionItemID = " _
    & Request.QueryString("AuctionItemID") _
    & " Order By WhenPlaced", DBConn)
DBCommand.Fill(DSPageData, _
    "BidData")
dgBids.DataSource = _
    DSPageData.Tables("BidData").DefaultView
dgBids.DataBind
DBCommand = New OleDbDataAdapter _
    ("Select Max(BidAmount) as MaxBid " _
    & "From AuctionItemBids " _
    & "Where AuctionItemID = " _
    & Request.QueryString("AuctionItemID") _
    , DBConn)
DBCommand.Fill(DSPageData, _
```

```
            "CurrentBid")
        If IsNumeric(DSPageData.Tables("CurrentBid"). _
            Rows(0).Item("MaxBid")) Then
            txtBidAmount.Text = DSPageData.Tables("AuctionItem"). _
                Rows(0).Item("BidIncrement") + _
                DSPageData.Tables("CurrentBid"). _
                Rows(0).Item("MaxBid")
        Else
            txtBidAmount.Text = DSPageData.Tables("AuctionItem"). _
                Rows(0).Item("MinimumBid")
        End If
        rngBidAmount.MinimumValue = txtBidAmount.Text
    End If
End Sub
```

The visitor can access this page only if they have first signed in:

```
If Len(Session("BidderID")) = 0 Then
```

If they haven't, we send them to the Sign-In page:

```
Response.Redirect("./index.aspx")
```

The page should also be entered only when the visitor selects an item from the DataGrid on the Auction Items page:

```
If Len(Request.QueryString("AuctionItemID")) = 0 Then
```

If they didn't, we send them back to that page:

```
Response.Redirect("./auction_list.aspx")
```

The rest of the code on the page should run only when the page is first loaded

```
If Not IsPostBack Then
```

We declare needed data objects

```
Dim DBConn as OleDbConnection
Dim DBCommand As OleDbDataAdapter
Dim DSPageData as New DataSet
```

and connect to our database

```
DBConn = New OleDbConnection("Provider=sqloledb;" _
    & "server=localhost;" _
    & "Initial Catalog=INETC18;" _
    & "User Id=sa;" _
    & "Password=yourpassword;")
```

retrieving from it all the data on the Auction Item selected by the visitor

```
DBCommand = New OleDbDataAdapter _
    ("Select ItemName, MinimumBid, OpenDate, " _
    & "CloseDate, BidIncrement, FullDescription " _
    & "From AuctionItems Where AuctionItemID = " _
    & Request.QueryString("AuctionItemID"), DBConn)
```

which is placed into our DataSet object:

```
DBCommand.Fill(DSPageData, _
    "AuctionItem")
```

We then use the data retrieved to populate our title label

```
lblTitle.Text = "<center>" _
    & DSPageData.Tables("AuctionItem"). _
    Rows(0).Item("ItemName") & "</center>"
```

and our information label:

```
lblFullInfo.Text = "<i>Date Opened: </i>" _
    & DSPageData.Tables("AuctionItem"). _
    Rows(0).Item("OpenDate") & "<br><br>" _
    & "<i>Date Closes: </i>" _
    & DSPageData.Tables("AuctionItem"). _
    Rows(0).Item("CloseDate") & "<br><br>" _
    & "<i>Minimum Bid: </i>" _
    & FormatCurrency(DSPageData.Tables("AuctionItem"). _
    Rows(0).Item("MinimumBid")) & "<br><br>" _
    & "<i>Bid Increment: </i>" _
    & FormatCurrency(DSPageData.Tables("AuctionItem"). _
    Rows(0).Item("BidIncrement")) & "<br><br>" _
    & "<i>Description: </i>" _
    & DSPageData.Tables("AuctionItem"). _
    Rows(0).Item("FullDescription") & "<br><br>"
```

Next, we need to retrieve the bid history for this auction item:

```
DBCommand = New OleDbDataAdapter _
    ("Select BidderName as [Name], " _
    & "Convert(varchar(30), WhenPlaced, 100) " _
    & "as [When Placed], " _
    & "'$' + Convert(varchar(30), BidAmount, 1) " _
    & "as [Bid Amount] " _
    & "From AuctionItemBids " _
    & "Inner Join Bidders On AuctionItemBids.BidderID = " _
    & "Bidders.BidderID Where AuctionItemID = " _
    & Request.QueryString("AuctionItemID") _
    & " Order By WhenPlaced", DBConn)
DBCommand.Fill(DSPageData, _
    "BidData")
```

We then bind our DataGrid to this DataSet object:

```
dgBids.DataSource = _
    DSPageData.Tables("BidData").DefaultView
dgBids.DataBind
```

Next, we need to set up our validation control to make sure that the visitor enters a valid bid. Therefore, we need to retrieve the current highest bid for this auction item:

```
DBCommand = New OleDbDataAdapter _
    ("Select Max(BidAmount) as MaxBid " _
    & "From AuctionItemBids " _
    & "Where AuctionItemID = " _
    & Request.QueryString("AuctionItemID") _
    , DBConn)
DBCommand.Fill(DSPageData, _
    "CurrentBid")
```

If a bid has been made, the value returned will be a number:

```
If IsNumeric(DSPageData.Tables("CurrentBid"). _
    Rows(0).Item("MaxBid")) Then
```

In that case, the lowest acceptable bid is based on the highest bid plus the bid increment:

```
txtBidAmount.Text = DSPageData.Tables("AuctionItem"). _
    Rows(0).Item("BidIncrement") + _
    DSPageData.Tables("CurrentBid"). _
    Rows(0).Item("MaxBid")
```

Otherwise, no bids have been made and the lowest bid is based on the MinimumBid field:

```
txtBidAmount.Text = DSPageData.Tables("AuctionItem"). _
    Rows(0).Item("MinimumBid")
```

To make sure the visitor doesn't change the text on the TextBox to a lower number, we also store this value in our validation control:

```
rngBidAmount.MinimumValue = txtBidAmount.Text
```

The next procedure fires when the visitor clicks one of the columns to sort the DataGrid.

```
Sub Sort_Grid(ByVal Sender as Object, _
    ByVal E as DataGridSortCommandEventArgs)
    Dim DBConn as OleDbConnection
    Dim DBCommand As OleDbDataAdapter
    Dim DSPageData as New DataSet
    Dim SortField as String
    If E.SortExpression.ToString() = "Name" Then
        SortField = "BidderName"
    ElseIf E.SortExpression.ToString() = "When Placed" Then
        SortField = "WhenPlaced"
    Else
        SortField = "BidAmount"
    End If
    DBConn = New OleDbConnection("Provider=sqloledb;" _
        & "server=localhost;" _
        & "Initial Catalog=INETC18;" _
        & "User Id=sa;" _
        & "Password=yourpassword;")
        DBCommand = New OleDbDataAdapter _
            ("Select BidderName as [Name], " _
            & "Convert(varchar(30), WhenPlaced, 100) " _
```

```
            & "as [When Placed], " _
            & "'$' + Convert(varchar(30), BidAmount, 1) " _
            & "as [Bid Amount] " _
            & "From AuctionItemBids " _
            & "Inner Join Bidders On AuctionItemBids.BidderID = " _
            & "Bidders.BidderID Where AuctionItemID = " _
            & Request.QueryString("AuctionItemID") _
            & " Order By " & SortField, DBConn)
        DBCommand.Fill(DSPageData, _
            "BidData")
        dgBids.DataSource = _
            DSPageData.Tables("BidData").DefaultView
        dgBids.DataBind
End Sub
```

Within this procedure, we will need data objects

```
Dim DBConn as OleDbConnection
Dim DBCommand As OleDbDataAdapter
Dim DSPageData as New DataSet
```

as well as a string to store the name of the sort field:

```
Dim SortField as String
```

We then place the name of the field that we need to sort by as determined by the name of the column selected by the visitor into our string variable:

```
If E.SortExpression.ToString() = "Name" Then
    SortField = "BidderName"
ElseIf E.SortExpression.ToString() = "When Placed" Then
    SortField = "WhenPlaced"
Else
    SortField = "BidAmount"
End If
```

Next, we connect to our database

```
DBConn = New OleDbConnection("Provider=sqloledb;" _
    & "server=localhost;" _
    & "Initial Catalog=INETC18;" _
        & "User Id=sa;" _
    & "Password=yourpassword;")
```

and retrieve the bid history sorted now by the field selected by the visitor:

```
DBCommand = New OleDbDataAdapter _
    ("Select BidderName as [Name], " _
    & "Convert(varchar(30), WhenPlaced, 100) " _
    & "as [When Placed], " _
    & "'$' + Convert(varchar(30), BidAmount, 1) " _
    & "as [Bid Amount] " _
    & "From AuctionItemBids " _
    & "Inner Join Bidders On AuctionItemBids.BidderID = " _
    & "Bidders.BidderID Where AuctionItemID = " _
    & Request.QueryString("AuctionItemID") _
    & " Order By " & SortField, DBConn)
DBCommand.Fill(DSPageData, _
    "BidData")
```

We then rebind our DataGrid to this DataSet object:

```
dgBids.DataSource = _
    DSPageData.Tables("BidData").DefaultView
dgBids.DataBind
```

The last procedure on this page fires when the visitor clicks OK, submitting a bid.

```
Sub SubmitBtn_Click(Sender As Object, E As EventArgs)
    Dim DBConn as OleDbConnection
    Dim DBCommand As OleDbDataAdapter
    Dim DSPageData as New DataSet
    Dim DBInsert As New OleDbCommand
    DBConn = New OleDbConnection("Provider=sqloledb;" _
        & "server=localhost;" _
        & "Initial Catalog=INETC18;" _
        & "User Id=sa;" _
        & "Password=yourpassword;")
    DBInsert.CommandText = "Insert Into AuctionItemBids " _
        & "(AuctionItemID, BidderID, BidAmount, WhenPlaced) " _
        & "values (" _
        & Request.QueryString("AuctionItemID") & ", " _
        & Session("BidderID") & ", " _
        & txtBidAmount.Text & ", " _
        & "'" & Now() & "')"
    DBInsert.Connection = DBConn
    DBInsert.Connection.Open
```

```
DBInsert.ExecuteNonQuery()
DBCommand = New OleDbDataAdapter _
    ("Select ItemName, MinimumBid, OpenDate, " _
    & "CloseDate, BidIncrement, FullDescription " _
    & "From AuctionItems Where AuctionItemID = " _
    & Request.QueryString("AuctionItemID"), DBConn)
DBCommand.Fill(DSPageData, _
    "AuctionItem")
lblTitle.Text = "<center>" _
    & DSPageData.Tables("AuctionItem"). _
    Rows(0).Item("ItemName") & "</center>"
lblFullInfo.Text = "<i>Date Opened: </i>" _
    & DSPageData.Tables("AuctionItem"). _
    Rows(0).Item("OpenDate") & "<br><br>" _
    & "<i>Date Closes: </i>" _
    & DSPageData.Tables("AuctionItem"). _
    Rows(0).Item("CloseDate") & "<br><br>" _
    & "<i>Minimum Bid: </i>" _
    & FormatCurrency(DSPageData.Tables("AuctionItem"). _
    Rows(0).Item("MinimumBid")) & "<br><br>" _
    & "<i>Bid Increment: </i>" _
    & FormatCurrency(DSPageData.Tables("AuctionItem"). _
    Rows(0).Item("BidIncrement")) & "<br><br>" _
    & "<i>Description: </i>" _
    & DSPageData.Tables("AuctionItem"). _
    Rows(0).Item("FullDescription") & "<br><br>"
DBCommand = New OleDbDataAdapter _
    ("Select BidderName as [Name], " _
    & "Convert(varchar(30), WhenPlaced, 100) " _
    & "as [When Placed], " _
    & "'$' + Convert(varchar(30), BidAmount, 1) " _
    & "as [Bid Amount] " _
    & "From AuctionItemBids " _
    & "Inner Join Bidders On AuctionItemBids.BidderID = " _
    & "Bidders.BidderID Where AuctionItemID = " _
    & Request.QueryString("AuctionItemID") _
    & " Order By WhenPlaced", DBConn)
DBCommand.Fill(DSPageData, _
    "BidData")
dgBids.DataSource = _
    DSPageData.Tables("BidData").DefaultView
dgBids.DataBind
DBCommand = New OleDbDataAdapter _
```

```
        ("Select Max(BidAmount) as MaxBid " _
        & "From AuctionItemBids " _
        & "Where AuctionItemID = " _
        & Request.QueryString("AuctionItemID") _
        , DBConn)
    DBCommand.Fill(DSPageData, _
        "CurrentBid")
    txtBidAmount.Text = DSPageData.Tables("AuctionItem"). _
        Rows(0).Item("BidIncrement") + _
        DSPageData.Tables("CurrentBid"). _
        Rows(0).Item("MaxBid")
    rngBidAmount.MinimumValue = txtBidAmount.Text
End Sub
```

We will need data objects to allow us to retrieve and insert data into our database:

```
Dim DBConn as OleDbConnection
Dim DBCommand As OleDbDataAdapter
Dim DSPageData as New DataSet
Dim DBInsert As New OleDbCommand
```

We start by connecting to our database:

```
DBConn = New OleDbConnection("Provider=sqloledb;" _
    & "server=localhost;" _
    & "Initial Catalog=INETC18;" _
    & "User Id=sa;" _
    & "Password=yourpassword;")
```

We then add the visitor's bid to the AuctionItemBids table through our Command object:

```
DBInsert.CommandText = "Insert Into AuctionItemBids " _
    & "(AuctionItemID, BidderID, BidAmount, WhenPlaced) " _
    & "values (" _
    & Request.QueryString("AuctionItemID") & ", " _
    & Session("BidderID") & ", " _
    & txtBidAmount.Text & ", " _
    & "'" & Now() & "')"
DBInsert.Connection = DBConn
DBInsert.Connection.Open
DBInsert.ExecuteNonQuery()
```

Next, we need to refresh the data on the page. We start by retrieving the data for the selected auction item

```
DBCommand = New OleDbDataAdapter _
    ("Select ItemName, MinimumBid, OpenDate, " _
    & "CloseDate, BidIncrement, FullDescription " _
    & "From AuctionItems Where AuctionItemID = " _
    & Request.QueryString("AuctionItemID"), DBConn)
DBCommand.Fill(DSPageData, _
    "AuctionItem")
```

and placing that data into our labels:

```
lblTitle.Text = "<center>" _
    & DSPageData.Tables("AuctionItem"). _
    Rows(0).Item("ItemName") & "</center>"
lblFullInfo.Text = "<i>Date Opened: </i>" _
    & DSPageData.Tables("AuctionItem"). _
    Rows(0).Item("OpenDate") & "<br><br>" _
    & "<i>Date Closes: </i>" _
    & DSPageData.Tables("AuctionItem"). _
    Rows(0).Item("CloseDate") & "<br><br>" _
    & "<i>Minimum Bid: </i>" _
    & FormatCurrency(DSPageData.Tables("AuctionItem"). _
    Rows(0).Item("MinimumBid")) & "<br><br>" _
    & "<i>Bid Increment: </i>" _
    & FormatCurrency(DSPageData.Tables("AuctionItem"). _
    Rows(0).Item("BidIncrement")) & "<br><br>" _
    & "<i>Description: </i>" _
    & DSPageData.Tables("AuctionItem"). _
    Rows(0).Item("FullDescription") & "<br><br>"
```

Next, we need to retrieve the bid history

```
DBCommand = New OleDbDataAdapter _
    ("Select BidderName as [Name], " _
    & "Convert(varchar(30), WhenPlaced, 100) " _
    & "as [When Placed], " _
    & "'$' + Convert(varchar(30), BidAmount, 1) " _
    & "as [Bid Amount] " _
    & "From AuctionItemBids " _
    & "Inner Join Bidders On AuctionItemBids.BidderID = " _
    & "Bidders.BidderID Where AuctionItemID = " _
```

```
    & Request.QueryString("AuctionItemID") _
    & " Order By WhenPlaced", DBConn)
DBCommand.Fill(DSPageData, _
    "BidData")
```

and bind our DataGrid to it:

```
dgBids.DataSource = _
    DSPageData.Tables("BidData").DefaultView
dgBids.DataBind
```

We also need to retrieve the current high bid for the auction item

```
DBCommand = New OleDbDataAdapter _
    ("Select Max(BidAmount) as MaxBid " _
    & "From AuctionItemBids " _
    & "Where AuctionItemID = " _
    & Request.QueryString("AuctionItemID") _
    , DBConn)
DBCommand.Fill(DSPageData, _
    "CurrentBid")
```

so that we can use it to set up the next lowest acceptable bid:

```
txtBidAmount.Text = DSPageData.Tables("AuctionItem"). _
    Rows(0).Item("BidIncrement") + _
    DSPageData.Tables("CurrentBid"). _
    Rows(0).Item("MaxBid")
rngBidAmount.MinimumValue = txtBidAmount.Text
```

Access Code Changes

C18.mdb

To make this solution work against an Access database instead of a SQL Server database, a few changes are needed. First, the connect string on all the pages needs to be changed to something like this, which uses the proper provider and the current path to the Access database:

```
DBConn = New OleDbConnection("PROVIDER=Microsoft.Jet.OLEDB.4.0;" _
    & "DATA SOURCE=" _
```

```
    & Server.MapPath("/INetBook/C18/" _
    & "Access/C18.mdb;"))
```

The other change needed applies to the queries used to bind the DataGrids on the Auction Items and Auction Item page. In SQL Server, we had a query like this:

```
DBCommand = New OleDbDataAdapter _
    ("Select '<a href="".auction_item.aspx?AuctionItemID=' " _
    & "+ Convert(varchar(50), AuctionItemID) + '"">' + " _
    & "ItemName + '</a>' as [Item Name], " _
    & "BriefDescription as [Description], " _
    & "Convert(varchar(30), CloseDate, 100) as [Closes], " _
    & "'$' + Convert(varchar(30), MinimumBid, 1) " _
    & "as [Minimum Bid] " _
    & "From AuctionItems Where CloseDate >= GetDate() " _
    & "Order By ItemName", DBConn)
```

Note the use of the Convert function, the "+" character for concatenation, and the GetDate function. These are all different in Access:

```
DBCommand = New OleDbDataAdapter _
    ("Select '<a href="".auction_item.aspx?AuctionItemID=' " _
    & "& AuctionItemID & '"">' & " _
    & "ItemName & '</a>' as [Item Name], " _
    & "BriefDescription as [Description], " _
    & "Format(CloseDate,""General Date"") " _
    & "as [Closes], " _
    & "Format(MinimumBid, ""Currency"") " _
    & "as [Minimum Bid] " _
    & "From AuctionItems Where CloseDate >= Now() " _
    & "Order By ItemName", DBConn)
```

Here the convert function either goes away or is replaced with the Format function. The concatenation character in Access is the "&" character. And the function Now returns the current system date and time.

CHAPTER

19

Providing Web Services

Web Services are a new technology available to Web developers that was not available with ASP. Web Services provide a mechanism for you to create a code library, or service, that you make available to other developers who may be on the same computer as you, on a different server than you are, on a machine somewhere else in the world, on a totally different operating system, or all of the above.

Web Services rely on standard XML formats to make calls to these libraries compatible with other operating systems and computer types.

Web Services can be used for a variety of purposes. For example, say that you created a great library that made it easy to charge shipping through UPS, FedEx, and USPS according to the zip codes of the sender and receiver. You could implement your library as a Web Service and charge developers for connecting to your service.

Since the code that runs your service runs on your own server, you can keep track of who is using your service. Plus, when you need to update your service, you can update it in a single place, your server.

Another good use of a Web Service is to integrate some difficult functionality into a wrapper that other developers at your company can connect to. For example, say that you were an expert at creating user accounts, folders, and other such activities on your company's servers and you needed this functionality for a variety of applications that were used on your Web servers. You could write code that simplified the process and place it into a Web Service. Then other developers could simply reference your library to take advantage of your code.

In this chapter, we will look at creating a Web Service and then using or providing the Web Service in a client application through an ASP.NET page. We will look at three Web Services. The first provides some simple data validation functions. The second provides string and date functions. And the third records page hits.

Note that the third Web Service uses the same database that was used in Chapter 8. Please refer to that chapter to review the structure of the database.

Sample Usage

Before we look at creating a Web Service and how to use one, let's review the sample pages that call our Web Services.

In this chapter, we employ three Web Services. The methods exposed in each service are demonstrated on a single page. Figure 19-1 shows the Data Validator Web Service in use.

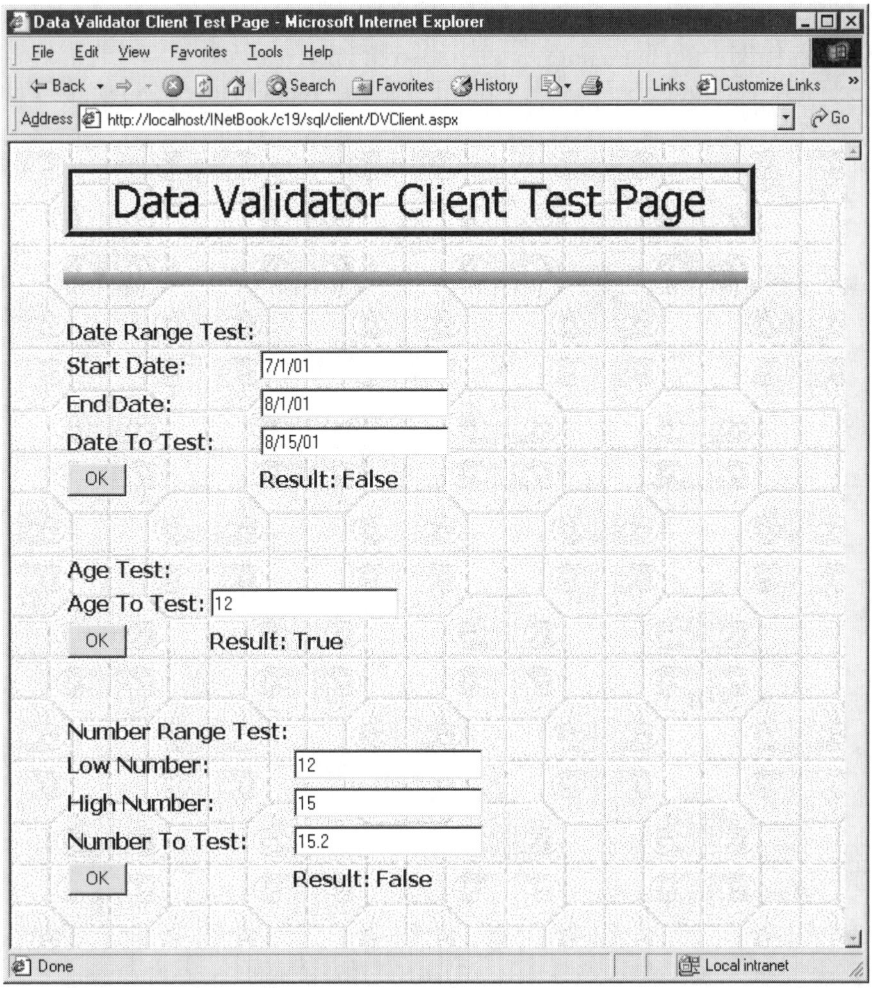

Figure 19-1 *Data Validator test page*

The Data Validator Web Services exposes three methods. The first method tests a date to see if it is between two other dates. It returns True if it is between the dates; otherwise, False is returned. In this example, the method returned False, since the date being tested was not between the two other dates.

The next method tests to see whether an age is in a valid range. In this example, 12 is considered valid but a number of 200 would not.

The third method tests to see if a number is in a range. Here it is not, so False is returned.

Figure 19-2 shows the second Web Service, String and Date Functions, in use.

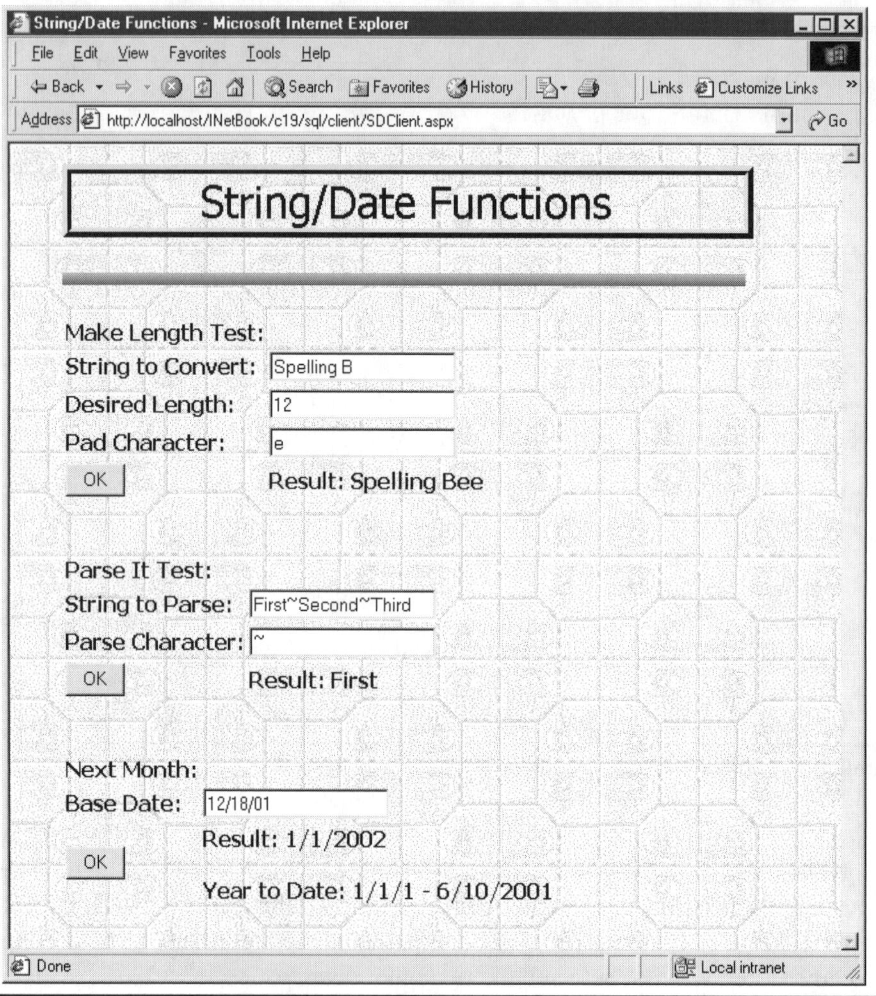

Figure 19-2 *String and Date Function Web Service in use*

The library contains four methods. The first method sizes a string to the desired length. It chops the string if it is too long and pads it with the specified pad character if the string is too short.

The second method parses text out of a string by using a parse character. In this example, "~" is the parse character. So all the text before that character is returned.

The other two methods in this library deal with dates. The first method returns the first day of the next month according to the date passed into it. The other method exposed in this library returns the current Year-to-Date range.

A test page that uses the third library is displayed in Figure 19-3.

The Usage Tracking Web Service contains a single method. This method records a page hit to the Usage Tracking database reviewed in Chapter 8.

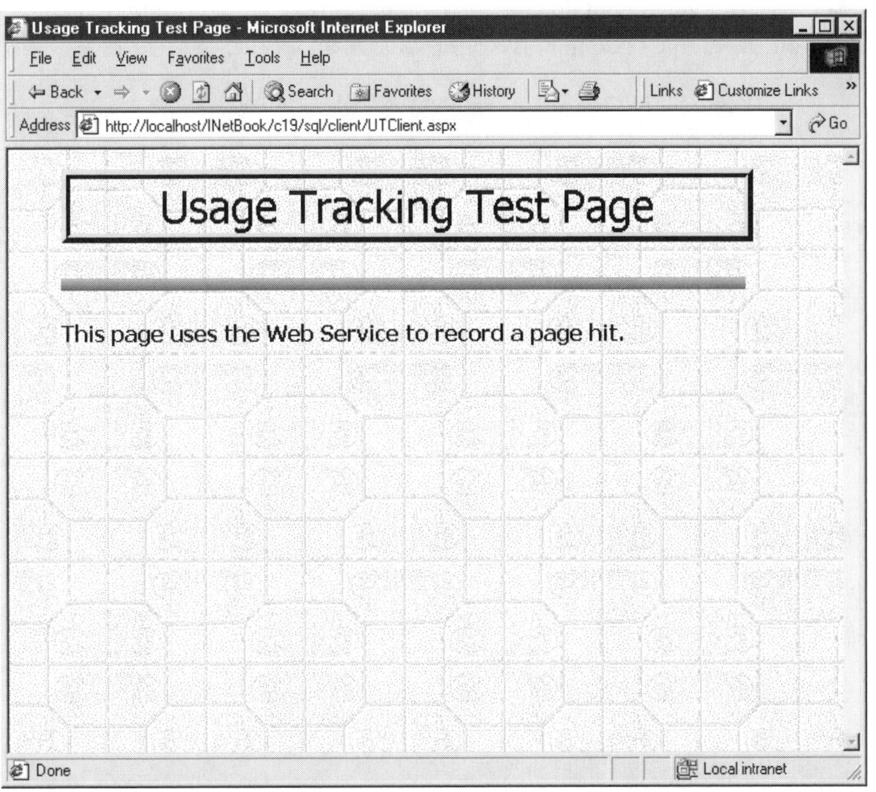

Figure 19-3 *Usage Tacking test page*

Creating the Web Services

The code for each of the Web Services used by the pages in the last section is contained in its own Web Service page. Those pages must end with the extension .asmx. In this section of the chapter, we will review the code in those pages. Then we will look at a simple way to test your Web Services before building pages that use them.

Data Validator Web Service

DataValidator.asmx

As with the other Web Services that we will review in this section, the code on this Web Service page must contain specific declarations, statements, and structure.

Here you see all the code that makes up this Web Service:

```
<%@ WebService Language="VB" Class="DataValidator"%>
Option Strict Off
Imports System.Web.Services
<WebService(Namespace:="http://localhost/" _
    & "wwwroot/INetBookC19/SQL/Server/")> _
    Public Class DataValidator
    <WebMethod()> Public Function _
        DateRange(DateToTest as Date, StartDate as Date, _
        EndDate as Date) as Boolean
        If DateToTest < StartDate or DateToTest > EndDate Then
            DateRange = False
        Else
            DateRange = True
        End If
    End Function
    <WebMethod()> Public Function Age(FieldToTest as Integer) _
        as Boolean
        If FieldToTest < 0 Or FieldToTest > 140 Then
            Age = False
        Else
            Age = True
        End If
    End Function
    <WebMethod()> Public Function NumberRange _
        (FieldToTest as Single, MinNumber as Single, _
```

```
        MaxNumber as Single) as Boolean
        If FieldToTest < MinNumber Or FieldToTest > MaxNumber Then
            NumberRange = False
        Else
            NumberRange = True
        End If
    End Function
End Class
```

First, note the absence of Script tags; none are required or allowed within a Web Service. The page does start with a compiler directive:

```
<%@ WebService Language="VB" Class="DataValidator"%>
```

This directive tells the compiler that this page is a Web service and that the language we will use is Visual Basic. Plus, we define the name of the class in this Web Service.

Next, I prefer to turn off Option Strict. You may prefer to have it turned on. I prefer to allow for the automatic conversion of my variables and concatenation:

```
Option Strict Off
```

Next, we must import this library into our Web Service:

```
Imports System.Web.Services
```

That is followed by the class definition. Note that the name here matches the name in the directive in the Class parameter. Also note the path to the Web Service location. You would change this to the location of your service:

```
<WebService(Namespace:="http://localhost/" _
    & "wwwroot/INetBookC19/SQL/Server/")> _
Public Class DataValidator
```

We then start by defining the methods within our Web Service. Note the WebMethod keyword in the declaration. This exposes your method beyond the public use of your own server and allows it to be called remotely. This method takes three date parameters as an Input and returns a Boolean:

```
<WebMethod()> Public Function _
    DateRange(DateToTest as Date, StartDate as Date, _
    EndDate as Date) as Boolean
```

We then test to see if the date to test is within the date range:

```
If DateToTest < StartDate or DateToTest > EndDate Then
```

If it isn't, we return False from our method:

```
DateRange = False
```

Otherwise, True is returned

```
DateRange = True
```

The next method tests to see if an age falls within an expected range:

```
<WebMethod()> Public Function Age(FieldToTest as Integer) _
    as Boolean
```

We perform that test here:

```
If FieldToTest < 0 Or FieldToTest > 140 Then
```

If it is not in that range, we return False:

```
Age = False
```

Otherwise, True is returned from this method:

```
Age = True
```

The third method in this Web Service class tests to see if a number is within a specified range:

```
<WebMethod()> Public Function NumberRange _
    (FieldToTest as Single, MinNumber as Single, _
    MaxNumber as Single) as Boolean
```

The test is performed here:

```
If FieldToTest < MinNumber Or FieldToTest > MaxNumber Then
```

And if it fails, False is returned

```
NumberRange = False
```

Otherwise, True is returned

```
NumberRange = True
```

String and Date Functions Web Service

StringDateFunctions.asmx

The String and Date Function Web Service exposes four methods that can be called through its service. The first method sizes a string to the specified length.

```
<WebMethod()> Public Function MakeLength _
    (StringToConvert as String, DesiredLength as Long, _
    PadCharacter as String) as String
    Dim TempString as String
    TempString = StringToConvert
    If TempString.Length > DesiredLength Then
        TempString = TempString.SubString(0, DesiredLength)
    Elseif TempString.Length < DesiredLength Then
        Do Until TempString.Length >= DesiredLength
            TempString = TempString & PadCharacter
        Loop
    End If
    MakeLength = TempString
End Function
```

The method expects three parameters. The first is the string to size, the second is the length that you want the string to size, and the third parameter is the character to use if the string needs to be padded

```
<WebMethod()> Public Function MakeLength _
    (StringToConvert as String, DesiredLength as Long, _
    PadCharacter as String) as String
```

We will use a temporary string

```
Dim TempString as String
```

to store the string that we need to convert

```
TempString = StringToConvert
```

Next, we check to see if the string is too long:

```
If TempString.Length > DesiredLength Then
```

If it is, we chop it to the desired length:

```
TempString = TempString.SubString(0, DesiredLength)
```

Next, we check to see if the string is too short:

```
Elseif TempString.Length < DesiredLength Then
```

If it is, we enter a loop that checks to see when the string is long enough:

```
Do Until TempString.Length >= DesiredLength
```

Within that loop, we pad the temporary string with the pad character:

```
TempString = TempString & PadCharacter
```

At the end of the procedure, we return the converted string:

```
MakeLength = TempString
```

The next method chops a string at the point where the specified character is found.

```
<WebMethod()> Public Function ParseIt _
    (StringToParse as String, ParseChar as String) as String
    If StringToParse.IndexOf(ParseChar) <> -1 Then
        ParseIt = StringToParse.SubString _
            (0, StringToParse.IndexOf(ParseChar))
    Else
        ParseIt = StringToParse
```

```
    End If
End Function
```

The procedure requires two parameters. The first is the string to parse, and the second is the parse character:

```
<WebMethod()> Public Function ParseIt _
    (StringToParse as String, ParseChar as String) as String
```

We then check to see if the parse character is found within the target string:

```
If StringToParse.IndexOf(ParseChar) <> -1 Then
```

If it is, we return the string before the parse character:

```
ParseIt = StringToParse.SubString _
    (0, StringToParse.IndexOf(ParseChar))
```

Otherwise, we return the entire string:

```
ParseIt = StringToParse
```

The next method returns the current year to date as a string.

```
<WebMethod()> Public Function YTD() as String
    Dim CurrentDate as Date
    YTD = "1/1/" & CurrentDate.Year & " - " & CurrentDate.Today
End Function
```

It does not take any parameters, and it returns a String:

```
<WebMethod()> Public Function YTD() as String
```

We start by dimensioning a date:

```
Dim CurrentDate as Date
```

That date is used to parse out the current system year and date into the return text:

```
YTD = "1/1/" & CurrentDate.Year & " - " & CurrentDate.Today
```

The other method in this Web Service class returns the first day of the next month in terms of the specified date.

```
<WebMethod()> Public Function NextMonth _
    (BaseDate as Date) as String
    Dim TheDate as String
    If BaseDate.Month = 12 Then
        TheDate = "1/1/" & (BaseDate.Year + 1)
    Else
        TheDate = (BaseDate.Month + 1) & "/1/" & BaseDate.Year
    End If
    NextMonth = TheDate
End Function
```

The method takes a single parameter, the start date, and returns the first day of the next month as a string:

```
<WebMethod()> Public Function NextMonth _
    (BaseDate as Date) as String
```

We declare a string variable

```
Dim TheDate as String
```

and check to see if the month of the date passed into this procedure is December:

```
If BaseDate.Month = 12 Then
```

If that is the case, we return the first date of next year:

```
TheDate = "1/1/" & (BaseDate.Year + 1)
```

Otherwise, we add 1 to the current month and combine that with the first day of the month and the year of the date passed into this procedure:

```
TheDate = (BaseDate.Month + 1) & "/1/" & BaseDate.Year
    End If
    NextMonth = TheDate
```

Usage Tracking Web Service

UsageTracker.asmx

The Usage Tracking Web Service contains a single method that records a page hit. This page imports the Web Services library, as we saw when we reviewed the first Web Service:

```
Imports System.Web.Services
```

It also needs to import two data libraries:

```
Imports System.Data
Imports System.Data.OLEDB
```

The single method in this class adds a record to the PageViews table, and if this is the first page viewed by the visitor, it also records a hit in the Visitors table.

```
<WebMethod()> Public Function RecordPageHit _
        (PageName as String, VisitorID as Long) as Long
        Dim DBConn as OleDbConnection
        Dim DBInsert As New OleDbCommand
        Dim DBCommand As OleDbDataAdapter
        Dim DSData as New DataSet
        DBConn = New OleDbConnection("Provider=sqloledb;" _
            & "server=localhost;" _
            & "Initial Catalog=INETC8;" _
            & "User Id=sa;" _
            & "Password=yourpassword;")
        DBInsert.Connection = DBConn
        DBInsert.Connection.Open
        If VisitorID = 0 Then
            DBInsert.CommandText = "Insert Into Visitors " _
                & "(DateEntered) Values (GetDate())"
            DBInsert.ExecuteNonQuery()
            DBCommand = New OleDbDataAdapter _
                ("Select Max(VisitorID) as MaxID " _
                & "From Visitors", DBConn)
```

```
            DBCommand.Fill(DSData, _
                "CurrentID")
            VisitorID = DSData.Tables("CurrentID"). _
                Rows(0).Item("MaxID")
        End If
        DBInsert.CommandText = "Insert Into PageViews " _
            & "(DateEntered, PageName, VisitorID) Values (" _
            & "GetDate(), '" _
            & PageName & "', " _
            & VisitorID & ")"
        DBInsert.ExecuteNonQuery()
        RecordPageHit = VisitorID
    End Function
```

The method requires two parameters. The first is the name of the page being hit, and the second is the visitor's ID. The method returns the visitor's ID:

```
<WebMethod()> Public Function RecordPageHit _
    (PageName as String, VisitorID as Long) as Long
```

Within this method, we will need data objects:

```
Dim DBConn as OleDbConnection
Dim DBInsert As New OleDbCommand
Dim DBCommand As OleDbDataAdapter
Dim DSData as New DataSet
```

We start by connecting to the database that we reviewed in Chapter 8:

```
DBConn = New OleDbConnection("Provider=sqloledb;" _
    & "server=localhost;" _
    & "Initial Catalog=INETC8;" _
    & "User Id=sa;" _
    & "Password=yourpassword;")
```

Our command object will use that connection object:

```
DBInsert.Connection = DBConn
DBInsert.Connection.Open
```

If the calling application passes a 0 in for the visitor's ID, it means this is a new visitor:

```
If VisitorID = 0 Then
```

In that case, we need to add a new record to the Visitors table:

```
DBInsert.CommandText = "Insert Into Visitors " _
    & "(DateEntered) Values (GetDate())"
DBInsert.ExecuteNonQuery()
```

We then retrieve the ID of the record we just added

```
DBCommand = New OleDbDataAdapter _
    ("Select Max(VisitorID) as MaxID " _
    & "From Visitors", DBConn)
    DBCommand.Fill(DSData, _
    "CurrentID")
```

and store it in the variable passed in:

```
VisitorID = DSData.Tables("CurrentID"). _
    Rows(0).Item("MaxID")
```

Now we can add a new record to the PageViews table

```
DBInsert.CommandText = "Insert Into PageViews " _
    & "(DateEntered, PageName, VisitorID) Values (" _
    & "GetDate(), '" _
    & PageName & "', " _
    & VisitorID & ")"
DBInsert.ExecuteNonQuery()
```

and return the ID of the visitor from this method:

```
RecordPageHit = VisitorID
```

Testing Your Web Service

Now that you have created your Web Service, you can use it in a client application. But that involves creating a client application and linking to your Web Service. We will do that in the next section.

But at this point, you really just want to test your Web Service to see if it works as you expect. If you browse to one of your Web Service pages, you will see that IIS generates a test page for you like the one displayed in Figure 19-4.

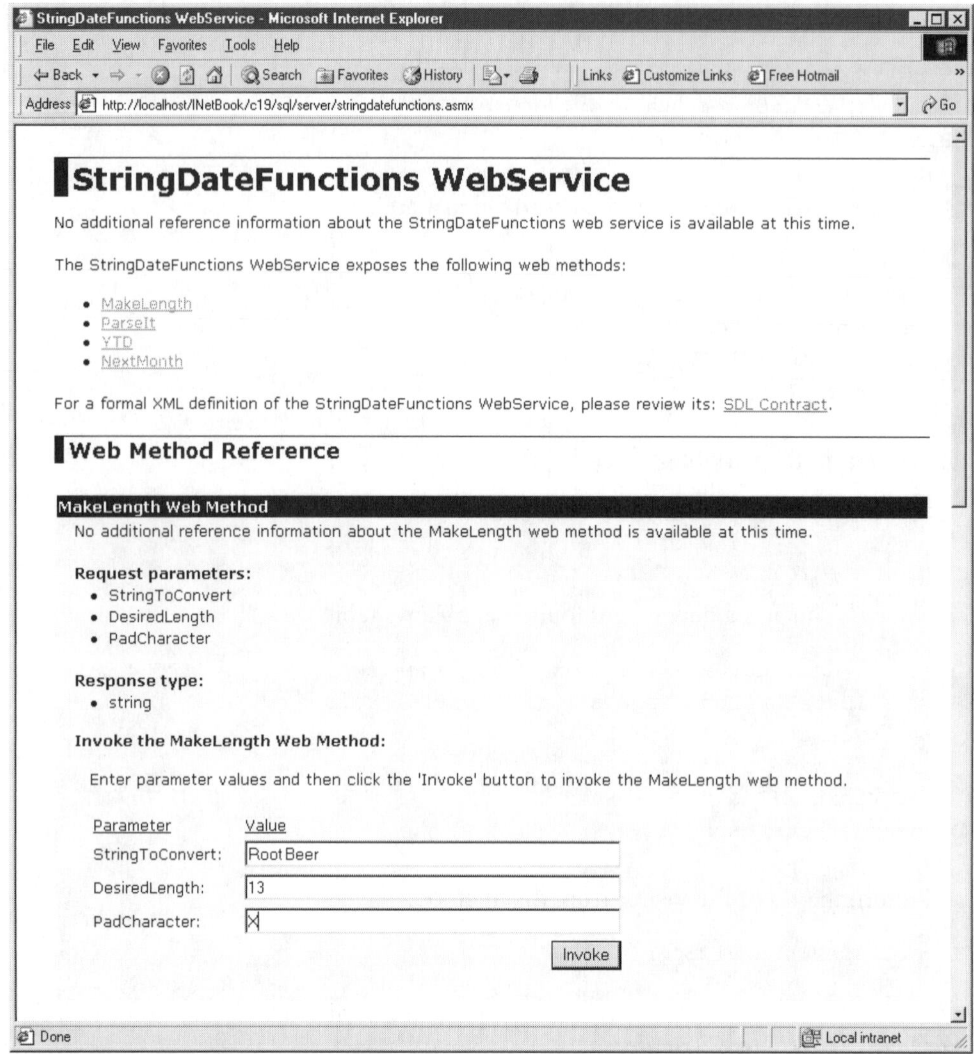

Figure 19-4 *Web Service test page*

The first thing you know if this page comes up when you browse to your Web Service is that your Web Service compiled. That means it did not contain any compile errors.

The page lists all the methods that are exposed in your Web Service. You can even test your methods on this page. You just enter values for the parameters and click the Invoke button. When you do that, your Web Service is called and the method is invoked. The return of your call is displayed in a Web page like the one displayed in Figure 19-5.

So, using this page allows you to thoroughly test your Web Service before creating a client or consuming application.

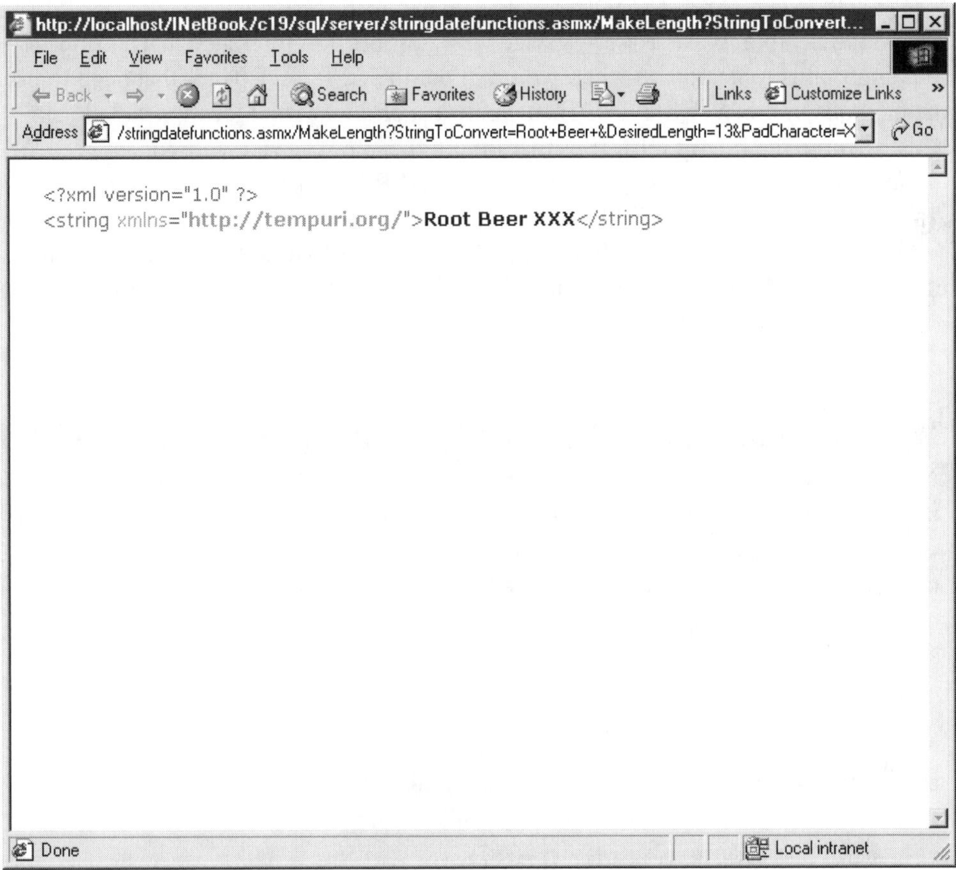

Figure 19-5 *Results of invoking a method*

Using a Web Service

In this section of the chapter, we will first look at what the client or consumer needs to do to reference your Web Service. Then we will look at the code that is used in the test pages to implement the Web Services.

Referencing a Web Service

For you to be able to use a Web Service, you first need to reference it. The first step in doing that is to decide on where you will put the ASP.NET pages that need to use the methods of the Web Service. Then create a subfolder at that location called "bin". This is where the binary DLL files that link to the Web Service will go.

Next, you need to mark the folder that the ASP.NET pages will go into as an Application through the IIS Manager.

Once you have set up your folders, you are now ready to use two command line utilities that will generate a class file and a DLL to reference the Web Service.

Take a look at Figure 19-6.

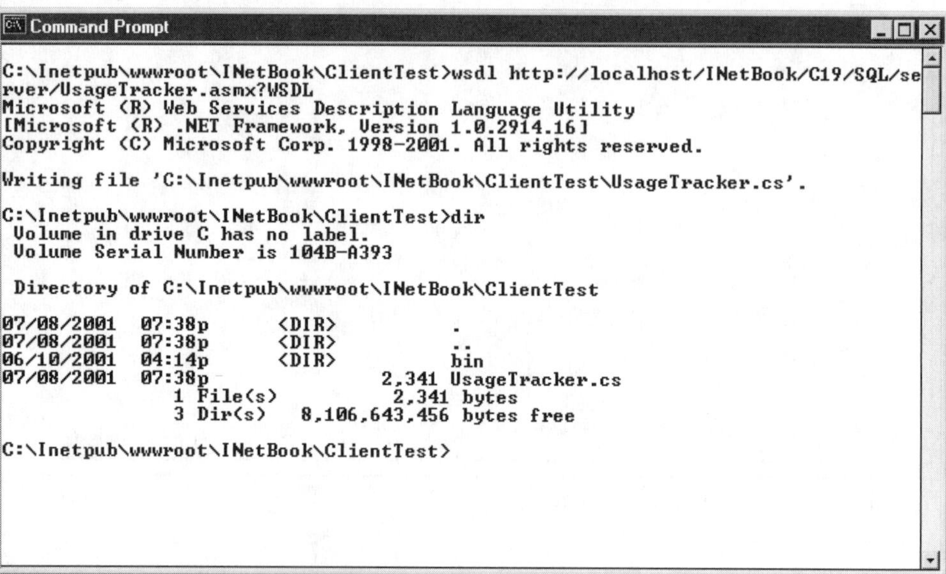

Figure 19-6 *Creating the class file*

Here we have opened a command prompt in the location where the ASP.NET pages will go to implement our Web Services.

We then issued this command—note that it is displayed across multiple lines but that it appears as a single line in the command prompt:

```
wsdl http://localhost/INetBook/C19/SQL/
    server/UsageTracker.asmx?WSDL
```

We use the WSDL program to generate a class file, cs. Most importantly, note the parameter. You would change this to point to the location of the .asmx file that contains the Web Service you are linking to. Note that you add the "?WSDL" to the end of the filename.

After that command completes, a .cs file is generated for the Web Service.

Next, we need to create a DLL for the referenced Web Service. Take a look at Figure 19-7.

Here, we used the CSC program to generate a DLL with this command line:

```
csc.exe /out:bin\UsageTracker.dll /t:library /r:System.XML.dll
    /r:System.Web.Services.dll UsageTracker.cs
```

```
Command Prompt

C:\Inetpub\wwwroot\INetBook\ClientTest>C:\WINNT\Microsoft.NET\Framework\v1.0.291
4\csc.exe /out:bin/UsageTracker.dll /t:library /r:System.XML.dll /r:System.Web.S
ervices.dll UsageTracker.cs
Microsoft (R) Visual C# Compiler Version 7.00.9254 [CLR version v1.0.2914]
Copyright (C) Microsoft Corp 2000-2001. All rights reserved.


C:\Inetpub\wwwroot\INetBook\ClientTest>cd bin

C:\Inetpub\wwwroot\INetBook\ClientTest\bin>dir
 Volume in drive C has no label.
 Volume Serial Number is 104B-A393

 Directory of C:\Inetpub\wwwroot\INetBook\ClientTest\bin

06/10/2001  04:14p      <DIR>          .
06/10/2001  04:14p      <DIR>          ..
07/08/2001  07:40p               4,608 UsageTracker.dll
               1 File(s)          4,608 bytes
               2 Dir(s)   8,106,639,360 bytes free

C:\Inetpub\wwwroot\INetBook\ClientTest\bin>_
```

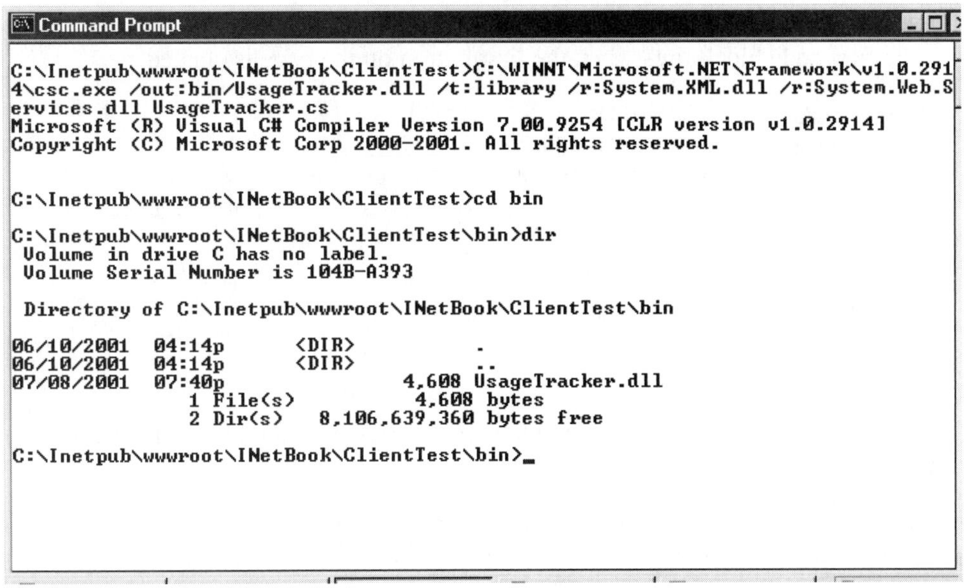

Figure 19-7 *Creating the DLL file*

Note that the command line is typed into the command prompt as a single line. Also note the out parameter:

```
/out:bin\UsageTracker.dll
```

Here we specify the name we want to call the DLL and that we want to put it into the bin subfolder. Also note that the command line program will compile the class that we generated in the last statement:

```
UsageTracker.cs
```

After that command executes, the DLL name we specified is created in the bin folder.

The same procedure needs to be performed for the two other Web Services that we reviewed earlier in this chapter. Once that is done, we can call the methods in the Web Services in the ASP.NET files located in the current folder.

Data Validation Client Test Page

DVClient.aspx

The code on the Data Validation test page calls the Data Validation Web Service to complete its functionality within its events.

The first code block fires when the first button on the page is clicked.

```
Sub SubmitBtn1_Click(Sender As Object, E As EventArgs)
    Dim MyDS as New DataValidator()
    lblResult1.Text = "Result: " & MyDS.DateRange _
        (txtTestDate.Text, txtStartDate.Text, txtEndDate.Text)
End Sub
```

It instantiates the Web Service

```
Dim MyDS as New DataValidator()
```

and calls the DateRange method with the results of that method being placed into a Label:

```
lblResult1.Text = "Result: " & MyDS.DateRange _
    (txtTestDate.Text, txtStartDate.Text, txtEndDate.Text)
```

The next procedure fires when the second button is clicked.

```
Sub SubmitBtn2_Click(Sender As Object, E As EventArgs)
    Dim MyDS as New DataValidator()
    lblResult2.Text = "Result: " & MyDS.Age _
        (txtAge.Text)
End Sub
```

It also creates an instance of our Web Service

```
Dim MyDS as New DataValidator()
```

and displays the results returned by the Age method:

```
lblResult2.Text = "Result: " & MyDS.Age _
    (txtAge.Text)
```

The other procedure on the page fires when the last Button control is clicked.

```
Sub SubmitBtn3_Click(Sender As Object, E As EventArgs)
    Dim MyDS as New DataValidator()
    lblResult3.Text = "Result: " & MyDS.NumberRange _
        (txtTestNumber.Text, txtLowNumber.Text, txtHighNumber.Text)
End Sub
```

We start by instantiating our Web Service

```
Dim MyDS as New DataValidator()
```

and calling the NumberRange method:

```
lblResult3.Text = "Result: " & MyDS.NumberRange _
    (txtTestNumber.Text, txtLowNumber.Text, txtHighNumber.Text)
```

String and Date Function Test Page

SDClient.aspx

The code on the String and Date Function test page fires when one of the three Buttons is clicked. The code invokes our String and Date Function Web Service and displays the results of calls to the four methods in that service.

The first procedure fires when the first Button control is clicked.

```
Sub SubmitBtn1_Click(Sender As Object, E As EventArgs)
    Dim MyDS as New StringDateFunctions()
```

```
    lblResult1.Text = "Result: " & MyDS.MakeLength _
        (txtStringToConvert.Text, _
        txtDesiredLength.Text, txtPadCharacter.Text)
End Sub
```

It instantiates our String and Date Function Web Service:

```
Dim MyDS as New StringDateFunctions()
```

Then it calls the MakeLength method and displays the value returned

```
lblResult1.Text = "Result: " & MyDS.MakeLength _
    (txtStringToConvert.Text, _
    txtDesiredLength.Text, txtPadCharacter.Text)
```

The next procedure fires when the second Button is clicked.

```
Sub SubmitBtn2_Click(Sender As Object, E As EventArgs)
    Dim MyDS as New StringDateFunctions()
    lblResult2.Text = "Result: " & MyDS.ParseIT _
        (txtStringToParse.Text, txtParseCharacter.Text)
End Sub
```

We start by instantiating the Web Service:

```
Dim MyDS as New StringDateFunctions()
```

We then call the ParseIt procedure and place the return of the call into a Label control:

```
lblResult2.Text = "Result: " & MyDS.ParseIT _
    (txtStringToParse.Text, txtParseCharacter.Text)
```

The final procedure is called when the third button is clicked.

```
Sub SubmitBtn3_Click(Sender As Object, E As EventArgs)
    Dim MyDS as New StringDateFunctions()
    lblResult3.Text = "Result: " & MyDS.NextMonth _
        (txtBaseDate.Text) & "<br><br>Year to Date: " _
        & MyDS.YTD()
End Sub
```

The procedure needs our Web Server:

```
Dim MyDS as New StringDateFunctions()
```

It then calls the two date functions in our Web Service. The results of those calls are placed into a Label control:

```
lblResult3.Text = "Result: " & MyDS.NextMonth _
    (txtBaseDate.Text) & "<br><br>Year to Date: " _
    & MyDS.YTD()
```

Usage Tracking Test Page

UTClient.aspx

The code on the Usage Tracking page calls the Usage Tracking Web Service when the page is loaded.

```
Sub Page_Load(ByVal Sender as Object, ByVal E as EventArgs)
    Dim MyDS as New UsageTracker()
    If Len(Session("VisitorID")) = 0 Then
        Session("VisitorID") = 0
    End If
    Session("VisitorID") = MyDS.RecordPageHit _
        ("Home", Session("VisitorID"))
End Sub
```

First, we instantiate the Usage Tracking Web Service:

```
Dim MyDS as New UsageTracker()
```

Then we check to see if this is the first page the visitor is viewing

```
If Len(Session("VisitorID")) = 0 Then
```

If it is, we set the ID of the Visitor to 0:

```
Session("VisitorID") = 0
```

We then call the Web Service to record the page hit and store the return in a session variable so that it could be used from other pages within the site:

```
Session("VisitorID") = MyDS.RecordPageHit _
    ("Home", Session("VisitorID"))
```

APPENDIX A

ASP.NET/VB Language Reference

In this appendix, many of the inherent methods and functions of ASP.NET are defined. Each procedure or method is listed with its description, any parameters, any return value, and a sample use.

Abs Returns the absolute value of a number.

Syntax:

```
X = Math.Abs(Num)
```

Num is a numeric value for which the absolute value needs to be determined. The method returns the absolute value of Num.

Example:

```
Label1.Text = Math.Abs(5)
Label2.Text = Math.Abs(-5)
```

This example will write the following output to a browser:

```
5
5
```

Asc Returns the numeric ASCII value of a character.

Syntax:

```
X = Asc(TheLetter)
```

TheLetter is the character for which you want to determine the ASCII value. The method returns the numeric ASCII value.

Example:

```
Label1.Text = Asc("B")
Label2.Text = Asc("?")
```

This example will write the following output to a browser:

```
66
63
```

Conversion Methods (CBool, Cbyte, Ccur, CDate, CDbl, CInt, CLng, CSng, CStr) Convert a variable of one type to a variable of another type.

Syntax:

```
X = CStr(ValueToConvert)
```

The syntax is the same for all the conversion methods. Passed to the method is the value you wish to convert. The method returns the converted number.

Example:

```
X = CInt("44")
```

X will contain an integer with the value 44.

Chr Converts an ASCII value to its character representation.

Syntax:

```
X = Chr(TheValue)
```

TheValue is the ASCII number you wish to return a character from. The method returns the value converted.

Example:

```
Label1.Text = Chr(72)
Label2.Text = Chr(74)
```

This example will write the following output to a browser:

```
H
J
```

DateAdd Adds a value to a date or time.

Syntax:

```
X = DateAdd(Part2Add, Number2Add, Date)
```

The first parameter is a number representing what you want to add to a date, such as days or hours. For this parameter, you can use DateInterval.Year, DateInterval.Month, DateInterval.Date, etc.

Num2Add is the quantity that you want to add. Use a negative number to perform date subtraction. Date is the date that you want to add to.

Example:

```
Dim x as Date
X = "5/15/1940 5:15"
Label1.Text = DateAdd(DateInterval.Hour, 4, x)
Label2.Text = DateAdd(DateInterval.Year, -3, x)
```

This example will write the following output to a browser:

```
9:15:00 AM
5/5/1937
```

DateDiff Subtracts two dates and returns the difference.

Syntax:

```
X= DateDiff(Part2Diff, Date1, Date2)
```

The first parameter is a number representing what you want to use to subtract, such as days or hours. For this parameter, you can use DateInterval.Year, DateInterval.Month, DateInterval.Date, etc.

The second parameter is the date that you want to subtract from the third parameter.

Example:

```
Dim x as Date, y as Date
X = "4/1/1952"
y = "3/1/2005"
Label1.Text = DateDiff(DateInterval.Year, x, y)
X = "1:15"
y = "1:25"
Label2.Text = DateDiff(DateInterval.Minute, x, y)
```

This example will write the following output to a browser:

```
53
10
```

DatePart Returns a portion of a date or time.

Syntax:

```
X = DatePart(Part2Return, Date)
```

The first parameter is a number representing what part you want to return, such as days or hours. For this parameter, you can use DateInterval.Year, DateInterval.Month, DateInterval.Date, etc.

The second parameter is the date that you want to parse from. The portion of the date requested is returned.

Example:

```
Dim x as Date
X = "4/1/1952 1:15"
Label1.Text = DatePart(DateInterval.Year, x)
Label2.Text = DatePart(DateInterval.Minute, x)
```

This example will write the following output to a browser:

```
1952
15
```

DateSerial Returns a date from the parts of year, month, day.

Syntax:

```
X = DateSerial(year, month, day)
```

The method returns the concatenation of the date parts.

Example:

```
Label1.Text = DateSerial("1955", "4", "22")
Label2.Text = DateSerial("2022", "8", "11")
```

This example will write the following output to a browser:

```
4/22/1955
8/11/2022
```

Day Returns the day portion of a date.

Syntax:

```
X = Day(Date)
```

The method returns the day of the Date.

Example:

```
Label1.Text = Day("5/1/1971 5:15:32")
Label2.Text = Day("9/21/2002 12:32:54")
```

This example will write the following output to a browser:

```
1
21
```

Do...Loop Repeats a chunk of code until a condition is met.

Syntax:

```
Do Condition
      'Code Block
Loop
```

The code will run until the condition is met.

Example:

```
Do Until Second(TimeOfDay) = 0
      Response.Write("Not Yet")
Loop
```

The text "Not Yet" will be written over and over again to the browser until the seconds on the system time are zero.

Fix Returns the integer portion of a number.

Syntax:

```
X = Fix(TheNumber)
```

X will be set to the integer portion of TheNumber.

Example:

```
Label1.Text = Fix(2.999)
Label2.Text = Fix(0.1)
```

This example will write the following output to a browser:

```
2
0
```

For...Each Allows you to iterate through a collection of objects.

Syntax:

```
For Eac MyItem in TheCollection
    'take action on the collection
Next
```

The code will perform the code block through each of the items in TheCollection.

Example:

```
For Each MyItem in MyCollection
    Label1.Text = Label1.Text & MyItem.Name
Next
```

This example will write the name of each item in the collection to a browser.

For...Next Iterates from one number to another performing a block of code with each cycle.

Syntax:

```
For TheNumber = Start to End
    'code block
Next
```

The block will iterate until TheNumber is equal to End.

Example:

```
For I = 1 to 5
    Label1.Text = Label1.Text & I
Next
```

This example will write the numbers 1 through 5 to a browser.

FormatCurrency Formats a number as currency.

Syntax:

```
X = FormatCurrency(Number2Format)
```

X is set to Number2Format converted to currency.

Example:

```
Label1.Text = FormatCurrency(2.999)
Label2.Text = FormatCurrency(0.1)
```

This example will write the following output to a browser:

```
$3.00
$0.10
```

FormatDateTime Formats a string in a date format.

Syntax:

```
X = FormatDateTime(TheDate)
```

X will be set to the formatted date version of TheDate.

Example:

```
Label1.Text = FormatDateTime("12/6/1989", 0)
Label2.Text = FormatDateTime("12/6/1989", 1)
Label3.Text = FormatDateTime("12/6/1989", 2)
```

This example will write the following output to a browser:

```
12/6/1989 12:00 AM
Wednesday, December 06, 1989
12/6/1989
```

FormatNumber Formats a number.

Syntax:

```
X = FormatNumber(TheNumber)
```

X will be set to the formatted version of TheNumber.

Example:

```
Label1.Text = FormatNumber(1234567)
Label2.Text = FormatNumber(.1)
```

This example will write the following output to a browser:

```
1,234,567.00
0.10
```

FormatPercent Formats a number as a percent.

Syntax:

```
X = FormatPercent(TheNumber)
```

X will be set to the value of TheNumber written as a percentage.

Example:

```
Label1.Text = FormatPercent(12.1)
Label2.Text = FormatPercent(.1877)
```

This example will write the following output to a browser:

```
1,210.00%
18.77%
```

Hex Returns a string representing the hexadecimal value of a number.

Syntax:

```
X = Hex(TheNumber)
```

X is set to a string containing the hexadecimal value of TheNumber.

Example:

```
Label1.Text = Hex(255)
Label2.Text = Hex(16)
```

This example will write the following output to a browser:

```
FF
10
```

Hour Returns the hour portion of a time.

Syntax:

```
X = Hour(TheTime)
```

X will be set to the hour of TheTime.

Example:

```
Label1.Text = Hour("5/1/1971 5:15:32")
Label2.Text = Hour("9/21/2002 12:32:54")
```

This example will write the following output to a browser:

```
5
12
```

If Provides for code to run depending on a condition.

Syntax:

```
If Condition1 Then
    'Code block
ElseIf Condition2 Then
    'Code block
Else
    'Code block
End If
```

If Condition1 evaluates to True, then the first code block will run. If not, the code will test Condition2. If Condition2 evaluates to True, then the second code block will run. Otherwise, the code in the third code block will run. The ElseIf and Else portions of an If statement are not required.

Example:

```
If Month(Today) = 9 then
    Label1.Text = "September"
Else
    Label1.Text = "Not September"
End If
```

This example will write, to a browser, "September" if the current month is September. Otherwise, "Not September" will be written.

InStr Searches for a string within a string.

Syntax:

```
X = Instr(String2Search, SearchString)
```

X is set to first occurrence of the SearchString within the String2Search. If the SearchString is not found, the method returns 0.

Example:

```
Label1.Text = Instr("Hello", "e")
Label2.Text = Instr("Hello", "R")
```

This example will write the following output to a browser:

```
2
0
```

InStrRev Same as Instr except that the search begins at the end of the string.

Syntax:

```
X = Instr(String2Search, SearchString)
```

X will be set to the last occurrence of the SearchString within the String2Search.

Example:

```
Label1.Text = InstrRev("Hello World", "l")
Label2.Text = InstrRev("Hello", "R")
```

This example will write the following output to a browser:

```
10
5
```

Int Returns the integer portion of a number.

Syntax:

```
X = Int(TheNumber)
```

X will be set to the integer portion of TheNumber.

Example:

```
Label1.Text = Int(2.999)
Label2.Text = Int(0.1)
```

This example will write the following output to a browser:

```
2
0
```

IsDate Tests a value to see if it is a date.

Syntax:

```
X = IsDate(TheDate)
```

X will be set to True or False depending upon whether TheDate is a date or not.

Example:

```
Label1.Text = IsDate("12/44/55")
Label2.Text = IsDate("12/14/55")
```

This example will write the following output to a browser:

```
False
True
```

IsNumeric Tests to see if a value is a number.

Syntax:

```
X = IsNumeric(TheValue)
```

X will be set to True or False depending upon whether TheValue is a number.

Example:

```
Label1.Text = IsNumeric("Hello")
Label2.Text = IsNumeric("33")
```

This example will write the following output to a browser:

```
False
True
```

LCase Converts text to lowercase.

Syntax:

```
X = LCase(TheValue)
```

X will be set to the lowercase text of the variable TheValue.

Example:

```
Label1.Text = LCase("HELLO")
Label2.Text = LCase("123")
```

This example will write the following output to a browser:

```
hello
123
```

Left Chops characters off the left side of a string.

Syntax:

```
X = Left(String2Chop, NumCharacters)
```

String2Chop is the string that you want to chop characters from. NumCharacters is the number of characters you want to chop. Returned to X will be the chopped string.

Example:

```
Label1.Text = Left("Hello", 2)
```

This example will write the following output to a browser:

```
He
```

Len Returns the length, in characters, of a string.

Syntax:

```
X = Len(TheString)
```

X will be set to the number of characters in TheString.

Example:

```
Label1.Text = Len("Hello")
Label2.Text = Len("Hello World")
```

This example will write the following output to a browser:

```
5
11
```

LTrim Returns a string without any leading spaces.

Syntax:

```
X = LTrim(TheString)
```

X will be set to TheString without any leading spaces.

Example:

```
X = LTrim("   Hello   ")
```

X will be set to the string "Hello   ".

Mid Returns characters from the middle of the string.

Syntax:

```
X = Mid(TheString, StartPosition, NumCbaracters)
```

TheString is the string to pull characters from. StartPosition is the spot to start retrieving characters from. NumCharacters is the number of characters to chop out of the middle. If the third parameter is left off, the method returns all characters after the start position.

Example:

```
Label1.Text = Mid("Hello", 2, 3)
Label2.Text = Mid("Hello", 2)
```

This example will write the following output to a browser:

```
ell
ello
```

Minute Returns the minute from a time.

Syntax:

```
X = Minute(TheTime)
```

X will be set to the minutes within the TheTime variable.

Example:

```
Label1.Text = Minute("5/1/1971 5:15:32")
Label2.Text = Minute("9/21/2002 12:32:54")
```

This example will write the following output to a browser:

```
15
32
```

Month Returns the month portion of a date as a number.

Syntax:

```
X = Month(TheDate)
```

X will be set to the Month of TheDate.

Example:

```
Label1.Text = Month("5/1/1971 5:15:32")
Label2.Text = Month("9/21/2002 12:32:54")
```

This example will write the following output to a browser:

```
5
9
```

MonthName Returns the month name for a number from 1 to 12.

Syntax:

```
X = MonthName(TheNumber)
```

X will be set to the text name of the month corresponding to the number in TheNumber.

Example:

```
Label1.Text = MonthName(3)
```

This example will write the following output to a browser:

```
March
```

Now Returns the current system date and time.

Syntax:

```
X = Now
```

X will be set to the current system date and time.

Example:

```
Label1.Text = Now
```

This example will write the current system date and time to a browser.

Oct Returns the octal value of a number.

Syntax:

```
X = Oct(TheNumber)
```

X will contain a string representing the octal value of TheNumber.

Example:

```
Label1.Text = Oct(9)
Label2.Text = Oct(12)
```

This example will write the following output to a browser:

```
11
14
```

Replace Replaces one character in a string with another.

Syntax:

```
X = Replace(String2Fix, Character2Replace, What2ReplaceWith)
```

X will contain a converted String2Fix that will have Character2Replace substituted with What2ReplaceWith.

Example:

```
Label1.Text Replace("Mississippi", "i", "o")
```

This example will write the following output to a browser:

```
Mossossoppo
```

Right Chops characters off the right side of a string.

Syntax:

```
X = Right(String2Chop, NumCharacters)
```

X will contain the right-most characters of String2Chop, depending on the number in NumCharacters.

Example:

```
Label1.Text = Right("Hello", 2)
```

This example will write the following output to a browser:

```
lo
```

RTrim Returns a string with any trailing spaces removed.

Syntax:

```
X = Rtrim(TheString)
```

X is set to TheString without any trailing spaces.

Example:

```
X = Rtrim("   Hello   ")
```

X will be set to the string "   Hello".

Second Returns the seconds from a time.

Syntax:

```
X = Second(TheTime)
```

Returns a number representing the number of seconds chopped from a time.

Example:

```
Label1.Text = Second("5/1/1971 5:15:32")
Label2.Text = Second("9/21/2002 12:32:54")
```

This example will write the following output to a browser:

```
32
54
```

Select...Case The Select…Case structure allows you to have code run depending on a condition.

Syntax:

```
Select Case X
    Case 1
        'first code block
    Case 2
        'second code block
    Case Else
End Select
```

The code will run a code block depending on the value of X. If X is 1, the first code block will run. If X is 2, the second code block will run. Otherwise, the Else code block will run.

Example:

```
X = 1
Select Case X
    Case 1
        Label1.Text = "This one."
    Case 2
        Label1.Text = "Not this one."
    Case Else
        Label1.Text = "Not this one."
End Select
```

This example will write the text "This one." to a browser.

Space Returns a number of spaces as a string.

Syntax:

```
X = Space(TheNumber)
```

X will contain a string of TheNumber spaces.

Example:

```
X = Space(5)
```

X will be set to the value "   ".

Sqrt Returns the square root of a number.

Syntax:

```
X = Math.Sqrt(TheNumber)
```

X will be set to the square root of the number.

Example:

```
Label1.Text = Math.Sqrt(9)
```

This example will write the following output to a browser:

```
3
```

StrComp Compares two strings and returns a value resulting from that comparison.

Syntax:

```
X = StrComp(String1,String2)
```

If the two strings are equal, X will contain 0. If string 1 is greater, X will contain 1. Otherwise, X will contain –1.

Example:

```
Label1.Text = StrComp("Hello", "Hello")
Label2.Text = StrComp("Hello", "World")
Label3.Text = StrComp("World", "Hello")
```

This example will write the following output to a browser:

```
0
-1
1
```

TimeOfDay Returns the current system time.

Syntax:

```
X = TimeOfDay
```

X will contain the current system time.

Example:

```
Label1.Text = TimeOfDay
```

This example will write the current system time to a browser.

TimeSerial Returns a time concatenated from an hour, a minute, and a second.

Syntax:

```
X = TimeSerial(Hour, Minute, Second)
```

X will contain the time corresponding to the values of Hour, Minute, and Second.

Example:

```
X = TimeSerial("5", "17", "32")
```

X will contain the time 5:17:32.

Today Returns the current system date.

Syntax:

```
X = Today()
```

X will contain the current system date.

Example:

```
Label.Text = Today()
```

The current system date will be written to the browser.

Trim Removes the spaces from both ends of a string.

Syntax:

```
X = Trim(TheString)
```

X will contain the string TheString with all the spaces removed.

Example:

```
X = Trim("    Hello    ")
```

X will be set to the string "Hello".

Ucase Converts a string to its uppercase value.

Syntax:

```
X = UCase(TheString)
```

X will contain the string TheString with the characters all in uppercase.

Example:

```
Label1.Text = UCase("hello")
```

This example will write the following output to a browser:

```
HELLO
```

Weekday Returns the numeric weekday of a date from 1 to 7.

Syntax:

```
X = WeekDay(TheDate)
```

X will contain a number between 1 and 7 according to the weekday of TheDate.

Example:

```
Label1.Text = Weekday("5/1/1971 5:15:32")
Label2.Text = Weekday("9/22/2002 12:32:54")
```

This example will write the following output to a browser:

```
7
1
```

WeekdayName Returns the name of a weekday according to its number.

Syntax:

```
X = WeekdayName(TheNUmber)
```

X will contain the name of the day matching the number, where Sunday is 1 and Saturday is 7.

Example:

```
Label1.Text = WeekdayName(1)
Label2.Text = WeekdayName(7)
```

This example will write the following output to a browser:

```
Sunday
Saturday
```

Year Returns the Year portion of a date.

Syntax:

```
X = Year(TheDate)
```

X will be set to the year portion of TheDate.

Example:

```
Label1.Text = Year("5/1/1971 5:15:32")
Label1.Text = Year("9/21/2002 12:32:54")
```

This example will write the following output to a browser:

```
1971
2001
```

APPENDIX B

Using the CD-ROM

On the CD-ROM that accompanies this book, you will find all the solutions discussed in Chapters 3 through 19. The structure of most of those chapters follows the outline discussed here. Note that since the files are stored on a CD-ROM, they will be marked as read-only. You will need to modify this when you copy the files to your hard drive so that the files can be changed. To do this, simply right-click the file and select Properties. Then uncheck the read-only attribute.

Each chapter has its own folder on the CD-ROM. For the chapters that have more than one solution presented in them, you will find a subfolder within the chapter folder that has the name of that solution. Then within that folder and within the chapter folder for the single-solution chapters, you will find a SQL folder and an Access folder.

The SQL folder contains the solution as it was designed to run with SQL Server. That folder also contains files needed to recreate the database in SQL Server. The Access folder contains the solution as it was designed to run with Microsoft Access. That folder also contains the Access database file.

The Access database contains all the tables and records that were populated to test the solution. You should be able to use the Access database without modification.

To use the SQL Server version of the solutions, you will need to recreate the tables and then import data into the tables. To do that, first create a new database in SQL Server. Then, with that database selected, select SQL Query Analyzer from the Tools menu, as is shown in Figure B-1.

You will then be in a new query window where we can create the table structure. From the File menu, select Open. Now browse to the .sql file that is located on the CD in the SQL folder of the solution you want to recreate. Open that file and you should see the SQL script for that database, like the one displayed in Figure B-2.

Make sure that the database you want the tables placed in is the active database in the drop-down menu in the toolbar. Otherwise, you may delete existing tables. Click the green arrow button to run the script. You should now be able to go back to the Enterprise Manager in SQL Server and see that the target database has the new tables. This is shown in Figure B-3.

But the new tables do not have any data in them. You need to import data into these tables from the .txt files that are in the same folder as the SQL script on the CD.

To import data into a table, right-click the table and select All Tasks followed by Import Data. Click Next on the Welcome screen to see the second page of the wizard displayed in Figure B-4.

This page of the wizard allows you to specify where you want to import data. Select Text File from the Data Source drop-down list. Then click the "…" button

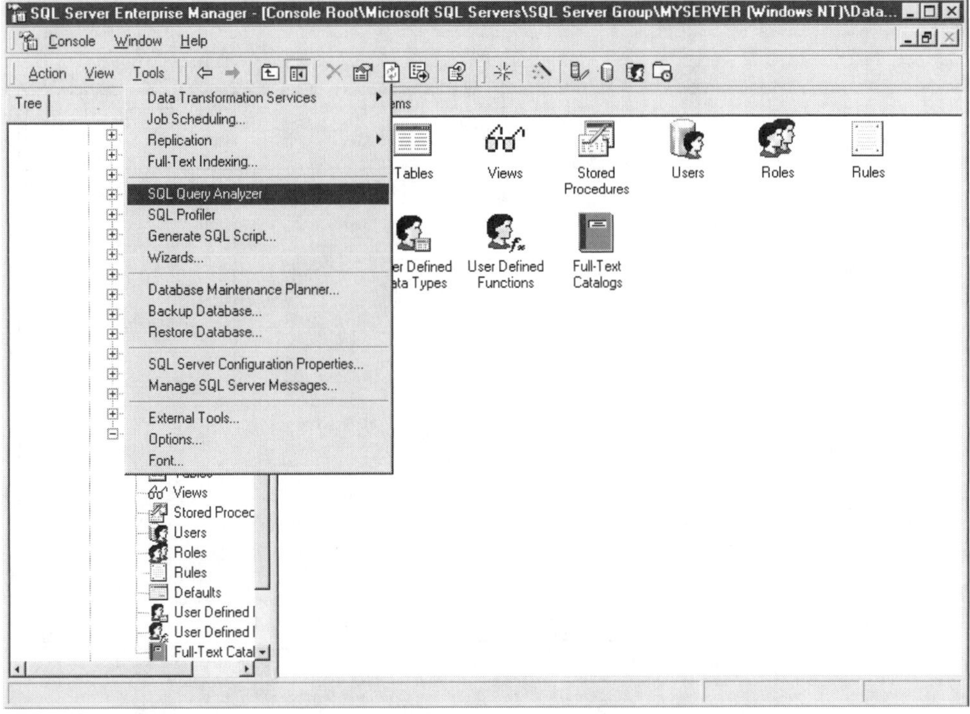

Figure B-1 *Selecting the SQL Query Analyzer*

to browse to the file where data is located. Again, these files end in .txt. You will find them in the SQL folder for the solution you are working with. The text files have the same name as the table. So if you are importing data into the Students table, browse to the file named Students.txt.

Once you have the file selected, click Next. You shouldn't have to make any changes on the next two pages of the wizard. Then you should see the page of the wizard displayed in Figure B-5.

Here you specify where you want the data to be placed. This would be on your SQL Server in the database that you just created tables in using the SQL script. Make sure it is selected in the Database drop-down list before clicking Next.

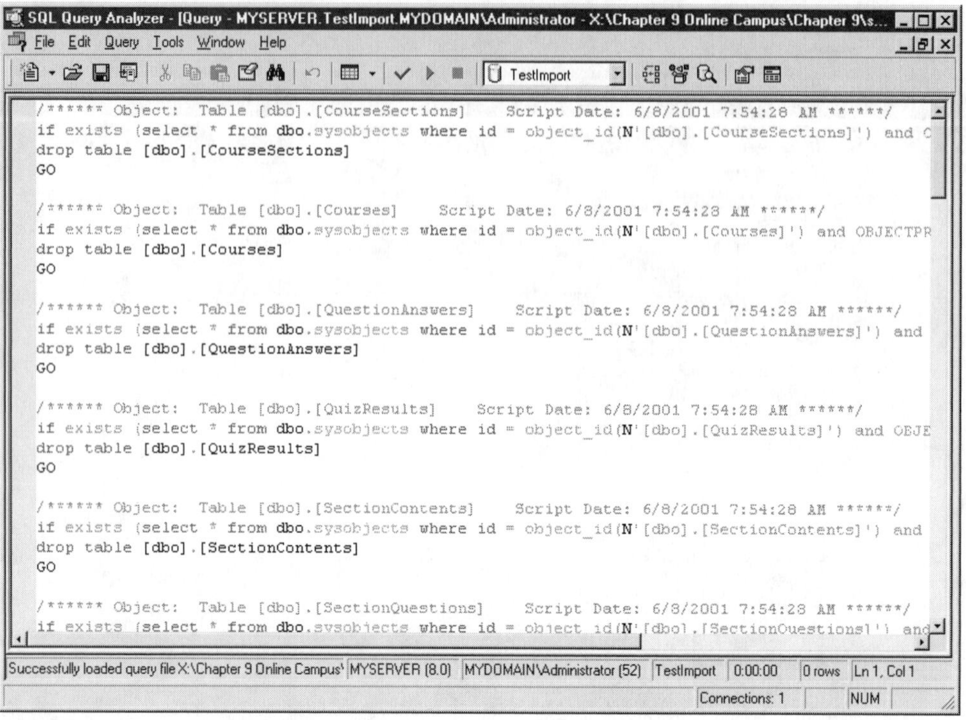

Figure B-2 *SQL Query Analyzer*

Next, you need to select the table that you want to place the data in, as is displayed in Figure B-6.

Pull down the list under Destination and make sure that, even though it says the correct table name, you find the correct table in the list. Click Next again, choose to run immediately, and keep going until you get to the Finish button. When you click that button, the table should be populated with the records that you just imported from the CD.

At this point, you have the structure of the database and the data in the database whether you are using Access or SQL Server. You now need to modify the connect string for either of these formats to match your own server settings.

If you are using Access, you will see a connect string like this in the code:

```
DBConn = New OleDbConnection("PROVIDER=Microsoft.Jet.OLEDB.4.0;" _
    & "DATA SOURCE=" _
    & Server.MapPath("/INetBook/C9/" _
    & "Access/C9OnlineCampus.mdb;"))
```

You will need to change this connect string to point to the location where you have placed the Access database within your Web root. And if you are using security with

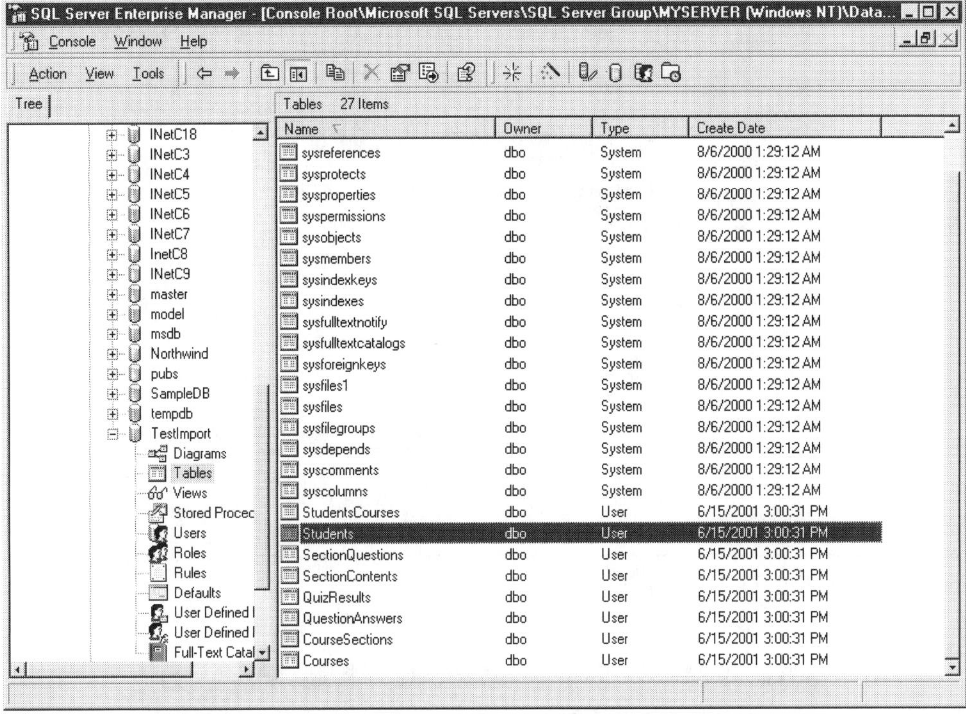

Figure B-3 *New tables created*

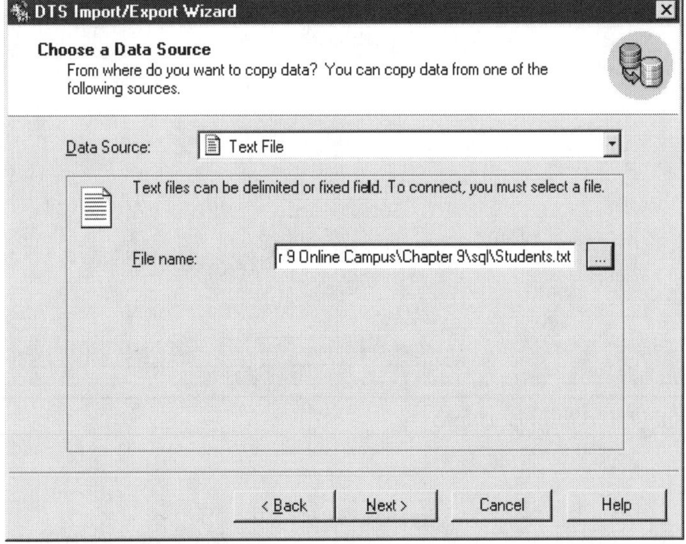

Figure B-4 *Selecting a data source*

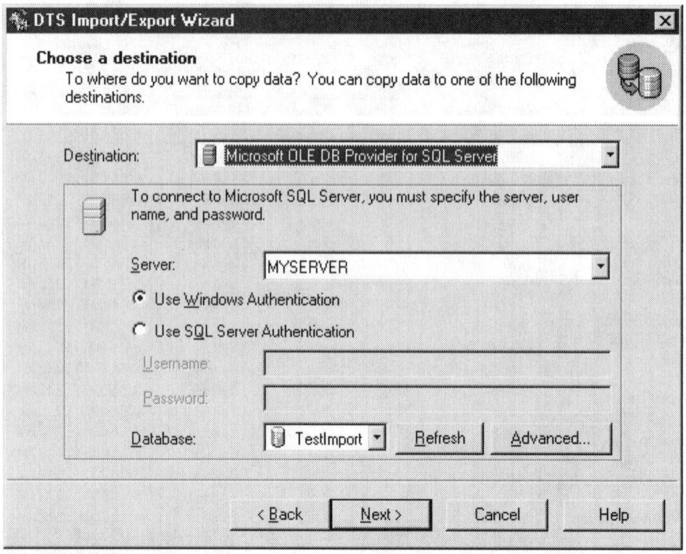

Figure B-5 *Selecting a destination*

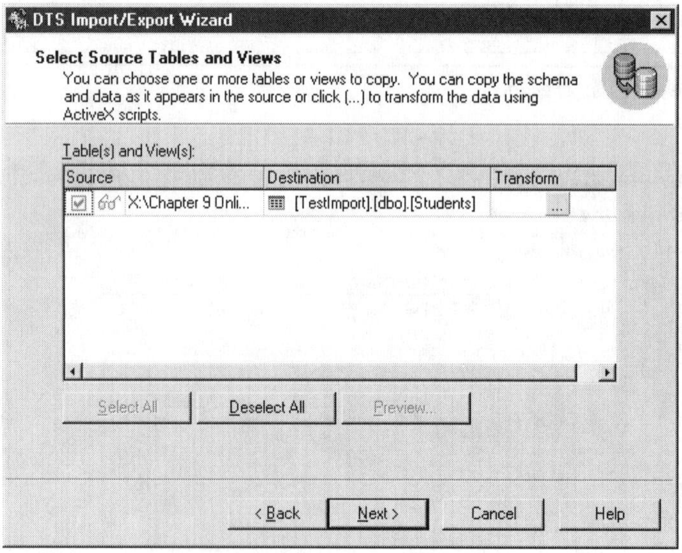

Figure B-6 *Select table to import into*

Access, which you definitely should be doing, you will also need to specify the user name and password used to connect to the database.

If you are using SQL Server, you will see a connect string in code like this one:

```
DBConn = New OleDbConnection("Provider=sqloledb;" _
    & "server=localhost;" _
    & "Initial Catalog=INETC9;" _
    & "User Id=sa;" _
    & "Password=yourpassword;")
```

Here the name of my server is "localhost" because the Internet and database server are on the same computer. You may need to change this to point to the computer that has your SQL Server. The name of the database in SQL Server in this connect string is "INETC9". If, when you set up this solution, you called the database something else, you will need to change it here.

And finally, you need to change the User ID and Password parameters to match those that allow access to your SQL Server installation.

Index

Symbols

A

C

D

E

F

G

H

I

J

K

L

M

N

O

P

Q

R

S

T

U

V

W

X

Z

INTERNATIONAL CONTACT INFORMATION

AUSTRALIA
McGraw-Hill Book Company Australia Pty. Ltd.
TEL +61-2-9417-9899
FAX +61-2-9417-5687
http://www.mcgraw-hill.com.au
books-it_sydney@mcgraw-hill.com

CANADA
McGraw-Hill Ryerson Ltd.
TEL +905-430-5000
FAX +905-430-5020
http://www.mcgrawhill.ca

GREECE, MIDDLE EAST, NORTHERN AFRICA
McGraw-Hill Hellas
TEL +30-1-656-0990-3-4
FAX +30-1-654-5525

MEXICO (Also serving Latin America)
McGraw-Hill Interamericana Editores S.A. de C.V.
TEL +525-117-1583
FAX +525-117-1589
http://www.mcgraw-hill.com.mx
fernando_castellanos@mcgraw-hill.com

SINGAPORE (Serving Asia)
McGraw-Hill Book Company
TEL +65-863-1580
FAX +65-862-3354
http://www.mcgraw-hill.com.sg
mghasia@mcgraw-hill.com

SOUTH AFRICA
McGraw-Hill South Africa
TEL +27-11-622-7512
FAX +27-11-622-9045
robyn_swanepoel@mcgraw-hill.com

UNITED KINGDOM & EUROPE (Excluding Southern Europe)
McGraw-Hill Education Europe
TEL +44-1-628-502500
FAX +44-1-628-770224
http://www.mcgraw-hill.co.uk
computing_neurope@mcgraw-hill.com

ALL OTHER INQUIRIES Contact:
Osborne/McGraw-Hill
TEL +1-510-549-6600
FAX +1-510-883-7600
http://www.osborne.com
omg_international@mcgraw-hill.com

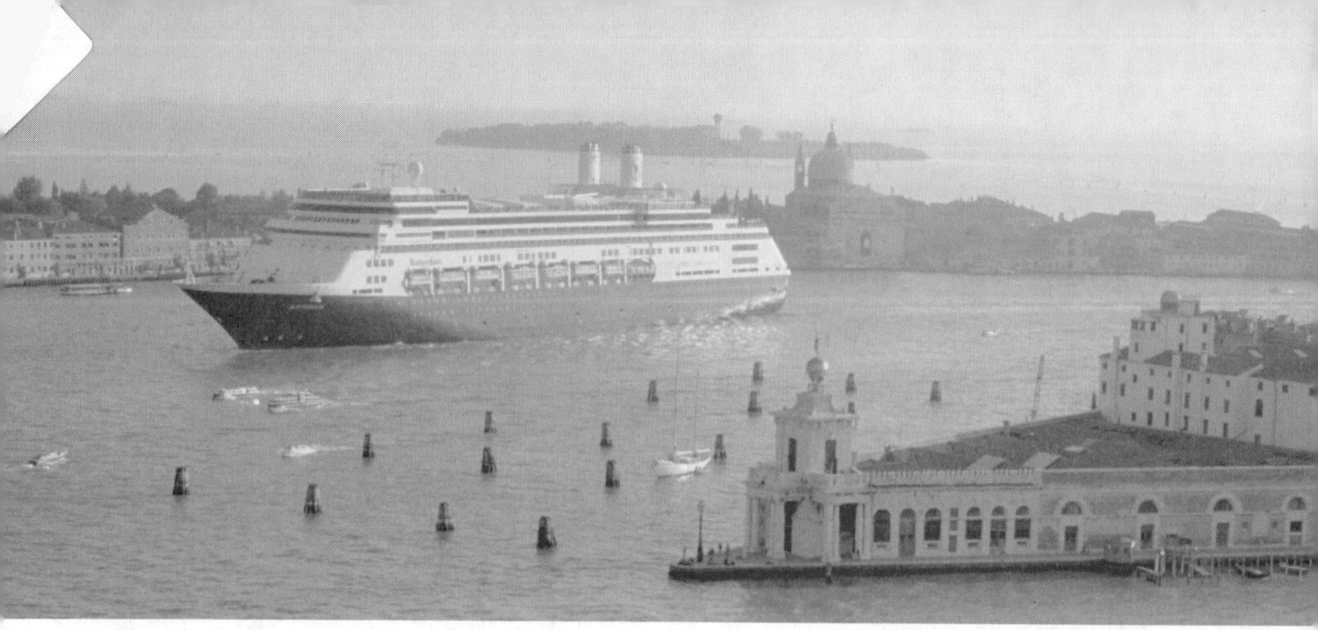

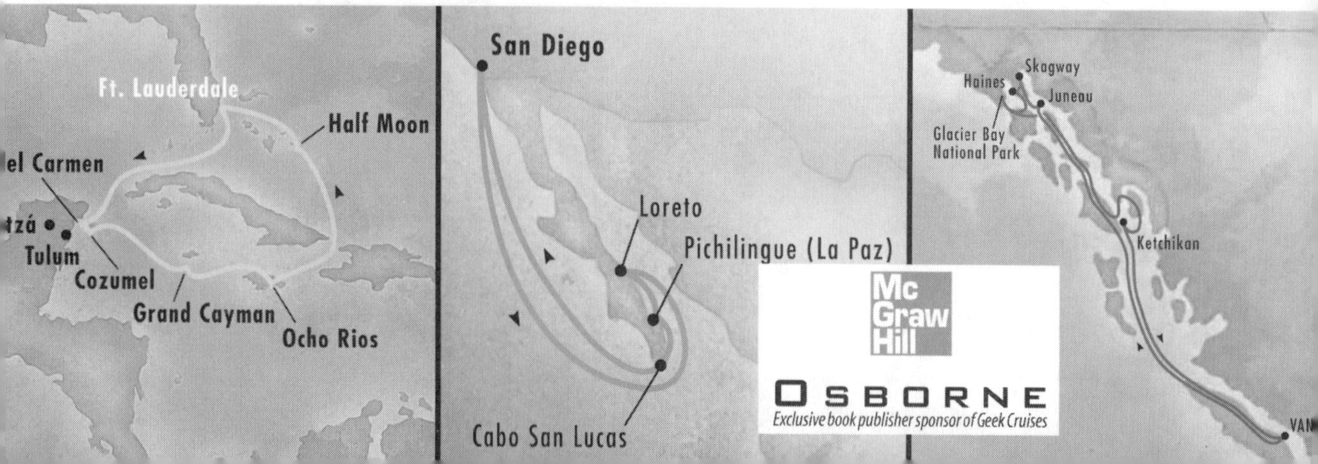

Ft. Lauderdale
Half Moon
el Carmen
Tulum
Cozumel
Grand Cayman
Ocho Rios
San Diego
Loreto
Pichilingue (La Paz)
Cabo San Lucas
Skagway
Haines
Juneau
Glacier Bay National Park
Ketchikan

LICENSE AGREEMENT

THIS PRODUCT (THE "PRODUCT") CONTAINS PROPRIETARY SOFTWARE, DATA AND INFORMATION (INCLUDING DOCUMENTATION) OWNED BY THE McGRAW-HILL COMPANIES, INC. ("McGRAW-HILL") AND ITS LICENSORS. YOUR RIGHT TO USE THE PRODUCT IS GOVERNED BY THE TERMS AND CONDITIONS OF THIS AGREEMENT.

LICENSE: Throughout this License Agreement, "you" shall mean either the individual or the entity whose agent opens this package. You are granted a non-exclusive and non-transferable license to use the Product subject to the following terms:

(i) If you have licensed a single user version of the Product, the Product may only be used on a single computer (i.e., a single CPU). If you licensed and paid the fee applicable to a local area network or wide area network version of the Product, you are subject to the terms of the following subparagraph (ii).

(ii) If you have licensed a local area network version, you may use the Product on unlimited workstations located in one single building selected by you that is served by such local area network. If you have licensed a wide area network version, you may use the Product on unlimited workstations located in multiple buildings on the same site selected by you that is served by such wide area network; provided, however, that any building will not be considered located in the same site if it is more than five (5) miles away from any building included in such site. In addition, you may only use a local area or wide area network version of the Product on one single server. If you wish to use the Product on more than one server, you must obtain written authorization from McGraw-Hill and pay additional fees.

(iii) You may make one copy of the Product for back-up purposes only and you must maintain an accurate record as to the location of the back-up at all times.

COPYRIGHT; RESTRICTIONS ON USE AND TRANSFER: All rights (including copyright) in and to the Product are owned by McGraw-Hill and its licensors. You are the owner of the enclosed disc on which the Product is recorded. You may not use, copy, decompile, disassemble, reverse engineer, modify, reproduce, create derivative works, transmit, distribute, sublicense, store in a database or retrieval system of any kind, rent or transfer the Product, or any portion thereof, in any form or by any means (including electronically or otherwise) except as expressly provided for in this License Agreement. You must reproduce the copyright notices, trademark notices, legends and logos of McGraw-Hill and its licensors that appear on the Product on the back-up copy of the Product which you are permitted to make hereunder. All rights in the Product not expressly granted herein are reserved by McGraw-Hill and its licensors.

TERM: This License Agreement is effective until terminated. It will terminate if you fail to comply with any term or condition of this License Agreement. Upon termination, you are obligated to return to McGraw-Hill the Product together with all copies thereof and to purge all copies of the Product included in any and all servers and computer facilities.

DISCLAIMER OF WARRANTY: THE PRODUCT AND THE BACK-UP COPY ARE LICENSED "AS IS." McGRAW-HILL, ITS LICENSORS AND THE AUTHORS MAKE NO WARRANTIES, EXPRESS OR IMPLIED, AS TO THE RESULTS TO BE OBTAINED BY ANY PERSON OR ENTITY FROM USE OF THE PRODUCT, ANY INFORMATION OR DATA INCLUDED THEREIN AND/OR ANY TECHNICAL SUPPORT SERVICES PROVIDED HEREUNDER, IF ANY ("TECHNICAL SUPPORT SERVICES"). McGRAW-HILL, ITS LICENSORS AND THE AUTHORS MAKE NO EXPRESS OR IMPLIED WARRANTIES OF MERCHANTABILITY OR FITNESS FOR A PARTICULAR PURPOSE OR USE WITH RESPECT TO THE PRODUCT. McGRAW-HILL, ITS LICENSORS, AND THE AUTHORS MAKE NO GUARANTEE THAT YOU WILL PASS ANY CERTIFICATION EXAM WHATSOEVER BY USING THIS PRODUCT. NEITHER McGRAW-HILL, ANY OF ITS LICENSORS NOR THE AUTHORS WARRANT THAT THE FUNCTIONS CONTAINED IN THE PRODUCT WILL MEET YOUR REQUIREMENTS OR THAT THE OPERATION OF THE PRODUCT WILL BE UNINTERRUPTED OR ERROR FREE. YOU ASSUME THE ENTIRE RISK WITH RESPECT TO THE QUALITY AND PERFORMANCE OF THE PRODUCT.

LIMITED WARRANTY FOR DISC: To the original licensee only, McGraw-Hill warrants that the enclosed disc on which the Product is recorded is free from defects in materials and workmanship under normal use and service for a period of ninety (90) days from the date of purchase. In the event of a defect in the disc covered by the foregoing warranty, McGraw-Hill will replace the disc.

LIMITATION OF LIABILITY: NEITHER McGRAW-HILL, ITS LICENSORS NOR THE AUTHORS SHALL BE LIABLE FOR ANY INDIRECT, SPECIAL OR CONSEQUENTIAL DAMAGES, SUCH AS BUT NOT LIMITED TO, LOSS OF ANTICIPATED PROFITS OR BENEFITS, RESULTING FROM THE USE OR INABILITY TO USE THE PRODUCT EVEN IF ANY OF THEM HAS BEEN ADVISED OF THE POSSIBILITY OF SUCH DAMAGES. THIS LIMITATION OF LIABILITY SHALL APPLY TO ANY CLAIM OR CAUSE WHATSOEVER WHETHER SUCH CLAIM OR CAUSE ARISES IN CONTRACT, TORT, OR OTHERWISE. Some states do not allow the exclusion or limitation of indirect, special or consequential damages, so the above limitation may not apply to you.

U.S. GOVERNMENT RESTRICTED RIGHTS: Any software included in the Product is provided with restricted rights subject to subparagraphs (c), (1) and (2) of the Commercial Computer Software-Restricted Rights clause at 48 C.F.R. 52.227-19. The terms of this Agreement applicable to the use of the data in the Product are those under which the data are generally made available to the general public by McGraw-Hill. Except as provided herein, no reproduction, use, or disclosure rights are granted with respect to the data included in the Product and no right to modify or create derivative works from any such data is hereby granted.

GENERAL: This License Agreement constitutes the entire agreement between the parties relating to the Product. The terms of any Purchase Order shall have no effect on the terms of this License Agreement. Failure of McGraw-Hill to insist at any time on strict compliance with this License Agreement shall not constitute a waiver of any rights under this License Agreement. This License Agreement shall be construed and governed in accordance with the laws of the State of New York. If any provision of this License Agreement is held to be contrary to law, that provision will be enforced to the maximum extent permissible and the remaining provisions will remain in full force and effect.